A BIBLICAL
THEOLOGY

OF THE

NEW TESTAMENT

FROM MEMBERS OF DALLAS THEOLOGICAL FACULTY

ROY B. ZUCK, *EDITOR*

DARRELL L. BOCK,
CONSULTING EDITOR

MOODY PRESS

CHICAGO

To Dr. Stanley D. Toussaint,
beloved colleague and esteemed professor
who taught the New Testament to each of
the contributors to the volume when they were students
at Dallas Theological Seminary
Dr. Toussaint served on the Dallas Seminary faculty
from 1960 to 1968 and from 1973 to 1993

Roy B. Zuck (A.B., Biola University; Th.M., Th.D., Dallas Theological Seminary), general editor, is Senior Professor Emeritus of Bible Exposition at Dallas Theological Seminary. He is editor of *Bibliotheca Sacra* and coeditor of *The Bible Knowledge Commentary*. He is also the author of *Open Letter to a Jehovah's Witness* and the Everyman's Bible Commentary on Job.

Darrell L. Bock (Th.M., Dallas Theological Seminary; Ph.D., University of Aberdeen), consulting editor, New Testament, is associate professor of New Testament studies at Dallas Theological Seminary and minister of the Word at Trinity Fellowship in Richardson, Texas. He is the author of *Proclamation from Prophecy and Pattern*.

CONTENTS

ABOUT THE EDITORS

ROY B. ZUCK (B.A., Biola Univ.; Th.M., Th.D., Dallas Theological Seminary) is department chairman and senior professor of Bible exposition at Dallas Theological Seminary. Most recently, he was listed in *Who's Who in American Education* (1991–92), *International Directory of Distinguished Leadership* (1994), and *Directory of International Biography* (1994).

Books written or edited by Roy B. Zuck: *A Biblical Theology of the Old Testament; Adult Education in the Church; Barb, Please Wake Up!; Basic Bible Interpretation; The Bib Sac Reader; The Bible Knowledge Commentary; Biblical Archaeology Leader's Guide; Childhood Education in the Church; Christian Youth: An In-Depth Survey; Church History Leader's Guide; Creation: Evidence from Scripture and Science; Communism and Christianity Leader's Guide; Devotions for Kindred Spirits; The Holy Spirit in Your Teaching; How to Be a Youth Sponsor; Job* (Everyman's Bible Commentary); *Reflecting with Solomon: Studies on the Book of Ecclesiastes; Sitting with Job: Selected Studies on the Book of Job; The Life of Christ Commentary; Vital Biblical Issues; Vital Contemporary Issues; Vital Ministry Issues; Vital Theological Issues; Youth and the Church; Youth Education in the Church*

DARRELL L. BOCK (B.A., Univ. of Texas at Austin; Th.M., Dallas Theological Seminary; Ph.D., Univ. of Aberdeen in Scotland) is professor of New Testament Studies at Dallas Theological Seminary. His books include *Proclamation from Prophecy and Pattern* (1987); *Luke*, 2 vols. (1994, 1995); and *Luke* (1994). He is also coeditor of *Dispensationalism, Israel, and the Church: The Search for Definition* (1992) and coauthor of *Progressive Dispensationalism* (1993), as well as a contributor to many other books.

FOREWORD

Systematic theology has been designated as the "queen of the sciences." It is the investigation of God and His universe. Thus, theology involves observing special revelation, God's inspired Word, and natural revelation—God's creation—and their relationship to each other. To examine special revelation, the theologian must investigate the contents of the Scriptures. This is exegesis. Then specific passages must be examined in light of the theological framework of the specific work of the writer of Scripture. This is biblical theology. This step attempts to prevent the theologian from taking passages out of context or bending passages of Scripture to fit a personal theology.

The role of biblical theologians is a difficult one. On the one hand, the exegete may think that some of the ramifications of the debate have not been taken seriously by biblical theologians. On the other hand, systematic theologians could think that the theological deductions of biblical theologians do not go far enough. It is a delight to see that in the present volume there has been a careful examination of the fruits of exegesis in an attempt to determine the theology of the writers of the New Testament. A good systematic theology is based on the fruits of good biblical theology, which in turn is based on good exegesis.

The present work deals not only with historical interpretations of the biblical texts but also with the contemporary discussion of those passages and Bible books. The authors discuss various views on passages that have a bearing on the theological teachings of the specific scriptural writers and have been fair in expressing these various interpretations and judicious in their critiques. In reading this work, one does not sense that the authors have axes to grind or hobby horses to pursue.

So many times theology is difficult to read, not necessarily because it is deep but because it is muddled with complex language. But this book is easy to read. This volume can be used by the church at large—it is not reserved for the intellectual few. It will serve as a handy tool for those who expound the Scriptures. Teachers and preachers will gain knowledge of the contents of particular problem passages in the New Testament and will also see the relationship of those passages to the development of the scriptural writers' theology and how it then contributes to the theology of the Bible as a whole.

With the present-day pandemic tendency to do what is expedient, this work is a welcome counterbalance. Christians should not be easily influenced by forces either secular or sacred but should follow biblical mandates. All too often Christians are encouraged to take actions on the basis of poor exegesis or sloppy theology. When believers read this book, they will gain insight into God's character and what He desires of them.

> HAROLD W. HOEHNER
> Senior professor and chairman
> New Testament Studies
> Dallas Theological Seminary

INTRODUCTION

Eugene H. Merrill introduced *A Biblical Theology of the Old Testament* with a definition of biblical theology and a discussion of its character in comparison to systematic theology.[1] In that work he defined biblical theology as tracing "the history of salvation a step at a time throughout the Bible, allowing the history to take whatever form appropriate at any given stage of revelation, recognizing how the doctrine developed as revelation progressed."[2] This definition of biblical theology reflects a concern to trace carefully the development of doctrine within the period of the Bible's production, a period covering more than a thousand years.

The issue of the progress of revelation over time is especially acute in the Old Testament, since its production spanned several centuries. However, when one comes to the New Testament, the issue of revelation's progress takes on a different dimension. This Testament emerged from start to finish within a fifty-year period. It reflects the most intense period of development for special revelation, since the New Testament covers the impact of Jesus Christ's life and ministry on God's plan. What the Old Testament looked forward to in promise, the New Testament claims has begun through fulfillment in Jesus. Hebrews 1:1–2 states it clearly, "In the past God spoke to our forefathers through the prophets at many times and in various ways, but in these last days he has spoken to us by his Son, whom he appointed heir of all things, and through whom he made the universe." In sum, the New Testament is about Jesus and how He completes the plan for the reestablishment of God's rule over His creation. But how should one organize material that is so tightly compressed and theologically loaded? What categories are best to use in synthesizing this material? If, as Merrill showed, biblical theology is distinct from systematic theology, what is its relationship to exegesis, the third member of the interpretive trinity? How does one get the building blocks for the Bible's theological message? Where does this volume on New Testament biblical theology fit? This in-

1. Roy B. Zuck, ed., *A Biblical Theology of the Old Testament* (Chicago: Moody, 1989), 1–6.
2. Ibid., 2.

troduction seeks to answer these questions by defining biblical theology's uneasy relationship to exegesis and systematics, while comparing where this volume fits with previous efforts to write a biblical theology for the New Testament.

BIBLICAL THEOLOGY'S RELATIONSHIP TO EXEGESIS AND SYSTEMATICS

Exegesis is the careful explanation of the meaning of a given text. The term comes from a Greek term, *exēgēsis,* that means "explanation."[3] Exegesis involves analyzing a text in its historical, cultural, and literary setting with concern for its lexical, grammatical, and theological content. The exegete focuses primarily on explaining the text's message for its initial audience. In a real way, exegesis is the foundation for both biblical theology and systematic theology. Yet anyone who has been a seminary student or has sat in a biblical studies class knows that often exegesis and theology seem to be operating on different agendas. This is simply because these disciplines are asking questions from differing perspectives. Understanding how each works helps relieve some of the tension felt in the differences of approach. There is nothing wrong with examining a text from various angles in order to appreciate the various dimensions of that biblical text.

When one compares biblical theology to exegesis and to systematic theology, it is clear that biblical theology occupies a "bridge" position between the other two ways of reading the Bible. All three disciplines make a valid contribution to theological study, though the assumption that allows biblical theology and systematic theology to work toward a unifying goal is that one divine Author stands behind the individual parts of Scripture. Without a commitment to the Author behind the human authors, all three disciplines lose any hope of producing a unified reading of the Bible's message. Doing biblical or systematic theology is problematic in a written document that might be randomly written and assembled, but the Bible is not an assortment of recorded individual religious experiences. The authors of this volume on New Testament theology share with those of the companion volume on Old Testament theology a commitment to a high view of the inspiration and authority of the Bible. Only such a view gives one any hope to hold together the distinct perspectives emerging from exegesis, biblical theology, and systematic theology.[4]

So how do exegesis, biblical theology, and systematics relate to each other? The history of interpretation shows that systematics and exegesis have always had a defined character, while biblical theology has not. The relationship of the three disciplines helps explain why. Systematics takes the whole of revelation and seeks to

---

3. Henry Liddell and Robert Scott, *A Greek-English Lexicon,* ed. Henry Jones (Oxford: Clarendon, 1968), 593.

4. For a different perspective that all but despairs of any hope of doing biblical theology and systematics, except in ecclesial contexts, see Heikki Räisänen, *Beyond New Testament Theology* (Philadelphia: Trinity Press Int., 1990). He focuses exclusively on a historical discipline that keeps history and theology completely distinct. Such a separation between history and theology and a lack of separation between orthodoxy and heterodoxy is precisely what theological studies must *not* maintain, though Räisänen's proposal is a natural consequence of viewing the biblical materials as part of a natural historical process instead of as superintended by God.

weave an inherent unity between the parts, using descriptive categories and subject topics that facilitate bringing the whole together. What emerges is the presence of a grid that explains how the parts fit together. The very building-block nature of the discipline means that various grids have been proposed. But the method in each case has been to work for a unity drawn from the whole of Scripture. In contrast, exegesis works minutely with the individual pieces of the text of Scripture, seeking to explain what each part says. Its terminology is often that of the text as defined by a very specific setting the passage originally addressed. Often background questions dominate the pursuit of original meaning or the quest for the historical starting point behind the message. The juxtaposition of these two other disciplines, along with the relatively recent age of biblical theology as a discipline, has caused biblical theology to be the struggling baby of the family.[5] It has often been squeezed out in discussion or else it has been pulled in two directions at once.

Biblical theology is an attempt to study the individual contributions of a given writer or a given period to the canon's message. It combines analysis and synthesis. Its intermediate position means that there has been much less attention paid to it than to systematics or to exegesis. When it has been taken seriously, the question has been which way its attention should be directed. Should biblical theology honor its commitment to synthesis and use the categories of systematics to describe its material? Or should it show its commitment to tracing the historical progress of revelation and use the categories of exegesis and the terms of a specific setting to present the biblical material? Should biblical theology be focused on the message of an original historical setting or the theological structures that addressed that specific setting? Like a rope being pulled by two powerful and related forces, biblical theology has always wrestled with its character as a fusion of synthetic and analytic concerns. As with the building of any bridge, it has slowly had to learn how to bear a lot of weight as theology proceeds from its historical base to its expression as principled propositions.

---

5. As a formal theological discipline, biblical theology is by far the youngest of the three ways of reading the text. Its identity, like any last-born child, has always been subject to sibling rivalry. The prominent early proposal to do biblical theology came from a lecture by Johann Philipp Gabler in 1787 at Altdorf in Germany. (The lecture is cited briefly and discussed in Werner Georg Kümmel, *The New Testament: The History of the Investigation of Its Problems*, trans. S. McLean Gilmore and Howard C. Kee [Nashville: Abingdon, 1972, 99–104].) Both systematics and exegesis were centuries older. Gabler described a discipline that would be historically focused and textually sensitive in contrast to the various developing systems of formal and philosophically oriented dogmatic theology that were so popular in this time. Gabler overplayed the tensions between history and the Bible, as well as dogmatics and biblical theology, by devaluing systematics too greatly, but his call for an intermediate discipline was helpful in allowing one to build one's reading of theology a step at a time with sensitivity to the historical character and progress of revelation, while being sensitive to the unique contributions of each portion of the Scripture. Ever since his work, biblical theology has struggled with whether it should look to exegesis, systematics, or history for its organizing principles.

NEW TESTAMENT THEOLOGIES: WHERE THIS VOLUME FITS

This pull on biblical theology is reflected in the various New Testament biblical theologies in circulation today. Since the New Testament was written in a more condensed time period than the Old, a "by time period" or diachronic organization of writing, as done in some Old Testament theologies, is not feasible. Other ways had to be tried. So a brief survey of the approach of other New Testament theologies can serve as a backdrop for where this present volume on New Testament biblical theology fits and how it resolves these tensions. The survey will be limited to treatments that were designed originally to address more than one writer of the New Testament. Four distinct approaches have been followed in the past.

First, some New Testament biblical theologies opted to organize themselves by author, but used systematics categories as a bridge to synthesis. Works by Alan Richardson and Charles Ryrie took this approach.[6] The value of such an approach is that those who work in systematics can see where New Testament material fits in the more synthetic scheme of things, but its weakness is that it moves to unify the distinct strands of New Testament emphasis too quickly and under categories distinct from those the individual writers used.

Second, other biblical theologies organized themselves basically by individuals, using the theological categories each one used. The individuals chosen may or may not have been writers of the New Testament. This choice brings historical concerns to the fore, as each individual is highlighted for his unique contribution to theology. Werner Kümmel and George Ladd focused on the teachings of Jesus, Paul, and John, while Ladd also covered the other major writers of the New Testament separately.[7] Ladd covered Jesus by uniting the treatment of the Synoptic Gospels into a single discussion of the major themes of Jesus' ministry. This is also a helpful way to proceed and the present volume basically takes that approach, but with two differences.

This volume separates the Gospels into individual treatments. Though there is value in attempting to present a unified theology of Jesus, the fact is that the Bible includes four presentations of Jesus through the eyes of His followers. The Gospels are their description of Him, and each description is distinct. The structure of the present volume seeks to honor the literary structure of Scripture, while noting the historical base behind that structure. Ladd's volume shows that the New Testament portrait of Jesus has many united features, especially in the Synoptic portraits, but what gets lost is the distinctive portrait each Gospel presents. So the contributors to this volume have opted instead to let the theology of each Gospel stand on its own.

---

6. Alan Richardson, *Introduction to the Theology of the New Testament* (New York: Harper, 1959); Charles Ryrie, *Biblical Theology of the New Testament* (Chicago: Moody, 1959).

7. Werner George Kümmel, *The Theology of the New Testament According to Its Major Witnesses: Jesus—Paul—John*, trans. John E. Steeley (Nashville: Abingdon, 1973); and George E. Ladd, *A Theology of the New Testament* (Grand Rapids: Eerdmans, 1974). A revised edition of Ladd's theology was published in 1993. It added individual, brief chapters on Matthew, Mark, and Luke to remedy the treatment of the Synoptic Gospels, but these overviews are so brief that only the most basic differences in perspective between the Gospels surface.

Though one could treat Paul's theology as a unit, his material is here separated into three major groupings. The Pastoral Epistles are so uniquely focused on ministerial and structural church concerns that it seemed they might get lost in a unified presentation of Paul's theology. In addition, the Prison Epistles have a more cosmopolitan flavor to them. It is likely that two of them, Ephesians and Colossians, were intended for more than one church community. So the Prison Epistles also have received a distinct treatment, reflective of their more regional character and the fact they all emerged from a single key period in Paul's life. The remaining letters are clearly focused on the individual communities to which they are written, and so they are treated as reflective of Paul's fundamental theological concerns. To prevent this material's separation from fragmenting the theological portrait of Paul, the different authors of these sections were asked to note connections to Pauline material in the other groupings where appropriate. The remaining groupings are also by author: John, Hebrews, James, Peter, and Jude.

A third approach to writing a New Testament biblical theology is to compromise between systematics' categories and the writers' categories. The volume by Donald Guthrie treats systematics' categories as the unifying structure and substructure, but discusses each category and subcategory an author at a time.[8] This also bridges the gap to the larger synthesis, but one loses the sense of coherence that reflects each author's contribution. For example, to determine John's teaching, one must read several separate theologically defined category discussions and then put them together. This present study does not go this way.

A fourth approach has been popular in Europe. It is historically and critically based, seeking to go behind the documents to the earliest history and theology reflected in them. Joachim Jeremias and Leonard Goppelt attempt to work back to the earliest forms of the traditions related to Jesus.[9] Since Jeremias wrote only an initial volume, his effort stops here. Goppelt went on to treat each New Testament author individually and focused more exegetically at locating the author in his original setting. These historical efforts tend to de-emphasize the biblical text's message, since they seek to reach back to the earliest expressions of the events associated with Jesus or become concerned with detailing the original setting of the teaching as specifically as possible. The speculative nature of such work seems not to be a topic for "New Testament" theology, since the Bible as it is today is treated as a foggy mirror back to the past. Formal, historical exegetical study, not a biblical theology, should treat these topics, so these issues are not pursued here. Background and introductory concerns are handled only to a limited degree.

---

8. Donald Guthrie, *New Testament Theology: A Thematic Study* (Downers Grove, Ill.: InterVarsity, 1981).

9. Joachim Jeremias, *New Testament Theology: The Proclamation of Jesus*, trans. John Bowden (New York: Charles Scribner's Sons, 1971); Leonard Goppelt, *Theology of the New Testament*, ed. Jürgen Roloff, trans. John Alsup, 2 vols. (Grand Rapids: Eerdmans, 1981, 1982). A proposed series of volumes being produced currently in the United Kingdom under the editorship of James Dunn is also taking this approach, concentrating heavily on the original setting.

Perhaps the consummate example of this approach comes from Rudolf Bult-mann.[10] He also attempts to place the New Testament historically in its world, but bases his work heavily on critical concerns. He is far more radical in his approach than Jeremias or Goppelt. He is so skeptical about the New Testament portrait of Jesus that he barely discusses a theology of Jesus.[11] Rather he pursues a division that is historically and ethnically based: the kerygma of the earliest church (i.e., the Jewish Christian community), the kerygma of the Hellenistic church, and then the theology of Paul. This approach sees much of the New Testament as a product of early church reflection, rather than stating concerns that reach back to Jesus. Even though this theology is probably the most widely read and influential in New Testament studies this century, it is far too skeptical in its handling of the documents, being too influenced by an excessive use of critical concerns.

In contrast, this volume works with the New Testament text as its reference point. A team of scholars was assembled based on their expertise in the given areas they were assigned. They are quite aware that much more could be said in each of the areas they address, but they were asked to highlight the major features of theological development within their areas. The historical concerns of exegesis or detailed attempts to reach back to the history that impacts the text or the specific original setting do not have a major place in this biblical theological treatment. The meaning of the scriptural text is the primary focus, especially how various passages on similar themes within each author's writing(s) fit together. This study seeks to surface the fundamental theological emphases of each New Testament writer. These studies work first with a biblical author's own categories, though many of the discussions proceed in groupings that can be easily related to more traditional systematics groupings. The goal has been to surface the basic theological structures and perspectives underlining the whole of an author's work. Details that fill in the basic structures raised by biblical theology can be found in exegetical commentaries on the key passages in question, while the way various passages fit into theological structures or systems that span the Bible can be examined in systematics discussions. Reading this volume should enable one to sense the unity between the authors of the New Testament, how they might say similar things in different ways, and where a biblical author has uniquely contributed to New Testament theology. Like light coming through a diamond, one should see both the diversity of color and the intensity of theological truth the New Testament offers.

10. Rudolf Bultmann, *Theology of the New Testament*, trans. Kendrick Grobel, 2 vols. (New York: Charles Scribner's & Sons, 1952, 1955). Similar in approach is Hans Conzelmann, *An Outline of the Theology of the New Testament*, trans. John Bowden (New York: Harper & Row, 1969). His approach also most parallels Bultmann's except that he has a separate section on the Synoptic Gospels and a section for John, while combining the theology of the primitive and Hellenistic communities. He is also less historically skeptical than Bultmann, though he is more skeptical than Goppelt or Jeremias.

11. In fact, one suspects that Jeremias and Goppelt may have written to attempt in part to challenge Bultmann at this point. See Bultmann, *Theology of the New Testament*, 3–32.

In the rich diversity of New Testament theology an inherent unity emerges around the activity of God through Jesus Christ. Promise is coming to fruition. Expectation is becoming reality. Salvation comes through Him, as He begins the work of reclaiming humanity for relationship with God. The creation groans for its final redemption and the Great Physician Jesus has come and will come to relieve its pain. The theology of the New Testament proclaims that message of hope through narrative, history, and argument. A biblical theology bridges the gap between the meaning of individual passages and the synthesis of theological proposition. The contributors of this volume offer this study with their hope that the reader will have a better appreciation of the richness and diversity of the biblical terrain, as well as the relationship between interpretation and theology. Sometimes standing on a high bridge allows one to see more clearly the sweep and progress of biblical hope. Sometimes by looking at the Bible from a new perspective old things are seen in a fresh way.

DARRELL L. BOCK

1

A THEOLOGY OF MATTHEW

DAVID K. LOWERY

Before considering particular aspects of the theological message of the gospel of Matthew, it will be helpful to think about the nature of the four gospels. Providing a brief definition of a gospel, however, is not so simple as it might seem since the Gospels function in a number of different ways. In one sense, the Gospels serve as biographies of Jesus. Matthew, for example, includes an account of events connected with the birth of Jesus, aspects of His life in public ministry, and His death. Like most biographies, it provides insight into its subject not simply by chronicling the words and deeds that were a part of that life but also by interpreting their significance for the reader.

Unlike most modern biographies, however, the Gospels are relatively brief. Matthew, for example, devoted several extended sections of his gospel to Jesus' teaching, but each can be read in a few minutes' time. That the gospel writer was presenting a summary of Jesus' teaching seems clear. Comparison of similar passages in the Gospels suggests too that each writer exercised freedom (in comparison to the constraints usually associated with modern historiography) in presenting and arranging this material. This freedom allowed each author, under the inspiration of the Holy Spirit, to highlight different aspects of Jesus' words and deeds. The result is that their accounts provide cumulatively a richer understanding of the significance of His life and ministry.

DAVID K. LOWERY, B.A., Th.M., Ph.D., is professor of New Testament studies at Dallas Theological Seminary.

Although Jesus is the focal point of the Gospels, an account of His life and teachings is not their sole concern. The Gospels also help readers understand some of the factors that led to the formation of the church, since the disciples whom Jesus drew around Him and whom He instructed became its founding members. Considering what Jesus said and did with His first disciples serves to answer in part a crucial question: "How did we get to where we are today?" The Gospels therefore are also pastoral homilies, sermons in writing that seek to gain from every reader an affirmative and practical response.

GOD

While Jesus' life and ministry are the focus of Matthew's gospel, he makes it clear that what Jesus said and did, as well as the events that conspired to bring Him to the cross, are a part of the plan and purpose of God. A primary means of making this point is in the frequent linkage of events in the life of Jesus to passages from the Old Testament. To one degree or another all the gospel writers portray Jesus' life and ministry as the fulfillment of Old Testament prophecy and expectation. But Matthew is particularly distinctive in this regard. His gospel is characterized by a series of Old Testament quotations introduced by a phrase using the verb "fulfill" in the passive voice (*plērothēnai*). The first occurrence illustrates the nature of these introductions: "All this took place to fulfill what the Lord had said through the prophet" (Matt. 1:22). This is followed by a quotation of Isaiah 7:14. The event or circumstance is said to have happened in accord with God's plan and purpose.[1]

Several of these citations are linked with the circumstances of Jesus' birth and the family's subsequent flight to Egypt and return to settle in Nazareth. From a human point of view these events seem oddly at variance with the auspicious beginning normally associated with a king, especially one who is divine. Even in His early days the "beloved Son" and His family had to flee persecution in Israel. They returned only to take up residence in the "backwoods" of Galilee, far removed from the center of political and religious influence in Jerusalem where a Davidic king would be expected to reside. But by means of these Old Testament citations Matthew showed that in these apparently spontaneous exigencies the purposeful hand of God may be seen fulfilling His plan in the life of Jesus.

That the purpose of God is achieved despite adverse circumstances and deplorable individual behavior is illustrated also by Matthew in the presentation of Jesus' genealogy. In the first verse of his Gospel, Matthew said Jesus is a descendant of both David and Abraham. The significance of those designations for Matthew's portrait of Jesus will be explored subsequently. For now suffice it to say that His Abrahamic and Davidic lineage involved not a few distressing twists and turns which nevertheless did not deter the outworking of the divine plan.

---

1. There are eleven citations like this (1:22–23; 2:5–6; 2:15; 2:17–18; 2:23; 4:14–16; 8:17; 12:17–21; 13:35; 21:4–5; 27:9–10). To this may be added 26:56, where no specific Old Testament passage is cited: "This has all taken place that the writings of the prophets might be fulfilled."

The mention of the four women in Jesus' genealogy (Matt. 1:1–17) is an illustration of this. Why Matthew chose to mention these women, contrary to the usual practice of citing men only, cannot be determined with certainty. But it is noteworthy that Tamar (v. 3), Rahab (v. 5), Ruth (v. 5), and Bathsheba (v. 6, named only as "Uriah's wife") were Gentiles, and, in the case of Tamar, Rahab, and Bathsheba, each was linked with acts of immorality. They serve to remind readers both that God has shown mercy to "unworthy" Gentiles in the past and also that the plan of God is not frustrated by human failure. The lineage of the Messiah is checkered with some dubious characters, the sort a selective genealogist might be inclined to leave unmentioned. Though they are not meant to be models of behavior (as will be seen, Matthew set forth the highest ethical standards), they are a reminder that the grace of God is often extended to the unlikeliest people who in turn serve to advance His purposes in the world.

This theme, that the plan of God advances by means of the unlikeliest people and in the face of inscrutable circumstances, appears repeatedly in Matthew's gospel. A classic text in this regard is Jesus' prayer of thanksgiving and praise to God: "I praise you, Father, Lord of heaven and earth, because you have hidden these things from the wise and learned, and revealed them to little children. Yes, Father, for this was your good pleasure" (11:25–26; cf. Luke 10:21). This statement is connected with the theme of the preceding section, the mission of the disciples (beginning at Matt. 9:35). It is both a reminder that the response accorded their preaching is inseparably related to the work of God in opening hearts and minds to the message they proclaimed and also a reminder that this grace is most often extended to those who are little esteemed by society at large.

The disciples themselves are a case in point. A motley band of diverse characters, they seem unlikely candidates for the role of representing Jesus and advancing His ministry. Yet these are the ones to whom God has given revelation concerning who Jesus is. This is brought out clearly in Matthew's account of Peter's confession. In reply to the question, "Who do people say the Son of Man is?" Peter answered: "You are the Christ, the Son of the living God" (16:13, 16). But Jesus' response makes it clear that Peter had not arrived at this fact by his own cleverness or intellectual ability, however considerable they may have been (v. 17). Peter was one of the "little children" mentioned by Jesus in 11:25, to whom God had revealed this truth. Notice Matthew's distinctive record of Jesus' words to Peter on this occasion: "Blessed are you, Simon son of Jonah, for this was not revealed to you by man, but by my Father in heaven" (16:17). It is God who reveals (the same verb, *apokaluptō,* is used in both 11:25 and 16:17) this truth to people in accord with His "good pleasure" (11:26).

The same view of the sovereign work of God revealing truth to some but not to others is also expressed by Jesus in answer to the disciples' question about His use of parables (13:10: "Why do you speak to the people in parables?"). He answered, "The knowledge of the secrets of the kingdom of heaven has been given to you, but not to them" (v. 11). The use of the passive verb ("has been given") in this statement is sometimes called a "divine passive."[2] In this way Jewish writers or speakers could refer to an action of God without explicitly mentioning His name, a manner of speech considered reverential.[3] But it was understood who carried out the action of the verb. The point once again is that the act of revelation whereby people understand and believe the message proclaimed by Jesus is something God does.

Whereas these statements may be discomfiting to those who think of themselves as masters of their own destiny, it is unlikely that Matthew recorded them solely for that purpose. Rather, these affirmations about God's sovereignty, particularly connected to a positive response to the message from and about Jesus, serve to quiet concerns the disciples may have had about their own suitability and effectiveness for the task entrusted to them. The reception accorded the message they proclaim is ultimately God's doing, not theirs. They had a ministry to discharge and were to do so in a manner pleasing to God, but the results were not their responsibility. This is a liberating concept, not only to those beset with self-doubt (moments of which the average individual called on to carry on Jesus' work would understandably have) but also to those besotted with self-confidence (Peter had his moments, as do others), who seek through winsomeness or manipulative skill to magnify the effect of the gospel among their hearers. To a beleaguered minority, which the church in the first century generally was, assurance about God's sovereignty was an encouraging word. Thinking of this sort could, of course, lead to passivity or produce an escapist mentality, but Matthew's presentation goes a long way toward precluding that eventuality.

For one thing, Matthew did not hesitate to record the fact that both John the Baptist and Jesus fulfilled the will of God and in doing so followed a path that led to martyrdom. The hand of God in this is seen at the very outset of Jesus' entrance into a life of public ministry. Immediately after Jesus' baptism, with the words of God, "This is my Son, whom I love; with him I am well pleased" (3:17) still ringing in the reader's ears, Matthew recorded the temptation of Jesus, introducing it with these words: "Then Jesus was led by the Spirit into the desert to be tempted by the devil" (4:1). Each of the synoptic writers recorded this in his own way, but Matthew's readers cannot miss the fact that the hand of God was in this experience of temptation for Jesus. He is led (a passive verb) by the Spirit (the agent of God)[4]

---

2. Cf. Friedrich Blass and Albert Debrunner, *A Greek Grammar of the New Testament and Other Early Christian Literature*, trans. Robert W. Funk from the 9th–10th German ed. (Chicago: Univ. of Chicago, 1961), 313; and Joachim Jeremias, *The Parables of Jesus*, 8th ed. (London: SCM, 1972), 203 n. 57.

3. This method of expression was also related to a concern not to take the name of God in vain (Ex. 20:7). An obvious preventive was to use the name of God as infrequently as possible. In this way there arose metaphorical circumlocutions (the abode of God, "heaven" in place of "God") and the use of the passive verb (avoiding the mention of God as the subject of the verb).

4. In Matthew 3:16 the Gospel writer modified mention of the Spirit with the genitive "of God," signifying either that the Spirit "belongs" to God (possession) or comes from Him (source). In either case, the Holy Spirit is the agent who carries out the will of God.

in order to be tempted (another passive verb, this time an infinitive of purpose) by the devil (the agent of the temptation). In view of the citations from Deuteronomy subsequently referred to by Jesus in the passage (4:4, 7, 10), the reader should think of the experience of Israel in the wilderness as the Old Testament counterpart to this trial of Jesus (cf. Deut. 8:2). But the reader may be excused if the story of Job also comes to mind. Although what happened to Job is shown clearly to be known by God, at least in that account Satan came to God, as it were, to seek permission for what ensued. In the case of Jesus, He was led into this temptation by the Spirit! The final petition of the Lord's (model) Prayer takes on special significance when seen in light of Jesus' experience in the wilderness: "And lead us not into temptation, but deliver us from the evil one" (Matt. 6:13). James correctly affirmed that God Himself does not tempt anyone (James 1:13), but Matthew leaves no doubt that He sometimes permits temptation to befall His children.

Matthew likewise made clear that trials may lead to martyrdom, as it did for John and Jesus. In Jesus' missionary charge to the disciples, Matthew included this word of warning from Jesus: "Do not be afraid of those who kill the body but cannot kill the soul. Rather, be afraid of the One who can destroy both soul and body in hell. Are not two sparrows sold for a penny? Yet not one of them will fall to the ground apart from the will of your Father" (10:28–29). If someone were to devise a "frightful sayings" category for biblical statements, this would be a candidate. Yet it too provides a word of assurance regarding the outworking of God's plan for His people in the world. The experience of opposition, persecution, even martyrdom, is not an indication that God has cut His people loose, or turned His back on them. They are experiences that happen, as they did to John and Jesus, to the choicest of God's servants. The sparrow does not fall apart from the will of God. But the sparrow does fall. Such is Matthew's vision of the will of God.

This is certainly not all Matthew wrote about the way God is carrying out His plan for this world through His servants in the church. But it is a reminder that the God whom Matthew portrayed often accomplishes His purposes in unexpected and, from a human point of view, sometimes perilous ways. In so doing, however, He is not a God removed from His people and indifferent to their plight. He is intimately concerned with their well-being, aware of their need, and solicitous for their care.

Several passages in the Sermon on the Mount make this point. As an introductory statement to the Lord's Prayer, the disciples were assured of God's knowledgeable concern for them: "Your Father knows what you need before you ask him" (6:8). This assurance is repeated a few verses later when the disciples were told that they need not worry about adequate food and clothing since, "Your heavenly Father knows that you need them" (v. 32) and "all these things will be given to you" (v. 33). In the same manner God is described as a giver of "good gifts" to those who ask Him (7:11). These "good gifts" include not only the necessities of physical life but also the spiritual blessings associated with the gospel (cf. the use of the same word, *agatha,* "good" in Rom. 10:15 [Isa. 52:7] and Heb. 10:1).[5]

---

5. The parallel statement in Luke's gospel (11:13) refers to God giving the Holy Spirit, the agent of the many "good gifts" connected with the blessings of salvation.

God's care for all members of the community of disciples is brought out also in the parable of the lost sheep (Matt. 18:12–14), recorded in a chapter containing various instructions about the maintenance of right relationships with those who are followers of Christ. This parable is introduced by a verse that emphasizes the importance to God of those who for various reasons might be little esteemed by others in the community. It is actually a warning: "See that you do not look down on these little ones. For I tell you that their angels in heaven always see the face of my Father in heaven" (18:10). While this verse has sometimes been understood to say that all Christians have a guardian angel assigned to their care, that is probably an overinterpretation of the statement. What is affirmed is that angels from the highest order (those nearest to God) carry out ministry to those poorly esteemed (*kataphroneō* means "to look down" or "treat with contempt"[6]) by human society. This is a reminder both that God's values differ from humanity's and also that one's estimate of the importance of others may differ from God's estimate and may therefore be in need of revision.

The parable of the lost sheep (18:12–14) is an illustration of this. Jesus focused on a member of the community who had gone astray (the descriptive word, *planaō*, means "lead astray" or "cause to wander," hence "deceive" or "mislead"). The response of some may be to say, "Good riddance" or "We're glad he's gone." But however prone some may be to treat this wandering one with contempt, Jesus' words here are a sharp reminder that to God, the weak and wavering person is important. This one should be solicitously sought and, if possible, saved from the error of his way. God is "not willing that any of these little ones should be lost" (18:14). This affirmation of God's concern for the lost is not limited to those who count themselves disciples. Matthew also recorded Jesus' words about God's care for the world generally as a basis for exhorting disciples to demonstrate love to all people, even adversaries: "Love your enemies and pray for those who persecute you, that you may be sons of your Father in heaven. He causes his sun to rise on the evil and the good, and sends rain on the righteous and the unrighteous" (5:44–45).

The point is clear enough. God bestows natural blessings comprehensively and unconditionally. In the same way, disciples are to love others, do what is best for them, and pray that the enemy may become an ally. There seems to be a certain dissonance in the comparison, however, because of the variance between the natural and the spiritual. Sun and rain can be seen and felt. Prayer is certainly less tangible. Giving bread to an enemy seems a more apt comparison, but the somewhat enigmatic illustration is common to Jesus' teaching style. It provoked thought and gave no place for complacency. And as is often the case, the Old Testament provided a point of connection that serves to illuminate and reveal the comparison's symmetry.

---

6. Walter Bauer, William F. Arndt, and F. Wilbur Gingrich, *A Greek-English Lexicon of the New Testament and Other Early Christian Literature*, 2d ed., rev. F. Wilbur Gingrich and Frederick W. Danker (Chicago: Univ. of Chicago, 1979), 420.

In the Old Testament God's ordering of sun and rain is not portrayed simply in terms of a natural blessing. Rather, the elements of nature also bear witness to God: "The heavens declare the glory of God; the skies proclaim the work of his hands. . . . Their voice goes out into all the earth, their words to the ends of the world" (Ps. 19:1, 4). The account of Paul's protest against the adulation directed at Barnabas and him likewise testifies to the witness of nature: "He has not left himself without testimony: He has shown kindness by giving you rain from heaven and crops in their seasons" (Acts 14:17).[7] The natural elements are a declaration of God to all humanity about Himself.[8] In their response of love to all people disciples similarly are to bear witness to God and manifest His kindness through their deeds. The comparison comes together then in the goal of the missionary enterprise, bringing people to a place where they too can glorify God and pray with meaning the opening petition of the Lord's Prayer: "Our Father in heaven, hallowed be your name" (6:9). But that is to anticipate another aspect of Matthew's theology. Before that is considered, however, attention must be given to the leading figure of Matthew's gospel.

CHRIST

The focus of the gospel of Matthew is the person of Jesus Christ. Some appreciation for who He is and what He does may be gained by considering the various titles given to Him. But titles alone do not exhaust Matthew's message about Jesus. The accounts of what Jesus said, did, and continues to do also give insight into who He is and show why He is the proper object of faith.

The first verse of the gospel contains four descriptive names or titles of Jesus: "Jesus Christ the son of David, the son of Abraham." The name given to Him at his birth, "Jesus," is the Greek form of the Hebrew name "Joshua," which means "the Lord saves." It was the name an angel of the Lord told Joseph to give to the son to be born to Mary, his betrothed (1:21). It was therefore chosen by God Himself, in whose behalf the angel spoke. The name described what Jesus was destined to do: "He will save his people from their sins" (1:21).

Accustomed to thinking of people having several given names, the last of which designates their family name, some may be similarly inclined to think of "Christ" as some sort of last or family name of Jesus. But it is actually a title or designation given to Him. Like the name "Jesus," it is also the Greek form of a Hebrew word—"Messiah"—and means "Anointed One," a person specially designated by God to carry out His will.

What God's will is for the Messiah is revealed in the testimony of the gospel to Jesus' life and ministry. The way in which the Messiah "will save his people from their sins" is quite different from what was most likely expected. Although it is difficult to determine with certainty what the general expectation for a messiah

---

7. Paul said much the same in his letter to the Romans (1:20).

8. In Isaiah 55:10–11, the word from God's mouth is likened to the rain from heaven which waters the earth.

was like among first-century Jews, it is probably fair to say that the idea of a suffering and humiliated one did not figure very largely in the public imagination.[9]

Matthew showed that those most closely associated with Jesus—His disciples—found His comments about His impending suffering and death objectionable (16:21–23) and grievous (17:22–23). Little wonder then that He generally sought to maintain a relatively low profile in the course of His ministry and attempted to limit the spread of reports about His miraculous deeds which might understandably feed nationalistic hopes for a political liberator.[10] But political liberation was not His immediate goal, notwithstanding His acknowledged kingly lineage.

"SON OF DAVID"

The third designation applied to Jesus in the first verse of the gospel focuses on His kingly lineage as a descendant of David with a rightful claim to Israel's throne. The ensuing genealogy makes this point emphatically by dividing Jesus' family tree into three generational blocks of fourteen names each,[11] a number which corresponds to the cumulative sum of the Hebrew letters in the name "David": daleth = 4; waw = 6; daleth = 4.[12]

This underscoring of Jesus' Davidic connections relates to the gospel's assertion that Jesus is indeed the King of Israel, though the display of His kingship differs markedly from the norm. He is a king characterized by humility, as Matthew quoting from Zechariah 9:9 declares: "Say to the Daughter of Zion, 'See, your king comes to you, gentle and riding on a donkey'" (Matt. 21:5). But He is nonetheless a king, a fact He acknowledged under interrogation by Pilate: "'Are you the king of the Jews?' 'Yes, it is as you say,' Jesus replied" (27:11). It is a truth with which He was mocked by the Roman soldiers: "Hail, King of the Jews!" (v. 29). And it is included in the announcement placarded above Him on the cross: "This is Jesus, the King of the Jews" (v. 37).

But if the kingship of His first coming is marked by humiliation, it will not be so at His return. Here Matthew portrays Jesus as the exalted King, seated on His throne in heavenly glory (25:31). He epitomizes the reversal that will characterize the people of God generally (19:28). No longer the One who is judged, He will dispense judgment and will vindicate the righteous (25:34, 40).

---

9. See Jacob Neusner, William Green, Ernest Frerichs, eds., *Judaisms and Their Messiahs at the Turn of the Christian Era* (New York: Cambridge Univ., 1987).

10. This is one factor in the question of why Jesus tried to keep His messiahship a secret, a phenomenon particularly associated with Mark's account of His ministry.

11. This arrangement counts Jeconiah twice in the process, at the end of the second block (1:11) and at the beginning of the third (v. 12), which ends with Jesus as the fourteenth (v. 16).

12. This literary convention, which the Jews called *gematria* (a borrowing from the Greek word for "geometry"), is curious to modern readers but relatively ordinary and generally comprehensible to both Jewish and Gentile readers in Matthew's day. See *Encyclopaedia Judaica* (New York: Macmillan, 1971), 7:369–74.

"SON OF ABRAHAM"

The fourth designation, "son of Abraham," is a further reminder that Jesus was a Jew, a descendant of Abraham, the father of the Israelite nation.[13] It may be too that readers are to think of the promise God made to Abraham, that "in you all the families of the earth will be blessed" (Gen. 12:3 NASB), and to see in the life and ministry of Jesus, Abraham's son, the fulfillment of that promise.

"SON OF GOD"

This is one of the more common titles for Jesus in Matthew's gospel and, some would say, the most important.[14] In the Old Testament, Israel as a whole (Hos. 11:1) and different groups or individuals within Israel, such as individual kings (2 Sam. 7:14) or priests (Mal. 1:6), were sometimes called sons of God. In the New Testament, Christians are also called sons of God (e.g., Rom. 8:14).

The significance of the idea of sonship applied to these various groups is that those who are called sons are expected to represent God their Father faithfully and to carry out His will. The same idea is central to the use of the title with regard to Jesus. Unlike anyone else, He faithfully carried out the will of God the Father, a fact poignantly affirmed in His prayer in Gethsemane: "My Father . . . may your will be done" (Matt. 26:42).

"Son of God" is thus first a functional description. It does, of course, have relevance for understanding Jesus' status and relationship to God, but the fact that others have been and will be called "sons of God" is a reminder that it is less an ontological statement or confirmation of His deity, and more an ethical or functional affirmation that Jesus did in fact carry out the will of His Father.

There is, of course, no question about His deity. His conception was "from the Holy Spirit" (1:20). He is called "Immanuel," which means "God with us" (1:23). He has been given "all authority in heaven and on earth" (28:18). But the designation "Son of God" gives particular attention to His manner of life. In this area too He showed Himself unique.

"SON OF MAN"

If any title rivals "Son of God" for place of greatest importance as a descriptive designation for Jesus, it is the title "Son of Man." Jesus used this designation of Himself more often than the other titles. Some would say it has no more significance than that of an ambiguous circumlocution, a roundabout way by which Jesus could say things about Himself without using the personal pronoun "I." The validity of this contention is illustrated by the fact that the gospel writers sometimes interchange "I" and "Son of Man" in their reporting of His statements.

---

13. The Jewish historian Josephus refers to him as "our father Abraham" (*Jewish Antiquities* 1.158; cf. John 8:39). In the New Testament another designation for Jesus is "seed of Abraham" (John 8:33, 37; Rom. 9:7; 11:1).

14. Jack Kingsbury, *Matthew: Structure, Christology, Kingdom* (Philadelphia: Fortress, 1975).

Two passages in Matthew 16 illustrate this. In the question Jesus put to Peter concerning His identity, Matthew wrote, "Who do people say the Son of Man is?" (16:13), while Mark has, "Who do you say I am?" (Mark 8:29), and Luke has, "Who do the crowds say I am?" (Luke 9:18). A few verses later Matthew recorded Jesus' first prediction of His impending death with the words, "He must go to Jerusalem and suffer many things" (Matt. 16:21), while Mark and Luke wrote, "the Son of Man must suffer many things" (Mark 8:31; Luke 9:22).

That the gospel writers exercised comparative freedom in interchanging the designation "Son of Man" with a personal pronoun does not mean the title had no theological significance for them. It means only that they had no doubt that readers would know that the designation applied to Jesus alone. The theological background to the term is likely found in Daniel 7:13–14, based on Jesus' statement at His trial before the Sanhedrin: "You will see the Son of Man sitting at the right hand of the Mighty One and coming on the clouds of heaven" (Matt. 26:64).

This passage neatly illustrates the dual significance of the designation as it is used in Matthew (and in the other Synoptic Gospels). Jesus was in the midst of the humiliation that would culminate in the cross; yet He referred to His future exaltation. Most of the other uses of this designation in the Gospel fall into one or the other of these categories, either the present humiliation of the Son of Man or His future exaltation in which He will manifest the prerogatives of deity. The reader of the gospel of Matthew can thus see in the use of this designation of Jesus that both aspects, the humiliation and the exaltation, are experiences of Jesus. These two experiences are temporally differentiated, however, so that humiliation characterized for the most part the course of His earthly life. But after the resurrection Jesus entered into His exalted role. All authority in heaven and on earth is given to Him (28:18), though the earthly manifestation of that exalted glory will be fully displayed only at His second coming. "At that time the sign of the Son of Man will appear in the sky, and all the nations of the earth will mourn. They will see the Son of Man coming on the clouds of the sky with power and great glory" (24:30). The assurance of this ultimate vindication despite the reality of His present humiliation may explain Jesus' preference for this enigmatic expression as His self-designation of choice, a title which in some measure captures the enigma of the Incarnation: God became man to be ultimately hailed as Lord of all.

"LORD"

One might be inclined to think that of all the designations applied to Jesus, the title "Lord" would connote as clearly as any the reality of His deity. In English translations of the gospel, this is probably true. But the Greek word *kyrios,* translated "Lord," has a broader range of meaning. It can be used simply as a term of courteous respect. For example, when the chief priests and the Pharisees came to Pilate to request that a guard be placed at Jesus' tomb, the report of their petition began with the (vocative of) address *kyrie,* which English translations appropriately render "Sir" (27:63). The Jews were not portrayed as according divine prerogatives to Pilate; they simply addressed him with respect.

On the other hand, *kyrios* is customarily used as the title of God in the Greek translation of the Old Testament, so that Old Testament citations in the gospel commonly refer to God in this way. This "divine" usage is significant in light of Jesus' discussion with the Pharisees about His sonship. The question is posed this way: "What do you think about the Christ? Whose son is he?" (22:42). When they rightly answered that He is David's son, Jesus posed a conundrum for them, based on Psalm 110:1: "How is it then that David, speaking by the Spirit, calls him 'Lord'? For he says, " 'The Lord said to my Lord: "Sit at my right hand until I put your enemies under your feet." ' If then David calls him 'Lord,' how can he be his son?" (Matt. 22:43–45). The superiority of Christ to David is certainly affirmed here, and the implication of Christ's deity, in view of the play on "Lord," is seen as well.

That Matthew saw divine prerogatives associated with the title "Lord" are clear from two passages concerned with Jesus as the Judge who determines individuals' destinies. According to 7:22, many will profess allegiance to Jesus and be numbered among His followers but they will ultimately be banished from His presence. "Many will say to me on that day, 'Lord, Lord did we not prophesy in your name, and in your name drive out demons and perform many miracles?' Then I will tell them plainly, 'I never knew you. Away from me, you evildoers!' " (7:22–23)

In this context, calling Jesus "Lord" formally identifies these individuals as followers of Christ, but ultimately this profession of faith is shown by their deeds to be false. It is noteworthy that the deeds that betray their false profession are not the miraculous and the spectacular. Their claims with regard to these deeds are not denied. Rather, they have not done the will of God (v. 21); the apparently prosaic and unspectacular deeds have been left undone. What that might mean is illustrated in part by the second passage of relevance to Jesus as Lord and ultimate Judge.

The account of the judgment of the nations, compared to a separation of sheep from goats, is also a passage distinctive to Matthew's gospel (25:31–46). Here too Jesus as the Judge of all humankind is hailed as "Lord" by both the blessed (v. 34) and the cursed (v. 41). What is cited as evidence for the reality of that profession is the attention given to those whom Jesus called "the least of these brothers of mine" (v. 40), with whom He identified so that He could speak of acts done to them as done to Him (cf. 10:42). Though the cursed hail Jesus as "Lord," they show by their deeds that they are not His sheep.

That both the blessed and the cursed acknowledge Jesus as Lord coheres with the conviction that "God exalted him to the highest place and gave him the name that is above every name that at the name of Jesus every knee should bow . . . and every tongue confess that Jesus Christ is Lord" (Phil. 2:9–11). "Lord," therefore, is a title associated with Jesus' exercise of divine prerogatives, suggestive of His deity.

"Lord" is also the designation Matthew seemed to regard as most appropriate on the lips of disciples. In addition to the two passages discussed above, comparison with two accounts also recorded by Mark and Luke illustrates this. The first is in the account of the stilling of the storm on the sea of Galilee (Matt. 8:23–27;

Mark 4:35–41; Luke 8:22–25). Although Jesus was with them, asleep in the boat, the disciples, afraid of perishing, called to Him for help. But each writer recorded a different form of address: for Luke, it is "Master" (Luke 8:24); Mark used "Teacher" (Mark 4:38); and Matthew wrote "Lord" (Matt. 8:25).

The same pattern occurs in the account of Jesus' transfiguration (Matt. 17:1–9; Mark 9:2–10; Luke 9:28–36). At the appearance of Moses and Elijah in conversation with Jesus, Peter made a proposal. Again, each writer recorded a different form of address consistent with what was used earlier: for Luke it is "Master" (Luke 9:33); for Mark, "Rabbi," a synonym for "Teacher" (Mark 9:5); and Matthew used "Lord" (Matt. 17:4).

Matthew seems to have been saying to his readers that a most suitable way to address Jesus is to call him "Lord." This title acknowledges both Jesus' authority and the responsibility disciples have to obey His commands (28:20).

OTHER DESIGNATIONS AND ROLES

This brief survey of names and titles or designations given to Jesus in the gospel of Matthew is not intended to suggest that understanding these alone will give exhaustive insight into His character and person. They represent but one avenue by which a reader may gain an appreciation for His life and ministry and in turn make an appropriate response. What Jesus said and how He conducted Himself are obviously also a crucial part of the process by which disciples form a right assessment of the Teacher and Master they are to emulate (10:25).

The mention of the role of teacher is a good example of this. Although Jesus was often called "Teacher" by those outside the circle of disciples (8:19; 9:11; 12:38; 17:24; 19:16) or addressed as "Rabbi" on two occasions by Judas (26:25, 49), Matthew never had the disciples referring to Jesus in this way. Yet it is clear that Matthew regarded Jesus as a teacher, or better "the Teacher," in view of the fact that he recorded Jesus applying this title to Himself on two occasions (23:10; 26:18)[15] and included in his gospel extended sections of Jesus' teaching. Matthew introduced his record of Jesus' Sermon on the Mount, for example, with the words "He began to teach them" (5:2), and Matthew noted at the conclusion of the sermon that "the crowds were amazed at His teaching, because He taught as one who had authority" (7:28–29). Clearly Jesus is a Teacher without peer, though in Matthew's gospel no disciple ever called him "Teacher."

The same is true regarding the designation "Servant." Jesus is never specifically called a "Servant," but the text of Isaiah 42:1–4 ("Here is my servant whom I have chosen," author's trans.) is applied to Him in connection with His healing ministry (Matt. 12:18–21). In addition, Isaiah 53:4 is cited in regard to Him in Matthew 8:17, also in connection with His ministry of healing. And Isaiah 53 may form

---

15. The usual word for "teacher," *didaskalos,* also occurs in Matthew 23:8. It probably is a reference to Jesus as well, although the fact that the Father is mentioned in verse 9, and Christ in verse 10, might suggest that the teacher of verse 8 is understood to be the Holy Spirit. The word in verse 10 to describe Christ as teacher, *kathēgētēs,* occurs only here in the New Testament.

the backdrop to His statement that the Son of Man "did not come to be served, but to serve, and to give his life as a ransom for many" (Matt. 20:28). Though the extent to which this portrait of Jesus is influenced by the Servant of Isaiah may be debated, it is clear that Matthew showed Jesus as One who was a servant. And Matthew set forth His example as a model for disciples to follow.[16]

Some interpreters of the gospel also think Matthew presented Jesus as the "Wisdom" of God, applying to Jesus a personification found in Proverbs 8:12–36 and developed in Jewish intertestamental literature (such as the Old Testament apocryphal book, Sirach).[17] If the support for this identification is not entirely convincing, it is nevertheless true that Jesus' manner of life illustrates the principles of wisdom, the application of God's revelation to the situations of daily life and, like wisdom, He invites others to emulate His manner of life (Matt. 11:28–30, cf. Sirach 51:23–30).

Matthew's portrait of Jesus ably shows Him to be "gentle and humble in heart" (Matt. 11:29), a description underscored by applying the words of Isaiah (42:2–3) to Him: "He will not quarrel or cry out; no one will hear his voice in the streets. A bruised reed he will not break, and a smoldering wick he will not snuff out" (Matt. 12:19–20). Yet Matthew also showed Jesus, even in His humility, as One already exercising great authority so that disease (8:1–4), infirmity (vv. 5–13), sickness (vv. 14–15), demons (v.16), the powers of the natural world (vv. 23–27), and death itself (9:18–26) submitted to His bidding.

To what extent these deeds are intended to be glimpses of His own authority (which the subsequent "investiture" at His resurrection simply acknowledges as now operative on a wider scale, 28:18), or whether they are meant to be seen as deeds done by means of the Spirit's power (12:28), is perhaps a question Matthew would regard as moot or inconsequential, if not simply pedantic. But the coming of the Spirit on Jesus at His baptism (3:16) and the pronouncement of God (v. 17) appear to be a commission and endowment with authority,[18] subsequently seen and acknowledged as from God (9:8). But trying to distinguish divine authority and the ministry of the Spirit may go beyond what it is necessary to know. Still, though references to the Spirit are relatively rare in Matthew's gospel, it is a subject of importance to consider.

THE HOLY SPIRIT

References to the Spirit occur only twelve times altogether in Matthew's gospel, with one-third of them in chapter 12. As might be expected in a gospel

---

16. The conjunction, "just as" (*hōsper*), which begins 20:28, introduces an example in light of the preceding admonition in verses 26–27.

17. Jack Suggs, *Wisdom, Christology, and Law in Matthew's Gospel* (Cambridge, Mass.: Harvard Univ., 1970); Frederick Burnett, *The Testament of Jesus-Sophia* (Washington, D.C.: Catholic Univ., 1981); cf. Celia Deutsch, *Hidden Wisdom and the Easy Yoke* (Sheffield, U.K.: Sheffield, 1987).

18. The pronouncement draws on two passages (Ps. 2:7; Isa. 42:1) which relate to the onset of divinely appointed roles.

concerned to interpret the significance of the life and ministry of Jesus, most of the references describe the work of the Spirit in relation to Him.

Mention has already been made of those references that speak of the Spirit as the life-imparting agent in Jesus' birth (1:18, 20). So too some consideration has been given to the significance of the coming of the Spirit on Jesus at the beginning of His public ministry (3:16; 12:18). In the only specific comment of Jesus about the relationship of the Spirit to His ministry, He attributed His performance of exorcisms to the agency of the Spirit: "I drive out demons by the Spirit of God" (12:28).[19] Whether this statement can be extrapolated to explain the performance of all His miraculous deeds may be debated, but there is nothing theologically problematic in doing so nor is it inconsistent with the portrait of Jesus in the wider context of the New Testament.[20]

In one of John the Baptist's announcements about Jesus, John told the people that Jesus "will baptize you with the Holy Spirit and fire" (3:11). It is possible that the association of fire with the Spirit is a reference to a cleansing or purifying work which the Spirit will accomplish. More likely, however, in view of the following verse (v. 12), which refers to burning chaff with unquenchable fire, two broadly summarizing aspects of Jesus' work are in view. John's statement appears to bring together distinguishing features of Jesus' first and second coming.[21] The baptism of the Spirit is associated with the blessings of salvation, and fire represents the awful destiny of those sent from the presence of Jesus the Judge (13:40–42; 25:41). The alternative experiences open to all humankind are thus represented in the references to the Spirit and fire.

John did not say when Jesus will baptize with the Spirit. A conclusion about this relates, in part, to some of the discussion earlier on the relationship of Jesus' authority to the role of the Spirit. While readers of the New Testament might be inclined to think that the baptism of the Spirit predicted by John was fulfilled initially at Pentecost (Acts 2) and thereafter in conjunction with the experience of conversion (1 Cor. 12:13), it may be that a preliminary or provisional "baptism" of the Spirit is associated with the disciples' commission to extend Jesus' ministry to Israel.

---

19. This quotation is drawn from the first part of a conditional statement ("if . . . then"), but it is clearly a proposition which hearers and readers are expected to regard as true.

20. Philippians 2:7, for example, refers to Jesus "making himself nothing." The statement might also be translated, "emptied himself" (NASB), in willingly becoming a man. The Greek word *keneō* has been taken to describe the decision by the Son willingly to forego the use of His own divine prerogatives in His incarnation. Thus when the disciples asked Jesus about the time of the end, this had not been revealed to the Son, who refused to avail Himself of His divine power and replied in effect, "I do not know" (Matt. 24:36).

21. It is possible that John himself did not recognize any temporal distinctions in the fulfillment of Jesus' work. This fact may account for his question concerning Jesus' messiahship (11:2–3). Languishing in prison, John may well have wondered why the vindication of the righteous and the judgment of the wicked did not proceed at a more rapid pace.

Matthew's account of this occurs in his tenth chapter. In the first verse he recorded that Jesus "gave them authority to drive out evil spirits and to heal every disease and sickness" (Matt. 10:1; cf. v. 8). Presumably the means by which the disciples were able to do this was the same as that of Jesus—the Holy Spirit (12:28) —though this is not explicitly stated at this point in the narrative.[22] However, the provision of the Spirit is mentioned later in the discourse in connection with the assurance that the disciples need not worry about how they should respond if they were arraigned before Jewish or Gentile courts because of their ministry (10:17–20).

The mention here of this ministry of the Spirit might be a further indication that the Spirit is indeed provisionally given in the course of this first mission of the disciples. A cautionary factor in coming too easily to that conclusion, however, relates to the fact that Jesus' instructions about the missionary enterprise that disciples are to undertake seems to anticipate a wider mission than the first one on which they were sent. In this first commission the disciples were to restrict their ministry to Israel (10:5), but the assurance of the Spirit's aid is in connection with witness before Gentile courts as well (v. 18). Jesus' remarks, therefore, seem to anticipate future missions, and it may be that some of these warnings and promises are meant to be construed in light of Pentecost.

The role of the Spirit as central to the missionary enterprise and indeed to the experience of forgiveness is made clear by what is said concerning blasphemy of the Spirit: "Every sin and blasphemy will be forgiven men, but the blasphemy against the Spirit will not be forgiven. Anyone who speaks a word against the Son of Man will be forgiven, but anyone who speaks against the Holy Spirit will not be forgiven, either in this age or in the age to come" (12:31–32).

These verses have understandably troubled readers of the gospel for a number of different reasons. First, one may wonder what constitutes blasphemy, or speaking against the Spirit, since it is never defined. Second, given the lack of definition, how can one know whether such an act has been committed, even inadvertently, and so become guilty of a sin for which there is no forgiveness?

In answering questions of this sort several factors are relevant. For one thing, an awareness of the immediate context of the statement is essential to a proper understanding of its meaning. In this case Jesus had been accused of carrying out His ministry of exorcism by means of Satan (12:24), which amounted to a repudiation of Him and His message.

A second factor of relevance concerns what information the wider context of the Scriptures might bring to bear on the interpretation of any given passage. One aspect of the ministry of the Spirit is to bear witness to Christ. This is evident from Matthew's gospel since the deeds Jesus did by means of the Spirit attested to His

---

22. There is no indication that Judas was precluded from this privilege. By all appearances he too was able to perform miracles. This would then be one illustration of the situation envisioned in 7:21–23. If, as seems likely, these miracles were done by means of the Spirit, it also sheds light on a passage like Hebrews 6:4, where those who have "shared" in the Holy Spirit may nonetheless find themselves numbered among the lost.

messiahship. When John sent emissaries to question Jesus about His messiahship, Jesus replied by pointing to the things He had done (11:2–6). Therefore, to deny that these deeds are done by the Spirit and are thus authenticating of Jesus is ultimately to reject Him as the emissary of God and to cut oneself off from the salvation He provides.

Of relevance also is the fact that what Jesus said here, He gave by way of warning. This is not presented as a pronouncement of doom at this point, even against those who have made this preliminary judgment regarding Jesus. It is a warning that to persist in this judgment is ultimately to reject the witness of the Spirit concerning Jesus, an act that leads to perdition for its advocates. This seems to be the focus of the passage.

If that is so, it is doubtful that anyone who is concerned about committing this sin has reason to be so. And concerning others it is difficult, if not impossible, to determine when someone reaches the point of fully and finally rejecting the ministry of the Spirit concerning Jesus. Suffice it to say, however, that those who have come to this point are unlikely to be worried about it. Anxiety about eternal destiny is not a characteristic typically associated with the lost. As Matthew reminded the readers of his gospel, "In the days before the flood, people were eating and drinking, marrying and giving in marriage, up to the day Noah entered the ark; and . . . that is how it will be at the coming of the Son of Man" (24:38–39).

This is not to say that people cannot cross a line from which there is no going back. Judas may be a case in point of one who did (27:3–4), and the writer of Hebrews (6:4–6) may be warning about this as well. But it is unlikely that Matthew included this passage about rejecting the witness of the Spirit as a word of condemnation delivered after the fact. It is rather a word of warning that the testimony of the Spirit about Jesus must not be rejected.

Two final passages regarding the role of the Spirit may be noted, before some concluding observations on this aspect of Matthew's theology are made. The Spirit's role in the inspiration of Scripture is referred to in 22:43, where David's statement in Psalm 110:1 is attributed to "speaking by the Spirit." And the personality of the Holy Spirit, in equality with God the Father and God the Son, is expressed in Jesus' command to baptize disciples "in the name of the Father and of the Son and of the Holy Spirit" (28:19). Baptism is a visual testimony to a disciple's entrance into a relationship with the triune God.

This is an appropriate place to consider Jesus' two affirmations about His presence with His disciples, since the Spirit seems to be the unmentioned agent of this presence. In 18:20, Matthew recorded this statement by Jesus, "Where two or three come together in my name, there am I with them." This statement clearly anticipated Jesus' absence physically while affirming His presence spiritually. Similarly, the concluding statement of the gospel is Jesus' word of assurance: "I will be with you always, to the very end of the age" (28:20). If one asks how or in what sense Jesus is present with His disciples, the answer would seem to be that it is by means of the Holy Spirit. Here then is another illustration of the ministry of the

Spirit in pointing to Christ. Though physically absent, Jesus is present by means of the Spirit, who bears witness to Him and continues to extend ministry to others in His behalf.

THE KINGDOM OF HEAVEN/GOD

Before noting what Matthew wrote about "the kingdom of heaven," or "the kingdom of God," some consideration needs to be given to the meaning of the terms themselves. Normally the English word "kingdom" denotes the idea of a physical or spatial realm, a region, including people and land, over which a king exercises authority. This meaning also applies to the words used for "kingdom" in the Old and New Testaments.

However, "kingdom" can also refer to the exercise of rulership or authority. In this use of the term there is more of a dynamic or active sense, referring to the imposition of the will of the ruler or his sovereignty over his subjects. The word thus has both a static or spatial idea associated with it and also a dynamic or spiritual sense. The English word "dominion" might illustrate these senses, since it can be used for both the exercise of authority and a region or realm in which this authority is exercised.

It is not always clear if one or the other or both aspects of the meaning of "kingdom" are referred to in a particular Bible passage. At the end of Psalm 103, for example, this statement appears: "The Lord has established his throne in heaven, and his kingdom rules over all" (103:19). But another translation renders the second part of the verse this way: "His sovereignty rules over all" (NASB). This second translation makes good sense in view of the following verses which refer to angels who "obey his word" (v. 20) and "servants who do his will" (v. 21). Yet some sense of spatial significance is suggested as well by the subsequent phrase, "everywhere in his dominion" (v. 22). Thus both aspects of the word may be relevant in a particular passage, though one sense may predominate in any given instance.

There is also a temporal duality associated with the use of the word in the Old and New Testaments. Usually the kingdom of God is spoken of as a present reality. According to the psalmist, for example, "All you have made will praise you, O Lord; your saints will extol you. They will tell of the glory of your kingdom and speak of your might, so that all men may know of your mighty acts and the glorious splendor of your kingdom" (Ps. 145:10–12).

But in other passages a future kingdom, or what might better be described as a future manifestation of God's kingdom, is referred to. Isaiah looked forward to one who "will reign on David's throne and over his kingdom, establishing and upholding it with justice and righteousness from that time on and forever" (Isa. 9:7). And Daniel recorded a vision of "one like a son of man . . . and to him was given dominion, glory and a kingdom, that all the people, nations and men of every language might serve him. His dominion is an everlasting dominion which will not pass away; and his kingdom is one which will not be destroyed" (Dan. 7:13–14).

Similar meanings are associated with what Matthew has said about the kingdom of God or the kingdom of the Son of Man. But before some of those particular statements are examined, a general comment about an expression that is distinctive to Matthew's gospel is in order. The concern is his use of the phrase "kingdom of heaven" in passages where Mark or Luke in their accounts refer to the "kingdom of God" (e.g., Matt. 13:31; Mark 4:30; Luke 13:18).

The use of a passive verb to describe the action of God was previously noted as one way a reverential Jew could describe something God had done without mentioning His name (since the subject is more easily omitted with a passive verb). The substitution of "heaven," the abode of God in place of the name of God, is another form of this reverence. Only in Matthew's gospel does this phrase occur. He also used the expression "kingdom of God" four times (12:28; 19:24; 21:31, 43), however, thus suggesting that the difference in nomenclature is more a matter of preference or deference than anything else.

Why "the kingdom of heaven" is mentioned routinely in Matthew's gospel but never in the others is uncertain. Probably Jesus used both expressions, but Mark and Luke simply chose to use consistently the phrase "kingdom of God" because it was less ambiguous for Gentile readers than the more Jewish expression, "kingdom of heaven." It is clear that Matthew regarded the two phrases as virtually synonymous from a passage like 19:23–24, where Jesus said to the disciples, "It is hard for a rich man to enter the kingdom of heaven . . . it is easier for a camel to go through the eye of a needle than for a rich man to enter the kingdom of God."

Unlike many of the Old Testament passages that refer to the kingdom of God as a present reality, the references in Matthew's gospel generally have in view either a kingdom yet future or an entrance into the kingdom which is yet future. However, one passage that refers to the kingdom as a present reality is 12:28, with Jesus' statement about His exorcisms: "If I drive out demons by the Spirit of God, then the kingdom of God has come upon you."

The statement is phrased in the form of a conditional proposition, but the conclusion is clear enough. Even the Pharisees conceded that Jesus drove out demons (12:24). The dispute concerns the means. They said it was done by Satan, but Jesus said it was done by the Holy Spirit. Of course, Matthew left no doubt about which contention is correct. Jesus was driving out demons by means of the Holy Spirit. If that is so, said Jesus, then the kingdom has come.

The verb "has come" (*ephthasen*) is written in the past tense. While it is true in the case of Greek verbs generally that the tense is more significant with regard to the way the action of a verb is portrayed than the time frame in which it is depicted,[23] it is difficult to escape the conclusion that the past tense verb here also affirms that the kingdom of God was somehow present in the ministry of Jesus.

23. The verb *ephthasen* (the present tense or lexical form is *phthanō*) is written in the aorist tense (and the indicative mood, the form normally used to make an assertion or statement). The aorist is probably the least significant of the tenses in the way the action of the verb is portrayed (rivaled perhaps by the future) since it is commonly used to assert only that something happened.

But in what sense was the kingdom of God present? Probably in the way envisioned by the psalmist when he said, "that all men may know of your mighty acts and the glorious splendor of your kingdom" (Ps. 145:12). In Jesus' ministry the power of the Spirit gave expression to and demonstrated the authority of God. God's sovereign rule was manifested in the ministry of Jesus. Because of this those who witnessed Jesus' ministry and heard His message were at the same time confronted with a call to submit to the rule and reign of God, to enter, in that sense, into the kingdom of God, where those who are God's servants carry out His will.

Seen in this light, the announcement of John the Baptist that the kingdom of God was near or close at hand (*engiken,* 3:2),[24] is also understandable. John sought to prepare people to hear and respond to the message and ministry of Jesus by calling for repentance. In this regard John's ministry was a reminder of a truth formerly expressed: "a broken and contrite heart, O God, you will not despise" (Ps. 51:17). John wanted to bring people to a place of repentance, an admission of spiritual impotence and an acknowledgment of the fact that purity of heart is the work of God alone. In a similar way Jesus (Matt. 4:17), the disciples (10:7), and later missionaries like Paul (Acts 28:31; cf. 20:21) preached a comparable "gospel of the kingdom" (24:14).

That the kingdom of God, as God's rule and reign, existed before the ministry of Jesus is at least implied in the parable of the tenants (21:33–41), which depicts Israel's insolence and selfishness in routinely rejecting the owner's servants, culminated in killing the owner's son (cf. 23:37). Jesus then told the leaders of Israel that "the kingdom of God will be taken from you and given to a people who will produce its fruit" (21:43).

Apparently this means that Israel's stewardship of the kingdom in her role as the representative and proclaimer of God's rule and reign, was being taken away and given to others. Further attention will be given to this passage subsequently when the respective situations of Israel and the church are considered. For now it is enough to observe that the notion of the kingdom of God is not depicted as a recent phenomenon in God's dealing with Israel. They have been long-standing beneficiaries of the blessings of God's realm, yet have offered little more than animosity and hostility in return.[25]

If the notion of the kingdom was not new to Israel, John's remarks about the nearness of the kingdom (3:2) nonetheless suggest that a distinctive stage in that unfolding drama was dawning in the ministry of Jesus. Jesus' statement that "from the days of John the Baptist until now, the kingdom of heaven has been forcefully

---

24. The verb used here, *engizō,* can refer to someone or something which comes near in a temporal and/or spatial sense. Both of these ideas are illustrated in Matthew 26:45–46. In the Garden of Gethsemane Jesus warned His disciples of His impending betrayal with the words "Look, the hour is near [*engiken*], and the Son of Man is betrayed into the hands of sinners" (v. 45). In the next verse He said of Judas, "Here comes [*engiken*] my betrayer" (v. 46).

25. That Jews thought of themselves as "subjects of the kingdom" is illustrated by Jesus' words in Matthew 8:12.

advancing, and forceful men lay hold of it" (11:12)[26] seems to reinforce that idea, although John's own place in relation to this new era is debated. For example, Jesus gave John the highest commendation when He said, "among those born of women there has not risen anyone greater than John the Baptist" (11:11a). Then Jesus added, "yet he who is least in the kingdom of heaven is greater than he" (v. 11b).

Does this mean that although John introduced this new phase of the kingdom, he was not himself a participant in it?[27] Probably not. While John was something of a hinge figure in the unfolding plan of God, the view that he was on one side or the other of an exact dividing line between successive eras likely reflects more a modern predilection for systemization than a distinction which the gospel writer himself maintained.[28] The point rather seems to be that although John could in one sense be regarded as a person without peer because of his role as the herald of the Messiah, to be a participant in the kingdom and a beneficiary of the blessings of God is in reality a far greater privilege. And yet to frame the comparison in this way does not necessarily signify that John was not a beneficiary of the latter blessing as well.

The kingdom can in fact rather broadly describe the blessings of God associated with salvation. In some passages, for example, entering the kingdom and gaining eternal life are treated as synonymous experiences. A rich young man asked Jesus what he must do to "get eternal life" (19:16). When he left, Jesus told His disciples that "it is hard for a rich man to enter the kingdom of heaven . . . it is easier for a camel to go through the eye of a needle than for a rich man to enter the kingdom of God" (vv. 23–24). In the account of the judgment of the Son of Man, the blessed are told to take their inheritance, "the kingdom prepared for you" (25:34) which at the end of the discourse is described as "eternal life" (v. 46). In that light, the parable of the hidden treasure and the parable of the pearl are understandable (13:44–46). Eternal life is a treasure of infinite value, a possession worth selling all that one has in order to obtain it (a fact the rich man could not accept).

The "knowledge of the secrets of the kingdom of heaven" (13:11) which had been given to the disciples thus amounts to a revelation of the truth of the gospel in relation to what God was doing in and through the life of Jesus. When heard and understood, the "message about the kingdom" (13:19) produces fruit in individual

---

26. The meaning of two words in this verse (the verb *biazetai* and its cognate noun, *biastai*), is debated. Are they to be taken in a negative or a positive sense? The NIV takes both as positive ("forcefully advancing" and "forceful men"). The NASB takes both as negative ("suffers violence" and "violent men"). Usage of the words elsewhere generally favors the NASB translation. But the parallel saying in Luke 16:16 and the idea that the kingdom of God is a power that cannot be deterred support a positive construal, at least of the first part of the statement.

27. See Richard France, *Matthew: Evangelist and Teacher* (Grand Rapids: Zondervan, 1989), 197–98.

28. Most interpreters have an understandable interest in specificity and exactness. It must be balanced, however, by a concern not to go beyond the statements of the verses themselves. Similarly, a desire for categorical or systematic neatness, though pedagogically welcome, is ultimately counterproductive if it misconstrues or exaggerates the message of the gospel writer.

lives (v. 23).[29] The term "kingdom" can thus be used rather broadly to describe the experience of salvation.

To enter into the kingdom of God is similar to entering into the experience of salvation. Both have spiritual and material implications, but the material aspects are thought of primarily in reference to a future experience. The expectation of receiving a transformed and glorified body is one illustration of this (e.g., Phil. 3:21). Paul, for example, referred to redemption as a present reality achieved by the death of Christ (Rom. 3:24), while at the same time recognizing that there is an aspect of the experience of redemption which awaits a future consummation, the redemption of the body (Rom. 8:23). There is thus what has been described as a "now, not yet" aspect associated with salvation as it is set forth in the New Testament.

This is also true with regard to the understanding of the kingdom of God. There is a present aspect related to the reality of entering into the sphere of God's rule and reign, which in one's present experience is for the most part a spiritual reality. But the future will also show that the kingdom of God has physical and material dimensions.

Jesus' comments about dining in the kingdom certainly point in that direction. He told a centurion that "many will come from the east and west, and will take their places at the feast with Abraham, Isaac and Jacob in the kingdom of heaven" (Matt. 8:11). And to His disciples, at the conclusion of their last supper together, He said, "I will not drink of this fruit of the vine from now on until that day when I drink it anew with you in my Father's kingdom" (26:29).

Similar material implications arise in connection with statements made about the future kingdom of the Son of Man. The existence and manifestation of this kingdom parallels Jesus' exercise of authority, so it too can be spoken of as having been present in Jesus' earthly ministry though its primary manifestation awaits His second coming.

That Jesus was invested with the power and authority of the Holy Spirit at the outset of His ministry has already been mentioned. Yet the final scene of the gospel alludes to Jesus' "formal" investiture with authority as the risen and exalted Son (28:18). On several occasions this authority and its future manifestation to all people is described. In His examination before the Jewish authorities, Jesus warned the high priest, as the representative of the Jewish people, that they would witness a visible display of His authority at His second coming (26:64). To His disciples earlier He referred to not just Israel but the world generally as a witness to His return in exaltation: "The Son of Man will appear in the sky, and all the nations of the earth will mourn. They will see the Son of Man coming on the clouds of the sky with power and great glory" (24:30).

---

29. Jesus' word about doing the will of God (7:21) is relevant to the question of what constitutes "fruit." Some details regarding ethical matters in Matthew will be offered later in this chapter. For now, Paul's word to the Romans that the kingdom of God is a matter of "righteousness, peace and joy in the Holy Spirit" (Rom. 14:17) can serve as a brief illustration of representative "fruit."

The beginnings of the kingdom of the Son of Man seem to coincide with the onset of Jesus' ministry. The explanation of the parable of the weeds (13:36–43) points in this direction as well. The Son of Man's field is the world in which He sows His disciples, the "sons of the kingdom" (v. 38). The devil is also active, sowing "the sons of the evil one" (vv. 38–39). But a separation will take place at "the end of the age" (v. 39) when "the Son of Man will send out his angels, and they will weed out of his kingdom everything that causes sin and all who do evil" (v. 41). The last verse of Matthew's gospel records Jesus' promise to the disciples that He will be with them to "the very end of the age" (28:20), when He will return. The explanation of the parable, therefore, seems to be a description of the situation that exists in the interim, when the kingdom of the Son of Man is also present.

Jesus' words at the end of chapter 19, however, point to the period which follows His return, and give some indication of the situation that will exist when the Son of Man visibly establishes His rule. The discourse is precipitated by the question of Peter who rightly declared that unlike the rich young man (19:16–22) the disciples "have left everything" to follow Jesus (v. 27).[30] "What," he asks then, "will there be for us?" (v. 27).

Jesus answered, "I tell you the truth, at the renewal of all things, when the Son of Man sits upon his glorious throne, you who have followed me will also sit on twelve thrones, judging the twelve tribes of Israel" (19:28). And as if to stress that the disciples' material sacrifice will be more than compensated for by the situation that will result, He added these words: "everyone who has left houses or brothers or sisters or father or mother or children or fields for my sake will receive a hundred times as much and will inherit eternal life" (19:29). The nature and grandeur of the recompense seems clear, even if the exact contours of it remain undefined.

That the disciples will be in a position to exercise authority in relation to the nation of Israel is affirmed, which implies the existence of both the nation and a context in which that rule can be manifest. Jesus' words here thus point toward a period following His return in which His rule and that of His disciples will be manifested in relation to the nation of Israel. This assertion has obvious significance for Matthew's viewpoint on the future of Israel, a subject which will be discussed later. For now, it may be seen to give material definition to that period which will follow Jesus' return, a period in which the kingdom of the Son of Man will be brought to completion.

The kingdom of the Son of Man thus appears to be one aspect of the earlier and more encompassing kingdom of God. Jesus as the Son of Man will be the focus of a particular era in the unfolding kingdom of God, but the kingdom is not exhausted by what Jesus says and does. Ultimately, the end of Christian experience is

30. In this respect the disciples illustrate the point of the parable of the hidden treasure and the parable of the pearl (13:44–46). In contrast to the rich young man, they "sold everything" to follow Jesus. For an indication of the conceptual association of "following Jesus" and "obtaining the kingdom," compare Matthew 19:29 and Luke 18:30.

described in words influenced by Daniel 12:3: "Then the righteous will shine like the sun in the kingdom of their Father" (Matt. 13:43). The words of Paul to the Corinthians echo a similar refrain: "Then the end will come, when he hands over the kingdom to God the Father after he has destroyed all dominion, authority and power. . . . When he has done this, then the Son himself will be made subject to him who put everything under him, so that God may be all in all" (1 Cor. 15:24, 28). In the end, God reigns.

The phrase "the kingdom of God" is thus a designation with some flexibility, whose features compare in some respects with what later literature in the New Testament relates to the experience of salvation. The difference is that the tenor of the remarks about the kingdom of God remind the readers that their focus is to be ultimately God and what He or His Son does. Discussion of salvation, on the other hand, more easily can focus on the object, people, rather than the subject, God, who does the saving. In that respect, talk about the kingdom of God is a healthy reminder of the proper focus of Christian living: "seek first his kingdom and his righteousness" (6:33).

MISSION

The subject of mission in Matthew is an appropriate point of transition for moving from discussion about God and His work to the disciples and their work, since the topic concerns an object, subject, and motivation which bring together God, His people, and those in need of salvation. It is also, by common consent, an issue of paramount importance to Matthew, shown by the place it occupies at the culmination of his gospel.

Jesus' command, which occupies center stage as Matthew brought his gospel to a close, is the mandate to "go and make disciples of all nations" (28:19). The context in which these last words are placed has the effect of making this commission a self-perpetuating decree since Jesus stipulated that the process of making disciples should include "teaching them to obey everything I have commanded you" (v. 20). Chief among the commands of Jesus which are to be taught and obeyed is the mission mandate.

Matthew had not waited until the end of his gospel to highlight the theme of mission in Jesus' teaching. Indeed, Jesus' first call to His disciples was a summons for them to join Him in the work of further disciple-making: "Come follow me . . . and I will make you fishers of men" (4:19). In this way the first and last words to His disciples became a command to enlarge and extend the company of their fellowship.

In each of the five major sections of the gospel which focus on presenting Jesus' teachings,[31] there are passages of specific relevance to missionary endeavor.

31. These sections with representative titles are as follows: (1) The Sermon on the Mount (chaps. 5–7), (2) The Missionary Discourse (chap. 10), (3) The Parables Discourse (13:1–53), (4) The Ecclesiological (or Community) Discourse (chap. 18), and (5) The Eschatological (or Olivet) Discourse (chaps. 24–25).

The second discourse (chap. 10, to which 9:35–38 is a prologue) is entirely given over to instructions and statements related to this theme. The importance of this subject for Matthew is clear.

For example, there is much in the first discourse, the Sermon on the Mount, that has relevance for those involved in disciple-making, not the least of which is information about the character and behavior expected of disciples. The Beatitudes (5:3–10) provide help in this way, as do the so-called antitheses ("you have heard . . . but I tell you," 5:21–48) and the discussion about true righteousness (6:1–18) which follows. In between these sections, however, is another passage that constitutes a commission in miniature, the declaration that disciples are to be the salt of the earth and the light of the world (5:13–16).

Salt and light are objects associated in the Old Testament with God's blessing. Though salt is a somewhat more enigmatic image, it is identified with God's covenant and prescribed as a regular element in worship (Lev. 2:13). The reference to the disciples as the light of the world is probably based on the role of the Servant of Isaiah: "I will also make you a light for the nations that you may bring my salvation to the ends of the earth" (Isa. 49:6).[32] These associations thus serve to remind the disciples whom they represent and what it is they mediate, namely, the salvation of God.

These statements, however, are also an affirmation that the disciples' realm of service is universal in its scope. The earth—the world—is the sphere of ministry for Jesus' followers. Jesus called them to be "fishers of men" without qualification concerning race or language. Although they were sent first to their kinsmen in Israel (10:5–6), these early references to the disciples' mission show that the commission to all nations which concludes the gospel is no afterthought or alternative plan but defines the original scope and intended sphere of ministry for disciples of Jesus.

One other passage in this first discourse may be mentioned as particularly relevant to disciples involved in missionary activity. That is, Jesus' words about avoiding worry with regard to the necessities of life (6:25–34). It is obviously a message of relevance to people generally, but one which is particularly applicable to disciples who will carry out ministry in accord with Jesus' directions recorded in chapter 10. He instructed them to make no material provision for themselves (10:9–10), but to rely on the hospitality of those who would receive their ministry (v. 11). Worry about one's welfare is understandable in view of such prospects or circumstances. Yet Jesus' words directed His disciples to be confident in God's knowledgeable care for them (6:31–32), thus freeing them to focus on the object of their calling—the advance of His kingdom and the accomplishment of His will (v. 33; cf. vv. 9–10).

The missionary activity of the disciples is the primary focus of the discourse in chapter 10. It is introduced by Jesus' expression of concern for the Jewish peo-

32. Light is also expressive of both the blessing of God's salvation and the righteousness it engenders (Isa. 62:1), though the imagery in Matthew likely evokes the Servant of Isaiah. Isaiah 49:6 is applied also to the ministry of Paul and Barnabas (Acts 13:47), and Jesus is "the light of the world" (John 9:5).

ple, whom He described with words drawn from the Old Testament (Num. 27:17; 2 Chron. 18:16) as "sheep without a shepherd" (Matt. 9:36). The initial focus of the disciples' ministry, like that of Jesus' ministry (15:24), was the people of Israel ("Go to the lost sheep of Israel," 10:6), but the references to ministry before Gentiles (10:18) implies that the broader audience of the world generally had not been lost sight of. Indeed, Jesus' exhortation to "ask the Lord of the harvest to send out workers into his harvest field" (9:38) likely has in view the world generally as God's field (cf. 5:45). But readers will soon see that the world is also the field of the Son of Man in which He sows the sons of the kingdom (13:38); and in His role as the One to whom all authority has been given (28:18), He will see that workers are sent into the field (vv. 19–20).

Chapter 10, however, is primarily concerned with the disciples' mission to Israel. It is sometimes taken as a description of an early concern for ministry to Jews which was later superseded by the mission to the world with which the gospel concludes. Some go so far as to say that Matthew regarded this ministry to Israel portrayed in chapter 10 as an era that is past. Besides the disciples' mission being broadened to encompass the world, Jews in this view are no longer regarded as those to whom the gospel should be preached.[33] Israel had her opportunity to listen and respond to the message of Jesus and the disciples, as chapter 10 shows. But for the most part Israel turned a deaf ear (as Matthew's gospel also demonstrates), and so she was set aside as an object of mission.

That such a view is an incorrect interpretation of the missionary message of Matthew's gospel will be set forth subsequently when the place of Israel in the plan of God is considered. Though the portrait of Israel's unresponsiveness and rejection of Jesus and the disciples is unflinchingly drawn by Matthew, it is mistaken to think that he saw Israel as no longer an object of mission.

Rather, chapter 10 serves to underscore the priority of Israel in the missionary task, a fact understood by Paul, the apostle to the Gentiles, who said that the gospel "is the power of God for the salvation of everyone who believes: first for the Jew and then for the Gentile" (Rom. 1:16). As seen in Acts, Paul routinely preached first to Jews in the cities he entered on his missionary journeys.

Several factors in Matthew's gospel indicate that he had a similar view. For one thing, it is not just in Matthew 10 that concern for ministry to Israel is expressed. At the end of chapter 23, with its series of woes Jesus pronounced on the Jewish religious leaders, Matthew recorded Jesus' affirmation that He would continue sending emissaries to Israel (23:34). The next chapter contains statements by Jesus in reply to the disciples' questions about various matters, including the end of the age. Jesus told them that the gospel "will be preached in the whole world as a testimony to all nations, and then the end will come" (24:14). It is possible that the phrases "the whole world" and "all nations" do not include reference to Israel, but the wording is oddly expansive if that is the case.

33. Douglas Hare and David Harrington, "'Make Disciples of All the Gentiles' (Mt. 28:19)," *Catholic Biblical Quarterly* 37 (1975): 359–69.

One of the more difficult verses in chapter 10 seems also to point in the direction of a mission to Israel that will continue until Jesus returns. It too is preceded by warnings of persecution and a word of assurance concerning vindication,[34] after which Jesus said, "I tell you the truth, you will not finish going through the cities of Israel until the Son of Man comes" (10:23). Although the coming of the Son of Man here has been subjected to some curious interpretations,[35] it seems best to see it as a reference to the same event described elsewhere in the gospel as occurring at the end of the age (24:26–31).[36] If so, Matthew may then have been interpreting this saying as a statement that the mission to Israel should be regarded as an ongoing enterprise, which only the return of Jesus at the end of the age will bring to a close. In light of this, it may be significant that Matthew did not include a report about the disciples' return from this mission and subsequent discussion with Jesus about it, as did Mark (6:30) and Luke (9:10). It may be a further (admittedly, rather subtle) indication that he regarded this mission to Israel as one that should continue.

Having discussed the subject of a mission to Jews, it may be appropriate to discuss the related question of what Matthew understood as the place or present status of Israel in the plan and purpose of God, since Israel for the most part rejected Jesus as the Messiah. It is a subject of no little controversy, particularly since Matthew has been seen as contributing to the anti-Semitism that has manifested itself at different times and in various places through the centuries.

ISRAEL

No one can deny that Matthew's gospel contains some scathing indictments of the Jewish religious leaders. Matthew 23 is almost wholly taken up with a litany of Jesus' woes against Israel's scribes and Pharisees, prompting one commentator to advise readers that "a Christian expositor is under no obligation to defend such a mass of vituperation."[37]

Nor is that the end of the matter. Attention has previously been given to Jesus' declaration to the Jewish leaders that "the kingdom of God will be taken from you and given to a people who will produce its fruit" (21:43). Earlier, Matthew re-

---

34. Similar warnings about persecution are recorded in 10:17–23 and 24:9–12, and the same statement assuring vindication is in 10:22 and 24:13.

35. This verse, for example, figured significantly in Albert Schweitzer's view that Jesus expected someone else to come as the Son of Man in the course of this first mission. Schweitzer regarded the fact that no one did as such a great disappointment to Jesus that it ultimately led him to the cross (*The Quest of the Historical Jesus* [London: Black, 1911], 358–60). More recently Donald Carson has taken this coming of the Son of Man to be an event fulfilled at the destruction of Jerusalem in A.D. 70 ("Matthew," in *Expositor's Bible Commentary* [Grand Rapids: Zondervan, 1984], 8:253).

36. Only Matthew 16:28 seems to be a reference to an event other than the Second Coming since Jesus told His disciples that "some who are standing here will not taste death before they see the Son of Man coming in his kingdom." In all three Synoptic Gospels this statement is followed by an account of the Transfiguration, suggesting that this event should be understood as a "preview" of Jesus' glory. Second Peter 1:16–18 also supports this understanding.

37. Francis Beare, *The Gospel According to St. Matthew* (New York: Harper & Row, 1981), 461.

corded Jesus' statement that "the subjects of the kingdom will be thrown outside, into the darkness, where there will be weeping and gnashing of teeth" (8:12). On another occasion, when Jesus had taken issue with Jewish scruples about cleanliness, His disciples asked Him, "Do you know that the Pharisees were offended when they heard this?" to which Jesus replied, "Every plant that my heavenly Father has not planted will be pulled up by the roots. Leave them; they are blind guides" (15:12–14).

These seem to be trenchantly blunt statements suggesting that whatever place Israel may have occupied as the chosen people of God is now a thing of the past. When those statements are combined with the account of Israel's cry of responsibility in connection with the death of Christ, the consequence seems dreadfully clear: "Let his blood be upon us and on our children!" (27:25). Can there be any doubt that Matthew portrayed Israel as a hopelessly reprobate people?

Yes, there can. In fact, Matthew holds out hope that Israel will one day welcome Jesus as her Messiah. Several references in Matthew's gospel point in this direction. One is in chapter 1, where the angel of God spoke about the work Jesus would accomplish. The angel told Joseph that Jesus "will save his people from their sins" (1:21). One interpreter has concluded that "this can hardly be taken to mean Jewish people in the context of the first gospel,"[38] though he adduces no evidence for this contention, possibly because the particular term used here to refer to "people" (*laos*) is used on every other occasion in Matthew (thirteen times, in fact) to refer to Jews.

By itself this bit of linguistic data may be a matter of relatively little consequence. But the first instance of Matthew's formulaic Old Testament quotations in Matthew 2:6 also refers to Jesus as one "who will be the shepherd of my people Israel" (2 Sam. 5:2; 1 Chron. 11:2). Is "Israel" here a covert reference to the church, or did Jesus' ministry to Israel in His first coming fulfill the expectations of the text? The answer seems to be no on both counts. When Matthew used the term "Israel" (thirteen times), it always meant ethnic Israel. And Jesus can hardly be said to shepherd a people who refuse to acknowledge His leadership.

Are their any indications that Matthew harbored hope for the future conversion of Israel? Two verses help answer this question in the affirmative. One has already been mentioned in relation to the discussion about the future role of the Son of Man and His kingdom, referred to in 19:28. Jesus told the disciples that "when the Son of Man sits on his glorious throne, you who have followed me will also sit on twelve thrones, judging the twelve tribes of Israel." The repetition of the number twelve is significant here, particularly since Matthew knew that Judas was no longer a member of the apostolic band (cf. 28:16, "Then the eleven disciples went to Galilee.").

The repeated reference to twelve draws attention to the twelve tribes, the complete company of the now scattered and dispersed nation of Israel. Jesus seems

---

38. Guenther Bornkamm, "The Risen Lord and the Earthly Jesus," in *Tradition and Interpretation in Matthew*, 2d ed., ed. Guenther Bornkamm, Gerhard Barth, and Heinz Joachin Held (London: SCM, 1982), 325.

to have been saying to His disciples that He will not fail to accomplish the task ordained for Him. He will save His people Israel. And He will become their shepherd in accord with the expectations established for Him.[39]

This obviously did not take place at His first coming. Is there any other indication in the gospel that this will be accomplished at His second coming? Here a second text is relevant. The last word in that woeful chapter 23 is a word of hope. Jesus spoke to the city of Jerusalem, saying to her people, "You will not see me again until you say, 'Blessed is he who comes in the name of the Lord' " (23:39). These words, drawn from Psalm 118:26, look forward to the acknowledgment by Israel that Jesus is indeed the Christ of God.

The statement could be construed as a condition ("if you say, then you will see"), but the first and last verses are a reminder that a major aspect of the psalm is expression of praise to God for His faithfulness: "Give thanks to the Lord, for he is good; his love endures forever" (Ps. 118:1, 29). And the general emphasis in the gospel concerning the faithfulness of God to His Word suggests that reading this quotation as a statement of assurance regarding Israel's future rightly apprehends the significance of these words.[40]

If, then, Matthew saw that a mission to Israel is to continue until Jesus returns and also held out hope for the ultimate success of that mission, does his gospel have anything to say about the relationship of Jews and Christians generally? This is another question which is subject to debate. However, it can be approached from the vantage point of a discussion about the law in Matthew.

THE LAW

The subject of the law in Matthew raises some challenging questions, but before launching into any of these it will be helpful to take a moment to define the term itself. Normally, the term "law" refers to the legislative aspect of the Old Testament, primarily expressed in the first five books of the Bible, the Pentateuch. The Sadducees, for example, held this part of the Bible to be authoritative in settling questions of theology and practice.[41]

The Pharisees, on the other hand, while accepting the authority of the Pentateuch and the rest of the Old Testament as important for theology and practice, looked with equal esteem to the scribal tradition of interpretation and application of the Scriptures. This tradition developed in response to questions about appropriate behavior on matters not specifically addressed by biblical texts.[42]

---

39. The prophecy of Ezekiel is of interest in this connection, especially chapter 34, which speaks of God assembling the scattered flock of Israel (v. 12) and appointing over them David as shepherd (v. 23), who will rule in an era of abundant blessing (vv. 25–29) in accord with God's promise (vv. 31–32).

40. Also see David K. Lowery, "Evidence from Matthew," in *A Case for Premillennialism*, ed. Donald K. Campbell and Jeffrey L. Townsend (Chicago: Moody, 1992), 165–80.

41. Josephus, *Jewish Antiquities* 13.297.

42. Ibid., 13.408.

In addition, the Pharisees recognized that the past national exiles were in part precipitated by the failure of Israel to live faithfully in accord with the Old Testament law which they had received. As a preventive against the repetition of such tragedies and to inculcate a concern for righteous living generally, the oral tradition also developed along lines that sought to protect people from ignorantly or unconsciously violating the law of God. This body of legal tradition could also be referred to as law, though in Matthew the term "tradition" (*paradosis*) is used to describe it (15:2–3, 6). The law thus normally refers to the legislative portion of the Old Testament.

Matthew's presentation of the issue of the law is fraught with intriguing tensions. For example, in the first part of the Sermon on the Mount, Jesus unequivocally stated that He had not come "to abolish the Law or the Prophets . . . but to fulfill them" (5:17). That seems to be a fairly clear statement about the continuing validity of the Old Testament generally, though one might say that the fulfillment of particular prophecies implies that in these cases, at least, immediate applicability has come to an end.[43]

The next verse also seems to take a long-term view regarding the law's validity, stating that "until heaven and earth disappear, not the smallest letter, not the least stroke of a pen, will by any means disappear from the Law until everything is accomplished" (5:18). Again, the phrase "until everything is accomplished" may allow room for maneuvering on certain points, but the longevity implied by the fact that heaven and earth will be around for a little while longer (at least until Christ's return) is difficult to escape.

The next verse seems equally stringent and unequivocal: "Anyone who breaks one of the least of these commandments and teaches others to do the same will be called least in the kingdom of heaven, but whoever practices and teaches these commands will be called great in the kingdom of heaven" (5:19). It is possible that "these commandments" anticipated the teaching of Jesus which would shortly follow. However, the context more likely points in the direction of Old Testament commands, though Jesus' next words about the disciples' righteousness exceeding that of the scribes and Pharisees (v. 20) may be intended to orient the reader to the antitheses that follow (5:21–48). It is difficult to escape the notion, however, that these verses amount to a ringing endorsement of the law and an affirmation of its enduring validity.

One problem with this view, however, lies in the fact that the extracts of Jesus' teaching which follow (5:21–48) seem on several occasions to go either beyond the prescriptions of the Old Testament law or simply to set them aside as no longer applicable. The remarks about oaths (5:33–37), for example, end up setting aside various Old Testament prescriptions about taking and keeping oaths (e.g., Lev. 19:12; Num. 30:2–15; Deut. 23:21–23; Ps. 50:14) and enjoining instead a candid yes or no, adding that anything more "comes from the evil one" (Matt. 5:37).

---

43. Jesus' birth in Bethlehem, for example, may be thought to have brought the prophecy in Micah 5:2 to an end by virtue of fulfillment (Matt. 2:6).

Of course, this might be seen as a positive way of saying that God is interested in integrity and simplicity in speech, while what the Old Testament legislation was concerned with was to limit duplicity. Jesus' teaching, therefore, represents the positive counterpart, the accomplishment of righteousness, in the face of the Old Testament attempt to limit evil. There is obviously something to this contention, but it is difficult to see how it does not in effect render obsolete certain portions of Old Testament legislation.

The same point of view appears in the next section which concerns the limits of retribution (5:38–42). The Old Testament stipulates retribution in what might be called retaliation in kind and degree: "An eye for an eye and a tooth for a tooth" (Ex. 21:24; Lev. 24:20; Deut. 19:21).[44] But Jesus proscribed retribution of any sort: evil deeds, He said, are not to be repaid in kind.[45] While this may be seen as a contrast between what was necessary to maintain the fabric of Old Testament society and the personal prerogatives open to those living in the era of the New Testament,[46] the fact remains that it produced a measure of tension with the contention that the law be fulfilled. Those familiar with the Old Testament who read Matthew 5 can be permitted a measure of bewilderment in sorting out the appropriate response to questions about the validity of the law for Jesus' disciples.

Before attempting a resolution of this issue, the question of the oral law and its treatment in Matthew can be added as a factor further complicating this quandary. In view of what Jesus said about the traditions of the Pharisees recorded in Matthew 15:1–20, the matter would seem to be clear-cut. In answer to His disciples' question about the Pharisees and their scruples Jesus said, "Leave them; they are blind guides" (v. 14).

But as a prefatory word to the pronouncement of the sevenfold woe on the scribes and Pharisees, Matthew recorded these words of Jesus "to the crowds and to his disciples: 'The teachers of the law and the Pharisees sit in Moses' seat. So you must obey them and do everything they tell you'" (23:1–3). Later in the same chapter is a statement in line with the affirmations of 5:17–20. Jesus told the scribes and Pharisees, "You give a tenth of your spices—mint, dill and cummin. But you have neglected the more important matters of the law—justice, mercy and faithfulness. You should have practiced the latter without neglecting the former" (23:23).

What should a disciple conclude about personally observing the law? Further, what should a Jewish Christian disciple conclude about the propriety of a relation-

44. It is not that the Old Testament texts cited "permit" retribution; they positively enjoin it.

45. Cf. Romans 12:17–21.

46. The sermon is directed to individual disciples, setting forth a manner of life applicable to those who are emissaries of God. It does not address the question of appropriate behavior in the face of threat or harm that concerns the welfare of others. A father or husband concerned about the well-being of his family may need to act differently (cf., e.g., Paul's comments in 1 Cor. 7:32–35 about the constraints of family responsibilities), as would one involved in restraining evil as a social servant (Rom. 13:4). But the fact remains that Jesus exemplified this spirit of nonretaliation in the course of His life and ministry and seems to have held it forth as the proper course of action for those involved in ministry on His behalf.

ship with Judaism which requires observation of the Old Testament law and, for all practical purposes, attention to the oral law as well? In light of the statements Matthew recorded, are Jewish religious leaders to be abandoned or obeyed? Jesus' advice regarding payment of the temple tax (17:24–27) may point the way to one resolution of this dilemma.

The collection of this two-drachma tax was apparently based on the stipulation of Exodus 30:11–16 that each Jew twenty years of age and older should make a half shekel offering "for the service of the Tent of Meeting" (Ex. 30:16). The payment of a Greek double drachma coin met this obligation since it was more or less equivalent in value to the Jewish half shekel.[47] Though this poll tax or obligatory offering may have been sporadically assessed in the course of Israel's history,[48] it seems to be regarded as based on the law and therefore an obligation viewed as justly due of Jews in Jesus' day for the support of the temple service in Jerusalem.

Peter, at least, when questioned on this point by the tax collectors, had no hesitation in affirming that Jesus paid the tax. But later Jesus put a question to him: "What do you think Simon . . . from whom do the kings of the earth collect duty and taxes—from their sons or from others?" (17:25). "From others," said Peter. " 'Then the sons are exempt,' Jesus said to him. 'But so that we may not offend them,' " He arranged (miraculously) for Peter to pay the tax on behalf of both of them (vv. 26–27).

In view of the way Jesus' reply to Peter is phrased, the sons who are exempt (*eleutheros*, "free" from obligation) refer to Jesus and Peter, the "we" of the sentence. They apparently represent the wider company of disciples associated with Jesus, whom He had earlier described as "my brothers" (12:49) or "sons of the kingdom" (13:38). The tax collectors, as representatives of Judaism, were those whom Jesus did not want to "offend." The word translated "offend" (*skandalizō*) is used several times in the following verses (18:6, 8–9, along with the use of the noun *skandalon* in v. 7) to stress the importance of doing nothing that would be a hindrance to or create an obstacle for another individual in his or her relationship with God.

What Jesus said to Peter was that the disciples should see themselves as free from this stipulation of the law, a prescription of the Old Testament. This may only be a remark made in view of the predicted demise of the temple (24:1–2). But it is difficult to escape the implication that what applies to a particular aspect of the law applies also to all of it. The extrapolation, therefore, is that the ordinances of the Old Testament, although valid for Israel, do not apply to Jesus and His disciples.

47. See Bauer, Arndt, and Gingrich, *A Greek-English Lexicon of the New Testament*, 192. One of the rights taken away from the Jews under Roman occupation was the mintage of coins, which explains the various references to foreign coins in the Gospels. The one drachma silver coin was the Greek counterpart to the Roman silver denarius. As a rough estimate of value, one or the other might be given as payment for a day's labor (cf. Matt. 20:2).

48. One account of its collection is recorded in Exodus 38:25–26. For a discussion of the history of this tax, see William Horbury, "The Temple Tax," in *Jesus and the Politics of His Day*, ed. Ernst Bammel and Charles Moule (Cambridge: Cambridge Univ., 1984), 265–86.

While that may in fact be a valid induction in theory, the practice which Jesus recommended, at least in this instance, is submission to a precept of the law. This was in order not to offend the Jews, those to whom both Jesus and His disciples were seeking to minister. Matthew's view on the matter may, therefore, be that although the particular ordinances of the law are not matters of obligation for Jesus and His followers, in order to maintain a relationship with Jews and the opportunity for ministry which that affords, the law should be observed. One who chooses not to submit to the law is free to do so ("the sons are exempt") but such a decision will offend the Jews and ultimately lead to the end of opportunities for ministry among them.

Some of the consequences of decisions like this may be seen in what is said about the relationship of different groups in the early church and the Jews. The community of Christians who remained in Jerusalem around James were apparently scrupulous with regard to their observance of the law (Acts 21:18, 20). Less careful on some matters or possibly less guarded in speech about some things was Stephen (Acts 6:13–14). In this respect, however, he is portrayed as speaking and acting in a manner similar to Jesus. Paul, on the other hand, seems to have accepted the fact that he was free from obligation to observe the law, although he willingly undertook its observance on some occasions, apparently to maintain opportunities of ministry to Jews (1 Cor. 9:19–21). This approach was inherently difficult to carry out, and it ultimately got him into trouble with certain Jews in Jerusalem who intended to put a stop to this kind of behavior and thus end his missionary career. They were prevented from achieving this objective only because of Roman intervention (Acts 21:27–32).

Vignettes such as these illustrate why different viewpoints on the role of the law are not easily sorted out. Although there may have been theoretical agreement about freedom from the law generally in the Christian community, there seems to have been significantly different approaches taken when it came to the matter of practical implementation. While Matthew might not have disputed the legitimacy of the approach practiced by Paul, the general orientation of Matthew's gospel seems to be more in accord with the way followed by James.

The retention of references to Jewish practices at various points in the gospel (e.g., temple worship, 5:23–24; almsgiving, 6:2–4; fasting, 6:16–18; temple taxes, 17:24–27; and Sabbath observance, 24:20) and the strong endorsement given to the practice of the law in 5:17–20 suggest that Matthew viewed sympathetically those who chose to live in light of the law and the precepts of Judaism. He, nonetheless, recognized that external observances alone were matters of indifference to God. This is shown by his emphasis on the necessity of having a righteousness that "surpasses that of the Pharisees and the teachers of the law" (5:20), a recognition that relationship with God is ultimately a matter of the heart which God alone can assess.

THE COMMUNITY OF DISCIPLES, THE CHURCH

The mention of righteousness, a significant term in Matthew's gospel, provides a point of transition to the subject of the disciples and the church. Before looking at the ethical or practical meaning of righteousness, however (and the ideas associated with it in Matthew), it would be helpful to consider how Matthew seemed to envision the relationship between the first disciples of Jesus and the church they subsequently composed.

That Matthew saw a correspondence between what he recorded of Jesus' teaching and instruction to the disciples and its relevance to the church is indicated by the gospel's conclusion, where disciples are told to teach others "everything I have commanded you" (28:20). That would seem to be a rather comprehensive endorsement for the applicability of all that Matthew included in his gospel. The fact that it is followed by the affirmation of Jesus' spiritual presence "to the very end of the age" seems to imply, as well, the enduring relevance of this instruction until Jesus' return.

There are some points of difficulty in that view, however, that complicate the facile application of Jesus' teaching to subsequent disciples. For one thing, Matthew had, for the most part, communicated Jesus' teaching in language that is relevant to Jewish religious and cultural practice. To a certain extent that is understandable, since this is the culture in which Jesus carried out His ministry and from which the disciples were drawn.

But what are Gentile Christians to make of injunctions that direct disciples to respond to an unrepentant brother as a "Gentile"[49] (18:17, although the association with "tax collector" helps make it a label of enduring transcultural relevance)? Or what significance does the command to "put oil on your head" while fasting (6:17) have for a predominately Gentile church where (at least judging by the silence of the epistles) fasting was not practiced?[50]

Yet these are fairly minor interpretive challenges of the sort the average Gentile would probably handle without too much difficulty. More significantly, what are readers to make of the fact that Jesus endowed His disciples with great authority, not only to "preach" (10:7) but also to "raise the dead" (v. 8)? To what extent did Matthew see these commands, which include the exercise of this miraculous authority, as also applicable to disciples beyond the sphere of the original Twelve?

49. The NIV frequently (though not always; cf. 20:25 "the rulers of the Gentiles lord it over them") translates the words *ethnikos* (an adjective) and *ethnos* (a noun) "pagans" as here in 18:17. This is a correct and helpful rendering for modern readers, although the fact remains that the Greek words were simply a reference to Gentiles generally.

50. Space does not permit an extensive discussion of the question of fasting, but it may be instructive to note that apparently Jesus and His disciples did not fast (9:14). Jesus explained this by the fact that mourning (= fasting) was inappropriate while the bridegroom (= Jesus) was present (v. 15). But the gospel closes with the affirmation, "I am with you always, even to the end of the age" (28:20 NASB). In light of this, the parables of the patch of cloth and the wineskins (9:16–17) which follow the question about fasting (vv. 14–15) may point to the inappropriateness of old covenant practices like this in the era of the new covenant.

What is said about Peter, following his confession of Jesus as the Christ (16:16), may be instructive in answering this question. Following an explanation of the divine enabling behind Peter's ability to make this confession (v. 17), Jesus made two statements about Peter. In a play on Peter's name using the Greek word for rock (*petra*), Jesus said, "On this rock I will build my church, and the gates of Hades will not overcome it" (v. 18).[51]

There is little dispute that this last affirmation is meant to be a word of assurance that the church will endure until Jesus returns, even in the face of Satan's opposition. But what does the first part of the statement mean? Was Jesus here declaring that Peter will be the foundation of the early church?

This text (in conjunction with the following verse) has been used by Roman Catholic interpreters to support the view that Peter was the first pope. As a counter to such argumentation, a body of Protestant interpretation has developed which argues that the "rock" to which Jesus referred was not Peter, but rather his confession of Jesus as the Christ. There is nothing inherently improbable about this second proposal, and a good case for this interpretation can be made.

However, the more natural reading of the text is to see that the play of words points to Peter as the rock. But in what sense is he the foundation on which the church is built? The answer to that question requires consideration of the next verse, Jesus' further statement concerning Peter: "I will give you the keys of the kingdom of heaven; whatever you bind on earth will be bound in heaven, and whatever you loose on earth will be loosed in heaven" (16:19).

The second part of this statement (the binding and loosing) appears again in 18:18 with reference to the disciples generally. This may be an indication that Peter was functioning here as the spokesman or representative of the disciples. If so, he would not be the sole beneficiary of this blessing but would share the role with the other disciples.

Peter, however, was given the keys of heaven. What is the significance of the keys? They open or close doors (cf. Luke 11:52). Matthew gives little indication of how this authority might have been exercised by Peter. The book of Acts, which gives attention to the development of the early church, records Peter's role in proclaiming the gospel to both the Jews and the Gentiles. In that light the role Jesus gave to Peter becomes clear.

51. This statement raises the interesting question of the language(s) spoken by Jesus. Most Jews in Jesus' day spoke Aramaic, a Semitic language kin to Hebrew. There is general agreement that this is the language Jesus, like most Jews, routinely used. However, Hebrew was apparently also known and used in scribal circles (probably the form which came to be known as mishnaic Hebrew), and it is not impossible that when Jesus debated with religious leaders in Jerusalem He also used some Hebrew of this sort in the process. The wordplay on Peter's name, however, is Greek. (His Aramaic name, Cephas, is the equivalent of the Greek, Peter). A knowledge of Greek could also be expected of Galileans who dealt more frequently with Gentiles (cf. 4:15, "Galilee of the Gentiles"), whose common language was Greek. When Jesus spoke with Pilate, for example, He probably did so in Greek (cf. the Epistle to the Romans, written in Greek to a people living in the capital of the Latin-speaking world). See S. Safrai and M. Stern, eds., *The Jewish People in the First Century* (Philadelphia: Fortress, 1987), 2:1032–37.

Peter preached the gospel to Jews on the day of Pentecost and 3,000 believed (Acts 2). On the birthday of the church, Peter functioned as the first "doorkeeper." As he declared the gospel, that "in the name of Jesus Christ [you may find] forgiveness of your sins" (2:38), many believed and were baptized. By means of Peter's ministry, a door was opened to many Jews who by faith in Christ were added to the church.

Peter was also the first doorkeeper for the Gentiles (Acts 10). Invited by Cornelius to come to his house and prepared by God to do so, he went. There Peter preached the gospel, and there also many believed and were brought into the kingdom of heaven. In both cases, it was Peter who initiated this new phase of gospel proclamation and opened the door for Jews and Gentiles.

In this capacity Peter functioned as the rock on which the church was built. He proclaimed the gospel, with the authority inherent in the message given him, and forgiveness of sins to all who believed—to the Jews first, but also to the Gentiles. In that sense, the sins which he proclaimed "loosed" by faith in Christ were loosed. To those who refused to believe, the sins which bound them remained (cf. Acts 2:40). In this way, Peter was the spokesman of God to both Jews and Gentiles, a role to which he was appointed by Jesus Himself.

Was Peter unique in this role? Yes, in the sense that he was the first, but others too proclaimed the gospel. Paul, for example, also preached the gospel. He too opened the door of faith to Jews and Gentiles (e.g., Acts 14:1). The foundation of the church was thus not laid by Peter alone.

In this regard Paul's words to the Ephesians are relevant, when he described the church as "built on the foundation of the apostles and prophets" (Eph. 2:20). Peter, indeed, was the first spokesman of the church to preach to Jews and Gentiles, but he was not the last. Nor was his authority unique. Others could proclaim with authority that those who believed the gospel could be assured that their sins were forgiven and could affirm with equal certainty that those who rejected the gospel message did so to their own peril and would remain bound by their sin (cf. Acts 13:38–41). Yet nothing can change the fact that Peter was the first doorkeeper for both Jews and Gentiles into the kingdom. It is this role that Matthew described in these words of Jesus about Peter, who became the pioneer for many who follow in his lead.

Our earlier question still remains. To what extent are the dispositions of authority which Jesus gave to the disciples in the course of their first missionary journey retained by them and transferable to subsequent disciples? The answer is a bit more complex than might first be imagined. As was mentioned earlier in the discussion of chapter 10, concerning the gospel's message about mission, Matthew (unlike Mark and Luke) provided no report about the disciples' return from this first journey through Israel, nor is there any account of what they were able to accomplish on it. There is, for example, no report about anyone being raised from the dead. If Matthew's gospel were all a reader had access to, the question about the extension of authority might remain unanswered. Yet to readers who also have access to Acts, the question of authority is clarified: disciples do retain the authority

Jesus gave them, even to raise the dead. Or at least Peter did, as Dorcas could attest (Acts 9:36–42).

Paul also had that authority, as Eutychus could also certify (Acts 20:7–11). Is, however, Paul, for want of a better description, representative of a second-generation disciple? Apparently not, at least in the way in which he saw his conversion and call to ministry. From Paul's point of view, he was made a disciple by Jesus Himself. No man instructed him (Gal. 1:11–24).

Paul's case, therefore, does not permit a clear answer to be given to the question about the transfer of authority. His own letters suggest that even in his case, however, the authority to do miracles waxed and waned, so that near the end of his life he at one point despaired of saving an ill comrade (Epaphroditus, who nevertheless recovered, Phil. 2:27). And Hebrews 2:3–4 seems to view this kind of authority as a phenomenon characteristic of the first generation or foundational ministry.

The outcome of this discussion, however, does not require alteration of the initial notion that Matthew did see the substance of Jesus' instructions and commands as applicable to the Christian community. In certain respects the first disciples were distinctive, and even among them Peter carried out a special task. But what Jesus said to them has application to subsequent disciples as well, who are to "obey everything I have commanded" (28:20).

This obedience, in fact, is the basic meaning of the term noted at the outset of this section, the word "righteousness."[52] In the Sermon on the Mount, this word is used with reference to the behavior of disciples (5:6, 10, 20; 6:1, 33), but it is also used with regard to Jesus (3:15) and John the Baptist (21:32).[53] It describes a manner of life lived in accord with God's will. As such, Jesus could tell the reluctant John that baptism was appropriate for Him as well as an expression of His submission to the will of God (3:15).

The first use of the word "righteousness" with reference to disciples is a reminder too that although righteousness, as it is used in the gospel, describes behavior, it is nonetheless an expression of the gracious enablement of God (5:6). A disciple is one who "hungers and thirsts," who earnestly desires to live a righteous life, but the One who satisfies that longing, who makes this righteousness a reality, is God.[54]

---

52. The adjective "righteous" (*dikaios*) is relevant here also since it is applied frequently to disciples (e.g., 10:41; 13:43, 49; 25:37, 46) as well as to God (20:4) and Jesus (27:19). Its meaning, however, is like that of the noun, "righteousness."

53. The NASB translation of this verse reads, "John came to you in the way of righteousness and you did not believe him." The NIV reads, "John came to show you the way of righteousness," which focuses more on John's message than on his manner of life. Perhaps this latter rendering is correct in view of the following phrase "and you did not believe him." The Old Testament background, however, inclines one to see "way" as a reference to manner of life (cf. Prov. 8:20). In either case, there is no question that John was portrayed with Jesus as one who illustrates a righteousness of life and submission to the will of God.

54. The Beatitudes routinely employ the "divine passive" verb, implying that it is God who will carry out the action referred to (see also nn. 2 and 3). The fact that these are future in tense may also indicate that the complete fulfillment of these desires will not be realized until the consummation of all things (cf. 13:43).

That is why it is also important to keep in mind the antecedent of the pronouns in the well-known statement of 6:33: "Seek first his kingdom and his righteousness." It is the advance of "His" kingdom, God's rule and reign, which disciples are to seek. And it is "His" righteousness, a manner of life in keeping with God's will, that Jesus sets before disciples as the proper objective of their lives.

Thus disciples are to so live that others may see their good works (5:16) and so that their Father in heaven, not they themselves, will be glorified (cf. 6:9; 15:31). As if to underscore this point, Matthew added what seems to be a contradictory statement a few verses later: "Be careful not to do your 'acts of righteousness' before men, to be seen by them" (6:1). Besides one's manner of life, its motivation is important to God. Why does a disciple do what he or she does? For self-advancement, personal gain, or glory? It is easy to forget that in the final analysis, it is not the commendation or the admiration of others which is significant, but the approval and praise of God (cf. John 12:43; Rom. 2:28–29). It is this singlemindedness of purpose that Matthew 6:33 holds before disciples.

This emphasis on attitude or motive, the spirit in which obedience is rendered, is also a reminder that however much attention is given in Matthew's gospel to deeds and behavior, there is the recognition that the righteousness that surpasses that of the Pharisees (5:20) affects the whole person, transforming not just external behavior but also the disposition of the heart as well (5:8). That Jesus referred to a member of the community as "ones who believe in me" (18:6) shows that Matthew had not lost sight of faith as the essential internal characteristic of the true disciple. To believe in Jesus is to accept the fact that He speaks and acts with the authority of God (8:8–10). In the religious leaders' statement to Jesus on the cross, they spoke the truth about Jesus while at the same time revealing their own failure to believe: "He saved others" they said, "he cannot save himself. He's the king of Israel; let him come down now from the cross and we will believe in him" (27:42). But because He came "to give his life as a ransom for many" (20:28), He could not come down from the cross. Only hours earlier He had explained the significance of His death to the disciples with the words, "This is my blood of the covenant, which is poured out for many for the forgiveness of sins" (26:28). By failing to believe Him, the religious leaders failed to obtain forgiveness. Faith then is that invisible disposition of the heart whose visible corollary or outward manifestation is righteousness of life.

A good illustration of this interplay between heart and life is found in the way Matthew's gospel calls attention repeatedly to the importance of regard for others, of mercy and compassion, of forgiveness and restoration as a distinguishing mark of one who does God's will. In the Beatitudes, which provide insights into characteristics of a disciple, Jesus referred to blessing for the merciful (5:7) and the peacemakers (v. 9). Being angry with a brother is tantamount to murder, and establishing reconciliation is a matter of the highest priority for a disciple (vv. 21–26). On the other hand, avenging evil or retaliation in kind is not to characterize the behavior of disciples (vv. 38–42; cf. 26:50–52). The enemy, in fact, is to be loved and prayed for (5:43–44).

Nowhere is the emphasis on forgiveness and reconciliation more pronounced than in Matthew 18, the so-called Ecclesiological[55] or Community Discourse. Concern for the well-being of the least member of the community is stressed by Jesus' identification of Himself with a little child (v. 5). Those who for various reasons might naturally invite contempt are to be the object of solicitous concern (v. 10). If one strays from the fellowship of the community, he or she is not to be ignored or dismissed but is to be diligently sought in order to be restored (vv. 12–14). If a brother has sinned, reconciliation must be attempted (v.15). Even if he must be disciplined by the church as a whole, and for the time being denied recognition as a brother in the fellowship, he is still to be loved and prayed for and his repentance sought (some tax collectors and Gentiles became, after all, pillars of the early church!).[56]

The sayings in verses 18–20 also apply to the practice of reconciliation. The church as a whole is to demonstrate the concern of God visibly for spiritual health and vitality in its members by confronting sin and urging the straying ones to seek repentance and restoration. Where such confrontation and discipline lead to repentance, the church as a whole can confidently declare that the individual has been "loosed" from that sin and forgiven, in accord with the will of God, and offered restoration to fellowship as evidence of that fact.

On the other hand, where an unrepentant attitude persists, the church can declare with equal certainty that such a person will reap the consequences of that sin, "bound" by a chain of his or her own making until he seeks the release and forgiveness that God makes available. In this capacity the church functions on behalf of God as His representative, just as Peter did as God's spokesman in a distinct though related capacity in the early days of the church's mission.

So too, just as prayer is to be made on behalf of those outside the church who oppose and oppress it (5:44), it also is to be offered concerning those inside (18:19–20) who by persistence in sin would harm not only themselves but also the community of which they are a part (cf. 1 Cor. 5:6–13). For these as well, the church collectively is to pray, confident that, in God's will, the errant brother will be restored and the forgiveness he needs will be given. In these deliberations concerning the well-being of individuals and the community as a whole, the church is assured of Jesus' abiding concern and spiritual presence (see also Paul's assurance of this, 1 Cor. 5:4). Indeed, to allay any question about forgiveness as a distinguishing characteristic of the church, the discourse concludes with Jesus' conversation with Peter about the extent of forgiveness (18:21–22) and the chilling account about

---

55. This word is from the word for church or community, *ekklesia,* which is mentioned twice in verse 17 (also 16:18).

56. Perhaps a word about church discipline is in order here. What is denied this unrepentant disciple is recognition as a brother in the fellowship. Tax collectors and pagans were admitted to the gathering of the church (cf. 1 Cor. 14:24–25) if they wished to attend, but it is unlikely that they shared in the observance of the Lord's Supper since, among other things, it was intended to give visible expression to the reality of Christian unity and fellowship. It is not unreasonable to imagine that the same practice would characterize the church's relationship with an unrepentant member until reconciliation was achieved.

the consequences of an unforgiving spirit in the parable of the unmerciful servant (vv. 23–35).

A strain runs through many of these sayings about the necessity of forgiveness that can be a bit unnerving to readers, namely, the recurring references to the consequence of an unforgiving or unmerciful spirit. In the parable of the unmerciful servant, for example, the final scene is of the unforgiving servant being turned over to the jailers until he should repay his impossible debt (v. 34; cf. v. 24), with Jesus intoning these words in conclusion: "This is how my heavenly Father will treat each of you unless you forgive your brother from your heart" (v. 35).

The same basic perspective occurs in the beatitude about the merciful which begins the Sermon on the Mount: "Blessed are the merciful, for they will be shown[57] mercy" (5:7). The implication is that the unmerciful will be shown no mercy by God (cf. James 2:13). This tone of judgment is also present in the exhortation to reconciliation (Matt. 5:21–26). It is implied by the petition in the model prayer ("Forgive us our debts as we also have forgiven our debtors," 6:12) and is made explicit in the two verses that immediately follow the prayer: "For if you forgive men when they sin against you, your heavenly Father will also forgive you. But if you do not forgive men their sins, your Father will not forgive your sins" (vv. 14–15).

Is Matthew teaching that salvation is by works? No, he knows that salvation comes from the grace of God. The disciples, amazed by Jesus' statement that "it is easier for a camel to go through the eye of a needle than for a rich man to enter the kingdom of God" (19:24), asked, "Who then can be saved?" (v. 25) Jesus simply replied, "With man this is impossible, but with God all things are possible" (v. 26). Salvation is not earned, but neither is it unrelated to deeds. Matthew, in fact, was probably doing several things with these statements about forgiveness. First, he was drawing attention to the importance of forgiveness by making it clear that failure to forgive can have awful consequences. Second, he was stripping away any illusions about what it means to be a disciple. Wanting to be a disciple and being one may be two different things. According to Jesus, a disciple "must deny himself and take up his cross and follow me" (16:24). In these statements about forgiveness Matthew was giving some direction as to what following Jesus entails.

Third, it is clear Matthew saw the danger of false profession and false discipleship. Some who call Jesus "Lord" will nonetheless be banished from His presence on the day of judgment (7:21–23). Judas is a stark reminder that even one of the original disciples (10:1), an apostle (v. 2), proved false (v. 4). Discipleship is not therefore merely a matter of profession, nor for that matter, is it verified by spectacular deeds of spiritual power (7:22). It is a matter of abiding faith (10:22; 24:10–13), often manifested in simple deeds of mercy (10:40–42; 25:35–40).

Does the God who demands forgiveness of disciples not extend it to them as well? Of course He does. Peter is a classic example. Jesus gave the stern warning to His disciples that "whoever acknowledges me before men, I will also acknowledge

---

57. This is another "divine passive" verb (see also nn. 2, 3, and 54).

before my Father in heaven. But whoever disowns me before men, I will disown him before my Father in heaven" (10:32–33).

Matthew did not often use this word for "disown" (*arneomai*). This particular form of the word occurs only four times: twice in 10:33, and then twice again, when describing Peter's denial of Jesus in the courtyard of the high priest (26:70, 72).[58] This terrible act seems to illustrate in awful measure the very thing Jesus had earlier warned against.

Is Peter then an example of an apostate disciple, one who will be disowned by Jesus before God? Though this has been contended,[59] it is an unlikely interpretation. Even if readers had only Matthew's gospel as a source of information about the early church (in itself an improbable eventuality), they would shortly learn of Judas' death (27:3–5) and then see that Matthew mentioned eleven disciples gathered before Jesus on the mountain in Galilee (28:16). One can conclude that Peter was still numbered among Jesus' followers.

A disciple can thus fail in the most abject manner, following an explicit and dire warning, and still experience forgiveness. Peter did. But Judas is a reminder of how close one can be to the kingdom without actually entering into it. And according to Jesus' warning, there will be "many" like him (7:22).

Jesus' words of warning are thus not theoretical or rhetorical. They are meant to clarify the will of God for disciples and to stress the importance of doing that will, as something that is essential, not optional. Jesus did not ignore the question of assurance, as earlier discussion has shown. But He had little time for complacency toward and indifference to doing the will of God in the community of disciples.[60] The standard is always held out before disciples in Jesus' life and teaching: "Be perfect, therefore, as your heavenly Father is perfect" (5:48). Wholehearted obedience is the desired ideal.

Yet, disciples fail. Even the first disciples had regular lapses of faith. The expression "O you of little faith" functions almost like a nickname for them (6:30; 8:26; 14:31; 16:8). Matthew's understanding and appreciation of this fact is illustrated in his presentation of Jesus' teaching regarding divorce and remarriage (5:31–32; 19:3–11). Whereas Mark and Luke chose to state only the unqualified ideal (that divorce is prohibited, Mark 10:11; Luke 16:18), Matthew also included a word of recognition that faith may not always triumph, that the "hardness of heart" (cf. 19:8) that existed under the old covenant has not been entirely eliminated in this era of the "now-but-not-yet-consummated" new covenant, and that marriages do fail. What then?

---

58. Matthew also used the intensive form (*aparneomai*), which has the same basic meaning, in the saying about disciples needing to deny themselves (16:24). It is also used of Jesus' prediction of Peter's disloyalty (26:34), Peter's vow to the contrary (v. 35), and his bitter remembrance of Jesus' words after his betrayal (v. 75).

59. Robert A. Gundry, *Matthew: A Commentary on His Literary and Theological Art* (Grand Rapids: Eerdmans, 1982), 548–49. (A new edition was published in 1994.)

60. Those who wish to be able to say with Paul that they "have not hesitated to proclaim . . . the whole will of God" (Acts 20:27), would do well to give Matthew's gospel due regard in their preaching and teaching routine.

This is a controversial subject, but Matthew seems to have said that Jesus recognized the right to remarriage for some who have been divorced. It is clear Jesus did not advocate divorce, for He stated the ideal in 19:6, "What God has joined together, let not man separate." In view of all that Matthew has included in his gospel regarding the importance of forgiveness, it should be clear that the first course of action for disciples is always forgiveness and reconciliation. But that is not always an attainable goal. Sometimes the "offending" partner does not seek forgiveness, nor is reconciliation always accepted.

The so-called "exception clause" in Matthew's gospel concerns the issue of "marital unfaithfulness" as a ground of divorce: "anyone who divorces his wife, except for marital unfaithfulness, and marries another commits adultery" (19:9; cf. 5:32). The word *porneia*, translated "marital unfaithfulness," is a general term for sexual immorality. Numerous attempts have been made to avoid the implication of the statement,[61] but the fact remains that the least problematic interpretation is the one that recognizes this for what it is, an exception to the ideal.

Jesus affirmed that there are situations involving marital unfaithfulness where for various reasons divorce occurs. It is a regrettable alternative and one which should be painstakingly avoided whenever possible. But when divorce occurs in such a situation, the exception grants the aggrieved partner the right to remarry.[62]

Here then is one illustration of a pastoral concern which sets before readers the highest standards—the accomplishment of the will of God—while at the same time recognizing that men and women, still awaiting the culmination of their experience of redemption, do not yet lead perfect lives. It is but one illustration of why forgiveness is essential in the Christian community.

ESCHATOLOGY

It seems appropriate to conclude this summary account of particular aspects of Matthew's message with a discussion of what he wrote about matters related to the close of the age. Attention has already been given to the conviction that Israel will remain a people whom God will not abandon, who will one day welcome Jesus as their Messiah. In the meantime, in this period between Jesus' ascension and His return, what are disciples expected to do and what should they expect to find?

When Jesus spoke about the coming destruction of the temple (24:2), the disciples asked Him, "When will this happen, and what will be the sign of your coming and of the end of the age?" (v. 3). His response constitutes the last extended teaching section in Matthew's gospel, commonly referred to as the Eschatological or Olivet[63] Discourse (24:4–25:46).

---

61. For a helpful discussion and evaluation of some alternative interpretations, see Carson, *Matthew,* 413–18.

62. The following verses (19:11–12) discuss the issue of never marrying, not the prospect of remaining single after divorce.

63. According to 24:3, Jesus was sitting on the Mount of Olives, the eastern hillside which affords a panoramic view of Jerusalem and the temple area, when the disciples asked Him this question.

It is a curious but instructive phenomenon that, as Matthew recorded it, Jesus' answer to the disciples' questions is rather indirect and unspecific. It may be an indication of the fact that disciples as a matter of course are given what they need to know, not necessarily what they want to know (cf. Deut. 29:29).[64] At any rate, Jesus told them that He does not know when the time of the end will be: "No one knows about that day or hour, not even the angels in heaven, nor the Son, but only the Father" (24:36).

He did, however, have some instruction and warning for them with regard to how they should conduct their lives in the period that remains until the end. To one degree or another, Jesus' advice and counsel in 24:4–14 is applicable to this intervening period, an era shared by both the disciples then and Matthew's subsequent readers until Jesus' return. Some of it is an echo of instruction also found in the second discourse concerning what disciples can expect to experience in the course of their missionary labors (cf. 10:17–22 and 24:9–14). Otherwise, these words appear to be a general picture of the grim and chaotic conditions that will characterize this period "of birth pains" until the end (cf. Rom. 8:18–25, esp. v. 22). In the midst of these times the gospel must be preached (Matt. 24:14).

Beginning at verse 15 and continuing through verse 25, however, the focus seems to shift to the period immediately preceding the end, just before Jesus' return. These words concern events in and around Jerusalem. In view of the disciples' question, this might be taken as a prediction of the destruction of Jerusalem in A.D. 70. But several factors suggest that an event of greater magnitude is being described here.

For one thing, if Matthew was reporting Jesus' prediction of Jerusalem's destruction in A.D. 70, it is difficult to escape the conclusion that he considerably exaggerated the extent of the catastrophe, the reported atrocities notwithstanding.[65] According to Jesus, "There will be great distress, unequaled from the beginning of the world until now—and never to be equaled again" (24:21; cf. Dan. 12:1).

Readers of Genesis 6 may wonder how the destruction of Jerusalem can be compared with the catastrophe of the Flood. But this is the sort of comparison envisioned, as the evocation of Noah's milieu at Matthew 24:37–39 shows. Even allowing for some metaphorical exaggeration, the destruction of Jerusalem in A.D. 70 is not easily squared with the description of events which Matthew portrayed. To see that disaster as a prefigurement or an anticipation of a yet future destruction seems more in keeping with the tone of the passage.[66]

---

64. That seems to apply in principle to material needs as well (cf. 6:31–33).

65. See the horrific details given in Josephus' account of the tragedy (*The Jewish War*, esp. 5.420—6.212 and the summary 6.429).

66. A problem with seeing Matthew's description as applicable to a period beyond the destruction of Jerusalem in A.D. 70 is the statement in verse 34, "this generation will certainly not pass away until all these things happen." Though this was spoken to Jesus' disciples, it may be that they function as representatives of a future generation of disciples, in line with the understanding that what Jesus said to His disciples also applies to those who follow in their train. It is a difficulty, but similar to the sort encountered in the interpretation of Matthew 10:23 (see the discussion under "Mission" above).

Jesus' citation of Daniel's reference to the "abomination of desolation" (Dan. 9:27; 11:31; 12:11) also orients the reader to think in terms of last things, since Daniel associated the appearance of this abomination with the time of the end and the resurrection of the righteous (12:2–3, 13). Drawing its name from the phrase used in Matthew 24:21, this period of time is sometimes also referred to as the "great tribulation" (*thlipsis megalē*; cf. Rev. 7:14), variously calculated, based on Daniel 9:27, as lasting from three and one-half to seven years.

At the end of that time ("immediately after the distress of those days," Matt. 24:29), Jesus, the Son of Man, will return. Verses 26–31 concern this event of universal dimensions (v. 30) which will lead to a separation of all humanity (v. 31; cf. vv. 41–42). The reality of this separation, and the judgment that it implies, is the subject explored in various ways in the remainder of the discourse.

In a sense Jesus' answer to the disciples' question about the time of the end posed in verse 3 is answered in verse 42: "keep watch, because you do not know on what day your Lord will come." Jesus was concerned that during the interim that awaits His return His disciples would be characterized by vigilance, manifested by faithfulness and diligence in carrying out His commands.

In that regard the period of delay that marks this interval until Jesus' return serves also as a part of the winnowing process that will also culminate in the separation of genuine and alleged disciples.

The three parables at the center of this discourse each refer to Jesus' delay and the spirit of lassitude or self-indulgence it may engender in false disciples. In the parable of the servant (24:45–51), the wicked servant said to himself, " 'My master is staying away a long time,' and he then begins to beat his fellow servants and to eat and drink with drunkards" (vv. 48–49). In the parable of the ten virgins "the bridegroom was a long time in coming, and they all became drowsy and fell asleep" (25:5). According to the parable of the talents, "after a long time the master of those servants returned and settled accounts with them" (v. 19).

Disciples should not be surprised if Jesus' return seems long overdue. In the purposes of God, "the master of that servant will come on a day when he does not expect him and at an hour he is not aware of" (24:50). In the meantime, disciples are to "keep watch," because they "do not know what day your Lord will come" (v. 42).

Will there be lapses of devotion and faithfulness in the case of genuine disciples? Yes. All the virgins awaiting the bridegroom's coming fell asleep. In the next chapter Matthew showed readers that despite Jesus' exhortations to vigilance (in this case, in prayer) disciples may fail (the same word, *gregoreō*, "keep watch," used in 24:42–43 and 25:13, is also in 26:38, 40–41). Matthew did not recount the disciples' failure to pray in Gethsemane to provide fodder for excuses, but to show how necessary is divine enablement if frail disciples are to remain faithful, and how hurtful to Jesus their apathy and indifference can be.

The reality of Jesus' abiding presence with His disciples and His identification with them is underscored in the final portion of this discourse, in the account of the judgment of the sheep and the goats (25:31–46). The principle that disciples are representatives of Jesus (and of God the Father) has been affirmed earlier in the conclusion to the Missionary Discourse, where Jesus told His disciples, "He who receives you receives me, and he who receives me receives the one who sent me" (10:40). This thought is repeated in the Ecclesiological Discourse: "And whoever welcomes a little child like this in my name welcomes me" (18:5). So Jesus' words in this final discourse, "whatever you did for one of the least of these brothers of mine you did for me" (25:40), should occasion no surprise. But it does, not only in the "cursed" (v. 41) but also for the "righteous" (v. 37): "Lord, when did we see you hungry and feed you or thirsty and give you something to drink?"

In this way, Matthew reminded his readers of at least two things. First, in the final analysis righteousness is not simply a matter of calculated behavior, even if it is conscious (though in this case the significance of the deed seems either to have been unperceived originally or subsequently forgotten by the "righteous"). Second, Jesus often identifies with those regarded as "the least." [67]

This reversal of values as it relates to people (18:4), status (20:26), and experiences generally (5:4; 16:23), pertains also to what Jesus said about the reward God promises to disciples. What has been mentioned previously about the grace of God in dealing with disciples applies to the subject of reward as well.

Jesus' parable about the workers in the vineyard is flanked on either side by the words, the "first will be last" (19:30) and "the last will be first" (20:16). As Jesus told it, the last ones called to work in the vineyard were given their "reward" (*misthos*) first (20:8), the recompense of a day's labor when all they invested was one hour. Those who labored all day for the same recompense complained (vv. 11–12), understandably, that this hardly seemed fair. But as the landowner pointed out, he had not been unfair[68] with those who agreed to the usual wage; he simply exercised his right to be generous with others.

Some of the terms in the parable (e.g., *apodidōmi, misthos,* v. 8) evoke words and ideas mentioned earlier in the Gospel (*apodidōmi,* 6:4, 6, 18; *misthos* 6:1–2, 5, 16) with reference to the hypocrites who carefully calculate their pretentious "acts of righteousness" (6:1) so they can receive the reward they seek: "to be honored by men" (v. 2 NASB). Jesus' words are meant to be sobering: "They have received their reward in full" (6:2, 5, 16). His words to disciples are in line with this parable: do what is right, without regard to the approval of people or a just recompense. Trust God that His reward will more than exceed the alternatives.

---

67. Just who "the least" are is uncertain, though the fact that Jesus described them as "the least of these brothers of mine" (v. 40) seems (in light of 12:50, "whoever does the will of my Father in heaven is my brother") to identify them simply as followers of Christ. It is possible, however, because of Jesus' instructions about missionary procedure in chapter 10, that itinerant missionaries needing food, clothing (v. 10) and even prison visits (v. 19) are in view. But the emphasis in this gospel on equality among the disciples ("you have only one Master and you are all brothers," 23:8) probably points in the direction of a more general application.

68. The adjective *dikios* (v. 4, "just" or "fair") and the verb *adikeō* (v. 13, "unjust" or "unfair") appear in the parable, possibly as a reminder to disciples that when it comes to reward, as is generally the case in a disciple's life, it is not a matter of justice or fairness but mercy and grace that characterizes relationship with God.

But what is God's reward? In 6:1, Jesus seemed rather indefinite when He spoke of a reward "from your Father in heaven." But the preposition *para* (rendered "from" in 6:1), often indicates simple spatial proximity,[69] such as when Jesus said, "I am telling you what I have seen in the Father's presence" (*para tou patras,* John 8:38). The ultimate reward of disciples may well be summed up by the experience of being "in the Father's presence" (*para tō patri,* cf. 6:1). The reward set before disciples thus seems to refer to being in the presence of God (cf. 5:8, "Blessed are the pure in heart, for they will see God"), an experience every Christian will enjoy (cf. 1 Cor. 4:5, where Paul wrote of the judgment when "each will receive his praise from God").

To what extent later disciples will be participants in Jesus' promise to the Twelve that they will rule and reign with Him (19:28; cf. Rev. 20:6) is not entirely clear. But His promise that "everyone who has left houses or brothers or sisters or father or mother or children or fields for my sake will receive a hundred times as much and will inherit eternal life" (Matt. 19:29) would seem to indicate that God's reward also includes material aspects, aspects that are readily comprehensible in the context of participation in the millennial rule and reign of Christ as the Son of Man (19:28; cf. Rev. 20:4).

It is difficult to conceive of a greater bliss than the enjoyment of the presence of God. In the final analysis, this is the reward Matthew held out to those who heed the message his gospel bears and who respond to Jesus' call to, "Take my yoke upon you and learn from me, for I am gentle and humble in heart, and you will find rest for your souls" (11:29). For those who do, they are assured of the presence of Jesus "to the very end of the age" (28:20). Beyond that is the assurance of the presence of God, the confidence that "the righteous will shine like the sun in the kingdom of their Father" (13:43).

The disciples' hope is in the person of God—that He will do what He says He will do. The language of "reward" is ultimately the assurance that God will be faithful to His word and will deal graciously with those who are Jesus' disciples.

---

69. See Bauer, Arndt, and Gingrich, *A Greek-English Lexicon of the New Testament,* 610.

2

A THEOLOGY OF MARK

David K. Lowery

For much of its history Mark's gospel has occupied a fairly inconspicuous place among the four Gospels generally. Among the Synoptic[1] Gospels (Matthew, Mark, and Luke) in particular, it has been less esteemed than its lengthier companions. The modest appreciation accorded Mark is somewhat understandable since only about 10 percent of the gospel's account contains information not found in Matthew and Luke. That this was the case may also have contributed to the judgment that Mark's gospel was essentially a condensation or abridgment of the longer Gospels, particularly Matthew. Augustine, in fact, referred to Mark as the "abbreviator" (*breviator*) of Matthew.[2]

But is this an accurate assessment of the relationship of Mark to the other gospels? Although it was more or less accepted as correct for about 1,800 years, the nineteenth century witnessed an era of biblical study that initiated a reassessment of viewpoint on many matters of interpretation, among them the question of the rela-

---

1. The first three Gospels are called "synoptics" (from the Greek word, *synoptikos*) because their depictions of Jesus' life and ministry employ a "similar viewpoint" of organization and style that differs from that found in John's gospel.

2. Augustine, *De Consensu Evangelistarum* 1.2. An English translation of Augustine's essay, "The Harmony of the Gospels," was made by S. D. F. Salmond in *Select Library of the Nicene and Post-Nicene Fathers of the Christian Church,* ed. Philip Schaff (New York: Scribner, 1908), 6:76–236.

DAVID K. LOWERY, B.A., Th.M., Ph.D., is professor of New Testament studies at Dallas Theological Seminary.

tionship of the Gospels. Out of that era emerged the consensus that Mark was probably not the "follower" of Matthew, as Augustine thought,[3] but the pioneer, the first writer of a gospel.

Several features of Mark's gospel suggest that this more satisfactorily fits the facts.[4] For one thing, if Mark was condensing or abbreviating Matthew, he did a rather inept job of it at various points. Actually on more than one occasion Mark's account of a particular incident in the life of Jesus is longer and more detailed than Matthew's. Rather, Matthew by comparison seems to have abbreviated and condensed the account.[5]

Related to this feature is the fact that if Mark was abbreviating Matthew, he seems to have had an unusual opinion about what is important and what is not. For example, although the Sermon on the Mount is the longest and generally regarded as the most important discourse in Matthew (chaps. 5–7), almost none of it appears in the gospel of Mark. If Mark, indeed, intended to summarize Matthew's gospel, but deleted almost all the Sermon on the Mount in doing so, he might well be thought to have lost his way somewhere in the process, particularly since his inclusion of the Parables Discourse (Mark 4) and the Eschatological Discourse (Mark 13) shows that he was not averse to inserting blocks of teaching material into his presentation. Most interpreters find it easier to conclude that Matthew subsequently provided additional examples of Jesus' teaching along the line begun by Mark, rather than that Mark simply passed over much of this in the process of writing an abridgment.

Another factor influential in the opinion that Mark's gospel was written first is the style of his Greek, the language in which the gospel was originally written. Although it is not readily apparent to the reader of an English translation, Mark's Greek style is often noticeably awkward in comparison to Matthew's. In the account of the feeding of the 4,000, for example, Jesus, concerned for the well-being of the crowd that had been with Him three days, implied that the disciples should provide food for the people before they departed to their homes. The disciples' reply is recorded in fairly straightforward Greek by Matthew: "Where could we get enough bread in this remote place to feed such a crowd?" (15:33). But the parallel

---

3. Ibid.

4. The question about the relationship of the Gospels and their interdependence is much debated and difficult to assess. The extent and degree of similarity in some cases (in certain instances, the Gospels' account of a statement or deed is identical) suggest literary dependence, namely, that the writer of one gospel saw fit to incorporate the other writer's report of a particular saying or event. It is possible, of course, that the gospel writers simply made use of the same information in the writing of their separate accounts, but the pattern of exact similarity coupled with periodic divergence has pointed to literary dependence as the more likely explanation.

5. One might compare, for example, the account of the Gerasene demoniac(s) (Matt. 8:28–34; Mark 5:1–20) or the account of Jairus' daughter and the woman with a hemorrhage (Matt. 9:18–26; Mark 5:21–43) to see that Matthew rather than Mark abbreviated the narrative. Held shows that this pattern recurs consistently in the narratives about Jesus' healing miracles (Heinz Joachim Held, "Matthew as the Interpreter of the Miracle Stories," in *Tradition and Interpretation in Matthew,* 2d ed., ed. Guenther Bornkamm, Gerhard Barth, and Heinz Joachim Held [London: SCM, 1982], 165–299).

statement at Mark 8:4 is a noteworthy example of rather jumbled Greek syntax, all the more curious if Mark had reference to Matthew's otherwise plain account.

It is possible that Mark intentionally adopted a somewhat primitive or "iconographic" style of writing in order to divert attention from himself as writer and to direct the focus of the reader to the subject matter at hand, the life and ministry of Jesus.[6] But if that is the case, in this instance at least it is counterproductive (as contrived self-effacement often is) since the average reader of Greek would probably have been put at a momentary loss by the awkwardness of the syntax. While it is impossible to prove that stylistic reasons do not account for this rough patch in the narrative, it seems more likely that it is simply a reflection of Mark's imperfect mastery of Greek, a medium which he chose to employ recognizing its suitability for reaching the most people, although it may not have been the easiest or most natural language for him to use.

That the gospel of Mark contains some passages of awkward Greek should not surprise or dismay the reader. On the contrary, it ought to be a source of encouragement. It provides another illustration of the fact that God often uses ordinary people (with sometimes less than ordinary skills) to accomplish extraordinary deeds.

Though primarily engaged in an oral rather than a written ministry, D. L. Moody was in certain respects a modern equivalent to Mark as a communicator of the gospel. His command of English was seemingly less than perfect and there were moments when he may have wounded the grammatical sensibilities of some of the more literate members of his audiences, but this inability never significantly hindered him in communicating the gospel with great effectiveness. In a similar way, Mark's occasional literary lapses have been no handicap to his communication in this gospel in which he skillfully set forth the life and ministry of Jesus.

Although much of what Mark recorded in his gospel is echoed in the gospels of Matthew and Luke, it would be wrong to conclude that Mark has nothing distinctive to say. While his gospel does not differ dramatically from the longer versions of his colleagues, his briefer account does have a power all its own that can be especially beneficial in the life of a self-satisfied or complacent reader.

Mark achieved this result by portraying the humanity and the humiliation of Jesus in bold, inescapable hues. In so doing he showed to great effect what Jesus meant when He said that "the Son of Man[7] did not come to be served, but to serve, and to give his life as a ransom for many" (10:45). In similar fashion the reader is left with the realization that following Jesus is an undertaking with profound implications: "If anyone would come after me, he must deny himself and take up his cross and follow me" (8:34).

6. See James Moulton and Nigel Turner, *Style*, vol. 4 of *A Grammar of New Testament Greek* (Edinburgh: T & T Clark, 1976), 27–28.

7. A discussion about the significance of the various titles associated with Jesus is included in the study of Matthew's theology. The meanings of these titles in the Gospels remain basically the same. For information about the ideas connected to these titles, the reader should consult the discussion of Christology in the chapters in this book on Matthew's or Luke's theology.

So that the reader may not despair in the face of this challenge and the realization of his or her own personal inability to meet it, Mark also portrayed the disciples in graphic and unsparing terms. Because of this, the reader, imbued with a spirit of self-sufficient triumphalism, may in fact be reluctant to identify with the disciples. But Mark intended that his readers would see themselves as one with the disciples.

On the whole, the disciples do not create a positive impression in Mark's gospel. No doubt this is partly due to the fact that they are shown for what they were—a fairly undistinguished group of people. Mark also underscored the frailty and fallibility of the disciples more decisively than did the other gospel writers. But the impressions left on the reader are salutary ones: disciples are ordinary men and women who routinely fail. Their confidence and trust cannot be in themselves; it must be in God.

GOD THE FATHER AND THE HOLY SPIRIT

Before attention is given to what Mark said about Jesus, some comments about his depiction of God the Father and the Holy Spirit are in order. Mark's presentation of both persons is in line with what is said about them in the other Gospels, though with less detail in keeping with the brevity of his gospel generally.

Mark showed that God is sovereignly at work accomplishing His will in the lives of Jesus, John the Baptist, the disciples, and even the opponents of Jesus. He did this by linking various events involving each to the fulfillment of Scripture. For example, when Jesus was accosted by His enemies in Gethsemane, He issued a rebuke of their duplicity and also a statement affirming that what was happening was in accord with the purposes of God: "Every day I was with you, teaching in the temple courts, and you did not arrest me. But the Scriptures must be fulfilled" (14:49).

The following verse describes the reaction of the disciples to Jesus' arrest: "Then everyone deserted him and fled" (v. 50). But Mark had prepared the reader to see this desertion also as a fulfillment of Scripture. A few verses earlier, Mark recorded Jesus' prediction to the disciples that "you will all fall away" (v. 27), an event Jesus associated with the words of Zechariah 13:7, "Strike the shepherd, and the sheep will be scattered."

Though Jesus earnestly sought to avoid the awful course set before Him in the experience of the Passion ("Take this cup from me," 14:36), He submitted, as the obedient Son, to the outworking of the will of God despite all its grievous implications for Him: "Yet not what I will, but what you will" (Mark 14:36).

The imprisonment and martyrdom of John the Baptist, treated by Mark in greater detail than elsewhere among the Gospels (6:17–29; cf. Matt. 14:3–12; Luke 3:19–20), is likewise said to be an event that occurred in accord with the Scriptures: "But I tell you Elijah has come, and they have done to him everything they wished, just as it is written about him" (Mark 9:13). What the relevant Scripture(s) might be Mark did not say, but 1 Kings 19:10 records the words of Elijah to God that his enemies "put your prophets to death with the sword." John's death at the hand of Herod's executioner (Mark 6:27) corresponds to those words of frustration from God's prophet Elijah.

All these references to events happening in accord with Scripture underscore the fact that the purposes of God are being carried out. They also give readers the assurance that the apparent triumph of God's enemies over John and Jesus is just that—it is only apparent, not real. Through it all, God's purposes are advancing. Jesus would give His life "as a ransom for many" (10:45). His "blood of the covenant, which is poured out for many" (14:24) would be effective in gaining redemption for people and bringing them into a new relationship with God. And the threefold predictions concerning His passion and death would be followed by His resurrection (8:31; 9:31; 10:32–34).

Thus the reader can see that Jesus' humiliation will issue in His vindication. This likewise is certain of accomplishment, because as Mark showed, it too is in accord with the Scriptures. Jesus pointed to His vindication in connection with the discussion about Christ being David's Son: "David himself, speaking by the Holy Spirit, declared: ' "The Lord said to my Lord: 'Sit at my right hand until I put your enemies under your feet' " ' " (12:36). In this quotation from Psalm 110:1, "the Lord" mentioned first is God the Father. It is to Jesus, as David's Lord ("my Lord"), that God gives the place of authority at His right hand. Jesus will occupy this position of authority until God sees to it that all the enemies of Jesus[8] are brought into submission to Him.[9] That Jesus looked forward to a comprehensive, ultimate vindication seems clear from the citation of this verse.

Actually the vindication of Jesus is referred to earlier by Mark in this same chapter, at the end of the parable of the tenants (Mark 12:1–9). There (in 12:10–11) Psalm 118:22–23 is quoted as an illustration that God will reverse the judgment of Israel's leadership concerning Jesus: "The stone the builders rejected has become the capstone; the Lord has done this, and it is marvelous in our eyes." "The stone" is Jesus, whom the parable depicts as the Son who is killed and thrown out of the vineyard by the tenants, the present leadership of Israel (Mark 12:8). The One who will occupy the place of preeminence ("the capstone") in the building established by God is this previously rejected stone, Jesus (cf. Eph. 2:20). It is another way of saying that Jesus will be vindicated by God in the presence of all people.

The mention of these few verses shows how Mark viewed the beginning and end of the life of Jesus as ordained by God and certain to be fulfilled. The empowering or enabling agent in the accomplishment of the will of God in Jesus' life was the Holy Spirit. Not only was the Holy Spirit active in the inspiration of Scripture, which spoke prophetically of Jesus (e.g., Mark 12:36 citing Ps. 110:1); but also the Spirit was the active agent in Jesus' life, coming on Him distinctively at

---

8. By extension, the enemies of Jesus are both enemies of God and also of God's people, the followers of Jesus, as well.

9. This particular theme also appears in Psalm 8:6 (in connection with the phrase "son of man," v. 4) and is developed by Paul in 1 Corinthians 15:25–28 and by the writer of Hebrews (Heb. 2:5–8).

His baptism (Mark 1:10), leading Him into testing (1:12), and empowering Him in the course of his ministry (3:29).[10] This same Spirit will likewise provide enablement for the disciples. Jesus promised them that in times of trial they need not worry "about what to say. Just say whatever is given you at the time, for it is not you speaking, but the Holy Spirit" (13:11).[11]

This emphasis on the sovereignty of God as a guarantee that what He says will be fulfilled does not mean that individuals are not responsible for their behavior, nor that everything God will accomplish is immediately achieved without regard for individual or personal endeavor. Mark, for example, made it clear that a recognition that the authority of God is at work in Jesus' ministry is one thing which has been revealed to the disciples ("the secret of the kingdom of God[12] has been given[13] to you," 4:11). Yet there were many important implications connected with that fact which the disciples did not comprehend, much to Jesus' dismay (4:13). This shows that the work of God in individual lives is not simply a passive affair.

The warning to Judas is a negative corollary of this fact. Although Jesus stated unequivocally the inevitability of Judas's betrayal, He did not suggest that because it accorded with God's sovereign purpose this eliminated or somehow excused human responsibility. On the contrary, Jesus' words are a chilling reminder that individual actions have important, sometimes even eternal, consequences: "The Son of Man will go just as it is written about him. But woe to that man who betrays the Son of Man! It would be better for him if he had not been born" (14:21).

GOD THE SON

Without doubt the central figure in Mark's gospel is Jesus. The "good news" concerns what He said and did (1:1). Although there is no question that Mark shared with the other gospel writers the conviction that Jesus was the divine Son of God, his portrait emphasizes more the humanity of Jesus. Through a series of un-

10. That Jesus performed His exorcisms by means of the power of the Spirit is implied by His response ("Whoever blasphemes against the Holy Spirit," 3:29) to the accusation that He had done them by means of Satan ("By the prince of demons he is driving out demons," 3:22).

11. This word of assurance concerns the enablement of the Spirit to deal with hostile situations involving threatening prosecution in court settings, where a disciple may be lacking representation or counsel (cf. the case of Paul versus Tertullus, Acts 24). It is not a blanket statement suggesting that a disciple need give no thought to preparation regarding his or her message or ministry.

12. For a discussion of the phrases "kingdom of God" and "kingdom of heaven" as references to the extension of the authority of God in individual lives and in the world generally, see chapter 1 on Matthew's theology.

13. This verb is passive. This particular form of the verb was commonly used by Jews in order to avoid the mention of God's name, since an active verb normally includes specification of a subject. Not using the name of God was an expression of reverence (it was also a way of insuring that the name of God would not be taken in vain [Ex. 20:7] on the logic that what is not mentioned cannot be misused—a dubious conclusion in itself). As a result, this use of a passive verb is sometimes referred to as a "divine passive." The verb "has been given" thus meant "God has given."

paralleled descriptions of Jesus' emotions in response to different events and circumstances, Mark enabled his readers to see with greater clarity the humanity of Jesus and to gain thereby a deeper appreciation for the faithfulness that characterized His years of ministry. Though Mark's mention of Jesus' initial testing by Satan is brief (1:12) in comparison to the fuller accounts in Matthew (4:1–11) and Luke (4:1–13), Mark's description of the whole of Jesus' ministry gives an extended insight into the opposition engendered by His commitment to doing God's will.

When, for example, Mark recounted, Jesus' healing of the man with the shriveled hand (3:1–5), he alone mentioned that Jesus was angered (v. 5) by the indifference of the religious leaders to the suffering of this man. The word used for "anger" (*orgē*) is often used elsewhere in the New Testament to describe the wrath of God against sin (e.g., Rom. 1:18), but this is the only instance in the Gospels in which this particular word is used to describe a response of Jesus.

Not only is it instructive as a revelation of God concerning sin, but it also illustrates a circumstance where anger is an appropriate response for those who would be like Jesus. His anger is due not to injustice against Him, but to a wrong done to someone else. This sheds light on the directive in Ephesians 4:26, "Be angry, and yet do not sin" (NASB). As a general rule anger, particularly in response to wrongs personally suffered, is inappropriate for the Christian (e.g., Eph. 4:31). But where injustice would frustrate the doing of good on behalf of someone else, anger can be a proper response.

Mark's record of another instance, employing a kindred word for anger (*aganakteō*, "to be indignant") also in relation to Jesus, is a further illustration of this point. In his account of the little children and Jesus (Mark 10:13–16), Mark alone described Jesus' emotion on this occasion. When Jesus saw the disciples rebuking those who tried to bring children to Him, "he was indignant" (v. 14).

In this instance Jesus' indignation was directed against His disciples whom He rebuked for their unjust behavior. Elsewhere the word describes the indignation of Jesus' opponents against Him (Matt. 21:15), or the indignation of the other ten disciples against the two (James and John) who sought places of honor in the kingdom (Mark 10:41). Instances like these illustrate self-centered indignation, motivated by personal interests or self-serving concerns. But Jesus' indignation arose not from any concern for personal advantage, but out of regard for the well-being of others. This too is an illustration of appropriate indignation, the kind Paul commended when he referred to the Corinthians' "indignation . . . to see justice done" (2 Cor. 7:11) when it concerned the righting of wrong on behalf of someone else.

Behind a discussion of this sort lies the conviction that these emotional notices, which Mark attached to his portrait of Jesus, are more than stylistic or literary features intended only to lend vividness to his narrative. It is not simply what Jesus said, but also how He lived which is instructive for disciples. That is why what Mark wrote about Jesus' reason for appointing the Twelve is noteworthy: it was not only so that He could send them out as His apostles but also so that "they might be with him" (3:14). The way He lived His life illustrated the message He proclaimed, thus providing an important lesson in discipleship which Mark passed on to his readers.

Jesus' anger or indignation at attempts to frustrate or hinder the extension of God's grace to people is but one emotion disclosed by Mark in his portrait of Him. In the same verse in which he mentioned Jesus' anger, Mark also referred to Jesus being "deeply distressed" (3:5) at the stubborn hearts of those opposing Him. Later when the Pharisees questioned Jesus in order to test Him, Mark wrote, "he sighed deeply" (8:12) before undertaking a response. These are not the emotions of a world-weary soul so much as the disclosure of sadness in the face of indifference to the grace of God. When Jesus visited the community in which He grew up and the people took offense at Him, He was "amazed at their lack of faith" (6:6). He also was experiencing difficult lessons about the hardness of human hearts (cf. Heb. 3:8).

The pathos of Jesus is also underscored in the account of His conversation with the rich young man who asked about eternal life (Mark 10:17–22). Mark alone mentioned that "Jesus looked at him and loved him" (v. 21). It is therefore a double sadness when the young man turned away "because he had great wealth" (v. 22). Narrated in this way, Mark's vignettes serve to show with greater effect the struggle and heartache experienced by Jesus in the course of His ministry.

Related to this presentation of Jesus' emotional response to situations is Mark's portrayal of a Christ who faced regular opposition or misunderstanding in the course of fulfilling His calling. At the beginning of His ministry Mark showed that Jesus encountered opposition that was to dog Him to the end of His days on earth. In the second chapter of his gospel, Mark related how the religious leaders concluded that what Jesus was saying and doing amounted to blasphemy, the dishonoring of God. For example, when Jesus granted forgiveness to the paralytic, the religious teachers asked, "Why does this fellow talk like that? He's blaspheming! Who can forgive sins but God alone?" (2:7). As Mark later showed, this was the charge the leaders of Israel ultimately used to condemn Jesus ("You have heard the blasphemy," 14:64).

The ultimate objective in their opposition took shape in the early days of Jesus' ministry. In narrating Jesus' healing of the man with the shriveled hand, Mark described the Pharisees and the Herodians as plotting together "how they might kill Jesus" (3:6). This kind of animus continued until a few days before His eventual crucifixion when Mark said that "the chief priests and the teachers of the law were looking for some way to arrest Jesus and kill him" (14:1), a prospect which eventually was brought to fruition in the cross.

However, not only did the religious and political establishment attempt to limit or halt the ministry of Jesus, Mark also gave a distinctive look at the misunderstanding Jesus' ministry engendered among members of His own family. There is no suggestion in the narrative that the family members were acting for any reason other than out of regard for Jesus, but it is nevertheless disquieting to read Mark's account that "they went to take charge of him, for they said, 'He is out of his mind' " (3:21).

When His family attempted to carry out this aim, Mark pointed out the distance between them and Jesus: "Then Jesus' mother and brothers arrived. Standing outside, they sent someone in to call him" (3:31). When the message was conveyed to Jesus that "your mother and brothers are outside looking for you" (v. 32), He asked, "Who are my mother and my brothers?" (v. 33). His answer, "whoever does God's will is my brother and sister and mother" (v. 35), suggests that His family's purpose in this instance placed them outside this circle.

That Mark later associated Jesus' sisters with the townspeople of Nazareth who took offense at Him ("Aren't his sisters here with us?", 6:3) also shows His family's misunderstanding. Added to this is the fact that Mark made no mention about any further contacts between Jesus and His family. All this serves to underscore the difficulties and personal hardships Jesus endured in faithfully carrying out God's will.

In truth, the disciples did not end up being much of a surrogate family either. Although they did discharge their commission to preach and heal (6:12–13), and though through their spokesman Peter they managed to confess Jesus as the Christ (8:29), in the end "everyone deserted him and fled" (14:50).

Undeterred by this pattern of human misunderstanding and failure, Jesus continued the itinerant ministry that characterized His work from the beginning. When His disciples told Him that "everyone is looking for you" (1:37), He simply replied, "Let us go somewhere else—to the nearby villages—so I can preach there also. That is why I have come" (1:38).

To make clear the authority with which Jesus taught and preached, Mark followed his first extended presentation of Jesus' teaching, the Parables discourse (4:1–34), with three successive examples of His power over tempestuous forces or powers at work in the world. The first example concerns authority over creation. In the storm at sea (vv. 35–41), He arose from His sleep in the stern of the ship to rebuke the wind and the waves: " 'Quiet! Be still!' Then the wind died down and it was completely calm" (v. 39).

After showing that Jesus has authority over the natural world and illustrating the power He had to bring order to manifestations of the chaos that exists there (cf. Rom. 8:20–21), Mark depicted Jesus' authority over the supernatural world, the realm of rebellious spirits (Mark 5:1–20). In the account of the demon-possessed man, Mark made it clear that the dominion of Satan, here represented by demonic hosts, is a kingdom of death and destruction. He described the tendency to self-destruction of this man, who "cut himself with stones" (v. 5). When Jesus permitted the demons afflicting the man to enter a herd of swine, "the herd . . . rushed down the steep bank into the lake and were drowned" (v. 13).

This is a dramatic illustration of the ruinous character of the kingdom of Satan and the ultimate havoc his rule would wreak were he free to fulfill his designs in the world. As Mark showed, however, the destructive power of Satan is ultimately subject to Jesus' healing and restorative power. Instead of following a course of self-destruction, the man was now "in his right mind" (v. 15) and set on a new course of behavior. Jesus told him to "go home to your family and tell them how much the Lord has done for you, and how he has had mercy on you" (v. 19). The man dutifully did this "and all the people were amazed" (v. 20).

The authority of Jesus does not extend only to elements in the natural and spiritual world. Death itself is subject to His bidding as Mark demonstrated in narrating the third example of His authority, the raising of Jairus' daughter (5:21–43). These three consecutive accounts serve to demonstrate further that the crowd in its initial impression of Jesus, mentioned in chapter 1, correctly assessed Jesus' ministry: "A new teaching—and with authority!" (1:27).

Yet in all of this there is the realization that Jesus' deeds were in some sense anticipatory, that the full manifestation of His authority on a universal scale, including the ultimate vanquishing of the powers of evil in the world, awaits fulfillment. Aspects of the two extended discourses that Mark included in his gospel (4:1–43; 13:1–37) speak to this point, addressing both the surety and the futurity of this rule. Also addressing this issue is the theme often referred to as "the messianic secret," Mark's recurrent citation of Jesus' warnings that reports about His deeds or knowledge about Him should not be publicized until such time (according to 9:9, after the resurrection) as it could be rightly understood.

THE MESSIANIC SECRET

A study published near the turn of the century called attention to the theological significance of this aspect of Mark's gospel[14] and initiated a discussion about its meaning which continues to the present time.[15] Although the other Synoptic Gospels also contain statements by Jesus that His identity not be made known (e.g., Matt. 16:20, "he warned the disciples not to tell anyone that he was the Christ") or that reports about His miracles not be publicized (e.g., Luke 8:56, "he ordered them not to tell anyone what had happened"), Mark gave more consistent attention to this theme. Why he did so is still a matter of debate, but this theme is coherent with his depiction of the extensive human misunderstanding concerning Jesus' life and ministry that marked His first coming.

As each of the Synoptic Gospel writers shows in his own way, the course of Jesus' ministry in His first coming was generally characterized by humble submission to fulfilling a life of service to God and people that ultimately led Him to the cross. Mark 10:45 is a virtual summary of Jesus' earthly life: "For even the Son of Man did not come to be served, but to serve, and to give his life as a ransom for many." The destiny of Jesus' first coming was fulfilled by His death, which achieved redemption for others. When the psalmist said, "No man can redeem the life of another or give to God a ransom for him" (Ps. 49:7), he spoke of all men except the Son of Man, who became the "one mediator between God and man, the man Christ Jesus, who gave his life as a ransom for all men" (1 Tim. 2:5–6).

In that sense the word "humiliation" appropriately summarizes the course of Jesus' earthly life. Yet the many descriptions of the greatness of His power and authority afford the reader insight into the profound character of that humiliation and

14. William Wrede, *The Messianic Secret,* trans. J. C. G. Grieg (Greenwood, S.C.: Attic, 1971).
15. See Christopher Tuckett, ed., *The Messianic Secret in Mark* (Philadelphia: Fortress, 1983).

show the voluntary and self-sacrificial nature of His life. These apparently disparate realities are brought together in the phrase "Son of Man," Jesus' usual self-designation. He said the Son of Man has authority (e.g., 2:10, 28), the Son of Man would suffer and die (e.g., 9:12; 10:33, 45), the Son of Man would be resurrected and exalted (e.g., 10:34; 13:26).

Mark showed that the manner in which Jesus' messiahship unfolded provided ample opportunity for misunderstanding. "Humiliation" is not a concept readily associated with those who possess power and authority. While it may not be entirely clear what the popular expectation of a Jewish messiah was,[16] it is probably fair to say that the idea of a self-sacrificial servant was not one very widely championed (or even considered).

This combination of great authority and abject humiliation in Jesus' life understandably bewildered even those closest to Him. Thus, the desire to limit pronouncement about His messiahship can be seen as a conscientious and compassionate course of action in view of the confusion and misunderstanding it would otherwise have produced. Mark's portrait of this phenomenon can thus be seen as historically coherent given the fact that humans then and now have certain expectations which they associate with the privileges of power and authority.

Since Jesus entered more fully into the "exaltation" aspect of His messiahship only after the resurrection, He counseled the disciples not to declare Him the Christ until that time (9:9). Then normal expectation and historical reality would correspond, though as chapter 13 makes clear, the manifestation of that reality is yet future.

There is still another reason why Mark gave attention to the "messianic secret" aspect of Jesus' life and ministry. Understanding the nature of His earthly humiliation as a necessary prelude to the exaltation into which He entered after His resurrection is essential to comprehending the nature of the ministry He left for His disciples to continue. They also would be endowed with great power and authority (3:15; 6:13). But as Jesus did, they too were to use this authority in the service of God and for the benefit of others. The disciples also were to see their lives as characterized by "humiliation," expressed in voluntary and self-sacrificial service (8:34). As in Jesus' case, the "exaltation" period is entered into at the end of one's earthly life, when death brings to a close the "humiliation" phase that characterizes the present course for followers of Jesus (8:35; 10:29–30).

There is a sense in which this aspect of Jesus' life and teaching as it applies to disciples is likewise susceptible to misunderstanding and confusion on the part of many. It too is a "secret" that needs to be comprehended from the vantage point of the resurrection and the ultimate vindication that God will accomplish in Christ. To misunderstand the nature of Jesus' messiahship is also to misunderstand the nature of discipleship, because one follows on the other. Thus to be privy to the one "secret" similarly has implications for understanding the other. Further attention to this

---

16. On the variety of views about messiah and kingdom in early Jewish literature see Michael Lattke, "The Jewish Background of the Synoptic Concept, 'The Kingdom of God,'" in *The Kingdom of God,* ed. Bruce Chilton (Philadelphia: Fortress, 1984), 72–91.

idea and related themes will be taken up when Mark's presentation of the disciples is considered subsequently. Before that subject is turned to, however, some issues related to the kingdom of God require discussion.

KINGDOM

The general outline of Mark's message about the kingdom of God is comparable to that found in the other Gospels. Also the ideas associated with the terminology are similar. The "kingdom" refers to the rule or reign of God. The primary representative of that kingdom in Mark's gospel is Jesus, who proclaimed "the good news of God: 'The time has come. The kingdom of God is near. Repent and believe the good news!'" (1:14–15).

Repentance involves a change of mind that manifests itself in a change of life. Believing the Good News means accepting or receiving what Jesus says, which has implications for the subsequent conduct of one's life. The gospel of Mark as a whole becomes something of a commentary on this message, giving definition to what it means to repent and believe. In the incident involving Jesus' family, for example, He said, "whoever does God's will is my brother and sister and mother" (3:35).

In the parable of the sower (which immediately follows the statement in 3:35), Jesus referred to understanding its message as an aspect of the "secret of the kingdom of God" (4:11) which had been given to His disciples. The seed which is sown is "the word" (v. 14) which Jesus proclaimed. Those described as "good soil, hear the word, accept it, and produce a crop" (v. 20).

The parable of the growing seed, distinctive to Mark (4:26–29), is a reminder to those who "scatter seed" that the life-giving power of God's Word is effective even if it is to a certain extent unfathomable. This, like the parable of the mustard seed which follows (vv. 30–32), shows that the progress of the kingdom is ultimately God's doing. However small and inauspicious it may seem, the kingdom will enjoy a grand and glorious final result. But that will be because the work of God, not only in name but also in fact, is finally His.

This point is reinforced by two incidents recorded in Mark 10. When a man asked what he must do to inherit eternal life (v. 17), Jesus told him to get rid of his possessions and "come, follow me" (v. 21). Shackled by his riches, the man sadly turned away. Later when Jesus told the disciples that "it is easier for a camel to go through the eye of a needle than for a rich man to enter the kingdom of God" (v. 25), they were amazed and asked, "Who then can be saved?" (v. 26). Jesus' reply fits the situation of people generally: "With man this is impossible, but not with God; all things are possible with God" (v. 27).

Mark did not include this account to cause anxiety or despair in the minds of his readers. To the contrary, if salvation and participation in the kingdom of God were in fact dependent on human capabilities, there would be ample ground for anxiety and despair. The point, however, is that God accomplishes salvation and brings people into the kingdom.

This does not mean individuals are only passive spectators in the process. In the ensuing conversation Peter rightly stated that he and the other disciples did what Jesus told the rich man to do—they left all and followed him (v. 28). Jesus did not dispute this; He simply assured Peter that whatever sacrifices may be involved in following Him, what is gained by doing so is incomparably greater (vv. 29–30).

At this point in the narrative Jesus' third prediction of His death is recorded (10:32–34). It serves to swing the focus of attention away from that just-mentioned glorious future and back to the self-sacrificial life that marks the present world for Jesus and those who follow Him. These two poles—humiliation and exaltation—come together again in the following account of the request of James and John (vv. 35–45).

Picking up on the prospect of the glorious future evoked by Jesus, James and John proposed to Him that He grant them the privilege of sitting in the places of honor at His side during His exaltation: "Let one of us sit at your right and the other at your left in your glory" (v. 37). In the discussion that developed out of Jesus' encounter with the rich man, a link had been drawn between sacrifice and glorious recompense (vv. 29–30). Here too Jesus pursued this connection with James and John.

Jesus had spoken for a third time about the humiliation and death that awaited Him in Jerusalem (vv. 32–34). Now He asked James and John if they were willing to undergo the same experience, "Can you drink the cup I drink or be baptized with the baptism I am baptized with?" (v. 38). They affirmed that they could,[17] and Jesus predicted that they would. But He also made it clear that when it comes to rewards it is not a simple measured transaction of "this for that," even if it is on the magnanimous order of 1 to 100 (v. 30). This is because, as Jesus explained, positions in the kingdom are not matters subject to negotiation or achievement. They are instead determined by God: "to sit at my right or left is not for me to grant. These places belong to those for whom they have been prepared" (v. 40). Here too a passive verb leaves unspoken the understood subject: God, not man (not even the Son of Man) decides these things.[18]

The extended passage (10:17–45) thus comes full circle with regard to viewpoints on the kingdom of God. It is God who enables people to enter the kingdom (vv. 23–27), and it is He who offers assurance of reward or final participation in it (v.40). Thus the beginning and the end of life in the kingdom is bound up with the authority of God.

Implicit in Jesus' reply to James and John is the assurance that He will reign over a kingdom. Following this discourse with James, John, and the other disciples,

---

17. The verb *dynamai* used in Jesus'question ("can you," v. 38) and the reply of James and John ("we can," v. 39) is related in spelling and meaning to the adjectives used in the statement in verse 27, which has relevance to the affirmation of James and John: "With man this is impossible [*adynatos*], but not with God; all things are possible [*dynatos*] with God."

18. In fact, the verb *etoimastai* ("have been prepared") is noteworthy not only because it employs the passive voice. It is also written in the perfect tense, which may indicate that decisions like this have already been made by God. At the very least, the perfect expresses that a reward will certainly be given; it is prepared and waiting for God's people.

is the account of the healing of blind Bartimaeus. In his appeal to Jesus he hailed Him twice by means of the royal epithet "Son of David" (vv. 47–48). The connection to a kingdom is explicitly made in the next chapter by the crowds who acclaimed Jesus at His Triumphal Entry: "Blessed is he who comes in the name of the Lord! Blessed is the coming kingdom of our father David!" (11:9–10).

But as Mark will show, the glorious manifestation of this kingdom awaits a future era. After a time of "distress unequaled from the beginning . . . and never to be equaled again" (13:19), "men will see the Son of Man coming in clouds with great power and glory" (v. 26). At this time the exalted Jesus will be vindicated before all people (cf. 14:62). The humiliation of the earthly Jesus will give way to the exaltation of the King of glory. Mark gave no further details about the configuration of this kingdom other than to assure readers once again (cf. 10:40) that it will be manifested, based on Jesus' certain affirmation: "Heaven and earth will pass away, but my words will never pass away" (13:31).

DISCIPLES

Mark's portrait of the disciples is, like his other characterizations in the gospel, sharply drawn. Although not persistently negative, it is fair to say that in comparison to the other gospel accounts Mark usually depicted the disciples in a rather unflattering light. Why Mark routinely drew attention to the disciples' shortcomings is not certain. There is little reason to doubt that it is an accurate representation since the descriptions in the other Gospels differ only in degree. Given the fact that Mark wrote his gospel to edify and strengthen the church, an explanation consistent with a general objective along those lines will more likely be correct. Before speculating about possible explanations, however, some of the concepts related to this question require consideration.

Mark applied several terms and phrases to the disciples which serve to illustrate their deficiencies rather plainly. For example, he showed how prone they were to misunderstanding. He used various terms to describe this failing, which was characteristic of the disciples at least until Peter's confession of Jesus as the Christ (8:29). Yet even after that, Mark demonstrated that the implications of Jesus' messiahship continued to be lost on the disciples who recoiled from the idea of a suffering and dying Messiah. As Jesus said to their spokesman,[19] Peter, "You do not have in mind the things of God, but the things of men" (8:33).

The first reference to the disciples' lack of understanding occurs in the Parables' Discourse (4:1–34). Jesus cited Isaiah 6:9–10 as an explanation of why He used parables, so that "they may be ever seeing but never perceiving, and ever hearing but never understanding; otherwise they might turn and be forgiven!" (4:12). The problem, as Mark indicated, was that the disciples had problems with understanding as well! True, "the secret of the kingdom of God has been given" to the disciples (4:11), but apparently there was a communication breakdown (or at

---

19. Mark included the observation that before rebuking Peter, "Jesus turned and looked at his disciples" as if to underscore the fact that what was true of Peter applied to them as well.

least a "slowdown") somewhere along the line because Jesus questioned why they did not understand the basic point of the parable: "Then Jesus said to them, 'Don't you understand this parable? How then will you understand any parable?' " (4:13).[20]

It is interesting to compare the parable of the sower in Matthew and Mark in relation to this point. Matthew began his account of the parable's explanation with these words: "When anyone hears the message about the kingdom and does not understand it, the evil one comes and snatches away what was sown in his heart" (Matt. 13:19). The parallel in Mark (4:15) is similar except that he did not include the phrase "does not understand,"[21] probably because his portrayal of the disciples shows this to be a characteristic of them as well.

The disciples also failed to understand that Jesus' miracles testify about Him. When the disciples saw Jesus walking on the water they were both terrified and amazed (6:50–51). The other gospel writers offered no further commentary, but Mark added a word of explanation: "for they had not understood about the loaves" (v. 52), a reference to the feeding of the 5,000 described in the preceding narrative (vv. 30–44).

In another context, when the disciples asked Jesus to explain what He meant by saying that cleanliness is more an internal than an external matter, He asked them, "Are you so dull? Don't you see that nothing that enters a man from the outside can make him 'unclean'?" (7:18). The NIV translation in this instance is a bit innocuous. The words for "dull" (*asynetos*) and "see" (*noeō*) both refer to understanding, or in this case, the lack of it, a point brought out more clearly in the NASB: "Are you so lacking in understanding? Do you not understand that whatever goes into a man from outside cannot defile him?"[22]

The discussion about the yeast of the Pharisees (8:14–21) can serve to bring to a close this look at one aspect of Mark's portrait of the disciples. Mark recorded Jesus' warning that they should "watch out for the yeast of the Pharisees and that of Herod" (v. 15). The disciples seemed a bit nonplussed by this remark and decided it related to the fact that "we have no bread" (v. 16). In response Jesus said, "Why are you talking about having no bread? Do you still not see or understand?" (v. 17). He then reviewed with them the feeding of the 4,000 (reported in the preceding narrative, 8:1–10) and asked them again, "Do you still not understand?" (v. 21).

It is once more instructive to compare Mark's account with Matthew who recorded this conversation as well (Matt. 16:5–12). Matthew also showed that the

---

20. There are actually two words for "understand" in this verse (v. 13, *oida* and *ginōskō*); there are three if the reference to Isaiah 6:9–10 is considered as well (v. 12, *syniēmi*). They are basically synonymous, since even the term used in the Isaiah quotation will be applied subsequently to the disciples (8:17, 21).

21. The verb in Matthew (*syniēmi*) is the same one used in the Isaiah 6:9–10 quotation, and the one Mark applied to the disciples in 6:52 and 8:17, 21. In Matthew's account, understanding is a characteristic of the "good soil" as verse 23 makes clear: "But what was sown on the good soil is the man who hears the word and understands it. He produces a crop, yielding a hundred, sixty or thirty times what was sown."

22. Matthew also recorded these words of Jesus to the disciples (Matt. 15:16), a reminder that Mark was not alone in showing the disciples' shortcomings.

disciples were befuddled by Jesus' remark about the yeast of the Pharisees[23] and deliberated instead about a lack of bread (v. 7). Matthew also recorded that Jesus asked them, "Do you still not understand?" (v. 9), but he placed less emphasis on the question than did Mark.[24] Matthew concluded by stating what Mark did not, namely, that "they understand" (v. 12). Thus while Matthew showed that the disciples were not the most perceptive individuals, he did indicate that they eventually arrived at a correct understanding. But on this point Mark remained silent.

At this juncture Mark's narrative includes the account of a unique event, the only example in the Four Gospels of a miracle accomplished in stages, the healing of a blind man at Bethsaida (Mark 8:22–26). When the blind man was asked what he saw after Jesus first touched him, he offered this description: "I see people; they look like trees walking around" (v. 24). Only after a second touch from Jesus is the reader told that the man "saw everything clearly" (v. 25).

Because Peter's confession of Jesus as the Christ follows this account in the narrative (8:27–30), some have suggested that Mark viewed this two-step miracle of the blind man's healing as illustrative also of the disciples' progress in understanding.[25] When first exposed to Jesus' teaching and miracles, their understanding approached the perceptive equivalence of the first step in the man's healing, when he saw people as trees walking around. But after a second course of instruction and miracle, as it were, the disciples at least saw things clearly enough to acknowledge Jesus as the Christ.

One can detect a corresponding pattern of repetitive miracle and teaching carried out in two phases in Mark's narrative. The first phase begins at the feeding of the 5,000 (6:30–44) and concludes with the peoples' acknowledgment that "he has done everything well" (7:37). A second phase then begins with the feeding of the 4,000 (8:1–10) and concludes with Peter's confession that Jesus is the Christ.[26]

A problem with this otherwise plausible explanation of Mark's narrative is that the disciples do not seem to be significantly more insightful in the remainder of the gospel. It is true that comments about their lack of understanding end with the discussion about bread. But unlike Matthew, Mark nowhere positively stated that the disciples arrived at a proper understanding of things. In fact, following Peter's confession, Jesus flatly said to their spokesman (after, Mark noted, looking at the disciples collectively), "You do not have in mind the things of God, but the things of men" (8:33). This can hardly be read as a ringing endorsement for insightfulness. The negative comments about them on related matters in the subsequent narrative suggest that interpreting the healing of the blind man as also illustrative of the disciples' progress in understanding overstates the evidence. More credible is the

---

23. Luke recorded only Jesus' statement, "Be on your guard against the yeast of the Pharisees, which is hypocrisy" (12:1).

24. Matthew used only the verb *noeō*, while Mark used both *noeō* and *syniēmi* in reporting Jesus' question. The verb *syniēmi* was used by Matthew in verse 12 to state that the disciples ultimately did understand the point of Jesus' warning.

25. See William Lane, *The Gospel According to Mark* (Grand Rapids: Eerdmans, 1974), 286–87.

26. Ibid., 269.

suggestion that it looks ahead to the era after the Resurrection as the period during which they "saw everything clearly,"[27] though this too may be a case of the practice of interpretation running ahead of reality, of finding more in the narrative of this miracle than is actually there.

At any rate, when it came to having a grasp of what Jesus was saying, or of seeing the significance of what He was doing, Mark made it clear that the disciples were often not much ahead of those outside their circle.[28] This is particularly noticeable when another phrase which Mark associated with them is examined.

On two occasions Mark connected the phrase "hardness of heart" with the disciples. In explaining their response of terror and amazement at seeing Jesus walk on the water, Mark wrote, "their hearts were hardened" (6:52). Later, in the discussion about the yeast of the Pharisees and Herod, Jesus asked them, "Are your hearts hardened?" (8:17).

These two instances might not be seen as a particularly trenchant commentary on the disciples' condition except for the fact that they occur between two similar attributions applied to another group hostile to Jesus. Those "looking for a reason to accuse Jesus" (3:2) evoked in Him anger and deep distress because of "their stubborn hearts" (v. 5). The phrase could also be translated "hardness of heart" (as in the NASB), since the noun Mark used (*pōrōsis*) is cognate to the verb (*pōroō*) used in the perfect participles applied to the disciples. In the next verse the reader discovers who these hard-hearted adversaries were. "Then the Pharisees went out and began to plot with the Herodians how they might kill Jesus" (v. 6).

Later the Pharisees once again shared the narrative scene with Jesus (10:2). They asked Him about the propriety of divorce, particularly as it concerned the regulation of the practice set forth in Deuteronomy 24:1–4. Jesus told them "it was because your hearts were hard[29] that Moses wrote you this law" (Mark 10:5). By extension, of course, Jesus' comment applied not only to the Pharisees but also to their predecessors during and after the time of Moses.

But as Mark showed, hard-heartedness was an affliction shared by Jesus' disciples also.[30] This is true of all people to one degree or another. The propensity to sin and self-centeredness characterizes the human condition generally. Although a process of transformation is initiated in those who enter into the new covenant, sin's deadly effect is not entirely eliminated until the transformation of the body that awaits Jesus' second coming.

In this respect, "hardness of heart" stands in comparison to the meaning of the term *sarx* (usually translated "flesh"). This term was used by Mark when he

27. Jack Kingsbury, *Conflict in Mark* (Philadelphia: Fortress, 1989), 102.

28. Though Mark did use the designation "the Twelve" routinely, he also saw the company of the disciples as wider than the Twelve. For example, those who are given the secrets of the kingdom of God are "the Twelve and the others around him" (4:10; cf. 3:34).

29. A different Greek word is used here (*sklērokardia,* also used in Matt. 19:8), but it is synonymous with the other expressions.

30. Mark 16:14 would be an additional illustration of this, but it is doubtful that 16:9–20 was part of Mark's original gospel. See notes 33 and 34.

described the disciples' failure to support Jesus with prayer during His travail in Gethsemane (14:32–38). As Jesus told them: "The spirit is willing, but the body [*sarx*] is weak" (v. 38). The other Gospels refrain from describing the disciples as "hard of heart," but not Mark. This provides another perspective on the nature of their relationship with Jesus that informs Mark's depiction of the disciples.

It would have been grim enough had Mark limited his portrait of the disciples' failings to comments about their capacity for misunderstanding, or their struggle with hardness of heart. But he did not. He also showed that they were subject to bouts of failing faith and its associated afflictions—cowardice, doubt, and fear.

In Matthew's gospel the disciples were sometimes referred to as "those of little faith." That is not flattering, but it is a step up from Mark's description. In Matthew's account of the storm at sea (8:23–27) Jesus responded to the disciples' appeal for deliverance from the threat of the waves with the words, "You of little faith, why are you afraid?" (v. 26). In Mark, on the other hand, Jesus posed the more disturbing question, "Do you still have no faith?" (Mark 4:40). This is particularly startling in the Greek text because the negative (*ouk*) used in the question usually anticipates an affirmative answer (thus, "yes, it is true that we still have no faith!").

But it is not by means of this question alone that Mark pointed to the disciples' lack of faith. In the same verse (4:40) Jesus also asked them, "Why are you so afraid?"[31] And in the following verse Mark described the disciples as "terrified" (v. 41).[32] That they are shown to be seized by fear also serves as an indication that faith was absent (or at best was frail and faltering), since faith and fear are elsewhere pictured as separate or conflicting experiences. Jesus, for example, said to the synagogue ruler who had been told that his daughter was dead, "Don't be afraid; just believe" (5:36).

Another illustration of this point is in the account of Jesus walking on the water (6:45–52). Once again the disciples were at sea and in desperate straits. After a prolonged struggle to maintain their course against the nighttime wind, Jesus approached them walking on the water. When the disciples saw Him, they thought He was an apparition or ghost and, as Mark wrote, "they cried out because they all saw him and were terrified" (vv. 49–50). But Jesus responded, "Take courage! It is I. Don't be afraid" (v. 50). As Mark later explained, their fear was a manifestation of related disabilities: "for they had not understood . . . their hearts were hardened" (v. 52).

The disciples' struggle with faith is also illustrated by another incident. Matthew (17:14–21) and Luke (9:37–43) also narrated this episode, but Mark

---

31. The word *deilos,* also used in the parallel question in Matthew 8:26, could be rendered "cowardly." It is used elsewhere in the New Testament only in Revelation 21:8 in describing those destined for the lake of fire.

32. The verb here is *phobeomai* ("to fear" or "be afraid"), but Mark intensified the statement by using the verb with a cognate accusative ("greatly afraid") and then added further intensification by attaching the comparative modifier *megan* ("very greatly afraid"). The translation "terrified" captures the idea well.

(9:14–29) gave it greater attention. On this occasion some of the disciples were unable to heal a boy with an evil spirit. As Jesus came on the scene, He was met by a man who explained the destructive effect a demonic spirit had on his son and summarily explained the disciples' dilemma: "I asked your disciples to drive out the spirit, but they could not" (9:18).

This report elicited from Jesus what might be called a lament or utterance of despair: "O unbelieving generation . . . how long shall I stay with you? How long shall I put up with you?" (v. 19). These questions could be a reference to the wearisome nature of ministry generally carried out for the benefit of antagonistic or unresponsive people. However, the fact is that the disciples' failure to render effective ministry in this instance was the immediate cause for Jesus' lamentation.

True, Jesus challenged the boy's father to believe: "Everything is possible for him who believes" (v. 23). And this evoked from the father that poignant and thoroughly human affirmation and appeal: "I do believe; help me overcome my unbelief!" (v. 24). But the narrative ultimately moved to the disciples, who were confounded by their inability in this instance: "Why couldn't we drive it out?" (v. 28). Jesus simply replied, "This kind can come out only by prayer" (v. 29).

The disciples seem to have lost sight of the fact that the authority given them was ultimately derivative. That is, it is God who accomplishes healing or deliverance, by means of the Holy Spirit. They were dependent on Him to carry it out successfully. Prayer is one expression of that dependence, an aspect of faith which the disciples either forgot or failed to learn.

A few verses later Mark referred to Jesus' second statement about His impending death and resurrection, but he explained that the disciples "did not understand what he meant and were afraid to ask him about it" (v. 32). Incomprehension and fear are also mentioned in conjunction with Jesus' third and final prediction of death: "the disciples were astonished while those who followed were afraid" (10:32).

The distinction Mark drew here between the Twelve and the larger company of those who accompanied Jesus is illuminated in part by His description of the women who witnessed Jesus' crucifixion: "Some women were watching from a distance. Among them were Mary Magdalene, Mary the mother of James the younger and of Joses, and Salome. In Galilee these women had followed him and cared for his needs" (15:40–41).

These same three women also figured in what seems to be the final scene in Mark's gospel as witnesses to the empty tomb (16:1–8). Their reaction is consistent with the portrait of disciples generally in this gospel: "Trembling and bewildered, the women went out and fled the tomb. They said nothing to anyone, because they were afraid" (v. 8).

Two of the oldest and generally reliable copies of the New Testament conclude Mark's gospel with this verse.[33] But if this is indeed the place where Mark

---

33. While there are a great number of copies of the New Testament in comparison to other ancient documents, it is nonetheless true that only copies and not the original edition of Mark's gospel (or any other part of the New Testament) are available. As the NIV notes before 16:9, "The two most reliable early manuscripts do not have Mark 16:9–20." The NASB notes similarly that "some of the oldest mss. do not contain vv. 9–20."

stopped writing, it is certainly a curious and troubling note on which to end, especially in comparison to the more positive conclusions of the other Gospels. Because it is such an unsettling ending, many interpreters believe that subsequent copyists added verses 9–20 to provide a conclusion more like that of the others.

One cannot be certain about matters like this,[34] but the abrupt conclusion at the end of 16:8 is consistent with Mark's portrait of the disciples as a group routinely characterized by disappointing behavior. Misunderstanding, hardness of heart, lack of faith, and fear seem to be the unhappy norm of the disciples in Mark's gospel.

Why would Mark choose to present the disciples in this light? Several answers might be given to this question in relation both to the life of Jesus and also to that of the disciples. For one thing, the bleak performance of the disciples provides a backdrop against which the faithfulness of Jesus can be more clearly seen. Surrounded by generally well-meaning but ultimately faltering and failing followers, Jesus nonetheless carried out the work He set out to do (10:45). He did so by depending on God the Father, expressing that dependence in prayer (1:35; 6:46; 14:32), and living a life in submission to God's will (14:36, 39).

The disciples, by contrast, are a reminder that even those chosen and given authority to carry on the work of Jesus must do so in dependence on God and with due recognition of their own propensity to misunderstanding, hardness of heart, lack of faith, and fearfulness. In other words, if God could use people like these first disciples to bring about the establishment of the church, those who follow in their train have reason to be encouraged. If God used such people to begin things, He can use their equally-prone-to-failure heirs to continue the work they began.

Mark's portrait of the disciples is also helpful for later followers who need to form a right estimate of themselves. Paul, for example, advised members of the church in Rome to "not think of yourself more highly than you ought, but rather to think of yourself with sober judgment, in accordance with the measure of faith God has given" (Rom. 12:3). Readers of Mark's gospel are given a good illustration of why it is inappropriate to think too highly of oneself in the lives of disciples who did so and failed miserably.

Instances such as this lend support to the contention that Mark's gospel was written in part to serve as a complement to the letters of Paul, reinforcing and amplifying aspects of the theology that is expressed in them.[35] Mark's portrait of the disciples, for example, is an apt illustration of Paul's words in 1 Corinthians 1:26–29: "Not many of you were wise by human standards. . . . But God chose the foolish . . . the weak . . . the lowly . . . so that no one may boast before him."

---

34. The process of evaluating variations in the readings of ancient documents for which copies alone remain is called textual criticism. It takes into account both the data from the existing copies to a particular reading and also an evaluation of the habits and tendencies of the copyists in arriving at a conclusion. Most questions about the text of the New Testament are smaller in scale (e.g., variations in wording in a verse) than the one about the ending of Mark. But none has a major bearing on the basic outline of Christian doctrine.

35. See Ralph Martin, *Mark: Evangelist and Theologian* (Grand Rapids: Zondervan, 1972), 140–225.

Mark's portrait of Jesus also accords well with Paul's contention to the Corinthians that "we preach Christ crucified" (1 Cor. 1:23). The Jesus of Mark's gospel exemplifies the trials and tribulations of a Messiah whose path was marked by humiliation. When Paul, for example, referred to his role as an apostle as being "the scum of the earth, the refuse of the world" (1 Cor. 4:13), the reader of Mark's gospel will see that, in that respect at least, the apostle was not much different from the Lord he represented. Jesus also was the object of insult and mockery (Mark 15:29–32).

In this sense Mark's gospel enables readers to form a proper estimate of themselves as servants of God. Its portrait of the disciples gives good reason for humility and dependence on God, while at the same time offering encouragement by showing that even a disappointing group like the first disciples, with all their shortcomings and failure, were nonetheless used by God to accomplish His purposes. If God used them, there is hope for subsequent generations who follow haltingly in their footsteps.

AUTHORSHIP

If indeed the person named Mark, who accompanied Paul and Barnabas on their first missionary journey, is the author of this gospel,[36] then appreciation for the fact that failure in faithfulness is not uncharacteristic of disciples would be understandable, since the Mark referred to in Acts seems to have had more than passing acquaintance with the subject. Paul and Barnabas were accompanied on the first leg of their missionary journey (from Antioch in Syria to Cyprus, Acts 13:1–12) by John Mark, who had returned with them from his home in Jerusalem to Antioch (12:25).[37] But when the time came to move on to Perga in Pamphylia (in present-day Turkey) Mark left them to return to Jerusalem (13:13).

This might not be considered problematic but for the contention it provoked subsequently between Paul and Barnabas when the subject of taking Mark along on a second missionary journey came up: "Barnabas wanted to take John, also called Mark, with them, but Paul did not think it wise to take him, because he had deserted them in Pamphylia and had not continued in the work" (15:37–38). In this way the reader learns that Mark's departure bore the stigma of desertion. He was not so much "honorably discharged" as he was "absent-without-leave," at least from Paul's point of view.

Paul and Barnabas saw the situation differently, to the point that "they had such a sharp disagreement that they parted company. Barnabas took Mark and sailed for Cyprus, but Paul chose Silas" (vv. 39–40). Paul presumably regarded Mark as an unsuitable companion for missionary work since he had failed in his first experience to see the work through to the end.

---

36. See Martin Hengel, *Studies in the Gospel of Mark* (London: SCM, 1985), 45–52.

37. "John" is Mark's surname. He was the son of a Mary from Jerusalem in whose house the church met (Acts 12:12).

Mark's cousin Barnabas (Col. 4:10), however, gave Mark another opportunity. References to Mark elsewhere in the letters of the New Testament suggest that the decision to do so proved to be a sound one.[38] Peter referred to him as "my son Mark" (1 Peter 5:13), a testimony to his relationship with Peter and a likely commendation of his contribution to the ministry in Rome as well.[39] Even Paul later came to appreciate Mark's contribution, referring to him in his letter to Philemon as "one of my fellow workers" (Philem. 24). And Paul's second letter to Timothy contains this tribute: "Get Mark and bring him with you, because he is helpful to me in my ministry" (2 Tim. 4:11).

These references show that although Mark's early venture in ministry could be described as a disappointing failure, it did not prove to be a debilitating experience nor did it represent the last word about him. Yet an appreciation for this failure in faithfulness, precipitated for whatever reasons (misunderstanding, fear, hardness of heart?), lends a measure of feeling to the bleak portrait of the disciples Mark painted for readers of his gospel.

The vividness of his presentation may owe something to a sympathetic understanding of his subjects. He knew their struggle. He had firsthand acquaintance with failure. He also knew that although human weaknesses may characterize (and even conclude) one phase of the story, they need not represent the last word. It may simply form the basis for a more satisfactory ministry later.

To that end, Mark's gospel effectively counters pretentiousness and presumption. If disciples are to continue the work Jesus began, they must depend on God if they are to succeed in the task before them. Disciples will also do well to remember that their example for ministry is One who did not assume the prerogatives of exaltation commensurate with His person or status, but instead accepted the role of a humble and humiliated servant. He came not to be served but to serve, even to the point of dying on behalf of others (Mark 10:45).

As there was vindication for Jesus and subsequent exaltation, so there will be vindication and exaltation for disciples who follow Him. But the focus of the present phase of Christian experience is servanthood. As a guide to the successful completion of that role and in appreciation for the spirit and faith it requires, Mark has written an eminently accomplished gospel.

---

38. It is possible that these references describe another person named Mark, since the name was common enough in the first century. But his mention with Barnabas in Colossians 4:10 makes it probable that the other notices refer to the same person as well. Bauer writes, "The same person is certainly referred to" (Walter Bauer, William F. Arndt, and F. Wilbur Gingrich, *A Greek-English Lexicon of the New Testament and Other Early Christian Literature*, 2d ed., rev. F. Wilbur Gingrich and Frederick W. Danker [Chicago: Univ. of Chicago, 1979], 492).

39. See Paul's similar commendation of Timothy in Philippians 2:22.

3

A THEOLOGY OF LUKE–ACTS

DARRELL L. BOCK

Of the 7,947 verses in the New Testament, Luke–Acts comprises 2,157 verses, or 27.1 percent.[1] By comparison, the Pauline Epistles have 2,032 verses and the Johannine writings have 1,407. In addition, only Luke–Acts tells the story of Jesus Christ from His birth through the beginning of the church into the ministry of Paul. This linkage is important for it gives perspective to the sequence of these events. Many Christians consider Matthew and Acts together, because canonically Matthew is the first gospel and Acts includes the history of the apostolic church. But the canonical link is Luke–Acts, not Matthew–Acts, since Luke authored both Luke and Acts. As such, it is appropriate that Luke–Acts should be treated as a unit.

With all the attention given to Jesus and the disciples in these two biblical books, one might think Luke's main subject is the history of Jesus and the church. However, Luke's main burden was much deeper. He portrayed the plan of God as worked out in fulfillment of divine promise. The inauguration of this fulfillment came through Jesus and through the church, which consists of both Jew and Gentile. The completion of this fulfillment will come when Jesus returns (Acts 3:18–26). These books stress the continuity of God's promise, and they present this progress in a pastoral way that instructs and comforts.

---

1. Kurt and Barbara Aland, *The Text of the New Testament*, trans. Erroll F. Rhoads (Grand Rapids: Eerdmans, 1987), 29.

DARRELL L. BOCK, B.A., Th.M., Ph.D., is professor of New Testament studies at Dallas Theological Seminary.

Luke wrote to Theophilus to give him assurance about the things he had been taught (Luke 1:4).[2] A major supposition of that assurance is the recognition that God was at work in recent events, events that were in fulfillment of God's promises (vv. 1–2). Two aspects of that claimed fulfillment, however, would be troubling: a dead Savior and a persecuted community of God that included Gentiles, when Israel held the hope of the promise. Since the church was undergoing persecution, as Acts so vividly portrayed, Theophilus, or anyone like him, might have wondered if that persecution was God's judgment on the church for being too racially broad with His salvation. Was God really at work in the church, and was Jesus really at the center of the plan? How did the promise become so broad and how could a dead Savior bring it to pass?

Luke–Acts assured Theophilus that persecution of the church was not a sign of judgment. Instead the persecution had been predicted and was a means by which the message could go out to even more people across the world. The work details how Jesus is at the center of God's plan, a plan that anticipated not only His death, but also more significantly His resurrection-ascension[3] to God's right hand where He offers the benefits of salvation as Lord to any who come to Him. Paul as the apostle to the Gentiles pictured the outworking of the broad mission of the promise. His role, like that of others in the church, was not undertaken on his own initiative, but was the direct result of the work of God. Thus God and His activity are at the center of Luke–Acts.

GOD'S PLAN OF SALVATION

THE GOD OF DESIGN AND CONCERN

At the beginning of his two volumes, Luke emphasizes that God has made promises. The material on the birth of Jesus in Luke 1–2 makes it clear that God is carrying out a plan according to His promise and that He will deliver His people. Luke 1:14–17 describes the mission of John the Baptist as Jesus' forerunner and the one who came in the spirit of Elijah to reconcile fathers and children to the way of God. John was to produce a "prepared people." Verses 31–35 describe Jesus as the promised Son and Messiah. He will sit on David's throne and rule over Israel. Verses 54–55 show that these events of mercy are grounded on God's promises

---

2. Most likely Luke–Acts was written in the early to mid-sixties. The final event of the book of Acts is Paul's imprisonment in Rome, which places Acts in at least A.D. 62. However, many argue that these books were written in the eighties, on the premise that Luke knew of the fall of Jerusalem in A.D. 70 as is suggested in Luke 19:41–44. The problems with this late-date view are why Luke stopped where he did in Acts and why the fall of Jerusalem is not discussed more directly. For a discussion of these introductory matters, see Donald Guthrie, *New Testament Introduction* (Downers Grove, Ill.: InterVarsity, 1970), 90–120; for a slightly later sixties date, see E. Earle Ellis, *The Gospel of Luke*, The New Century Bible (Greenwood, S.C.: Attic, 1974), 50–62; for a date in the eighties, see Joseph Fitzmyer, *The Gospel According to Luke I–IX*, The Anchor Bible (Garden City, N.Y.: Doubleday, 1981), 35–59.

3. The expression "resurrection-ascension" reflects the fact that Luke regards these events as fundamentally one event, even though they were separate events. Acts 2:20–36 shows how closely Luke linked these two events.

made to Abraham. Verses 68–75 speak of the raising up of a horn of salvation out of the house of David as promised by the prophets. Jesus' task is to deliver God's people from their enemies, so that His people might serve Him without fear in holiness and righteousness. Also mentioned in this passage is God's promise to Israel's "fathers" or patriarchs. Luke 2:34 states that Jesus will bring division in Israel. Thus the infancy material overviews the plan of God and various elements in it. It does not relate the parts of the plan in detail to each other; rather, it introduces them as any overview might do. The key note is that God fulfills His promises in Jesus. God is a God of design and concern.

Acts reinforces this picture. Acts 2:17–21 speaks of the pouring out of the Holy Spirit as a fulfillment of God's promise about the last days. Verses 38–40 make the point that forgiveness of sins and the Spirit are available to those who respond to God's call. Acts 3:22–26 indicates that Jesus is the promised Prophet like Moses who must be heeded (Deut. 18:15).[4] Acts 13:22–33 portrays Jesus as the promised Savior descended from David. Acts 23:4–8 speaks of Paul on trial for the hope of the promise of resurrection. Acts 26:22–23 argues that the prophets and Moses testified of Christ and His subsequent mission. In the middle of Luke–Acts stands Luke 24:44–49. Its theme is the same. Jesus' death, resurrection, and the church's message of repentance and the forgiveness of sins to all men reflect Old Testament promise. So also the promise of the Spirit is the "Father's promise."

God is graciously at work to save a people for Himself. A forerunner, the Messiah, fulfillment of promises to Israel, the execution of a plan revealed in the prophets, the inclusion of the Gentiles, and division in Israel—all these are in His plan.

Enhancing the picture of God's design are those elements of the plan (*hē boulē*) that are called "foreknown" (*proginōskō*), "foretold" (*prokatangellō*), "predestined" (*proorizō, procheirizomai,* and *procheirotoneō*), "promised" (*hē epangelia* and *epangelomai*), ordained (*tassō*), or things that are "worked out through God's choice" (*hoizō*). Included in these descriptions are Christ's crucifixion (Acts 2:23), the promise of the Spirit to those near and far off (v. 39), Christ's suffering and return (3:18–20), the persecution of Jesus and the community (4:27–28), the witnesses who testify to Jesus (10:41), the Gentiles appointed to eternal life (13:48), His sovereignty over men (17:26), a judgment day and a Judge (17:31), and the appointment of Paul as a witness to the Gentiles (22:10, 14). Behind the events recorded in Luke–Acts stand the presence of the sovereign God and His compassionate acts.

GOD'S DIRECTION OF THE PLAN

How does God direct His plan? God administers it through four means: revelation, divine intervention, the work of human agents, and the work of Christ Him-

---

4. The title "Prophet like Moses" is also purposeful. Deuteronomy expected a series of prophets to come that would provide a line of communication between God and Israel. They would function as Moses did, by revealing God's will. But "*the* Prophet like Moses" above any others was Jesus, as Acts 3 indicates.

self. Revelation fundamentally involved the declared promise of the Old Testament, a theme so pervasive that it will receive more attention later.

God also revealed His plan through angelic announcements. John's mission was revealed to Zechariah by the angel Gabriel (Luke 1:11–20). Gabriel also declared Jesus' mission to Mary (vv. 26–38). Jesus' birth was announced by angels to shepherds (2:9–14). Angels proclaimed Jesus' resurrection to women (24:1–7) and the promise of Jesus' return to the disciples (Acts 1:10–11). Philip was directed to the eunuch by an angel of the Lord (8:26). Cornelius was instructed about Peter by "an angel of God" (10:3–7), and an angel announced that Paul would survive a shipwreck (27:23–24).[5] At key points in the story God intervened and provided direction. Each of the events of Acts is a turning point in God's direction of the church's expansion.

Besides providing revelatory detail to the direction of events, divine intervention came in two additional ways. Some people were aided by angelic mediation, usually in deliverance from prison (Acts 5:19; 12:7–15). In one case Philip was relocated after ministering to the eunuch (8:39). A more direct means was visions, which also brought instruction. Stephen saw his heavenly reception as he observed the Son of Man rising to meet him (7:55–56). Saul was called through a heavenly appearance of Jesus (22:6–10; 26:13–18). In addition, Ananias was directed to lay hands on Saul (9:10–16). This double appearance to both parties—Saul and Ananias—shows God's direct hand in choosing Saul, something that the multiple telling of His appearance to Saul also emphasizes. Another double intervention is Cornelius being directed to send for Peter, while Peter had a vision in which God declared that all foods are clean. This intervention makes the point that Gentiles are welcomed in God's plan (10:3–7, 10–16). Paul was directed to Macedonia in a similar way (16:9–10), and he was called to preach in Corinth (18:9–10). All these examples from Acts show how God sovereignly directed the foundational events of the church, especially those related to her expansion into the Gentile community.

Besides angelic hosts, human agents were another major vehicle God used. God worked through Jewish prophets of piety like Simeon and Anna (Luke 2:25–38). He used John the Baptist (7:24–30), the disciples (9:1–6; 10:1–12), the testimony of the church (Acts 4:24–31; 5:38–39), and the activity and witness of the apostolic band (1:8). His agents included the work of church prophets such as Agabus and the daughters of Philip (11:27–30; 21:9–10), as well as missionaries including Barnabas (13:1), Paul (13:13), Timothy (16:1–3), and Silas (16:22). In Acts much of this ministry is Spirit-directed as Acts 1:8 makes clear, so even the agents in their activities relied on God's provision.

Of course, the most significant revelation is Jesus Himself. His ministry is often summarized in the predictions about the Son of Man (Luke 9:22, 44; 17:24–25; 18:31–33; 22:22), in which His betrayal, death, and resurrection are the main focus. It was God's will and plan that these events occur (22:42; Acts 2:23). The re-

---

5. Interestingly in the appearances to Philip and Cornelius, "an angel of the Lord" appeared, whereas Paul saw an angel. Since Luke made it clear when the Lord Jesus appeared, as Acts 9 shows, this "angel of the Lord" was another unnamed angelic being.

jection of Jesus (4:27–28) and His resurrection are part of the revealed promise (13:32–37; 24:14–15; 26:22–23, which stresses the promise according to the prophets and Moses).

PROMISE AND FULFILLMENT

Within God's plan, Luke set forth Christ's role as the fulfillment of promise. This perspective is evident not only in the references to fulfillment, as noted earlier, but also at key structural points in the two books. First, the Lucan prologue clearly speaks of fulfillment in the first verse. Luke described Jesus' activities as events "fulfilled among us" (*peplērophorēmenōn en hēmin*). Second, the prologue to Acts speaks of the completion of God's plan in terms of times and seasons, a phrase that indicates a set schedule (Acts 1:6–7). Verses 4–5 repeat the reference to the coming of "the gift my Father promised," that is, the Holy Spirit, a promise introduced in Luke 24:49. So both prologues discuss the same theme.

"The gift my Father promised" links the closing chapter of Luke with the opening chapter of Acts (Luke 24:49 with Acts 1:4–5). Like an unbreakable chain, Luke related the promise of God about the Holy Spirit, and this theme ties the two volumes together. Preceding the reference to the promise of the Spirit's enabling power is a summary of the center of the plan as promised in Moses, the prophets, and the Psalms (Luke 24:44–47, "the Lucan Great Commission"). In this passage three infinitives are prominent. Christ would suffer (*pathein ton christon*), on the third day He would rise (*anastēnai ek nekrōn*), and forgiveness of sins would be proclaimed in His name to all the nations (*kērychthēnai . . . metanoian eis aphesin hamartiōn*). Here several themes come together. The work of Christ, His exaltation, and the message of repentance for forgiveness, which is available to people of every race are key Lucan themes. As important as the cross is to salvation, for Luke the exaltation of Jesus is even more crucial, since it not only shows that Jesus is alive but also is the basis of His investiture into authority (Acts 2:30–36).

Just as Luke 24 summarizes the plan, so Acts 1:8 outlines the progress of the early church. Here geographical advance is described. The message went from Jerusalem to Judea and Samaria and then to the ends of the earth. Spirit-enabled and Spirit-directed, the church took up the mission described in Luke 24:47 and carried it out from generation to generation.

OLD TESTAMENT FULFILLMENT

Luke spoke of the fulfillment of three themes that were predicted in the Old Testament: Christology, Israelite rejection and Gentile inclusion, and justice at the end. The warnings to heed the prophets are a recognition that irreversible authority resides in the message about Jesus. The prophets are to be believed (Luke 16:31; Acts 3:22–26; 13:27, 32, 40–41; 26:27). At the center of this message from the Old Testament was Christology, as Luke 24:44–47 reveals.

This Christological emphasis also permeates the infancy material. John the Baptist is the forerunner, as Malachi 3:1; 4:5–6 promised (Luke 1:14–17; Luke 3:4–6 adds the reference to Isaiah 40:3–5). Jesus is the promised Davidite, the Son of God, who will rule over Israel forever (Luke 1:31–35). God's accomplishment of this plan reflects His mercy promised to Abraham and to the fathers (vv. 46–55). The promise of the "raised horn" from the house of David is found in Jesus (vv. 68–79). The title "raised horn" alludes to Psalm 132:17, which in turn alludes to 2 Samuel 7, which records the Davidic Covenant. Psalm 132 is part of another key allusion in Acts 2:30, thereby linking the infancy declaration to the key introductory speech in Acts. Promise also pervades the end of Acts. Christ's death and resurrection and the spread of the gospel to Gentiles were predicted of Moses and the prophets (26:22–23). Moses and the prophets also testified to Jesus and the kingdom (28:23). "The Way," as Christianity is called in Acts, is in accord with the Law and the Prophets (24:14).

Numerous Lucan texts also speak of Israelite rejection and Gentile inclusion. Luke 2:34 introduces the point of division and rejection. Luke's quotation of Isaiah 40 emphasizes the theme of the appearance of salvation before all flesh (Luke 3:4–6). Current Jewish rejection was like the pattern of ancient Israel. Certain passages raise the specter of the covenant curses for unfaithfulness, stated in Deuteronomy. Other Lucan texts recall that Israel had earlier responded with unfaithfulness (Luke 11:49–51; 13:31–35; Acts 3:23; 7:51–53; 28:25–28).

The reality of judgment at the end is stressed in the Old Testament allusions to the eschatological discourses of Luke 17:20–37 and 21:5–38. In addition, the apostles stressed the reality of coming judgment (Acts 2:38–40; 3:23; 17:26–31). The God of design and concern has carried out His plan in Christ Jesus and through Him in the church. Luke also noted other points of fulfillment from the hand of God in these events. John's birth (Luke 1:20, 59–64), Christ's mission and message (4:17–21), the times of the Gentiles (21:24), the Passover meal in the future kingdom (22:16), Judas (Acts 1:16–20), and the apostles' preaching ministry (13:47) are other events that picture fulfillment.

THEMES THAT REVEAL THE PLAN'S OUTWORKING

"Today" passages. Numerous other concepts relate to God's outworking of His plan. One theme is the emphasis on fulfillment "today" (*sēmeron*). This expression is unique to Luke. The theme begins with the announcement of Jesus' birth (Luke 2:11). In Jesus' synagogue speech, in which He outlined His mission, He spoke of Isaiah 61:1–2a and 58:6 as being fulfilled "today" (Luke 4:21). As a result of the paralytic's healing and receiving the forgiveness of sins, the people said they had seen "remarkable things today" (5:26). The journey of Jesus to Jerusalem was put in terms of what must happen "today" and tomorrow (13:32–33). Jesus declared the immediacy of salvation to Zacchaeus when He told the tax collector that salvation had come to his house "today" (19:5, 9). A variation of this theme was the lament over Jerusalem and her failure to know what had come to her "this day," that is, on the day of Jesus' Triumphal Entry into Jerusalem (19:42). To the thief on the cross, Jesus promised that "today" the lowly but repentant man would be with Him in paradise (23:42–43). The emphasis on "today," besides un-

derscoring fulfillment, also highlights the immediacy and availability of that blessing. Right now God makes available such blessings and promises. Such immediacy informs the background of other elements of the plan. Salvation is here and now.

John the Baptist. John the Baptist was a bridge in God's plan. The "last of the old order," he was also the transition to the new. Luke 1:14–17 made this role clear when John was called "the one who goes before the Lord God in the spirit and power of Elijah." Malachi 3:1; 4:5–6 had predicted that such a one would come in the end. Jesus pointed out that John had an "Elijah-like" ministry in his preaching of repentance and his call to people to turn to God (Luke 7:27). His role was to make ready "a prepared people" (*laon kateskeuasmenon*), a phrase unique to Luke that has a rich Old Testament background. The language recalls verses like Isaiah 43:7, where Israel is prepared for the Lord, and 2 Samuel 7:24, where the reference is to a prepared people in the context of Davidic hope. Luke 1:76–77 summarizes the mission of this prophet as preparing God's way, recalling the preparation language of verses 16–17. According to verses 76–77, John also presented "the knowledge of salvation in the forgiveness of their sins." Luke 3:1–6 underscored John's role as forerunner by referring to Isaiah 40. John affirmed that he was not the Christ and that one greater than him was coming who would bring the Spirit (Luke 3:15–18).

In Luke 7:19–35 a question was raised about John's ministry. In Jesus' answer, He affirmed that John was related to Elijah, and He also made a comparison between the old era and the new. Whereas John was the greatest born among women up to that point, the least in the kingdom is greater than John (v. 28). In other words, the difference between the two eras is so great that the greatest of prophets, even a prophet of the eschaton, is less than any member of the new era of fulfillment! In Luke 1–2, John is a bridge figure, but in Luke 7 he pictured the old era only. Together the two passages show that John was a bridge in the plan of God, which with Jesus' coming leaped forward to a significantly higher plane.

Jesus' mission. An examination of Christology later will detail Jesus' role in God's plan. This section is concerned only with "mission statements," in which Jesus or others described His mission or spoke of Himself as sent (*apostellō*) by God. These statements represent Jesus' timeless mission. They describe what He was called to do in His life and what those who followed His message are called to proclaim in His name. The statements represent why He came and why He is raised. Jesus said that He was sent to preach release to the captives, as well as to offer sight to the blind and forgiveness to the oppressed (Luke 4:18–19). Jesus was sent to release the needy from the burden of sin. In this text Jesus appealed to the Old Testament year of Jubilee. Like that event, the current period is one in which people can be graciously released from debts (Lev. 25:1–12; Deut. 15:2–3; Ps. 82:1–2; Isa. 52:7; 61:1–2).

Comparing Himself to a physician sent to make the sick well, Jesus said His mission was to call sinners to repentance (Luke 5:32). This is one of many places where Luke emphasized repentance. Jesus offers spiritual restoration to those who recognize they are spiritually sick. Jesus was sent as the Father's representative

(10:16) to seek and save the lost (19:10). Acts 3:20 speaks of the sending of the appointed Christ in the future, while 3:26 emphasizes that He was sent to bless those Jews who turn from their evil. In His earthly ministry He was sent to "the people of Israel" (10:36). These mission texts describe a ministry of compassion and forgiveness made available through Jesus to those who seek relief from their spiritual needs. The God of design and concern makes His will known through Jesus.

Geographical progression. The advancement of God's plan into fulfillment receives attention in the Lucan portrait of geographical progression that pervades the two books. In Jesus' initial mission He moved from Galilee to Jerusalem (Luke 4:14–15; 9:51). In fact, of the gospel writers only Luke stressed repeatedly that Jesus was headed for Jerusalem (9:51; 13:33; 17:11; 18:31). This progression is reviewed in Acts 10:35–39. The advance of the church is similar. Acts 1:8 speaks of movement from Jerusalem to Judea and Samaria and then to the ends of the earth. The book of Acts follows that movement, as Judea and Samaria are mentioned in Acts 8:1, and as the missionary journeys of the book extend the church's outreach far into Gentile regions. Paul's long journey by ship to Rome in Acts 27 seems to highlight how difficult it was to get to the capital of the empire. Though Rome was at the ends of the earth, the message of salvation was penetrating the entire inhabited world.

"It is necessary." Perhaps no theme underscores divine design more than the Lucan "it is necessary" (*dei*) theme. This Greek word is used 99 times in the New Testament, of which 40 are in Luke–Acts. The references cover a wide variety of topics. Christ *must* be in the Father's house (Luke 2:49). He *must* preach the kingdom (4:43). He *must* heal women tormented by Satan (13:16). In looking at events associated with His death or His return, certain things *must* precede the end (21:9). A Passover lamb *must* be sacrificed, as Jesus and His disciples gathered for a final meal (22:7). The Son of Man or the Christ *must* suffer, perish in Jerusalem, and be raised (9:22; 13:33; 17:25; 24:7, 26; Acts 17:3). The Scriptures *must* be fulfilled in that Jesus *must* be numbered with transgressors (Luke 22:37, quoting Isa. 53:12), and certain events predicted of Christ *must* occur (Luke 24:44). Judas's fall was a *necessity* according to Acts 1:16. The gospel *must* go to Gentiles after the Jews rejected it (13:46). Entrance into the kingdom to come *must* come through trials (14:22). Christ *must* remain in heaven till the appropriate time (3:21). Paul *must* suffer for Jesus' name sake (9:6, 16), he *must* stand trial before Caesar (25:10; 27:24) , and he *must* go to Rome (19:21) where he *must* witness (23:11). Much in God's plan was carried out by commissioned agents, some of whom knew what they must do.

Other categories of necessity (*dei*) do not reflect this plan, but grow out of its nature as directed by God. Ethical necessity also exists. In critiquing the Pharisees, Jesus noted the *necessity* of justice (Luke 11:42) and the appropriateness of healing on the Sabbath (13:16). It was *necessary* to respond with joy to the prodigal son who repented (15:32). It is *necessary* to respond to Jesus with belief, since there is no other name under heaven by which it is *necessary* to be saved (Acts 4:12;

16:30–31). Persistent prayer is *necessary* (Luke 18:1). One *must* obey God, not man, when magistrates ask that believers not proclaim Christ (Acts 5:29). Jesus promised that in times of persecution the Spirit would give what is *necessary* to speak (Luke 12:12). Again Luke showed that the Lord is a God of design.

The kingdom. Another key theme in Luke–Acts is the kingdom. This is a vast concept with many elements in it that relate to other areas. Here the major features are surveyed.⁶ Four points about God's kingdom program should be noted: the kingdom as present, the kingdom as future, the kingdom promise as political, and the kingdom promise as spiritual. The presence of the kingdom is suggested in Luke by the picture of John the Baptist as the bridge into the new era (Luke 7:28). John was pictured as the last prophet of an old age and the new age of the kingdom has come, since the least in the kingdom is greater than John.

Jesus gave instructions to the seventy-two disciples to proclaim that the kingdom was near (Luke 10:9). The debated term here is *ēngiken*. Does it mean "to draw near" or "to arrive"? Lexically the term can carry either meaning.⁷ But the use of the preposition *epi* ("upon") makes it likely that the sense in Luke 10:9 is "to arrive" or "to approach" (cf. Matt. 26:45–46). This is confirmed by the fact that Luke normally used the term this way (12:33; 15:1; 18:40; 22:47; 24:15; Acts 21:33).

The picture of a current ruling authority is presented in Luke 10:18–19. Jesus said He saw Satan falling like lightning, a clear image of his defeat. Jesus expressed this picture as a result of the miraculous activity of the seventy-two and related it to the authority He bestowed on them (v. 19). In Judaism there was the belief that with Messiah's coming Satan's rule would end (1 Enoch 55:1; Jubilees 23:29; Test. of Simeon 6:6).

The third passage dealing with this theme in Luke 10–11 is 11:20–23, where Jesus made the point in verse 20 that if He were casting out demons by the finger of God, "then the kingdom of God has come upon you" (NASB, *ephthasen eph' humas*).⁸ The allusion to the finger of God points to a formative era like the Exodus, since the allusion is to Exodus 8:19. Also verses 21–23 show that arrival is meant, since Jesus is the stronger one who plunders Satan's house. This picture of victory and authority parallels other New Testament passages (Eph. 4:7–10; Col. 2:14–15). All these texts point to a plundering and victory that has already occurred.

In Luke 17:21 Jesus said that the kingdom was in the midst of the Pharisees (*entos humōn*), that is, the kingdom was in their presence. It was "within your

---

6. For more details, see Darrell L. Bock, "The Reign of the Lord Christ," in *Israel, the Church, and Dispensationalism,* ed. Craig A. Blaising and Darrell L. Bock (Grand Rapids: Zondervan, 1992).

7. J. A. Fitzmyer, *The Gospel According to Luke X–XXIV,* 848.

8. This term clearly means arrival in this tense and context (Rom. 9:31; Phil. 3:16; 1 Thess. 2:16). See W. Kümmel, *Promise and Fulfillment,* trans. Dorothea M. Barton, Studies in Biblical Theology 23 (Naperville, Ill.: Allenson, 1957), 105–9. In the LXX, this verb with *epi* means "to reach" or "to happen to" (Dan. 4:24, 28). Thus, a past-tense translation is justified here.

reach in the present."⁹ The parable of the ten minas (19:12–27) is also instructive. Like the nobleman, Jesus has gone away to receive a kingdom, and, having already received that kingdom, He will return. In other words, His departure, not His return, initiates His reign. Luke 22:69 is another key verse. Here Jesus said, "from now on" (*apo tou nun*) the members of the Sanhedrin will see the Son of Man seated at the right hand of power (Mark 14:62). The "right hand" is an allusion to Psalm 110:1, which portrays investiture. It pictures Jesus' rule at the side of God in a "coregency" in which He is actively distributing salvation benefits to those who believe (Acts 2:30–36). Psalm 110:1 is a text that the New Testament relates to Davidic sonship and the promise to David, as Luke 20:41–44; 22:69; and Acts 2:30–36 show (Heb. 1:5–13).

The distribution of the Holy Spirit, as recorded in Acts 2, and Peter's explanation of that event show that Jesus is now at the side of God the Father. As Lord, Jesus is exercising salvific authority and the prerogatives of rule from God's side. Thus in Luke's view, the kingdom is present not in its final form but in an inaugurated form, in which the promises of the last days have begun to be fulfilled. Further fulfillment is anticipated in the future.

This second, future form of the kingdom receives detailed attention in several Lucan texts. Most crucial are the two eschatological discourses in Luke 17:22–37 and 21:5–38. In these passages the kingdom is still anticipated, and the passage depends heavily on the Old Testament.¹⁰ This is the kingdom of culmination foreseen in many Old Testament prophecies. Peter spoke of the return of Jesus from heaven, when He will bring about the "period of restoration" (*chronon apokatastaseōs*; Acts 3:20 NASB). This restoration involves all the things God spoke through the mouth of the prophets. Here is hope for the world and particularly for Israel, since this verse recalls the disciples' question in Acts 1:6 about the time of the restoration of Israel (*chronō* and *apokathistaneis*). The future kingdom is first and foremost the realization of Old Testament kingdom promises.¹¹

In certain verses, Luke described the kingdom in political terms. Luke 1:32–33 points to Jesus ruling from the Davidic throne over the house of Jacob forever, and verses 51–55 relate the messianic task in direct terms to Israel, Abraham, and His seed. Mary's hymn is expressed in the tone of Jewish messianic national hope. In Luke 1:69 Zechariah referred to salvation from a horn out of the house of David. That Davidic-led salvation combines political and spiritual elements is seen in the rest of the hymn (1:69–79). In this last hymn, the career of the promised Son of David is summarized. Some of what the Son of David does meets with fulfill-

---

9. I. Howard Marshall, *Commentary on Luke*, New International Greek New Testament Commentary (Grand Rapids: Eerdmans, 1978), 476. Note also the present tense in the verse. The verse cannot mean that the kingdom is "within you." Jesus would never have said this to the Pharisees who rejected Him.

10. The day of the Lord and kingdom imagery dominate these texts. For example, in Luke 21:25–27 alone, there are allusions to Isaiah 13:10; Ezekiel 32:7; Joel 2:30–31; Psalm 46:2–3; 65:7; Isaiah 24:19 (LXX); Haggai 2:6, 21; and Daniel 7:13.

11. For more details, see Bock, "The Reign of the Lord Christ," in *Israel, the Church, and Dispensationalism*, which discusses the connection of Acts 3 to Acts 1 in detail.

ment in His first coming (vv. 78–79), while other elements anticipate Jesus' activity in the future (vv. 71–75).

Some aspects of the kingdom are spiritual rather than political. In the same infancy texts, Jesus' mission is described as a visitation from "the rising sun," which shines on those in darkness and those seated in the shadow of death (Luke 1:78–79). Jesus' task is to lead them "into the path of peace." This imagery comes from Isaiah 9:1–2; 58:8; 60:1–2; and Psalm 106:10, 14 (LXX). It is spiritual in focus. Some argue that the kingdom is not present until both political and spiritual elements are present, but Luke's view of the presence of the kingdom speaks against this distinction. Luke's kingdom comes in two phases, "already" and "not yet." It has been "inaugurated" already, but it is not yet "consummated." The kingdom is present, but not all its promises have come. What is to come relates to the Old Testament and its covenant promises to the nation Israel. What is present now is related to the church and the exercise of her mission by the Spirit's power.

The Holy Spirit. Another key element in God's plan is the Holy Spirit's work. The Spirit's role indicates the inauguration of the fulfillment of God's promises (Acts 2:17–33 appeals to the fulfillment of Joel 2:28–32; also see Acts 2:38–40). John the Baptist, summarizing Old Testament hope and announcing what the "stronger One to come" would bring, promised the coming of the Spirit with Jesus' coming as the Christ (Luke 3:15–18). In fact, the provision of the Holy Spirit was evidence of Jesus' superiority to John. With Jesus' own reception of the Spirit at His baptism came one of two divine endorsements of Jesus (Luke 3:22, alludes to Psalm 2:7, thus marking Jesus as the messianic Son, and to Isaiah 42:1, which pictures Him as the beloved Servant).

The Spirit's activity extends to the community and includes a variety of functions. Luke did not emphasize the individual reception of the Spirit as much as he pointed to its corporate reception. This community reception was promised in Luke 24:49, which states that the Father's promise of the Holy Spirit looks back both to John the Baptist's pronouncement about the Christ to come and to the promise of new covenant hope. In Acts 1:4–5 Jesus repeated the promise. The initial bestowal in Acts 2 was so important to Luke that he alluded to it in numerous passages. Acts 10:44–47 notes a similar bestowal on the Gentiles, comparing it to the original provision in Acts 2 (cf. 11:15–16; 15:8). Another community reception of the Spirit that involved those who knew only of John's baptism is recorded in Acts 19:6. It pictures the initial movement from the forerunner into the believing community. In Acts 19 the old age is swallowed up into the new. The last of the transition groups comes in. This communal pouring out of God's Spirit not only shows the presence of the "last days" (2:17), but also indicates (when He was poured out again in Acts 10) that Gentiles and Jews are equal in God's plan (11:15–18). They participate in the same new community. In fact, Acts 11:15 looks back to Acts 2 as the beginning (*en archē*). A new community, which came to be known as the church, emerged from this special work.[12] The reception of the Spirit represents the presence of both blessing and enablement, since the Spirit is also called "power from on high" (Luke 24:49; cf. Acts 1:8). The beginning of a new period in God's work had dawned.

What functions does the Spirit have in this plan? The Spirit's primary activity is filling (*eplēsthē pneumatos* and its variations). Filling is a general Lucan term for presence and enablement. Before he was born, John the Baptist was filled with the Spirit (Luke 1:15). In fact, while still in the womb, he testified to Jesus with joy (v. 44). Filling here was enablement to testify to Jesus, the ability to function as a prophet. Elizabeth and Zechariah were filled and gave praise to God (vv. 41, 67). Filling was related to testimony and praise.

In Acts 2:4 all the believers were filled with the Holy Spirit. Again there was enablement to testify to Jesus and to offer praise (v. 11). Here filling also described the Spirit's reception by the community, the Spirit's "outpouring" (*ekcheō apo tou pneumatos mou*) according to Joel 2. Later in Acts, the Spirit's filling again enabled believers to testify to Jesus, whether through an individual like Peter (Acts 4:8) or by means of the entire praying community (v. 31). Another phrase, *plēreis pneumatos* ("full of the Spirit"), is parallel in force. In Acts 6:3, 5 the phrase refers to the mature quality of the seven who were chosen to help the widows. This term speaks here of an abiding quality of spirituality. Stephen, one of these men (v. 5), was full of the Spirit at the time of his martyrdom, and in a vision he saw the standing Son of Man. Stephen testified to this vision as he died (7:55–56). Though Stephen was stoned for blasphemy, he was full of the Spirit, was received by Christ, and was vindicated in heaven. Saul was enabled for ministry and filled with the Spirit through the laying on of hands by Ananias (9:17). Barnabas is described as full of the Spirit, as he showed maturity and ministered encouragement to believers (11:24). Paul, filled with the Spirit, pronounced judgment on Elymas (13:9–11). A variation of the phrase appears in the description of Apollos, who was "fervent in spirit" (*zeōn tō pneumati*, 18:25).

The Lucan phrase "filled with the Spirit" describes an important role for the Spirit in God's plan. It is the gift of enablement, either bestowed initially, as in Acts 2:4, or in a later moment of special spiritual direction. Usually the gift describes enablement to testify to Jesus boldly. On a few occasions the phrase describes an individual's general spiritual character. The words show that the Spirit is the driving power behind the early church's effectiveness. Jesus gave the Spirit not only to show that the promise was being fulfilled, but also to equip the church to perform its mission of taking the gospel message to the world.

The Spirit performs other functions in God's plan for His community. Through prophets He speaks to Israel (Acts 1:16, David; 4:25, David; 28:25, Isaiah) and to the church of the apostolic era (Acts 11:28; 21:10–11, Agabus; 21:4, disciples). These prophetic utterances of the church involved information about

---

12. The term *church* is not used in Luke's gospel, but it appears twenty-three times in Acts. The uses in Acts 5:11 and 7:38 are ambiguous, since they could mean "assembly," which is the normal meaning of the Greek term *ekklēsia*. By Acts 8:1, 3, the technical meaning of "church" was clearly present. Of the twenty-three uses in Acts, eighteen occur after Acts 10.

things like famine as well as exhortation and advice. In at least one instance, Paul seemed to have had a choice about an issue the Spirit raised, since the Spirit-led Agabus pleaded for Paul not to go on to Jerusalem where he would face Jewish rejection (21:11). Paul decided to go anyway and the passage ends on the note, "the Lord's will be done" (v. 14). Apparently the Spirit's prophetic exhortation and warning here was something about which Paul could reflect. He chose to go, knowing he would face rejection. Those present responded and agreed that what would happen would occur in the the the will of God.

In Acts 5:3, 5 the Holy Spirit guarded the community from the lie of Ananias and Sapphira. In executing judgment in the community, the Spirit jealousy guarded the church's integrity. He sees what happens in the church.

The Spirit guided the believing community as she made decisions and took action. In the letter emerging from the Jerusalem Council, the leaders declared that the decision made was that of the community and the Spirit (15:28). The Spirit gave elders to the Ephesian community (20:28). The Spirit comforted or encouraged the church as she grew (9:31). The Spirit enables obedience, especially under the pressure of persecution (Luke 12:12; Acts 5:32; 6:10). The provision of the Spirit is God's way of empowering the church to complete her task.

Whether leading the way in discipline, guidance, the supply of leadership, or encouragement, the Holy Spirit in Acts was a driving force in the new community. Along with the presence of the Holy Spirit, God called those in the new community to lead lives honoring to Him. In the emerging church, God through His Spirit is at work in molding a new, exemplary group of faithful people. That is a part of His plan as well. The God of design and concern has called His people to a life of discipleship and service, a life that differs from the world's way of selfish living.

The new community's ethic. One of God's goals within His plan is to call His people to a righteous life, a life that honors Him. Design and compassion provided the enablement, but with that provision comes a call for believers to live in light of God's goodness. The call to discipleship contrasts with the Jewish leaders' way to God. Most of these passages come in the "Jerusalem journey" section of the gospel (Luke 9:51–19:44). As Jesus headed toward the place of suffering, He instructed the disciples on what God desired of them and what He planned for them. When Jesus condemned the current ways of official piety, He issued a call to new piety and prepared them for His absence.

Luke's look at the Jewish leadership in Jesus' day provides the negative portrait against which Christian discipleship is defined. The note of trouble for those leaders came early. John the Baptist stated that the axe of judgment sits at the root of the tree, ready to be wielded against anyone who does not respond with repentance (Luke 3:7–9). Genealogy is no guarantee against judgment. God wants responsive people with hearts open to Him.

No section is stronger in its condemnation of the old way than Luke 11:37–52. Here Jesus, like a classic Old Testament prophet, railed against the hypocrisy of the Pharisees and scribes. Jesus said they were morally filthy inside, no matter how clean they were outside. They followed all kinds of tithing rules about herbs, but neglected justice and love. They loved the attention of the first seats and thought they led others, but in fact their teaching was like an open grave, leading to death. They burdened others with their rules, but did not lift a finger to help those so burdened. They thought they had the key of knowledge, but instead their way of thinking was a wall that prevented entry. Their actions were like the nation's failure in earlier eras to heed God's message. Jesus' imagery is strong here. This long condemnation destroys the popular portrait of Jesus as a mild-mannered teacher who avoided confrontation. Though not blatantly immoral, the Jews had a form of piety that was not honoring to God at all. That is what Jesus condemned here. By contrast, the new community is not to be selfishly and arrogantly pious.

Jesus' warning about the wrong way continued in Luke 14:7–14, where He admonished His host and the guests at a meal not to seek places of honor. The next passage shows that many, who think they will be present at the great banquet will miss it (vv. 15–24). Jesus also condemned self-righteousness (Luke 16:14–15), a flaw seen in the Pharisee in contrast to the tax collector-sinner (18:9–14). Here the humble sinner was commended. Jesus' confrontation closed with a word of weeping lament (Luke 19:39–44) and with His cleansing of the temple (vv. 45–48). The way to please God was not found in the Jewish leadership.

The way to God stands in contrast to the way sought by the Jewish leaders. His new way is a life of love and service. His followers are called to a unique kind of love. Luke 6:27–36 is a declaration to love in a way different from that of sinners. While Paul defined the attributes of love in 1 Corinthians 13, Jesus described here in concrete terms what love is and how it acts. Love is giving. It reaches out to enemies as well as friends. It is vulnerable and sensitive to others, treating them as one wishes to be treated. Love exposes itself again and again to abuse by turning the other cheek in the hope of helping others. It is generous and expects nothing in return. In short, love continually and consistently displays mercy, compassion, and honesty. It is slow to judge others (Luke 6:37–42). It senses responsibility for others. It does not dictate to them, but aids them. This love recognizes that similar spiritual dangers and faults exist anywhere, especially in oneself. The disciples' major responsibility is to deal with their own faults first and then to help others deal with theirs.

Love for one's neighbor is described in Luke 10:25–37. Here the issue is not who one's neighbor is but rather the challenge to be a neighbor. Such was the Samaritan to the man who fell among the thieves. Love for Jesus is exemplified in Mary seated at His feet (vv. 38–42). This pictures the dedicated disciple, as does responding to the call to pray (11:1–13).

Love for God expresses itself in a variety of ways besides listening to and talking with God. The disciple gives all of himself to the Lord (9:57–62; 14:25–35). This means that generosity is the characteristic of his life and that life is not defined by excessive attachment to material things (12:13–21; 16:1–32). The disciple is called to confess Christ and fear God (12:4–12), to seek the lost (15:1–32), to have faith (17:5–6), and to view his spiritual labor as his duty (17:7–10). Fundamentally discipleship involves giving to God and to others.

The God of design and concern has devised His plan, in part, to produce such transformed people. Such ethics are to typify the community He has molded and saved through Jesus Christ. Such a life pictures promise realized and enablement received. As seen in Luke 1:73–74, God made an oath to Abraham "to rescue us from the hand of our enemies, and to enable us to serve Him without fear, in holiness and righteousness before Him all our days." That is a key goal of the plan at an individual level.

God and Christ's direct intervention. A final way that Luke reveals God's plan is through the direct intervention of God and His representative. Early on in Acts, an opponent, Gamaliel, stated the driving observation of the second volume as the Sanhedrin deliberated about how to handle the apostles (Acts 5:38–39). The respected rabbi states that if this movement is of human origin, then it will fail of its own accord. But if it is of God, then nothing can destroy it. To oppose it is to become an enemy of God. This statement poses the choice for the reader of Acts: the new movement is either divine or human in origin. Luke showed his preference even in the way the question is framed. Luke had Gamaliel state the divine option with a first-class condition (*ei* plus a present indicative), a grammatical touch that has Gamaliel present the divine option with more certainty than the other approach.

With this question posed, Luke described a series of events that reveals God's hand in the activity and that indicates the presence of a movement of God. Such activity extended beyond the numerous miraculous signs done in Jesus' name. For example, before Gamaliel's speech, the prison doors had been opened, so that Peter and his company were released (Acts 5:5:17–20). This act is probably what gave Gamaliel pause. Stephen's reception into heaven at the time of his martyrdom was yet another sign that God was with this movement and believers were on the side of God (7:55–56). God's direction of Philip also makes this point (8:26–29). The reversal of Saul's life vocation from persecutor to persecuted witness for the Lord involved an appearance by Jesus (9:1–31). In fact, it took a second appearance to Ananias to insure that Saul was properly received (9:10–16). God was directing in amazing ways and in surprising directions. The opening up of the door to Gentiles also required a combination of visions, divine activity, and the public bestowal of the Spirit to make sure all saw what God was doing (10:1–11:18). In a very real sense, Luke's argument for the church's direction and activity is very simple. God made us do it. This guidance required engaging in such practices as giving the gospel to Gentiles. It also declared freedom from the law's dietary restrictions. In fact, in some cases when these visions initially came there was resistance (9:12–16; 10:13–16), but God insisted, so the new community responded with obedience.

In the second half of Acts, such direction continues. God directly protected Peter and judged Herod in a picture of how the judgment of God functions (12:1–23). Such direction continues in Paul's ministry. Whether in mission (13:1–3; 16:6–10) or in travel (27:1–28:10), God actively directs and protects His witness. Luke is showing that this new movement is of God; He has a plan. He has watched over His newly forming community and has sovereignly directed its mission, growth, and practice.

In examining how Luke portrayed God and His plan, it is important to see these themes as they are developed in Luke–Acts. Theophilus and others like him could be reassured as they examined what God is doing in Christ (Luke 1:3–4). But details in the basic categories of the plan need examination as well. Who is this Jesus who saves (Christology)? How does He do it? How does one respond to Him (soteriology)? What institution does God work through? What is that community's structure and task (ecclesiology)? Where is the plan of God headed and how is it structured (eschatology)? This study turns to these questions to fill out the picture of Lucan theology, a picture that focuses on the salvation of a caring, gracious God of design.

CHRISTOLOGY

THE PERSON OF CHRIST

From Messiah-Servant-Prophet to Lord. A study of Lucan Christology indicates that Luke consciously revealed who Jesus is with a step-by-step approach. Luke's presentation of Jesus begins mostly in regal and prophetic terms and ends with an emphasis on His lordship. In the infancy section, Jesus is described as Son and as King (Luke 1:31–35). There is some ambiguity in this initial description of Jesus as "Son," since a regal figure could be described as God's "son." In the Old Testament the Davidic successor was said to have God as his Father, as promised in the Davidic Covenant (2 Samuel 7:14). The dynastic Davidic ruler inherited the hope of this promise (Ps. 2:7). But Jesus' unique birth by the Spirit makes it clear that "something more" is here, but it is not explicitly clear in this initial context of Luke 1–2 what that "something more" is since the passage emphasizes Jesus as a Davidic, regal figure. Mary and those around her took the promise only in messianic terms. What that "something more" involved became clear as Luke developed his description of Jesus. In short, Luke built his Christology "from the earth up," though in the infancy section, it is suggested that this Child is unique, coming from heaven itself.

Other regal references in Luke 1–2 include the mention of the presence of the "horn of salvation" (*keras sōtērias*) in the house of David (1:69). This title alludes to Psalm 132:17 and brings in the hope of Davidic promise. The picture of the "morning star" that shines in darkness (Luke 1:78–79) also indicates that fulfillment is present (Isa. 9:1–2; 58:8; 59:19; 60:1–2). The grouping of three titles in Luke 2:11—"a Savior," "Christ," "the Lord"—sums up the descriptions in the infancy portrait. Of these titles, only "Lord" is not defined through an appeal to the Old Testament in this introductory section. Luke 2:34–35 pictures Jesus as the one who divides Israel. Here the conceptual imagery comes from Isaiah 8:14. The pain that Jesus' ministry would cause Mary is the first hint of trouble, alluding to His suffering. Jesus would be like a rejected prophet, as well as a rejected messianic King.

The first reference to Jesus' self-understanding came in Luke 2:49. Here Jesus spoke of "my Father's house" (*eis tois tou patros mou*). Jesus' first words about His relationship to God speak of an intimacy that reveals filial and familial self-consciousness. Luke thus showed that Jesus knew He had a special relationship to God. This is Luke's first indication of where things are headed. Important is the fact that this infancy material is only in Luke.

In the baptism of Jesus, regal and servant categories come together as the divine voice spoke about Jesus for the first time (3:22). "You are My Son, whom I love; with you I am well pleased" refers to Psalm 2:7 and Isaiah 42:1, bringing together the king and the servant imagery. The prophetic and regal marriage continues in Luke 4:18–19, where Isaiah 61:1–2 and possibly Isaiah 58:6 are cited in another passage that has detail unique to Luke's gospel. Though strictly speaking Isaiah 61 is probably not a "servant song," the prophetic figure in that chapter serves much like the servant in earlier Isaianic passages, so the parallel could be made. The citation pictures Jesus in an anointed prophetic mode, as Luke 4:24–27 makes clear. However, the anointing by the Spirit, which Jesus declared was fulfilled, also alludes back to Jesus' baptism. This anointing was of Jesus as King and Prophet. (In Luke 3:21–22, Ps. 2:7 points to the King, while Isa. 42:1 looks to the Suffering Servant who declares and brings God's deliverance.) This union maintains the Lucan focus up to this point. The imagery of Luke 4 pictures the Old Testament declaration of Jubilee, a release from debts and a declaration of freedom (Lev. 25:1–12; Deut. 15:2–3). It pictures one released to serve God, because of who Jesus is. He is the center of God's plan.

Jesus is superior to the greatest figure of the old era, John the Baptist (Luke 7:18–35). Jesus is more than a prophet, though that is how the populace viewed Him (9:7–9). He is the Christ (9:20). At His Transfiguration, He was presented, as in His Baptism, as "Son," but He was also called "elect" (the One "whom I have chosen," Luke 9:35). In addition there is the call to hear Him. Here Psalm 2:7; Isaiah 42:1; and Deuteronomy 18:15 come together. Jesus is King, Servant, and Prophet, but not just any prophet. He is the "prophet like Moses," who has ushered in a new era.

In Luke 9–19, predictions of the Son of Man's suffering are evident (9:22, 44; 18:31). But other descriptions of Jesus as the Son of Man also are present (9:58; 11:30; 12:10; 19:10 give descriptions of His present ministry; and 9:26; 12:8, 40; 17:22, 24, 26, 30; 18:8 give descriptions of His ministry when He returns). The title "Son of Man" is also ambiguous in Luke until Jesus used it in Luke 21:27, with clear reference to Daniel 7:13–14. This title pictures the authority He has received from the Father to serve over a kingdom. This position is made clear in the present ministry texts, which state that the Son of Man can forgive sin, and in the texts describing His return to judge. However, that "Son of Man" ministry also involves seeking the lost and suffering rejection, as well as returning to judge the world. The texts on the suffering Son of Man point out that the road for Jesus led to the cross. These images are still rather regal, since they look at rule, but such total authority also suggests something more.

Luke 19–20 include a series of parables in which Jesus is portrayed as "Lord." In these pictures that summarize His ministry, Jesus functions as an intermediary with authority. Jesus receives a kingdom and then grants authority to others (19:11–27). He is heir to the vineyard, "the son" who is slain so that the vineyard goes to others (20:9–19). Jesus' central role is clear in these parables.

The key passages for Lucan Christology come in the middle of his two books as Jesus headed for death followed by resurrection. In Luke 20:41–44 Jesus raised a question (cf. Ps. 110) that stumped the religious leaders. He asked how Messiah can be called David's son, since David himself called Messiah his "Lord"?[13] Jesus did not answer the question. He simply raised the messianic dilemma. The suggestion is that "Lord" is a better title than Davidic son.

The answer began to come in Luke 22:69. Answering the question of whether He is the Christ, Jesus replied using the title "Son of Man." He said "from now on" the Sanhedrin would see the Son of Man seated at the right hand of God. This alludes to Psalm 110. The picture is of Jesus seated in authority at God's side, invested as a regal figure and ruling with Him. The implications of this reply are staggering and Jesus' own response led to His being condemned for blasphemy. Jesus was claiming that He could go directly into God's presence and sit and rule with Him at His side, alluding again to Psalm 110. This title of "Lord" was a more important title than Messiah, for it pictured Jesus' total authority and His ability and right to serve as an equal with God the Father.

This emphasis is confirmed in Acts 2. Here as Peter reviewed the events surrounding Jesus' death and resurrection, he also appealed to Psalm 110 in Acts 2:32–36. Jesus is the Lord at God's right hand. Peter explained how the resurrection and exaltation of Jesus led to His being seated at the right hand of the Father and to the distribution of the Spirit as promised in Joel 2. The citation of Joel alludes to the initial fulfillment of the new covenant and the presence of the new era. Joel urged men to "call on the name of the Lord" (Acts 2:21). The "Lord" to be called on here is Jesus (2:34–38).

In addition, Jesus' position at the right hand of God is an initial fulfillment of a promise made to David that one of his descendants would sit on his throne. Here Peter alluded to Psalm 132:11, which in turn alludes to the promises of 2 Samuel 7 and the Davidic Covenant. In Acts 2, the Psalm 132 allusion leads into the discussion of Psalm 110 about the descendant of David. Peter linked the two psalms in fulfillment. Each of Peter's allusions to these psalms uses the word "sit" (*kathisai* in Acts 2:30 and *kathou* in v. 34). So the two images are one and meet their initial realization in Jesus' resurrection-ascension. Jesus is portrayed as ruling at God's side as the Mediator and intermediary source of divine blessing, an act that is an initial realization of promises made long ago. In Peter's speech the title "Lord" in verse 36 is in the emphatic position. Jesus' authority over salvation is absolute and the title "Lord" is the comprehensive Christological title that summarizes that total authority over salvation's benefits and as the One who rules at God's side.

13. The question is framed in a theoretical way here, so that a direct allusion to Jesus is only implied. As stated, it is a messianic question, not a Christological one. Jesus was asking, "What title is best for the Messiah?"

The significance of Jesus' title of "Lord" appears again in Acts 10:36–42, where Peter made the point that Jesus is Lord over all humanity (Rom. 10:12 is similar in meaning). Since Jesus is Lord over all, Peter could proclaim to Cornelius and other Gentiles that the gospel is available to all. This is one of the most central points in Luke–Acts. Christology is the ground for the scope of the salvation message, and the fact that Jesus is Lord and that He has authority over salvation to distribute its benefits is one of the crucial theological conclusions of Luke's two books.[14] The movement from regal-prophetic categories to the title "Lord" is one of the most basic theological themes in Luke–Acts. It reveals that Jesus, being intimately related to God, functions with a full array of divine prerogatives. In fact, the identity is so strong that one now acts in the name of Jesus Christ. Jesus even bears the title "Lord," the title normally used of Yahweh. The exalted position of Jesus can be seen through comparison with Old Testament statements about Yahweh. In the Old Testament, such actions occurred in the name of Yahweh, so the transition to "in the name of Jesus" is significant. To act "in the name" is a major Lucan theme that stresses Jesus' total authority to exercise divine prerogative (Acts 2:38; 3:6, 16; 4:7, 10, 12, 18, 30; 5:40–41; 8:12, 16; 9:15, 27–28; 10:43, 48; 15:26; 16:18; 19:13, 17; 21:13; 22:16; 26:9). Acts 15:17 speaks of the name of God in a similar way. Jesus' name means that when one deals with Him, that person deals with one who has the authority of God.[15] In short, to deal with Jesus is to deal with God.

Having noted this fundamental Christological progression in Luke–Acts, it is necessary to examine the variety of Christological titles in Luke, since his portrait of Jesus is multifaceted.

THE TITLES OF JESUS

Savior. Though it is popular today to refer to Jesus as Savior (*sōtēr*), Luke rarely used this title. It appears in the infancy summary in Luke 2:11, when the angel announced Jesus' birth. The deliverance alluded to in the title is clarified by the hymns and declarations of the infancy material. That deliverance is both national and spiritual (1:70–75, 77; 2:30–32).

14. Much debate exists today in American evangelical circles over "lordship salvation." Clouding the debate is the failure to define carefully the biblical meaning and emphasis of Jesus' title of "Lord." The emphasis in the title is the *position* into which it places Jesus and the benefits He possesses as a result. Jesus is the One with whom men must deal, and His authority over salvific blessing is absolute. In addition, the scope of this authority and the absence of racial distinction that emerges from it receives emphasis in the New Testament. That He is Lord of all races with authority over salvation's benefits, as Acts 10 and Romans 10 make clear, is the point of the title. All other developments of the title's force with reference to the offer of the gospel deal with the implications of the term and not its central biblical force. They run the risk of putting too much meaning into the term, when it is applied to the offer of the gospel. See Darrell L. Bock, "Jesus as Lord in Acts and in the Gospel Message," *Bibliotheca Sacra* 143 (1986): 146–54.

15. Luke never called Jesus God directly. He presented Jesus' position more subtly through the use of the title "Lord." Luke showed that Jesus does what God does and carries the authority God has. In contrast to John's gospel, which makes the identification explicit, Luke left the conclusion to the reader. This approach is another example of Luke's Christology built "from the earth up."

A similar picture is seen in Acts 5:31 and 13:23–25, passages that present Jesus as the Savior of Israel. Jesus is the exalted Savior lifted up to the right hand of God to give repentance and forgiveness of sins to Israel. He is the Savior promised to David, one who is his descendant and to whom John the Baptist pointed (Luke 3:15–18). For Luke, Jesus is the Savior and the Christ, the One to come who brought the Spirit. So for Luke the title Savior has particular reference to God's whole program of promised deliverance, as well as to Israel, to exaltation, to forgiveness, and to the offer of the Spirit.

Christ. Though the title "Lord" points up Jesus' ultimate authority as ruler, "Christ" (*christos*) is Luke's most frequent title for Jesus and serves as his foundation point in building his "from the earth up" Christology.[16] The title "Christ" refers to Jesus as the promised Anointed One ("Messiah" in Hebrew means "Anointed One"). The first use of the title in Luke is in the angelic confession (Luke 2:11), and its force is clearly defined in Luke by the description of Jesus' role in 1:31–35. Here is a regal deliverance figure promised to David. The hope He stirs for the redemption of the nation was noted by Simeon (2:26).

John the Baptist refused the title for himself and spoke of One who would come after him (3:15–16). The promise that would reveal His presence is the distribution of the Spirit. A key usage of the word "Christ," unique to Luke, occurs in Luke 4:41. Demons confessed that Jesus is the Son of God, and then Luke explained that they "knew that He was the Christ." In this way Luke shows Jesus' sonship is linked to the promise of the Messiah. "Christ" was also the title used by Peter in his confession (9:20). The role the title plays in this scene shows its foundational character, since Jesus revealed more of God's plan after this confession. As already noted, the issue of Jesus' identity as Christ was at the center of a key question asked by the Jewish leaders and was a key issue at Jesus' trial (22:67). The issue of Jesus as Christ the King continued to be central in His movement toward crucifixion (23:2, 35, 39). In reflecting on the resurrection, Luke made the point (in material unique to him) that Christ's suffering was necessary and was foretold (24:26, 46). In this concept of a suffering messiah, the Christian portrait of Messiah clashed with Jewish expectation. To Jews, a suffering messiah was incongruous, an impossibility. They thought that the nation might suffer, but not their Deliverer. However, His suffering and death make it possible for Him to purchase a people who will serve the Lord (Acts 20:28 does not use the term "Christ," but does use the image of purchase). Then being exalted as Christ, He can bring both deliverance and forgiveness of sins.

In the book of Acts a number of things are said to happen "in the name of Christ": baptism (2:38), salvation (4:10), healing (9:34), peace (10:36), baptism of the Spirit (10:48), risking of life (15:26), and exorcism (16:18). Several things

16. To speak of Luke's Christology as built "from the earth up" is important. Luke brings the reader along a step at a time to understand who Jesus is. The three titles of Christ, Prophet, and Servant were understandable to the reader and made good starting points. To claim that Jesus is Lord was a more radical claim that Luke gradually revealed.

were predicted about the "Christ": resurrection (2:31), suffering (3:18; 17:3; 26:23), and being appointed for humankind (3:20). Christ was the subject of the apostles' preaching (5:42; 8:5; 9:22; 17:3; 18:5; 28:31). Because of all He is and all He does, He is to be the object of trust (24:24).

Son of David. This title is another way of presenting Jesus as a regal authority. This emphasis is also part of the Christological foundation Luke presented in the infancy material. Jesus' connection to David was noted numerous times (Luke 1:27, 32, 69; 2:4, 11). Of these passages, the most descriptive ones are 1:32, 69. Here one reads of Jesus occupying the throne of David and emerging from David's house to rule and deliver. When blind Bartimaeus asked for healing, he addressed Jesus as Son of David (18:38–39). The relationship between a regal role and healing is not clear, though some have suggested that in Judaism Solomon was believed to have possessed miraculous skill, as well as wisdom.[17] The question Jesus raised about David's Son in 20:41–44 focused on His messianic connection.

In Acts 2:25–31 Peter made the point that David as a prophet anticipated that his son would be resurrected (Ps. 16:8–11). Peter used this passage to explain that Jesus' resurrection was a part of God's promise. Acts 13:22–23 also refers to the promise to Israel of a Savior from David's lineage. Acts 13:34 added a note, citing the promise of Isaiah 55:3. The promises given to David are also promises to the nation Israel and to Paul's audience, since Paul noted that David's "holy and sure blessings" belong to the nation. In Paul's exposition that followed, part of the holy things promised through the Messiah were the forgiveness of sins and justification. So part of the promises to David are inaugurated through Jesus' resurrection.

The final passage relating to David is Acts 15:16, which refers to the promise of the rebuilt Davidic booth made in Amos 9:11.[18] Jesus' resurrection and recent events in the church showed that God was rebuilding the Davidic house. So James argued that Gentile involvement in that process should not surprise anyone. It was a

---

17. The claim that this expectation is late must deal with a text like Josephus, *The Antiquities of the Jews* 8.2.5, pars. 45–49. This description of Solomon, who is said to have passed on incantations and other means of healing, does not mention a figure like him to come, but it does show that Solomon was regarded as a healer. As such it lays the basic foundation for the pattern to be established. See D. C. Duling, "Solomon, Exorcism, and the Son of David," *Harvard Theological Review* 68 (1975): 235–52; and Klaus Berger, "Die königlichen Messiastraditionen des Neuen Testaments," *New Testament Studies* 20 (1973–74): 1–44.

18. In fact, though Amos 9 is cited, the introductory formula makes use of Luke's generalized appeal to the prophets, showing that this is not the only text James could have appealed to, but is one example from many. The distinction is important, because James's rendering of the text is close to the LXX, which differs from the MT. But James's point is that the Bible as a whole teaches this point, as the introductory formula shows. He picked a well-circulated example, and could have appealed to other texts, had he wanted to develop the argument. The use of the formula also suggests that James had in view a current aspect of fulfillment, not a future one. On the introductory formula, see Luke 18:31; 24:25, 27, 44; Acts 3:18, 21; 10:43; 13:27; 15:15; 24:14; 26:22, 27; 28:23.

part of the promise as well.[19] Thus the title "Son of David" is a major link in the chain that points to God's completing His promise.

Son of God and King. Another title of Jesus used by Luke is "Son of God" (*ho huios tou theou*). This full form rarely appears. As noted earlier, the title is used in Luke 1:35 in association with the Virgin Birth. The term is a foretaste of Luke's high Christology, but its sense is so ambiguous in this initial setting that it is difficult to express its clear intent without the help of Luke's later development.[20] The title is used by Satan at the temptations as the claimed title of Jesus ("If you are the Son of God," 4:3, 9). A significant use of the title appears in 4:41, where it is linked to and explained by the title "Christ." The linkage shows that the title does have regal overtones for Luke. Demons called Him the "Son of the Most High God" (8:28). The title seems predominant when spiritual beings addressed Jesus. The use acknowledges that Jesus possesses a high level of authority. "Son of God" was a position in dispute at Jesus' trial, as seen in Luke 22:70.

The use of the simple title "Son" is more complex. Sonship is associated with the Virgin Birth in Luke 1:31–32, expressing a unique origin of the "Son." Jesus spoke of God as His Father (2:49). Again "Son" suggests a unique relationship to God. "Son" is the title in the heavenly voice at Jesus' baptism and transfiguration (3:22; 9:35). These are the only occurrences of this title in the gospel of Luke.

Acts 9:20 is the only place where the full title appears in Acts.[21] Early in Luke the term "Son" may be ambiguous as to whether it stresses a regal position or unique Sonship, but in Acts it clearly describes the exalted Messiah who sits next to God the Father with total authority. As such, it is a title of high Christology. This is confirmed by the reference to Psalm 2:7 in Acts 13:33. This allusion looks back to the Father's voice at Jesus' baptism and transfiguration. An examination of Luke's two volumes shows that although "Son of God" is not used frequently in Luke, the title did ultimately express Jesus' unique relationship to God the Father, though in some contexts it might have been simply another way of saying Jesus is the King or the Christ.

19. The force of this text is debated. The pattern of Lucan fulfillment and citation in Acts suggests that here is another text Luke saw as being initially fulfilled in Jesus' first coming (see Darrell L. Bock, "Evidence from Acts," in *A Case for Premillennialism,* ed. Donald K. Campbell and Jeffrey L. Townsend [Chicago: Moody, 1993]). Even if the fulfillment in view here were looking to the future, it does not alter the basic point that the Davidic connection for Luke is one of promise and fulfillment.

20. As noted earlier, in the original setting the title is surrounded by regal imagery, which the title "Son of God" can also bear. Thus, in the original setting the title could be perceived as meaning either King or unique Son of God. Mary initially took it as the former. Later events showed that it meant something more. These Christological distinctions may seem like hair-splitting, but they are important. Luke was showing that the disciples gradually came to see who Jesus is, and the gospel writer told the story in such a way that the development could be experienced by his readers. To remove the distinctions is to remove one of the theological achievements of Luke's work.

21. This assumes that the disputed variant in Acts 8:37 is not original to Acts. If this other verse is genuine, then a second use of the full title exists in a confession of faith.

Jesus was called the "King" (*ho basileus*) at the time of His triumphal entry (Luke 19:38, which alludes to Ps. 118:26). "King" is the title discussed in the legal proceedings surrounding Jesus' trial before Pilate (Luke 23:3: "Are you the King of the Jews?") and in connection with His death (vv. 37–38). One thief recognized he was dying with a king, for he asked to come into Jesus' kingdom (v. 42) and was promised paradise that day. Some Jews in Thessalonica accused Christians by saying the believers called Jesus a king (Acts 17:7).

Prophet. In the midst of the messianic Christology, one should be careful not to miss Luke's focus on Jesus as prophet (*prophētēs*). The outstanding example of this "submerged" category is Luke 4:16–30. Here Jesus said He fulfilled Isaiah 61:1–2a, in which Isaiah described a prophet who would be anointed by God and would bring the message of hope to God's people.[22] However, Jesus is more than a prophet, for He brings the salvation He proclaims. Jesus' prophetic function receives confirmation in Luke 4:24, when He said that a prophet is without honor in his own country. In addition, the comparison to the period of Elijah and Elisha also makes the prophetic connection clear (Luke 4:25–27).

Much popular speculation about Jesus centered in a prophetic confession. Luke 9:7–9, 19 shows the strength of such speculation, as did the popular reaction to Jesus' raising the son of the widow of Nain ("A great prophet has appeared among us," 7:16). For many, Jesus was only a prophet. But even that was doubted by the Jewish leaders as His associations led them to question that Jesus held that position (v. 39). Luke 7:36–50 is significant because the leaders claimed Jesus' willingness to receive anointing from a woman of questionable reputation showed He was not a prophet. And yet, as a prophet, He knew all the while what they were thinking! This point of irony, expressed with literary flair, affirms that Jesus is a prophet.

Disappointed that Jesus had been crucified, one of the Emmaus followers called Jesus a "prophet powerful in word and deed" (24:19). These men also had hoped Jesus would redeem Israel (v. 21). Luke loved to place Prophet-Redeemer themes side by side. Jesus was both, not one or the other.

The prophetic description of Jesus received more emphasis as the narrative moves on. Luke 9:35 ("Listen to him") points to Jesus as the "prophet like Moses" by alluding to Deuteronomy 18:15. The disciples needed to hear what Jesus said, since He is the bearer of a New Way, as was Moses. In particular, the message of the Messiah's suffering needs to be heard (9:43–45). The title "prophet like Moses" indicates that Jesus not only brought the message of God but also introduced a new era. These descriptions of Jesus receive attention in Acts 3:22–23 and 7:37.

One other point emerges from the prophetic theme. As a prophet, Jesus shared the fate of earlier prophets, namely, national rejection. Luke 13:33 brings this point out explicitly, and it is implicit in 11:47–51. It is particularly seen in the

---

22. This text is used in a typological-prophetic way. It refers to a type of prophet of which Jesus is the most representative example.

teaching of His journey toward Jerusalem (Luke 9–19), when Jesus as a prophet, rebuked the Jewish leaders and called disciples to righteousness. Many of the passages in Luke 9–14 are strong prophetic rebukes of current religious practice. There is a piety that is false and dishonoring to God, no matter how good it may seem outwardly. Such hypocrisy received stronger judgment in this section than did blatant sin, possibly because hypocrisy is deception. Luke 11:39–52 presents Jesus at His prophetic best.

Son of Man. This key title (*ho huios tou anthrōpou*) is the way Jesus preferred to speak of Himself. Late in the gospel (21:27), Jesus indicated that "the Son of Man" alludes to the authoritative figure of Daniel 7:13–14, who received authority from the Ancient of Days over the kingdom. In Daniel, the term is not a title but a description, "one like a son of man," that is, a human. The title "Son of Man" is prevalent in all three gospels. Though Mark emphasized the suffering Servant, Luke's treatment is divided between uses that describe Jesus' current ministry, suffering, and return.

As the "Son of Man," Jesus has a wide variety of ministries. He has authority to forgive sins, a claim that stirred much reaction, since in the Jewish view only God could do that (Luke 5:24). This claim shows the extent of the authority suggested in the title. He is Lord of the Sabbath (6:5). Jesus recognized that some will be hated for the Son of Man's sake (v. 22). Though Jesus has authority, some reject Him. The Son of Man came eating and drinking, an allusion to His open lifestyle and particularly to His associating with tax collectors and sinners, another area where he differed from the leaders, who tended to be separatistic (7:24). Rejection again is the note when Jesus lamented that the Son of Man had nowhere to lay His head (9:58). Because of His rejection, it is hard to follow in the footsteps of the Son of Man. In Luke 11:29–31, the Son of Man gave no sign to that generation except that of Jonah. Verse 32 explains that this sign is the message to repent, not of Jesus' resurrection, for it was Jonah's preaching in Nineveh to which Jesus drew attention. Men may speak against the Son of Man, but if they speak against the Holy Spirit, that is, reject the Spirit's testimony about Jesus, they cannot be forgiven (12:10). The mission of the Son of Man is to seek and save the lost (19:10).

Most of the Son of Man sayings pertaining to His suffering are predictions or point to the necessity of His suffering (9:22, 44; 18:31; 22:22; and 24:7, a passage unique to Luke, that notes the fulfillment did come). Jesus added tension to the point of Judas's betrayal by noting the disciple betrayed the Son of Man with a kiss (22:48). Here the hypocrisy of the disciple is contrasted to the submission of the Son to His calling, despite His high position. Luke 22:69 affirms that the result of Jesus' suffering is His glorification: "From now on the Son of Man will be seated at the right hand of the power of God." Only Luke, among the Synoptic Gospels, omitted the reference to Jesus' coming back in the clouds; his focus was on Jesus' current authority.

The apocalyptic Son of Man is a figure with great authority who judges. He will be ashamed of those who are ashamed of Him (9:26). Those who confess Him, He will confess before the angels (12:8). He will come when He is not expected

(v. 40). Luke 17 includes several facts about His return. Many long to see His days (v. 22), yet when He comes it will be like lightning and the judgment in the days of Noah (vv. 24, 26). When He is revealed, that is, when He returns, He will judge (v. 30). Later Jesus asked whether the Son of Man will find faith on earth when He returns (18:8). Will people continue to wait for His return? Luke 21:27 notes Jesus will ride the clouds as He returns (cf. Dan. 7:13–14), a figure of speech that was an Old Testament picture of deity (Ex. 34:5; 14:20; Num. 10:34; Ps. 104:3). People are to watch so that they have the strength to stand before the Son in that day (Luke 21:36).

When Stephen was martyred, he saw Jesus, standing as the Son of Man to receive him (Acts 7:56). Here Jesus, functioning as Judge, welcomed Stephen into heaven, showing that despite earthly rejection, Stephen was honored in heaven. The Son of Man for Luke is a title that allowed Jesus to describe Himself, since only He used the title. Included in the title is authority, rejection, and reign.

Lord. The pivotal role of the key title "Lord" (*kyrios*) has received attention already. As the title of Jesus, the term is much more prevalent in Acts than in Luke. There are numerous uses of the term "Lord" in the gospel of Luke, but they are used as a title of respect to one who is viewed as socially superior, much as people today use the word "Sir." In everyday Greek usage the title often referred to a master or to a leader who had authority over another. The Christological use of the title first appears in Luke 2:11 and reappears in 24:3. Its use is ambiguous in certain gospel texts like Luke 5:8, where Peter distinguished himself from the righteousness of Jesus.

The force of the title is made clear in Acts 2:21 when Peter cited Joel 2:32, "Everyone who calls on the name of the Lord will be saved." In that Old Testament passage "Lord" translates the Hebrew "Yahweh." The call was the cry of one needing God to deliver him from peril, namely, the day of the Lord. In Acts 2:36–39, Peter made the point that Jesus is the Lord to whom one calls. So "Lord" refers to Jesus' authority. Jesus resurrection-ascension, revealed in Acts 2:30–33, testifies to His lordship. The essence of Jesus' lordship is His authority over salvation and the right to distribute its benefits. He also has such authority over people of all races (Acts 10:35–36).

The centrality of the title becomes clear when one sees how many verses speak of people believing in the Lord (Acts 5:14; 9:42; 16:30–31; 18:8; 20:21). These texts show the title was appropriate to confess in response to the gospel, whether one was a Jew or a Gentile. The confession recognized Jesus' right to distribute the benefits of salvation, His authority over them, and His authority over humanity. Jesus is the one with authority over salvation, who is worthy to receive honor and to be followed. To come to God, a person must come through Jesus (Acts 4:10 says the same thing, while not using this title).

Servant. Another title that Luke used with interesting variation is "servant" (*pais*). Only in Acts did Luke use this term to refer to Jesus. These involve allusions to the servant passages in Isaiah. But before considering those passages in Acts, two other occurrences of the term are significant. In Luke 1:54 Israel is called

God's servant. Having Old Testament precedent (Isa. 49:3), this points to the special role Israel had as an object of God's grace and as His representative. God was helping His servant Israel by bringing justice to His people (Luke 1:52–53) and by being merciful (vv. 54–55). In Luke 1:69, Zechariah called David God's servant for similar reasons. He was God's regal representative ruling over His people, and he was the recipient of God's promises. Out of the lineage of this servant, the promised Deliverer came.

Luke presented Jesus as the glorified Servant, not the suffering Servant. Jesus is God's Servant glorified (Acts 3:13) and exalted (v. 26). This is the emphasis in Isaiah 52:13–53:12 as well. For Luke, the fact that Jesus was vindicated and exalted to rule was as important as the fact that He suffered. What good is His death without His exaltation? Nonetheless, Jesus as the rejected Servant is also a part of this theme. Luke 22:37 cites Isaiah 53:12, where it is noted that Jesus' death must be fulfilled, as Isaiah declared that Jesus would "be numbered with the lawless." The title "your holy Servant Jesus" in Acts 4:27 and the allusion to Isaiah 53 in Acts 8:32–33 refer to Jesus' rejection. Jesus suffered as the Servant. Acts 4:30 simply notes that "your holy Servant Jesus" performed healing and signs through His disciples. This corporate identity with Jesus is also brought out in 13:47 where servant imagery from Isaiah 49:6 was applied to Paul and Barnabas. They were a light to the nations to "bring salvation to the ends of the earth." The mission of the Servant, Jesus Christ, is the mission of His servants (cf. Luke 2:30 about Jesus). They are to be one in their goals.

Some observe that it is significant that the idea of substitutionary imagery from Isaiah 53 was not applied directly by Luke to Jesus. This is really an insignificant complaint. What Luke was stressing is the person of salvation more than the means of salvation. Luke was certainly aware of Jesus' substitutionary death (Luke 22:19; Acts 20:28), but he did not highlight it. Preferring to stress the position and person of Jesus, Luke did not detail the means of His work as much as Paul did. The two emphases show how various parts of the New Testament message supplement each other.

Less frequently used titles. Other titles of Jesus appear in Luke–Acts with less frequency. Some refer to His authority. For example, Peter spoke of Jesus as the "Prince" or "Leader" (*archēgos*, Acts 5:31). This depicts a royal figure who leads the way for His people in redeeming them. The redemptive emphasis is seen in its use alongside the title "Savior" in the same verse. The demons confessed that Jesus is "the Holy One of God" (*ho hagios tou theou*, Luke 4:34). These spiritual beings were silenced by Jesus, who had authority over them. (A similar title was used in Acts 3:14–15.) Jesus was called a "judge" in Acts 10:42 and 17:31. Another title of respect is "Master" (*epistatēs*) used in Luke 5:5; 8:24, 45; 9:33, 49; 17:13. This title indicates little more than that Jesus was held in high regard.

A centurion referred to Jesus' innocence by affirming that He was "a righteous [*dikaios*] man" (Luke 23:47). In Acts 4:11 Peter spoke of Jesus as the "rejected stone" (*ho lithos ho exouthenētheis*), an allusion to Psalm 118:22.

Still another title referred to Jesus' role as instructor. Twelve times He was called "Teacher" (*ho didaskalos*, Luke 7:40; 9:38; 10:25; 11:45; 12:13; 18:18; 19:39; 20:21, 28, 39; 21:7; 22:11). This title is the most popular title used by the scribes and Pharisees for Jesus, though others also used it occasionally. It described Jesus as a "rabbi," at least of sorts, since He did not receive official training.[23]

In summary, Luke used numerous titles to describe Jesus. Most suggested His authority or His role as the promised regal Messiah. He also exercised a prophetic role. In addition, some day He will return and judge. He is at the center of God's plan. For Luke, the person of Jesus is as crucial as His work. Because of who Jesus is, He is able to save, and He is worthy of people's trust. Because of who Jesus is, one must respond to Him. For not only is He a prophet and the Messiah, but also He will return to judge all as they stand before Him. In fact, even now He sits at the right hand of God exercising authority and distributing the benefits of salvation, even the Spirit of God, to those who call on Him for salvation. In Luke, when a person responded to Jesus, it is more to who Jesus is than to what He has done. What Jesus does is also of importance to Luke, but Luke's priorities are shown by how little time he spent explaining how Jesus saves when the gospel is given. Nonetheless, an examination of Jesus' work reveals the ground of human salvation.

THE WORK OF JESUS

Earthly ministry. Much of Jesus' ministry revolved around teaching and miracles. Several summaries in Luke's gospel, as well as a major summary in Acts, point up this fact (Luke 4:15, 31–32, 44; 6:17–19; 7:22; Acts 10:36–38). In particular, Jesus' teaching often included parables. The gospel of Luke has a concentration of parables in the "journey section" (Luke 9:51–19:44).[24] There are thirty-five parables or pictorial aphorisms in Luke, with nineteen of them unique to his gospel.

Jesus' miracles served as signs that attested to God's vindication of Jesus' identity and claims (Acts 2:22; 10:38). When John the Baptist's disciples asked Jesus if He was "the one who was to come" (Luke 7:20), an allusion to His messianic position, He pointed to a series of miracles (v. 22) that allude to Old Testament promises of what would happen in the eschaton (Isa. 29:18–19; 35:5; 42:6; 61:1). His reply indicated that His healing ministry marked the beginning of the eschaton.[25] Such activity also depicted the fall of Satan, as indicated in Luke 10:18 and 11:14–23. This event indicates that Jesus' coming impacts heavenly realities and also portrays the beginning of the eschaton. The new era is a special era for Luke, and Jesus' work is particularly unique.

23. Luke never used the title "rabbi," probably because it would have been unknown to some in his audience and because it would have made Jesus seem too Jewish for Luke's Greek audience.

24. The exact end of the journey section is disputed, but in 19:45 Jesus arrived, whereas in 19:28–44 He was still approaching Jerusalem (see v. 41).

25. This does not mean the hope of the eschaton is exhausted by this fulfillment. Here is another "already" element in Luke's eschatological portrait. The eschaton had started, but there is more to come.

The message of Jesus has two parts: a message of hope and a call to a life of ethical honor before God. Luke 4:16–30, which summarizes His message of hope, is a representative presentation of Jesus' preaching. Luke's record here includes more than is found in the other Gospels (cf. Mark 6:1–6). He declares that the time of Jubilee is present and that the Anointed One has appeared. Jesus was commissioned to preach to the poor, proclaim release to the captives, give sight to the blind, release the oppressed, and offer forgiveness. "The poor" refers especially to the materially impoverished (cf. 1:53; 6:24), as well as to the spiritually poor. Luke established such a spiritual element in the definition when he referred to the humble in the context of covenant promise, who are exalted, while the proud are brought down (1:49–54). Luke's concern for such material categories is seen in Luke 6:20–26 (1 Cor. 1:26–29 is similar). This group seems to have been the most responsive to Jesus. He said the message is for them. Such people understand what it is to stand humbly before God.

The Sermon on the Plain summarizes Jesus' ethical message (Luke 6:20–49). The sermon closely parallels the Matthean Sermon on the Mount (Matt. 5–7), except that Luke omitted those elements that focused on Jewish issues.[26] Luke's including the Sermon in a form that relates to Gentiles shows the message is timeless. The Beatitudes (Luke 6:20–22) stress the present situation of His disciples: poor, hungry, weeping now, and rejected. But all will be changed later (vv. 23–26). The ethic of love (vv. 27–36) is the cornerstone of the community's ethic, both as individuals and as a body. Jesus' new commandment to "love one another" is similar in force (John 13:34). Jesus' disciples are to display a slowness to judge and an awareness of one's own faults (Luke 6:37–42). A person's character is reflected in his or her actions, revealing the character of the heart, just as fruit reveals the nature of the tree (vv. 43–46). Foolishness is a failure to respond to Jesus' teaching, while wisdom means responding to it (vv. 47–49).

Part of Jesus' work is to reveal the way to God (4:17–19) and the will of God (6:20–49), but more detail comes from several of Jesus' parables. Some parables explain why Jesus spent time with tax collectors and sinners (15:1–32). God is committed to finding the lost. The way to God is open to all, but the message must go out so that all can hear. When Jesus associated with social outcasts, the Pharisees repeatedly grumbled at these relationships (5:27–32; 7:36–39; 15:2–3). The parables of the lost sheep, lost coin, and lost son (chap. 15) were Jesus' apologetic for spending time with such people. His commitment and labor reflected the love of God in seeking out the lost. This series of three parables is unique to Luke's gospel.

Other parables outline God's plan and the coming change of focus from Israel to the Gentiles because of rejection by the nation Israel. The parable of the tenants (20:9–18) overviews the rejection of God's messengers all the way back to the Old Testament prophets. However, the slaying of the Son caused the owner to give the vineyard to others. The rejected stone is the head stone, and those on whom it falls

---

26. It is debated whether the sermons in Luke and Matthew are the same. This writer prefers to see them as the same, with Luke presenting a scaled-down form. But the point is valid, even if a different version of the same teaching is in view.

are crushed (Ps. 118:22; Isa. 8:14; Dan. 2:34, 44). Everyone knew against whom Jesus spoke when He made that remark.

Other passages deal with key elements in the will of God and in discipleship. Another uniquely Lucan parable, the parable of the rich fool (12:13–21), teaches that Jesus' followers should avoid being overly dependent on wealth. At least twice Jesus stressed the importance of prayer for His disciples (11:1–13; 18:1–8). He often spoke of the crucial need for faithfulness among those who await His return (12:35–48; 19:11–27). Above all, Jesus made it clear that discipleship is a total commitment of one's life and self to God. In terms of God's expectation and will, there is no minimal discipleship; what He desires is everything (9:23–26, 57–62; 14:25–33). In short, one is to love God with everything he or she has. Such a focus means His followers will also love their neighbor (10:27–28).

The Cross. Alongside Jesus' teaching, there stands His work on the Cross. Often this is the only thing people consider when they speak of Jesus' work. It also has an important role for Luke, though he did not give it the detailed attention Paul did.

Luke stressed that Jesus is the "righteous Sufferer *par excellence.*" This is indicated by allusions to the Psalter in Luke 23, where psalms of lament about suffering Old Testament saints are applied to Jesus. He fit this pattern of suffering and fulfilled it (Luke 23:34–36, 46 allude to Pss. 22:18; 31:5). All through this chapter Luke stressed that Jesus is innocent (Luke 23:4, 14–15, 20, 22, 47). Luke 23:47 is the climactic declaration that Jesus suffered innocently in that He suffered as a "righteous [*dikaios*] Man."

Jesus' righteous suffering is also a major theme in the apostles' speeches in Acts. The sufferer is vindicated, according to Acts 2:23–24, since God raised Him from the dead and death could not hold Him (Pss. 18:4–5; 116:3–4). Other Lucan passages repeat this theme (Acts 4:10; 5:30). Acts 3:14–15 makes the point that He is "the Holy and Righteous One." Jesus was rejected and that is clearly shown by the fact that His death occurred "on a tree" (5:30; 10:39; 13:29), a picture of rejection. In 13:29 the reference to the tree alludes to the cursed death described in Deuteronomy 21:23 (cf. Gal. 3:13).

Two passages—Luke 22:20 and Acts 20:28—speak of Jesus' death in terms similar to Paul's. At the Last Supper Jesus shared a cup that commemorated "the new covenant in my blood which is poured out for you" (Luke 22:20, accepting the longer reading of this verse). Here several ideas come together. Jesus' death inaugurated the benefits of the new covenant. Jesus died for the benefit of His disciples. His death cleared the way for people to be rightly related to God, a relationship in which God also pours His Spirit on them. Luke later alluded to this provision of the Holy Spirit as the "promise of the Father" (24:49; Acts 1:5). Jesus' death opens the door to many benefits to the one who comes to Him.

The second key text is Acts 20:28. Luke 22:20 looked forward to the Cross, whereas Acts 20:28 looks back. The church has been purchased with Jesus' blood. Jesus is again portrayed as a sacrifice whose death made possible the new community, "the church of God." The Lucan treatment of the Cross does not emphasize how the Cross provides forgiveness. Luke simply pointed repeatedly that the Cross has made it possible for humans to be related to God, since death did not end the story. After death, came vindication in His resurrection. Some have said that Paul saw "the Christ of the Cross," whereas Luke saw "the Christ of glory." Once again, the authors of Scripture complemented each other.

Resurrection-Ascension. Jesus' resurrection receives strong emphasis in Luke –Acts. In addition, many of the speeches of Acts center on the significance of the Ascension. Luke is the only New Testament author to describe the Ascension. When he discussed it, he was also pointing up the significance of His resurrection, which is why we have hyphenated the two events. For Luke they are distinct, but linked. Jesus' reception into heaven to the right hand of God had a great impact on Luke's view of His work. Numerous passages in Acts indicate that the Resurrection indicates vindication (2:23–24; 3:14–15; 4:10–12; 5:30; 17:31). Also, His resurrection resulted in His being positioned at God's right hand, so He could pour out the Holy Spirit and exercise authority (2:30–34). As already noted, Jesus' resurrection is the basis on which His disciples can minister in His name. Jesus remains in heaven until His return (3:21). But when He returns, He will rule on earth and judge all humanity (3:20–21; 17:30–31).

A dead Savior is no savior at all. If Jesus were still in a grave, He could do no one any good. But raised and ascended to the side of the Father, Jesus is able to empower His children and enable His church. He reigns, seeing all that everyone does and thinks. For Luke the death and resurrection of Jesus are important, but more important is His reign, both presently and in the age to come. For Luke, Jesus is not passively sitting in heaven awaiting His return; He lives and rules in anticipation of a more visible rule to come. All are and will be subject to Him.

The two-stage kingdom reign of Jesus. It is impossible to consider the work of Jesus without considering His rule. The basic outline of Jesus' rule has been discussed in relation to Luke's concept of the kingdom. Under the current heading, more specifics can be noted. The rule of Jesus is reflected in Luke's writing by what is done "in His name" or "through Jesus." To do something "in Jesus' name" is to do it in His authority, that is, in view of the fact that He reigns. Such texts are limited to Acts, which shows how important a turning point His resurrection was.

Numerous passages speak of salvation or forgiveness of sins in His name (Acts 2:21 [this refers to Jesus as is seen in v. 38]; 4:12; 10:43). Others speak of baptism in Jesus' name (2:38; 8:16; 10:48; 19:5). These references to water baptism refer to the public confession of Jesus that expresses concretely the presence of inner faith in Christ. Water baptism pictures the spiritual washing that comes from forgiveness as well as the coming of the Spirit. This public identification with Jesus pictured God's saving act and showed that the one who was baptized acknowledged what God had done in Jesus. In the first century, the rite of baptism and what it represented are seen as a unit and are interchangeable (1 Peter 3:21–22 is similar in perspective and shows how Peter saw this connection). A third group of passages speak of healing done in Jesus' name (Acts 3:6, 16; 4:9–10), and a fourth group refers to signs and wonders through His name (4:30). Some preached in His name (8:12) or spoke boldly in His name (9:27–28).

Early in Acts, healing and other acts of ministry were the focus. But later the emphasis was on Jesus' followers suffering shame and imprisonment in or for His name (5:41; 9:14, 16; 15:26; 21:13). This suffering referred not to Jesus' activity, but to the consequences of identifying with Him in a world that rejects Him. Also 15:14 does not mention Jesus, but the benefits of identifying with Him are noted. The concept that the Gentiles are "a people for His name" (15:14 kjv), where His name describes God the Father (cf. v. 17), shows that Jesus gives anyone who believes access to the Father. Jesus is active in dispensing the benefits of salvation and is involved in the rites where identification with Him is demonstrated. The Spirit and forgiveness are the preeminent gifts Luke mentioned as a result of one's coming to the Father through Jesus.

As noted earlier in the discussion on the kingdom, Jesus' future rule is described primarily in terms of His work as judge, when He returns to gather His people (Luke 17:22–37; 21:5–36; Acts 1:11; 3:19–20; 10:42; 17:31). Luke did not give much detail about God's future program other than to make one very important note that Jesus will fulfill the rest of the Old Testament promise about the restoration of all things at that time (Acts 3:20–21).[27]

SOTERIOLOGY

Soteriology is a vast field in Luke's writings. In discussing salvation, two categories are basic. "Objective salvation" refers to what God has done, and "subjective salvation" refers to the responses of people that permit them to share in the benefits God has provided. Objective salvation involves God's work, but related to salvation is the delivery of the message about that work. This preaching reveals salvation's content. So this section of the chapter will first examine the act of proclaiming the good news, giving attention to the scope of salvation, including both Jews and Gentiles and other specially mentioned groups. Also requiring attention is the means by which God supported the message and gave it authentication. With such background in place, the treatment of objective salvation follows. Then we will examine subjective salvation, the response to the message God desires. The benefits received in salvation will be discussed next, followed by a consideration of some tangential issues in soteriology (e.g., How does the salvation message relate to promise? What is Luke's view of the law?).

THE ACT OF PROCLAIMING GOOD NEWS

The gospel. In Acts the word gospel (*euangelion*) is used only twice. Peter noted that the "message of the gospel" went to the Gentiles through him (15:7).

27. The language of Acts 3:20–21 recalls the language of Acts 1:6–7, so that when Peter spoke of the restoration of all things in Acts 3, he included events surrounding the restoration of the kingdom to Israel, which the disciples asked about in Acts 1. The link between Acts 1 and 3 link is defended in Bock, "Evidence from Acts," in *A Case for Premillennialism*.

Acts 10:34–43 is a good example of the message Peter preached. Paul said that his life was given over for the testimony of "the gospel of God's grace" (20:24).

The use of the verb (*euangelizō*) is more plentiful in Luke–Acts than elsewhere in the New Testament. Angelic announcements of John's and Jesus' births were said to be "good news" (Luke 1:19; 2:10). John's message was the preaching of good news (3:18). This word is especially used of Jesus' message to the poor (4:18; 7:22), His preaching the message of the kingdom (4:43; 8:1; 16:16), or preaching the gospel (9:6; 20:1).

In Acts the content of the good news is more specific. The apostles proclaimed the message that "Jesus is the Christ" (Acts 5:42). Other verses also point out that Jesus was the focus of the apostles' preaching (8:35; 10:36; 11:20; 17:18). Some passages call this message the preaching of the Word (8:4; 15:35), while others refer to the promise of the fathers (13:32). Still another speaks simply of the kingdom and Jesus (8:12). However, the most common expression is simply to preach the gospel (8:25, 40; 14:7, 21; 16:10).

According to Acts 14:15 Barnabas and Paul said that the gospel meant turning from "worthless things," idols, "to the living God who made heaven and earth and sea and everything in them." The gospel is an invitation to come to the living Creator God and enter into a dependent relationship with Him. At the center of the gospel stands the person and work of Jesus. He is the promised one, the Christ. The promise of the fathers finds fulfillment in Him. The kingdom is bound up with Him. Peace is through Him. Through a myriad of equally valid images, the gospel points to Jesus as people are invited to come to know God through forgiveness. This call to be related to God through Christ summarizes the gospel as presented in Luke's writings. It is the offer of forgiveness and then life.

Preaching. The noun "preaching" (*kērygma*) is rare, appearing in Luke's writings only in Luke 11:32, where the message of repentance Jonah preached is compared to Jesus' message. The verb "to preach" (*kērussō*) is more frequent. John the Baptist preached a baptism of repentance (3:3). Jesus preached in the synagogue about the arrival of the "acceptable year of the Lord," a picture of forgiveness made through His appeal to the Old Testament image of Jubilee (4:18–19; Lev. 25, esp. v. 10). Jesus preached the good news of the kingdom in the synagogues of Judea (vv. 43–44; 8:1; 4:18–30 is a good example). The disciples also preached the kingdom (9:2). On occasion, the verb *kērussō* is used to describe how others told people about what Jesus had done for them (8:39). As such, the term means the same as giving testimony. Jesus also noted that a day will come when everything people said secretly will be preached from the rooftops (12:3). This does not refer to the preaching of salvation, but to judgment in the eschaton.

In Acts, Christ is the one preached (8:5; 9:20, the "Son of God"; 10:36–39, in a ministry summary). Acts 10:42–43 gives a very significant summary of the apostles' preaching. As witnesses they were commissioned to testify that Jesus is the One God ordained to judge the living and the dead. To Jesus all the prophets bear witness that "everyone who believes in Him receives forgiveness of sins through his name" (10:43). Both apostolic witness and Old Testament prophetic witness testify to Jesus.

A nonsoteriological use of *kērussō* is in 15:21, which refers to the fact that Moses was being preached every Sabbath in the synagogues. And, of course, Paul presented Jesus or the kingdom (19:13; 20:25; 28:31). As Luke–Acts progresses, the message of salvation became more focused on Him than on anything else.

Teaching. Jesus is described as one whose teaching (*didachē*) brought astonishment because of its authority (Luke 4:32). Of course illustrations of His teaching are seen all through the gospel of Luke. He taught with sayings, parables, and prophetic actions, along with a few major discourses (4:16–30; 6:20–49; 11:37–52; 15:1–32; 17:20–37; 21:5–36; 22:14–38). The topics range from salvation out of sin to life with God, from Jesus' current ministry to His return. Jews who were saved on the day of Pentecost followed in the apostles' teaching (Acts 2:42). The consternation of the Jewish leadership (5:28) and the astonishment of the synagogue audiences (13:12) greeted the apostolic message as well. In Athens, Paul's message of the resurrection was called a "new teaching" (17:19).

Like the cognate noun *didachē*, the verb *didaskō* is used by Luke to summarize Jesus' and the apostles' teaching. Jesus taught in the synagogues on the Sabbath; in public settings as on a boat by the shore, in towns and villages; and in the temple (Luke 4:15, 30; 5:3, 17; 6:6; 13:10, 22, 26; 19:47; 20:1; 21:37). Luke was particularly fond of Jesus' teaching at meals (5:29; 7:36; 9:16; 11:37; 12:37; 13:29; 14:1, 8–9; 22:14; 24:30). Only once was teaching requested of Jesus, when His disciples asked Him to teach them about prayer (11:1). Jesus' opponents acknowledged that He is a teacher, while accusing Him of stirring up Judea and Galilee (20:21; 23:5). He told His disciples that the Spirit would teach them what to say when they faced persecution (12:12).

In Acts the emphasis on teaching sometimes looked back at Jesus the teacher (Acts 1:1). The apostles taught the people about the Resurrection and the name of Jesus, which annoyed the authorities (4:2, 18; 5:21, 25, 28, 42). Barnabas and Saul taught the disciples in Antioch, where disciples were first called Christians (11:26; 15:35). Some Judaizers were wrongly teaching that Gentile Christians needed to be circumcised (15:1). Paul taught in various locales, including Corinth (18:11) and Ephesus (v. 25). In Ephesus he taught "the way of the Lord" (v. 25) and to the Ephesian elders he summarized his teaching of repentance toward God and faith in the Lord Jesus (20:20). Paul's opponents charged him with teaching against the people and Moses (21:21, 28). Acts closes with Paul teaching about the Lord Jesus Christ (28:31).

Teaching in Luke–Acts is seen as a broad term encompassing much more than the offer of the gospel, whereas preaching in Luke–Acts tends to be limited to the salvation message. As Luke–Acts progressed, Luke's presentation of the gospel message became more focused on Jesus. That message is still one message and one hope, because of its link to God's promise, but the center of the promise residing in Jesus emerged most clearly after His resurrection.

THE SCOPE OF SALVATION

The promise for Jews and Gentiles. Luke emphasized that what Jesus provided is available to all people. This point gradually emerges in the infancy narrative's overview of salvation. Zechariah spoke of Jesus, the "horn" in David's house (Luke 1:69), as a rising light (Num. 24:17; Isa. 9:2–7) that would shine on those who sit in darkness and death (Luke 1:78–79). Such activity is a fulfillment of God's promises. Angels told the shepherds that Jesus came to bring peace on earth for all those who are the object of God's good pleasure (2:14). Not every person automatically receives these benefits, but God in Jesus makes them available to those who respond and are a part of His special people. The scope of this provision became clearer still in 2:30–32, where Jesus is said to be a light for revelation to the Gentiles, as well as glory for Israel. This language is rooted in Isaiah (Isa. 42:6; 46:13; 49:9). Thus the universality of God's work is noted early in Luke's introductory section in language that recalls Old Testament promises about Messiah and His rule.

The body of Luke's gospel made the same point. In an extended citation unique to Luke, the gospel writer included Isaiah 40:3–5, when he described John the Baptist's ministry. The citation ends with the words "all mankind will see God's salvation" (Luke 3:6). Here the scope of salvation is made clear. The wording actually is not a direct citation as much as a summary of Isaiah 40, drawing on the imagery that comes from Isaiah 40:10–11, since the reference to "God's salvation" summarizes the picture of Isaiah 40:10–11 in the Masoretic text, while Isaiah 40:5b in the Septuagint has already made the summarizing translation. This universal note occurs also in Luke 24:47, where the message of the new community is the preaching of repentance to all the nations. This message is said to be predicted by the Old Testament (vv. 44–47). In extending salvation to the Gentiles, God's promises about the Messiah are being initially realized.

Acts continued this Gentile emphasis by citing Jesus' words that the message is to go to the ends of the earth (Acts 1:8). The dramatic vision given to Peter (Acts 10:9–16) showed God's direction and intervention to guarantee and endorse this expansion, while Peter in his speech in Cornelius' house said that "God accepts men from every nation" (v. 35) and that salvation through Christ is available to "everyone" (v. 43). Acts 28:28 also makes explicit the fact that the message is for Gentiles. This Gentile inclusion is a key theme in Luke. Its tie to the Old Testament hope struck a note of continuity in God's plan. To Jews in the community, this inclusion would be a difficult point, since Israel is God's special people. Therefore Luke spent much time on this theme.[28]

Numerous texts picture this expansion of the gospel to Gentiles. Luke 7:1–10 described a Gentile centurion whose faith exceeded anything found in Israel. A demon was exorcised from a man in the Gentile region of Gerasene by Jesus

---

28. Other New Testament books also indicate the church's struggle with implications of Gentile inclusion. Romans, Galatians, and Ephesians also deal with additional issues that such inclusion raised.

(8:26–39). Jesus led a mission to Samaria, a region of a mixed race (9:51–56). In the parable of the Good Samaritan a man responded to God's will properly in the treatment of others (10:25–37). Jesus spoke of people coming from east, west, north, and south to dine at the banquet table in the kingdom to come (13:22–30). In another parable, people from the highways and hedgeways were invited to share in the banquet that Jesus brings (14:15–24). In the episode of the ten lepers, only the Samaritan leper responded with gratitude for the healing he received (17:11–19). In the parable of the tenants (20:9–19), the vineyard was to be given to others after the son was slain (v. 16). Jesus went so far as to call the current age the "times of the Gentiles" (21:24).

Acts continues this emphasis. Acts 9:15 describes the call to Saul to bear Jesus' name before the Gentiles. Acts 10–11 shows how God directed Peter to Cornelius. God is the one who brought in the Gentiles. Of course, much of the rest of Acts showed how Gentiles were receptive to the gospel. If anyone had been disturbed by the racial breadth in the new community, according to Luke there was only one figure to blame and that was God Himself. Luke's emphasis on the universality of the gospel was an effective apologetic claim against any who thought the gospel message in the church had become too broad, too generous, or too gracious.

To the poor, sinners, and outcasts. Special attention is given to the poor in Luke's gospel. Mary's hymn in Luke 1:46–55 sets the tone for this theme. Her reference to God's lifting up and blessing the poor (vv. 52–53) does not mean all the poor. It refers primarily to the *'ănāwîm* of the Old Testament, those pious poor who humbly relied on God (vv. 50–55; cf. 2 Sam. 2:5; Job 5:11; 12:19; Pss. 103:11, 13, 17; 89:10; 107:9). This distinction is an important one for Luke, since the focus on the poor was not a political manifesto. What the passage does indicate is that often the poor are more dependent on God and in tune with His will than the rich. The focus on the poor was reinforced in three representative presentations of Jesus' preaching (Luke 4:18; 6:20–23; 7:22). In all these passages salvation is offered to the poor. Jesus mentioned the poor explicitly when He thanked the Father for those who were His ministering disciples (10:21–22). The poor are those who should be invited by the disciples and who are to be invited to the eschatological banquet table (14:13, 21–24). Salvation for Lazarus the beggar concludes the focus on this theme (16:19–31), while the widow with her small copper coin of contribution also reinforces this theme (21:1–4). For Luke, the "lowly people" are especially noted as candidates for God's grace. (The book of James is parallel here.)

Sinners also received special mention in Luke. Jesus' enemies frequently complained about Jesus making Himself available to such people (5:27–32; 7:28, 30, 34, 36–50; 15:1–2; 19:7). Each time Jesus vindicated His behavior by word and/or deed. Such grumbling showed that the Jewish leaders misunderstood Jesus' mission to call the spiritually sick to be healed through repentance (5:30–32).

Another group of rejected people were the tax collectors, regarded in the culture as social outcasts and traitors. The passages dealing with this group often overlap with the passages dealing with Jesus' treatment of sinners: 5:27–32 (Levi); 7:29,

34; 18:9–14 (prayer of the publican); 19:1–10 (Zacchaeus). These passages show that the gospel penetrated the hearts of those who lived on the fringe of humanity. Whether rich in sin (the tax collector) or poor in life (the *'ănāwîm*), the gospel can transform the lives of those who respond to it.

THE AUTHENTICATION OF THE MESSAGE

Three levels of authentication. Along with the message came authentication. By what authority did Jesus perform His works and proclaim His message? When this question was raised by the Jewish leaders, Jesus did not reply other than to point to the same authority John the Baptist obviously had (Luke 20:1–8). Other evidence demonstrated that Jesus is who He claimed to be. Jesus was authenticated through signs and wonders (Acts 2:22; 10:38), through His fulfilling of promises given in the Scriptures and through the presence of the Holy Spirit.

The subject of scriptural fulfillment has been discussed already, but a key passage pointing to this theme is Luke 4:18–21, in which Jesus publicly proclaimed that the Scriptures attest to His ministry. Luke 24:44–47 is similar in force.

In addition, Jesus' work and message were authenticated through miracles. When John asked if Jesus is the coming One, He answered by pointing to the miracles of His ministry (7:18–23). These actions allude to passages in Isaiah that point to the end (Isa. 26:19; 29:18–19; 35:5–7; 61:1). Jesus' answer was that His work indicates the nature of the time and the nature of His person. He is the promised "One to come." Luke 11:14–23 explains what His miracles mean. God the Father exercised His power through Jesus, a power that demonstrates His superior strength, in which He portrayed Himself as the strong man pilfering Satan's house (vv. 21–22). In fact, Jesus said that if His miracles were by the finger of God, then the kingdom of God had come (v. 20).

This picture of authority is also seen in the ministry of the disciples. Jesus gave authority to the Twelve (9:1–2) and to the seventy-two (10:1). The Eleven received unique authority both now in relationship to the present kingdom and will receive it over Israel in the kingdom to come (22:29–30). Such authority, which gave them the power to exorcise demons, caused the disciples to marvel and rejoice (10:17–20). Jesus' reference to Satan falling like lightning shows the current victory this authority represents (v. 18; Eph. 1:19–23; 1 Peter 3:20–21). Similar authority existed through the apostles and others in the early church. God performed miracles through a number of individuals: apostles (Acts 2:43; 5:12); Peter and John (4:16, 22); Stephen (6:8); Philip (8:6, 13); Paul and Barnabas (14:3; 15:12). Such healings occurred in the name of Jesus (3:6, 16; 4:10) and demonstrated that there is no other name under heaven by which people can be saved (4:12). The apostles (4:33), Stephen (6:8), Philip (8:13), and Paul (19:11) are said to have miraculous power (*dynamis*), though that power stemmed not from them but from Jesus (3:12; 14:8–18). Such exercises of authority accompanied the message and indicated the approaching arrival of God's promise, as the missions of the Twelve and the seventy-two indicated (Luke 9:1–2; 10:8–12).

A final authentication of the gospel message was the presence of "power from on high," that is, the Holy Spirit (Luke 3:15–18; 24:49; Acts 1:8; cf. Acts 2:14–22, 32–36; 10:38; 11:15–16). Pentecost authenticated not only Jesus' resurrection but also the presence of the promise of God. The Spirit's activity and testimony declared that Jesus was alive and that God was at work through those in the church.

The miracles of Jesus and His disciples. What Jesus offered in His person and message was pictured in the miracles He and His followers performed. The nature of miracles as "picture" as well as event emerges in Luke 5:1–11, where a miraculous catch of fish also prompted Jesus' remark that the disciples' will be "catchers of men." The miracle portrays a deeper reality and inspires wonder. Salvation's scope is revealed in these miracles. To appreciate the extent of salvation, it is important to look at the theology of this aspect of ministry, which authenticated, pictured, and explained what Jesus was doing.

The scope of Jesus' healing could easily be regarded as part of His work and could have been discussed earlier. However, the truths about salvation pictured by His miracles show their importance to the present theme. Jesus' healings covered a vast range of situations: the sick (Luke 4:18, 40–41; 5:31–32; 7:22); evil spirits (4:31–37; 8:26–39; 9:42; 11:14–20; 13:32); fever (4:38–39); leprosy (5:12–16; 7:22; 17:11–19); paralysis (5:17–26); a withered hand (6:6–11, on the Sabbath); epilepsy (9:37–43a); dropsy (14:1–6, on the Sabbath); blindness (4:18; 7:22; 18:35–43); a constant flow of blood (8:43–48); deafness (7:22); and resuscitation from the dead (7:11–17, 22; 8:40–42, 49–56). All these maladies picture the destructive presence of sin and chaos. The healings show Jesus' power to reverse these effects and to declare the healed one saved (5:24).

Jesus' authority, however, goes beyond dealing with human misery. He also controls creation, as seen in the nature miracles. He directed His disciples into finding a large catch of fish (Luke 5:1–11), He calmed a storm (8:22–25), and He fed the 5,000 (9:10–17).

In a revealing section in Luke's gospel, Jesus brought restoration in all kinds of ways (8:22–56). He calmed the storm, exorcised demons, healed the flow of blood, and resuscitated one from the dead. Whether over nature, spiritual forces, disease, or death, Jesus has the authority to deliver and overcome those forces that harm or destroy people.

The reactions produced by His miracles are interesting. Usually the reaction was in the form of a question or an emotional response. Seeing a man exorcised of a demon, the crowd asked, "What is this message?" and "By what authority does He do this?" (4:36). Reacting to the catch of fish with a sense of his own sinfulness, Peter asked Jesus to depart (5:8–9). After Jesus healed a man with leprosy, news about Him spread (5:15); and after He healed a paralytic, people glorified God (5:26). Some thought Jesus' power to restore the widow's son to life pointed to the presence of a prophet (7:16). When confronted with the calming of the storm and knowing that God controls the weather, the disciples asked, "Who is this?"

(8:25).[29] Another crowd was gripped with fear after the demoniac was healed (8:37). The parents of a resuscitated child were amazed (8:56). After another exorcism by Jesus, multitudes marveled (11:14). A large crowd gave praise to God when a blind man was given sight (18:43). Even demons confessed Jesus' authority (4:34, 41). Clearly the people were impressed that someone of unusual authority and power was present, though many never thought He was more than a prophet (9:18–19).

Equally impressive is the scope of the disciples' work. They also healed the sick (Luke 9:1–2; 10:9) and exorcised demons (9:1, 42, 49; 10:17). In Acts, God healed a lame man through Peter and John (Acts 3:1–10, 16; 4:8–10) and another cripple through Paul and Barnabas (14:8–18). Saul regained his sight (9:17–18). Aeneas, a paralytic, walked (9:32–35) and Dorcas was resuscitated (9:36–43), as was Eutychus (20:7–12). Exorcisms occurred (16:16–18). Publius's fever was cured (28:7–10). The power of Jesus attested the authenticity of the ministry of these men who preached Jesus; His power showed that their message came from God. Alongside these miraculous works of ministry came other authenticating signs. On three occasions, angels delivered the apostles from prison (5:17–26; 12:6–11; 16:24–34). Apostolic judgment brought death or other consequences (5:1–11; 19:13–20). People survived shipwreck and snakebites (27:23–44; 28:3–5). The scope of this exercise of power is impressive.

The important point was not so much the miracles themselves as what they portrayed (Luke 10:18–20). Jesus' power was expressed through His appointed messengers which showed that He was raised and active. The forces that oppose people meet their defeat and death through Jesus. He can deliver. In other words, physical salvation portrays spiritual salvation. The account of Acts 3:1–4:21 makes this connection clear as Peter moved from a discussion of physical healing to a declaration of spiritual salvation. What Jesus and His disciples did indicated what God was doing. The message of hope they brought in the gospel was (and is) true.

THE OBJECTIVE ASPECT OF SALVATION

Words for salvation. Several words are used in Luke and Acts to speak of salvation. The best way to examine this subject is to look at the salvation word group: *sōtēr, sōzō, sōtērion,* and *sotēria.* The term *Savior* (*sōtēr*) was discussed earlier in the section on Christ. Three times this word is used of Christ (Luke 2:11; Acts 5:31; 13:23), and once it refers to God (Luke 1:47).

The verb "to save" (*sōzō*) means to deliver from calamity. Numerous miracles picture this concept. When Jesus healed the man with the withered hand, He asked the Pharisees and teachers of the law whether it was lawful on the Sabbath "to do good or to do evil [harm], to save life or destroy it" (Luke 6:9). For Jesus the answer was to save life, which is what the miracle of physical deliverance pic-

---

29. The exact force of this question is purposely open and ambiguous. One should not see the disciples asking too much here, since in Elijah's day famine began and ended through the power of God. Here is another place where Luke leaves the narrative tantalizingly unclear and lets the reader reflect on the question as his account proceeds.

tured. The same was true of the demon-possessed man (8:36), the bleeding woman (v. 48), Jairus' daughter (v. 50), the Samaritan leper (17:19), and the blind beggar (18:42). These miracles were audiovisuals of God's power and authority.

The sinful woman who anointed Jesus' feet was saved because of the attitude reflected in her action (7:50). In the parable of the sower (8:4–15), Jesus explained that rejecting the Word, by which He meant the message of the kingdom (v. 10), resulted in lack of salvation (v. 12). To save one's life, a person must lose it (9:24). Those who place their lives in His hands can be delivered.

Hearing Jesus' teaching, some concluded that few would be saved and so a listener asked Jesus about it (13:23). He answered that entry is through a narrow door, a reference to responding to the message on God's terms, and not human terms. Jesus added that people will come and enter in from all directions, an allusion to all races, yet some who will expect to sit at the banquet table with the patriarchs and prophets will be missing (13:24–30). Another parable speaks of a filled house (14:23), also suggesting that though many reject the gospel, many others will respond. The point of both remarks is that though many Jews will miss out on the promise they expected to share in for failing to respond to Jesus, the place of God's blessing will be full of God's people.

A similar question from one of the disciples raised the issue of who could be saved (18:26). The question was asked in response to Jesus' remark that a rich man entering the kingdom is like a camel passing through a needle's eye (v. 25). Here Jesus noted that what is impossible for man is possible with God. Peter then remarked that the disciples had left all for Jesus. In turn, Jesus responded positively, describing the rich reward that would be theirs for their response, a reward that includes eternal life (vv. 27–30). Though Peter said that the disciples had forsaken "all," they, including Peter himself, failed at certain points to be "total" disciples. Nonetheless basic dependence on God was there, so Jesus responded positively to the claim that the disciples had left all.[30] These disciples, and people like Zacchaeus, picture what the mission of Jesus is about, namely, to seek and save the lost (19:10).

There is irony in the final use of the verb "to save" in Luke's gospel. As Jesus was crucified, people mocked Him, calling on Him to save Himself (23:35, 37, 39). Of course Jesus' death was laying the groundwork by which He could save sinners. He was doing what they mocked Him for not doing!

In Acts, the use of the term for physical deliverance occurs in 27:20, 31 (and perhaps 16:30). Most uses are summary descriptions that occur along with acts of healing or preaching (2:47; "no other name by . . . which we must be saved," 4:12; about the house of Cornelius, 11:14; of the lame man at Lystra, 14:9; of Gentiles like Cornelius, 15:11). In his message on the day of Pentecost, Peter said those who call "on the name of the Lord will be saved" (2:21), a quotation of Joel 2:32 (cf. Rom. 10:13). The Lord to whom one calls, Peter explained, is Jesus (Acts

---

30. What Jesus' reply means here is that the remark to "leave all" is figurative for placing God first or relying on God alone.

2:36). He saves by providing forgiveness, sparing from wrath, and giving the Holy Spirit (vv. 38–40).

Another key summary occurs in Acts 16:30–31. The Philippian jailer was overwhelmed by his circumstances and asked what he needed to do to be saved. All he may have meant was how his physical life could be spared. Paul responded by speaking of spiritual life, by calling for faith in "the Lord Jesus" (v. 31). Ultimately, life is retained through Him, so Paul answered a question even more fundamental than the one the jailer asked.

Thus the verb "to save" is used in a variety of ways. First, some occurrences refer only to physical deliverance (Acts 27:20, 31). Second, some occurrences suggest both physical and spiritual deliverance. Often miracles of physical deliverance pictured spiritual deliverance. Though Luke 5:17–26 does not use the term "save," the incident recorded there pictured this connection when Jesus healed the paralytic. Jesus asked whether it was easier to tell the man to get up and walk or to tell him his sins were forgiven (v. 23). There is irony in the question. In one sense it was "easier" for Jesus to say one's sins are forgiven, since that cannot be seen, while making a man walk can be observed. And yet, forgiving sin in reality is the "harder" thing to achieve. But how can one show that forgiveness is present? Such a claim can only be pictured. So to show His authority to forgive, the "harder and more visible" act, physical healing, was accomplished. One reality pictured the other. Miracle becomes a metaphor for salvation. All Jesus' miracles should be seen in this light. Third, other verses refer directly to spiritual salvation (Luke 19:10; Acts 2:40; 4:12). When spiritual healing is present, Jesus stands active at the center of salvation.

The meaning of the various forms of the noun *sotērion* and *sotēria* differ little from the verb *sōzō*. When the prophet Simeon saw Jesus, he could say he had seen God's salvation (*sotērion*, Luke 2:30). Luke 3:4–5 cites Isaiah 40:3–5 to describe John the Baptist's ministry, noting that the forerunner's activity of clearing the path occurs so that "all mankind will see God's salvation." Salvation had come to the Gentiles in the message about Jesus (Acts 28:28). So from the first of Luke to the last of Acts, God's saving activity is in view.

The other noun (*sotēria*) is rarely used in Luke–Acts, but its usage is significant. In a key text, Luke 1:69, 71, 77, the focus is on the Davidic "horn" of salvation, who delivers from all enemies and who is associated with the hope of forgiveness and the arrival of peace with God, through rescuing people out of darkness (cf. Col. 1:12–14). In this description of salvation, physical and spiritual deliverance are discussed side by side as part of Jesus' messianic task. Jesus brings both. Also national and spiritual hope are tied together. Personal salvation ultimately results in peace on earth.

Zacchaeus, rejected by society, responded to Jesus' teaching and so he was welcomed before God (Luke 19:1–10). As already noted, Acts 4:12 points out that salvation is only through Jesus. The hope of deliverance for Israel was expressed in Paul's apostolic message in Antioch of Pisidia (13:26). In fact, Paul's entire speech recorded in Acts 13:16–41 is representative of a Pauline message on salvation, just as Luke 4:16–30 is an example of Jesus' preaching. Paul's mission was to bring salvation to the Gentiles and to the ends of the earth (13:47 alludes to Isa. 49:6). The remaining two uses of *sotēria* in Acts (7:25; 27:34) refer to physical deliverance.

Without doubt, salvation is a key concept in Luke. Salvation is centered in Jesus. It possesses spiritual qualities, but eventually it will impact the human structures on earth (Luke 1:68–79). It is offered to all races (Acts 10–11). It is possessed by those who respond to Jesus. It is at the center of the apostolic message, and in it is everlasting life.

The work of salvation: The Cross and Jesus' resurrection-ascension. Luke highlighted who Jesus is more than how He saves, but the basic outline of His work is still present. Many of the points to be made here were discussed earlier in connection with Jesus' work on the cross. Here focus is on the Old Testament allusions, since they vividly explain various aspects of Jesus' work.

There are two probable allusions to Isaiah 53 in Luke's passion material. One is explicit. Luke 22:37, portraying Jesus as the innocent sufferer, cites Isaiah 53:12 (He "was numbered with the transgressors"). Jesus noted that His fate was a necessary part of God's plan. Jesus died as a social criminal between two thieves in fulfillment of this promise (Luke 23:32, 39–43). In addition, Luke noted that He died a cursed death on a tree (Acts 5:30; 10:39; 13:29 using Deut. 21:23).

The second passage alluding to Isaiah 53 is more debated because it is conceptual and also involves a passage that is missing in some Greek manuscripts of Luke's gospel. On the cross, Jesus interceded for forgiveness for His enemies (Luke 23:34). This also recalls Isaiah 53:12, which says the Servant "made intercession for the transgressors." The connection between Luke 23:34 and Isaiah 53:12 is not verbal, but nonetheless it is likely. The text is probably original to Luke, since it has a parallel in Acts 7:60, where Stephen interceded for His enemies. Such parallelisms are frequent between Luke and Acts. These two allusions to Isaiah 53 relate Jesus to the figure of the Suffering Servant, especially in portraying His death as unjust. Jesus died like a sinner, numbered with transgressors. Yet in the midst of it all, Jesus' compassion for His enemies shone forth in His prayer for them. In praying for His enemies, Jesus applied the principle He enunciated in Luke 6:27–36, namely, to love one's enemies.

Repeatedly, Luke 23 affirms Jesus' innocence. Pilate mentioned it three times (vv. 4, 14–15, 22), and in one of his references Pilate reported that Herod too had found Jesus innocent (v. 15). In addition, a centurion at the cross proclaimed Jesus' innocence (v. 47, a remark unique to Luke). The term chosen by the soldier is *dikaios*, which can be translated "innocent" or "righteous." Either term makes good sense here, but the slightly broader term "righteous" seems preferable. The soldier was probably not interested merely in the legal status of Jesus, but in His character, which made such a verdict likely. According to the lips of one of His executioners, Jesus died a righteous man. The testimony of an enemy is often worth more than the protestations of many friends.

Luke's record of the crucifixion reflects imagery from the Psalter and Isaiah. Five such allusions exist. Jesus not only requested forgiveness for His enemies (Luke 23:34 alluding to Isaiah 53:12), but Luke noted that they cast lots for His clothes, recalling Psalm 22:18 (21:19 LXX). In Luke 23:35, the onlookers' mocking cry that Jesus save Himself recalls Psalm 22:6–7 (21:8–9 LXX). The offer of wine (Luke 23:36) finds a parallel in Psalm 69:21–22 (68:21–22 LXX). Psalms 22 and 69 are psalms of lament, portraying an innocent sufferer's cry to God for vindication from his enemies. These allusions show that Jesus died in the pattern of suffering like that of the saints of old.[31] It also shows that He trusted in God the Father for vindication.

The fourth allusion to the Psalter is in Luke 23:46, which records Jesus' final words in which He committed His spirit into God's hands. The language recalls Psalm 31:5 (30:5, LXX). This "last word" of Jesus differs from the record in the other Synoptics (Mark 15:34–37; Matt. 27:46), where Jesus quoted Psalm 22:1 (21:2, LXX), though Mark noted that Jesus made two cries. Only Luke recorded the details of the second cry. Psalm 22:1 expressed a painful cry of anguish, which Jesus offered from the cross. Psalm 22 is another psalm of lament. Psalm 31 is also a psalm of lament, but verse 5 from that psalm is an expression of trust. Thus, Jesus knew that His fate and vindication were in God's hands. With this cry He rested Himself in the care of the Almighty. The vindication, if it was to come, must come from the mighty God who cares for His own.

Of course, the vindication did come in Jesus' resurrection. The enemies had mocked Jesus by urging Him to get down from the cross (Luke 23:33–38). But God did something more; He took Him out of death. With vindication came benefits to be bestowed on those allied to Him. Numerous verses indicate that with Jesus' resurrection-ascension came the opportunity for forgiveness. Forgiveness is included in the message (24:47), is pictured in baptism (Acts 2:38), results from repentance (3:19), was offered to Israel (5:31), comes through Jesus' name as the prophets promised (10:43), comes through Him by faith (13:38), means that sins are washed away when one calls on His name (22:16), and comes as a result of turning from Satan to God (26:18). According to Luke, forgiveness is the key emphasis which Jesus' work on the cross and His resurrection can bring. When Jesus cried out, it was as if He interceded for all. To gain access to that forgiveness, all one needed do is respond to His offer.

---

31. Thus, the use of the Old Testament here is a case of typological-prophetic fulfillment, where Jesus fits the patterns of suffering of the earlier era, but in a unique way because of the nature of His work. So when Jesus completed the typico-prophetic pattern, the way in which He fulfilled the text is true only of Him. Many New Testament texts, when utilizing this type of fulfillment, speak of a unique fulfillment in Him and note that the text does not refer to anyone else. This is true in the sense Jesus "fully fulfills" the text in a way no one else does. So He is the "righteous Sufferer" or the "Servant." On this category of Old Testament fulfillment, see Darrell L. Bock, "The Use of the Old Testament in the New," in *Foundations for Biblical Interpretation* (Nashville: Broadman, 1994).

Other benefits of Jesus' resurrection-ascension include the outpouring of the Holy Spirit (Acts 2:30–36), the offer of the times of refreshing along with the yet-future times of renewal (3:19–21), the realization of the Abrahamic covenant (vv. 25–26), the offer of salvation in His name (4:12), the availability of justification (13:23, 38–41), and the appointment of Jesus as Judge (17:31). God is at work through Jesus.

According to Luke 22:19–20 the new covenant was inaugurated by Jesus' death.[32] The supper portrayed a broken body and life's blood shed on behalf of "you," a reference to disciples. The church is a community purchased by the blood of "his own" (Acts 20:28), that is, the blood of God's Son. As such, the community is precious, and those who are elders must care for it as a special gift. Rich benefits come from the hand of the innocent one who was vindicated by God and now rules at God's side as Lord.

THE SUBJECTIVE ASPECT OF SALVATION

The subjective aspect of salvation refers to the personal appropriation of salvation. Luke used a variety of concepts to express this fundamental response. The variety is important to maintain, for each term helps focus on different aspects of one's response. Salvation is not to be seen as the accumulation of these various responses. Rather the one true response to the message has these elements bound up in it, though each term highlights an ingredient in that response. Any one term can summarize a genuine response, while highlighting an element in it. Luke wished to show the multidimensional character of response to the gospel. The three key terms are repentance, turning, and faith.[33] Luke wanted His readers to appreciate what God graciously offers, how simply it can be received, and how deep the response itself is.

Repentance. A key concept for Luke is repentance, whether expressed by the noun "repentance" (*metanoia*) or the verb "to repent" (*metanoeō*).[34] The Greek verb means "to change one's mind," but in its Lucan usage it comes very close to

---

32. These verses are part of a significant textual problem in Luke. Many omit them, but 1 Corinthians 11:23–26 contains a summary of these remarks as reflected in the early church's tradition that is very close to that in Luke. Since this summary includes this remark, it was probably also present in Luke's version, given the fact that Paul's account of the Last Supper account is closer to Luke's version than it is to the other Synoptics.

33. This variety is important to note in light of current discussions about the gospel. The biblical writers seem to be more free in using a variety of images to discuss and summarize the offer of salvation than many seem to be today. Any one of these terms is sufficient for Luke. To insist that one term is better than another is to make distinctions the biblical writers did not make. The variety exists to allow the one gospel message to be presented with different emphases to address particular concerns at a given moment.

34. Luke is the theologian of repentance. He used the noun eleven times in Luke–Acts, exactly half of the twenty-two New Testament uses of the noun. The verb appears fourteen times in Luke–Acts out of thirty-four New Testament occurrences, with twelve of the others being in the book of Revelation.

the Hebrew verb for repent which literally means "to turn or turn around" (*šûb*). That the Hebrew sense of the term is primary is clear from Luke 24:44–47, where the message of repentance is seen as fulfilling Old Testament promise that such a message would be preached to all the nations.[35] So repentance is a reorientation, a total shift of perspective from where one was before repenting.[36] This prophetic force is introduced in the section where John the Baptist preached "a baptism of repentance for the forgiveness of sins" (Luke 3:3). A change of perspective, involving the total person's point of view, is called for by this term. In fact, John called for the Israelites to bring forth fruit worthy of repentance (3:8). This passage is significant for it separates repentance from what it produces, and also expresses a link between repentance and fruit. One leads to the other. That this change of perspective finds concrete expression in life is clear from the dialogue that follows in Luke 3:10–14, a passage unique to Luke. When people asked what they must do in response to John's call to repent, he told them to live with kindness and compassion toward others. John's message only prepared one for the gospel, so it is illustrative, not defining. Nevertheless, the passage reveals the basic character of repentance, though the gospel makes the ultimate basis of repentance clearer.

A central passage picturing repentance is Luke 5:30–32. Here Jesus described His mission as calling sick "sinners" to repentance. Though this passage has parallels in Matthew 9:13 and Mark 2:17, only Luke mentioned repentance here. Jesus used the term to describe His own mission, thus showing that it is an appropriate concept to use today in presenting the appropriate response to His mission and work.[37] To repent includes an awareness that as a sinner one has an unhealthy relationship with God that needs the "medical attention" of the Physician. Repentance involves recognizing that a person is spiritually sick and impotent, unable to help oneself. Repentance is turning to Jesus for spiritual healing, for treatment of one's heart and life, knowing that only He can give "the cure." One goes to the physician, so the doctor can diagnose and treat the disease. Repentance is similar with regard to sin and how it corrupts one's standing before God. Jesus makes it clear that humankind has a disease and that only He can treat it. Care of sin is to be placed in His hands. Part of the change of perspective in repentance is to see sin differently and to recognize it is deadly when left untreated. So the sinner who

35. Leonhard. Goppelt rightly points out that merely speaking of "a change of mind" is an insufficient definition of this term's force in the New Testament, because of this Old Testament backgound (*Theology of the New Testament*, 2 vols., trans. John Alsup, ed. Jürgen Roloff [Grand Rapids: Eerdmans, 1981], 1:34–36).

36. Today much energy is spent trying to determine if faith is active or passive or whether it precedes, is simultaneous with, or follows repentance. The sequence, though a significant theological discussion, is not as important to the biblical texts as the fact that both occur as a part of a genuine response to the gospel message and that either term (faith or repentance) can adequately summarize an appropriate response. The fact that either term is adequate to summarize the response shows that either term is sufficient to use in the gospel offer, provided, of course, the terms are defined biblically.

37. This passage is one of several "mission statements" in Luke which summarize why Jesus came. Also Luke 19:10 is conceptually parallel to Luke 5:30–32.

repents to receive salvation comes to Jesus, knowing that only He can heal the relationship to God and deal with sin and its consequences.[38]

Such transformation in a sinner was a cause for joy to Jesus, for heaven rejoices to see such repentance (15:7). In fact, the term He used in His Great Commission to the disciples about their future message was repentance (24:47). This verse shows that the term is an appropriate summary for the offer of the gospel today.

Acts reinforces this point. According to apostolic preaching, repentance is available for both Jews and Gentiles. It is for Israel and is related to Christ (Acts 5:31); it is for Gentiles, leading to life (11:18); and it was prepared for by John's baptism of repentance (13:24; 19:4). So repentance is offered to Jews and Greeks though Jesus (20:21). In fact, in 26:20 Paul told Agrippa that those who repent should "prove their repentance by their deeds," a comment similar in tone to Luke 3:3–14. This parallelism shows a continuity between John the Baptist and Paul. Deeds are the natural, expected product of genuine repentance.

The verb "to repent" (*metanoeō*) is similar in force. A call to repent is the natural response to the miracles Jesus performed (Luke 10:13). Jesus' message is compared to Jonah's call to the Ninevites, showing that repentance in the New Testament has Old Testament roots (11:32). Jesus warned that people will perish if they do not repent (13:3, 5). But joy in heaven results when anyone does repent (15:7, 10). The rich man in Hades held out the hope that a messenger from the dead would convince his brothers to repent of the way they treated others, that is, to respond with a different way of life (16:30). Abraham, however, replied that a resurrection would not be convincing. Nonetheless, the discussion shows the centrality of repentance as an appropriate summary term for response. Luke 17:3–4 uses "repent" in a nonsoteriological sense (repentance of personal acts done to another).

In Acts the verb *metanoeō* is used in summary calls that invite one to enter into forgiveness (Acts 2:38; 3:19; 17:30; 26:20). Peter urged Simon, the sorcerer, to repent and seek forgiveness (8:22). Excluding Simon from sharing in the benefits of the Spirit may well indicate that Simon was lost and that the belief he exercised earlier (v. 13) was less than genuine.[39]

Three portraits of repentance exist in Luke's gospel. Already noted was that of the physician calling the sick to repent (5:30–32). A second portrait is the prodigal son returning to his father (Luke 15:11–32). The attitude of the son is the key. Here he came pleading no rights; he simply sought his father's mercy. He asked to be received not as a son, but only as a servant. Recognizing that what he had done

---

38. A distinction between sin and sins here is crucial. The orientation of repentance in a saving response to the gospel message is a fundamental reorientation, but it does not mean perfection or even continual advance. It does not mean a believer ceases to struggle with sin or sins in the spiritual life. A believer will have setbacks, as Peter's denials show (Luke 22:54–62). But repentance does mean that a person knows that the answer to the sin problem (and how one sees sin) comes from Jesus, and not from one's conscience, works, or any other such anthropocentric source.

39. This passage is debated. Some see Simon as saved, but headed for severe believer judgment. However, the strength of Peter's rebuke and the absence of the provision of the Spirit suggest the conclusion that Simon was unsaved.

was wrong, he entrusted himself to his father's care. That humble reliance is a change of perspective, the essence of repentance.

The third portrait, that of the tax collector in contrast to the Pharisee (18:9–14), is similar to the prodigal. Standing before the throne of heaven, realizing he could bring nothing to commend himself to God, the tax collector rested on His mercy. The beating of his breast graphically portrays his sense of regret for his sin and his sense of need for God's mercy. Not an emotion, repentance in Luke is a change of perspective. What the emotive picture evidenced was that this man knew he was in need of God's mercy, but the attitude, not the emotion, is the point.

In summary, Luke saw repentance as a change of perspective that transforms a person's thinking and approach to life. It applies to Jews and Gentiles. The term summarizes the appropriate response to the message of Jesus and the apostles. Bringing forth fruit is a natural outgrowth of repentance. Just as a good tree brings forth good fruit, so genuine repentance produces change in one's life (6:43–45).

Turning. Another key term in Luke pertaining to the response to salvation is "turning." The noun "turning" (*epistrophē*) is used only once. In Acts 15:3 it refers to the act of conversion by Gentiles. The report alludes back to the results of the first missionary journey. The verb "to turn" (*epistrephō*) is more frequent. John the Baptist's ministry was to turn Israel to God (Luke 1:17). Luke 17:4 speaks of a brother who turns ("seven times comes back [turns] to you") to seek forgiveness for sin. This example does not refer to initial salvation. Predicting that Peter would turn from his failure of denial, Jesus then called on the apostle to "strengthen" the brethren (22:32). Here again, "turning" refers to how a believer rebounds from sin. "Turning" is the reversing of estrangement as one recognizes and accepts that he has done wrong. In this sense it is similar to repentance, but it is a more vivid term, since it portrays a reversal of direction.

The word "turn" is used similarly in Acts. In 3:19, turning is associated with repentance: "Repent, then, and turn to God." Forgiveness is the result. This verse points up a slight difference between repentance and turning. Repentance is the change of perspective and turning follows, as one's direction changes as well. Other summaries in Acts also use the term. Gentiles, seeing Aeneas healed by Peter, "turned to the Lord" (9:35). Gentiles in Antioch "believed and turned" to God (11:21). In this passage "belief" functioned in a manner similar to repent in 3:19. These terms are used interchangeably to refer to the same saving act, though they highlight different elements of that response. Whether repentance or faith, the product is a turning to God. That entire single act saves and produces a reorientation toward God.

So Barnabas and Paul urged the Gentiles in Lystra to turn from idols to God (14:15). Again this passage shows the reversal of direction necessary for salvation of unbelievers estranged from God. The focus of turning always comes back to God. Gentiles are said to be "turning to God" in Acts 15:19, where the term alone is sufficient to describe the response that saves.

The most important passage on turning to God is 26:18, 20. Paul related the Lord's call for him to turn the Gentiles from Satan to God, to receive forgiveness of sins and inheritance that comes by faith in God (v. 18). This passage is important, because all the terms appear together here. In fact, people are to repent and turn, performing good deeds. So the urging of a response and of a result are proclaimed as the essence of Paul's call and thus of his message. Paul called on Jews and Gentiles to "repent and turn to God" (v. 20), so they could receive benefits from God that come by faith. He also told them to perform deeds worthy of repentance.[40]

Repentance for Luke is to express itself concretely and visibly in the life of the responder.[41] Fruit shows the presence of a life-giving root. That root can be biblically described as planted by faith, repentance, or turning. Each of these three terms points to approaching God and resting in His provision and mercy. "Repenting" emphasizes what is left behind as one looks at life, sin, and God in a new way, "turning" alludes to a person's taking up a new direction, and "believing in God" focuses where one's attention ends up as one has a new orientation.

A negative use occurs in Acts, when Luke described the Jews' failure to "turn" because of the hardness of their hearts (28:27). Here a failure to turn was caused by a refusal to respond.

Faith. Two other terms used frequently in Luke–Acts are faith (*pistis*) and "to believe" (*pisteuō*). Luke's usage of these words varies between the act of trust and the trust that saves. All occurrences of the words suggest a reliance on another to provide something one cannot provide for himself. The paralytic's friends had faith in Jesus that He could heal their friend (Luke 5:20). Because of the centurion's "great faith" (7:9), he understood Jesus' authority to heal (vv. 7–8). Jesus spoke of the faith of the sinful woman who washed His feet (v. 50). Each act of faith expressed itself in concrete action. On the other hand, the disciples' lack of faith showed that they questioned God's ability to watch over them. As a result, they were nervous and panicked (8:25). The woman with the continual flow of blood understood that Jesus could heal her and in faith she touched His garment (v. 48). Jairus was challenged by Jesus to believe (v. 50).

Faith can be increased, as indicated by the apostles' request, "Increase our faith!" (17:5–6). This request means that faith can always have more depth, though Jesus' reply emphasized the importance of faith's presence, no matter how small, rather than its quality. The Samaritan leper (v. 19) and the blind beggar (18:42) also acted out of faith in approaching Jesus.

Peter's faith failed, as Jesus predicted (22:32). The possibility of lapsed faith in the face of persecution was so real that Jesus asked if faith would be found on earth when He returns (18:8). The faith described in these last two examples refers not to initial faith but to the continuation of faith. Lapses of faith can and do occur, but ideally faith should be constant. Such constant faith involves a fundamental orientation and trust that a person possesses, a basic recognition that if provision for deliverance in any situation is to come, Jesus must provide it. So faith is to continue; if it does not, spiritual catastrophe is the result.

40. Again this is parallel to Luke 3:3–14.

41. This shows that such exhortation is appropriate and has apostolic sanction.

The usage of the noun "faith" (*pistis*) in Acts is similar. Faith comes through Jesus and was the basis of the lame beggar's healing by Peter (Acts 3:16) and of Paul's healing of the man in Lystra with crippled feet (14:9). Stephen was a man "full of faith," a spiritually mature man, whose faith was exemplary and constant (6:5). At times the Christian movement was called "the faith" (6:7; 13:8; 14:22; 16:5). Gentiles had faith (14:27) and were cleansed by faith (15:9). Faith's object is Christ (20:21; 24:24), and faith is the subjective means that sanctifies (26:18).[42]

In Luke's gospel the verb "to believe" (*pisteuō*) is similar in force. Positive and negative examples abound. Zechariah did not believe the angel Gabriel (Luke 1:20), but Mary did believe the same angel (v. 45). Zechariah was incredulous that God could do what was announced; Mary believed, and, as a result, she became a vessel for God's use. In the parable of the sower the devil is said to prevent belief (8:12), while faith on the part of others is portrayed tragically as short-lived (v. 13). Jairus was told that Jesus could raise his daughter (v. 50). Luke noted that many people believed John's message (20:5). Jesus declared that whatever He might say in His defense, the Jewish leaders would not believe (22:67). Jesus asked the Emmaus travelers if they believed all that the prophets spoke (24:25). Faith responds to content and results in concrete reaction. It includes perception, but this perception produces a product.

Most uses of the verb *pisteuō* in Acts are summaries of people's responses of belief. In a few passages the church is described as a community that believed (2:44; 4:32). The participle describes the respondents as "believers" (5:14; 15:5). Usually the word refers to someone or something who is trusted: belief was in the message (4:4); in the good news (8:12–13); in the Lord, with faith in Him produced by a miracle (9:42); in the Lord, with forgiveness as a result (10:43); in Christ (11:17); in the Lord (11:21; 14:23; 16:31); in God (16:34; 27:25); in Jesus (19:4); in the Old Testament promise (24:14); and in the prophets (24:14). Those who believed included the Bereans (17:12), Athenians (17:34), Corinthians (18:8), Ephesians (19:18), Jews (21:20), and Gentiles (21:25). In Acts 13:12 no object of faith is mentioned, but the proconsul of Cyprus believed as a result of the sorcerer Bar-Jesus being blinded. Belief justifies (v. 39), but those who do not believe will perish (v. 41). All those whom God has ordained to eternal life believe (v. 48). And belief is by God's grace (15:11; 18:27).

Faith, that is, simple belief, expresses itself concretely. Numerous pictures provided in Jesus' ministry are illustrative. They show that faith acted. Faith was the recognition and persuasion that God had something to offer that one must receive and embrace. So in Jesus' miracles, individuals moved to receive what He offered. Faith is active, not passive. It understands, receives, and embraces. The one who welcomes God's message receives what God offers and responds to the gospel. He or she acknowledges that God through Jesus has dealt with the effects of sin and that only He can provide what is needed to reverse sin's presence and eradicate its penalty.

---

42. One unusual usage of the noun *pistis* is in Acts 17:31, where it means proof or assurance.

THE BENEFITS OF SALVATION

Forgiveness. Besides the presence of the indwelling Spirit, Luke enumerated numerous benefits that come from salvation. The first is forgiveness (*aphesis*). In Luke the knowledge of forgiveness is available through the preaching of the "prophet of the Most High," namely, John the Baptist (Luke 1:76–77), who in turn pointed the way to the Davidic "horn" (v. 69) who will bring salvation to the nation of Israel (v. 68) and light to all those who sit in darkness (v. 79). This knowledge and experience of salvation comes through the forgiveness of sins.

John the Baptist's baptism for the forgiveness of sins (3:3) was not the same as Christian baptism, since it could not yet picture the cleansing provided by the Cross. Rather, John's baptism represented a turning to God as a preparation for the arrival of the promised Messiah. The humility reflected in the partaking of this baptism paved the way for divine forgiveness. To the synagogue crowd, Jesus proclaimed a release (*aphesin*) for the captives and liberty for those who are oppressed (4:18). Here His words harked back to the imagery in Isaiah 61:1 and 58:6. This "second exodus" imagery, as Jesus announced in the synagogue, pictured God's people released from enemies, which included Satan and sin, as Jesus' later mission made clear (Luke 10:9; 18; 11:20–23; 22:20). Luke 24:47 summarizes the disciples' message, a message about repentance and the forgiveness of sins. The Acts passages are all familiar summary passages. In Acts 2:38 forgiveness is related to repentance and pictured in baptism; in 5:31 forgiveness is available to Israel; in 10:43 forgiveness is based on faith; in 13:38–39 forgiveness is available through Jesus based on the faith that frees one from bondage, a freedom that the law could not provide; and in 26:18 those who turn from Satan to God receive His forgiveness.

Life. Another key benefit of salvation is life (*zoē*). A scribe asked Jesus about inheriting eternal life (Luke 10:25), actually concerned about being assured of participating in the final resurrection (Dan. 12:3). Jesus replied that he should love God and his neighbor, a reply that well summarizes the message of the law. To do this would bring life (Luke 10:28). This reply, though soteriological in nature, reflects the pre-Cross setting it depicted. The scribe's failure to respond to Jesus' message showed that he erroneously thought he could earn salvation through his own achievements.

A negative statement about life is given in Luke 12:15. Life does not consist in one's possessions. The parable of the rich fool (vv. 16, 21) illustrates this truth and calls on one to be rich toward God.

Luke 18:18 repeats the question of 10:25, "What must I do to inherit eternal life?" Now the answer is supplied in 18:29–30. Anyone who leaves all for the sake of the kingdom will receive many benefits in this life and eternal life in the age to come. Jesus' reply indicated that the disciples had already done this and so they had received the benefits named here. This response, together with Jesus' remarks in 10:25–28, show the point that one does not earn salvation, but must come to God for it. Luke 18 teaches that total sacrifice for Jesus does pay off. The premise behind this passage is basic to understanding the absolute character of Jesus' remarks.

In the first century any confession of Jesus would probably have resulted in rejection by some in one's family, since most Jews were rejecting Jesus. Coming to Jesus in faith would automatically mean a person would be rejected by relatives who did not believe in Him. If one feared family more than God, then the response to the gospel would be a refusal to come to Jesus. To give over all meant being willing to leave all earthly ties behind for a new set of relationships, namely, the one God calls for through Jesus. So Jesus noted that although a disciple lost a family, what was gained was a new family, along with eternal life.

In Acts, life described resurrection (Acts 2:27–28). Because of what Jesus provides He is called "the author of life" (3:15). The apostolic message is called the "words of life" (5:20), and repentance leads to life (11:18). Paul stated that since the Jews refused to respond to his message they did not consider themselves worthy of eternal life (13:46). So he turned to Gentiles, who were appointed to it (v. 48). In 17:25 life is probably not soteriological but refers instead to the physical life God gives all men, since the verse also speaks of God's giving "life and breath and everything" to all.

Gift. A number of times Luke referred to "the gift" (*dōrea*), by which he meant the Holy Spirit (Acts 2:38; 8:20; 10:45; 11:17). Particularly significant here is the parallel between Acts 2 and Acts 10–11, since what was given to the Gentiles was also what the disciples received at Pentecost.

Peace. Another benefit of salvation is peace (*eirēnē*). Like a rising star, Jesus, as the promised One from the house of David (Luke 1:69), shines as light and reveals the way of peace (v. 79). What is meant here is that Jesus makes possible a reconciled relationship between God and humanity. Jesus, as Savior, Christ, and Lord, brings peace to men of God's good pleasure (2:14). The offer of peace is part of the kingdom message (10:5–6). In a counter note, Jesus said that He came not to bring peace but division (12:51). This remark is simply a recognition that some would accept what He offered and others would not. With that reality is the recognition that division within families would come, as verses 51–52 indicate. Of course, this is precisely what did happen in many Jewish families. Peter said his message was "the good news of peace through Jesus Christ" (Acts 10:36).

Grace. Grace (*charis*) is another salvation benefit mentioned by Luke, though he used the word with some variation of force. Grace refers to unmerited favor, a gift one receives from God at the moment he genuinely believes. Mary was the object of God's favor as God prepared to use her as a vessel through whom Jesus would enter the world (Luke 1:30). In two verses that describe Jesus' growth (2:40, 52), grace, that is, God's favor, is said to rest on Him. In 6:32–33, in a nontheological use, the term "grace" is translated as "credit." Here Jesus asked what is the merit of a person loving only those who love him or her.

In Acts grace rests on people and communities. Acts 4:33 speaks of grace resting on all the believers. Stephen was full of grace (6:8), and Stephen spoke of God's favor on David (7:46). Paul and Barnabas had been committed to God's grace by the church at Antioch for their first missionary journey (14:26). Later they were sent to Antioch (15:40). The most common use of the word "grace" is as a description of salvation or its message (11:23; 13:43; 14:3; 15:11; 20:24, 32). Acts 18:27 spoke of belief through grace, that is, they were enabled by God to believe. Salvation is a gift of God in which He bestows rich blessings and favor on those who seek His aid. Those who come to Him humbly in faith for deliverance they cannot supply for themselves receive His unmerited favor, and heaven rejoices at the provision of the gift (Luke 15:7, 10).

OTHER POINTS OF SOTERIOLOGY

The message of salvation and promise. Much of this subject has already been discussed in connection with other themes about salvation. The purpose of this section is to highlight that in Luke–Acts God's promise is portrayed as having already come and also as still yet to come with a judgment tied to what remains. Acts 2 emphasizes what is already fulfilled and Acts 3 discusses what is yet to come.

Jesus' message focused on the offer and approach of the kingdom. He coupled that offer with exhortations about the ethic that was appropriate for those who are associated with the kingdom. The discussion on the kingdom considered these points, which also relate to the topic here.

The apostles' message emphasized the realization of God's array of promises, particularly as they relate to Jesus Christ, the Lord. Salvific benefits are available through Him now, and judgment and consummation are yet to come. This is all in line with the hope of the Old Testament as discussed in the sections on God's plan, the kingdom, and Old Testament fulfillment. In addition, Paul argued in his defense speeches that he was simply preaching the hope of the Old Testament and the hope of resurrection (Acts 23:6; 24:14–16; 25:8; 26:6–8, 22–23). The scope of this message includes all people. Therefore, there should be no bigotry in the church or in the offer of the gospel.

In the face of promise, one other contrasting dimension merits discussion. It is that the hope of the gospel is offered in the face of approaching judgment. Speaking of an axe lying at the root of a tree, John the Baptist warned that judgment was imminent (Luke 3:7–9). Though the actual judgment John referred to will come later, the fate of one's relationship to that judgment is decided in this life. So judgment is encountered directly in the message, along with the opportunity for deliverance from it. When Jesus' message was rejected or when He anticipated rejection, He pronounced woes on His hearers to make the consequences clear (6:24–26; 10:13–15; 11:42–44, 46–52). Without repentance, Jesus said, deliverance was impossible (13:3–5). In the story of the rich man and Lazarus, judgment is seen in the fate of the rich man (16:19–31). Vultures hovering over dead bodies graphically depict the death and judgment that comes with Jesus' return as the judging Son of Man (17:37). Similar warnings in Acts invoke the imagery of the day of the Lord (Acts 2:40), and the "covenant curses" of the Torah that promise being "cut off" (3:23, taken from Lev. 23:29). In addition, two texts refer to Jesus as the Judge (Acts 10:42; 17:30–31).

With the offer of salvation, each individual faces life or death. A person may choose to be rightly related to God or to face eternal judgment. Jesus gives opportunity to receive life, forgiveness, peace with God, and the presence of His Spirit. His death and resurrection have shown that He died for others and is ruling at God's right hand, ready to distribute salvific benefits to those who come to Him. As already discussed, Luke used three terms to describe the appropriate response: repent, turn, and believe. Anyone of these terms can summarize the response that gains life, humbly coming to God for deliverance which only He can give. When a sinner repents, heaven rejoices and God receives the sinner with open arms, for to seek and save the lost is at the center of Jesus' mission (Luke 15:7, 10, 18–24; 19:10).

The law. An examination of the law in Luke–Acts is related to soteriology, because a dispute over the relationship of the law to grace was a central conflict in the early church (Acts 15). Luke indicated that the law has certain points of value for the church. A discussion of the law in Luke–Acts considers its use in Jesus' ministry and in the church. Law in Luke–Acts does not have simply one function, nor is it simply abrogated. What is said about the law depends on the perspective from which it is addressed. Luke–Acts can refer to law as a moral guide which still has instructive value, to law as containing promise which is fulfilled, or to law as regulation of membership and ethnic regulation within the community. In this last sense Acts 15 shows that law is abrogated. A Gentile does not need to be circumcised or change one's choice of food (in other words, become a Jew) to come to Christ.

Certain Lucan passages emphasize continuity betweeen the old era and the new era introduced by Jesus. Luke 10:25–28 indicates that the moral essence of the law is to love God and one's neighbor. Here is life. The law, having an ethical goal, is concerned with how others are treated. All the law is summed up in this focus, and Jesus endorsed it as a message worthy of the one who wishes to have a right relationship with God. Such a description fits what other New Testament texts say when they describe a believer who has embraced God's grace (John 21 with Jesus' questions to Peter; 1 Cor. 2:9; James 2:5; 1 John 4:19). Of course, if one loves God, he or she will respond to Jesus' call to enter into a relationship with Him through responding to Jesus' message.

In another context Luke affirmed that the law has abiding value. In Luke 16:17, Jesus stated that the law will not fail. Here the focus is on law as promise, since the verse follows a remark about John the Baptist's message and the newly arrived kingdom message (v. 16). In other words, the law as promise will not fail. Yet another example is that Moses and the prophets revealed the type of moral life God desires (v. 29). If one is to respond to God and undertakes to examine the law carefully, one can see the hope (and accountability to God) it proclaims. The law indicates promise, since Moses and the prophets witnessed to Christ (Luke 24:27, 44). The continuity of the new era to the law is found in its ethical call to love and its anticipation of God's promise.

Other passages point to discontinuity between the law and the present age (though in some cases the discontinuity pertained to how the law was interpreted in the Jewish tradition or by the leaders). The Pharisees and teachers of the law thought that the authority to forgive sin was limited to God, but Jesus noted that He, as the Son of Man, possessed such authority (Luke 5:17–26). In 5:27–32 Jesus challenged how the Pharisees and teachers of the law viewed associating with sinners. Jesus showed that the person who is sensitive to the message of God's hope could and should relate to sinners the hope of God's promise, as His own example proved (also see Luke 15). An explanation for the difference in perspective about sinners comes in 5:33–39, when Jesus responded to questions about His associations with sinners by using proverbs that showed how what He taught was new. It could not be mixed with Judaism, the old cloth or old wineskin. He also noted that those who liked the old, Judaism, would not like the new, the message of Jesus. The two approaches could not be syncretized, for they are distinct. That Jesus' objection here is with the interpretation of the law as opposed to law itself is clear from Luke 16:19–31, where the law should have taught the rich man to care for those in need (cf. Deut. 14:29). When the rich man wished to warn his relatives, it was to tell them, in part, that they should not respond as he had to the one in need (Luke 16:24–29).

Another key pair of texts pertain to laboring on the Sabbath, where two aspects of the law were more directly challenged (6:1–5, 6–11). In verses 1–5, Jesus pointed out that David was allowed to do what the law specifically prohibited when he and his companions ate the consecrated bread (Lev. 24:5–9; 1 Sam. 21:6). Jesus then affirmed that He and His disciples could pick the heads of grain (Sabbath labor in Jewish tradition) because He, the Son of Man, has authority over the Sabbath. Jesus is like David and more than David. Verses 6–11 affirm His right as Lord over the Sabbath to "labor" on the Sabbath in order to heal. There is irony and vindication when God honored Jesus' "labor" of commanding the man with the withered hand to "stretch out" his hand (cf. 13:10–17; 14:1–6).

In 11:41–42 Jesus argued that the Pharisees' perception of the law was distorted. By tithing herbs and neglecting justice and love, they were ignoring the law's ethical thrust. Luke 16:16 teaches discontinuity, for here Jesus noted that the law and the prophets were until John.[43] In contrast to the era of law stands the present era of proclaiming the kingdom. The law is viewed as a period that has passed away, even though verse 17 makes it clear that the law does not fail, in the sense that it reaches its realization in the kingdom preaching about Jesus. Thus Luke 16:16–17 place discontinuity and continuity side by side.

The picture in Acts is similar. Law is juxtaposed as both continuous and discontinuous. Apparently what the church said stirred the charge that the disciples did not uphold the law (Acts 6:11–14, against Stephen; 18:13 and 21:21, against Paul). The church's reply was that the law was upheld because the promise of the law was proclaimed, either in resurrection or in hope in general (23:6; 24:14–21). What Paul preached was what the Law and the Prophets taught (24:14; 25:8; 26:22). Paul seemed to be highlighting the law as read in light of the prophets. The law reflects the moral will of God and anticipated that deliverance and justice would some day come from Him. Paul even emphasized that he said nothing against the Jews, and so he called

---

43. This phrase has no verb in Greek.

on his listeners to consider his message and ask themselves if they believed the prophets (26:26–28; 28:17). Seeing the law as promise is evident in Acts 3:12–26, where Peter declared the hope of Jesus by appealing only to passages from the Torah (Acts 3:13, the promise of the God of Abraham [Ex. 3:6, 15]; Acts 3:22, Deut. 18:15–20; Acts 3:23, Lev. 23:29; Acts 3:25, Gen. 22:18; 26:4). In highlighting the promise of the second Moses, Peter was declaring that in Jesus a new era had come.

Nonetheless, the church, at least in Jerusalem, kept portions of the law as a means of staying in contact with Jews, for the sake of the gospel. The apostles frequented the temple (3:1). They went to the synagogue on the Sabbath (13:14). Jewish believers were sometimes circumcised (16:3). Paul took vows and honored them (18:18; 21:23–24). In fact, they advised all believers, both Jews and Gentiles, to refrain from certain items. Such action was to "do well," for it avoided giving offense (15:23–29).

The law, however, was not binding on Gentiles, since Peter affirmed that to insist that believers keep the law would place a burden on their necks (15:10). Peter argued that even their ancestors, the fathers of Israel, were not able to bear this burden. The law was not to be followed as a way of salvation. It might instruct and guide, but it was not binding for the church. Nothing made this distinction clearer than the vision from God Himself in which He showed Peter that all foods are considered clean. This vision stood in clear contrast to what the law taught (Lev. 11; Acts 10:9–16). Peter's hesitation to believe the vision only underlined the contrast contained in this instruction and the fact that the "end of the law's reign" was something God insisted on, despite the apostle's objection.

In short, the Mosaic Law had ended because God brought its role to an end! God as Lord of the law had indicated dramatically that the law had served its purpose when it had yielded the stage to the realization of hope. With the hope now realized in Jesus, the resurrection, and the inauguration of the kingdom program, it no longer played a central role in marking out what the people of God should eat or do to establish their association to Christ. The only function remaining for the law was its call to love God and to love one's neighbor, which also meant responding to Jesus, the one who embodied the message of God's offer of peace to the fallen world (Luke 1:68–79, esp. vv. 78–79). Coming to Him meant embracing light and entering a new era of relating to God.

ECCLESIOLOGY

A look at Lucan ecclesiology requires an examination of the relationship between Israel and the church. After this study, there will be a survey of the major ecclesiological characters in Luke–Acts. Such an inquiry is necessary because Luke often revealed his theology through the examples of the individuals he discussed. This inquiry will be followed by an overview of the activity, structure, titles, and ethic of the church—God's new community—for in these elements one can see how Luke saw the church and where she fits in God's plan.

ISRAEL AND THE CHURCH

The church. A consideration of Israel's relationship to the church requires defining the church, examining the role of the apostles, and considering what is actually said to Gentiles and to Israel about God's promise.

The church in Luke's thinking relates to some things old and new. It is tied to old things because it shares in promises made and bestows that message to the world. It is tied to things new because it is an entirely new structure through which God is now working. The apostles proclaimed in the synagogues that Jesus is the fulfillment of the Old Testament law, so any Jew responding to promise should come to Jesus. The apostles' contention was that the natural end of Judaism is to be found in Jesus. The apostles, early in Acts, do not appear to see themselves as called to be separate from Israel. They went to the temple and met there (Acts 3:1–10; 4:1–2; 5:12). Their practices were sensitive to Jewish concerns (15:1–35; 21:17–26). Later in Acts, Paul preached in the synagogues to Jews everywhere he went (13:14–48; 28:17). Even when Paul turned his back on the Jews to go to the Gentiles, he still went to the synagogue or to the temple in the cities to which he traveled (13:46–14:1; 18:6 with 21:26; 28:28 followed by the note in v. 30 that he preached to all). The point of continuity was the message of promise-fulfillment whose roots reached back into the Old Testament and the nation of promise (Luke 24:44–49; Acts 3:13–26; 10:42–43; 13:23–39). The Jews who heard Paul were being told that if they followed through on their commitment to God, they would embrace the message of promise inaugurated and become members of the new community.

However, events forced the church to become distinct, because of the depth of Jewish rejection. As a result, the church emerged as an independent community outside the synagogue. In Luke's view, Christians did not leave the synagogues; they were forced out. Acts outlines this development and shows that Christians did not turn their backs on Israel, but, rather, the synagogue failed to embrace the promise given to the Jewish fathers. Such argumentation is especially central to Peter and to Paul's apologetic in their speeches (2:42–47; 4:23–37; 13:1–3; 20:17; 23:6; 24:14–16; 25:8; 26:6–8, 22–23).

Luke saw the new community as something novel. This is why in Acts 11:15 Peter could refer to the events in 2:1–4 as "the beginning." Now in Lucan terms, it is the beginning of the realization of promise, as Peter's remarks relate to the first distribution of the Spirit (Acts 2:14–36), an act that recurred for Gentiles in Acts 10. So what emerged as the church had its origin in the coming of the Holy Spirit. Acts 11:15–18 makes the bestowal of the Spirit the starting point for this new era and this new group of faithful people. Luke explained how this group became distinct from Judaism and yet had the right to proclaim promises that used to be the unique property of the synagogues. God is present in this new community. The additional point about this new people in Acts 11 is that God has included Gentiles in this circle of blessing through direct intervention (vv. 11–18). The events of the founding of the church in Acts 2 have a parallel in the events at Cornelius' house in

Acts 10:1–11:18, thus showing beyond dispute that God had acted to include the Gentiles.

Such inclusion was suggested in remarks earlier in Acts (i.e., before chap. 10), even though their full force was not realized at the time by the speakers. The promise was for Israel and also for those "far off" (2:39; cf. Eph. 2:11–17). In fact, it is for "all the families of the earth" (Acts 3:25 NASB). Even Jesus had spoken of the Old Testament teaching that the message of repentance would go to all nations (Luke 24:47). In this sense there was continuity between the new community and the Old Testament, yet there was discontinuity as well.

God had to press the point to make discontinuity clear and to show that Gentiles were to be included. He had to use a vision to show Peter that no man is unclean and that the church is to show no partiality (Acts 10:28, 34). All are welcome and have access to the Spirit, whether Jew or Gentile (10:35, 47; 11:18). But Gentiles do not have to become Jews first and then Christians (15:1–29). The new institution, having a beginning, did not require a total link to the old era other than to share in the promise to which it always looked. This promise stands inaugurated, but it is not completed. God still has work to do.

Previously, in the section on the bestowal of the Holy Spirit, the Spirit's provision was seen to be central in Luke's theology. The Spirit's coming is clearly central to the church. John the Baptist alluded to it (Luke 3:15–18), and Jesus told the disciples to wait for it (24:49). The event is described in Acts 2:1–4 and explained later by Peter in vv. 17–21, where he cited Joel 2:28–32. Here is a sign of the inauguration of the last days. The Spirit's bestowal is the essence of the new covenant promise. In his exposition, Peter made clear that the events of Acts 2 initially fulfilled Joel. Peter used a strong fulfillment formula to introduce the citation, saying of the present event that "this is what was spoken" (*touto estin to eirēmenon*, v. 16) by God through Joel long ago. This fulfillment formula would be familiar to Peter's Jewish audience as indicating fulfillment, as its use at Qumran to indicate fulfillment shows (1QHab). When Peter cited Joel, he also added within the citation an additional reference to prophesying, to highlight the connection to what was occurring and to describe what had just resulted from the pouring out of the Spirit. The verb for pouring out, *ekcheō*, is used again in Acts 2:33 with *execheen*, thus linking the citation's fulfillment to the event with Pentecost. Because Jesus ascended, the promised Holy Spirit was poured out. This was the promise of God that had now come for those near and those far off (vv. 30–33, 38–39). The centrality of the Spirit's bestowal is also indicated in two other outpourings: 10:45 ("the gift of the Holy Spirit had been poured out") and 19:6 ("the Holy Spirit came on them"). The repetition of the event shows its importance to Luke.

Thus, the essence of the church is that she is a Spirit-indwelt community. This indwelling is not limited to her leaders and is not something that came and went. Instead, it includes the entire membership and continues permanently, just as Joel said the Spirit would come on all God's children (Acts 2:17). The indwelling described here is new and unprecedented, though it was anticipated in the promise of Joel. The church is something new and something old, new because of its quality and scope, and old in that God said the Spirit would come and relate the church's gifts and blessings of forgiveness to existing covenants and promises tied to the hope of the Christ and His resurrection.

One other feature made it new. The Spirit's indwelling came because of Jesus' rule *in abstentia,* which means that the Messiah is ruling now not on earth from a national throne, but from God's side in heaven. A future, earthly rule was not excluded by this new dimension, as Acts 3:19–21 shows. Peter's remark about "the times of restoration" of all the Old Testament prophets promised shows that the development of Old Testament promise in Jesus' ministry did not cancel out what had been promised earlier. The program of promise as presented, explained, and expanded by Jesus and the apostles complements earlier Old Testament revelation and anticipates the decisive rule of Christ on earth, what Revelation 20 defines as the Millennium. This future period will bring in the final phases of the promise's realization that Luke alluded to in Acts 3:21, a realization that eventually will culminate in the new heavens and new earth.

So the church age represents a sneak preview of Christ's coming earthly rule. The transforming presence of God's Spirit in His people shows that He is active in fulfilling His promise to vanquish the enemies of the people of God, as He enables them to serve Him in holiness, gives them life, and spares them from the judgment to come (Luke 1:74–75, 78–79; 3:7–18; 11:14–23; Acts 2:30–39). The Spirit-indwelt community pictures to some degree, but not fully, what the greater kingdom and rule of Christ will be like when He returns to earth to bring all righteousness. However, only in this coming return will Jesus' foes and the enemies of the people of God be totally vanquished, as the restoration of all things comes and Israel's promises are fully realized (3:21).

So Luke saw two phases of rule, of which the church is the first. The two periods, though distinct, are related. The church, though it lives in an era of fulfillment, also awaits the consummation of God's promises. For Luke, the uniqueness of the church is not so much that she is Spirit-indwelt, for that was anticipated by the new covenant. Rather, she is Spirit-indwelt in a way that includes Gentiles (cf. Eph. 3:4–6; Col. 1:24–29). In this new institution, the church, the Mediator Jesus Christ rules from heaven through the work of His Spirit to bring righteousness to people on earth. Though He is not directly manifest on earth, He dispenses blessing to His children. The next phase of God's rule will differ because the Mediator will be present on earth and His rule will be comprehensive, including the redemption of all earth's social institutions and national entities.

It is interesting to note that in Acts the term for church (*ekklēsia*), when it refers to this new community, appears only in narrative notes and summaries by Luke (Acts 8:1, 3; 9:31; 11:22, 26; 12:1, 5; 13:1; 14:23, 27; 15:3–4, 22, 41; 16:5; 18:22; 19:32, 39, 41; 20:17). The one exception comes in Paul's remark to the Ephesian elders (Acts 20:28). The new community's identity emerged slowly as her distinctness became clearer through the movement of events. Even the name "Christians" came after the church had spread to Antioch (11:26), and another frequent term used to refer to her was as a "sect" (*airesis*) of the Nazareans or of the "way" (24:5, esp. v. 14; 28:22, where Jews in Rome had been warned about this new "sect"). The term sect was also used to refer to groupings within Israel (5:17; 15:5; 26:5), so it was not necessarily negative. It simply noted a distinct group was emerging. Even outsiders had trouble noting that the distinction was becoming a chasm (23:27–29). Acts notes the growing division with sensitivity and tries to explain what factors created it.

The apostles. The importance of the present church age was underscored by various authenticating signs, as discussed earlier in the section on soteriology. Here may be noted the twofold role of the apostles as overseers and witnesses to the formation of this new entity. The function of overseeing is evident in the passages that refer to the presence of the apostles at new phases of expansion in the church. Acts 8:14–25 records Peter and John's approval of the work of Philip in Samaria. Paul contacted the apostles after His call (9:26–27). Peter carried the gospel to Gentiles (10:23–48). The apostles sent Barnabas to Antioch (11:22). The Jerusalem Council was mainly an apostolic gathering, though others (including James, Paul, and Barnabas) were involved (15:1–35). Paul reported to James and the elders of Jerusalem about his Gentile mission (21:17–19). From the beginning, the church had structure, authority, and accountability. In Acts this authority was mostly in the hands of the apostles.

One other passage, Luke 22:29–30, shows a distinct feature about the apostles' role. Here Jesus offered the Eleven kingdom authority, with the opportunity to sit at His banquet table and additionally to "sit on thrones judging the twelve tribes of Israel." This passage looks ultimately to the future coming consummation, when Messiah will reign on the earth. The seat at the banquet anticipates a kingdom celebration after Jesus' victorious return. Though the apostles had authority in the early church, they will also have authority in the kingdom to come.[44] Their authority then will expand and extend over all Israel. This expanded exercise of authority is yet future because such a banquet or such "apostolic rule" over Israel's twelve tribes is not seen in Acts. No allusion to a current apostolic rulw over Israel appears there. The apostles had oversight over the church, but one day, interestingly, they will help rule Israel.

The apostles were qualified to exercise leadership over the church because they were appointed to be witnesses (*martyres*) to Jesus. Luke 24:48 anticipated this development, and Acts 1:8 formalized this call to be witnesses. The qualifications for this special function included being personal acquaintances with Jesus and His ministry, and being a witness to His resurrection (Acts 1:21–22). References to the witnesses abound as they testified to various events in Jesus' life, including His resurrection (2:32; 3:15; 13:31); His death, resurrection, ascension (5:32); and His ministry, crucifixion, and resurrection (10:39). Not all witnesses were apostles, though most were. Though Paul was a witness (22:15; 26:16), his "apostolic" role is a much-discussed issue in Acts.[45] Stephen also received the title of "witness,"

---

44. Though one could biblically speak of the Millennium here, Luke did not use this term, so it is best, since the topic is the theology of Luke–Acts, not to use this technical term here.

45. This issue will be discussed later, when the major personalities in Acts are considered.

and he clearly was not an apostle (22:20). Despite these minor exceptions, the church expanded under the leadership of the apostles, who had oversight over the church. As reliable witnesses of what they had seen firsthand, they proclaimed the the message about Jesus. They took the message to a broader audience and formed a new community by God's direct intervention.

Israel and the church. In the early chapters of Acts the Jews' reception of the gospel message was strong and troubled the Jewish leaders. But later, Jewish reaction and persecution set in so that the church was scattered. In some locales the message was taken out of the synagogue and offered directly to Gentiles, who responded favorably (13:46: 18:6; 28:28). This pattern of mixed Jewish reception, persecution, and turning to the Gentiles was especially common in Paul's ministry. The apostles began in the synagogues because they believed the message of Christ was for those in Israel. Local churches developed by necessity, the necessity of survival in the face of rejection. These realities caused Luke to speak repeatedly in Acts of the church's messengers "turning to the Gentiles" and "warning Israel." These themes often appear side by side, and they dominate the last third of the book of Acts. They show how the church was not Israel and how that distinction became a reality historically.

From the start God's plan was to include Gentiles. Luke 2:32 and 3:6 appeal to Isaiah to make the point that God sent Jesus to bless Gentiles too. First, the appeal to Isaiah 42:6 meant that Jesus would be a light to the Gentiles. This servant-light image pictures the inclusion of Gentiles in the blessing of the light (cf. Luke 1:78–79). The quotation of Isaiah 40:5 in Luke 3:6 showed that God's salvation would be available to all. John the Baptist's ministry would prepare the way for God's coming in Jesus so that all people might have the opportunity to come to God.

Illustrations of this universally available salvation abound. The centurion was commended for having a faith greater than anything seen in Israel (Luke 7:9). Gentiles are pictured as parading to the banquet table (14:16–24). In a particularly significant parable overviewing God's plan, the vineyard of promise and blessing is described as taken from Israel and given to others (20:9–18). Others recieve what Israel once had. The fact that the current period is called "the times of the Gentiles" (*kairoi ethnōn*, 21:24) also points to God's present focus on the Gentiles.

Two facts show that Israel has a future as well. Jesus' eschatological discourse in Luke 21:5–36 with its "day of the Lord" imagery, points to Israel's future vindication, since that was what the "day" was all about. Also Peter's speech recorded in Acts 3:12–26, which refers to the future fulfillment and completion of all the Old Testament promises (v. 21), indicates that she is only temporarily set aside. But the current focus on Gentiles also helps show that a distinction exists between Israel and the church.

The apostles were slow, however, in turning to the Gentiles, though Jesus had commanded the disciples to preach forgiveness of sins to all the nations starting from Jerusalem (Luke 24:47). What the disciples seem to have understood by this was a call to preach the message in every nation to Jews of the diaspora. However, that is not what God meant. So He seized the initiative in Acts 10. Through a vision to Peter, He showed that Gentiles were intended.

This vision is important because it is Luke's (and God's) answer to the Jewish charge that what the church offers is not really God's promise, because that promise is for Israel. God's offer of salvation and a share of His promise to Gentiles needed explaining, because some Jewish Christians were nervous about opening the gospel to Gentiles without making them respond to the law and many Jews had rejected the Christian claims outright. Acts 15 shows the concern of Jewish Christians, while the persecution of the church in Acts comes almost entirely from Jewish sources. On the other hand, Gentiles might have been disturbed too. Having entered into God's blessings, they saw the violent response of Jews to something that was originally for Jews. Some Gentile believers might have concluded they were in the wrong place at the wrong time, or at least, in the wrong way. Or they may have thought Jesus was not for them, or that they needed to heed the law. Luke's answer to this problem was short and simple. God made disciples go to the Gentiles.

As a result, Gentiles, starting in Acts 10, became more and more the center of evangelistic success. Three times Luke highlighted Paul's turning to Gentiles (13:46–49; 14:27; 28:25–29). Sometimes Jewish unbelief preceded this turn in Paul's ministry, but the call to the Gentiles was a part of the church's mission regardless of Jewish response. Nonetheless, the juxtaposition of Jewish rejection and Gentile reception recalls an element in Pauline theology, the turning to Gentiles as a means to making Israel react (Rom. 11:11–14).

Warnings to Israel also were frequently given. John the Baptist spoke of the axe at the root of the tree, warning that having the right racial ancestry was not enough (Luke 3:7–9). In bitter pronouncements of woe against the Jewish leaders Jesus told them they were not on the path to life and were preventing others from getting there (11:37–52). In the parable of the barren fig tree Jesus threatened to cut down the tree of Israel which had not borne fruit (13:6–9). The judgment was delayed, but its potential reality still was present.

That threat was carried out later. The first hint was Jesus' declaration that Israel's house was desolate (13:35). This language recalled the judgment of the Exile stated in Jeremiah 22:5 (cf. Jer. 12:7). Rejecting God's way and living under sin, the prospect of covenant curse—God's judgment—could only follow. However, this does not mean that Israel is permanently rejected, just as the Exile was not permanent. But those in the period of judgment would have no hope unless they responded to the Lord. The nation's history of rejection of the Lord was evidenced by the fact that she had slain prophets and God's messengers even before Jesus came to them (Luke 13:31–33). This critique of the nation is common in Luke and recalls the message of the Old Testament prophets against the nation. This historical critique of the nation means that Luke shared the "Deuteronomistic perspective" of Israel's history, because the appeal for judgment was based on the covenant curse that would come on the nation for unfaithfulness, as promised in Deuteronomy 28–32.

Jesus did not relish such judgment. He wept over Jerusalem because she had not recognized that in Jesus, God was coming to her in a "visitation" (cf. Luke 19:41–44). Similarly, as Jesus journeyed to the cross, He warned the daughters of Jerusalem to weep and mourn because judgment was coming on the nation (23:27–31). This passage, unique to Luke, alludes to several Old Testament passages in painting the horror of judgment in terms that recall the day of the Lord (Jer. 19:9, 41, 43; Isa. 54:1; Hos. 10:8). The allusions refer to the approaching fall of Jerusalem that came in A.D. 70. The vineyard, given to others, fits this theme as well (Luke 20:9–18).

Luke made the same point in Acts. In Acts 3:23 Peter spoke of the curse of being "cut off," by citing Leviticus 23:29. Failure to heed the apostles and prophets results in judgment. Stephen's dying words related how the nation had always resisted God and, as a result, brought judgment on herself (Acts 7:51–53). Stephen's remarks recall Jesus' stinging rebuke in Luke 13:31–33.

Too much, however, should not be made of this emphasis that the nation is "cut off." All through the book of Acts, the apostles always went to the Jews first and then to the Gentiles (Rom. 1:16). The offer to enter into participation in the promise was always made to the nation Israel, despite her rejection of Christ. Nowhere was that offer withdrawn in the book of Acts. Opportunity to receive the message still existed. However, the pattern of response was clear. Usually the offer was rejected, though others responded (2:41, 47; 4:4; 5:14; 6:7). Those who responded picture a faithful remnant in the nation who clung to the nation's hope. In fact, it could be argued that this Jewish remnant was a point of connection between the promise of the old era and the realization of the new, since this group most clearly had moved from one period into the other. They represented those Jews who clearly saw what God was doing and so responded to the gospel message.

So the new community saw herself as called to obey God by continuing to preach the message of Jesus to the people of the nation, even in the face of the leadership's opposition. In fact, much of Acts 3–5 is concerned to show that God gave His endorsement to those being persecuted for preaching Jesus. Peter noted that the new community will obey God, not man (4:19). Rabbi Gamaliel noted that if this movement is of God, the Sanhedrin will not be able to stop it, while if it was not, the movement would die out on its own (5:38–39). The new community's growth and survival in the narrative is Luke's answer to these alternatives. Even while in prison, God directs the apostles through the angel to take the message to the people of Israel in the temple (5:19–20). The church considered it an honor to be able to share the message and asked for boldness to do the job (4:23–30; 5:41).

However, since most Jews did not respond, the messengers of the gospel turned to others. As recorded in Acts 13:41–45, Paul turned and offered a warning to Jews. Jewish jealousy and persecution would not stop the message, but it did mean danger for those who rejected it. Paul and Barnabas shook the dust from their feet (v. 51), a sign of judgment (cf. Luke 10:11–15). Later Paul left the synagogue in Corinth to continue his evangelistic work (Acts 18:5–11). Finally, Paul turned again to the Gentiles (28:25–28), explaining to the nation his move by using the language of Isaiah 6:9–10 to describe the dull hearts of many (or even of most) in the nation. Though not a rejection of the nation nor of Jewish mission, Paul's remark did warn of severe obduracy and thus of possible judgment that the nation faced during the period of the prophets.

Luke was saying to his readers that the gospel might not be going to Israel as much as it seemed it might, but that was not the church's fault or intention. Such a failure had not halted God's plan, nor did such failure represent a departure from God's plan. The Gentiles are also included. They are responding. God is building a new institution, the church, which now proclaims the promise and in which both believing Jews and Gentiles are blessed (Eph. 2:11–22). The new community had attempted to offer the promise to Israel. That new community had taught and preached in her synagogues, but the church mostly met persecution and expulsion.

God presented His message to Israel but she, especially as represented in her leadership, rejected it. Since Israel's house was "desolate," in its place had come a new house, the church, in which God's Spirit indwells all who come to seek refuge in salvation through Christ. Jew and Gentile alike share in God's benefits. The temple is no longer a place to go see the Shekinah. Rather, the Shekinah has come to indwell believers. God is not through with Israel; He has just set her aside. In her stead has come a new entity whose origin is traced in the momentous events recorded in Acts 2. The Holy Spirit, once promised to Israel, still had come, despite the nation's refusal. That promise resides in the church until Jesus returns to set all things straight again and bring Israel back into the fold (Acts 3:19–21).

PERSONALITIES IN THE EARLY CHURCH

Peter. Undoubtedly, the key disciple in Luke's writings is Peter. He was the representative disciple, as well as the leading apostle. A key incident early in Jesus' ministry occurred in Peter's boat (Luke 5:1–11). The miraculous catch of fish caused him to confess his sin and to ask Jesus to depart, since he considered Jesus too holy to be in their presence. But Jesus communicated reception, mentioning that the fish caught in the net were nothing compared to the people Peter and others like him would catch for God. They would become fishers of men. The recognition of sin's presence enables one to serve. Peter represents confessing disciples who enter humbly into service for God and are accepted by Him.

Another indication of Peter's leading position was his confession of Jesus as the Christ (9:18–20). In another incident Peter spoke for the disciples by raising a question about the meaning of a parable (12:41). Peter recognized the difficulty of what Jesus had asked a rich man to do, in telling him to sell all and follow Him (18:22), so Peter probingly affirmed that the disciples had done that very thing (v. 28). Responding positively, Jesus spoke of the rewards such a response brings both now and in the age to come (v. 30). Jesus' remark showed that the "all" language of His call to the rich man did not mean that the absolute standard was impossible. As Jesus said, "What is impossible for man is possible with God" (v. 27). The disciples, despite their many moments of failure and lack of faith, had a fundamental association with Jesus that God recognized.

Another incident showing that failure does not mean disqualification is Peter's denial of Jesus (22:31–34, 54–62). Here is an example of a disciple in severe failure, who regretted his fall and was enabled by God to continue to serve. Peter had come to learn that assuming one will always remain faithful can lead to spiritual failure. One must recognize the strength of sin and the necessity of dependence.

Peter was a representative disciple. He learned about his sin. He confessed Christ. He had made fundamental commitments to Jesus, in the midst of a world with other values. He sometimes failed. But in it all he recognized that Jesus is the answer. There was nowhere else to turn. He learned to rely on the One he confessed as the Messiah. In this focus Peter is exemplary.

Peter also was the leading apostle. He preached to the unsaved, exercised apostolic oversight among believers, and witnessed to Jesus. He was the leader in early church events, including the choosing of a replacement for Judas (Acts 1:15–22), explaining Pentecost (2:14–40), speaking of a healing (3:12–4:12), or exercising judgment against members of the community (5:1–11). He challenged the religious authorities, who tried to prevent Peter and others from speaking about Jesus (5:29–32). He took the gospel to the Gentiles and defended this expansion before Jewish believers (10:1–11:18). Peter modeled carrying out God's will boldly and bearing His message powerfully.

Stephen. Stephen is a key transition figure whose ministry is told briefly (Acts 6:8–7:60). He is the first Hellenistic Christian whose words are recorded in Acts. He had less patience for the veneration of the temple than perhaps did his Jewish Christian colleagues, but his understanding of Old Testament history paralleled that of Jesus (Luke 11:47–52; Acts 6:9–12). Stephen knew that God could not be confined to a single location, something the Old Testament prophets also knew (Isa. 66:1). In Acts 7 Stephen outlined Israel's history of rejection of the Lord, an act ironically repeated by the nation when the people stoned Stephen. In Acts 6 Stephen was a part of a group that raised questions about the church's treatment of widows. He then became part of the solution to the problem as he served the widows in the church. His bold preaching and selfless service are models to the church of an active member filled with God's Spirit (6:3, 5; 7:55), wisdom (6:3), faith (v. 5), and grace and power (v. 8). His martyrdom showed the length to which a disciple should be prepared to go in proclaiming Jesus. Jesus' standing to greet him at his death (7:55–56) shows heaven's welcome of such a saint, where Jesus received him as the reigning Son of Man.

Philip. Another Hellenist who was prepared to share Christ is Philip. An active witness for Christ in Samaria (8:5–13), he explained Christ from the Old Testament to the Ethiopian eunuch (vv. 26–40). The cameo descriptions of figures like Stephen and Philip indicate what God can do with people among the multitudes in the new community. Such people grew into maturity and benefited the church through active service, including evangelism.

Barnabas. Barnabas was the exemplary encourager, witness, and servant. Nothing he did was for himself. He freely gave of his resources to the church (4:36–37), thus providing an example of how one with material means can serve the church. He confirmed Paul to the disciples, when some had doubted Paul's sincerity (9:26–27). He was an encourager and teacher at Antioch (11:22–30). He engaged in a missionary journey with Paul (13:1–15:12). Even when Paul had doubts about John Mark, Barnabas continued to offer encouragement that eventually bore fruit (15:36–40; 2 Tim. 4:11). In a church under pressure, where it would have been easy for some to complain or blame, Barnabas, by example and word, continually encouraged others to serve.

James. By Acts 15 James, the half-brother of the Lord, had become the leader of the Jerusalem church and the representative of Jewish Christian interests. He played a crucial role at the Jerusalem council (15:13–21). His citation of the teaching of Amos, as one example among the prophets about Gentile inclusion in God's blessing, seals the decision that Gentiles need not be circumcised. The citation of Amos 9:11–12 was a clear stroke of genius. Besides mentioning the rebuilding of the Davidic house and Gentiles seeking the Lord in a context of fulfillment, James cited the text in its Greek form, showing his desire to reach an agreement with those concerned about the Gentiles. James had a spirit that desired a thought-through, theologically sound unity. Lest anyone at the council object about the use of Amos with this emphasis, he introduced the citation by noting that many prophets had taught the same thing. When he said, "the words of the prophets are in agreement with this" (Acts 15:15), he was affirming not only what Amos taught, but also what the prophets as a whole taught. Amos is but one rendering that could be used to teach the theme.[46] Thus James, representing the theologically conservative Jewish camp, supplied the final touch that resulted in a resolution to the problem.

When Paul returned to Jerusalem, James advised him to carry out purification rites (Acts 21:17–24). Taking the advice, Paul reflected sensitivity to Jewish Christian concerns. In this way Paul followed principles he taught in his own writings (1 Cor. 9:19–23). James was the representative of traditional Christian interests, but he was not a hard-nosed, stubborn leader. He examined what God was doing and studied the Scriptures to determine the best way to proceed. His commitment was not to rules or to blind tradition, but to God's message and will. He wished it to be carried out in the church with sensitivity to others. He worked for unity. Here is another example of leadership, in which cooperation was exercised in the midst of recognizing nonessential differences of emphasis.

Paul. The major personality in the second half of the book of Acts is Paul. Converted while an arch rival of the church, Paul represents the truth that God can transform even the most hostile heart. As a young Jewish leader, he took delight in

---

46. The use of the plural "prophets" in the introductory formula is one reason the long debate over the difference in wording between Amos in the Hebrew and the Septuagint is really not important to James's argument. By citing the Septuagint, James was citing one well-circulated example of his point. If pressed, he could have noted many other Old Testament passages. For more on this passage and how it is fulfilled, see Darrell L. Bock, "Evidence from Acts," in *A Case for Premillennialism.*

Stephen's martyrdom and sought to put Christians in jail (Acts 7:58–8:3). Paul thought he was protecting God's honor from being defamed. But, ironically, God, taking the initiative yet again in Acts, transformed this archenemy of the gospel into one of its chief proponents. God was honored by Saul in a way Saul had never imagined. The account of Paul's conversion is so crucial to Luke that the story appears three times (9:1–19; 22:6–16; 26:12–18). Paul's conversion illustrates the dramatic reversal God's grace can achieve. He also represents the church's mission to Gentiles (9:15–16). Saul later became known as Paul and went from persecutor to persecuted. Carrying out his commission is the burden of Acts 11–20, while the theological basis that vindicates his mission appears in Acts 15.

In fact, the account of Paul's ministry has two parts: his journeys (Acts 11–20) and his trials (Acts 21–28). His journeys describe what he did, while his trials explain why he did it. Through Paul's arrest and persecution, the gospel went to Rome. The movement showed that even events that on the surface seem to be hindrances to the gospel helped accomplish its advance. Paul got to Rome, despite great risk. His long journey depicts the gospel getting to the ends of the earth through God's sovereign protection (Acts 27).

In his mission Paul preached Christ, planted churches, and performed miracles. This combination shows that he was engaged in all the ground-breaking activities of the apostles. In fact, Paul may well be the key to the otherwise enigmatic Acts 19:1–7 episode, in which the Spirit came on those who knew only about John the Baptist. Paul was used by God in bestowing the Holy Spirit on them (v. 6), much as Peter was used in Acts 10. Scholars have discussed whether Luke considered Paul to be an apostle. In Acts 14:14 Paul shared this title with Barnabas, but this is not necessarily conclusive, since all that may be meant here is a broader use of the term, which suggests Paul was an authoritative representative of the church who planted churches. Barnabas's inclusion in the remark suggests that this is the sense in Acts 14. Luke answered the question of Paul's position and role not by giving him titles, but by showing how Paul's ministry was like that of the other apostles. Paul's miracles and events like the one in Acts 19:1–7 make this point.

So Paul preached the promise of the resurrection (23:6; 24:15; 26:6–8, 22). From the early days of his conversion, he shared Jesus (9:27–29). In his trial Paul declared his innocence and affirmed that he suffered innocently with a good conscience (23:1; 24:12–21; 25:8). He was guilty of no offense and none of the charges against him could be proved. As with Jesus, others too declared Paul's innocence, including scribes (23:9), Claudius Lysias (23:29), Festus (25:25), and Agrippa (26:32). Paul was an innocent sufferer. Justice may not always be carried out on earth, but the Lord noted Paul's faithfulness. Acts ends triumphantly, even though Paul was in prison, because the message still went out openly. Paul's own words in Philippians 1:12–19 describe the mood in which the book of Acts concludes. Even in chains, Paul could rejoice because the gospel was being preached. A witness and a sufferer for Christ, Paul is an example to all believers, especially those who face negative reaction to the gospel.

Paul's speeches differed, depending on his audience. His message, as summarized in Acts 13:16–41, is a typical synagogue speech, in which the emphasis is on God's promise to the nation about a future Son of David and the opportunity for Jews to share in its fulfillment. Acts 17:22–31 records a representative speech to pagans for whom the gospel was a completely new idea. In Athens, Paul began by speaking of the sovereign God, who is Creator and Judge of all men. He was interrupted, so no one can know exactly how his message would have ended, though one can be sure he was headed toward mentioning Jesus Christ, whom God has "appointed" as the coming Judge (17:30–32). Later Paul addressed the elders of the Ephesian church. The contents of this speech (20:18–35) look most like portions of his letters. Here he exhorted the leaders to be faithful in their oversight of the church, just as he had been with them. They were to guard the truth, watch for error, and offer gentle care to the flock. The church is precious, having been purchased with Christ's own blood. They were to lead it accordingly, knowing that God's grace would strengthen them for their tasks. They were to help the weak, for as Jesus taught, it is more blessed to give than to receive. Paul's three messages recorded in Acts 13, 17, and 20 picture him in three distinct roles: preacher-evangelist, apologist-evangelist, and church leader.

Paul's defense speeches differed from his earlier discourses. He gave defenses to the Jews (22:1–21), to the Sanhedrin (23:1–10), Felix (24:10–21), Festus (25:8–11), and Agrippa (26:1–32). In those speeches Paul spoke of his faithfulness to God and to his racial heritage. He upheld the Law and the Prophets. He believed, as the Old Testament teaches, in promise and resurrection. He did not ask for the role he had, for God called him in a vision. He was compelled to preach Christ as the fulfillment of promise and to carry out a mission to Gentiles. If Paul was "guilty" of anything, it was that he was an obedient vessel for God, faithfully proclaiming God's promise.

Paul's career is a capsule portrait of grace. The opponent of God's people became their servant. He was a Jew burdened for saving Gentiles. He was victorious in persecution. Though he was imprisoned, the Word of God was free. Paul pictures the triumph of God's sovereign direction.

Paul also pictures, with Barnabas, the messenger of God who is a light to the world through the message preached to it (Acts 13:47). Interestingly, in this passage the task of Isaiah's servant, normally associated with Jesus (Acts 8:32–35), extends to those who represent Him and preach the message about Him.

Summary. Events in the early church and the difficult lives of the church's major early characters do not seem on the surface to favor the spread of the gospel. But every apparent setback was a catalyst to the church's growth. Suffering is not to be shunned and neither is rejection. It is part of how the gospel spreads. The early church understood this lesson for in her praying, the community asked not to be spared of suffering, but to have boldness in speaking the Word of God (4:24–31). The lessons in the lives of the believers and leaders of the book of Acts can be summarized in the call to be strong, faithful, generous, and unified as the church seeks to fulfill her mission of proclaiming Jesus in the strength of God's Spirit.

THE NEW COMMUNITY

Her activities. The early church was an active community. Many of her activities have already been discussed. Her missionary activity and the proclamation of Jesus as the Christ are the outstanding features of the book of Acts. This preaching moved from Jerusalem (Acts 2–5), into Samaria (Acts 8), then to Gentiles (Acts 10–11), into various missionary journeys (Acts 13–20), and finally by trial to Rome (Acts 21–28). Along with the message came authentication by miracles. Numerous summary statements underline the church's proclamation role as she was characterized as a "bearer of the Word" (2:47b; 5:14; 6:7; 9:31; 11:21; 12:24; 13:49; 16:5; 19:20). In various ways these verses speak of the Word growing as a result of the church's activities.

Besides proclamation, the church also enjoyed communal life. The believers became a caring community, who worshiped, studied, and prayed together. Acts 2:42–47 summarizes the variety of activities in which the church engaged. The believers shared possessions, met needs, broke bread in their homes, praised God, shared in apostolic teaching, had fellowship, and prayed together. Acts 4:23–31 records the early church's exemplary prayer for boldness in speaking the Word. Acts 4:32–37 indicates how they shared possessions with each other to meet their needs. Acts 6:1–6 portrays how they creatively accepted appropriate criticism about the treatment of widows and then let those who raised the problem assist in solving it. Even physical needs were the object of the church's attention. One local community sent material aid and food to another community in need (11:29). The church prayed, supported, and commissioned a missionary endeavor (13:1–3). The church was active in outreach and in supporting the growth of its members.

The church also engaged in instruction, which led to theological reflection. Two scenes indicate the apostles had to give thought to what God was doing through them. In Acts 11:1–18 Peter submitted an oral report about what God did for the Gentiles. Later in Acts 15 further questions about this same issue needed further reflection. Here the church came together and hammered out a solution to a difficult theological problem. The discussion centered around a reflective evaluation of experience measured by a look at the Scriptures. The decision also reflected sensitivity to all concerned.

The church disciplined her members. This is seen in a grim way in the experience of Ananias and Sapphira, who lied and were struck dead (5:1–11). Peter, functioning like a prophet, described their deceit as against the Spirit of God, a reference to the fact that the community is indwelt by God and thus is special in the sight of God (vv. 3, 9). The penalty's immediacy probably has more to do with the young age of the church than anything else. But here God went to great lengths to show how important honesty and purity are to Him. Accountability for sin is graphically portrayed here. Also revealed is that God does see everything that happens in his church. Sin and deceit are an offense to Him.

The church sought to minister to her members and reach out to the world. Ministry involved meeting both physical and spiritual needs. The whole person was cared for in the individual churches and across communities. In addition, the gospel was preached whether locally or by missionaries to faraway lands. The believers in the churches of Acts did not limit their vision to their own neighborhoods. Their call was to preach the gospel to the ends of the earth, and each community sought to do so. Alongside various activities was preaching, worship, and a desire to represent the Lord boldly. This required a clear message, an active communal life, theological reflection, and support for righteous living. The many dimensions of church activity created an effective community that accomplished much despite initially small numbers.

Functions in the new community. Luke mentioned five church functions, which are either offices or other organized roles. Some were permanent, others were temporary. The first, that of apostle, is most frequently discussed by Luke. The Twelve who were chosen for this role were named in Luke 6:12–16. They were not all successful, since Judas Iscariot was in their midst. He pictures someone who participates in the community, but is not a genuine member. Such people sometimes even reach prominence in the church. When the church replaced Judas, Peter described the qualifications of an apostle (Acts 1:12–26).[47] This office was not to continue into succeeding generations, since a requirement was that one had to have been with Jesus and to have seen Him after His resurrection (vv. 21–22). These authoritative representatives laid the foundation of the church and exercised oversight over the various communities, as already noted. But with the passing of the Twelve, this office passed away in its most technical sense. Paul and Barnabas were also called apostles in Acts 14:14, but this use is not the most narrow use of the term, since Barnabas is included (cf. 1 Cor. 9:1–6). Here it refers to authoritative representatives who planted churches in new areas.

The second function, the role of witness, has been discussed earlier. This is a major Lucan category and often is used along with the title of apostle in describing one of the functions of an apostle. But others also were witnesses. Stephen and Paul are singled out (22:15, 20; 26:16). The disciples were commissioned witnesses (Luke 24:48), and the Lord's commission was repeated in Acts 1:8. The witnesses attested to Jesus' miracles (2:22), His resurrection (v. 32), His crucifixion and resurrection (3:15; 5:30–32), and His postresurrection appearances (13:31).

Third, Luke briefly mentioned prophets. Agabus predicted famine in Judea and warned Paul about traveling to Jerusalem (Acts 11:27–30; 21:7–14). Philip's four unmarried daughters were prophetesses to the church (21:9). Though not members of the church, Simeon and Anna were also prophets who spoke to all who passed by about the new baby Jesus (Luke 2:25–38). They represented pious Jews who awaited the time of promise and who responded to Jesus. Finally, the praise

47. There is no indication that the appointment of Matthias was an error by the church. Acts 1 has no hint of criticism about it. The discussion before the vote is bathed in Scripture, prayer, and dependence on the Lord. Luke also noted that he was added to the Eleven. Luke solved the issue of Paul's authority in another way. Luke did not argue about Paul's title. The historian simply showed that whatever the apostles did, Paul did as well. Anyone who wished to criticize Paul or doubt his ministry would have to recognize that his activity was no different in scope from that of Peter. So this was a powerful argument against rejecting Paul.

associated with the tongues-speaking of Acts 2 was called prophecy by Peter (vv. 11, 17–18). So sometimes the activity was present without the office being present.

Fourth, the seven men of Acts 6:1–6 were perhaps not precursors of deacons, since Luke did not mention that connection anywhere. These men represent those who ministered to believer's physical and other needs so that the leaders of the Jerusalem church could concentrate on ministering the Word.

Fifth, Luke mentioned the leaders of a local community in Ephesus (20:17–35). These elders were charged with oversight in a local area with responsibility to serve believers.[48] There were several such leaders rather than one.[49] They were to instruct and lead the local congregations. They gave the church a structure for accountability, as well as instruction and direction.

As the church grew, new functions emerged and organizational structure developed for the sake of efficient, effective service. Such development is seen in Acts 6:1–6. Leaders of spiritual quality developed. However, Luke spent little time discussing the structure of the church. Instead he stressed her activities and effectiveness.

Descriptions of community members. Luke had a few titles by which he referred to those who follow Jesus. By far the most common title is disciple (*mathētēs*), which simply means "learner." It reflects the fact that one who responds to the gospel is walking with God and is learning from Him. "Disciple" is used thirty-seven times in Luke and twenty-eight times in Acts. Some disciples were not real believers, since Judas was a disciple. There are false disciples and poor disciples. But the term itself describes a person who is dependent on and instructed by Jesus, or who at least appears to be in such a position.

Another common title used by Luke is believers (*hoi pisteuontes*). This term, occurring more in Acts than in Luke's gospel, became equivalent to "disciple." Eventually "believers" replaced "disciple" in other New Testament writings because the former focused on the fundamental characteristic of trust. The words "believe" and "believers" occur in Acts 2:44; 4:32; 10:43; 11:21; 13:39; 18:27; 19:18; 21:20, 25; 22:19.

The title "Christian" was used in a derogatory way by the enemies of the gospel. It described those who so identified with Jesus Christ that they were given His name. At least this seems to be the implication of the passive verb in Acts 11:26. The disciples were first called Christians in Antioch, and Agrippa also used the term (26:28). Believers were so clearly related to Jesus that outsiders knew the connection.

A final title for the movement was "the Way." This title expresses the notion that in this movement points the way to God (Acts 9:2; 18:25–26; 19:9; 22:4;

---

48. Probably these elders were over believers in a given area rather than over "one congregation" in Ephesus. Ancient house churches could hold only about fifty or so people, so it is quite possible that there were numerous meeting areas around a city the size of Ephesus.

49. The church's structure in the book of Acts assumes a level of mutual accountability within given communities. The sharing of teaching and direction among several leaders shows this trait.

24:14, 22). However, the church's faith and commitment, not her titles, were the important issue for Luke. That, along with her ethics, marks the church out as a unique institution among men. Both her deliverer and her messengers are light to a needy world (Luke 1:78–79; Acts 13:47).

THE ETHICS OF THE COMMUNITY

Total commitment. The ethics of the church community found expression in her discipleship. At salvation, a believer becomes a disciple, but discipleship is a walk that lasts the rest of one's life. Since each Christian must still deal with the presence of sin, his or her walk has successes and failures. For Jesus, the life of a disciple required total commitment (Luke 9:23; 14:25–33). This was something the disciples struggled to learn, but Jesus made it clear the requirement was absolute. Nonetheless, Jesus dealt graciously with His followers' lapses. On numerous occasions the disciples failed to understand what Jesus was doing and He rebuked them, but He called them to learn and respond more appropriately the next time (8:24–25; 9:46–50, 51–55). The disciples were also willing to learn. They were committed to Christ, for which He commended them (18:28–30).

Love for God and for one's neighbor. Jesus' basic commandment to His followers was for them to love God and others. This ethic was always a part of God's plan and revelation, since it is called the essence of the law (Luke 10:25–28). In one significant passage Jesus juxtaposed a discussion of love with the issue of faith, showing how closely these two ideas are tied together (Luke 7:37–50; cf. 1 Cor. 2:9; 9:21; an idea called the Law of Christ in James 2:5, 8; 1 John 4:18).

Another section of Luke's gospel is particularly clear in setting forth a focus on love for God and for others. In three consecutive passages Luke detailed loving one's neighbor (10:25–37), showing devotion to Christ (10:38–42), and speaking to God (11:1–13). The parable of the Good Samaritan is Jesus' response to an attempt by a scribe to limit his own ethical responsibility by asking, "Who is my neighbor?" Jesus told the parable to make one point: The question is not to determine who one's neighbor is, but rather to be a neighbor to all. Loving others has no limitations, something Jesus elaborated on in Luke 6:27–36, where one is to love even one's enemy. This love, because of its unusual quality, is different from the way the world ("a sinner") loves (vv. 32, 33, 34). As Jesus said, a distinguishing mark of sonship is this unusual kind of love (v. 35).

When Martha was preparing a meal for Jesus, she was disturbed that Mary was not helping. She complained to Jesus, but He rebuked her, noting that Mary had made the better choice (10:38–42). Jesus' point was that it is better to sit and hear His teaching, for that reflects devotion to Him.

Sensing that communicating with God was key to their spiritual walk, Jesus' disciples asked Him how to pray (11:1–13). Jesus' model prayer reflects a respect for and reliance on God for every daily need. It also shows that the only way to be protected from sin is if one asks for the Father's help in avoiding temptation and follows Him. Jesus also urged them to trust God to give them what is best. Together, these three passages (10:25–37; 10:38–42; 11:1–13) emphasize treating others well, being in contact with Christ, and praying often to God the Father.

Prayer. Besides the focus on prayer recounted in Luke 11, other passages show this emphasis. In Luke 18:1–8, Jesus told a parable to stress that His disciples should pray for God's justice and not lose heart. Just as the judge determined to give the persistent widow justice, so God will execute justice when He returns. The passage is often read in a general way, but its focus is on keeping an eye out for God's vindication of the saints at His return (v. 8). But Jesus wondered whether many, in fact, will be waiting for His return (v. 8).

Luke 18:9–14 contrasts two attitudes in prayer, one of which is commended and the other of which is rejected. The Pharisee prayed proudly, almost as if his relationship with God did Him a favor. Jesus condemned such arrogance. By contrast, the tax collector prayed humbly, approaching God on the basis of His grace and knowing that one cannot demand anything of God. God honors such humility in prayer.

Jesus urged His disciples to pray that they would "not fall into temptation" (22:40), a phrase that recalls the petition of the Lord's Prayer. They failed to learn the lesson during Jesus' passion (vv. 41–46), but in Acts 4:23–31, the believers were praying, showing that they were ready through the power of God to stand up for the Word.

Luke also underscored the importance of prayer by showing how significant events were associated with prayer. Jesus' baptism (Luke 3:21) and a miracle of Jesus (5:15–16) were accompanied by prayer. The choice of the Twelve came after Jesus spent an evening in prayer (6:12). The Transfiguration was accompanied with His praying (9:29), as was the return of the seventy-two (10:17–21). Both at Gethsemane and the cross, Jesus expressed humble dependence on God through intercession (22:39–46; 23:34, 46).

The church learned from Jesus' example of prayer. The descent of the Spirit was asked for through prayer, even though it was promised (Acts 1:7–14). Decisions were made in prayer (1:23–26). Miracles were done in conjunction with prayer (3:1). The vision about the mission to the Gentiles came to Peter as he prayed (10:9–11). Peter's deliverance from prison came during prayer (12:5). Paul and Barnabas's mission to the Gentiles was bathed in prayer (13:2–3). Prayer was clearly of supreme importance to Luke.

Perseverance in suffering. Jesus fully expected His disciples to suffer rejection for their association and identification with Him. He constantly called on them to persevere in the face of such rejection. One of the obstacles that could prevent them from bearing fruit was the pressure of the world. On the other hand, fruit could appear as they received the Word with patience (Luke 8:13–15). The exhortation for them to take up their cross daily (9:23) has already been noted. But Luke is the only Gospel writer to emphasize that this is a daily task. The question of whether the Son of Man will find faith on earth when He returns has already been noted (18:8). The call to endure to the end also was made in the Olivet Discourse (21:19). The road of His followers is difficult and so they should be prepared to experience opposition, as should any believer. More than that, they should continue to trust Him through all the adversity.

Watchfulness, patience, and boldness. Jesus told His followers that pressure against them would be intense. This was especially true in the first century, for if a person within a Jewish family decided to follow Jesus, one could be dismissed from the family and excommunicated from the synagogue. Therefore Jesus told believers to be bold and patient.

He exhorted them not to fear those who killed the body, but rather to fear the one who can cast into hell (Luke 12:1–12). In addition, Jesus promised the aid of the Holy Spirit to help believers give the right kinds of responses when they would be brought before government or synagogue leaders. Jesus told them to be prepared to stand before earthly authorities and confess Him. Peter (Acts 3–4), Stephen (Acts 6–7), and Paul (Acts 21–26) did so.

Jesus also told various parables on stewardship to warn those associated with the church to be faithful in carrying out their responsibilities. Luke 12:35–48 records a parable in which Jesus taught that people will be accountable to Him when He returns. Three levels of punishment will be meted: dismemberment (v. 46), "many blows" (v. 47), and "few blows" (v. 48). Others will be rewarded with more responsibility (vv. 43–44). Dismemberment figuratively speaks about the severe punishment given to the person who denies Christ by actions that blatantly disobey what He asks for from those who profess Him. It pictures being cast out with the unfaithful into hell.[50] Many lashes will be given to those who do not obey but have knowledge. Few lashes will be meted to those who do not obey but who are ignorant. The obedient will receive the reward of additional responsibility.

A similar parable is that of the ten minas (19:11–27). Here too Jesus urged His hearers to watch and be faithful. Those who do something with the opportunity they have from the Lord will receive blessing. Those who do not trust God and fail to see Him as gracious, will end up with no blessing (v. 26). When the Lord returns, he will require accountability. One should be bold, patient, and obedient.

Steadfastness in praying for the Lord's return is also stressed in the parable of the persistent widow, already noted (18:1–8). Being able to read the weather, but not the signs that Jesus performed points up the need for all to be watchful spiritually (12:54–56). These words were a rebuke of people's refusal to see Jesus' authority in His works. Finally, Jesus warned the disciples to read the times that point to the approach of the end much as one "reads" the leaves of a fig tree (21:28–36). All these passages stress the importance of living in light of the end. One could place such texts in a discussion of the believer's response to eschatology hope. But for Luke the believer is called to live his life in light of the approach of the end, so placing this subject here in the context of discipleship is also important.

Faith and dependence. Individuals must approach God humbly, recognizing that because of their sin they are "sick" and in need spiritually (Luke 5:31–32).

---

50. Jesus said that these individuals will be cast out among the "hypocrites," where there will be "weeping and gnashing of teeth" (Matt. 24:51), a Matthean figure for rejection and the reaction on being rejected (cf. Matt. 8:12; 13:42, 50; 25:30).

Having come to the Father for help, the believer is not to be anxious but is to rest in the care of His gracious Father (12:22–34). Here Jesus stated that God's children are much more important to the Father than the other parts of creation. In fact, since the Father knows His children have need of things, they need not be anxious. Faith helps remove anxiety.

Another picture of faith is the example of the prodigal who returned to his father, asking nothing but to rest in his mercy (15:17–21). The response of the father as he ran to meet his son is as important as the turning of the son to him. Here the humility of genuine repentance and return were met with total acceptance. One can trust the heavenly Father, who runs to the penitent to meet the one who turns to Him.

A prime example of humility is Jesus' prayer at Gethsemane (22:39–46). Jesus desired that events be different from the death He was to face, but in the end He asked for the Father's will, not His own. He trusted in God's sovereign care. Equally exemplary was Paul's willingness to die (Acts 21:13–14). Those who know they are in God's hands can face any opposition.

Joy and praise. Luke frequently mentioned praise as the appropriate response to God's work. John the Baptist's birth was a cause for praise, as was the birth of Jesus (Luke 1:14; 2:10). Joy was an initial response of some people to the Word (8:13). The seventy-two returned from their mission with joy (10:17). Heaven rejoices when sinners repent (15:7, 10). The disciples were filled with joy when they saw the resurrected Jesus (24:41) and witnessed His ascension (24:52). Philip's ministry in Samaria was a cause for joy (Acts 8:8). Peter's release from prison brought joy to the servant girl Rhoda (12:14). Paul's converts rejoiced (13:52), as did those who heard of Gentiles being converted (15:3). God's works bring joy; believers are to enjoy what God is doing in drawing people to Himself.

Testimony and witness. This theme has already been examined. It is at the center of the church's mission; all believers are called to share in witnessing of Jesus' work. A basic passage here is Luke 24:44–49.

Wealth and possessions. Luke wrote more on the topic of wealth than any other New Testament writer. The first mention of this topic is in Luke 1:50–53, where the hymn of Mary contrasted the powerful and the humble. God said He would bring blessing on the poor and judgment on the rich. This first reference was given in the context of God's covenant with His people (vv. 50, 55). God's promises come to those who fear Him; therefore, the hymn is not saying that God blesses all the poor without regard for their spiritual condition. Only certain poor, the pious poor, can claim these promises. Mary's references to the poor may allude to the 'ănāwîm, the pious poor described in the Psalter and elsewhere (1 Sam. 2:5; Job 5:11; 12:19; Pss. 89:10; 103:11, 13, 17; 107:9).

The poor are mentioned again in Luke 4:18, in which Jesus said he came "to preach good news to the poor." In addition, Jesus' beatitudes focused on the poor and the deprived (6:20–23). These passages suggest that the poor may have an inherently clearer understanding of what it means to depend on God for needs.

Luke also wrote about wealthy and poor people, whose generosity is commendable. The women who supported Jesus' ministry received a brief mention in 8:1–3, a passage unique to Luke's gospel. The wealthy Zacchaeus, standing in contrast to the wealthy young ruler of Luke 18:18–23, was commended when he declared that he had changed the way he handled his tax collecting (19:1–10). A poor widow was said to have given more than anyone else because she gave of her life when giving two copper coins worth little more than a few pennies (21:1–4)! In Acts 4:32–37 Luke applauded the sharing that occurred in the church, singling out wealthy Barnabas for special attention.

Three passages focus on money directly. Luke 16:1–13 records the parable of a shrewd manager, who, faced with dismissal, became generous and forgave some of the debts of those who owed his master money. Jesus lauded this generosity as wise (v. 8). Then Jesus added that a person cannot serve both God and money (v. 13). He called the disciples to be generous with their resources, for generosity makes friends (v. 9). He also noted how the handling of money is an indicator of responsibility and trustworthiness (vv. 10–12).

The failure of money is precisely the point of the parable of the rich fool in Luke 12:13–21. Here a man experienced a rich harvest. There was no greed in him initially, only good fortune. Yet when fortune came, he planned selfishly and foolishly. When God required his soul, the man was rich toward himself but not toward God. In his death he was left with nothing. Such are the dangers of attachment to wealth.

A negative example also is seen in Luke 16:19–31. Here the rich man who showed no concern for the beggar Lazarus ended up in Hades where he suffered torment. In contrast the poor man, Lazarus, was at Abraham's side enjoying fellowship and comfort with his ancestors. Because "a great chasm" separated the two, it is impossible for them to change places. The passage warns the rich to be generous, for God knows what one does with his wealth (16:19–23). In the Old Testament, God had declared His desire that men be generous to the needy. The picture of eschatological reversal between the poor and the rich, like that found in this parable, is seen in Luke 1:53 and 6:20–26.

Yet another negative example regarding wealth is Ananias and Sapphira, who lied about their donation and incurred the swift and total judgment of God, who took their lives (Acts 5:1–11). Wealth can be a potential obstacle to discipleship, as it was for the seed that fell among the thorns (Luke 8:14).

Money, like any other God-given resource, is to be used wisely and generously. Having money is a risk, for it can give a false sense of security and lessen one's dependence on God. Money can create an excessive attachment to the world and greed, both of which Jesus condemned (Luke 9:57–62; 12:13–21). It also is a barometer of whether one wishes to serve self or others. The statements in Luke about money are not unique, for Paul's advice about money is similar (1 Tim. 6:6–10, 17–19). It is far better to trust God than money (Luke 12:22–34).

Hindrances to discipleship. Besides money and attachment to the world, Luke commented on other hurdles to discipleship. The cost of discipleship is often not counted sufficiently, so failure results (Luke 9:23–26, 57–62; 14:25–35). God is to be first. Because suffering is a potential reality (12:1–10; 21:12–17), it takes patience and endurance for believers to stand for the Lord (8:15). Much of Luke 9:51–19:44 is dedicated to explaining what the disciples' walk with Him is to be like. In fact, the section exists to explain how the disciples should live in light of the reality of Jesus' coming departure (setting up the section, 9:22, 44–45; then 9:51, 58; 13:33; 17:11, 25; 18:31–34; 19:41–42). The disciples' piety is to stand in contrast to the false piety displayed by the Pharisees and scribes. The walk that pleases God loves selflessly and serves constantly, suffering rejection and loving those who reject. The believer's distinctive walk with the Lord and love are to stand out in contrast to the often self-directed love of the world (6:27–36).

Commitment to the lost. Another key to discipleship is the believer's role in helping the church accomplish her mission. Luke 24:46–47 and Acts 1:8 record Jesus' commission to the church, while Luke 3:6 promised that in Jesus, the world would see God's salvation. God's commitment to the lost is noted in His consistent concern for outcasts and sinners, even when others object (5:27–32; 7:28–35; 15:1–32). When the church was slow to take up her task to reach all nations, God took the initiative, by giving a vision to guide her (Acts 10:9–22). He also used persecution to spread the church out to locales beyond Jerusalem where the Word of God grew (Acts 6–8). Members did not cower at the adversity; they asked for boldness to stand in the face of it (4:23–31). Individuals walking with God desired to make Him known to those who needed Him. This is the challenge of the disciple: to share Him with others.

This ministry was shared by all the people, and all types of people participated in its benefits. Peter, a self-confessed sinner, was a major leader (Luke 5:8). Lepers, paralytics, tax collectors, the blind, lame, deaf, and poor were included (5:12–16, 17–26, 27–32; 7:22–23). A woman of suspect reputation responded to the Lord. This was a beautiful account of the sacrifice of response, faith, and love (Luke 7:36–50). In the account, this woman said not a word, yet her anointing of Jesus spoke volumes about the gratitude she felt for receiving forgiveness. Anyone can be included in God's blessings. This woman is one of four "silent witnesses" in Luke whose acts speak more than a thousand words could (the others are Mary, 10:38–42; Lazarus, Luke 16:19–31; and the widow, Luke 21:1–4).

Luke also noted the active role women had in Jesus' ministry. Elizabeth and Mary exchanged notes of praise (Luke 1:39–45). Anna the prophetess announced to all at the temple about Jesus as Israel's hope (2:36–38). Women offered monetary support to Jesus, including a woman from inside Herod's palace (8:1–3). A poor widow who gave little actually gave all (21:1–4). Women went to Jesus' tomb to anoint His body, and they were the first to hear that He was raised (24:1–12). In the book of Acts, other women had important roles in the church's mission. Mary, the mother of Mark, hosted a house church (Acts 12:12). Rhoda announced Peter's release (12:13–17). Lydia helped plant a church and hosted it (16:14–15). Priscilla, with her husband, aided a community and corrected Apollos, teaching him "the way of God more adequately" (18:26; cf. vv. 2, 18). Philip's daughters were prophetesses (21:9). Nowhere in Luke did a woman have an official role in the church's organizational structure, but they were active and very effective in many aspects of the church's work.

Summary. Discipleship is both demanding and rewarding. According to Luke, it is people-focused, showing love for God and then treating others with love that parallels the love of the Father. In Acts, one sees little of the church serving itself and much of the church reaching out to those who needed the Lord. For Luke, the people in the highly effective early church looked outward. They were not cloistered constantly; they were penetrating the world and sharing the gospel, even though it involved great risk. The church did not withdraw from those outside her; she engaged the world. Trusting God, they were not afraid of what that path meant for them. Such is the picture of the effective, exemplary community of Acts, which took the message of God's plan and promise to a dark and dying world (Luke 1:79). The picture of the church in Acts is not so concerned with structures, strategies, and offices as it is concerned about attitudes, allegiances, growth, character, and outreach.

ESCHATOLOGY

THE BASIC STRUCTURE

A look at Luke's eschatology shows a fundamental two-part structure with the second half divided into three parts. The basic division is between promise and fulfillment (Luke 7:28; 16:16). In the "period of anticipation" are the Old Testament promise and the ministry of John the Baptist. The forerunner was a part of the promise period as indicated in Luke 7:19–20, 28; 16:16. With Jesus' ministry one enters the "period of realization." This fulfillment has three parts: transition, the "already" (church age), and the "not yet" (Christ's return to reign).

The transition is shown in passages like Luke 11:20 and 17:21. They indicate that God's current activity for His people had taken on a new level of intensity with Jesus' coming. One can speak of the kingdom arriving, in that the King was exercising His power and reflecting His authority. This fact was discussed in the section on Christology and the work of Jesus. It is transition, because the covenant's salvific blessings, most notably the "promise of the Father," the Holy Spirit, was not yet available to all who believed (3:15–18; 24:49). This promise of the new covenant (Luke 22:20) could not be realized until the covenant was activated by Jesus' sacrifice. So the arrival of the central promised blessings of the period of realization did not come until the Spirit arrived. The Spirit's arrival completed the period of transition, in terms of bringing initial fulfillment of promised blessing to those who acknowledged that Jesus is the promised Messiah.

The descent of the Holy Spirit on Pentecost, made possible by Jesus' resurrection-ascension, marks the arrival of the "already" period of promise. Jesus functions now as Lord-Messiah, distributing blessings promised in the Old Testament and holding all people accountable for responding to Him ("from now on," Luke 22:69; "exalted to the right hand of God" as Psalm 110 promised, Acts 2:32–36;

the pouring out of the Holy Spirit as Joel promised, Acts 2:1–4, 16–21; and coming to judge, Acts 2:40; 10:42; 17:30–31). Acts 11:15 referred back to the event on the Day of Pentecost as "the beginning." Here the hope of the new covenant was inaugurated, made possible by Jesus' death (Luke 22:20). These current blessings are part of the eschaton because in Luke's view they represent the initial line of Old Testament promises that God fulfilled. In the Holy Spirit, God is at work in His people. Jesus rules with sovereignty over these benefits as the Mediator of divine blessing. The kingdom has come because the power of God is expressed through Jesus by means of His Spirit.

But there also is a "not yet" element in Luke's eschatology. Here is the hope of consummation, in which God's promises will be brought to full realization. All the Old Testament promises made to Israel will be fulfilled (Acts 3:19–21) and God will "restore everything" (v. 21). The promise of a period of the restoration of all things recalls the language of the disciples' question in Acts 1:6, a question Peter himself answered in this Acts 3 speech. It is the promise of salvation for Israel, expressed in Luke 1:69–75. This helps explain where the rule of Jesus over the nation (Luke 1:31–35) is headed. Jesus will return to the earth to rule directly over all. He will exercise His sovereignty, not only in salvific benefits, but also as "judge of the living and the dead" (Acts 10:42; cf. 17:31). At that time, realization of Jesus' promise to the apostles that they will rule over the twelve tribes of Israel arrives, as they help administer righteousness and justice (Luke 22:30). The numerous pictures of the banquet table celebration relate ultimately to this yet-future age, when those who will share in the consummation of the promise will rejoice (13:22–30; 14:15–24; 22:16, 20).

Luke 22:16 is particularly significant. Jesus said He would not eat the Passover meal again with His disciples until He does so in the kingdom. This remark suggests that Jesus anticipated that promises to Israel will be fulfilled, that her major feast (the Passover) will continue to be celebrated, and that the apostles will be present at the celebration. Details about establishing this period are given in Luke 17:22–37 and 21:5–33. In these passages the coming final judgment is compared to what would happen soon, namely, the fall of Jerusalem in A.D. 70. In Luke 21, Jesus discussed what will happen first "before the end" (vv. 5–9) and what will occur "before" those events that come "before" the end (vv. 12–19, i.e., the events of vv. 12–19 come before those of vv. 5–9). He also declared what will happen to Jerusalem until the times of the Gentiles are fulfilled as a pattern of what the end is like (vv. 20–24). Then Jesus summarized what the End will look like (vv. 25–28). So the first judgment, which involves Jerusalem, is a picture of what the final judgment on the world will be like (see more on Luke 21 below).

An inauguration (of the present age) is related to Jesus' ascension, and the consummation (in Jesus' future reign) is related to His return. Jesus is at the center of these plans. His return, followed by the consummation, provides perspective on how one should live now. For in the consummation, there is accountability, judgment, and reward. Judgment will be for those who do not know Jesus or who blatantly disregard Him (Luke 12:45–46; 13:25; 17:37; 19:24–26; Acts 10:42;

17:30–31). Reward is for those who obey, while punishment is for those who fail to respond to the call of the Master (Luke 12:42–44, 47–48; 14:14; 19:17–19).

IMMINENCE AND DELAY

One of the great tensions in New Testament eschatology is the fact that Jesus' return, which is said to be soon, is accompanied with the fact that the church has a mission to the whole world. Added to this is the fact that Jesus has not yet returned. This tension is reflected in Luke. In Luke 18:8 Jesus spoke of the "speedy" vindication that will come to God's children. This highlights the theme of imminence that Luke associated with Jesus' return.

Perhaps Luke 18 sees imminence and vindication at two levels. One set of events lays the groundwork for ultimate vindication. Jesus' current rule means that He is present to give aid to His children now, as they face opposition from the world. Final vindication will come, but Jesus' presence with His own now means that the groundwork of vindication is already present. This reality is seen in two "death scenes" in Luke–Acts. One involves a thief crucified with Jesus and the Lord's promise that "today" the thief would be with Jesus in paradise (23:42–43). In the other scene Jesus welcomed the martyr Stephen (Acts 7:55–56). Strictly speaking this is not the full vindication spoken of in Luke 18:8, since the enemies are not yet dealt with, but it does represent an initial form of vindication. End time vindication is both "soon" and "not yet."

Another text often thought to teach imminence (and particularly problematic, if it has that sense) is Luke 21:32, where Jesus said that "this generation" will see God's promises being completed. The "generation" in view may be the generation of the end (looking back to events about Jerusalem's end in v. 20 or to the events of v. 25). That is, once the end-time events start, it will take only one generation's duration to establish His rule. When Jesus comes, the end will come quickly. Thus the text teaches how "instantaneous" the return is, not how imminent. Another way to take the verse is to see the reference to generation, not so much as chronological as moral. So this "evil" generation, which is what the unredeemed creation consists of, will pass away when Jesus returns. Such a use of the term "generation" occurs in Luke 9:41 and 11:29. If this is the sense, then imminence is not in view either; instead what is emphasized is that at the end, judgment comes. Either view of this verse is possible.

Luke 21 is complicated, because two events are described simultaneously in the first part of the discourse. Luke 21:5–24 covers two periods. Verses 5–19 describe mostly the situation that came with the fall of Jerusalem in A.D. 70. This fall was also discussed in Luke 19:41–44. Its grisly judgment in turn pictures what the end will be like. The earlier judgment "patterns" what the end judgment will be like, providing an illustration of it. Luke 21:20–24 describes both events as one. Luke clearly included the earlier event when he, alone among the Synoptic writers, referred to Jerusalem's "desolation" and did not mention the abomination of desolation. The shorter term in Daniel refers to a variety of desecrations, as opposed to a specific desecration (Dan. 9:27; 11:31; 12:11). All the desecrations involve the temple, but Daniel 11:31 refers to temple destruction and a cessation of sacrifices, as opposed to a desecrating sacrifice. It broadens the allusion to include the fall of Jerusalem. However, Luke 21:25–36 describes the events of the end only.

The details in Luke 21:25–28 are discussed more fully in Luke 17:22–37. The return of the Son of Man to earth will take place instantly and in a way that is obvious to all (17:24). It will come after the Son of Man suffers (17:25). Suddenly, as judgment comes, some will be taken and others will be left. Some will be preserved; others will be judged. The vultures (17:37) indicate that the major picture of this aspect of the return involves judgment. If one asks where those who are taken go, as the disciples asked (v. 37), the reply is only that vultures are there.

In Luke 21 Jesus spoke of two events, both future when He spoke, but one of which (the destruction of Jerusalem in A.D. 70) is now past and one of which is yet future. In good prophetic style, Jesus united two events that picture the same reality. One mirrors the other. The fall of Jerusalem, occurring in the lifetime of many of the disciples, guaranteed the coming reality of the end-time judgment on the world. The events are so similar, it is easy to see how they could be confused. In fact, describing the two events together would have made it difficult to distinguish the two events until one of them had occurred.[51] But the mixing together of these events also means that this discourse was very relevant to the disciples. They would need to stand firm in persecution, but they also could know that when the Lord returned, those who stand opposed to God's people will be judged. Vindication for the saints will come.

Other verses state that a time of delay would come. In Luke 19:11 the people expected the immediate arrival of the consummated kingdom. But in the parable of the ten minas that followed (vv. 12–27), Jesus made the point that in the interim between His departure and His return the disciples are to be faithful. More indicative are warnings in the Olivet Discourse itself. Luke 21:8–9 show that the events described in the first section are not yet part of the time of the end. Verses 20–24 suggest that Jerusalem would fall before the end would come. Only with the cosmic signs and the Son of Man's return will the end come (vv. 25, 28, 31). Then redemption draws near. In fact, verse 24 refers to the entire present age as "the times of the Gentiles."

Similarly, Peter later declared that delay is actually evidence of God's patience and desire to save (2 Peter 3:9). The return of Jesus and all the events associated with it are next on God's calendar (and so at least in this sense they will occur "soon"), but also in the interim believers are to be faithful and to watch for His return (Luke 21:34–36).

Luke's treatment of eschatology is not exhaustive. Other New Testament writers described events that Luke did not mention at all. Luke's eschatology focuses on the saints' final vindication in terms of Old Testament promises. His focus on the authority and victory of the returning Son of Man shows where the resolution

---

51. The prophetic model for this type of presentation can be seen in the prophets' descriptions of the exiles' return from captivity as salvation. These images also portray endtime salvation. This typological-prophetic "pattern" or mirroring is normal Old Testament style.

of all things resides. Similarly, Paul remarked that God has summed up all things in Christ (Eph. 1:9–10). Salvation moves toward its completion, which means not only deliverance for the saints, but also vindication before their opponents as well.

PERSONAL ESCHATOLOGY

In Luke's "personal eschatology" Jesus briefly described what happens when people die. Two passages are to be noted: Luke 23:42–43 and Acts 7:55–56. They speak of people at death who were immediately aware that they were entering God's presence. The thief who confessed Jesus while hanging on the cross heard the Lord promise that "today" he would be with Him in paradise. Even as Jesus died on the cross, He drew people to Himself and promised them life in God's presence. In Acts Stephen saw heaven open up and Jesus, standing as the Son of Man, waiting to welcome him. The arms of heaven are open to receive His children. Death is consumed by eternal life (1 Cor. 15:54–55).

THE MIGHTY GOD WHO SAVES

Luke's two volumes are about the mighty God who saves and who does so through Jesus Christ. Mary sang of the "Mighty One" who had done great things (Luke 1:49). In her hymn she spoke of the hope of salvation, which Luke then described in his two books. Jesus is now seated at the right hand of the mighty God (22:69). This is the God for whom impossible things are possible (1:37; 18:27). He can save individuals and transform hearts. His plan will be accomplished. When God revealed to Peter that salvation was available to all, Peter could not resist serving God's plan (Acts 11:17).

God is also the Savior, as Mary said (Luke 1:47). His intricate plan "redeemed his people" (v. 68) through a "horn" raised up from the house of David (v. 69). God is calling people (Acts 2:21, 39; 15:14) and in Jesus Christ they see God's salvation (Luke 2:30).

These promises express God's lovingkindness and grace. It is by His "tender mercy" that "the rising sun will come to us from heaven to shine on those living in darkness and in the shadow of death, to guide our feet into the path of peace" (1:78–79). He cares for His own daily (12:24–28), and He desires to reach those who are lost (chap. 15). God visits people in Jesus Christ (1:68; 7:16; Acts 15:4) whether they see it or not (Luke 19:41–42). God's Word reveals that through Jesus Christ, He is mighty, saving, and compassionate. His arms are open to any who turn to Him. Jesus is Lord of all, so the gospel can go to all. The hard times of the church are not signs of God's judgment against her because she has been too generous in offering salvation directly to Gentiles, but, rather, they are opportunities to stand up boldly for Him as God spreads His Word through the testimony of those who faithfully witness to the fulfillment of God's promises. This is the story of reassurance Theophilus needed to hear (Luke 1:4). But Luke's message and theology were not for Theophilus alone. The church has the responsibility to carry this message to a world that needs such deliverance and reassurance. People need to come to God through Christ to meet, both now and forever, the mighty God who saves.

4

A THEOLOGY OF JOHN'S WRITINGS

W. HALL HARRIS

Johannine theology is, in essence, Christology.[1] The person of Jesus Christ is at the heart of everything the Apostle John wrote. Whether in the gospel of John with its unique emphasis on the Word made flesh, in the Johannine epistles with their emphasis on the Word of life amid the controversy of church schism, or in Revelation with its vision of the exalted Christ (Rev. 1:12–16) and His ultimate triumph, the primary goal of the apostle was to explain to his readers who Jesus is. An attempt to discuss the theology of the Johannine writings by dividing it into the traditional categories of systematic theology (e.g., anthropology, soteriology, pneumatology, eschatology) will inevitably produce some distortion because John did not organize his material along these lines. Instead he had one central focus, and that was Jesus Christ. Much of what John wrote about Jesus, particularly in the gospel and the three epistles, was tempered by years of reflection and Christian experience, but always at the center was Christ Himself.

This is not to say, however, that John said nothing about anthropology, soteriology, pneumatology, or eschatology. It simply means that whatever he said about these and other topics is almost always related to his Christological emphasis.

---

1. In his brief discussion of Johannine theology C. K. Barrett notes how the interpretation of the gospel of John must be fundamentally Christological in nature (*The Gospel According to St. John*, 2d ed. [Philadelphia: Westminster, 1978], 96–97).

W. HALL HARRIS, B.A., Th.M., Ph.D., is professor of New Testament studies at Dallas Theological Seminary.

Any attempt to treat these individual aspects of Johannine theology must therefore be somewhat repetitive since all point back to Christ. In the following discussion the major emphases of Johannine theology will be considered along with the structures and techniques employed by the Evangelist to communicate those emphases to his readers.

The first major theological theme to be examined is Christology. This will include not only a general overview of John's perspective on the person of Jesus Christ, but also specific examinations of key titles of Jesus in the Johannine writings. Next, the perspective of the fourth gospel on Jesus' glorification will be examined. This consists not only of His exaltation to the Father, but also of His death, resurrection, and ascension. This will be followed by a consideration of John's emphasis on the Holy Spirit as Jesus' replacement after His departure, and then a discussion of polarization in Johannine theology—John's use of paired opposites or antitheses such as light and darkness, belief and unbelief, heaven and earth, and flesh and spirit. Such paired opposites are tremendously important for an understanding of Johannine theology not only because of the striking impact they have on the reader, but also because they underscore John's presentation of Jesus as the Messiah and the Son of God in antithetical choices—the reader of John's gospel must choose for Jesus or against Him, with this choice determining his or her eternal destiny.

The next subject to be examined is John's doctrine of salvation in its various aspects. After Christology, this is the second most important theme in the Johannine writings. The discussion will consider John's theology of the Cross, including his emphasis on Jesus' death as part of God's plan, the voluntary nature of Jesus' death, and its sacrificial aspects. Attention will be given to the development of the disciples' faith in Jesus in the fourth gospel, beginning with their faith in Jesus as Messiah and culminating with the confession of Thomas that Jesus is Lord and God (John 20:28). Following this will be a discussion of regeneration in the Johannine writings and an extended section on belief. Then the unique Johannine emphasis on eternal life as a present experience available to believers will be examined.

The last major section discusses Johannine eschatology, including the tension between "future" eschatology and so-called "realized" eschatology in the gospel of John. Although some other topics could be discussed, these have been selected as the central themes of the Johannine writings around which all else revolves.

THE GOSPEL OF JOHN

CHARACTERISTICS OF JOHANNINE NARRATIVE STYLE AND THEOLOGICAL EMPHASES

John's narrative style differs noticeably from that of the Synoptic Gospels. Several of the stylistic techniques employed by John contribute to the theological emphases the Evangelist wished to make. The most important of these are the use of extended discourse material, the frequent use of wordplays and misunderstood statements, and the use of irony.

Discourse material as a stylistic characteristic of John's gospel. The long running discourses which occur, for example, in John 3:1–21, 31–36; 4:4–42; 5:16–47; 6:25–71; 7:14–36; 8:12–59; and 12:44–50 as well as the prolonged Upper Room Discourse (chaps. 14–17), present extended sections of Jesus' public teaching and private conversations. This is in contrast to the short, pithy sayings of Jesus that are characteristic of the Synoptics.[2] Choosing to present such a fuller account of Jesus' own teaching allowed the Evangelist to keep before the reader the claims of Jesus as He presented them in His own teaching. Sometimes this includes the imagery and symbolism used by Jesus Himself to get His point across. Examples of this are the repeated use of "water" in connection with the Holy Spirit (3:5; 4:10; 7:38–39) and Jesus' description of Himself as the Bread of Life (6:26–59).

Wordplays and misunderstood statements. In addition to the inclusion of extended discourses, John also made use of a number of wordplays involving double meanings. Some examples of this are the Greek word *katelaben* in 1:5 which may mean either "overcome" or "understand"; the word *anōthen* in 3:3 meaning both "from above" and "again"; the description of the water in 4:10–11 as both "flowing" and "living" (*zōn*); and Jesus' statement in 7:8 that He is not "going up" (*anabainō*) at that time, which referred immediately to Jerusalem, but in reference to Jesus' "time" being fulfilled could also refer to His return to the Father.

To get his theological point across John often combined the use of double meanings with the "misunderstood statement"—a statement made by Jesus which was taken by His hearers to refer to an earthly situation, while Jesus really spoke of a heavenly or eternal truth. This is illustrated in John 3:3–4 where Jesus' remark about being born "from above" (see NIV text note) is understood by Nicodemus to refer to a second physical birth. Other misunderstandings are also found in 2:19–22; 4:10–11; and 6:32–34. When they occurred, they gave Jesus the opportunity to explain clearly what He really meant. This brings the theological point across more forcefully than a simple declarative statement would have done.[3]

John's use of irony. A number of times John recorded individuals making statements about Jesus that are derogatory, sarcastic, or incredulous. In John 4:12, for example, the Samaritan woman asks, "Are you greater than our father Jacob, who gave us the well and drank from it himself, as did also his sons and his flocks and herds?"[4] By way of irony, such statements are true or more meaningful than

---

2. The difference in style may be partly accounted for by the probability that the fourth gospel originated as a series of sermons by the apostle John about the life and ministry of Jesus before being committed to writing. This would have given John the opportunity to present Jesus' teaching in fuller form rather than extracting key summary statements as the Synoptic writers often did.

3. These wordplays and misunderstood statements have their origin in the teaching of Jesus Himself, but among the gospel writers only John made extensive use of them.

4. The woman's question in Greek anticipated a negative answer, which is not obvious in the NIV translation. The NASB reads, "You are not greater than our father Jacob, are You?"

the speaker realized at the time. Yet the reader of the gospel, having at least some idea of who Jesus is at this point, realizes the statement to be true and is able to give assent to it. In the case of 4:12, Jesus really is greater than Jacob.

Other examples of ironic statements in the gospel of John are found in 7:35, 42; 8:22; and 11:50. The last is the well-known statement by Caiaphas, "You do not realize that it is better for you that one man die for the people than that the whole nation perish." Caiaphas spoke only in political terms (cf. 11:48): the death of Jesus would save the Jewish nation from Roman reprisals which would surely follow if Jesus or His followers instigated a popular uprising. Nevertheless, the reader of the gospel, who knows that Jesus really will die vicariously for the sins of others, can see the irony in Caiaphas's statement.[5] These ironic statements are not explained by the Evangelist. He left it to his readers to see their significance for themselves. Such use of irony heightens the emphasis on who Jesus is and draws attention once more to the question by now familiar to the student of the fourth gospel, "Who is Jesus?"

THE CONTRIBUTION OF THE STRUCTURE OF
THE GOSPEL OF JOHN TO ITS THEOLOGICAL EMPHASES

Even a superficial examination of the gospel of John reveals the basic structure: a twofold division with the first section (1:19–12:50) relating a selected number of sign-miracles which testify to who Jesus is, and the second section (13:1–20:31) containing a large amount of discourse material (the so-called Upper Room Discourse) and the passion narrative.[6] Prior to the first section is a prologue (1:1–18) which introduces most of the major themes of the fourth gospel. The second section is followed by an epilogue (21:1–14) which repeats a number of these themes.

The sign-miracles and John's presentation of Jesus. Seven of Jesus' sign-miracles are recorded in the first major section of the gospel of John.[7] The first is the changing of water into wine (2:1–11), described in 2:11 as the "beginning" (*archē*) of Jesus' signs. The second is the healing of the nobleman's son (4:46–54). The healing of the paralytic at Bethesda (5:2–9) is the third, followed by the feeding of the multitude (6:1–14) and Jesus walking on the sea (6:16–21). The sixth is the healing of the man born blind (9:1–7), and the seventh is the raising of Lazarus (11:1–44). Theologically, all of the signs point to who Jesus is. He is not simply a prophet or a miracle worker, nor merely the expected Messiah, but the Word Incarnate Himself as described in the prologue (1:1–18) and affirmed by Thomas at the gospel's climax (20:28). During the earthly ministry of Jesus the signs led to belief

---

5. Cf. 1 John 2:2.

6. C. H. Dodd has referred to the first major section as "the Book of Signs" (*The Interpretation of the Fourth Gospel* [Cambridge: Cambridge Univ., 1953], 289). Raymond A. Brown calls the second major section "the Book of Glory" (*The Gospel According to John (i–xii)*, The Anchor Bible [Garden City, N.Y.: Doubleday, 1966], cxxxviii–cxxxix).

7. The seven sign-miracles are discussed at greater length in the section dealing with the person of Jesus.

on the part of some, but rejection on the part of others (1:11–12). The author of the Gospel wanted his readers to see and believe, so that they may receive eternal life through Jesus Christ and be strengthened in their faith in Him (20:31). The structuring of the first major section of the gospel around the seven sign-miracles helps keep before the readers the question, "Who is Jesus?" At the same time, the last of the seven, the raising of Lazarus (11:1–44), prepares the way for the passion narrative and the account of Jesus' own resurrection. Although not described by John as one of the sign-miracles, the resurrection of Jesus functions similarly to the previous signs in that it leads those who observe it and understand its significance to believe (John 20:8).

Discourse material as a structural element. Interspersed with the sign-miracles is a large amount of didactic material in the form of discourses by Jesus with various individuals and groups. These provide dramatic interludes which support the theological insight provided by the sign-miracles. At the same time, the discourses often advance the reader's theological insight into the person of Jesus (as in 4:4–42), His work (as in 6:25–71), and His claims (in 8:12–59). Embedded within the discourse material of the gospel of John are most of the "I am" statements, which echo to some degree Exodus 3:14.[8] Also to be included as discourse material is the lengthy Upper Room Discourse of John 14–17.[9]

These major structural elements in the fourth gospel contribute to the major Christological and soteriological emphases in Johannine theology. In reference to the former, they keep constantly before the reader the question "Who is Jesus?" Regarding the latter, they present discourses and dialogues between Jesus and various individuals who were confronting the issue of what to make of Him (e.g., Nicodemus in chap. 3, the woman at the well in chap. 4, the paralytic in chap. 5, and the man born blind in chap. 9). This is very much in keeping with John's purpose for writing his gospel as reflected in John 20:31.

THE JOHANNINE EPISTLES: THEOLOGY IN CONTROVERSY

John's theological emphases in his epistles grow out of a pastoral concern for his readers. This concern is motivated by a major theological controversy over the person of Jesus in the churches of Asia Minor to which the apostle addressed the letters. The controversy had progressed so far that a serious schism had already taken place, resulting in the departure of a large number (perhaps even a majority) of professing Christians (cf. 1 John 2:19) from these churches. John's purpose in writing was to reassure the readers, as those who had been left behind, that they had in fact remained true to the apostolic confession of who Jesus is and indeed possess eternal life (1 John 2:21, 24). The readers needed such reassurance in the face of continued controversy with the secessionist opponents, whose inadequate and het-

---

8. The only exception to this would be John 18:5, which is found in the narrative of Jesus' arrest. Strictly speaking, this is not a discourse. All of the "I am" statements are discussed more fully in the section dealing with the deity of Jesus.

9. It is perhaps more descriptive to call this material Jesus' Farewell Discourse to His disciples, since it focuses on the contents rather than the location where it was given.

erodox Christology denied the full humanity of Jesus and the importance of His earthly life and ministry as an example for believers to follow (cf. 2:26; 4:2–3). So deceptive was the defective Christology of the opponents and so serious its consequences that John could label its proponents as antichrists (2:18, 22; 4:3). John's message to the churches was urgent because there was considerable danger that more people would be taken in by the teaching of the opponents (2:26; 3:7).

John made it clear that the secessionist opponents, regardless of what they might claim about a relationship with God, had never actually belonged to the true fellowship of believers at all. This is demonstrated by their withdrawal from fellowship: "They went out from us, but they did not really belong to us. For if they had belonged to us, they would have remained with us; but their going out showed that none of them belonged to us" (2:19). In fact, the opponents belonged to the world and not to the fellowship of Jesus' true followers: "They are from the world and therefore speak from the viewpoint of the world, and the world listens to them" (4:5).[10]

Within this setting it is not surprising that John's tendency to use polarized imagery (antitheses or opposites), already found in the fourth gospel, would come to the forefront. Several contrastive images are employed to impress on the readers the drastic differences between their theology and that of the secessionist opponents. John used pairs of opposites like light and darkness and especially love and hate to describe the contrast between his readers and the opponents. Even the terminology of antichrist is brought into play in an attempt to emphasize the gulf separating the readers as genuine believers from the opponents who were not (2:18, 22; 4:3). For John the Christological and moral issues at stake were clear and there was no middle ground; one either sides with the opponents and their heterodox Christology or with the apostles and the orthodox view of who Jesus is. No other alternative is presented.

REVELATION: LANGUAGE, IMAGERY, AND THEOLOGY

A reader of average intelligence otherwise unfamiliar with the Bible, if asked to read the gospel of John or any of Paul's epistles, might be unable to decipher some details but would have no doubt about the major thrust of what he or she was reading. In fact, summaries of these books given by two such readers could be expected to be reasonably similar. The same, however, cannot be said for the book of Revelation, which is most likely to leave the unprepared reader wondering what it is all about. Summaries of the book would in all probability differ widely in all but the most obvious and general details (and for that matter commentaries on Revelation do reflect tremendous disparity).

What is the reason for this? In large part it is because Revelation is often seen as an example (in fact, the only New Testament example) of a literary genre known as apocalyptic. Symbolism and imagery are widely used in apocalyptic literature

10. The "world" as distinguished from the followers of Jesus is clearly seen in Jesus' prayer for His disciples in John 17:1–26, especially verses 6–19.

much as contemporary symbols appear in editorial or political cartoons. Readers in the first century, whether Jews, Hellenistic pagans, or Christians, were more well-versed in apocalyptic imagery than the average reader today.

THE USE OF SYMBOLIC LANGUAGE IN REVELATION

Interpretive difficulties begin when one must decide how far to take the apocalyptic symbolism literally and how far to take it figuratively. For example, there is little doubt that when John referred to "a Lamb, looking as if it had been slain, standing in the center of the throne" (Rev. 5:6) the lamb symbolically refers to the Lord Jesus Christ. The description of the Lamb as "slain" refers to the sacrificial death of Jesus on the cross and suggests a connection with the "Lamb of God" imagery used by John the Baptist in the gospel of John (John 1:29, 36). This in turn leads back to the Old Testament imagery of the Passover lamb (Ex. 12:21–28) and the Suffering Servant who is "led like a lamb to the slaughter" (Isa. 53:7).[11] Once the referent of the "Lamb" has been identified as the Lord Jesus Christ with the help of the qualifications attached to the initial reference, further mention of the Lamb does not need to be qualified. The reader is expected to know that the symbolism will be consistently used throughout the remainder of the book, and with one exception that is exactly what is found. All the following usages of "lamb" in Revelation do in fact refer to the Lord Jesus Christ with the exception of one in Revelation 13:11. In this context it is clear that the term "lamb" is not a reference to Jesus, since the verse contains a description of the second beast, also known as the false prophet (19:20), who supports the antichrist.

More difficult to interpret is the symbolic language used in the description of the locusts who will plague the earth after the sounding of the fifth trumpet (Rev. 9:1–12). The description is quite detailed: the locusts are said to look "like horses prepared for battle" (v. 7). They have "something like crowns of gold" on their heads, and "their faces resembled human faces" (v. 7). The locusts have "hair like women's hair" and teeth "like lions' teeth" (v. 8). They are equipped with "breastplates like breastplates of iron" (v. 9) and "tails and stings like scorpions" (v. 10). Are we to understand this description literally, as referring to real beasts with an appearance similar to that described by John in his vision? Or, as some have suggested, do we have a first-century description of armored attack helicopters? Probably neither is the case. Furthermore, though parts of John's description of the locusts bear similarities to a plague of locusts prophesied by Joel (Joel 2:1–10), the Old Testament prophecy differs in considerable detail from that found in Revelation. It is better to understand the language of Revelation as symbolic; the origin of the locusts, mentioned in Revelation 9:2–3, provides an important clue to the interpretation. They come from the cloud of smoke which rises from the abyss, suggesting demonic torment. The demonic nature of the locusts is confirmed in verse 11, which states that they have as their king the angel of the abyss, known as

---

11. Most of the apocalyptic symbolism used by John in Revelation finds its roots in the Old Testament, which often provides the interpretive key necessary to understanding the imagery.

Abaddon in Hebrew and Apollyon in Greek. Further symbolic interpretation of the details of John's prophetic vision may be less certain, but in broad outline the vision refers to a plague of demons loosed on the earth to torment the earth's inhabitants for five months (v. 10).

It is important to note that a symbolic interpretation of the language used in Revelation does not detract from its futuristic and prophetic nature. The events and persons described by John in his vision are real, even if described in symbolic terms, just as the symbolic description of Jesus as "the Lamb" changes nothing about the fact of His present glorified existence in heaven and future return to earth.

IMPORTANT DIFFERENCES BETWEEN
REVELATION AND OTHER APOCALYPTIC LITERATURE

For all its similarities to other works of apocalyptic literature, the book of Revelation has important differences. A significant fact often overlooked by those who place Revelation in the same category as other nonbiblical apocalyptic productions is that the author of Revelation expressly considered his work prophecy. "Blessed is the one who reads the words of this prophecy, and blessed are those who hear it and take to heart what is written in it" (Rev. 1:3). This claim is repeated in 22:7, 10, 18–19. Extrabiblical apocalyptic works were frequently pseudonymous, written in the name of some notable historical figure in an attempt to add authority or gain the reader's interest, but the author of Revelation clearly identified himself as "John" (1:1, 4, 9; 22:8) and did not feel the need for added authority. What he wrote is authoritative because it is revelation from God; no human authority is needed.

Additional significant differences between Revelation and other works of apocalyptic genre should be noted. First, Revelation includes pastoral letters to the seven churches of Asia Minor (Rev. 2–3), an element found in no other apocalyptic work. Second, most nonbiblical apocalyptic literature is generally pessimistic about the present age, seeking relief in the age to come. Revelation, on the other hand, is realistic about the presence of evil in the world, especially as it breaks out just before the return of Christ, but is equally clear about who the final Victor will be. Third, Revelation is integrated with the redemptive program of God in history as presented in the rest of the Bible. It tells "the rest of the story" following the ascension and exaltation of Jesus at the close of the gospel narratives.

Thus the book of Revelation serves as an appropriate conclusion not only to the Johannine writings of the New Testament but also to the entire Bible. Its theological emphases are sometimes conveyed by symbolic language, but are no less real nor inspired than the propositional theology found in the epistles of Paul. This book conveys important truths about the Lord Jesus Christ and the final stages of human history.

JOHANNINE CHRISTOLOGY: THE PERSON OF JESUS

As already stated, Christology is at the forefront in all the Johannine writings of the New Testament. What is arguably the major theme of the gospel of John concerns the revelation of who Jesus is: the Son of God, sent from the Father, who is Himself deity.[12] If the climax of the fourth gospel occurs in 20:28 when Thomas proclaimed of Jesus, "My Lord and my God," the primary thrust of the entire work is summed up in 20:31, which indicates that the purpose for the gospel of John is to lead the reader into a proper understanding of who Jesus is and thus have eternal life.

Likewise, Christology is also of primary importance in the Johannine epistles. First John 1:1 declares, "That which was from the beginning, which we have heard, which we have seen with our eyes, which we have looked at and our hands have touched—this we proclaim concerning the Word of life." The "Word of life" is none other than Jesus Himself, and John wrote to affirm the orthodox Christology of the letter's recipients in contrast to the heterodox Christology propounded by their secessionist opponents. Thus a proper understanding of who Jesus is, especially in regard to the importance of His earthly life and ministry, is at the heart of the controversy that lies behind all three of the Johannine epistles. Christology is also important in Revelation. In fact, the entire contents of the book are described as "the revelation of Jesus Christ, which God gave him to show his servants what must soon take place" (Rev. 1:1). John's vision of the exalted Christ dominates the opening chapter of the book (1:12–18). The theme of the book is the ultimate victory of Jesus Christ over all enemies and the establishment of His earthly kingdom.

THE PERSON OF JESUS IN THE GOSPEL OF JOHN

The confession of Thomas in John 20:28 dramatically underlines who Jesus is. But testimony about the person of Jesus is not limited to the closing chapters of the fourth gospel. It is found throughout the book, especially in the testimony of John the Baptist and Nathanael in the opening chapter of the gospel, in the seven sign-miracles of John 2:1–11:44, and in the lengthy discourses of Jesus Himself with both His opponents and His disciples.

Testimony about Jesus by John the Baptist and Nathanael. One of the first indications of Jesus' identity encountered by the reader of the gospel of John is the testimony of John the Baptist. John's testimony is mentioned in the prologue (John 1:6–8, 15) and resumed immediately in the remainder of chapter one (1:19–35). The Baptist first appeared, giving testimony to representatives of the Jewish leadership in Jerusalem as to who he is not (1:19–27). On that occasion John the Baptist denied that he is the Messiah or Elijah or the eschatological Prophet.[13] Positively, the Baptist identified himself as one who cries out in the desert, "Make straight the way for the Lord," in the words of Isaiah 40:3 (see NIV note). As to the reason for his baptizing activity, John answered indirectly by saying that a greater one would come after him (John 1:26–27). John's reply to the Jewish authorities is clarified in

12. John 20:31 strongly suggests that the main purpose of the fourth gospel is to affirm Jesus as the Christ (i.e., Messiah), the Son of God.

13. This refers to the "prophet like Moses" promised in Deuteronomy 18:15–18.

the following verses (vv. 29–34). John came as a witness to the Messiah, the One who was to come. John himself did not know who this person would be (v. 31), but carried out his baptizing activity so that the Messiah might be revealed to Israel. When the Baptist saw the Spirit descending on Jesus (v. 33), then he recognized Jesus as the one he came to identify. John the Baptist summarized his testimony in verse 34: "I have seen and I testify that this one is the Son of God" (cf. 20:31).

When two of the Baptist's disciples heard his testimony, they left his company and followed Jesus instead (1:37). One of these, Andrew, then found his brother Simon Peter and announced, "We have found the Messiah" (v. 41). Thus within the opening chapter of John's gospel, Jesus is identified as both Son of God (v. 34) and Messiah (v. 41), and both of these titles recur a significant number of times in the fourth gospel. Furthermore, Jesus' link to the promises of the Old Testament is affirmed when Philip announced to Nathanael, "We have found the one Moses wrote about in the Law, and about whom the prophets also wrote—Jesus of Nazareth, the son of Joseph" (v. 45). After Nathanael met Jesus for himself, he declared that Jesus is the Son of God and the King of Israel (v. 49). This adds further emphasis to John the Baptist's testimony; now two witnesses have testified that Jesus is the Son of God.

The seven sign-miracles and the person of Jesus. After the first of the sign-miracles in the gospel of John, the changing of water into wine at the wedding feast in Cana (2:1–11), the point of the miracle is stated (v. 11): through it Jesus revealed His "glory" and His disciples believed in Him. Thus the first sign-miracle had the same purpose as that of all the following sign-miracles, namely, to reveal the person of Jesus. Scholarly interpretations of John 2:1–11 to the contrary, the author of the fourth gospel does not put primary emphasis on the replacing of the water for Jewish purification, or on the change from water to wine, or even on the quality of the resulting wine. John did not focus on Mary and her intercession, or on why she made the request, or whether she pursued it further after Jesus' initial response. Nor did John focus on the reaction of either the master of the feast or the bridegroom. The primary focus, as for all the Johannine sign-miracles and discourses, is on Jesus as the one sent by the Father to bring salvation to the world. What shines through is His "glory" (*doxa*), and the only reaction emphasized is that of His disciples when they believed in Him (cf. 20:31).

Likewise the second sign-miracle, the healing of the nobleman's son at Cana (4:46–54), also testifies to the person of Jesus. It occupies an important transitional spot in the narrative. The stress on the necessity of trusting in Jesus summarizes and culminates the previous material in chapters 2–4, while the stress on Jesus as the Giver of life introduces one of the most important themes of the next section (chaps. 5–10). In chapters 2–4 the reader sees how people responded to Jesus. While Nicodemus responded inadequately (at least at this point), the Samaritans showed a proper response (4:42). And of course His disciples had placed their trust in Him at the wedding at Cana (2:11). In the following chapters (5–10) Jesus is portrayed as the Giver of life (though this has been foreshadowed in chaps. 2–4; note the introduction of the living water in chap. 4). Jesus is also the Bread of life (chap. 6), the Giver of the water of life (chap. 7), and the Light of life (chap. 8).

The third sign-miracle, the healing of the paralytic at Bethesda (5:1–47), emphasizes the importance of trusting in the person of Jesus. In 5:1–15 Jesus healed the paralytic and ordered him to stop sinning (5:14). To those held in the bondage of death and sin the Son offers life, and the only danger is that an individual will ignore that offer. To do so would be not to trust in the Son. And something worse, condemnation at the Last Judgment (5:29) would surely befall such a person.

The fourth and fifth sign-miracles are both recounted in chapter 6. The fourth sign-miracle, the multiplication of the bread (6:1–15), brings the reader face-to-face with the supernatural again, but this time on a far "grander" scale than the changing of water into wine at Cana, the healing of the nobleman's son at Cana, or the cure of the paralytic at Bethesda in Jerusalem. This is the only event in the entire public ministry of Jesus before the passion week recorded in all four gospel accounts. Again, as with the other sign-miracles, revelation about the person of Jesus took place, as explained in the so-called "Bread of life" discourse which follows the fifth sign-miracle (6:25–71). Jesus called on the crowd to believe in the One whom the Father has sent (6:29), calling for personal response and belief. His statement, "I am the bread of life" (6:35), reveals Jesus as the Giver and Sustainer of eternal life, much as the references to "living water" do in John 4.

The fifth sign-miracle, Jesus walking on the water (6:16–21), is a less "public" sign directed at His disciples. Many have characterized this as a nature-miracle, emphasizing Jesus' sovereignty over nature, in which the disciples were rescued from the storm. But John did not even mention Jesus' calming of the storm (as the Synoptic accounts do), nor whether Jesus got into the boat (v. 21 only states that the disciples wanted to receive Him into the boat; one may assume He got in, but John 6 does not actually state this). Why then did John include this miracle, and why here, when the Bread of life discourse which comes next (6:22–71) would follow so naturally after the miraculous feeding in 6:1–15? The most likely answer to these questions can be found in Jesus' use of the expression "I am" in 6:35, 41, 48, and 51. Jesus is the one who bears the divine name (cf. Ex. 3:14). For John, this story takes on the character of a theophany, not unlike the Transfiguration recorded by the Synoptics. After Jesus multiplied the bread and fish, the crowd attempted to crown Him king (6:15). And in the Bread of life discourse, which follows the fifth sign-miracle, many of even Jesus' disciples were unable to accept what He said about Himself (vv. 60, 66). But to Jesus' disciples in the boat (probably to be identified with the Twelve [cf. v. 67], not the crowds), Jesus privately manifested Himself as much more than a political messiah. What He is can be summed up only by the phrase "I am." These disciples knew that to some extent already; they had placed their trust in Jesus as Messiah (2:11). But they needed a reminder that their ideas about the person and work of Jesus were not to be conditioned by the ideas of the general population, to which they had just been witness.

The sixth sign-miracle is the healing of the man born blind (chap. 9). This sign has messianic significance. In the Old Testament God Himself is associated with the giving of sight to the blind (Ex. 4:11; Ps. 146:8). In a number of passages in Isaiah (29:18; 35:5; 42:7) giving sight to the blind was considered a sign of messianic activity. In fulfillment of these prophecies Jesus gave sight to the blind man. As the Light of the world (John 8:12; 9:5), Jesus has defeated the darkness (cf. 1:5). Thus this miracle has particular significance for John as one of the seven sign-miracles he employed to point to Jesus' identity and messiahship. John developed the antithesis of light and darkness at considerable length in his gospel.

The seventh sign-miracle, the resurrection of Lazarus (11:1–44), occurred at the culmination of Jesus' public ministry and serves as the transition to the Farewell Discourse and the passion narrative in the fourth gospel. Above all it confirms Jesus' claims to messiahship and to equality with God (cf. 5:18). There are interesting parallels between this miracle and the healing of the man born blind (chap. 9). Just as that miracle illustrated Jesus as the Light of the world (8:12; 9:5), so the raising of Lazarus in 11:1–44 is an illustration of Jesus as the Life (cf. 14:6). These two themes, light and life, were both used in the prologue (1:4) to describe the relationship of the Word to humanity. Just as the preincarnate Word gave physical life and light to humankind in creation (1:2), so Jesus as the Word Incarnate gives spiritual life and light to people who believe in Him.

The discourses of the fourth gospel and the person of Jesus. In addition to the sign-miracles, another striking feature of the gospel of John are the lengthy discourses of Jesus. Some of the most prominent of these are Jesus' conversations with Nicodemus (3:1–21) and with a Samaritan woman (4:4–26); with the Jewish leadership (5:16–47) and with the crowds in Capernaum (the "Bread of life" discourse, 6:25–59); again with the Jewish leadership (the "Light of the world" discourse, 8:12–59) and with some Pharisees (the "Good Shepherd" discourse, 10:1–21); and finally Jesus' Farewell Discourse to His disciples (13:31–17:26). Some of these discourses are related to sign-miracles: the "Bread of life" discourse (6:25–59) is related to the fourth sign-miracle, the multiplication of the bread (6:1–15), and the "Light of the world" discourse (8:12–59) is associated with the sixth sign-miracle, the healing of the man born blind (9:1–41).

The discourses, like the sign-miracles, contain important revelation about who Jesus is. In the discourse with Nicodemus (3:1–21) Jesus is seen as the revealer of God's truth (v. 12), sent from God (v. 17), the Son of Man who came down from heaven (v. 13). In the discourse with the Samaritan woman (4:4–26) Jesus identified Himself as the Messiah (vv. 25–26) and in verse 13 as the Giver of the water of life (i.e., the Holy Spirit; cf. 7:38–39). The discourse with the Jewish leadership in 5:16–47 reveals the relationship of the Son to the Father, emphasizing the Son's dependence on the Father (vv. 19, 30) and the authority given the Son by the Father to execute judgment (vv. 22, 27). The "Bread of life" discourse (6:25–59) contains more revelation about Jesus as the Son (vv. 27, 40, 53), including His heavenly origin (vv. 33, 38, 51, 58), His being on a mission sent from the Father (vv. 29, 44, 57) and His being approved by the Father (v. 27). Jesus is the only one who has seen the Father (v. 46; cf. 1:18).

Many of the same themes appear in the "Light of the world" discourse in 8:12–59. Jesus is sent by the Father (vv. 16, 18, 29, 42) and reveals the Father (vv. 19, 28, 38, 40). No one is able to accuse Jesus of sin (v. 46). At the conclusion of the discourse Jesus revealed His preexistence and identified Himself with God (v. 58). The Good Shepherd Discourse (10:1–21) again shows Jesus in His relationship with the Father (10:15), with special emphasis on His voluntary sacrifice of His life on behalf of others (vv. 10–11, 15, 17–18).

The Farewell Discourse to the disciples (13:31–17:26) reveals much about the person and work of Jesus. As the Son, Jesus is to be glorified (13:31–32; 16:14; 17:1–2, 5, 10, 22, 24), a reference both to His approaching death on the cross and to His resumption of preincarnate glory. Again Jesus is the one sent by the Father (16:5; 17:3, 8, 18, 21, 23, 25) and to reveal the Father (14:6, 9–11; 15:15; 16:15, 25; 17:6, 8, 26). In this discourse Jesus spoke repeatedly of His return to the Father (14:2, 12, 28; 16:5, 10, 28; 17:11, 13) and of His complete obedience to Him (14:10, 24, 31; 15:10; 17:4). Jesus is the only way to the Father (14:6; 17:2).

CHRISTOLOGY IN THE JOHANNINE EPISTLES

In the Johannine epistles the issue of Jesus' identity again comes to the forefront with primary emphasis on Him as the "Word of life" (1 John 1:1) and as the Son of God (2:22–23; 3:23; 4:15; 5:5, 10, 12–13). First John includes twenty-two references to the Son. A correct understanding of Jesus' person and work is essential for believers, and 1 John presents this in the framework of an apostolic response to a dispute between orthodox Christians and heterodox secessionists who had left the churches to whom the Johannine epistles are addressed and had withdrawn from fellowship with them. The Apostle John did not address the opponents directly in an attempt to refute their faulty view of who Jesus is. Instead, he wrote to the true believers who remained faithful to the apostolic testimony about Jesus (of which they were reminded in 1 John 1:1–4) to reassure them that they were on the right side in the controversy regardless of what the opponents might say. Naturally a proper view of who Jesus is, especially with regard to His earthly ministry and full humanity, is a central theme of the first epistle under these circumstances. The same controversy lies behind 2 John and 3 John. However, it is not developed at length in these epistles because of the brevity of the letters and their purpose, namely, to address specific situations that had arisen as a result of the controversy.

CHRISTOLOGY IN REVELATION

Like the other Johannine writings, from a theological standpoint the focus in Revelation is Christological. John introduced the book as "the revelation of Jesus Christ, which God gave him to show his servants what must soon take place" (1:1). Unlike the gospel of John, which shows Jesus in His humiliation and tells of His return to the Father through crucifixion, death, resurrection, and exaltation, Revelation shows the exalted Christ, who has been restored to the glory He had with the Father "before the world began" (cf. John 17:5). The book of Revelation focuses particularly on the return of Jesus Christ to establish His kingdom on earth and His victory over the satanic forces which will arise to oppose Him at His return.

THE DEITY OF JESUS

The following sections examine the titles and formulas found in the Johannine literature of the New Testament which are most important for understanding the person of Jesus.

Explicit claims of deity. The clear and climactic assertion of Jesus' deity in the gospel of John is found in Thomas' exclamation in John 20:28, "My Lord and my God!" This is not the first time such an identification of Jesus occurs in the fourth gospel, however. It is introduced in the prologue and repeatedly emphasized throughout the gospel. John 1:1 makes three assertions about the Word (the *Logos*, identified as Jesus in 1:14). First, before the created order existed, the Word already existed. Second, the Word was in intimate personal relationship with God. Third, the Word was fully deity in essence (the NEB provides a helpful translation here: "What God was, the Word was"). Again at the end of the prologue a similar point is made about who Jesus is. "No one has ever seen God, but God the One and Only, who is at the Father's side, has made him known" (1:18). Thus at the very outset of his gospel, John set forth his understanding of the person of Jesus Christ. This understanding is amplified and repeated throughout the remainder of the fourth gospel, reaching its climax in the confession of Thomas in 20:28. Contributing to John's affirmation of the deity of Jesus are the seven sign-miracles of John 2:1–11:44 (discussed in the preceding section), the nonpredicated "I am" statements of the gospel of John (8:24, 28, 58; 13:19; and perhaps 18:5), and statements relating to the identity of Jesus and the Father. The use of the expression *ho ōn* ("him who is") in Revelation 1:4, 8; 4:8; 11:17; 16:5 also points to the deity of Jesus.

The sign-miracles and the deity of Jesus. The preceding general section on the person of Jesus in the Johannine writings discussed at some length the seven sign-miracles of John 2:11–11:44. Each of these has its place in John's narrative as an expression of some facet of Jesus' person and work, but, in addition, all point to Jesus' heavenly origin, divine authority, and full deity. This is explicitly stated by Jesus Himself in John 10:37–38: "Do not believe me unless I do what my Father does. But if I do it, even though you do not believe me, believe the evidence of the miracles, that you may learn and understand that the Father is in me, and I in the Father." The sign-miracles themselves provide testimony as to who Jesus is.

The "I am" statements and the deity of Jesus. The "I am" statements are unique to John's gospel. As first-person statements by Jesus they form a significant part of His self-revelation. These statements are important for two reasons. First, a number of them make significant predications about Jesus by using metaphors (e.g., "I am the bread of life," 6:35). Second, the phrase "I am" is used in the Old Testament as a description of God Himself (Ex. 3:14; cf. Isa. 46:4). A number of the "I am" statements in John's gospel (8:24, 28, 58; 13:19; and perhaps 18:5) are absolute (i.e., without a predicate) and strongly suggest an allusion to Exodus 3:14.

There are seven "I am" statements which make predications about Jesus in the gospel of John. Jesus used this construction to make assertions about Himself as the Bread of life (6:35), the Light of the world (8:12), the Door (10:7; NIV "gate"), the Good Shepherd (10:11), the Resurrection and the Life (11:25), the Way, the Truth, and the Life (14:6), and the Vine (15:1). Each of these metaphors illustrates some aspect of Jesus' person and work. As the Bread of life, Jesus is the Provider and Sustainer of all life. As the Light of the world, Jesus is the Giver of moral light—but He is also the Light who came into the world at its creation (1:4) and who continues to shine in the darkness (1:5). Many of the abstract concepts about the *Logos* mentioned in the prologue to the gospel of John are made concrete by the "I am" statements that follow. Important as these are for understanding who Jesus is and what He came to do, they stop short of explicitly identifying Him with the name of Yahweh as found in the Old Testament.

The absolute (nonpredicated) "I am" statements go further, however. Four of these statements make explicit claims to Jesus' identification with God (8:24, 28, 58; 13:19). The clearest and most remarkable of these is John 8:58, "Before Abraham was born, I am!" This was Jesus' reply to His opponents' exclamation, "You are not yet fifty years old . . . and you have seen Abraham!" (v. 57). Jesus' statement clearly alludes to Exodus 3:14, and the response of His opponents makes it clear that they understood Jesus' words as a claim to identification with deity. They prepared to stone Him for what they understood to be blasphemy (v. 59).

The three remaining nonpredicated uses of the phrase "I am" (8:24, 28; 13:19) must be seen against the background of 8:58. Although it might be possible to understand these statements as simple affirmations ("I am He"), in the contexts in which they occur they seem to imply more. In 8:24 and 28 Jesus was discussing who He is. He told His opponents that He is from above, not from this world, and that if they do not believe that He is the one He claims to be ("I am"), they will die in their sins (v. 24). At stake in this context is the urgent necessity of believing in Jesus for salvation and the need for forgiveness of sins. Jesus said that when He would be "lifted up" (in His crucifixion, resurrection, and ascension), He would draw all people to Himself (8:28; cf. 12:32), and in that moment it will be clear to those who have eyes to see that He truly bears the divine name ("I am") and that He has the power to raise people to the Father. But if they refuse to believe—refuse to see—then there is no other way (cf. 14:6) that leads to the Father above, and people will go to their graves permanently separated from the gift and Giver of eternal life.

Similarly in John 13:19 Jesus had told His disciples of His betrayal beforehand, in order that when it happened their faith might be strengthened (that they already believed seems clear from numerous previous statements in the gospel, such as 2:11). What they would believe when they looked back on His prediction of betrayal is given in the final clause of 13:19: "that I am" (NIV "that I am He"). The expression here is almost certainly to be understood as an absolute statement without a predicate as in 8:28. On later (postresurrection) reflection concerning Jesus' prediction of His betrayal, the disciples would conclude that He had been in complete control of the situation as only God Himself could be.

Less certain as an absolute claim to identification with God is Jesus' statement "I am He" in John 18:5. Jesus may simply have been identifying Himself as the person Judas and the soldiers were seeking. Based on the response in 18:6 to Jesus' statement, however, some interpreters see this scene as similar to a theophany, where Jesus revealed to His enemies for a moment who He really is, and they prostrated themselves at His feet. It may well be that in verses 5–6 John recorded an incident in which the opponents of Jesus recoiled from surprise or abhorrence of what they perceived to be blasphemy. But for the reader of the gospel, who already knows who Jesus is and that His claim to identification with God is true, the reaction of the enemies is highly ironic. The betrayer Judas himself fell down at Jesus' feet before the soldiers led Him away to His trial and crucifixion.

Statements relating to the identity of Jesus and the Father. Statements regarding the identity of Jesus and the Father in John 10:30 and 17:22 also point to Jesus' deity. Some interpreters have understood Jesus' words in these passages to affirm merely a oneness of will, action, or purpose. But within the framework of John's gospel the Word is declared to be essentially God (1:1), and the confession of Thomas in 20:28 provides the climax. As already seen in 8:58, Jesus alluded to His identification with God by appropriating the divine name (cf. Ex. 3:14) and the Jewish opponents responded by attempting to stone Him. A similar response to Jesus' statement "I and the Father are one" occurs in John 10:30. This suggests that Jesus' opponents understood the statement as a blasphemous (to them) assertion of deity on Jesus' part. It is important to note that although the statements in 10:30 and 17:22 regarding the relationship of Jesus to the Father do imply Jesus' deity, they stop short of complete identity. The word for "one" used by Jesus in John 10:30 is neuter rather than masculine in form, thereby preserving the distinction between Jesus and the Father established in the prologue to the fourth gospel (1:1b, "the Word was with God") and maintained throughout.

The deity of Jesus in Revelation. In the book of Revelation the use of the expression *ho ōn* ("him who is" in 1:4, 8; 4:8; 11:17; 16:5) also points to the deity of Jesus because it too alludes to the self-designation of God in Exodus 3:14. There are also three "I am" statements in Revelation (1:8; 21:6; 22:13) which are followed by the same predicate ("the Alpha and the Omega"). Of these, the first is probably best understood as an utterance of God the Father (1:8), while the last (22:13) is said by the exalted Jesus (cf. 22:16). It is difficult to be sure whether in 21:6 Jesus or the Father is speaking, but it is probably best to see a reference to the Father here. In any case, the interchangeability of speaker between 1:8 and 22:13 (Jesus and the Father) constitutes an implicit ascription of deity to Jesus.

THE HUMANITY OF JESUS

Jesus' humanity in the gospel of John. The gospel of John is noted for its portrayal of Jesus as very God. However, it should not be overlooked that this gospel also presents strong statements in support of Jesus' humanity. John 1:14, while affirming that "the Word became flesh and made his dwelling among us," nevertheless presumes that the flesh the Word became was real and that He bore a humanity like all other descendants of Adam.

There are other indications of Jesus' humanity in the fourth gospel as well. The followers of John the Baptist regarded Him as a rabbi (1:38) and so did Nicodemus (3:2) and Jesus' own disciples (9:2; 11:8). John recorded that Jesus, wearied from the journey to Sychar in Samaria (4:6), experienced thirst (v. 7). Standing by the grave of Lazarus, Jesus was so deeply moved that He wept (11:33–35). He was again troubled after His entry into Jerusalem (12:27). Taking the role of a servant, Jesus washed His disciples' feet (13:1–12).

Thus it is clear that John's gospel portrayed Jesus' humanity as true and real. The Johannine epistles continue this affirmation and even expand on it.

Jesus' humanity in the Johannine epistles. The opening verses of 1 John are clear in their insistence on what has been heard, seen, and even touched concerning the Word of life (1 John 1:1–4). This precedes a specific rejection and condemnation of those who denied that Jesus is the Christ (1 John 2:22) and that He had come in the flesh (1 John 4:2–3; 2 John 7). Many who have studied the Johannine writings see this as combating some form of Docetism, a heresy that denied the reality of Jesus' incarnation. If these opponents were attempting to draw a distinction between the heavenly Christ and the human Jesus, preferring the former to the latter, this would be a seriously inadequate Christology which warranted the label "antichrist" (1 John 2:18, 22; 4:3; 2 John 7).

Jesus' humanity in Revelation. Revelation, because it focuses on the ascended and exalted Christ, finds little room for expression of the humanity of Jesus. Nevertheless, two references to the death of Jesus (Rev. 1:7, 18) indirectly point to His humanity.

The sinlessness of Jesus. While the Johannine literature portrays Jesus as fully human, it is also important to note that it also affirms that He was without sin. In His dispute with the Jewish leaders (John 8:31–59) Jesus asked, "Can any of you prove me guilty of sin?" (v. 46). To this there was no reply. Instead they changed the subject: "Aren't we right in saying that you are a Samaritan and demon-possessed?" (v. 48). Further support for Jesus' sinlessness is found in His claims to be one with the Father, a claim which of necessity excluded sinfulness (10:30; 17:22). The same emphasis is found in First John. Jesus Christ is "the Righteous One" (1 John 2:1), and John stated explicitly, "But you know that he appeared so that he might take away our sins. And in him is no sin" (3:5).

JESUS AS SON OF GOD

The Johannine writings include considerable emphasis on the title "Son of God." John 20:31 explicitly states that the purpose of the gospel is "that you may believe that Jesus is the Christ, the Son of God, and that by believing you may have life in his name." In addition to the use of the title itself, there are numerous times when Jesus is called "the Son" without further qualification. There are also more than 100 instances in the fourth gospel when Jesus addressed God directly or referred to Him as His Father. The concept of sonship when applied to Jesus thus becomes one of the dominant themes of the gospel of John.

For John, Jesus is the Son of God in a unique sense. Unlike Paul, John never used the Greek word *hyios* ("son") to describe believers in their relationship to God. Instead, believers are referred to as "children of God" in both John's gospel and his epistles (*tekna theou,* John 1:12; 11:52; 1 John 3:1–2, 10; 5:2). The phrase *hyios theou* is reserved by John as a description of Jesus in His unique relationship to the Father. This is emphasized in John 3:16, 18 where Jesus is described as God's "one and only Son" (NIV; NASB "only begotten Son"). Throughout the entire gospel of John the uniqueness of Jesus' relationship to the Father is maintained.

Jesus as Son of God in the gospel of John. First, John emphasized that Jesus as the Son of God has been sent into the world by the Father. This is clearly stated in John 3:17 ("For God did not send his Son into the world to condemn the world, but to save the world through him") and is repeated in 3:34; 5:36–38; 6:29, 57; 7:29; 8:42; 10:36; 11:42; 17:3, 8, 18, 21, 23, 25; 20:21. In the last of these references Jesus commissioned His disciples, telling them, "As the Father has sent me, I am sending you." The mission on which Jesus was sent from the Father was thereby transferred to the disciples, who were to continue it. References to Jesus as sent by the Father are also found in 1 John 4:9–10, 14.

Second, just as Jesus spoke of being sent by the Father, He also spoke of His return to the Father. On the eve of Jesus' passion John mentioned that Jesus knew it was time for Him to leave this world and go to the Father (13:1). Many references to Jesus' departure from the world and return to the Father occur in His Farewell Discourse (chaps. 14–17). Jesus promised that the disciples would perform miracles that would exceed His own because He was returning to the Father (14:12). He expected His disciples to rejoice over His return to the Father (v. 28). Jesus mentioned His return to the Father in connection with the sending of the Spirit (16:10) and the completion of His earthly mission (v. 28). After His resurrection Jesus told Mary, "I have not yet returned to the Father" (20:17).

Third, Jesus as Son of God is always portrayed by John as dependent on the Father. This is clear from John 5:19: "The Son can do nothing by himself; he can do only what he sees his Father doing, because whatever the Father does the Son also does." This is found as well in John 5:30; 14:31; and 15:10. Related to this theme are statements that reflect the absolute unity of the Son and the Father (10:30; 17:11; see also 14:11, 20).

Fourth, as Son of God Jesus is the revealer of the Father. This is first mentioned in the closing verse of the prologue to John's gospel: "No one has ever seen God, but God the One and Only, who is at the Father's side, has made him known" (1:18). Like many of the other themes found in the prologue, Jesus' role as revealer of the Father is reiterated throughout the fourth gospel. Jesus is said to be the only one who has ever seen the Father (6:46). When asked by the Pharisees, "Where is your father?" Jesus replied, "If you knew me, you would know my Father also" (8:19). A similar reply is made to Philip's request, "Show us the Father" (14:8–9). Jesus answered, "Don't you know me, Philip, even after I have been among you such a long time? Anyone who has seen me has seen the Father." Just as He is the revealer of the Father, in the preceding context Jesus had just affirmed that He is the only way to the Father (14:6). Along the same lines Jesus also reveals the Father's words: "everything that I learned from the Father I have made known to you" (15:15). Jesus does not speak on His own authority; He speaks what the Father has commanded Him (12:49). To His disciples Jesus added, "These words you hear are not my own; they belong to the Father who sent me" (14:24).

Fifth, as Son of God Jesus is the object of the Father's love. The Father's love for the Son leads Him to place everything in Jesus' hands (3:35). The Father loves the Son and shows Him everything He does (5:20). Jesus stated that the Father loves Him because He was willingly laying down His life only to take it up again (10:17). The loving relationship between the Father and the Son extends beyond the bounds of time and eternity. Jesus prayed that the disciples may see the glory given to Him by the Father because the Father loved Him before the creation of the world, that is, in eternity past (17:24). This relationship of love between the Father and the Son also becomes the pattern for the Father's love for believers (17:23) and the believers' love for each other (13:34–35).

Jesus as Son of God in the Johannine epistles. The role of Jesus as Son of God also receives special emphasis in 1 John. The Son is mentioned twenty-two times. The central point in the dispute between the recipients of the epistle, who held an orthodox Christology, and their opponents, who held an inadequate and heretical view of Christ, is that Jesus is the Son of God (1 John 2:22–23; 3:23; 4:15; 5:5, 10, 12–13). The sending of the Son into the world is emphasized (just as in the gospel of John) in 1 John 4:9–10, 14. The Son's mission into the world from the Father is said to be to destroy the devil's work (3:8). The prologue of the epistle states that believers have fellowship with the Father and with His Son Jesus Christ (1:3). As Son of God, Jesus made propitiation for sins (4:10; "an atoning sacrifice"). The Father bears testimony to the Son as the Source of eternal life (5:9–12). The purpose of the epistle is found in 5:13: that those who believe in the Son of God might have assurance of eternal life. First John 5:20 states that the Son of God has come and given His followers understanding and that believers are in His Son Jesus Christ.

Jesus as Son of God in Revelation. Jesus is given the title Son of God only once in Revelation. This is in the letter to the church at Thyatira (2:18). The description which follows ("whose eyes are like blazing fire and whose feet are like burnished bronze") alludes to the vision of the exalted Jesus in 1:14–15.

JESUS AS SON OF MAN

The Son of Man in the gospel of John. Though the title "Son of Man" is more prominent in the Synoptic Gospels than in the gospel of John, the title does occur in several important passages in the fourth gospel (1:51; 3:13–14; 5:27; 6:27, 53, 62; 8:28; 9:35; 12:23, 34; 13:31). In a number of these instances the expression "Son of Man" is equivalent to the pronouns "I" or "me" when spoken by Jesus (e.g., 8:28, "when you have lifted up the Son of Man"; also see 6:53 and 9:35).

This is the same usage found in the Synoptic Gospels. Other occurrences of the phrase (1:51; 3:13–14; 6:62) are more indirect and might be understood as referring to someone other than Jesus except for the context.

One of the most important aspects of the "Son of Man" theme found in John's gospel is an emphasis on the descent and ascent of the Son of Man, which implies both preexistence and exaltation. Examples of this are in John 1:51; 3:13; and 6:62. In 1:51 Jesus spoke of angels ascending and descending on the Son of Man (rather than the ascent and descent of the Son Himself). Most interpreters agree that this is an allusion to Jacob's ladder, which was "resting on the earth, with its top reaching to heaven, and the angels of God . . . ascending and descending on it" (Gen. 28:12). The last two words of this verse ("on it") may also be translated "on him" (i.e., Jacob). A later work records rabbinic arguments about this point, some of which may date back to the time of Jesus (*Genesis Rabbah* 68:18; 69:7). In John 1:51 Jesus alluded to this incident in Jacob's life, drawing a parallel between Himself and Jacob as recipients of God's revelation. Jesus thereby assured the disciples that they would receive divine confirmation that He really is the Messiah sent from God. No longer is Bethel the place of God's revelation, as it was for Jacob. Now Jesus Himself is the "place" of God's revelation, just as later in John's gospel Jesus replaced the temple in Jerusalem (2:19–22) and Mount Gerizim in Samaria (4:20–24). The fulfillment of Jesus' promise to the disciples takes place in the remainder of the fourth gospel, especially in Jesus' death, resurrection, ascension, and exaltation through which He accomplished His return to the Father.

Jesus told Nicodemus, "No one has ever gone into heaven except the one who came from heaven—the Son of Man" (3:13). The following verse speaks of Jesus' return to heaven through crucifixion, resurrection, and exaltation ("the Son of Man must be lifted up," v. 14). This represents a further unfolding of the theme introduced in 1:51. Again the themes of divine revelation (to Nicodemus, but also to "everyone who believes," 3:14) and Jesus' upcoming suffering, death, and exaltation are connected with the title "Son of Man."

Jesus also spoke of His return to heaven: "What if you see the Son of Man ascend to where he was before!" (6:62). Here the preexistence of Jesus is explicitly stated, consistent with the presentation of the preexistent Logos in the prologue (1:1–14). The concept of descent and ascent connected with the title "Son of Man" is central to John's understanding of who Jesus is—the connecting link between earth and heaven (cf. 3:16). It is reflected in John's presentation of the Incarnation ("the Word became flesh," 1:14). It reflects Jesus' own consciousness of having come from God and returning to God (13:3). It is even possible to understand the entire fourth gospel as structured around the theme of Jesus' descent (1:19–12:50) and ascent (13:1–21:23), with the turning point being the arrival of Jesus' "hour" (12:20–36).

Related to the emphasis on descent and ascent connected with the Son of Man sayings in the gospel of John are statements concerning the glorification of the Son of Man (12:23; 13:31). This glorification began on earth, but continues in eternity. It is John's unique way of describing Jesus' suffering, death, resurrection, and ascension with their ultimate consequences. The hour of Jesus' glorification is the hour of His crucifixion, because for John the glory of the Cross has eclipsed its shame and humiliation. John's concept of Jesus' glory extends beyond the Son of Man sayings, however. It is also found in the prologue ("we have seen his glory," 1:14) and is repeated elsewhere (e.g., 2:11; 7:18; 8:50; 11:4; 12:41; 17:1–5, 22, 24).

Along the same lines are statements relating to the lifting up of the Son of Man (3:14; 8:28; 12:32–34). It is clear that the "lifting up" refers to Jesus' crucifixion, because 12:33 explains, "He said this to show the kind of death he was going to die." This also follows from the comparison with Moses lifting up the serpent (3:14) and Jesus' statement to His Jewish opponents that they would lift up the Son of Man (8:28). More than Jesus' crucifixion alone is in view, however, as 12:31 suggests. The glorification of the Son of Man involves not only His crucifixion but also His resurrection, ascension, and exaltation to "where he was before" (6:62).

Other passages in the gospel of John demonstrate the authority of the Son of Man. He has authority to give eternal life (3:14–15; 6:27) and to exercise judgment (5:25–27), a prerogative of God which indicates that the Son of Man is not merely human, but divine.

The Son of Man in Revelation. The phrase "Son of Man" occurs twice in Revelation (1:13; 14:14). These usages, similar to each other, differ from the use of the phrase as a title in the gospel of John. Instead, the exalted Jesus is described as "someone 'like a son of man'" (1:13), an allusion to the vision of Daniel 7:13. The expression refers to the figure in the vision rather than being a title.

In summary, Jesus' self-designation "Son of Man" in the Johannine literature involves allusions to the vision of Daniel 7:13, but it is also connected with the heavenly origin and preexistence of the Son, and His glorification and return to the Father through death, resurrection, ascension, and exaltation. The title is also used in connection with the Son's authority to give eternal life and to execute judgment.

JESUS AS MESSIAH

Of the four gospels only John used the transliterated form of the Hebrew or Aramaic term for Messiah (*Messias,* 1:41; 4:25) and, at the same time, gave the Greek translation (*Christos*). The word *Christos* occurs seventeen times and the compound title with the name Jesus (*Iesous Christos*) occurs twice. The question of Jesus' messiahship comes up repeatedly in the gospel of John. John the Baptist insisted that he was not the Christ (1:20, 3:28); the disciples confessed that Jesus is the Messiah (1:41); and the messiahship of Jesus was discussed by the Jewish leaders (7:52), the common people (7:25–31, 40–43; 12:34), and the Samaritans (4:29–30).

Jesus as Messiah in the gospel of John. Yet the messiahship of Jesus described in the gospel of John differs somewhat from that portrayed by the Synoptic Gospel writers. Both instances when the title Messiah is explicitly applied to Jesus occur early in the fourth gospel (1:41; 4:25). According to John's account, the first disciples recognized the messiahship of Jesus almost immediately when they met

Him initially, while the Synoptic Gospels mention nothing of this until Peter's confession at Caesarea Philippi (Matt. 16:16). Although some have argued against the historicity of the fourth gospel at this point, there is an explanation which does not place the Johannine account at odds with the Synoptic one. In John 1:41 Andrew told his brother Peter, "We have found the Messiah." Immediately after that, Philip told Nathanael, "We have found the one Moses wrote about in the Law, and about whom the prophets also wrote" (1:45). This suggests that the early disciples of Jesus understood messiahship against its Old Testament background rather than in a political sense. There is no indication from the context that this observation by the disciples is anything more than a first impression. The scope of who Jesus really is and what that would mean for them was an insight that would grow with time and that expressed itself later in Peter's confession recorded in the Synoptics. John was simply giving their first impressions, which the Synoptic accounts omitted. In John 4:25 the term "Messiah" was used by the Samaritan woman in a general sense, as her uncertainty about the exact mission of the coming one indicated ("When he comes, he will explain everything to us"). In any case, the title "Messiah" would not have conveyed to the Samaritans the political misunderstandings it would have held for the Jews.

In two places in his gospel, John gave information about contemporary Jewish messianic expectations. Some believed the Messiah would appear suddenly from an unknown origin (7:27), and some believed He would perform miraculous signs (v. 31). Others understood from the Law that the Messiah, when He came, would remain forever (12:34). John evidently included these (mistaken) insights to show that Jesus was not the Messiah the common people were expecting, and thus it is not surprising that they rejected Him (cf. 1:11–12). The belief that the Messiah would appear from a secret place excluded Jesus because His (supposed) origin was known (Nazareth). The belief that the Messiah would remain forever excluded Jesus because He predicted His departure (i.e., His approaching death on the cross). In both of these dialogues John showed that Jesus really is the Messiah and that the expectations of the people were mistaken. In 7:29 Jesus answered the question of origin by appealing to His heavenly origin, which really was unknown. In 12:35–36 Jesus pointed out that spiritual enlightenment (which He Himself provides) is needed to understand a suffering and dying Messiah.

A further use of the title Messiah is found in the confession of Martha (John 11:27) where it is linked with the title Son of God ("'Yes, Lord,' she told him, 'I believe that you are the Christ, the Son of God, who has come into the world'"). Again it is clear that political concepts are excluded in 11:27 because the two titles ("Christ" and "Son of God") are linked, and Martha made reference to Jesus' heavenly origin. Similarly, John recorded Jesus' rejection of the attempt to make Him king after the feeding of the 5,000 (6:15), a further exclusion of political implications.

The title Messiah is also found in John 20:31, which is viewed by most interpreters as a major statement of purpose for the writing of the Gospel. Again as in 11:27 this title is linked with the title Son of God ("But these are written that you may believe that Jesus is the Christ, the Son of God, and that by believing you may have life in his name."). Although more emphasis in the fourth gospel is placed on Jesus as Son of God, the affirmation of His messiahship plays an important part. One gets the picture from John's gospel that Jesus is the Messiah, not in the sense of popular political expectations, but in a different sense which is related to His divine Sonship and is in line with Old Testament rather than first-century Jewish expectations.

Jesus as Messiah in the Johannine epistles. In the Johannine epistles the term *Messiah* is used as a title associated with Jesus. The combined form "Jesus Christ" is found in 1 John 1:3; 2:1; 3:23; 4:2; 5:6, 20; and in 2 John 7. Important for the understanding of Jesus' role as Messiah are 1 John 2:22 and 4:3 (see also 2 John 7) where John's opponents were denying that Jesus is the Messiah. As stated earlier, many interpreters see some early form of Docetism here, a heresy that distinguished the human Jesus from the heavenly Christ and placed faith in the latter to the disregard of the former. John emphasized that such a view is not only unacceptable Christology, but is an evidence of the presence of antichrist (1 John 4:3). It is a basic tenet of the Christian faith to accept Jesus as the Messiah (5:1).

Jesus as Messiah in Revelation. Only three references to the term Messiah are found in Revelation (Rev. 1:1–2, 5). All of these are combined with the name Jesus and used as a title similar to the combined form "Jesus Christ" in the Johannine epistles.

Messiah and King of Israel. Closely related to Jesus' description as Messiah in the Johannine literature is the title "King of Israel," which occurs in John 1:49 and 12:13. In 1:49 Nathanael exclaimed that Jesus is both Son of God and King of Israel. In 12:13 the crowd at the Triumphal Entry shouted, "Blessed is he who comes in the name of the Lord! Blessed is the King of Israel!" This is followed almost immediately in John's account by the citation of Zechariah 9:9, the same prophetic passage quoted by Matthew in connection with Jesus' Davidic kingship (Matt. 21:4–9). Therefore, it seems clear that the title "King of Israel" for John carries connotations of Davidic kingship and that Jesus is understood to be the heir and successor to the Davidic throne. This is indirectly supported by the question raised by the multitude about Jesus' origin: "How can the Christ come from Galilee? Does not the Scripture say that the Christ will come from David's family and from Bethlehem, the town where David lived?" (John 7:41–42). In John's narrative the question reveals ignorance about Jesus' true origin, an ignorance that becomes ironic because the reader of his gospel is expected to know that Jesus really did come from Bethlehem (and before that, from heaven). Although the question itself reveals popular ignorance, it assumes the reader has knowledge of the accounts of Jesus' birth in Bethlehem and of His descent from David found in the Synoptic Gospels.

JESUS AS THE LOGOS

The Greek term *logos* occurs many times in the gospel of John in several of its normal senses (e.g., "statement" or "saying" in John 4:39, 50; 6:60; 7:36;

15:20; 18:9; 19:8; God's "word" as revelation in John 10:35; God's "word" revealed through Christ, John 17:14). But the most significant use of *logos* in John's gospel occurs in the prologue (1:1–18) in 1:1 ("In the beginning was the Word") and 1:14 ("The Word became flesh"). Here the term is used as a technical designation for Jesus Himself, and much scholarly effort has been devoted to understanding the background and use of *logos* in these two verses.

It has not been proven beyond doubt whether the term *logos,* as John used it, derives from Jewish or Greek (Hellenistic) backgrounds or from some other source. Nor is it plain what associations John meant to convey by his use of it. Readers are left to work out the precise allusions and significance for themselves. John was working with allusions to the Old Testament, but he was also writing to an audience familiar with Hellenistic (Greek) thought, and certain aspects of his use of *logos* would occur to them. Both backgrounds are important for understanding this title as John used it in 1:1, 14.

The Greek background of the term. As a Greek philosophical term, *logos* referred to the "world-soul," that is, the soul of the universe. This was an all-pervading principle, the rational principle of the universe. It was a creative energy. In one sense, all things came from it; in another sense, people derived their wisdom from it. These concepts are at least as old as the Greek philosopher Heraclitus (6th century B.C.), who wrote that the *logos* is "always existent" and "all things happen through this *logos.*"[14] In later Hellenistic thought these concepts persisted but were modified somewhat. Philo of Alexandria, the Jewish philosopher of the early first century, frequently mentioned the *logos* (it appears over 1,400 times in his writings), but he was concerned with his Platonic distinction between this material world and the real, heavenly world of ideas. The Stoics, another group of Hellenistic philosophers, developed the concept of *logos.* They abandoned Plato's heavenly archetypes in favor of the thought (closer to Heraclitus) that the universe is pervaded by *logos,* the eternal Reason. The Stoics, convinced of the ultimate rationality of the universe, used the term *logos* to express this conviction. For them it was the "force" that originated, permeated, and directed all things. It was the supreme governing principle of the universe. But the Stoics did not think of the *logos* as personal, nor did they understand it as one would understand God (i.e., as a person to be worshiped). In fact, they did not even think of a single *logos,* but of *logoi spermatikoi* ("seminal Reasons"), the forces responsible for the creative cycles in nature. Later Stoics considered the *logos* to be the "world-soul" in a pantheistic sense.

Thus John was using a term that would be widely recognized in Hellenistic circles. But the average person would not know its precise significance, any more than most people today would precisely understand terms like "relativity" or "space-time continuum." But it would clearly mean something very important.

The Jewish background of the term. Recently more attention has been given to Jewish sources as a background for John's use of *logos* in his gospel prologue. First, there is the Old Testament to consider. The words of John 1:1 ("In the begin-

14. Heraclitus *Fragmenta* 1, 50, 54, 114.

ning") inevitably recall Genesis 1:1. But the use of *logos* in John 1:1 also suggests Genesis 1:3 ("and God said") as well as Psalm 33:6 ("By the word of the Lord were the heavens made"). There is also the near personalization of wisdom in Proverbs 8:22–31. In many places the Targums (Aramaic translations of the Old Testament, first oral and later written) substitute *Memra* ("word") as an intermediary for God. For example, in Exodus 19:17, "And Moses brought the people out of the camp to meet God" (NASB). The Palestinian Targum reads, "to meet the Word of God." Targum Jonathan uses this expression some 320 times. Some say this is not significant because *Memra* does not refer to a being distinct from God. It is just a way of referring to God Himself. But this is the point; people familiar with the Targums were familiar with *Memra* as a designation for God. John did not use the term *logos* the way the Targums used *Memra*, but to those familiar with the Targums, *logos* would have aroused similar associations, with which John would be in agreement.[15]

The use of the term in the prologue to John's gospel. Why did John choose to call Jesus the Logos in the prologue to his gospel, and what did he mean by it? As to why the term was used, the answer probably lies with John's audience. John gave no explanation of the Logos, apparently assuming his readers would understand the idea. Greek readers would probably think he was referring to the rational principle that guided the universe and would be shocked to find that this Logos had become not only personalized but incarnate (John 1:14). Jewish readers would be more prepared for some sort of personalized preexistent Wisdom, but they too would be amazed at the idea of incarnation. John presented Jesus as the true Logos as preparation for his own presentation of Jesus as the Son of God. After John 1:14, John never again used the absolute, specific, unrelated term *logos*. After this the Greek word is always modified or clarified by the context, and does not occur again in the gospel to refer to Jesus as the Logos. There is no need for this since in 1:14 the Word is now incarnate as Jesus of Nazareth, and from this point on He is called Jesus. In other words, Jesus and the Logos are identical; the Logos is the preexistent Christ.

John's Logos-Christology has three main emphases. First, John 1:1 outlines the relationship of the Word to God. John 1:1a ("In the beginning was the Word") forms a clear statement of preexistence. John 1:1b ("the Word was with God") distinguishes God (the Father) from the Word, showing that the two are not interchangeable, and yet suggesting there is a personal relationship between the two. John 1:1c ("and the Word was God") affirms the full deity of the Word, and yet implies that there is more to God than the Word alone.

Second, John 1:3 gives the relationship of the Word to Creation: "Through him all things were made; without him nothing was made that has been made." The Logos is clearly separate from Creation since He was the Agent who brought it about.

15. See further M. McNamara, "Logos of the Fourth Gospel and *Memra* of the Palestinian Targum, Ex. 12:42," *Expository Times* 79 (1967–1968): 115–17.

Third, John 1:14 shows the relationship of the Word to humanity: "The Word became flesh and made his dwelling among us." This simple statement sums up the Incarnation. The word "flesh" is not used here in the Pauline sense of "sinful flesh" because the notion of sinfulness is incompatible with John's presentation of Jesus (John 10:30; 17:22; 1 John 2:1; 3:5). Rather, it refers to the humanity of Jesus in His humiliation. Thus the Logos terminology of John's prologue affirms both the full essential deity of Jesus (1:1) and His full humanity (1:14).

Other Johannine references to the term. The title Logos also appears in 1 John 1:1 with similar meaning. In particular, Jesus is called the Logos of life, emphasizing His role as Giver of life similar to the statements in the prologue of the gospel (see John 1:4, 9). First John 1:1 also implies the Incarnation and places the Logos in a historical framework through its emphasis on eyewitnesses who have heard, seen, and handled the Word.

The term *logos* also appears once in Revelation in the same sense as in the prologue to the fourth gospel. In Revelation 19:13 Jesus Christ is called the Logos of God. This use of the Logos terminology shows a close link between the gospel of John and Revelation and is one of the indications of common authorship.

JESUS AS THE LAMB OF GOD

One of the titles applied to Jesus in both the gospel of John and Revelation is "the Lamb" (John 1:29, 36; Rev. 5:6, 8, 12–13; 6:1, 16; 7:9–10, 14, 17; 12:11; 13:8; 14:1, 4, 10; 15:3; 17:14; 19:7, 9; 21:9, 14, 22–23, 27; 22:1, 3). The Greek words for "lamb" are different, however: the gospel uses *amnos* while Revelation uses *arnion*. The imagery is certainly related but is not identical.

The Lamb of God in the gospel of John. Jesus is called "the Lamb of God" twice in the gospel of John, both times by John the Baptist (John 1:29, 36). On the first occasion this is clarified with the additional description, "who takes away the sin of the world" (1:29). Connected as it is with Jesus' baptism by John (mentioned indirectly in vv. 32–34) and the beginning of Jesus' public ministry, the title says something significant about Jesus' mission. That this mission is primarily redemptive accords well with the taking away of sin and also with other statements later in John's gospel: "For God did not send his Son into the world to condemn the world, but to save the world through him" (3:17); and "Now we have heard for ourselves, and we know that this man really is the Savior of the world" (4:42).

The Lamb imagery in the gospel of John suggests allusions to two Old Testament contexts. One of these is the "Suffering Servant" passage in Isaiah 53:7: "he was led like a lamb to the slaughter, and as a sheep before her shearers is silent, so he did not open his mouth."[16] All of the Servant songs occur in Isaiah 40–55. John the Baptist quoted from this section of Isaiah (40:3) in John 1:23 in the same context as the "Lamb of God" statements. In addition, Jesus is related to the Suffering Servant later in the gospel of John: John 12:38 is a quotation of Isaiah 53:1. All of

---

16. The Greek word for "lamb" used in Isaiah 53:7 in the Septuagint (the Greek translation of the Old Testament) is the same as the word used in John 1:29, 36 (*amnos*).

this suggests the Suffering Servant is in the background of John the Baptist's use of the title "Lamb of God" to describe Jesus in John 1:29, 36.

Another possible Old Testament allusion suggested by the Lamb imagery in the fourth gospel is the Passover lamb. Passover symbolism is certainly present in the gospel of John, especially in relation to the death of Jesus. According to John 19:14, Jesus was condemned at noon on the day before the Passover at the very time the priests began to slay the paschal lambs in the Jerusalem temple. Furthermore, hyssop was used to give Jesus a sponge of wine while He was on the cross (John 19:29); hyssop was also used to smear the blood of the Passover lamb on the doorposts (Ex. 12:22). Also John 19:36 sees a fulfillment of Old Testament Scripture in that none of Jesus' bones were broken; according to Exodus 12:46 no bone of the Passover lamb was to be broken. True, the Old Testament did not regard the Passover lamb as a sacrifice per se, but as a symbol of God's deliverance. Nevertheless, by Jesus' time the sacrificial imagery in the Passover lamb began to merge with the symbol of deliverance (cf. 1 Cor. 5:7, "For Christ, our Passover lamb, has been sacrificed") so that the Passover lamb imagery was appropriate to apply to Jesus' sacrificial death.

Both sets of imagery, the Suffering Servant background from Isaiah 53:7 and the Passover lamb imagery from Exodus 12:46 and elsewhere, are in the background of John the Baptist's designation of Jesus as "the Lamb of God, who takes away the sin of the world" (John 1:29). The Passover lamb imagery may carry slightly more emphasis in light of John's later use of this imagery in connection with Jesus' crucifixion.

The Lamb imagery in Revelation. Jesus is called "the Lamb" twenty-seven times in Revelation (5:6, 8, 12–13; 6:1, 16; 7:9–10, 14, 17; 12:11; 13:8; 14:1, 4 [twice], 10; 15:3; 17:14; 19:7, 9; 21:9, 14, 22–23, 27; 22:1, 3). In each of these instances the Greek word *arnion* is used. Other Jewish apocalyptic literature in the first century refers to a conquering lamb who will destroy evil in the world. The Testament of Joseph 19:8 (one of the Testaments of the Twelve Patriarchs) speaks of a lamb who overcomes evil beasts and crushes them underfoot.[17] First Enoch 90:6–12 contains an extended discussion of the Maccabees as horned lambs. None of this imagery is particularly helpful for understanding John's use of "the Lamb" as a title for Jesus in Revelation, but it is possible that John was aware that he was using a standard apocalyptic term that would be understood as such.

More to the point is the Old Testament background already discussed in relation to the "Lamb of God" in the gospel of John. Both sets of imagery, the Suffering Servant from Isaiah 53:7 and the Passover lamb from Exodus 12:46 and elsewhere, form the background to the lamb imagery in Revelation as well. Here, however, there is one significant difference. The Lamb in Revelation 5:6 has already been sacrificed and is now "standing in the center of the throne." The sacrifice of the Lamb has already taken place; now He is exalted and victorious over all His enemies. With this imagery John has brought together one of the central themes

17. There is the possibility that a later Christian made additions to the Jewish work.

of the entire New Testament, namely, victory through sacrifice. Indeed, whenever the Lamb appears in Revelation He is always victorious. For example, the Lamb in 5:6 was described in the previous verse as "the Lion of the tribe of Judah," who "has triumphed." One of the major accomplishments of this use of imagery is to unite the victorious Christ of Revelation with the sacrificial Victim of the four gospels. He is one and the same, and even though triumphant in Revelation, He still carries the marks of His sacrifice ("looking as if it had been slain," Rev. 5:6).

THE GLORIFICATION OF JESUS IN THE GOSPEL OF JOHN

In the gospel of John Jesus' glorification collectively describes His death, resurrection, ascent, and exaltation. This is clear in a passage like John 7:39 where John wrote in an explanatory note that "Up to that time the Spirit had not been given, since Jesus had not yet been glorified." Here the "glorification" presupposes Jesus' death, resurrection, and return to the Father.[18] "Glorification" in relation to Jesus' death, resurrection, and return to the Father is also mentioned in John 12:16: "Only after Jesus was glorified did they [the disciples] realize that these things had been written about him and that they had done these things to him."

The background to such an understanding of Jesus' death, resurrection, ascension, and exaltation may be found in John's use of the term "glory" (*doxa*) in the fourth gospel. It occurs for the first time in John 1:14 where the Evangelist testified concerning the Incarnate Word, "We have seen His glory, the glory of the One and Only, who came from the Father, full of grace and truth." Jesus is presented in the gospel of John as the full and complete Revelation of God's presence and nature (e.g., John 1:18). This self-revelation of God in the person of Jesus took place not only through Jesus' earthly lifestyle, but also through the sign-miracles He performed (2:11; 11:4, 40). John mentioned this in his explanatory comment following the miracle of the water turned into wine at the wedding feast in Cana. "This, the first of his miraculous signs, Jesus performed at Cana in Galilee. He thus revealed his glory, and his disciples put their faith in him" (2:11). But Jesus' glory did not begin with His incarnation or His public ministry, including the sign-miracles. For John, this glory was always possessed by the preincarnate Christ in eternity past. In His prayer in John 17 Jesus referred to this preincarnate glory. "And now, Father, glorify me in your presence with the glory I had with you before the world began" (17:5). This glory, John said (12:41), was also spoken of by the prophet Isaiah in the Old Testament (Isa. 6:1–3).

With this background in mind John's presentation of Jesus' death, resurrection, ascension, and exaltation as glorification can be evaluated. For John, the manifestation of glory that began at Jesus' incarnation (John 1:14) and continued in the sign-miracles (2:11) was supremely manifested in Jesus' sacrificial death on the cross. In 12:23 Jesus announced that the hour had come for the Son of Man to be glorified. The following two verses make it clear that this is ultimately a reference

18. Elsewhere Jesus, in His Farewell Discourse, told the disciples that the Holy Spirit would not come unless He went away (John 16:7, a reference to His departure through death).

to Jesus' death on the cross, which would result in many people believing in Him. Jesus compared His own death to the "death" of a grain of wheat which, after falling into the ground, produces many other grains of wheat (v. 24). This sacrificial death was part of Jesus' mission from the beginning. As Jesus declared, "it was for this very reason I came to this hour. Father, glorify your name" (vv. 27–28). In the same context Jesus referred to His death as being "lifted up from the earth" (v. 32), which John interpreted as a prophecy of the kind of death He was to die, namely, crucifixion (v. 33). A Johannine wordplay is present here, since "lifting up" refers not only to Jesus' elevation on the cross but also to His exaltation as well.[19] For John, Jesus' death is part and parcel of that exaltation, as much as His resurrection and return to the Father's side. The same imagery of glorification in relation to the impending death of Jesus is also seen in John 13. After Judas's departure, Jesus declared, "Now is the Son of Man glorified and God is glorified in him. If God is glorified in him, God will glorify the Son in himself, and will glorify him at once" (13:31–32). Here Jesus was speaking proleptically of His death and return to the Father. The departure of the traitor Judas to perform his act of betrayal (v. 30) was the immediate cause of Jesus' arrest, trials, and crucifixion. Then Jesus informed His disciples that He would be with them only a little longer (v. 33), again a reference to the immediacy of His death. In this context Jesus spoke of glorification no less than five times, twice of God being glorified in the Son and three times of His own glorification.

However, John's presentation of Jesus' glorification did not end with His death on the cross. It involved a return to the preincarnate state of glory which Jesus experienced with the Father (17:5) following the humiliation of the Incarnation and His suffering and death. This return to the Father involved not only Jesus' death on the cross, but also His resurrection and ascension to the presence of the Father as well. Jesus' statement to the disciples in John 13:33, "Where I am going, you cannot come," implies not only that Jesus was about to depart through death, but that He was going back to the Father.[20] In fact, the entire movement of John's gospel may be thought of as Jesus' descent followed by His ascent. This movement is expressed in the prologue to the gospel (1:1–18) and reiterated in the remainder of the work. In the prologue, the preincarnate Word, who was in the presence of the Father (v. 1), came down into the world but was rejected by it (vv. 9–10), and then went back to the presence of the Father again ("at the Father's side," v. 18). The same movement is found again in the remainder of the gospel of John. Jesus is the one who has come down from heaven (3:13), but He was rejected by His own people who preferred the darkness to the light (v. 19; cf. 1:10). This rejection characterized Jesus' entire public ministry. As the Evangelist summarized, "Even after Jesus had done all these miraculous signs in their presence, they still would not believe in him" (12:37).

19. The same wordplay with the same double meaning is found in the "lifting up" of the Son of Man in John 3:14–15.

20. Later, of course, after Jesus had prepared a place for them, the disciples would be able to join Him there (John 14:2–3).

After this, the upward movement of Jesus' return to the Father began, predicted already by Jesus in John 12:32 ("when I am lifted up from the earth"). For John, the crucifixion of Jesus is an integral part of this upward movement. Jesus lay down His life, but He did so voluntarily, only to take it up again (10:17–18). Pilate presented Jesus to the Jewish people as King (19:14), the Jewish leaders categorically and finally rejected Him (v. 15), and then He was displayed as King on the cross for all the world to see (vv. 19–20). The upward movement continued with Jesus' resurrection and ascension (20:17) in which He returned triumphant to the Father's side (cf. 1:18).

The word "hour" (*hōra*, 2:4; 4:21, 23; 5:25, 28; 7:30; 8:20; 12:23, 27; 13:1; 16:21; 17:1) conveys an important concept in the gospel of John relating to Jesus' exaltation. It refers to the special time in Jesus' earthly life when He was to leave this world and return to the Father (13:1), the hour when the Son of man was to be glorified (17:1). This was accomplished through His suffering, death, resurrection (and ascension, though this was not emphasized by John). John 7:30 and 8:20 imply that Jesus' arrest and death are included in His "hour." John 12:23 and 17:1, referring to the glorification of the Son, imply that the resurrection and ascension are included as well. In John 2:4 Jesus' remark to His mother indicates that the time for this self-manifestation had not yet arrived; His identity as Messiah was not yet to be publicly revealed.

THE SPIRIT/PARACLETE IN THE JOHANNINE WRITINGS

THE HOLY SPIRIT IN THE GOSPEL OF JOHN

Much of the material concerning the Holy Spirit in the gospel of John is found in the Farewell Discourse of Jesus to His disciples in chapters 14–17. Here Jesus spoke of the Spirit as a "Paraclete" (*paraklētos*). Before this, six passages in the fourth gospel include significant statements about the Holy Spirit.

The Spirit in the opening chapters of John's gospel. Jesus' baptism by John the Baptist is the first reference to the Holy Spirit in the gospel of John (1:29–34). The major difference between John's account of Jesus' baptism and that of the Synoptics is that John recorded the reaction of John the Baptist himself. He said he saw the Spirit come down from heaven as a dove and remain on Jesus (1:32). The act of baptizing is not even mentioned, although it is clearly implied from the context. The dove is mentioned in the Synoptic accounts of Jesus' baptism as well. John the Baptist said he would not have recognized Jesus, except that God revealed to him that the one on whom the Spirit descended would baptize with the Spirit (v. 33). The account in the fourth gospel does not mention the voice from heaven at Jesus' baptism, as do the Synoptics (Matt. 3:17; Mark 1:11; Luke 3:22).[21] But the Baptist,

---

21. This omission does not imply that John's account contradicts that of the Synoptics. John was more interested in the personal recollection of John the Baptist concerning the prophetic revelation he received. Since the Baptist's conclusion is the same as the pronouncement from heaven ("this is the Son of God") and since John 1:29–34 is presented not as a direct account of Jesus' baptism but as the Baptist's recollection of it, the voice from heaven is not mentioned.

as a result of the revelation he received, came to the same conclusion: "I have seen and I testify that this is the Son of God" (John 1:34). Thus the Evangelist's account of Jesus' baptism by John is not an alternate version to that of the Synoptics. It implies a second personal and supplementary revelation to the Baptist himself. He then became a witness to the identity of Jesus as the Messiah.[22]

Two times in John the Baptist's account he made mention of the Spirit "remaining" on Jesus (1:32–33). This is extremely important as a description of the Spirit's relationship to Jesus because permanence is implied. The Greek phrase *menein en tini* used here means "an inward, enduring personal communion."[23] The phrase is used elsewhere in the fourth gospel to describe the permanent mutual indwelling relationship of the Father and the Son (John 14:10–11, "it is the Father, living in me"). This relationship between the Father and the Son becomes the paradigm of the believer's relationship in God the Father (1 John 4:15, "God lives in him and he in God"), in Jesus (John 6:56, "remains"; 15:6, "remain"), and even in Jesus' word (8:31, "hold to"). The phrase *menein en* is used in 1 John 3:24 ("lives") to describe the indwelling of God in the believer through the Spirit, and repeatedly in John 15:4–11 ("remain," etc.) to describe the relationship of Jesus to His disciples. It is significant that this phrase also describes the Spirit of truth as permanently remaining with believers in John 14:17 ("he lives with you"). As the one on whom the Spirit permanently resides, Jesus is able to dispense the Spirit to others (John 1:33, "he who will baptize with the Holy Spirit"; note also 15:26; 16:7; 20:22).

The remaining references to the Spirit in the opening chapters of the gospel of John are found in discourses by Jesus. Jesus told Nicodemus, "no one can enter the kingdom of God unless he is born of water and the Spirit" (3:5). Although the reference to water is debated (whether it refers to physical birth or baptism), the thrust of the passage is clearly on the regenerating power of the Spirit in believers. This idea is reinforced in the following verse, where Jesus drew an analogy between what is born of flesh and what is born of the Spirit (v. 6). The point Jesus was making is that like begets like. Contrary to Paul, John did not use the word "flesh" here with negative moral connotations in opposition to "spirit." John was simply pointing out that spiritual birth does not come through human means.[24] Regeneration can be achieved only through the work of the Holy Spirit, not by any human effort. The entire spiritual existence of the believer depends on the work of the Holy Spirit. It should not be surprising that Nicodemus misunderstood this radical assertion. Nevertheless, Jesus expected Nicodemus to have understood at least part of this: "You

22. Note John 1:31 ("the reason I came baptizing with water was that he might be revealed to Israel") and the repeated use of the word "witness" (NASB; cf. NIV "testimony," 1:32; "testify," 1:34).

23. Walter Bauer, William F. Arndt, and F. Wilbur Gingrich, *A Greek-English Lexicon of the New Testament and Other Early Christian Literature,* 2d ed., rev. F. Wilbur Gingrich and Frederick W. Danker (Chicago: Univ. of Chicago, 1979), 504.

24. In the statement "the Word became flesh" (John 1:14), certainly the Evangelist would not have wanted to suggest anything morally negative about Jesus as the Incarnate Word.

are Israel's teacher . . . and do you not understand these things?" (v. 10). Of the Old Testament passages that relate water and spirit, the most important is Ezekiel 36:25–27, where "water" indicates cleansing from impurity and "spirit" refers to the indwelling Holy Spirit who will enable people to follow God and obey Him more fully.

Another reference to the Spirit is found in the concluding words of John 3: "For the one whom God has sent speaks the words of God, for God gives the Spirit without limit" (v. 34). The first part of the verse clearly refers to Jesus Himself as "the one whom God has sent." The latter part of the verse has sometimes been understood to refer to believers as the recipients of the Spirit in unlimited measure, but it is far more probable that these words also refer to Jesus. Verse 34 occurs toward the end of the final section in the fourth gospel dealing with the witness of John the Baptist to Jesus (3:27–36). It is not entirely clear whether verses 31–36 are to be taken as the words of John the Baptist or the Evangelist, but in either case they contain testimony about Jesus as Messiah and Son of God. Thus it is better to understand the latter part of verse 34 as referring to Jesus as well. He has been given the Spirit without limit as part of all things the Father has placed in His hands (v. 35).

In Jesus' dialogue with the Samaritan woman in John 4, He made a statement about the nature of God Himself. "God is spirit, and His worshipers must worship in spirit and truth" (v. 24). Although neither of these two uses of the word "spirit" refer directly to the Holy Spirit, the notion that worship must take place in spirit and truth presupposes the activity of the Spirit of truth who leads believers into true worship.

Following the Bread of Life discourse, Jesus told some of His disciples who were grumbling, "the Spirit gives life; the flesh counts for nothing" (6:63). Already seen in John 3 is the Spirit's role in the giving of spiritual life. Likewise in the Old Testament the Spirit of God was associated with the giving of life (Gen. 1:2; Ezek. 37:1–14). Jesus Himself, as the One on whom the Spirit remains (John 1:32–33) and the One to whom God gives the Spirit without limit (3:34), now said, "The words I have spoken to you are spirit and they are life" (6:63). The words He spoke were the product of the life-giving Spirit and, properly understood and accepted, they produce eternal life in the hearer. If Jesus' words are thus understood and appropriated, the hearers would recognize Him to be the true Bread from heaven who gives His flesh for the life of the world (v. 51).

The promise of the Holy Spirit is made in John 7:38–39. After Jesus' statement about streams of living water in verse 38, the Evangelist added an interpretive comment, "By this he meant the Spirit, whom those who believed in him were later to receive" (v. 39). The close connection between water and Spirit is similar to that found in 3:5. John 7:39 also affirms that the Spirit would not be given to believers until Jesus was glorified (cf. 20:22), a reflective comment that illustrates the postresurrection point of view of the Evangelist. The implication of John's comment in 7:39 is that the disciples did not understand Jesus' remarks at the time He made them, but understood them later with the insight they received after His resurrection (cf. 12:16). It is generally agreed that the "streams of living water" mentioned in 7:38 refer to the Holy Spirit (given the connection between water and the Spirit in 3:5). This leads to the further observation that the "living water" Jesus offered the Samaritan woman (4:10) should also be understood as a reference to the Spirit. This accords well with Jesus' later remarks to the woman about the need for true worship to take place "in spirit and in truth" (vv. 23–24).

It is much more difficult to decide who is the source of the "living water" which represents the Holy Spirit in John 7:39. The NIV punctuation of verses 37–38 suggests that the final "him" in verse 38 is the believer: "Whoever believes in me . . . streams of living water will flow from within him." Although John 4:14 is often suggested as a parallel, nowhere else in the Johannine literature of the New Testament is there a reference to the believer being the source of the Spirit poured out for others. John did, however, portray Jesus in this role (6:35; Rev. 22:17). Thus it is better to understand Jesus Himself as the source of the living water (the Holy Spirit), as suggested by the NIV marginal reading for John 7:37–38: "If anyone is thirsty, let him come to me. And let him drink, who believes in me. As the Scripture has said, streams of living water will flow from within him."

The Paraclete passages in the Farewell Discourse. In John 14:16 Jesus promised that in response to His disciples' love as shown by their continued obedience, He would ask the Father, who would send "another Paraclete" (*allon paraklēton*). This implies that a Paraclete had already been with the disciples. It seems best to understand the previous Paraclete as a reference to Jesus Himself, since "another Paraclete" was to come when He departed. First John 2:1 presents Jesus as a Paraclete in His role as Intercessor in heaven. Here the implication is that Jesus had also been a Paraclete to the disciples during His earthly ministry. Much is often made of the word "other" (*allos*) here, that it should be understood to mean "another of the same kind." Not all commentators agree on a sharp distinction between the two words *allos* and *heteros* ("another of a different kind") in this context. But on the whole Jesus, although He did not speak of Himself in the fourth gospel as a Paraclete, nevertheless performed actions for His disciples that a Paraclete would perform.

It is important to note that John's comparison of the Holy Spirit as Paraclete to Jesus' own role as a Paraclete while with the disciples strongly implies that the Spirit must be as personal as Jesus Himself is. In addition, the range of functions the Holy Spirit performs for the disciples after Jesus' departure (John 14:26; 15:26; 16:8–15) point to the Spirit's personal nature.

The Greek word *paraklētos* ("paraclete") itself is difficult to translate. The English translation "Comforter" is traditional; apparently it goes back to John Wycliffe. Most would agree that this is not the idea of the Greek term, but would not agree on how in fact it should be translated. Perhaps the best suggestion is Goodspeed's, who concludes that the word meant a person called to someone else's aid in court, a helper, intercessor, pleader, or character witness. "Defender" comes close to conveying this idea, but more than just a defense witness is in view. Jesus' statements about the coming Paraclete teaching and reminding the disciples go beyond this meaning and call for a broader translation. Goodspeed suggests "Helper" as a translation in the gospel of John and "One who will intercede for us" in 1 John 2:1.[25] Clearly the referent in all the uses of *paraklētos* in the Gospel of John is the Holy Spirit (cf. John 14:26), while in 1 John 2:1 the referent is Jesus Himself.

In addition to the title "Paraclete," the Holy Spirit is mentioned once directly in Jesus' Farewell Discourse (John 14:26), and the title "Spirit of truth" occurs three times (14:17; 15:26; 16:13). Above all else the Holy Spirit in the Farewell Discourse is portrayed as the Spirit of witness or testimony. His chief function is to bear witness to Jesus (15:26; 16:13–15). This includes bringing glory to Jesus by bearing witness to Him (14:14). Alternatively the Spirit is said to bear witness to the truth, because Jesus Himself is truth (14:6). Therefore the Spirit may be called the Spirit of truth (16:13), that is, the Spirit who communicates truth to the disciples, and His function is to guide the disciples into all the truth (16:13). One may even go so far as to say that the Spirit is the truth (1 John 5:6 NIV; 5:7 NASB) just as Jesus is the truth (John 14:6).

For John, truth is not merely something to be known or believed, but something to be practiced (7:17). When the apostle wrote of the Spirit guiding the disciples into all the truth (16:13), he did not mean truth in the broad or exhaustive sense as it is used today (i.e., the truths of modern science, medicine, technology, etc.). He was speaking of the experience the disciples had undergone in their understanding of who Jesus was while He was with them compared to their understanding of who Jesus is after His death, resurrection, and glorification. This is what Jesus had promised the disciples: "He [the Spirit] will teach you all things, and bring to your remembrance all that I said to you" (14:26 NASB). This is exactly what happened to the apostles. Only after Jesus' resurrection did they come to understand the truth that Jesus had taught them and acted out before their eyes (2:22).

The world, on the other hand, cannot receive the Spirit or know anything about Him; it is only to the followers of Jesus that the testimony of the Spirit can come (14:17). This is parallel to the manifestation of Jesus Himself not to the world, but only to believers (v. 22). The Spirit's testimony to the world comes through His joint witness with Jesus' disciples (15:26–27). This appears to be the case even in the one passage about the Paraclete concerned with His conviction of the world (16:8–11).

The coming of the Holy Spirit to the followers of Jesus depended on His departure and return to the Father (16:7). Again this is consistent with the interpretive comment the Evangelist made in 7:39: "Up to that time the Spirit had not been given, since Jesus had not yet been glorified." On other occasions the Spirit is said to be a gift from the Father (14:16, 26) sent by the Son (14:26; 15:26; 16:7). Whatever else is meant by the difficult statement that the Spirit "goes out from the Father" (15:26), it implies that the Spirit shares the same essential nature as the Father. In fact, John was indicating here the parallelism between the mission of the Son, sent from God (3:17, 34; 5:36–38; 6:29, 57; 7:29; 8:42; 10:36; 11:42; 17:3, 8, 18, 21,

25. E. J. Goodspeed, *Problems of New Testament Translation* (Chicago: Univ. of Chicago, 1945), 110–11.

23, 25; 20:21), and the mission of the Son's replacement, the Holy Spirit, who would be "another Paraclete" to the disciples and who would enable them to carry on Jesus' mission after He returned to the Father. Thus although it is not explicitly stated, the passage has strong Trinitarian implications.

Finally, Jesus in His Farewell Discourse mentioned the Holy Spirit's indwelling of believers: "he lives with you and will be in you" (14:17). In the previous verse Jesus promised His followers that the Spirit would be with them forever, suggesting the permanent nature of the Spirit's indwelling of believers. This is consistent with Jesus' own statements about the security of His followers (10:27–30).

The Johannine foreshadowing of Pentecost. The final mention of the Holy Spirit in the fourth gospel is in 20:22: "And with that he [Jesus] breathed on them and said, 'Receive the Holy Spirit.'" It is common for this statement to be understood as John's version of Pentecost, the fulfillment of Jesus' promise in the Farewell Discourse (16:7) to send the Holy Spirit after His return to the Father. It is better, however, to view Jesus' action in breathing on the disciples as symbolic of the outpouring of the Spirit at Pentecost rather than as an actual bestowal of the Spirit at the time of this postresurrection appearance to the disciples. The disciples' behavior in the remainder of the gospel of John does not reflect the confident and powerful behavior they exhibited following the day of Pentecost according to Acts 2. In fact, if John 20:22 represents an actual bestowal of the Holy Spirit in some sense, one of the Twelve, Thomas, was not even there to receive the Spirit at the time (v. 24). Jesus had already made other proleptic statements in the gospel of John, notably with regard to His glorification that followed His death, resurrection, and return to the Father (17:1–5). It should not be surprising to find Him doing the same in relation to the giving of the Spirit.

THE HOLY SPIRIT IN THE JOHANNINE EPISTLES

Four passages in 1 John mention the Holy Spirit. Two of these deal with the assurance of believers that God resides in them. First John 3:24 states, "And this is how we know that he lives in us: we know it by the Spirit he gave us." Similarly 1 John 4:13 appeals to the presence of the Spirit in the lives of believers as assurance of their relationship to God. This language is similar to that of John 15:1–17, in which Jesus discussed the "abiding" of the disciples (NIV "remain"; Gk., *menō*). This followed Jesus' promise to the disciples of "another Counselor" (the Holy Spirit, 14:16) and preceded Jesus' discussion of the work of the Holy Spirit in relation to the disciples and the world (16:5–16).

As in the gospel of John, the role of the Spirit in witness is stated in 1 John 5:6: "And it is the Spirit who testifies, because the Spirit is the truth" (cf. John 15:26; 16:13–15). The following verse, 1 John 5:7, although difficult, clearly reiterates the role of the Spirit along with water and blood as witnesses to Jesus Christ (cf. 5:6, 10).

A sharp contrast between truth and falsehood is set up in 1 John 4:1–6, culminating in the recognition by believers of "the Spirit of truth and the spirit of falsehood" (4:6). Acknowledgment that Jesus Christ has come in the flesh provides a test by which the Spirit of God may be recognized (4:2). The need for such recognition grew out of a schism within the churches to which John was writing, which divided the recipients of the letter (genuine Christians) from their secessionist opponents, whose Christology was heterodox (2:19, 26). But John was not writing primarily to refute the views of the opponents; rather, he sought to reaffirm and encourage the orthodox Christians who had not departed from the apostolic faith. In such a context the opponents' wrong Christology (4:2-3), refusal of apostolic authority (v. 6), and lack of love (vv. 7-12) demonstrated that they did not possess the Spirit of God at all (vv. 3, 6, 8). They represented the spirit of antichrist, not the Spirit of God (v. 3).

THE HOLY SPIRIT IN REVELATION

In the book of Revelation the Holy Spirit is the Spirit of prophecy. This is foreshadowed in John 16:13 where the general statement, "he will tell you what is yet to come," is comprehensive enough to include the eschatological teaching of Revelation which balances and complements the emphasis in the gospel of John on eternal life as a present experience of believers (Rev. 1:19; 4:1; also see 1:1; 22:6).

At the conclusion of each of the letters to the seven churches, the recipients are exhorted to listen to what the Spirit says to them (2:7, 11, 17, 29; 3:6, 13, 22). This is consistent with the Johannine emphasis on the role of the Spirit in revelation (John 14:26; 16:13; 1 John 2:27). Furthermore, since the letters to the churches are from the exalted Christ, the same relationship between what Christ says and what the Spirit says is found in Revelation as in John 16:13-15: "He [the Spirit] will not speak on his own; he will speak only what he hears. . . . I [Christ] said the Spirit will take from what is mine and make it known to you." The words of the Spirit are the words of Christ. Thus John spoke of being "in the Spirit" when he received the messages to the seven churches (Rev. 1:10) and the visions of the remainder of the book (4:2). Likewise he was carried away "in the Spirit" to see the woman on the scarlet beast (17:3) and the New Jerusalem coming down out of heaven from God (21:10). John left no doubt that what he had seen and written did not come from himself, but had been revealed to him by the Holy Spirit, just as Jesus promised when He said, "he will tell you what is yet to come" (John 16:13).

One unique aspect of the portrayal of the Holy Spirit in the book of Revelation is the reference to the "seven spirits of God" (Rev. 1:4; 3:1; 4:5; 5:6). Since John referred to the Spirit in the singular elsewhere in Revelation (1:10; 2:7, 11, 17, 29; 3:6, 13, 22; 4:2; 17:3; 21:10), there is no reason to think that he held to a plurality of Spirits. The seven spirits are mentioned in relation to the seven stars (3:1), the seven lamps (4:5), and the seven horns and seven eyes (5:6). It is therefore probable that the number seven is representative of perfection, and the NIV marginal note "sevenfold Spirit" at Revelation 1:4; 3:1; 4:5; and 5:6 is an acceptable interpretation. The connection of the number seven with the Spirit may be based on an allusion to Isaiah 11:2, where the Spirit is described in terms of attributes: "The Spirit of the Lord will rest on him [Jesus]—the Spirit of wisdom and of understanding, the Spirit of counsel and of power, the Spirit of knowledge and of the fear of the Lord." These attributes (beginning with the "Spirit of the Lord") add up to seven.

POLARIZATION IN JOHANNINE THEOLOGY

The imagery of opposites is an important aspect of Johannine theology. Paired opposites—such as light and darkness (John 1:5), heaven and earth (3:12; 8:23), flesh and spirit (3:6), and belief versus unbelief (3:18)—are striking in their impact when encountered by the reader. These pairs of polar opposites have often been described as dualistic, but this may be misleading if dualism is understood in a philosophical sense. For example, John did not place light and darkness on the same level. In the Johannine frame of reference, darkness is not the counterpart of light but its absence, the separation from and removal of the One who is the Light of the world. By means of polarized imagery John was able to emphasize to his readers that they, like all people, face alternative choices. When it comes to one's response to Jesus, these choices are of enormous importance because they determine one's eternal destiny. To John, there was no middle ground.

LIGHT AND DARKNESS

One of the primary contrasts in the Johannine literature is between light and darkness. This imagery is found extensively in the gospel of John and is repeated in 1 John. As to the origin of this contrasting imagery, the author of the gospel of John may have had in mind the significance attributed to light in the Hellenistic world. It is possible that his language was chosen to appeal to the interested pagan, but at the deeper level the concept of "the true light" in the prologue to the gospel of John (1:9) owes nothing to Philo.[26] John's thought is biblical and eschatological; in the Old Testament a parallel can be found to every Johannine use of "light" (*phōs*).

Light and darkness imagery in the gospel of John. The first mention of light (and darkness) in the fourth gospel is found in 1:5: "The light shines in the darkness, but the darkness has not understood it." The Greek verb *katelaben,* translated by the NIV as "understood," may also be translated "overcome," and Carson calls the entire verse "a masterpiece of planned ambiguity."[27] On one level the verse may be read simply as an echo of the Creation (Gen. 1:2–3) since John 1:3 declares the role of the preexistent Son in Creation. In this case the darkness did not "overcome" the light. But "the Word became flesh" (John 1:14), that is, the "true light" (*to phōs to alēthinon*) has already come into the world with the coming of Jesus Christ (v. 9). Jesus Himself stated later, "I am the light of the world" (8:12; 9:5). Thus John 1:5 may also be understood in terms of salvation: Jesus as the Light of the world came into the world, but the world did not understand Him or His message. Thus the NIV translation of *katelaben* in 1:5 implies more than just a cosmic struggle between light and darkness at the creation; it foreshadows the rejection theme made explicit in verses 10–11.

The contrast between light and darkness, with Jesus as the Light and with evildoers affiliated with the darkness, is repeated and amplified in John 3:19–21. This is one of the most important sections in the gospel of John for understanding

---

26. *De somniis* 1.75 refers to the "archetypal light" (*phōtos archetypon*).

27. D.A. Carson, *The Gospel According to John* (Grand Rapids: Eerdmans, 1991), 119.

the light/darkness polarization in Johannine theology and also for understanding John's gospel itself. The coming of the light (Jesus Christ) into the world has precipitated a judgment (3:17–18). The judgment consists in a person's response to the light, that is, to Jesus. One is faced with only two alternatives: to come to the light (i.e., to believe in Jesus; 1:12; 3:18) or to shrink back into the darkness and thus incur condemnation (i.e., to reject Jesus; 3:17). Just as John would refer to those who believe as possessing eternal life already in the present (5:24), so he would also speak of those who reject the light (i.e., Jesus) as being already condemned (3:18).

This decision, to come to the light or remain in the darkness, is presented again in 8:12 ("Whoever follows me will never walk in darkness, but will have the light of life."); in 9:4–5 ("As long as it is day, we must do the work of him who sent me. Night is coming, when no one can work. While I am in the world, I am the light of the world."); in 12:35–36 ("Walk while you have the light, before darkness overtakes you"); and in 12:46 ("I have come into the world as a light, so that no one who believes in me should stay in darkness."). After Judas Iscariot departed from the Upper Room, the Evangelist stated, "And it was night" (13:30). As the Light of the world was about to depart and return to the Father, the darkness had come at last (cf. Luke 22:53). Again the contrast in imagery is clear. For John, Jesus is the Light of the world, and those who believe in Him come to the light and walk in the light. At the opposite extreme is Judas Iscariot, who rejected Jesus, cast in his lot with the powers of darkness, departed into the darkness, and was swallowed up by it. If there is a middle ground between these two opposite responses, John gave no indication of it.

Light and darkness in the Johannine epistles. The polarization between light and darkness found in the gospel of John is carried over into John's epistles and Revelation. Eschatological overtones of the light/darkness imagery can be seen in 1 John 2:8: "the darkness is passing away, and the true light is already shining" (cf. Rom. 13:12). This is consistent with the Johannine emphasis on eternal life as a presently available experience for believers, although with a future consummation. Following the return of Jesus to the Father, the Light of the world continues to shine; the darkness did not succeed in overcoming it. Yet the darkness has not yet fully passed away in the present age.

The statement "God is light" (1 John 1:5) is metaphor. Nevertheless, in the same verse the contrasting theme of darkness appears in opposition to the light: "in him there is no darkness at all." The absolute nature of the polarization is also indicated: for John, light and darkness are mutually exclusive and cannot coexist. Nothing that has anything to do with darkness can have anything to do with God. Thus in the following verse (1:6), the person who claims to have fellowship with God and yet walks in the darkness has, by implication, no relationship with God at all, regardless of what he or she might claim.

In 1 John 2:9–11 the imagery of light and darkness is used again to describe the state of an individual who makes a claim which is shown to be either true or false depending on one's love for fellow believers. It is clear that the person who "is still in the darkness" (v. 9), who "is in the darkness and walks around in the darkness" (v. 11), is not a genuine believer in Christ at all, no matter what he or she might claim. This is strongly supported by the previous light and darkness imagery in 1 John 1:5–7, as well as in John 3:19–21. The darkness has "blinded" this individual (1 John 2:11), a situation analogous to the spiritual blindness of the Jewish leaders attacked by Jesus in John 9:39–41. On the other hand, the person who obeys Jesus' command to love one another by loving his neighbor "lives in the light, and there is nothing in him to make him stumble" (1 John 2:10). This individual is one who has come to Jesus as the Light of the world and now lives in the light "so that it may be seen plainly that what he has done has been done through God" (John 3:21).

Light and darkness imagery in Revelation. The reiteration of the imagery of God as light in Revelation 21:23 reflects a concept that the end of all things will be like the beginning: the light which shone out of the darkness on the first day of creation (Gen. 1:3) will shine forth once more when the last things are fulfilled (Rev. 22:5). This has its Old Testament roots in Isaiah 60:19.

HEAVEN AND EARTH (ABOVE AND BELOW)

Another major contrast in the gospel of John is between heaven and earth, or that which is above and the world below. Jesus stated this contrast succinctly in His reply to the Jewish leaders as He taught in the temple, "You are from below; I am from above. You are of this world; I am not of this world" (John 8:23). Such imagery is prevalent throughout the fourth gospel. It is implied in the prologue by the indirect reference to Jesus' departure from heaven ("the Word was with God," John 1:1) and entry into the world below ("the true light that gives light to every man was coming into the world," John 1:9). In John 3:13 the same theme is explicitly stated in connection with the Son of Man, described as "the one who came down from heaven."

In the Bread of Life discourse the contrast between heaven and earth is expressed a number of times. In John 6:33 Jesus declared both His heavenly origin and His mission on earth: "For the bread of God is he who comes down from heaven and gives life to the world." It occurs again in John 6:38 in relation to Jesus' earthly mission: He was sent by the Father to do the Father's will, which is that all who believe in the Son should have eternal life (vv. 39–40). This is reiterated in 6:50–51 ("here is the bread that comes down from heaven, which a man may eat and not die") and once more in 6:58 ("This is the bread that came down from heaven").

The contrast between heaven and earth is implied in 6:62 when Jesus said, "What if you see the Son of Man ascend to where he was before!" It lies in the background of the wordplay on "going up" in 7:8, by which Jesus referred specifically to an upcoming visit to Jerusalem, but the reader of the fourth gospel also realizes that Jesus would soon be "going up" to heaven, returning to the Father who sent Him. Again, the reader of the gospel realizes when Jesus answered His opponents in John 7:28 ("Yes, you know me, and you know where I am from. I am not here on my own, but he who sent me is true"), He was referring not to His earthly origin, but to the fact that He came down from heaven. Jesus also referred to His return to heaven in 7:33. The contrast is implied again in Jesus' response to the Pharisees in 8:14, "I know where I came from and where I am going. But you have no idea where I come from or where I am going." The earth and heaven imagery is clearly presented (as below and above) in 8:23, and implied in 8:42 ("I came from God and now am here."); 9:39 ("For judgment I have come into this world."); 10:36 ("what about the one whom the Father set apart as his very own and sent into the world?"); and 12:46 ("I have come into the world as a light."). These last four references all imply a contrast between the world of humanity (the earth below) and the world above (heaven) from which Jesus came.

In Jesus' Farewell Discourse the contrast between heaven and earth is implied several times (14:2, 28; 16:5, 10) and is explicitly mentioned by Jesus in 16:28: "I came from the Father and entered the world; now I am leaving the world and going back to the Father." Earth is contrasted (by implication) with heaven as the place where the Father is. Jesus declared, "I have brought you glory on earth by completing the work you gave me to do" (17:4). This is made more explicit in verse 11 where Jesus again spoke of His departure from the world: "I will remain in the world no longer, but they [the disciples] are still in the world, and I am coming to you" (cf. v. 13). In His interview with Pilate, Jesus proclaimed, "My kingdom is not of this world . . . my kingdom is from another place" (18:36). Later Jesus told Pilate, "You would have no power over me if it were not given to you from above" (19:11).

After examining the heaven/earth imagery in the gospel of John, it is clear that much of it is vertical imagery, revolving around the use of terms like "above" and "below" (8:23), "descending" and "ascending" (3:13; 6:33, 50–51, 58, 62), and "earth" (as opposed to heaven, 17:4). On other occasions the vertical element is not emphasized; it is merely asserted that Jesus came into the world from somewhere outside it (1:9; 9:39; 10:36; 12:46; 16:28; 17:11; 18:36). In either case, it is clear that John was writing in terms of opposites.

FLESH AND SPIRIT

Less extensive but still present in John's theological framework is a contrast between flesh and spirit. The term "flesh" (*sarx*) is not used by John to convey the idea of sinfulness, as it often does in Paul's writings. Crucial in this regard is John 1:14 which asserts, "the Word became flesh and made his dwelling among us." Because of its association with Jesus, no connotation of sinfulness is attached to the term "flesh" in the Johannine literature. Rather, it is indicative of weakness and humiliation as seen in 1:14. It simply affirms that in the Incarnation Jesus became fully human.

The strongest statement of the contrast between flesh and spirit is in John 3:6 where Jesus told Nicodemus, "Flesh gives birth to flesh, but the Spirit gives birth to spirit." Flesh is therefore limited; it cannot attain spiritual life with its own abilities or resources. Rather, it is necessary for a person to be "born from above" (John 3:3, 7 NIV margin), that is, to undergo a spiritual birth corresponding to physical birth.[28] To some extent the contrast between flesh and spirit in this context is parallel to the contrast between heaven and earth explicitly mentioned in 3:12, where Jesus said, "I have spoken to you of earthly things and you do not believe; how then will you believe if I speak of heavenly things?"

Similar to the contrast between flesh and spirit found in John 3:6 is Jesus' statement in 6:63, "The Spirit gives life; the flesh counts for nothing." Jesus' point to the disciples is that by understanding His teaching only in human terms, they missed the point and began raising the kinds of objections mentioned in 6:42, 52, 60. The polarization is absolute. When it comes to matters of the Spirit, that is, spiritual truth, mere human understanding is not only useless but is also distracting. Again in the immediate context, as in John 3:12, the contrast between heaven and earth is also present (6:62).

BELIEF AND UNBELIEF

Belief and unbelief (or rejection of Jesus, or refusal to believe) are often mentioned separately in the gospel of John. On a number of occasions, however, the two are juxtaposed, creating another of the Johannine polarizations. The first of these is in John 3:12 where Jesus told Nicodemus, "I have spoken to you of earthly things and you do not believe; how then will you believe if I speak of heavenly things?" Jesus had been discussing the need for a new spiritual birth in order to enter the kingdom of God (3:3–8). He had mentioned the rejection of His testimony by the Jewish people (v. 11). In verse 12 the contrast between belief and unbelief occurs in the same phrase as the contrast between heaven and earth ("earthly things . . . heavenly things"), adding further emphasis to the imagery. Later in the same context belief and unbelief are mentioned again in mutually exclusive terms, the former leading to freedom from condemnation and the latter leading to condemnation. John 3:18 states, "Whoever believes in him is not condemned, but whoever does not believe stands condemned already because he has not believed in the name of God's one and only Son." This is followed in verse 19 by a contrast between light and darkness, again adding emphasis to the polarization between belief and unbelief. Once more for John there was no middle ground.

The contrast between belief and unbelief is repeated again in slightly different terms in John 3:36: "Whoever believes in the Son has eternal life, but whoever rejects the Son will not see life, for God's wrath remains on him." Here the contrast is between belief in the Son and rejection of the Son (which is the equivalent of unbelief). The contrast between belief and unbelief is also found at the end of chapter 5 as Jesus spoke to His opponents, the Jewish leaders. Jesus warned them, "If you believed Moses, you would believe me, for he wrote about me. But since you do not believe what he wrote, how are you going to believe what I say?" (5:46–47). Here the issue is belief in the testimony of Moses concerning the Messiah and belief in the words of Jesus Himself. The Jewish leaders rejected both.

28. There is a wordplay in John 3:3, 7 involving the Greek word *anōthen*, which may mean both "from above" and "again," thus accounting for Nicodemus's misunderstanding of Jesus' reference to a spiritual birth.

In the Bread of Life discourse Jesus again brought up the subject of belief in Himself as the one God had sent (6:29). The contrast between belief and unbelief surfaces again in verses 35–36 as Jesus declared, "I am the bread of life. He who comes to me will never go hungry, and he who believes in me will never be thirsty. But as I told you, you have seen me and still you do not believe."

At the conclusion of the section in the gospel of John which deals with the seven sign-miracles (1:19–12:50), the Evangelist picked up on the contrast between belief and unbelief in the teaching of Jesus Himself as a way of summarizing the results of Jesus' public ministry. John noted that the Jewish people still refused to believe in Jesus even after all the miraculous signs He had worked among them (12:37). This was in fulfillment of Isaiah's prophecy (Isa. 53:1) about the rejection of the Lord's messenger (John 12:38). John attributed this unbelief to spiritual blindness and deadness brought on by God Himself as judgment (vv. 39–40). In contrast to the response of unbelief, John noted that many even among the leadership did in fact believe in Jesus (v. 42). John then quoted Jesus Himself that belief in the Son also involves belief in the Father (v. 44). Jesus drew on the contrast between light and darkness to drive the point home: "I have come into the world as a light, so that no one who believes in me should stay in darkness" (v. 46). Then, returning to the theme of rejection, Jesus declared that whoever rejects Him will be condemned at the final judgment (v. 48). Here in the final summary of Jesus' public ministry John wove together two pairs of polar opposites: belief and unbelief and light and darkness. Rejection of the Son has serious consequences, and the Evangelist wished to communicate this as strongly as possible.

The contrast between belief and unbelief, so prominent in the first major section of the gospel of John, virtually disappears in the second section. It is not difficult to see why this is the case. The first major section deals with the public ministry of Jesus where He is frequently in dialogue with His opponents (cf. 1:11). The second major section of the gospel concerns Jesus' private teaching to His disciples (chaps. 13–17) and the passion narrative (chaps. 18–20). The disciples, with the exception of Judas Iscariot who departed (13:30), were regarded as believers, so that the theme of belief and unbelief no longer needed to be emphasized. In the passion narrative the emphasis is on belief, not unbelief (20:8, 27, 29, 31).

LOVE AND HATE

Another pair of opposites in the Johannine literature, less obvious than some of the others but extremely important for an understanding of Johannine thought, is love and hate. These are juxtaposed on only one occasion in the gospel of John, but are repeatedly related in 1 John. The reason for this lies in the nature of the dispute in 1 John, a dispute over Christology between the orthodox Christians to whom the letter is addressed and their heterodox opponents. Since for John genuine love for God is expected to result in obedience to God's commands and love for fellow-believers (1 John 3:10), the opponents' lack of love and failure to obey demonstrate conclusively that they were not genuine believers at all (2:19, 23; 3:6, 8–9; 4:8).

Love and hate in John's gospel. In John's gospel almost all the references to love and hate appear in Jesus' Farewell Discourse. This is not surprising, since in this discourse Jesus was addressing His disciples rather than opponents.[29] The first mention of the disciples' love appears in John 13:34–35, where Jesus gave His disciples the new commandment to love one another. The model for their love is Jesus' love for them ("as I have loved you," v. 34). The love the disciples were to have for one another would testify to everyone that they were followers of Jesus (v. 35).

In the following chapter a number of passages relate the disciples' love for Jesus to their obedience of Him. Jesus stated the relationship between love and obedience explicitly in 14:15: "If you love me, you will obey what I command." Love is further linked to obedience in 14:21 ("Whoever has my commands and obeys them, he is the one who loves me.") and 14:23 ("If anyone loves me, he will obey my teaching."). The reciprocal of this is expressed by Jesus in 14:24, "He who does not love me will not obey my teaching." From a human standpoint it is difficult to know if an individual genuinely loves Jesus or not, but it is easy to tell whether an individual is obedient to Jesus' teachings. The two outward signs of genuine love for Jesus mentioned so far are the disciples' love for each other (13:35) and their obedience to Jesus' commands (14:15, 21, 23). The same theme appears in John 15:10 although the wording differs slightly. Jesus declared, "If you obey my commands, you will remain in my love, just as I have obeyed my Father's commands and remain in his love." The command Jesus specifically mentioned in the immediate context is (as in 13:34–35) that the disciples love one another as He has loved them (15:12, repeated in 15:17). Thus as in John 14:15, 21, 23 and negatively in 14:24, obedience (specifically obedience to the command to love one another) demonstrates the genuineness of an individual's love for Jesus.

Immediately following the repetition of the command to love one another in John 15:17, Jesus introduced the theme of the world's hatred for the disciples: "If the world hates you, keep in mind that it hated me first" (v. 18). Thus for the first and only time love and hate are mentioned in immediate proximity to one another in the gospel of John. Jesus then explained to His disciples why the world would hate them. "If you belonged to the world, it would love you as its own. As it is, you do not belong to the world, but I have chosen you out of the world. That is why the world hates you" (v. 19). Although the juxtaposition of love and hate does not occur frequently in the fourth gospel, it is significant among the Johannine opposites because as it occurs in John 15:17–19 it provides a "litmus test" of genuine love for Jesus. On the one hand genuine followers of Jesus will love one another, while on the other the world will hate them because they no longer belong to it. This theme will be developed at much greater length in the Johannine epistles: genuine Christians with their orthodox Christology are expected to show their love for one another in concrete terms, while the secessionist opponents, who claimed to love God, are proven false by their failure to love the brethren (cf. 1 John 3:17–20).

---

29. The first mention of the disciples' love in John 13:34 follows the departure of the traitor Judas Iscariot in 13:30.

The hatred of the world for believers is expressed by Jesus again in John 16:1–4. Here Jesus predicted persecutions for His followers because of the world's hatred for them. Finally in 16:27 Jesus declared to His disciples, "the Father himself loves you because you have loved me and have believed that I came from God." Thus there is also a relationship between loving Jesus and believing His claims.

Love and hate in the Johannine epistles. In his epistles John developed the contrast between love and hate extensively. The first passage in which love is mentioned is 1 John 2:5 (in relation to obedience as in John 14:21, 23). The apostle explicitly stated in 1 John 2:3, "We know that we have come to know him [Jesus Christ; cf. 2:1–2] if we obey his commands." Thus for the genuine believer, obedience to Christ's commands (especially the command to love one another; cf. the "new command" in 2:7–8) provides a ground for assurance that an individual truly has a relationship with Christ. In verse 4 John illustrated the opposite situation. The person who claims to have a relationship with Christ but does not obey His commands is a liar, that is, the person has claimed to have a relationship with Christ which he or she does not really have. The love mentioned in verse 5 and described as God's love is made complete in the person who obeys Christ's word.

As in John 14:15, 21, and 23 obedience is linked to genuine love; obedience to Jesus' commands indicates the genuineness of the love professed for Him. The Apostle John went a step further in 1 John 2:6 by proclaiming, "Whoever claims to live in him must walk as Jesus did." Obedience to Jesus' commands involves imitation of His behavior during His earthly ministry. A person who claims to be obeying Jesus' commandments and yet follows a lifestyle contrary to what Jesus would have done during His time on earth is a liar (cf. v. 4). Likely, the secessionist opponents with their heterodox Christology were making just such a claim, resulting in confusion for the genuine Christians to whom John was writing. In all probability the opponents rejected the importance of Jesus' behavior during His earthly life as an example for Christians to follow because their Christology denied or downplayed Jesus' full humanity.[30]

Immediately following this passage the first love/hate contrast occurs in 1 John 2:9–11. In these verses obedience to Jesus' commandment to love one another becomes an indicator of the genuineness of an individual's claim to be in relationship with Christ (the light/darkness imagery of the passage has been discussed above). The person who claims to be "in the light," that is, in relationship with Christ, yet hates his brother, is still "in the darkness"; his claim is invalid. On the other hand, the person who loves his brother "lives in the light"; he has come to the Light (cf. John 3:21) and now lives in it. In the following verse John returned to the case of the first individual and amplified it further. Such a person is not only "in the darkness," but also "walks around in the darkness" and "does not know where he is going, because the darkness has blinded him" (1 John 2:11). Such an individual

---

30. The opponents' Christology is often described as Docetic, involving some sort of a distinction between the heavenly Christ and the human Jesus, perhaps with a denial of the reality of the Incarnation.

exhibits a spiritual blindness comparable to Jesus' opponents in the gospel of John (see especially John 9:39–41). Just as the Jewish leaders, Jesus' opponents during His earthly ministry, demonstrated their spiritual blindness by their rejection of Him, so the secessionist opponents in 1 John demonstrated their spiritual blindness by their rejection of John's readers, refusing to love them.

In 1 John 2:15 love and hate are not opposed to one another, but rather two different objects of love are contrasted: "If anyone loves the world, the love of the Father is not in him." The opponents were guilty of love for the world. But as the Apostle John declared, love for the world and love for the Father are mutually exclusive. Once again, regardless of what such a person might claim, love for the world demonstrates that any claim to love God is invalid.

In 1 John 3:11–20 love and hate are juxtaposed a number of times within the same passage in relation to love for the body. John began by reiterating Jesus' commandment to the disciples to love one another (v. 11; cf. John 13:34–35). In the following verse Cain's murder of his brother Abel serves as a negative example of hatred for one's brother (1 John 3:12). In light of this, John reminded his readers that they should not be surprised at the world's hatred of them (v. 13). Verse 14 makes two assertions: first, love for one's brothers is evidence of eternal life (cf. 1 John 2:3 and John 14:15, 21, 23). Second, the person who does not love [his brothers] remains in death (i.e., spiritual death). For the Apostle John, this second point is another description of the secessionist opponents who had rejected his readers and refused to love them as brothers, and thus were still in a state of spiritual death. First John 3:15 simply carries the same thought further by asserting that whoever does not love his brother is a murderer (just as Cain; cf. v. 12) and no murderer has eternal life in him.

After discussing the negative example of hatred (Cain plus the secessionist opponents) John turned to the positive example of Jesus Christ Himself, who "laid down his life for us" (v. 16). From this example of sacrificial love it follows that believers ought to lay down their lives for one another. John spelled this out concretely in 3:17–18. A fellow believer in material need is to be assisted; the apostle's readers are to love one another not "with words or tongue but with actions and in truth." This love for brothers demonstrated in action is thus a further ground for assurance of a genuine relationship with God (3:19–20).

Similar thoughts are presented in 1 John 4:7–12. Although hate is not mentioned, love for the family of God is contrasted with the absence of love. The former demonstrates that an individual "has been born of God and knows God" (v. 7); it is a thorough description of a person who has been born spiritually and has a genuine relationship with God. In contrast, "Whoever does not love does not know God" (v. 8). In verses 9–10 God's sending of His Son to provide an atoning sacrifice for sins is used as a positive example of love (cf. John 3:16). Believers ought to be motivated by this demonstration of God's love to love each other (1 John 4:11–12).

John returned to this theme in 4:16–5:3. When John wrote, "Whoever lives in love lives in God, and God in him" (4:16), he was simply saying again that love for the brethren demonstrates that a person has a genuine relationship with God. Anyone who claims to love God and yet hates his brother is a liar (4:20; cf. 1:6; 2:4, 9–11; 3:14–15; 4:8). The new commandment itself (cf. John 13:34–35) is rephrased by the apostle: "Whoever loves God must also love his brother" (1 John 4:21).

The commandment for believers to love one another is mentioned again in 2 John 5–6, where it is again related to obedience: "And this is love: that we walk in obedience to his commands" (2 John 6). The command is to love one another (v. 5) and to walk in love (v. 6). Love for fellow believers is also in view in 3 John 5–8, where service to the brethren, especially material assistance for traveling missionaries, is commended and encouraged further.

SALVATION IN THE JOHANNINE WRITINGS

The outworking of God's plan of salvation is one of the major themes of John's gospel. John constantly kept before his readers the question "Who is Jesus?" Related inextricably to the answer is the mission on which the Son was sent by the Father. No clearer expression of this may be found than in John 3:16–17: "For God so loved the world that he gave his one and only Son, that whoever believes in him shall not perish but have eternal life. For God did not send his Son into the world to condemn the world, but to save the world through him." The Johannine Epistles and the book of Revelation also emphasize the sacrificial nature of Jesus' death as part of God's plan of salvation.

THE DEATH OF JESUS IN THE JOHANNINE WRITINGS: JOHN'S THEOLOGY OF THE CROSS

Just as John's presentation of the person of Jesus has distinctive features and emphases, so also does his presentation of Jesus' death on the cross and its benefits. In particular, John viewed Jesus' crucifixion as an integral part of His mission, the means by which He accomplished His return to the Father from whom He was sent. This is echoed in Jesus' prayer in John 17:4: "I have brought you glory on earth by completing the work you gave me to do." John picked up on this theme of completion when, as Jesus was hanging on the cross, John wrote, "Later, knowing that all was now completed, and so that the Scripture would be fulfilled, Jesus said, 'I am thirsty'" (19:28).

Jesus' death in the gospel of John as part of God's plan. Because Jesus' sacrificial death on the cross is central to God's plan to save the world through Him, it is not surprising to find that the gospel of John views the ultimate arrest, trials, and crucifixion of Jesus as no accident, but as foreordained. Throughout the fourth gospel Jesus continually makes reference to the coming of His "hour," beginning with the announcement in 2:4 to His mother at the wedding feast in Cana, "My hour has not yet come" (NASB; NIV translates "hour" as "time"). Jesus reiterated this to His brothers as the reason He would not yet go up to Jerusalem (7:6, 8). After Jesus did go up to Jerusalem, John noted that the Jewish authorities were unable to seize Him because His hour had not yet come (v. 30). The same explanation is given by the Evangelist as the reason Jesus was not seized while teaching in the temple treasury (8:20). At the culmination of Jesus' public ministry, when some Greeks asked to see Him, He replied, "The hour has come for the Son of Man to be glorified" (12:23). Immediately following this remark Jesus noted that a grain of wheat must fall into the earth and die in order to bring forth much fruit (v. 24). Jesus' impending death would bring forth a plentiful harvest of people who would come to believe in Him. A few verses later Jesus considered whether to pray for the Father to spare Him from the coming of the hour—His impending death. He concluded, "No, it was for this very reason I came to this hour" (v. 27). The mission of Jesus (cf. 3:17) had always included the cross, and this lay before Jesus from the beginning of His ministry.

In 12:32 Jesus again referred to His death: "And I, when I am lifted up from the earth, will draw all men to myself." The Evangelist's note in the following verse makes it clear that this is ultimately to be understood as a reference to the manner of Jesus' death (i.e., by crucifixion), although there is room for a Johannine wordplay on the meaning of "lift up."[31] Besides referring to Jesus being "lifted up" on the cross, it can also refer to His exaltation to the right hand of the Father—an exaltation which for John is an integral part of Jesus' return to the Father. Again in John 12:35–36 Jesus indicated that He, as the Light of the world, was soon to be withdrawn from the world, a further prediction of His approaching death.

In Jesus' words to His disciples in the Upper Room there are several explicit references to His impending death, all of which indicate it was completely within the plan of God. One of the most dramatic of these is John 13:1, where John wrote that "Jesus knew that the time had come for him to leave this world and go to the Father." Jesus' arrest, trials, and crucifixion did not take Him by surprise. It was the way through which He was to accomplish His return to the Father. Another indication that Jesus' death was completely according to plan is His prediction of Judas's betrayal before it occurred (13:21–27). At several other points within the discourse Jesus alluded to His approaching death (John 13:36; 14:2, 12, 19, 28; 16:5, 16, 28).[32] In Jesus' prayer at the conclusion of the discourse, He again announced that His hour had come (17:1) and He referred to the completion of the work God had sent Him to do (v. 4). Statements concerning His departure from the world and return to the Father became even more explicit (vv. 11, 13). All the foregoing evidence makes it abundantly clear that in John's gospel the death of Jesus was no accident or quirk of fate, but an integral part of God's plan for salvation and the culmination of the mission on which He sent the Son. Fully aware that His earthly mission would end on the cross, Jesus set Himself to this purpose without wavering.

31. The same wordplay on "lifting up" is found in John 3:14 and 8:28.

32. Scholars disagree on where Jesus' Farewell Discourse begins. Following the standard chapter divisions would suggest 14:1, but a better case can be made for 13:31. Judas, the betrayer, went out into the night in 13:30. At that point Jesus began His address to those who would remain faithful to Him. See Carson, *The Gospel According to John*, 476–77.

Jesus' death in the gospel of John as voluntary. Along with those passages in John's gospel that depict Jesus' death on the cross as a foreordained part of God's plan of salvation are those passages that indicate that Jesus went to His death voluntarily. Some of the clearest statements of this are found in the Good Shepherd discourse (John 10:1–21). Jesus first mentioned the voluntary nature of His death in verse 11: "I am the good shepherd. The good shepherd lays down his life for the sheep." This is repeated in verse 15: "just as the Father knows me and I know the Father—and I lay down my life for the sheep." Even stronger is Jesus' statement in verses 17–18: "The reason my Father loves me is that I lay down my life—only to take it up again. No one takes it from me, but I lay it down of my own accord." Jesus' willingness to give up His life voluntarily is also indicated in the words, "Greater love has no one than this, that he lay down his life for his friends" (15:13).

Throughout the passion narrative in John's gospel the voluntary nature of Jesus' death is implicit. One gets the strong impression that Jesus—rather than Judas, Annas, or Pilate—was the One in control of the events as He was moving inexorably toward the cross. At Jesus' arrest, Judas, the soldiers, and officials who had come to take Him fell to the ground when Jesus identified Himself (John 18:6). Jesus practically ordered His captors to let His disciples go free (v. 8). When interviewed by Pilate for the second time Jesus told him, "You would have no power over me if it were not given to you from above" (19:11). From the cross Jesus handed over His mother to the care of one of His disciples (vv. 26–27). Finally, even Jesus' death itself was voluntary: when He knew that all was completed (v. 28) He said, "It is finished" (v. 30) and gave up His spirit before the soldiers came to break His legs. Even the very moment of Jesus' death was His own choice.

Jesus' death in the gospel of John as sacrificial. The language and imagery of sacrifice is connected with Jesus' death in a number of passages in the gospel of John. At the beginning of Jesus' public ministry John the Baptist declared that He is the Lamb of God (John 1:29, 36). Although the title "Lamb of God" was discussed at length earlier, it is significant to note that sacrificial imagery is associated with the title regardless of whether its background is the Suffering Servant motif of Isaiah 53:7 or the Passover lamb of Exodus 12:1–28. The Baptist's qualifying statement, "who takes away the sin of the world," which accompanies the title in John 1:29, is a clear indication of the sacrificial imagery present in the context.

Another passage that involves sacrificial imagery in relation to the death of Jesus is John 6:51 in the Bread of life discourse. Jesus declared, "This bread is my flesh, which I will give for the life of the world." This verse looks at Jesus' death (the giving of His "flesh") regardless of any secondary allusions the statement may contain. Because this is said to be given for the "life of the world," a sacrificial motif is in view here.[33]

---

33. "World" and "Savior" are related in John 4:42. Also 1 John 2:2 includes the explicit statement of Christ's sacrifice "for the sins of the whole world."

Jesus' death in the Johannine epistles and Revelation as sacrificial. Two passages in 1 John introduce the idea of propitiatory sacrifice in relation to the work of Jesus Christ. The first of these is 1 John 2:1–2, where Jesus is described as "the Righteous One" and is said to be "the atoning sacrifice for our sins, and not only for ours but also for the sins of the whole world." The word translated by the NIV as "atoning sacrifice" should be understood technically to mean "propitiation."[34] The concept of propitiation involves more than simply canceling out sin and thus purifying the sinner. It involves the actual turning aside of wrath, which in this case is the wrath of God directed at sinners. It is significant that in the immediate context of 1 John, Jesus Christ is described as "an Advocate" (1 John 2:1 NASB; NIV translates "one who speaks . . . in our defense"). An advocate is needed only if the wrath of God directed against sinners is a present reality. The same idea of propitiatory sacrifice is present in the other passage, 1 John 4:10. This passage is particularly significant because God Himself provided the propitiatory sacrifice by sending His Son (cf. John 3:16–17). In neither 1 John 2:2 nor 4:10 is the death of Jesus explicitly mentioned, but there can be little doubt that Jesus' death on the cross is the occasion of the propitiation described in these verses. In 1 John 1:7 "the blood of Jesus, his Son" purifies believers from sin, and "blood" is a clear reference to Jesus' death.

In Revelation the sacrificial imagery already encountered in the gospel of John and the Johannine epistles is continued. As stated earlier, the Lamb imagery so prevalent in Revelation (the title is used of Jesus twenty-seven times) conveys the unmistakable idea of sacrifice, particularly since in Revelation 5:6 John wrote that he saw "a Lamb, looking as if it had been slain, standing in the center of the throne." Another passage in Revelation that includes sacrificial imagery is Revelation 1:5, which describes Jesus as the one "who loves us and has freed us from our sins by his blood." Again the blood refers to Jesus' death on the cross, and the release from sin conveys the idea of atonement. The two concepts taken together convey a sacrificial image.

THE DEVELOPMENT OF THE DISCIPLES' FAITH IN JESUS IN THE GOSPEL OF JOHN

In one sense it is legitimate to view Jesus' disciples in the gospel of John (with the exception of Judas Iscariot) as believers in Him from near the beginning of His public ministry. In another sense, however, it is also clear that the disciples' faith in Jesus grew and developed as they observed the progress of His public ministry. The course of this development may be traced in the gospel of John.

Shortly after Jesus' baptism by John the Baptist, two of the Baptist's disciples became disciples of Jesus (John 1:35–39). After spending a day with Jesus one of the two, Andrew, went immediately to find his brother Simon Peter and announced, "we have found the Messiah" (v. 41). It is difficult to be sure exactly what Andrew and the other unnamed disciple who had been followers of John the

---

34. The same Greek word is used in Romans 3:25 which the NIV marginal note translates as "the one who would turn aside his [God's] wrath, taking away sin."

Baptist expected in the Messiah. The Baptist himself had been their teacher, and his own messianic expectations were firmly rooted in the Old Testament (cf. v. 23). Thus it is reasonable to assume that they expected a Messiah who would fulfill the Old Testament prophecies and restore Israel. This much at least they believed about Jesus when they acknowledged Him to be the Messiah.

The next insight into the disciples' concept of who Jesus is occurs in the interview with Nathanael. Philip, when he went to find Nathanael, declared, "We have found the one Moses wrote about in the Law, and about whom the prophets also wrote—Jesus of Nazareth, the son of Joseph" (1:45). This confirms the strong Old Testament roots of the first disciples' messianic expectations. Nathanael's initial response was skeptical, especially concerning Jesus' hometown, Nazareth (v. 46). After meeting Jesus, Nathanael thought otherwise, however, for he proclaimed to Jesus, "Rabbi, you are the Son of God; you are the King of Israel" (v. 49). Now three new titles for Jesus had been introduced. "Rabbi" indicated that Nathanael looked on Jesus as a teacher and spiritual leader. "Son of God" is more difficult to clarify; it is altogether too easy to read into Nathanael's use of this title the full content as implied by John's statement of purpose at the conclusion of the gospel (20:31). It is more likely that Nathanael did not have such a comprehensive view of who Jesus was when he made this declaration, particularly as he linked the title "Son of God" with another title, "King of Israel." It is probable that Nathanael used the title mainly in light of its messianic implications, implications drawn from such Old Testament passages as 1 Samuel 26:17, 21, 25; 2 Samuel 7:14; and especially Psalm 2:7, which link divine sonship and the Davidic succession. It is doubtful that Nathanael understood "Son of God" in its fullest sense of the relationship between the Father and the Son, which is foreshadowed in the prologue and made explicit later in the fourth gospel. Nevertheless, Nathanael spoke "truer than he knew," and the reader of John's gospel who has any inkling of the later usage of the title "Son of God" would recognize that Nathanael had done so.

The third title used by Nathanael, "King of Israel," was applied to Jesus again in John's gospel at the Triumphal Entry into Jerusalem (John 12:13). In the context in which Nathanael used it this title is almost certainly messianic, although Jesus later explained to Pilate that His kingdom was not of this world (18:36). To sum up, Nathanael had taken a considerable step of faith in his confession of who Jesus was, a step based on Jesus' demonstration of supernatural knowledge (cf. 1:48). Nevertheless, most if not all of his confession was an acknowledgment that Jesus is the Messiah, God's anointed, and heir to the Davidic kingship.

The next comment John made regarding the faith of the disciples is in John 2:11. Following Jesus' miraculous transformation of water into wine at the wedding feast in Cana, Jesus revealed His glory and His disciples put their faith in Him. Certainly the disciples were not the only witnesses of the miracle; John explicitly stated that the servants who had drawn the water that was turned to wine knew what had happened. What the servants thought of this, or what they believed about Jesus, is not stated. However, Jesus "thus revealed His glory" (2:11), and presumably the disciples, since they had already concluded that Jesus was the Messiah, interpreted the sign within this framework as they put their trust in Him. The sign-miracle performed by Jesus at Cana was not without precedent in Israel's history; Moses and Aaron, for example, had performed miracles at the court of Pharaoh at the time of the Exodus (Ex. 7:8–13) and later Elijah (1 Kings 17:8–24; 18:20–40) and Elisha (2 Kings 4:1–7, 18–37; 5:8–14) had also performed miracles. Jesus' disciples would have viewed the miracle at the time as divine confirmation of Jesus' messiahship in line with their original expectations. Only later, after Jesus' resurrection, would they have come to understand that "one greater than Moses" was there.

Another possible insight into the disciples' developing faith in Jesus is in John 2:17. After Jesus' cleansing of the temple (vv. 13–22), John noted that "His disciples remembered that it is written: 'Zeal for your house will consume me'" (v. 17). These words are quoted from Psalm 69:9, in which David cried out in despair to God because of persecution he was enduring for the sake of God and His temple. John did not clarify whether the disciples remembered this at the time of the temple-cleansing or later, after Jesus' resurrection.[35] If Jesus' disciples remembered the words of Psalm 69:9 at the time or shortly thereafter, it is probable that they focused on the zeal demonstrated by Jesus for His Father's house and saw in it a further confirmation that Jesus is the promised Messiah.

Another passage that might give insight into how Jesus was viewed during His ministry is John 3:31–36. In this passage Jesus' heavenly origin is mentioned explicitly (v. 31) as is His relationship with the Father (v. 35). Furthermore, belief in the Son is said to result in eternal life, while rejection of the Son leaves one under the wrath of God (v. 36). If these statements about Jesus' identity were known to His disciples at the time, they would provide evidence of a much fuller understanding of the person of Jesus before His resurrection than has been suggested so far. This is not likely, however, for several significant reasons. First, although the words are often taken as a continuation of the Baptist's testimony in 3:27–30, they are more likely an explanatory expansion added by the Evangelist summarizing not only the Baptist's words but also the response of Nicodemus to Jesus in the preceding conversation. Second, even if they are the words of the Baptist, they were not spoken to Jesus' disciples but to the disciples of the Baptist (vv. 25–26). Whether any account of them got back to Jesus' disciples at the time cannot be known. Third, John the Baptist had already been shown to possess prophetic ability to receive revelation from God (1:33), and these words, if attributed to him, would constitute another example of that. There is no indication that the disciples would have shared this insight at the time, unless Jesus Himself had revealed it to them. Whether they would have understood it is another matter.

By John 5:16–18 elements of the unique relationship between the Father and the Son began to appear in Jesus' public teaching; the Jewish authorities were beginning to persecute Jesus because "not only was he breaking the Sabbath, but he was even calling God his own Father, making himself equal with God" (5:18). In

---

35. In the case of Jesus' statement about the destruction of the temple in John 2:19, the Evangelist made it clear that the disciples did not recall Jesus' words until after He was raised from the dead (2:22). No such clarification is given in the case of 2:17.

Jesus' reply to His accusers (which was almost certainly witnessed by His disciples) He elaborated on the relationship the Son has with the Father, including the authority of the Son to give life (v. 21) and to execute judgment (v. 22). From this point on in the gospel of John such elements became a regular feature of Jesus' public teaching and thus were known to His disciples. Following Jesus' saying about eating His flesh and drinking His blood (6:53–58), many of His disciples began to grumble (vv. 60–61) and no longer followed Him (v. 66). Simon Peter's confession at this time as spokesman for the Twelve provides an indication of their level of understanding: "Lord, to whom shall we go? You have the words of eternal life. We believe and know that you are the Holy One of God" (vv. 68–69). This confession acknowledged Jesus as the Giver of eternal life. It also acknowledged that He is "the Holy One of God," which in this context was probably a messianic title, although its use as such is not clearly attested elsewhere. Presumably the Twelve (with the exception of Judas) gained a clearer understanding of what this entailed after Jesus' resurrection than they had at the time.

John 11:7–16 records the disciples' misunderstanding concerning Jesus' words about the death of Lazarus. While this does not tell much about the disciples' level of understanding regarding who Jesus is, it does indicate that much of what Jesus said to the disciples could have been misunderstood by them at the time. Thomas appeared at this point as the supreme pessimist (v. 16). His words are somewhat ironic because ultimately Jesus died so that the disciples might go free, a point not missed by the Evangelist as he recorded Jesus' words at His arrest: "If you are looking for me, then let these men go" (18:8).

By the time of Jesus' Triumphal Entry into Jerusalem (12:12–19) the disciples still did not understand the full significance of what was happening. After the crowd greeted Jesus with palm branches and proclaimed, "Blessed is he who comes in the name of the Lord! Blessed is the King of Israel" (v. 13), an Old Testament quotation from Zechariah 9:9 was introduced which prophesied that the messianic King would come riding on the colt of a donkey. John stated that at the time the disciples "did not realize that these things had been written about him [Jesus] and that they had done these things to him" (v. 16). Only after the resurrection ("after Jesus was glorified") did they realize the significance of what had happened. A superficial reading of what the disciples did not understand at the time produces a contradiction. If the phrase "that they had done these things to him" refers to the actions and words of the crowd at the Triumphal Entry, it is difficult to see how the disciples did not understand these actions as having messianic significance. This is particularly true as Nathanael had long before, near the beginning of Jesus' public ministry, used exactly the same title of Jesus, "King of Israel," as did the crowd, and there (1:49) the title was clearly messianic. If the disciples did not now pick up on the significance of such messianic imagery, their understanding of who Jesus is would seem to have regressed rather than developed.

Since the quotation from Zechariah 9:9 is introduced after the proclamation by the crowds and before the statement about the disciples' failure to understand, it is better to see the Evangelist's retrospective statement about the disciples' degree of understanding as referring to actions predicted in the prophetic quotation rather than to the actions of the crowd at the Triumphal Entry. This would mean that the disciples did in fact grasp the messianic significance of the crowd's actions and the use of the title "King of Israel" at the time, in line with their previous messianic expectations concerning Jesus. What they failed to understand before Jesus' resurrection, then, was the true nature of His messiahship: it was to consist in humility and sacrifice ending in His death, rather than in militaristic, nationalistic, or political aspirations. In fact, this was something they could not understand until after Jesus had been glorified and the Holy Spirit had come (John 14:26).

Even on the eve of Jesus' arrest and crucifixion, as He spoke to the disciples in the Upper Room, it is evident that they had not understood the necessity of His death nor the full truth about who He was. They did not understand the significance of Jesus' actions in washing their feet (13:2–17). They were bewildered by Jesus' prediction that one of them would betray Him (vv. 18, 21–30). In fact, Jesus explicitly said He was telling them of His betrayal in advance, so that when it happened they would believe (v. 19). What they would believe when they looked back on the prediction of betrayal is given in the final clause of verse 19: "that I am" (NIV "that I am He"). This is one of four absolute "I am" statements in the gospel of John without a predicate (cf. John 8:28). As a deliberate allusion to Exodus 3:14 it implies Jesus' deity. The disciples had no idea of this at the time. On later (postresurrection) reflection concerning Jesus' prediction of His betrayal, the disciples would conclude that He was in complete control of the situation as only God Himself could be.

Later in the Farewell Discourse (John 13:31–17:26) several of the Twelve asked questions or made requests that reflected their level of understanding at the time. Thomas's question, "Lord, we don't know where you are going, so how can we know the way?" (14:5) indicates lack of understanding regarding Jesus' departure through death. Philip's request, "Lord, show us the Father" (v. 8), indicates that the disciples had not at this time grasped the true nature of Jesus' relationship to the Father. This is confirmed by Jesus' response in verses 9–14. The question by Judas (not Iscariot), "But Lord, why do you intend to show yourself to us and not to the world?" (v. 22), missed the point that Jesus' relationship to the world and to His disciples would be fundamentally different after His resurrection. A similar misunderstanding among several of the disciples is indicated in 16:17–18.

In 16:29 Jesus' disciples professed to understand at last and to believe that He came from God. In reply to this Jesus seemingly acknowledged their belief ("You believe at last!" v. 31). This is almost certainly another example of irony. Jesus did not need their professions to know what was in their minds. He knew, in fact, that the hour of testing which was coming would find them scattered, as He predicted (v. 32). Thus even at this point, on the eve of Jesus' arrest, trials, and crucifixion, the disciples apparently did not understand the necessity of His death or who He really is.

Only after Jesus' resurrection did His disciples begin to understand who He really is. One of the first was the "beloved disciple," traditionally identified as the

Apostle John. On reaching the empty tomb and looking inside, he "saw and believed" (20:8). Although John did not specify precisely what it was that he believed at the time, the context makes it almost certain that it included Jesus' resurrection from the dead. Whether anything more was involved concerning the person of Jesus is not clear, but it is evident that the Evangelist introduced here the theme of "seeing and believing" which would reach its climax in John 20:28 with the confession of Thomas.

Thomas's confession was readily accepted by Jesus, indicating that he really had now believed. Jesus then commended others who would likewise believe without the benefit of seeing (v. 29). Whatever may be said (or speculated) concerning the disciples' previous belief in Jesus as the Messiah, clearly after the resurrection their faith now included belief in Jesus' deity (Thomas's use of "my God" to address Jesus in 20:28 indicates this). Here is the final realization of the statements about the Word introduced in the prologue to the gospel of John (1:1, 14). Jesus' repeated teaching about the relationship of the Son to the Father and His repeated use of "I am" statements without predicates all led up to this confession by Thomas, as did the seven sign-miracles. This same confession also related to John's purpose in writing his Gospel: "But these are written that you may believe that Jesus is the Christ, the Son of God, and that by believing you may have life in his name" (20:31).

In spite of the fact that the disciples had repeatedly heard Jesus speak of His unique relationship with the Father and had also heard Him allude to His impending death by crucifixion, they did not understand the true nature of Jesus' person and work until after His resurrection.

REGENERATION IN THE JOHANNINE WRITINGS

The new birth in the gospel of John. The only explicit mention of the new birth is found in Jesus' dialogue with Nicodemus (3:1–21). In reply to Nicodemus' questions, Jesus told him, "I tell you the truth, no one can see the kingdom of God unless he is born again" (v. 3). Nicodemus's reply, "How can a man be born when he is old? . . . Surely he cannot enter a second time into his mother's womb to be born!" (v. 4), indicates that he understood Jesus' comment on a human, physical level. Nicodemus's misunderstanding gave Jesus opportunity to clarify what He meant. He was speaking of the need for a new spiritual birth rather than a second physical birth (vv. 6–8). The misunderstanding and its resulting clarification are reflected in a wordplay in verse 3 (repeated in v. 7). As stated earlier, the Greek word *anōthen,* translated "again" in the NIV, may mean either "again" or "from above." Although Nicodemus understood it to mean "again," leading him to conclude that Jesus was speaking of a second physical birth, Jesus' reply in verses 6–8 shows that He referred to the need for a spiritual birth, a birth "from above." This new birth was not to be the result of any human action (cf. v. 6), but is the work of the Holy Spirit (v. 8). Supernatural activity by the Spirit of God is required to bring about this new spiritual birth within an individual. It did not consist in merely greater insight or understanding but in a complete transformation of the individual (cf. 2 Cor. 5:17).

In John 3:5 Jesus declared that the new spiritual birth is a prerequisite for entry into the kingdom of God. The need for a new spiritual birth is implicitly stated in the prologue to the gospel of John: "Yet to all who received him, to those who believed in his name, he gave the right to become children of God—children born not of natural descent, nor of human decision or a husband's will, but born of God" (1:12–13). These verses link the new birth with receiving Jesus and believing in His name. This implies that the new birth is an initiatory process which occurs at the time of belief.

The new birth in the Johannine epistles. The same concept of the new spiritual birth is found numerous times in 1 John. Those whose righteous behavior emulates that of Jesus are said to have been "born of him" (1 John 2:29). John asserted that "No one who is born of God will continue to sin" (3:9, cf. 3:6; 5:18). Although this verse has sometimes been misunderstood as teaching sinless perfection, it is highly unlikely that such is in view here, because elsewhere in 1 John the author acknowledged that genuine believers do on occasion commit sins (2:1). Differences in the Greek verb tenses have also been suggested as an explanation for the apparent contradiction regarding believers' sin. It is difficult to see how John could express such a major point with a grammatical subtlety, however. The answer to the apparent contradiction more likely lies in the situation addressed in the Johannine epistles. A serious Christological schism existed in the churches to which John was writing. It concerned the humanity of Jesus and the importance of His earthly life and ministry as an example for believers. John's secessionist opponents had claimed to be without sin (1 John 1:8, 10); in reply to this John reassured his readers that if they do sin, Jesus Christ remains their Advocate (2:1–2 NASB). On the other hand, the opponents were denying the need for a moral lifestyle because they rejected the significance of Jesus' earthly life and ministry (as well as His sinless humanity) as an example for believers to follow. Their failure to act righteously provided an outward indicator of their inward spiritual state: "No one who continues to sin has either seen him or known him" (3:6). To his readers John wrote, "Dear children, do not let anyone lead you astray. He who does what is right is righteous, just as he [Jesus] is righteous. He who does what is sinful is of the devil, because the devil has been sinning from the beginning" (vv. 7–8). John stated the conclusion in verse 10: "This is how we know who the children of God are and who the children of the devil are: Anyone who does not do what is right is not a child or God; nor is anyone who does not love his brother." John's point to his readers concerns how they may identify the opponents; conduct is a clue to paternity. Those who have been genuinely born of God, who have truly experienced the new spiritual birth, will generally behave in certain recognizable ways, and those who have not been reborn will also behave in recognizable ways. This is not to say that the believer will never sin, as John already acknowledged in 2:1. It is simply to say that in the midst of the sharp controversy over orthodox versus heterodox Christology, how one behaves is a reliable indicator of one's allegiance (to God or to the devil).

Other references to the new spiritual birth are found in 1 John 4:7 and 5:4. Again, 1 John 4:7 must be read in light of the controversy within the churches in

Asia Minor. John was not claiming that to act in love is all that is necessary to be born of God and to know Him. He was simply asserting once more that conduct is a clue to paternity; the recipients of the letter may recognize fellow believers by their love for one another (cf. John 13:34–35), while the opponents may likewise be recognized by their lack of love. The spiritual birth is linked to victorious living in 1 John 5:4, where John asserted that everyone born of God overcomes the world.

BELIEF

For John, one's knowledge of God begins with an act of personal faith in Jesus Christ (John 1:12). This involves acknowledging who Jesus is and is related to the purpose of the fourth gospel (20:31). Belief does not depend on the actual physical seeing and hearing of Jesus alone; many who saw Jesus in the flesh did not believe (6:64, 66), and believing in the fullest sense is possible only after Jesus was "lifted up" (i.e., crucified; cf. 8:28).[36] Ultimately, a blessing is reserved for those who have not seen and yet have believed (20:29).

On the one hand, believing involves a new and different kind of seeing, as illustrated by the incident of the man born blind and its conclusion (9:1–41). The blind man's physical eyes were opened, and his "inner eyes" were opened as well, for he ultimately came to personal faith in Jesus (v. 38). On the other hand the Pharisees, who possessed physical sight, were spiritually blind and continued, ironically, to plunge headlong into spiritual darkness (vv. 39–41).

This "inner sight" or belief is ultimately the result of God's enablement rather than a matter of human achievement. As Jesus said, "This is why I told you that no one can come to me unless the Father has enabled him" (6:65). The distinctive Johannine use of *pisteuein* ("to believe") with the preposition *eis* emphasizes the strongly personal character of belief, a trusting relationship with a person. It is not, however, an automatic grammatical indication of genuine faith; this must be contextually determined.

The Johannine epistles are particularly concerned to reassure the readers of their genuine belief in light of the Christological controversy that had split the churches in Asia Minor to which they were addressed. The Apostle John gave a number of indications of genuine faith intended to reassure his readers and help them identify their heterodox opponents. To understand the subject of belief in the Johannine epistles and the gospel of John, it is important to note that John expected genuine belief to result in some behavioral indications. Once a person has come to faith in Jesus, John's expectation was that such a person's faith will continue to grow and develop. The experience of the Twelve in the gospel of John (with the obvious exception of Judas Iscariot, who was never a believer to begin with) provides a significant model for this. There is no distinction in the Johannine writings between genuine belief and discipleship. It is expected that believers will be disciples of Jesus and will continue to grow in their relationship with Him. For John

---

36. See the previous section, "The Development of the Disciples' Faith in Jesus in the Gospel of John."

there are only two categories of people: those who come to the light, and those who remain in darkness (cf. John 3:19–21).

Belief in Jesus in the gospel of John. Interestingly *pistis,* the Greek noun for "belief," does not occur in John's gospel, although the verb *pisteuō* ("believe") is used nearly 100 times both alone and with various prepositions. Since the purpose of the gospel of John is "that you may believe that Jesus is the Christ, the Son of God, and that by believing you may have life in his name" (20:31), it is to be expected that this concept would receive much emphasis in the gospel. The avoidance of the noun form is more difficult to explain, especially since it is frequently used in the rest of the New Testament (some twenty times in the Synoptic Gospels and 140 times in Paul's epistles).[37] The most common suggestion, which is probably correct, is that John wanted to stress the act of believing more than the content.[38] In the gospel of John belief is viewed in terms of a relationship with Jesus Christ, which begins with a decision to accept rather than reject who Jesus claims to be. This leads to a new relationship with God, as John 1:12 states: "Yet to all who received him, to those who believed in his name, he gave the right to become children of God."

One of the favorite constructions of John to indicate belief is the verb *pisteuō* plus the preposition *eis.*[39] Some scholars have conjectured that this particular construction originated in early Christian circles to distinguish between intellectual assent and personal trust. Others have found a parallel to this usage in the Dead Sea Scrolls, in which members of the community are said to have faith in their leader (1QpHab 8:2–3, referring to the Teacher of Righteousness), but it is uncertain whether this refers to their belief in him or their faithfulness to him. What is clearer is that in the Johannine writings (regardless of where he got the phrase) *pisteuō* with *eis* refers to belief in a person. Thirty-one times it describes belief in Jesus, three times it refers to belief in the name of Jesus, and twice it reflects belief in the Father. Believing in Jesus is equated with coming to Him in the parallelism of John 6:35, where Jesus said, "He who comes to me will never go hungry, and he who believes in me will never be thirsty" (the same parallel between coming to Jesus and believing in Him is repeated in 7:37–38). Regardless of whether the opening clause of 14:1 is understood as indicative or imperative, belief in Jesus is compared to belief (NIV "trust") in God. When the crowd who followed Jesus to Capernaum after the feeding of the 5,000 found Him, they asked, "What must we do to do the works God requires?" (6:28). Jesus' reply indicated that belief in Him was what God expected: "The work of God is this: to believe in the one he has sent" (v. 29).

37. The noun form occurs in the remaining Johannine literature very infrequently: once in 1 John and four times in Revelation.

38. There is actually some development within the gospel of John regarding the content of belief. The disciples started out believing that Jesus was the Messiah (1:41) and ended up affirming that He is Lord and God (20:28). John's purpose in writing was of course that his readers would make the latter confession about Jesus, but the disciples' relationship of faith in Jesus grew and developed as they came to a more complete understanding of who He is. See the previous section, "The Development of the Disciples' Faith in the Gospel of John."

39. This construction is used thirty-six times in the gospel of John and three times in 1 John.

Another construction used by John, which is often compared to *pisteuō* with *eis* is the verb *pisteuō* with the dative case, which occurs about twenty times in the gospel of John and twice in 1 John. Although this construction may also refer to genuine faith on the part of an individual, there is a difference in emphasis. *Pisteuō* with the dative is used both for believing in a person (Moses, 5:46; Jesus, 8:31; the Father, 5:24) and in a thing (the Scriptures, 2:22; Jesus' words, 4:50; 5:47). The element of personal trust and commitment is less emphatic here; the context suggests that mere assent or acceptance of a message is more in view.

A few other constructions with *pisteuō* are used in the Johannine writings. In John 4:41–42 the verb is used with the preposition *dia* and the accusative case to mean "believe on account of." Here the accusative object of the preposition specifies the ground or basis of faith: "And because of his words many more became believers" (v. 41). The same usage is found in 14:11, "believe on the evidence of [*dia*] the miracles themselves." *Pisteuō* is also used many times in an absolute sense without any object specified (e.g., 1:50; 3:12; 4:48, 53; 5:44; 6:36), and the context must determine the nuance. It is also followed occasionally by clauses, usually giving the content of the belief.

Significantly most of the uses of the verb *pisteuō* in the gospel of John occur within the first twelve chapters (seventy-four times out of ninety-eight). In chapters 13–21 only four uses of *pisteuō* with *eis* occur, out of thirty-four uses in the entire gospel. This is perfectly understandable since chapters 1–12 deal primarily with the sign-miracles and discourses where the issue is who Jesus is and the necessity of believing in Him, whereas chapters 13–21 record Jesus' Farewell Discourse to His disciples (who have already believed in Him) and the events of the passion.

Expressions related to believing in the gospel of John. A number of similar or parallel expressions related to belief are also found in the gospel of John. In John 1:12 "receiving" Jesus is virtually equivalent to "believing in His name" due to the parallelism of the verse. Something similar occurs with the parallelism of "knowing" (*ginōskō*) and "believing" in John 17:8, where Jesus stated, "They knew with certainty that I came from you, and they believed that you sent me." In this case certain knowledge is virtually equated with belief regarding the Father's sending of the Son. The same parallelism between knowing and believing may be seen by comparing John 14:7 and 10.

Another concept related to believing in the gospel of John is "seeing." This is most clearly noted in Jesus' comments following the healing of the man born blind. Jesus' remark in response to the man's confession of faith is paradoxical: "For judgment I have come into this world, so that the blind will see and those who see will become blind" (9:39). Jesus was speaking not only of the restoration of physical sight to the blind but also of the giving of spiritual vision as well. While the blind man who had just professed to believe in Jesus had received both physical and spiritual sight, the Pharisees who possessed physical sight were struck with spiritual blindness (cf. 12:39–40). The theme of judgment mentioned here links this passage with 3:19–21 with its light and darkness imagery. The Evangelist's summary of the results of Jesus' public ministry in 12:37–41 also refers to the spiritual blindness of the Jewish leadership as a deliberate judgment of God (v. 40).

This relationship between seeing and believing is also implicit in the exchange between Jesus and Thomas in 20:24–29. When the other disciples informed Thomas that they had seen the resurrected Lord, Thomas replied, "Unless I see the nail marks in his hands and put my finger where the nails were, and put my hand into his side, I will not believe it" (v. 25).[40] After Jesus appeared to Thomas He told him, "Because you have seen me, you have believed; blessed are those who have not seen and yet have believed" (v. 29).

Genuine belief versus inadequate belief in the gospel of John. The fourth gospel makes reference both to genuine belief in Jesus—the sort that produces eternal life—and a less than adequate faith in Jesus that does not. Only a careful reading of the context distinguishes between these two types of faith, not (as some have supposed) a technical distinction between the Greek phrases John used for belief. It has been said that whenever the Evangelist wished to refer to genuine saving faith he used the construction *pisteuō* with the preposition *eis.* On the other hand, it is argued, the use of *pisteuō* plus the simple dative case supposedly refers to an inadequate or superficial faith. From a linguistic standpoint such a distinction does not hold. Examples may be found in John's gospel of both constructions which violate this distinction. *Pisteuō* with *eis,* which allegedly indicates genuine saving faith, almost certainly refers to inadequate faith in John 2:23. The people in question believed on the basis of the miraculous signs they had witnessed. It is true that to believe on the basis of miraculous signs is better than not to believe at all (cf. 10:38). Nevertheless, Jesus' response to these converts was enough to call their faith into question: "But Jesus would not entrust himself to them, for he knew all men" (2:24). The Greek text contains a wordplay: the verb translated by the NIV as "believed" in verse 23 and "entrust" in verse 24 is the same, namely, *pisteuō.* If these were genuine believers, Jesus' refusal to entrust Himself to them is extremely difficult to explain, especially since the gospel of John places people in only two categories: those who come to the light, and those who choose to remain in darkness (cf. 3:19–21).

On the other hand, *pisteuō* and the simple dative case, which supposedly refers to an inadequate faith, is used of faith that is clearly genuine in John 5:24, where Jesus said, "whoever hears my word and believes him who sent me has eternal life and will not be condemned; he has crossed over from death to life." There are in fact different nuances attached to both expressions (see above), but the distinction is not between genuine faith and inadequate faith.

Inadequate faith is also the point of John 6:60–66. After hearing Jesus speak of their eating His flesh and drinking His blood, many of His disciples began to grumble (v. 60). In responding to them Jesus noted, "Yet there are some of you who do not believe" (v. 64). After this John added the comment that Jesus had known from the beginning which of them did not believe (probably an allusion to 2:24–25) and who would betray Him. The mention of the betrayer, Judas, in con-

---

40. The English word "it" is supplied by the NIV translators and has no Greek equivalent.

nection with these false disciples puts them in the same category with him. The only real difference is that Judas was also one of the Twelve. Proof that Jesus' evaluation of these false disciples was correct is indicated by their actions. "From this time many of his disciples turned back and no longer followed him" (6:66). Perseverance with Jesus is an outward sign of genuine belief.

Another passage that deals with inadequate faith in the gospel of John is 8:31-59. In verses 31-32 Jesus told those Jews who had believed Him, "If you hold to my teaching, you are really my disciples. Then you will know the truth, and the truth will set you free." The Jews who had believed were apparently part of the group mentioned in verse 30, which says that "many put their faith in him." Problems arise in the interpretation of the passage, however, for it soon becomes apparent that the Jews who had believed Jesus (v. 31) were still regarded by Him as slaves of sin (v. 34), as having no room for His word (v. 37), as offspring not of Abraham (v. 39) but of the devil (v. 44), and as liars (v. 55). Ultimately, they attempted unsuccessfully to stone Jesus for blasphemy (v. 59).

Some have attempted to explain the discrepancy between the attribution of faith to these Jews in John 8:31 and their subsequent behavior as a difference in meaning between two Greek constructions used by John to indicate faith, *pisteuō* and the preposition *eis* in verse 30 versus *pisteuō* and the simple dative case in verse 31. As already seen, however (although there are indeed different nuances between the two constructions), the difference is not one of genuine saving faith versus inadequate faith. Others have attempted to explain the contradictory behavior described in 8:33-58 by suggesting that some Jewish leaders genuinely believed in Jesus, whereas most of the Jewish authorities did not believe and were thus the object of Jesus' comments in verses 34-58. While such a "division of the house" is perhaps possible, there is no real contextual indication that in verses 34-58 Jesus was addressing anyone other than "the Jews who had believed him" (v. 31).

The easiest explanation is that whatever these Jewish leaders had believed about Jesus, He did not regard it as adequate to place them among His followers.[41] His initial reply to them indicated that the genuineness of their faith would be demonstrated if they continued to be obedient to His teaching (8:31; NIV "if you hold to my teaching").[42] This is completely consistent with the perspective elsewhere in John's gospel, "If anyone loves me, he will obey my teaching . . . he who does not love me will not obey my teaching" (14:23-24). It is also the perspective of the Johannine epistles, where, as noted, conduct becomes the clue to paternity. Perseverance is the outward sign of genuine belief; real disciples will continue on with Jesus (1 John 2:19; 2 John 9). Failure to do so indicates that any faith expressed was not really genuine.

41. It is possible, for example, that these Jewish leaders had believed that Jesus was the Messiah in some sense, but rejected His claims to be the Son of God. Jesus' claim to deity is certainly an issue later in the passage, for after Jesus' use of the "I am" formula in John 8:58 the Jewish authorities attempted unsuccessfully to stone Him for blasphemy.

42. The Greek word is *menō,* an important Johannine term for remaining or continuing in permanent relationship.

Belief in the Johannine Epistles. The concept of belief presented in the Johannine epistles is similar to that in the gospel of John. The verb *pisteuō* occurs nine times in 1 John and the noun *pistis* occurs once (5:4). Three times in 1 John *pisteuō* with the preposition *eis* is used (5:10 [twice], 13). Twice *pisteuō* is used with the simple dative case (4:1; 5:10).[43] The remaining uses are either absolute (with no object specified) or are followed by the accusative (4:16) or by clauses specifying the content of the belief (5:1, 5). It is important to note, however, that although there are only ten references to the verb *pisteuō* and the noun *pistis* in John's epistles, genuine saving faith is discussed by other terms and other imagery. These will be discussed in turn.

The first mention of belief in 1 John actually occurs in 1:6–7: "If we claim to have fellowship with him yet walk in the darkness, we lie and do not live by the truth. But if we walk in the light, as he is in the light, we have fellowship with one another, and the blood of Jesus, his Son, purifies us from all sin." In these two verses John employed no less than three sets of images referring to genuine belief: claiming to have fellowship with God, living by the truth, and walking in the light. "Walking in darkness" as the antithesis of walking in the light denotes the person who has not come to the light, that is, one who has not come to Jesus, the Light of the world (cf. John 3:19–21). This person, for John, is an unbeliever regardless of whatever claims one may make about having fellowship with God.

First John 2:3–4 also speaks of genuine belief versus unbelief: "We know that we have come to know him if we obey his commands. The man who says, 'I know him,' but does not do what he commands is a liar, and the truth is not in him." This is exactly parallel to Jesus' statements about genuine love for Him resulting in obedience (John 14:23–24). It is to be expected that genuine faith will result in a lifestyle obedient to Jesus' commands (especially the commandment to love one another; 1 John 2:7–11). This is reiterated in 1 John 2:6, where claiming "to live in him" is another reference to genuine saving faith, which will result in an imitation of Jesus' own manner of life.

Another phrase synonymous with genuine belief is in 1 John 2:9, "to be in the light." The person who makes this claim (to have come to Jesus as the Light of the world and thus "to be in the light") and yet continues to hate one's brother is really still in the darkness. Such a person has not come to the Light at all, regardless of his or her claim. This is completely consistent with the light and darkness imagery of John's gospel and with the concept of spiritual blindness which accompanies the absence of spiritual light (cf. John 9:39–41).

A phrase related to genuine belief (although not exactly synonymous with it) is found in 1 John 2:19. Speaking of the secessionist opponents whom he labeled "antichrists," John declared, "They went out from us, but they did not really belong to us. For if they had belonged to us, they would have remained with us; but their going showed that none of them belonged to us." By his use of the phrase

---

43. A further example of *pisteuō* and the simple dative case is 1 John 3:23, but there are textual variants within the verse.

"belong to us" John referred to those who belonged to the company of genuine believers as opposed to the opponents with their false Christology.

Also indicative of genuine faith is the description of believers as "children of God" in 1 John 3:1–2. Believers are also described as "righteous" (v. 7) and as those who are "born of God" (v. 9). Again John stressed that one's behavior is an outward indication that enables both the genuine believer and the unbeliever to be recognized: "This is how we know who the children of God are and who the children of the devil are: Anyone who does not do what is right is not a child of God; nor is anyone who does not love his brother" (v. 10). John also described genuine believers as "those who belong to the truth" (v. 19).

The first actual use of the verb "believe" (*pisteuō*) occurs later in the chapter. "And this is his [God's] command: to believe in the name of his Son, Jesus Christ, and to love one another as he commanded us" (v. 23). John reassured his readers that they had indeed obeyed this command and thus were those who "live in him," as the presence of the Spirit in their lives testified (v. 24). John referred here to the mutual indwelling of God and the believer, promised by Jesus in John 14:23.

A negative reference to belief occurs in 1 John 4:1: "do not believe every spirit, but test the spirits to see whether they are from God." Since John then referred to false prophets who had gone out into the world, it is probable that the spirits he referred to are the spirits that governed the prophets and their messages. The false prophets (and the spirits behind them) constitute another reference to the secessionist opponents with their heretical Christology. The pressing issue before John's readers was how they could recognize such messages as originating from God or from the spirit of the antichrist (cf. v. 6). "Being born of God" and "knowing God" (v. 7) are further descriptions of genuine belief that have occurred before in the epistle (2:3–4; 3:9). In this context John spoke of "believing" the love that God has for the readers as believers (4:16, "rely on").

In 1 John 5:1 John related believing that Jesus is the Christ with being born of God; both are descriptions of genuine belief. In 5:5 the person who believes that Jesus is the Son of God is said to have overcome the world. Similarly verse 10 sets up another antithesis between belief and unbelief: "Anyone who believes in the Son of God has this testimony in his heart. Anyone who does not believe God has made him out to be a liar, because he has not believed the testimony God has given about his Son." The testimony is said to be that God has given eternal life in His Son. The readers as genuine believers fall within the category of those who have the testimony (and thus possess eternal life in the Son). The opponents, on the other hand, have not believed God and thus have made God out to be a liar (cf. 1:10). They do not have the Son of God and, therefore, neither do they have eternal life (5:12). The final reference to belief in 1 John 5 is aimed at reassuring the readers as those "who believe in the name of the Son of God" that they do in fact possess eternal life (v. 13). In the remainder of chapter 5 John repeated some of the phrases he had used previously for genuine belief: "born of God" (v. 18), "children of God" (v. 19), knowing Him who is true (v. 20), and being in Him who is true (v. 20).

Believing and abiding. One of the most important terms John used to express the permanency of relationship between the believer and God is the Greek verb *menō*. It is variously translated by the NIV as "dwell in" (John 5:38), "remain" (15:7), "live" (1 John 2:10, 14), and "continue" (2 John 9).[44] It is not possible to offer a single translation which does justice to every context in which the word is found, but one of the most versatile translations is "reside," which conveys the nuance of permanence without the implication of possible departure implied by "remain."[45]

On one level John used this word to describe the indwelling of various attributes and gifts of God in the believer and reciprocally the residing of the believer in various attributes. God's word or Jesus' word is said to reside in the believer (John 5:38; 15:7; 1 John 2:14, 24). Reciprocally the believer is said to reside in Jesus' word (John 8:31). God's love resides in believers but not in unbelievers (1 John 3:17), while reciprocally the believer is said to reside in Jesus' love (John 15:9–10) and God's love (1 John 4:16). God's truth resides in believers (2 John 2) as does God's anointing (1 John 2:27) and God's seed (3:9). Eternal life does not reside in a murderer, but by implication does reside in believers (v. 15). On the other hand, believers are said to reside "in the light" (2:10; cf. John 12:46 where believers do not remain in darkness). The one who remains in the teaching of Christ "has the Father and the Son" while the one who does not remain "does not have God" (2 John 9).[46]

On another level John used the verb *menō* to describe the mutual indwelling of the Father, the Son, and the believer. Sometimes this is expressed in terms of the mutual relationship between Jesus and the believer. In the Bread of Life discourse Jesus declared, "Whoever eats my flesh and drinks my blood remains in me, and I in him" (John 6:56). On another occasion Jesus told His disciples, "Remain in me, and I will remain in you" (15:4). In 1 John 4:15 the mutuality of relationship between God the Father and the believer is emphasized. "If anyone acknowledges that Jesus is the Son of God, God lives in him and he in God." The verb *menō* is also used to describe the mutual relationship between the Father, the Son, and the believer. "See that what you have heard from the beginning remains in you. If it does, you also will remain in the Son and in the Father" (1 John 2:24).[47] In John

---

44. The KJV generally employs the translation "abide" for *menō*.

45. In the following discussion of examples of Johannine usage, "remain" is used only when it is clear from the context that some change of status is in view or when the text of the NIV is quoted.

46. "Remain" is used here as a translation for *menō* because this refers to the secessionist opponents whose false Christology had led them to depart from the churches in Asia Minor to which John was writing. Their failure to "remain" in the teaching of Christ, and their subsequent departure from fellowship, demonstrated that they were never genuine believers to begin with (1 John 2:19).

47. Virtually the same thought is expressed in John 14:23, where the cognate noun form *monē* ("abode") is used instead of the verb *menō*.

14:10 Jesus used *menō* to describe His relationship with the Father, obviously a permanent relationship.[48]

The relationship between Jesus and the Father is the model for the relationship between Jesus and His disciples. It is, therefore, not surprising that when Jesus spoke to His disciples about the status of their relationship to Him in His Farewell Discourse (John 15:1–17), He used terminology that implied the mutuality and permanence of their relationship. Thus *menō* is used eleven times in those seventeen verses. Mutuality of relationship is explicitly stated by Jesus (vv. 4–5). The presumption is that the disciples present as Jesus spoke would indeed remain and continue. The prime example of one who did not remain is Judas (v. 6), who had already departed from Jesus' presence (13:30). For John, Judas's failure to remain with Jesus demonstrates that he never genuinely belonged to Jesus in the first place, just as in 1 John 2:19 the departure of the opponents with their errant Christology demonstrates that they never genuinely belonged to the group of believers to whom John wrote.[49] Regarding the secessionist opponents mentioned in 1 John, a similar thought is expressed by the apostle in 2 John 9: "Anyone who runs ahead and does not continue [*menōn*] in the teaching of Christ does not have God; whoever continues in the teaching has both the Father and the Son." John's expectation was that genuine believers (disciples) would continue with Jesus. In John 8:31 Jesus declared, "If you hold [*meinēte*] to my teaching, you are really my disciples," and it quickly became clear that those to whom He was speaking were not genuine disciples of His (vv. 37, 40, 42, 44, 47, 52, 59). As already noted in the discussion of belief in the Johannine epistles, John expected genuine faith to result in a lifestyle obedient to Jesus' commands (especially the commandment to love one another; 1 John 2:7–11).

ETERNAL LIFE

Eternal life in the gospel of John. The concept of eternal life is introduced in the prologue to the gospel of John: "In him was life, and that life was the light of men" (1:4). Jesus Himself is the source of eternal life ("everlasting life" NIV), who is Himself "life" (*zōē*, 3:16; 10:10; 20:31), and whose life is the life of God (5:26). Outside the New Testament the phrase "eternal life" itself is found only once in the Septuagint (Dan. 12:2) in a context that is clearly eschatological. It occurs once in Philo as well[50] but does not occur in pagan religious or philosophical writers until long after the New Testament period.

The author of the gospel of John explicitly states that to have "eternal life" means to be raised up by Jesus Christ at the last day (John 6:40, 54; cf. 6:39, 44; 11:24; 12:48). The righteous will come forth to experience eternal life (5:29; literally "to a resurrection of life"; NIV "to live"); the unrighteous will be raised to eter-

---

48. This permanent relationship between Jesus and the Father is also expressed in John 17:21–23 although the verb *menō* is not used.

49. *Menō* is also used in 1 John 2:19.

50. *De fuga et inventione* 78.

nal judgment. Thus what is translated by most English versions as "eternal life" or "life everlasting" really means "the life of the age to come." This is consistent with the usage of the phrase in Daniel 12:2 as well as other intertestamental sources (Testament of Asher 5:2; Psalms of Solomon 3:16; 2 [4] Esdras 7:12–13; 8:52–54). Likewise it is found in this sense in other New Testament writers. In discussions about conditions of entry into the reign of God, the rich man in Mark 10:17 asked, "Good teacher . . . what must I do to inherit eternal life?" (*zōē aiōnios*, the same phrase used by John). Such a contrast between the present life and the life of the world to come may also be seen in John 12:25: "The man who loves his life will lose it, while the man who hates his life in this world will keep it for eternal life."[51]

Yet for John eternal life is not limited to the age to come; it is something that extends back into the present age and is currently available for believers to experience. According to Jesus, "whoever hears my word and believes him who sent me has eternal life and will not be condemned; he has crossed over from death to life" (5:24). One of the major purposes for the Son's mission into the world from the Father is that "whoever believes in him shall not perish but have eternal life" (3:16). The following verse restates the purpose of God in sending His Son; the parallelism suggests that providing eternal life to those who believe is equivalent to saving the world (cf. 3:17). Jesus' purpose in coming down from heaven is again stated in the Bread of life discourse: "For the bread of God is he who comes down from heaven and gives life to the world" (6:33). This involves the satisfaction of spiritual hunger and spiritual thirst (v. 35). John 10:10 also relates the mission of the Son to the present provision of eternal life, as Jesus declared, "I have come that they may have life, and have it to the full." The Father Himself is the source of this life, but He has granted the Son to have life in Himself (5:26). Because of this Jesus could declare, "I am the resurrection and the life" (11:25; cf. 14:6). Jesus' prayer includes a virtual definition of eternal life. "Now this is eternal life: that they may know you, the only true God, and Jesus Christ, whom you have sent" (17:3).

These two aspects of eternal life, present and future, are closely associated in John 5:21–30. The Father raises the dead and gives them life, and the Son is also able to give life to whomever He pleases (v. 21). The Father has entrusted all judgment to the Son (v. 22). Whoever believes has eternal life in the present and will not face condemnatory judgment, but has already crossed over from death to life (v. 24). Those who are spiritually dead are now hearing the voice of the Son; the ones who respond receive eternal life (v. 25). Yet there is a future resurrection for the physically dead as well, followed by judgment (vv. 28–29).

In writing of eternal life as a future blessing in the age to come, John is in agreement with the Synoptic Gospels. The emphasis on eternal life as a present reality experienced by the believer differs from the Synoptics and is a unique contribution of John. These two are not disparate and contradictory; rather the future aspects of eternal life are a continuation of that aspect of eternal life experienced in

---

51. Cf. the similar sayings in the Synoptic Gospels: Matthew 10:39, 16:25; Mark 8:35; Luke 9:24, 17:33.

the present. As Jesus said in John 11:26, "whoever lives and believes in me will never die," that is, the person who believes and thus possesses eternal life in the present age will continue to possess it in the age to come, and therefore it may be said that he or she "will never see death" (cf. 8:51).

Eternal life in the Johannine epistles. In John's epistles the concept of eternal life parallels what is already seen in his gospel. If anything, Jesus' role as Source and Giver of eternal life is magnified in 1 John, where Jesus is initially described not just as the "Word" (following John 1:1, 14), but as the "Word of life" (1 John 1:1). Jesus is the one who has life in Himself, and who came to dispense it to all who believe in Him. John told his readers, "we proclaim to you the eternal life, which was with the Father and has appeared to us" (1 John 1:2). In the midst of a serious Christological controversy, where some professed members of the churches to which John wrote had withdrawn from association with the readers (2:19), John reminded his readers that eternal life had been promised to them (v. 25). Here it sounds as if eternal life is something in the future, not yet received by the readers. But this is simply a reflection of the twofold emphasis already encountered in the gospel of John on eternal life as both future, in the age to come, and at the same time a present experience for believers. The present aspect of eternal life is also mentioned in 1 John: "We know that we have passed from death to life, because we love our brothers" (3:14; cf. John 5:24). By the quality of love which Christians express in the church they may know they already experience eternal life.

Another indication of the believer's present experience of eternal life comes through the indwelling Spirit (1 John 4:13). Crucial to possessing eternal life is the acknowledgment that Jesus is the Son of God (v. 15). Again, for John, the eternal life God gives is in His Son, so that the one who believes in the Son has eternal life, and the one who does not believe does not possess eternal life (5:11). As in John 17:3, the believer's possession of eternal life is inseparably linked to one's relationship to Jesus Christ. This is true to such an extent that John could say at the conclusion of his epistle, "we are in him who is true—even in his Son Jesus Christ. He is the true God and eternal life" (1 John 5:20). Eternal life, for John, is a relationship with the Father and the Son. It begins in the present when a person comes to faith in Jesus Christ, but it continues uninterrupted into the age to come.

Eternal life as the possession of the "overcomer" in Revelation. In Revelation the Apostle John emphasizes eternal life as a future blessing in the age to come, the inheritance of those who "overcome" (cf. Rev. 21:7). "Overcomers" are genuine believers who have been given to drink of the water of life in the present (v. 6) and who receive the promised blessings of eternal life in the future as well (v. 7). They are contrasted with "the cowardly, the unbelieving, the vile, the murderers, the sexually immoral, those who practice magic arts, the idolators and all liars" (v. 8) who will experience the second death in the lake of fire.

The promises made to the "overcomers" in the letters to the seven churches (Rev. 2:1–3:22) also point to the future blessings of eternal life and correspond to the description in 21:6–8. Overcomers will be given the right to eat from the tree of life which is in the paradise of God (2:7). As genuine believers these individuals will not be hurt by the second death (v. 11; cf. 21:8). Overcomers will share Christ's authority over the nations (2:26–27; 3:21). Their salvation is secure (3:5).[52]

Other individuals were also addressed in the letters to the seven churches. There were some in the church at Pergamum who led others into the sins of idolatry and immorality (2:14). Others in the same church held to Nicolaitan teachings (v. 15).[53] In the church at Thyatira the false prophetess Jezebel misled some into sexual immorality (v. 20). Those unwilling to repent were to be judged (vv. 22–23). The seven churches addressed in Revelation were not without problems, and not all who claimed to belong to these churches were genuine believers ("overcomers").

ESCHATOLOGY IN THE JOHANNINE WRITINGS

ESCHATOLOGY IN THE GOSPEL OF JOHN

At the outset of a discussion of Johannine eschatology it is helpful to make some general observations. Many New Testament scholars have argued that the fourth gospel, in particular, has a completely different approach to the last things than that found in the Synoptic Gospels.[54] While the Synoptics are structured around a horizontal dimension between present and future, Johannine narrative centers around a vertical dimension between heaven and earth (or above and below; cf. John 3:12–13, 31; 8:34).[55] It is true that for John the vertical dimension occupied much of his attention. Jesus stated that He came from above (3:13; 6:62; 8:34), often spoke of being sent by the Father (3:17, 34; 5:36–38; 6:29, 57; 7:29; 8:42; 10:36; 11:42; 17:3, 8, 18, 21, 23, 25; 20:21), and talked of returning to the Father (13:1; 14:12, 28; 16:10, 28; 20:17). However, it would be a misrepresentation of John's eschatology to overlook the horizontal dimension as well, or to assume that the vertical dimension is present in the gospel of John to the exclusion of the hori-

---

52. These promises are not made to "overcomers" as a special group of "faithful" Christians (as opposed to Christians who are not faithful). John elsewhere defined what he meant by the term "overcomer" when he asked, "Who is it that overcomes the world? Only he who believes that Jesus is the Son of God" (1 John 5:5).

53. The teachings of the Nicolaitans may have been connected with some form of immoral behavior in view of the strong condemnation in Revelation 2:6.

54. Perhaps the most widely known approach to eschatology in the gospel of John is that of C. H. Dodd in *The Interpretation of the Fourth Gospel* (Cambridge: Cambridge Univ. Press, 1953), usually referred to as "realized eschatology." This theory holds that the kingdom of God is to be seen as completely "realized" in the present age in the ministry of Jesus and has nothing to do with future apocalyptic fulfillment. Such a position is refuted in the following discussion.

55. See Donald Guthrie, *New Testament Theology* (Downers Grove, Ill.: InterVarsity, 1981), 798–801. Also see George E. Ladd, *A Theology of the New Testament* (Grand Rapids: Eerdmans, 1974), 302–3, and George R. Beasley-Murray, *John,* Word Biblical Commentary (Waco, Tex.: Word, 1987), lxxxv–lxxxvii.

zontal one. There are clearly horizontal elements in the fourth gospel, as seen in the following examples.[56]

A continuing mission for the disciples. First, although John neither presented teaching about the church as explicitly as Matthew (e.g., Matt. 16:18–19) nor mentioned the so-called "Great Commission" (Matt. 28:19–20), he did speak of a mission for the disciples after Jesus' departure. Jesus told them, "As the Father has sent me, I am sending you" (John 20:21). In 20:23 Jesus spoke of the disciples after His departure as forgiving or not forgiving the sins of others, an authority reminiscent of the "keys of the kingdom of heaven" given to the disciples in Matthew 16:19.

Eternal life as a future possession. Second, while eternal life in the gospel of John is normally presented as a present reality available to the believer (cf. 5:24), on one occasion it seems to refer primarily to the age to come as a contrast to the present age. Jesus said, "The man who loves his life will lose it, while the man who hates his life in this world will keep it for eternal life" (12:25). This saying is found in a similar form in the Synoptic Gospels (Matt. 10:39; Mark 8:35; Luke 9:24) where it refers in each case to life in the world to come.

The future return of Christ. Third, the gospel of John speaks of the future return of Christ. Some of the statements in John are somewhat ambiguous and may refer to the coming of the Paraclete rather than the return of Jesus (e.g., 14:18). Other statements may refer to Jesus' appearances to the disciples after His resurrection rather than to a future return (e.g., 16:16). A clear reference to Jesus' future return is found in 21:22, however, where Jesus said to Peter regarding the fate of the beloved disciple, "If I want him to remain alive until I return, what is that to you?" A future parousia is clearly indicated here because a rumor spread among the disciples that the beloved disciple of whom Jesus spoke would not die (21:23).

The future resurrection of believers. Fourth, the gospel of John teaches a future bodily resurrection of believers in addition to a spiritual regeneration in the present age. Jesus said, "And this is the will of him who sent me, that I shall lose none of all that he has given me, but raise them up at the last day" (6:39). Similar statements are made in 6:44 and 54. In another passage where Jesus spoke of resurrection as a present spiritual reality (5:25), He then referred to the future bodily resurrection of "all who are in their graves" (5:28–29). Although some would attribute the juxtaposition of Jesus' teaching about a present spiritual regeneration and a future bodily resurrection to the work of a (somewhat inept) editor, there is a much simpler explanation. John was completely consistent here with the Synoptic

---

56. Rudolf Bultmann claimed that many of the elements in the gospel of John that reflected a future eschatological fulfillment (e.g., 5:28–29; 6:39–40, 44, 54) were the addition of a later redactor (editor) of the gospel who wished to make it conform to Synoptic apocalyptic (*Theology of the New Testament,* trans. K. Grobel [New York: Scribner, 1955], 39). Bultmann's approach to the eschatology of the fourth gospel has been strongly criticized by D. Moody Smith, Jr. (*The Composition and Order of the Fourth Gospel: Bultmann's Literary Theory,* Yale Publications in Religion 10, ed. D. Herne [New Haven, Conn.: Yale Univ. Press, 1965]), among others.

Gospels and the rest of the New Testament, which speaks of the new life Jesus offers to believers as being experienced in two consecutive stages. The first is spiritual regeneration in the present age; the second is bodily resurrection to life in the age to come. Some of the benefits and blessings of the life of the age to come are available now to the believer in Christ. This creates a certain tension between the "now" (the believer's present experience) and the "not yet" (the promise of future participation in the eschatological realization of the kingdom of God) which is common to the New Testament. In John's gospel there is emphasis on the present experience of eternal life, but this does not exclude or nullify the future fulfillment.

The future judgment. Fifth, the fourth gospel also speaks of a future (eschatological) judgment. This is affirmed by Jesus in John 12:48: "There is a judge for the one who rejects me and does not accept my words; that very word which I spoke will condemn him at the last day." A similar concept is found at the conclusion of the Sermon on the Mount in Matthew 7:22 where Jesus stated that people will be turned away on the day of judgment because they have not put His words into practice. In John 5:28–29 Jesus declared that the righteous will be resurrected to eternal life, but the wicked will be resurrected to face condemnation. Again this looks at the future fulfillment of a process of judgment that, according to John 3:18–19, has already begun in the present age. "Whoever believes in him [Jesus] is not condemned, but whoever does not believe stands condemned already because he has not believed in the name of God's one and only Son. This is the verdict: Light has come into the world, but men loved darkness instead of light because their deeds were evil." The future condemnation is determined already, based on the response of an individual to the person of Jesus. This is again similar to Jesus' statement in Matthew 10:32–33, "Whoever acknowledges me before men, I will also acknowledge him before my Father in heaven. But whoever disowns me before men, I will disown him before my Father in heaven." In the person of Jesus people are confronted with a choice that determines their eternal destiny. This is true to such an extent that Jesus could say that the person who responds to Him possesses eternal life already in the present, having crossed over from death to life (John 5:24).

Realized eschatology in the gospel of John. The problem of so-called "realized" eschatology in the gospel of John can be seen in microcosm in John 5:20b–30.[57] On the one hand, there are statements that speak of the parousia (Christ's second advent) as a future event in the traditional sense. "For an hour is coming, in which all who are in the tombs shall hear His voice, and shall come forth; those who did the good deeds, to a resurrection of life, those who committed the evil deeds to a resurrection of judgment" (5:28–29 NASB).[58] Alongside these on

---

57. The most important scholarly work on this topic is G. Stählin, "Zum Problem der johanneischen Eschatologie," *Zeitschrift für die neutestamentlichen Wissenschaft* 33 (1934): 225–59. Later discussions have not gone much beyond it.

58. The NASB is used for this and several following citations (as indicated) because its wording at this point follows the original Greek more closely.

the other hand are statements that seem to speak of the full realization for believers of salvation in the present. For example, "Truly, truly, I say to you, he who hears my word and believes him who sent me, has eternal life, and does not come into judgment, but has passed out of death to life" (5:24 NASB). There is an obvious tension between these statements that must be reconciled; judgment cannot be both present and future at the same time.

On closer examination, however, the apparent tension between present and future in these verses is not so great as it may seem. The resurrection mentioned in John 5:28–29 is not a general resurrection followed by judgment with some participants rewarded and others punished. Instead, it is a differentiated resurrection, with some resurrected to life and others resurrected to receive judgment. The judgment leading to these respective destinies has already taken place: it has occurred in the present life as the individual has responded to Jesus Christ. For John, one's future destiny is determined by trusting or rejecting Jesus. This is clearly indicated in John 3:18–19. "He who believes in Him is not judged; he who does not believe has been judged already, because he has not believed in the name of the only begotten Son of God. And this is the judgment, that the light is come into the world, and men loved the darkness rather than the light; for their deeds were evil" (NASB). To reject Jesus Christ and the free gift of eternal life that He offers is to place oneself under judgment, a judgment that will be worked out at the last day. Conversely, to place one's faith in Jesus is to escape future judgment and receive instead eternal life. But the response of faith not only guarantees eternal life in the future, for eternal life is a present reality which the believer can begin to experience from the moment of belief. These two perspectives, eternal life as a present reality and as a future inheritance, are both illustrated in Revelation 21:6–8. There the exalted Christ stated, "To him who is thirsty I will give to drink without cost from the spring of the water of life" (v. 6). This alludes back to the statements Jesus made in the gospel of John which offered eternal life as a present experience (John 4:10, 13–14; 7:37–39). The exalted Christ then spoke of the future experience of eternal life as an inheritance for believers (Rev. 21:7) in connection with the future judgment of unbelievers (v. 8).

This is consistent with John 5:29, which makes the resurrection to life depend not on faith but on doing good. The phrase "those who have done good" in 5:29 appears nowhere else in the gospel of John. In 3:20–21 doing evil is contrasted not with doing good, as in 5:29, but with practicing the truth ("whoever lives by the truth" NIV) and coming to the light. To practice the truth, according to John 6:29, means simply to believe in Jesus. Thus "those who have done good" (5:29) are the ones who have believed in Jesus, exempting themselves from future judgment and receiving eternal life in the present.

John 5:28, however, precludes a totally "present" eschatology which would disallow a future bodily resurrection, a view that apparently was in circulation at the time 1 Corinthians was written (1 Cor. 4:8; 15:12–19). This misunderstanding is also reflected in the assertion quoted and refuted in 2 Timothy 2:18 that the resurrection had already taken place.

Thus John's gospel preserves the tension between present and future found in the rest of the New Testament. Although there are differences of emphasis between John and the Synoptic Gospels, the eschatological perspective found in the fourth gospel is complementary to that of the Synoptics, not contradictory. The gospel of John does speak of a future return of Christ, a future bodily resurrection, and a future judgment, as do the Synoptics. Jesus' earthly ministry is presented as having both present and future implications for humanity.[59]

ESCHATOLOGY IN THE JOHANNINE EPISTLES

The Johannine epistles include references to a future parousia of Christ. John warned his readers to "continue in him [Jesus], so that when he appears we may be confident and unashamed before him at his coming" (1 John 2:28). Jesus' return was not explained; it was assumed. It was taken as common knowledge among the readers. The reference to shame ("and not shrink away from Him in shame at His coming" NASB) implies a negative judgment resulting in Christ's rejection of the individual involved. Again this is future. John was not suggesting that a believer in Christ could ultimately be rejected by Him at the final judgment. The author was addressing his readers as faithful Christians who had held to the apostolic teaching in the face of heretical opponents who had taught otherwise. These opponents had failed to "remain" because they did not really belong to Christ in the first place ("their going showed that none of them belonged to us," 2:19). John was reminding his readers that (just as in his gospel) one's response to Jesus in the present determines one's future destiny. To accept the false teaching of the opponents would be to reject Jesus and incur condemnation at the future judgment, for it would show that the person had never really belonged to Christ at all. To remain faithful to the apostolic teaching about the person of Jesus, on the other hand, would assure confidence before Christ in the day of judgment.

Another reference to the return of Christ is in 1 John 3:2. "But we know that when he appears, we shall be like him, for we shall see him as he is." As in other New Testament passages, the return of Jesus Christ in the future is presented as a motive for moral purity in the present (cf. v. 3). First John 3:2 is a clear statement of the expectation of Christ's future return; in no way can it be understood as referring to a "spiritual" return of Christ in the present age, for believers are not yet "like" Him.

---

59. C. F. D. Moule has argued that the tension between present and future in John's eschatology may be explained as a shift in emphasis between sayings directed at individuals and sayings directed at the church collectively ("A Neglected Factor in the Interpretation of Johannine Eschatology," in *Studies in John Presented to Prof. J. N. Sevenster on the Occasion of His Seventieth Birthday*, Supplements to *Novum Testamentum* 24 [Leiden: E. J. Brill, 1970], 155–60). The gospel of John does exhibit a strong emphasis on an individual's relationship with Jesus Christ.

ESCHATOLOGY IN REVELATION

In its emphasis on eschatology, the book of Revelation differs from the other Johannine writings of the New Testament. While the gospel of John emphasizes eternal life as a present experience of the believer and 1 John mentions the second coming of Christ a few times, eschatology is the central theme of the last book of the Bible. To a certain extent it is helpful to see the eschatological emphases in the gospel of John and Revelation as complementary. The gospel of John emphasizes the reaction of individuals to the person of Jesus in the present and how that affects their future destiny, while the book of Revelation portrays the future consummation of all things, telling "the rest of the story." The perspective in Revelation is futuristic, focusing on the events that will surround the second advent of Christ and the establishing of His earthly kingdom. Nevertheless, some material is directed to the specific first-century situation of the seven churches in Asia Minor, which are addressed in Revelation 2–3.

As the last book of the Bible, it is appropriate that Revelation should present the final fulfillment of Old Testament prophecy regarding the establishment of God's kingdom on earth. Much attention is focused on the Great Tribulation just before the Second Advent. Revelation also specifies the length of the millennial kingdom as 1,000 years (20:1–6) and distinguishes it from the eternal state which follows (21:1–22:5).

The eschatological judgments of Revelation. Central to the theology of Revelation are the series of seal, trumpet, and bowl judgments (chaps. 6–16). John's apocalyptic portrayal of God's righteous judgment began with the throne room vision in chapters 4–5. In chapter 5 John recorded how he was introduced to the seven-sealed scroll (v. 1). The Lamb, who was found worthy to open the scroll (vv. 6–10), was identified with the Lion of the tribe of Judah (v. 5) thus portraying the Lord Jesus Christ as both sacrificial and triumphant.

The divine judgments described in chapters 6–16 are future events which immediately precede the second coming of Christ. Interpreters of Revelation have often noted a connection between the events related in these chapters and the last seven years of Israel's history prophesied in Daniel 9:27 (the "seventieth week"). The apostle John did not clearly state that the events described in Revelation 6–16 occupy the entire seven-year period immediately preceding Christ's return, however. These judgments, in fact, appear to be confined only to the second half of this final seven-year period. This period of three and one-half years was described in Matthew 24:21 as a time of "great distress."[60] The apostle John refers to this period as "the great tribulation" (Rev. 7:14).

The relationship of the seals, trumpets, and bowls of Revelation 6–16 is also crucial to an understanding of the book and its message. Although some interpreters have insisted that the trumpets and bowls recapitulate some or all of the seal judg-

60. For a comparison of the order of events in Revelation 6–16 and the order of events in Matthew 24–25, see J. Dwight Pentecost, *Things to Come* (Findlay, Ohio: Dunham, 1958), 280–82.

ments, the contents of the respective seals, trumpets, and bowls argue strongly against this. The seventh seal actually contains the seven trumpets (8:1–2). The connection between the seventh trumpet (11:15) and the seven bowls (16:1–21) is not as clear. There are similarities between the seven trumpet judgments and the seven bowl judgments. However, due to the climactic nature of the bowl judgments and the analogous relationship between the seventh seal and the seven trumpets, it is preferable to distinguish between the trumpets and bowls. The seven bowls would thus be contained in the seventh trumpet.

The seals, trumpets, and bowls may be outlined briefly as follows. The first seal is marked by the appearance of a rider on a white horse who will represent the Antichrist (6:1–2). The second reveals a rider on a red horse who will have power to take peace from the earth (vv. 3–4). The third seal introduces a rider on a black horse with scales in his hand (vv. 5–6). This represents severe famine, which often accompanies political upheaval and war. The fourth seal reveals a pale horse whose rider John identified as Death, with Hades following close behind (vv. 7–8). Death for one-fourth of the inhabitants of the earth will result from the previous judgments of war and famine, as well as from plagues and attacks by wild beasts. The fifth seal involves a cry from heaven for vengeance by the martyrs who will lose their lives in the Great Tribulation (vv. 9–11). The sixth seal reveals cataclysmic disturbances on earth and in the heavens (vv. 12–17).

The final words of verse 17 raise the question, "Who can stand?" Would it be possible for anyone to be saved during these terrible judgments? John answered this question in chapter 7, which forms a parenthesis in the description of the judgments. Two groups of people saved from the Great Tribulation were mentioned specifically: 144,000 saved from Israel (vv. 1–8) and those of all nations who are saved but martyred (vv. 9–17).

After this interlude, the seventh seal will be opened and the seven trumpet judgments revealed (8:1–7). The first trumpet will bring hail and fire mixed with blood, which will destroy a third of the vegetation on the earth (vv. 6–7). The second trumpet announces a large body falling from heaven which will destroy a third of the sea creatures and ships (vv. 8–9). The third trumpet reveals a corresponding destruction of the earth by a blazing star which will poison much of the fresh water on the planet (vv. 10–11). The fourth trumpet will bring attenuation of the light of the sun, moon, and stars (v. 12). After the fourth trumpet will come a minor interlude which will proclaim that the next three trumpet judgments will be even more severe than the previous ones (v. 13). This warning is confirmed by the judgment of the fifth trumpet, which will involve demonic torment of the remaining population of the earth for a period of five months (9:1–11). The sixth trumpet signals the marshaling of a vast army of 200 million in the vicinity of the Euphrates River, which will kill a third of the remaining inhabitants of earth (vv. 12–19). In spite of this terrible judgment the survivors will not repent, but will persist in their idolatry and immorality (vv. 20–21).

The sounding of the seventh trumpet will be preceded by another interlude (10:1–11:14) similar to the one preceding the opening of the seventh seal. During this interlude an angel will announce that there will be no more delay; the mystery of God which He had announced to His prophets will soon be fulfilled (10:6–7). With the sounding of the seventh trumpet there will be another interlude before the introduction of the bowl judgments in chapter 16. In chapters 12–13 seven of the most important characters of the Great Tribulation are introduced.[61] Chapters 14–15 describe various other details of the scene in heaven and on earth immediately before Christ's return. The chronological description of the judgments resumes in chapter 16.

The first bowl judgment will result in a plague that will produce painful sores on those who bear the mark of the Antichrist (16:1–2). The second bowl judgment will destroy all life in the sea (v. 3). The third bowl will poison the remaining sources of fresh water (vv. 4–7). The fourth bowl will intensify the heat of the sun so that people will be scorched (vv. 8–9). The fifth bowl will bring darkness on the earth (vv. 10–11). With the sixth bowl the Euphrates River will be dried up to prepare the way for an invading army from the East (vv. 12–16). The seventh bowl will involve a final series of catastrophes including lightning, thunder, earthquake, and huge hailstones (vv. 17–21). With the completion of the seventh bowl the stage is set for the second coming of Christ (chap. 19), but before this event another parenthesis describes the fall of Babylon (chaps. 17–18).

The destruction of Babylon. The final destruction of Babylon is described in chapters 17–18 of Revelation. The great prostitute described in the vision of 17:3–6 is identified as Babylon in verse 5 and as "the great city that rules over the kings of the earth" (v. 18). The seven heads of the beast on which the woman will sit are identified with seven hills, which are also said to be seven kings (v. 9). It is not clear whether the seven hills are to be identified with the seven kings, or are merely associated with them in some way. Some have suggested the seven kings represent seven successive kingdoms, but seven contemporaneous kingships may be in view. Many interpreters have understood the reference to the seven hills as a reference to Rome, in which case the term "Babylon" as used in Revelation 17–18 must be understood as symbolic. On the other hand, the detailed description of Babylon's destruction in chapter 18 has suggested to some a reference to the literal city of Babylon. A third possibility is that the term "Babylon" may be a symbolic reference to another great city, neither Rome nor Babylon, that is, the world capital at the time these prophecies are fulfilled. The difficulty of specifying precisely the referent of the term "Babylon" in Revelation 17–18 illustrates again the difficulty involved in interpreting the imagery and symbolism used in apocalyptic literature. It can be affirmed that Revelation 17–18 speaks of the future literal destruction of a world capital, even though one cannot specify with absolute certainty which city is in view.

The Millennium. Chapter 20 describes the reign of Christ on earth for a thousand years. It represents the final fulfillment of many Old Testament prophecies

---

61. For a discussion of these characters, see John F. Walvoord, *The Revelation of Jesus Christ* (Chicago: Moody, 1966), 187–224.

which spoke of a messianic reign of righteousness on the earth (Pss. 2; 24; 72; 96; Isa. 2; 9:6–7; 11–12; 63:1–6; 65–66; Jer. 23:5–6; 30:8–11; Dan. 2:44; 7:13–14; Hos. 3:4–5; Amos 9:11–15; Mic. 4:1–8; Zeph. 3:14–20; Zech. 8:1–8; 14:1–9). The events described in Revelation 20 are chronologically sequential to the second coming of Christ in chapter 19 and portray a literal earthly kingdom ruled by Jesus Christ for a thousand years.[62] John recorded that during this period Satan will be bound and prevented from deceiving the nations (20:1–3). John then described the resurrection of the martyrs from the Great Tribulation, who "came to life and reigned with Christ a thousand years" (v. 4). The scene then shifts to the end of the thousand-year reign of Christ on earth (vv. 7–10). Satan, who had been bound during the Millennium, will be released to stir up rebellion once more (vv. 7–8). The defeat of these rebellious armies will be instantaneous (v. 9). After the destruction of his followers, Satan himself will be consigned to the lake of fire (v. 10, "the lake of burning sulfur").

The Great White Throne judgment. The judgment described in the last five verses of chapter 20 marks the end of the Millennium and the transition to the eternal state. Again, these events are sequential to the events of the Millennium that preceded them. John described how the earth and the sky[63] will flee from the presence of the one who will sit on the throne, "and there [will be] no place for them" (v. 11). This indicates the end of the present heaven and earth will prepare the way for the new heavens and the new earth of the eternal state (cf. 21:1). John described the resurrection and judgment of the remaining dead in 20:12–15. These will include the unrighteous dead of all ages, who will not yet have been resurrected for judgment.[64]

The new heavens and the new earth. John concluded his prophecy with a vision of the new heavens and the new earth of the eternal state which will follow the Millennium (21:1–22:5). The apostle stated that the first heavens and the first earth will pass away (21:1). This implies that the new heavens and the new earth of the eternal state is not a renovation of the present heavens and earth, but a new creation. John gave little description of what the new heavens and new earth will look like. One of the few comments is in verse 1: there will no longer be any sea. Much of the remainder of chapter 21 and the first five verses of chapter 22 describe not the new earth in general but the New Jerusalem. John described the New Jerusalem as it will appear in the eternal state. This is much the same as it would have appeared in the Millennium, but the author's perspective at this point was that of the final, ultimate consummation of all things. John's description of the city in these verses emphasizes its beauty and majesty. Some of these elements might have symbolic

---

62. For one of the best defenses of this interpretation of the Millennium, see Jack S. Deere, "Premillennialism in Revelation 20:4–6," *Bibliotheca Sacra* 135 (1978): 58–73.

63. The same Greek word, *ouranos*, is translated by the NIV as "sky" in 20:11 and as "heaven" in 21:1.

64. Old Testament saints and church saints had been raised at the Rapture, just prior to the Tribulation. This resurrection was not explicitly mentioned in Revelation. John described the resurrection of the Tribulation saints (martyrs) in Revelation 20:4.

meaning, but John did not elaborate on their interpretation. The New Jerusalem will be the future residence of the saints of all ages and the unfallen angels.

The final admonitions by the apostle John. The concluding words of the apostle John in Revelation are also appropriate to the conclusion of the entire Bible (22:6–21). The angel affirmed to John the reliability of the words of this book (v. 6). The theme of Revelation is again repeated: "Behold, I am coming soon!" (v. 7). The appropriate response to the words of this prophecy was worship of God (vv. 8–9). The prophecy was not to be sealed up, but to be made public (vv. 10–11). A direct admonition from Jesus Christ Himself is given (vv. 12–16), echoing the words of verse 7. The open invitation to come and take the free gift of the water of life (v. 17) reiterates an important Johannine theme found in the fourth gospel. John's closing words give a warning to those who would add to or subtract from the words of the prophecy (vv. 18–19). A final prayer for Jesus to come quickly (v. 20) and a brief benediction (v. 21) conclude the book.

The theological message of Revelation. The stated purpose of Revelation was to reveal events that will take place at the time of the second coming of Jesus Christ (1:19). This serves to complete Old Testament prophecies concerning the establishment of God's kingdom and the accomplishment of His purposes for humanity. Like the remainder of the Johannine writings, Revelation is strongly Christological in its emphasis. From John's initial vision of the exalted Christ in chapter 1 to the establishment of the new heavens and the new earth in chapter 22, the central message of the book concerns the return of Christ and the consummation of His rule. In spite of suffering, persecution, and even martyrdom, God's people ultimately share in Christ's triumph. This message of encouragement and reassurance is as applicable to the church today as it was toward the close of the first century. Christians may rest assured that they are on the winning side; no earthly or demonic powers will be able to resist the victorious Christ when He returns.

5

A THEOLOGY OF
PAUL'S MISSIONARY EPISTLES

DAVID K. LOWERY

Webster's dictionary defines "irony" as "incongruity between the actual result of a sequence of events and the normal or expected result." That is an apt description of the life and ministry of the apostle Paul. He is first mentioned in Acts (7:58) in connection with the stoning of Stephen, "giving approval to his death" (8:1). Thereafter, he "began to destroy the church. Going from house to house, he dragged off men and women and put them in prison" (8:3). But that sequence of events is remarkably different from the last word in Acts about Paul, that "boldly . . . he preached the kingdom of God and taught about the Lord Jesus Christ" (28:31).

Paul himself testified to this irony in his letter to the Corinthians when he wrote, "I am the least of the apostles and do not deserve to be called an apostle, because I persecuted the church of God. But by the grace of God I am what I am, and his grace to me was not without effect" (1 Cor. 15:9–10). Indeed, the persecutor of the church became an outstanding missionary of it and left a legacy in writing to the churches he founded that was early recognized as having abiding significance and authority. Even within the canon of the New Testament the letters of Paul are associated with the "other Scriptures" (2 Peter 3:16). And some of the oldest

DAVID K. LOWERY, B.A., Th.M., Ph.D., is professor of New Testament studies at Dallas Theological Seminary.

copies of the New Testament (such as papyrus 46, a second-century manuscript[1]) and early arrangements of the canon (such as the second-century list of Marcion[2]) give pride of place to Paul's writings.

Paul's first six letters were written in the course of three missionary journeys, within a period of about ten years (A.D. 48–58). If the letter to the Galatians was written to the churches of Antioch, Iconium, Lystra, and Derbe (Acts 13–14), the six letters were written in an easily remembered sequence. After his first journey he wrote one letter, Galatians. On his second journey he wrote two, 1 and 2 Thessalonians. In his third journey he wrote three, 1 and 2 Corinthians and Romans.

One problem with this neat arrangement concerns the proper placement of the letter to the Galatians. It is possible that the letter was not written to churches founded on the first journey located in the southern region of Galatia (Acts 13–14), but to churches established during the course of the second missionary journey in the northern territory. According to Acts 16:6, "Paul and his companions traveled throughout the region of Phrygia and Galatia, having been kept by the Holy Spirit from preaching the word in the province of Asia." He returned to this northern territory at the beginning of the third journey, traveling "from place to place throughout the region of Galatia and Phrygia, strengthening all the disciples" (Acts 18:23). If the letter was written to the churches in this northern part of the country it would have been written in the course of the third journey, possibly during his stay in Ephesus, before the writing of 1 Corinthians, or later while in Corinth, just before the writing of Romans. Most interpreters of Galatians incline to the view that Paul was writing to churches in the northern region,[3] though a good case can be made in support of the southern view.[4] The alternative decisions lead to a different understanding about when the letter was written and what that may indicate about development in Paul's theological perspective on certain matters (e.g., the relationship of Christians to the Mosaic Law), but a decision about the destination of Galatians does not significantly alter the interpretation of the letter's message.

Paul wrote these letters as a founding pastor concerned about the well-being of the churches planted through his ministry. Usually there were particular issues he felt compelled to address. Sometimes, as in the case of 1 Corinthians, he answered

---

1. The manuscript includes eleven of Paul's letters and Hebrews. The date usually assigned to it is about A.D. 200 (Bruce M. Metzger, *The Text of the New Testament,* 3d ed. [New York: Oxford Univ., 1992], 265). However, on the basis of the scribe's writing style, a date as early as A.D. 80–100 has been proposed (Y. K. Kim, "Palaeographical Dating of p 46 to the Later First Century," *Biblica* 69 [1988]: 248–57).

2. The primary source for information about Marcion is Tertullian (*Against Marcion* 5). Marcion's collection included ten letters of Paul in the following order: Galatians, 1 and 2 Corinthians, Romans, 1 and 2 Thessalonians, Ephesians, Colossians, Philippians, and Philemon. Though Marcion may have made this arrangement himself, he probably adopted the order and contents of an existing edition. See Harry Gamble, *The New Testament Canon* (Philadelphia: Fortress, 1985), 41–42.

3. For example, H. D. Betz, *Galatians* (Philadelphia: Fortress, 1979), 3–12; and John M. G. Barclay, *Obeying the Truth* (Philadelphia: Fortress, 1988), 7–8.

4. F. F. Bruce, *The Epistle to the Galatians* (Grand Rapids: Eerdmans, 1982), 3–18.

specific questions from the church. More often, he tackled false teaching or improper conduct that threatened the stability of the Christian community. It is important to keep this point in mind as the discussion of the theology of these letters develops. Because they address selected issues, the letters individually and collectively do not present a comprehensive or systematic theology. The writing that comes closest to a systematic theological presentation is Romans, the one letter among the six written to a church Paul did not found. Even in the case of Romans, however, the focus is not on theology generally, but a presentation of the message of salvation. Though Paul had not visited the church, he hoped it would welcome him as an apostle of God and support him in his plans to do church-planting in the western regions of the Roman Empire. As the church at Antioch had functioned as the base of Paul's missionary ventures in the course of the first three journeys in the eastern regions of the empire, so Rome was a logical base of operations for ministry reaching to the western extremity, Spain (Rom. 15:23–24). Romans thus served in part as a letter of introduction, setting before the Roman church the message of salvation Paul preached, a message he believed the Romans would readily affirm and support (vv. 14–16).

GOD THE FATHER

In his opening words to the Roman church the apostle Paul said he was "set apart for the gospel of God" (1:1). The message he preached was God's revelation about Himself to people—who He was, what He had done, what He was doing and what He would do, and how people should respond in light of this revelation. Paul thus used the word "gospel" in a broad sense, encompassing the whole of God's revelation about Himself and His work in the world. This breadth is illustrated by his statement to the Roman church, "I am eager to preach the gospel also to you" (1:15), implying that the gospel message is larger than the extensive discussion about salvation that is a part of that letter.

An important part of the gospel concerns the character of God, what theologians sometimes refer to as His attributes. The references to God's character in Paul's letters not only describe who God is but also what He does, since character and behavior are closely bound. Paul's references to God's character enable his readers not only to understand God and their relationship to Him better, but also to see that many of these attributes are to become characteristic of them as well. Paul, for example, commended the Thessalonians because they "became imitators of us and of the Lord" (1 Thess. 1:6; cf. Eph. 5:1). Knowing who God is and what He does provides a context for meaningful relationship with Him, and it also serves as a guide to the way in which His children are to live as representatives in the world.

FAITHFULNESS

A fundamental aspect of God's character is faithfulness (*pistia*), the assurance that He will do what He says. On several different occasions in these letters Paul affirmed God's faithfulness. He assured the Thessalonians that God would complete the work of salvation begun in them: "The one who calls you is faithful and he will do it" (1 Thess. 5:24). Similarly, he wrote the Corinthians that "God, who called you into fellowship with his Son Jesus Christ our Lord, is faithful" (1 Cor. 1:9). This is a reminder that confidence about salvation is grounded in God alone. Because temptation is part of human experience, self-confidence and presumption invite disaster, as Paul illustrated in the history of Israel (1 Cor. 10:1–12). But it does not have to end that way for "God is faithful; he will not let you be tempted beyond what you can bear" (10:13a). Human strength will fail but "he will provide a way out so that you can stand up under it" (v. 13b).

The contrast between human failure and divine faithfulness is even more sharply drawn in a question in Romans, given in a context dealing with God's promises to Israel: "What if some did not have faith? Will their lack of faith nullify God's faithfulness?" (3:3). This is the first example in a series of rhetorical questions in this letter that accept the premise as true but deny a presumed conclusion as false. In the case of this question, most would agree that the majority of the Jews in Paul's day (and still today) had rejected the gospel of God. It would be reasonable to expect that God would then reject them. Paul returned to this issue later in the letter (Rom. 9–11), but for the moment he categorically denied the expected conclusion that God would be unfaithful to Israel: "Not at all!" (3:4). God continues faithful to His word and the fulfillment of His will. As Paul later affirmed, "Israel will be saved" (11:26), "for God's gift and his call are irrevocable" (v. 29). This confidence in God's faithfulness formed the foundation of Paul's ministry and enabled him to preach a sure and certain message (2 Cor. 1:18).

RIGHTEOUSNESS

Closely related to the characteristic of faithfulness is the attribute of righteousness (*dikaiosynē*). Righteousness exists when there is conformity to a standard. For example, in the Old Testament the Israelites were told to use righteous weights, that is, measures that conformed to a particular standard (Deut. 25:15). A merchant was not to have a fifteen-ounce weight to use as a balance for the sale of a pound of material (v. 13). Nor was a buyer to carry a seventeen-ounce weight to use as a standard for purchasing products sold by the pound. A pound weight was to be sixteen ounces, which was a righteous or just weight.

Similarly, people who conform to a particular standard can be described as righteous. The standard to which God's people must conform is His will, primarily as it is expressed in the commands and prohibitions of the Scriptures. God also is said to be righteous when He acts in conformity with His stated will, doing what He says He will do.

A defense of God's righteousness is called a theodicy. In relation to two areas in particular, Paul engaged in theodicy and dealt with the issue of God's righteousness. One concerned the question of God's faithfulness to Israel and her place in the plan of salvation, addressed in chapters 9–11 of Romans. In this discussion Paul raised the question, "Is God unjust?" (9:14) in the execution of this plan of salvation. Paul answered with an unequivocal denial, "Not at all!" And yet it is clear that Paul did see Israel in the era after the first coming of Christ as a people partially and temporarily rejected by God (11:7, 15). The resolution to the question of God's righteousness (v. 12), however, was that this rejection was partial and temporary. Ultimately, God would show Himself true to His word and accomplish the salvation of Israel (vv. 26–27).[5]

A second question also concerned God's plan of salvation, but it revolved around the issue of God's just punishment of sin. Paul phrased the question this way: "If our unrighteousness brings out God's righteousness more clearly, what shall we say? That God is unjust in bringing his wrath on us?" (3:5). The truth in the first premise is that humanity's failure provides a backdrop against which the righteousness of God can be seen to better effect. But Paul dismissed the implication that therefore people should be exempt from the consequences of sin as perverse nonsense (3:6–8).

Another form of this question appeared later in this letter in a context affirming the sure and certain accomplishment of God's plan of salvation: "Then why does God still blame us? For who resists his will?" (9:19). This is a reversal of the usual form since the premise is in the second position. Paul would agree with the truth of the premise (that no one resists God's will), but he would again deny the conclusion (that because of that people are blameless). In fact, Paul's message was that everyone is blameworthy (3:23). According to Paul, people who are left to pursue their own course of life would all be headed in a direction away from God and His will and on a road leading to self-destruction (vv. 11–12). Because God does intervene (and because no one resists His will) some are turned from the road that ends in death to the path that leads to life. When Paul wrote about this irresistible will of God, he accentuated the aspect of God's mercy which he saw as humanity's only hope (9:15–16). At the same time, he did not deny the reality that some people are their rebellion to God (vv. 17–18).

The other question related to this issue of God's righteousness is the reversal of a perspective that looks at His mercy and asks instead if He can be relied on to punish sin. It takes two forms. On the one hand is the question of whether God will punish the sin of those who persecute His people. To the suffering Thessalonians Paul wrote, "God is just: He will pay back trouble to those who trouble you. . . . He will punish those who do not know God and do not obey the gospel of our Lord Jesus Christ" (2 Thess. 1:6, 8).

On the other hand, because God does forgive, how can He be said to punish sin justly? Paul answered this question by pointing to Jesus' atoning death in the place of sinners. His death was a proof of God's righteousness. "He did this to demonstrate his justice, because in his forbearance he had left the sins committed beforehand unpunished—he did it to demonstrate his justice at the present time, so as to be just and the one who justifies the man who has faith in Jesus" (Rom. 3:25–26).

---

5. For more discussion of these verses, see S. Lewis Johnson, Jr., "Evidence from Romans 9–11," in *A Case for Premillennialism,* ed. Donald K. Campbell and Jeffrey L. Townsend (Chicago: Moody, 1992), 199–223.

This last verse is a reminder that righteousness is not only a characteristic of God, but is also a status He gives to people, bound up in the forgiveness for sin received by those who believe. We will look at that aspect of the experience of salvation later when we discuss the human dimension of Paul's message about soteriology.

WRATH

God's wrath is not a characteristic that occupies much attention in contemporary theological discussions. Perhaps this inattention is a matter of relief for some who consider talk about it a vestige of the "fire-and-brimstone" preachers of an era fortunately past. But in his missionary letters Paul frequently mentioned God's wrath (*orgē*). As the apostle told the Romans, the reality of God's wrath was the reason people needed to receive His righteousness (1:17–18).

Wrath is the response of God to sin. It has both a present and a future aspect. Paul referred to both in his letter to the Thessalonians. First, he assured the Thessalonians that they would escape the future expression of God's wrath, reminding them that "God did not appoint us to suffer wrath but to receive salvation through our Lord Jesus Christ" (1 Thess. 5:9). This was a reassuring repetition of his previous description of Jesus, as One "who rescues us from the coming wrath" (1:10).

But God's wrath is also a present reality from Paul's point of view. He saw his kinsmen, the Jews, as suffering the wrath of God because of their hostility to the church and their opposition to the spread of the gospel. According to Paul, "the wrath of God has come upon them at last" (2:16).

What Paul meant by that declaration is not entirely clear. But some insight may be provided by his comments in Romans about the expression of God's wrath in the present time. There he said that "the wrath of God is being revealed from heaven against all the godlessness and wickedness of men who suppress the truth by their wickedness" (Rom. 1:18). This "suppression of the truth" is similar to what he had told the Thessalonians the Jews were guilty of doing in their opposition to the gospel (1 Thess. 2:15–16). God's wrath manifested itself, according to Paul, in the fact that He permitted people to indulge their sinful practices in increasingly greater degree. Three times in the following verses Paul intoned the refrain "God gave them over": to "sinful desires" (Rom. 1:24), to "shameful lusts (v. 26), and to "a depraved mind" (v. 28).

God's wrath on the Jews may refer to Paul's understanding that He has given over many of his kinsmen to a deepening rejection of the gospel, what Paul called "a hardening in part until the full number of the Gentiles has come in" (11:25). With regard to this hardening he quoted Deuteronomy 29:4 and Isaiah 29:10, "God gave them a spirit of stupor, eyes so that they could not see and ears so that they could not hear, to this very day" (Rom. 11:8).

Though Paul believed that this present manifestation of divine wrath confirmed both Gentiles (Rom. 1) and Jews (Rom. 11) in their rejection of the truth, he did not allow it to deter him from preaching the gospel to both groups. He did so with the confidence that however dire the plight of individuals may be, God's grace can rescue them from the consequences of their sin and give them an escape from both the present and future consequences of His wrath (10:12–13). As he told the Romans, "God has bound all men over to disobedience so that he may have mercy on them all" (11:32).

MERCY AND GRACE

Mercy (*oiktirmos*) and grace (*charis*) reflected for Paul the twin aspects of God's character that resolve the dilemma of humanity's sinfulness and God's righteousness. If God were characterized by righteousness alone, all the world would justly be condemned (Rom. 3:19–20). Paul saw in the people of Israel an illustration of humanity's dilemma. Freed from bondage in Egypt, the people soon turned from the worship of God to idolatry. To Moses God said, "Your people whom you brought out of Egypt have become corrupt. They have been quick to turn away from what I commanded them and have made themselves an idol cast in the shape of a calf. . . . Now leave me alone that my anger may burn against them and that I may destroy them" (Ex. 32:7–8, 10).

But when Moses interceded for the people, God relented and said to him, "I will have mercy on whom I will have mercy and compassion on whom I will have compassion" (33:19). Paul pointed to this verse as a summary statement of the solution to humanity's dilemma (Rom. 9:15). God's mercy, His undeserved and unmerited favor, provides a way of deliverance "through the redemption that came by Christ Jesus" (3:24). In the final analysis, for Paul salvation does not "depend on man's desire or effort, but on God's mercy" (9:16).

God's grace and mercy became the basis on which Paul urged people to commit themselves wholeheartedly to the Lord and the accomplishment of His will. This is illustrated by complementary passages in the letter to the Romans. At one point Paul exhorted people to "offer the parts of your body to him as instruments of righteousness . . . because you are . . . under grace" (6:13–14). Later he wrote, "I urge you, brothers, in view of God's mercy, to offer your bodies as living sacrifices" (12:1). Paul viewed the experience of salvation from beginning to end as an expression of God's mercy and grace and as such he urged people to respond with wholehearted trust and obedience to God and His will.

POWER

God's power (*dynamis*) is mentioned often in Paul's letters. It is a characteristic displayed in many ways, including the evidence throughout creation, the witness of natural revelation: "For since the creation of the world God's invisible qualities—his eternal power and divine nature—have been clearly seen, being understood from what has been made, so that men are without excuse" (Rom. 1:20). Creation bears testimony to the reality of God's power and makes people accountable to acknowledge Him properly.

God's power was also evident in the miracles Paul and others performed as a validation of their role as God's representatives (the word *dynamis* was used to refer both to God's power itself and to a miracle, a visible example of this power; cf. Acts 14:3). When Paul dealt with the Galatians about the issue of the law, he asked them, "Did God give you his spirit and work miracles among you because you observe the law, or because you believe what you heard?" (Gal. 3:5). When the Corinthians struggled with contentions about Paul's apostleship, he reminded them that "the things that mark an apostle—signs, wonders and miracles—were done among you" (2 Cor. 12:12).

However spectacular these miracles were (see Acts 14:8–11), Paul regarded Christ's resurrection as the preeminent display of God's power (Rom. 1:4; 1 Cor. 6:14; 2 Cor. 13:4) and Christ Himself as the ultimate embodiment of that power (1 Cor. 1:24), who one day will "put all his enemies under his feet," even death (15:25–26).

Meanwhile, God's power is manifested in the experience of salvation. As Paul told the Romans, "I am not ashamed of the gospel, because it is the power of God for the salvation of everyone who believes" (Rom. 1:16). He told the Corinthians that "the message of the cross is foolishness to those who are perishing, but to us who are being saved it is the power of God" (1 Cor. 1:18). The gospel is God's power because when the message is believed God begins a process that culminates in people becoming like Christ Himself. Because of this, Christ is called the "firstborn" (Rom. 8:29) or "firstfruits"[6] (1 Cor. 15:20), as the one who presently exemplifies the power of God that will one day be experienced by all Christians (v. 23).

The gospel is the means by which people experience God's power and Paul was the human agent who proclaimed it, but the divine Agent who applies that power is the Holy Spirit. As Paul told the Corinthians, "My message and my preaching were not with wise and persuasive words, but with a demonstration of the Spirit's power, so that your faith might not rest on men's wisdom, but on God's power" (2:4–5). The miracles authenticating Paul's message were done "through the power of the Spirit" (Rom. 15:19). Paul's prayers also show that he regarded the Spirit as the Agent of God's power, as this benediction in Romans illustrates: "May the God of hope fill you with all joy and peace as you trust in him, so that you may overflow with hope by the power of the Holy Spirit" (v. 13).

In this connection Paul sometimes referred to Christ as the mediator of God's power, though the Holy Spirit is probably to be understood as the unmentioned Agent. When Paul told the Corinthians that the "power of our Lord Jesus" (1 Cor. 5:4) would be present in their assembly, the ministry of the Spirit as Christ's representative was likely in mind.

This is probably also the case when later he reminded the Corinthians of an important lesson he had learned about his own weakness and God's provision for it. Paul explained how he had prayed that a "thorn in my flesh" might be removed (2 Cor. 12:7–8), but was told instead by the Lord, "My grace is sufficient for you,

---

6. This term referred to the first crops or animals, which were to be given as a sacrifice to God. Paul often used it as virtually equivalent to the word "first" (e.g., Rom. 16:5; 1 Cor 16:15) but with the added understanding that the people referred to belong to God.

for my power is made perfect in weakness." As a result Paul concluded, "I will boast all the more gladly about my weakness, so that Christ's power may rest on me" (v. 9). The phrase "rest on me" could be translated "live in me" since the phrase is used to describe the place where someone lives.[7] The "power" resting on Paul was the abiding presence of the Holy Spirit, providing divine enablement to carry out the life and work God had called him to do (cf. Rom. 8:9–11).

GLORY

God's glory (*doxa*) is a characteristic associated with His presence. It may be called a visible sign of His presence. Paul linked God's presence and glory in his correspondence to the Thessalonians when he described the fate of those who rejected the gospel: "these will pay the penalty of eternal destruction, away from the presence of the Lord and from the glory of His power" (2 Thess. 1:9 NASB).

A visual manifestation of God's glory is brightness or radiance. Paul compared the radiance reflected in the face of Moses after experiencing the presence of God on Mount Sinai (Ex. 34:29–35) with the greater and abiding glory associated with the Spirit's ministry in the new covenant (2 Cor. 3:6–18). That comparison did introduce a transition in the understanding of visible manifestation, however. Instead of a brightness or radiance indicating God's presence and reflecting His glory, Paul described the ministry of the new covenant as a character-changing experience in which people "are being transformed into his likeness with ever-increasing glory" (v. 18).[8] This display of God's character in Christian experience is the primary manifestation of His glory in the present time, the era of the new covenant.

These two manifestations, radiance and character, are brought together in the culmination of salvation. Then the process of character transformation will be completed and the presence of God for Christians will be immediate, as it is now for Christ, "the Lord of glory" (1 Cor. 2:8; 2 Thess. 2:14), who is "the image of God" (2 Cor. 4:4). As Paul told the Romans, God intends Christians "to be conformed to the likeness of his Son" (Rom. 8:29). To experience the end result of that process is to be "glorified" (v. 30). Alternatively, when Paul referred to falling short of "the glory of God" (3:23) he described failure to gain access to this divine presence, in short, failure to obtain salvation (cf. 5:2).

Because the Spirit is the empowering Agent of this character transformation in Christian experience, Paul occasionally used the term "glory" as a reference to the Spirit's work. When, for example, he wrote that "Christ was raised from the dead through the glory of the Father" (Rom. 6:4), the word "glory" is a shorthand

---

7. Walter Bauer, William F. Arndt, and F. Wilbur Gingrich, *A Greek-English Lexicon of the New Testament and Other Early Christian Literature,* 2d ed., rev. F. Wilbur Gingrich and Frederick W. Danker (Chicago: Univ. of Chicago, 1979), 298.

8. This idea of individuals presently reflecting God's presence is also mentioned by Paul in his letter to the Corinthians in connection with a discussion about proper behavior in worship (1 Cor. 11:2–16). He wrote that "a man ought not to cover his head, since he is the image and glory of God" (v. 7). The man is to function as the representative of God and is to reflect His character and thus His presence.

description of the Spirit's work (cf. Rom. 1:4). Similarly, he described the era of the new covenant as a period characterized by the glorious ministry of the Spirit (2 Cor. 3:8), because the Spirit is the Agent producing transformation in God's people (3:18).

Another concept associated with glory is the idea of approval or praise. Paul reminded the Thessalonians that when he ministered among them he was not looking for "glory from men" (1 Thess. 2:6), that is, people's praise or approval.[9] The only approval or praise that mattered to Paul was from God (1 Cor. 4:5). On the other hand, giving glory to God distinguished people who had a relationship with Him from those who did not. When Paul described those who rejected the truth about God, he said, "they neither glorified him as God nor gave thanks to him" (Rom. 1:21). In contrast to this was an individual of faith like Abraham, who "gave glory to God" (4:20). People thus give glory to God by what they say and do, that is, by expressing praise and thanks to Him and by representing Him in reflecting His character and doing His will.

WISDOM

Paul began the doxology that concludes his presentation of God's plan of salvation for Jews and Gentiles in Romans by extolling God's wisdom (*sophia*): "Oh, the depth of the riches of the wisdom and knowledge of God!" (11:33). And he ended the letter with a similar doxology "to the only wise God" (16:27). Wisdom refers to the skillful accomplishment of God's work in the world, particularly as it concerns the manner in which salvation is achieved (cf. Eph. 3:8–10).

Paul referred to this divine characteristic frequently in his correspondence with the Corinthians. Since they seemed to be highly impressed with human wisdom, Paul underscored its limitations, notably the inability of human wisdom to comprehend God and experience His plan of salvation. "For since in the wisdom of God the world through its wisdom did not know God, God was pleased through the foolishness of what was preached to save those who believe" (1 Cor. 1:21). Paul described the gospel as "God's secret wisdom, a wisdom that has been hidden and that God destined for our glory before time began" (1 Cor. 2:7; cf. Rom. 16:25–26).

God's wisdom is then particularly displayed in His plan of salvation. Because the central figure in this plan of salvation is Christ, Paul described Him as "the wisdom of God" (1 Cor. 1:24). Christ "has become for us wisdom from God" (v. 30) for through His death He made salvation possible, and through His life He showed how to live according to God's will. The one who implements the wisdom of God is the Spirit. "'No eye has seen, no ear has heard, no mind has conceived what God has prepared for those who love him—but God has revealed it to us by his Spirit'" (2:9–10). The Spirit enables people to receive the wisdom of God, the gospel (vv. 11–15), and to benefit from it in daily experience by being "wise about what is good" (Rom. 16:19).

---

9. The idea of failing to gain God's approval may also be a part of the meaning of Romans 3:23.

CHRISTOLOGY

Much of what Paul said about Christ was in the context of discussions about salvation (soteriology), the nature of the church (ecclesiology), and future events (eschatology). Since each of these areas will be considered subsequently in this chapter, what Paul said about Christ in those contexts will be taken up under the separate topics. Thus the focus of the present section will be on the significant ideas associated with the various names or titles associated with Jesus in these letters.

GOD

Though Paul usually reserved the name God (*theos*) as a designation for God the Father, the doxology in Romans 9:5 seems to be an instance in which he applied the name to Christ, as one "who is God over all, forever praised! Amen." However, since punctuation was not used in the Greek text, the statement could also be translated "Christ, who is over all. God be forever praised!" or "Christ, God who is over all be forever praised!" Nevertheless, word order in the phrase suggests that Paul meant to affirm the divine nature of Jesus by this ascription. The relative silence on this point elsewhere in these letters probably shows that the deity of Jesus was not a question or matter of dispute in the churches Paul founded.

SON OF GOD

As in the Gospels, the expression "Son of God" primarily identifies Jesus' role as the Representative of God who faithfully carries out His will. But in contrast to the Gospels, the emphasis is less on Jesus' humble submission and obedience in fulfilling God's will and more on Jesus' exalted status as the one who carries out God's work in the present era. Paul, for example, said that Jesus was "declared with power to be the Son of God by his resurrection from the dead: Jesus Christ our Lord" (Rom. 1:4). In this sense the designation "Son of God" is similar in meaning to the title "Lord." Both are linked with the authority Jesus exercises as the Representative of God the Father in the present era. As Paul told the Corinthians, "he must reign until he has put all his enemies under his feet" (1 Cor. 15:25).

LORD

In the Old Testament, Lord (*kyrios*) is a common designation of God. In the New Testament this title is routinely given to Jesus as the Provider of salvation (e.g., Paul applied Joel 2:32 to Jesus in Rom. 10:13, "Everyone who calls on the name of the Lord shall be saved."). The confession "Jesus is Lord" is used by Paul as a summary statement of faith for those saved: "If you confess with your mouth, 'Jesus is Lord,' and believe in your heart that God raised him from the dead, you will be saved" (Rom. 10:9). Similarly when he told the Corinthians that "no one can say, 'Jesus is Lord,' except by the Holy Spirit" (1 Cor. 12:3), he was not denying the possibility of false profession. Rather, he was affirming the role of the Spirit in bringing people to a confession that epitomized their faith.

Also associated with the idea of Jesus as Lord is a recognition of His authority over people. When Paul, for example, advised Christians about how wisely to handle various debatable issues of personal conviction and behavior (Rom. 14–15), he reminded his readers that in the final analysis the only one to whom they were accountable in these matters was the Lord. "Whether we live or die we belong to the Lord. For this very reason, Christ died and returned to life so that he might be the Lord of both the dead and the living" (14:8b–9). In a similar vein he told the Corinthians, "I care very little if I am judged by you or by any human court. . . . It is the Lord who judges me" (1 Cor. 4:3–4).

Paul linked Jesus' authority over the lives of Christians to ethical behavior generally (7:10). He told the Corinthians that "the body is not meant for sexual immorality, but for the Lord" (6:13) and added that "he who unites himself with the Lord is one with him in spirit" (v. 17). Paul also expressed the close connection between a Christian's relationship with Jesus as Lord and a Christian's manner of life by using the brief phrase "in the Lord" (en kyriō) to modify a variety of actions. Paul spoke of people who were faithful (4:17), worked (Rom. 16:12), stood firm (1 Thess. 3:8), provided leadership (5:12), were confident (Gal. 5:10), and were to be received "in the Lord" (Rom. 16:2), to cite only a few examples.[10] By doing so, he linked behavior to the primary relationship that shapes a believer's views and actions. It was, in short, a summary reminder that behavior is defined by the Christian's relationship with the Lord.

But not only must Christians who must take account of Jesus' lordship. The universal dimensions of His rule will be seen when "he has destroyed all dominion, authority and power. For he must reign until he has put all his enemies under his feet" (1 Cor. 15:24b–25). Then the distinctive lordship of Jesus will come to an end and "the Son himself will be made subject to him who put everything under him, so that God may be all in all" (v. 28).

JESUS

The name Jesus means "God saves." As Paul told the Thessalonians, "God did not appoint us to suffer wrath but to receive salvation through our Lord Jesus Christ" (1 Thess. 5:9). Earlier in the letter he referred to Jesus as the One "who rescues us from the coming wrath" (1:10). Only infrequently (about ten times in these letters) did Paul refer to Jesus without also using the ascription "Christ" or "Lord." The subject in most of these passages is Jesus' death (Rom. 8:11; 2 Cor. 4:10–11, 14; 1 Thess. 1:10; 4:14), a reminder both of His humanity and also of the costly way in which He accomplished salvation (Rom. 3:25–26).

This may be a clue to understanding the one passage at variance with this pattern, Paul's warning that "no one speaking by the Spirit of God says, 'Jesus be cursed'" (1 Cor. 12:3). A denunciation of this sort may have been on the lips of false teachers who denied Jesus' humanity. The earliest Christological heresy, do-

---

10. The phrase occurs only one time outside of Paul's letters in the New Testament (Rev. 14:13). Even Paul's secretary sent greetings "in the Lord" (Rom. 16:22).

cetism (from *dokeō,* "to seem" or "have the appearance"), denied Jesus' humanity, arguing that He only seemed to be, but was not in fact, human. The pattern of Paul's references to Jesus and His death firmly rebutted a falsehood of that kind.

CHRIST

Paul's references to Jesus as "Christ" (*christos*) also serves to remind readers of Jesus' humanity, especially His role as the Jewish Messiah. When Paul listed for the Romans some distinctive privileges of Israel as the people of God, he concluded by noting that "from them is traced the human ancestry of Christ" (Rom. 9:5; cf. Eph. 2:12). This affirmation was also made earlier in the letter (Rom. 1:3) when Paul connected his proclamation of the gospel with the fulfillment of promises regarding Christ made by Old Testament prophets. He referred to Jesus as One "who as to his human nature was a descendant of David" (1:3). The fulfillment of the prophetic statements about Christ was important to Paul because he found in them assurance for Israel's salvation. As he wrote later in this letter, citing Isaiah 59:20, "The deliverer will come from Zion; he will turn godlessness away from Jacob" (Rom. 11:26). Paul looked forward to the day when Israel would receive Jesus as Christ.

While Paul thought it important that Gentile Christians understand their debt to Israel as the people from whom Christ came (cf. Rom. 11:18), Christ's humanity also serves as an example for Christian life and practice. Because he was concerned that the Corinthians were prone to self-serving, self-centered behavior, Paul stressed Christ's self-sacrificial life, culminating in His death on the cross. "Christ crucified" (1 Cor. 1:23) epitomized Paul's message: "I resolved to know nothing among you except Jesus Christ and him crucified" (2:2). In a similar way he reminded the Romans that "we who are strong ought to bear with the failings of the weak and not to please ourselves. . . . For even Christ did not please himself" (Rom. 15:1, 3a).

The prophetic fulfillment connected with Christ's life and His self-sacrificial example for living are brought together in Paul's call for unity in the church: "Accept one another, then, just as Christ accepted you" (15:7a). The benefits of Christ's ministry are experienced by both Jews and Gentiles. "For I tell you that Christ has become a servant of the Jews on behalf of God's truth, to confirm the promises made to the patriarchs so that the Gentiles may glorify God for his mercy" (vv. 8–9a), a truth demonstrated by the Old Testament texts subsequently cited (15:9b–12; cf. Gal. 3:28; Eph. 2:11–22).

Though Paul linked these themes of servanthood and fulfillment to his references to Christ, he also used the title as a virtual name so that it is often interchangeable or freely combined with the other designations previously discussed. One remaining designation, however, stands apart. Though limited in its application and frequency, it is relevant to an understanding of Paul's Christology. This is his reference to Christ as the "last Adam" (1 Cor. 15:45).

THE LAST ADAM

Paul referred only once to Jesus as "the last Adam" (1 Cor. 15:45). However, he did compare and contrast Christ and Adam at different times in Romans and 1 Corinthians.[11] When he described Christ as "the last Adam" in Corinthians, the adjective "last" underscores the difference between the two men. Paul viewed Adam as the one whose act of disobedience brought sin and death to all people (Rom. 5:12; 1 Cor. 15:21–22). The obedience of Christ, on the other hand, brought life and the promise of resurrection and eternal life to all those associated with Him (Rom. 5:17; 1 Cor. 15:21–22).

The focus of discussion in 1 Corinthians 15 is the resurrection (v. 12). Earlier in the passage Paul had contrasted the effect of Adam and Christ on humanity: "For since death came through a man, the resurrection of the dead comes also through a man. For as in Adam all die, so in Christ will all be made alive" (vv. 21–22). This contrast is continued in Paul's reference to Christ as the last Adam. "So it is written: 'The first man Adam became a living being'; the last Adam, a life-giving spirit" (v. 45). In the series of opposites developed in the preceding verses, Adam is associated with mortality (perishable, v. 42; dishonor, weakness, v. 43; natural body, v. 44) and Christ with immortality (imperishable, v. 42; glory, power, v. 43; spiritual body, v. 44). Just as Adam was an earthly man who brought death to all those associated with him (v. 22a), so Christ is a heavenly Man who brings life to all those connected with Him (v. 22b). Adam represents the first creation, formed by God from the dust of the earth (v. 47a). Christ represents the new creation, those resurrected by God's power. The destiny of the resurrected is heaven, where Christ now is and from where He will come to claim "those who belong to him" (v. 23).

PNEUMATOLOGY

If Paul thought of God the Father and God the Son as existent in heaven, the Holy Spirit is seen as the member of the Trinity present in the world. The Holy Spirit is the divine person who presently carries out the will of God the Father and God the Son. For Paul, the Holy Spirit is the primary Agent at work in the ministry to which he had been called, a ministry he described as "proclaiming the gospel of God, so that the Gentiles might become an offering acceptable to God, sanctified by the Holy Spirit" (Rom. 15:16).

When some questioned the validity of Paul's apostleship, he referred to the Corinthians as "a letter from Christ, the result of our ministry, written not with ink but with the Spirit of the living God" (2 Cor. 3:3). Though he described himself with others as "ministers of a new covenant" (v. 6), it could also be said that he and his fellow ministers of the the new covenant carried out "the ministry of the Spirit" (v. 8). The Holy Spirit is the Agent who performed Christ's work in Paul's ministry, a fact he routinely acknowledged (Rom. 15:17–19; 1 Cor. 2:1–4; 2 Cor. 3:4–6).

---

11. The comparison between Christ and Adam will also be considered later in this chapter in the discussion about Paul's doctrine of salvation.

Because Paul's references to the Holy Spirit often appear in a discussion about salvation, much of Paul's thought about the Spirit receives treatment under the topic of soteriology. It may be helpful now, however, to look at Paul's understanding about the Spirit's ministry in the progress of God's revelation through different eras.

THE HOLY SPIRIT AND THE NEW COVENANT

For Paul, the Spirit's present ministry represented a distinctive difference between the era of the old covenant (*palaios diathēkē*, 2 Cor. 3:14) and the new (*kainē*, 2 Cor. 3:6). The old covenant was characterized by a revelation of God's will summed up in the Mosaic Law, a revelation that people often failed to observe (Jer. 31:32). Paul regarded the revelation of the law as "holy, righteous and good" (Rom. 7:12). The repeated failure of people to live according to these stipulations was not due to a shortcoming of the law. Rather, it testified to human weakness and inability (Rom. 8:3). The new covenant, which the Old Testament prophets looked forward to (e.g., Isa. 59:20–21; Jer. 31:31–34; 32:37–40; Ezek. 16:60–63; 37:21–28), was regarded by Paul as initiated by Christ and carried on by the Spirit (Rom. 8:3–4; 2 Cor. 3:4–18). He therefore concluded that the old covenant and the stipulations associated with the Mosaic Law had been superseded by the ministry of Christ and the Spirit (Rom. 10:4; Gal. 3:25).

This did not mean, however, that commandments or stipulations were no longer associated with the new covenant. On the contrary, Paul's letters are full of commands and exhortations for the churches. The significant difference is that in the new covenant era the ability to live in light of this revelation of God's will is made possible by the Spirit's ministry. Paul associated the Holy Spirit with the whole experience of salvation, making it possible not only for a person to have a relationship with God but also to live in accord with God's will as it is set forth in the New Testament.

This does not mean that Paul's view of human weakness changed. Apart from the Spirit, people are still powerless when faced with performing God's will. Human nature did not change in the passing away of one era and the arrival of another. Unique to the new covenant is the work of Christ and the wide and extensive involvement of the Holy Spirit in the experience of salvation (Rom. 8:3–4).

SATAN AND EVIL SPIRITS

While it may seem unusual to discuss Paul's references in these letters to Satan and evil spirits under the heading of pneumatology, he did use the word *pneuma* to describe the existence of supernatural beings active in the world but different from the Holy Spirit. When he reminded the Corinthians, for example, of the many and varied gifts or abilities given by the Holy Spirit to members of the church, he mentioned "distinguishing between spirits" (1 Cor. 12:10) as one of the abilities given by the Spirit.

Presumably not all who represented themselves as speaking for God did so truthfully. Paul alluded to this fact later in this letter when he argued for the validity of the resurrection. If Christ were not raised, he said, "we are then found to be false witnesses about God, for we have testified about God that he raised Christ from the dead" (1 Cor. 15:15). In a similar vein he warned the Corinthians later about accepting the testimony of false apostles (2 Cor. 11:13) and of receiving "a different spirit from the one you received" (11:4). Paul regarded the church as a mixed community, composed of true and false brothers (2 Cor. 11:26; Gal. 2:4).

Paul described all these individuals with the defining word "false" (*pseudō*), from the word *pseudos* meaning "lie" or "deceit." In writing to the Thessalonians, Paul used this word with reference to Satan's activity, warning his readers that "the coming of the lawless one will be in accordance with the work of Satan displayed in all kinds of counterfeit [*pseudos*] miracles, signs and wonders" (2 Thess. 2:9). This lawless one seems to be the quintessence of false witnesses, false brothers, and false apostles, and is often described as the Antichrist.[12] What should be noted, however, is the fact that Paul attributed the Antichrist's power to Satan. The author of this deceit is the Devil.

In 2 Corinthians Paul referred to Satan as "the god of this age" who "has blinded the minds of unbelievers, so that they cannot see the light of the gospel of the glory of Christ" (4:4). The "god of this age" attempted to frustrate every endeavor to rescue those under his thrall, and Paul recognized his continuing attempts to oppose the work of the gospel both to those associated with the church and those outside. As Paul reminded the Romans, it is a program that has proceeded with considerable success as people have "exchanged the truth of God for a lie, and worshiped and served created things rather than the Creator" (Rom. 1:25). For Paul, idolatry testified to Satan's deception. He told the Corinthians that "the sacrifices of pagans are offered to demons, not to God" (1 Cor. 10:20).

Ultimately, however, Satan's numerous deceits will be eliminated. As Paul told the Thessalonians, this "lawless one" who will epitomize the work of Satan is doomed, "whom the Lord Jesus will overthrow with the breath of his mouth and destroy by the splendor of his coming" (2 Thess. 2:8). The word translated "breath" (the extended phrase is reminiscent of Isa. 4:11) is *pneuma,* and may allude to a future demonstration of the Spirit's power as Christ's Agent to sweep away all opposition before Him.

Anthropology

Anthrōpos is the common Greek word for a human being, regardless of race or gender. Paul used the word this way as well. When he described the life of Jesus in comparison to the life of Adam, for example, he used the word (often, as in this instance, translated "man") with reference to both Adam and Jesus ("sin entered the world through one man," Rom. 5:12; "the gift that came by the grace of the one man, Jesus Christ," v. 15).

People, especially in their present life and future prospects, were of utmost importance to Paul. As he told the Corinthians, "we endanger ourselves every

---

12. Bauer, Arndt, and Gingrich, *A Greek-English Lexicon of the New Testament,* 76.

hour" (1 Cor. 15:30) in the course of a ministry that sought to proclaim the gospel to as wide an audience as possible ("I worked harder than all of them [i.e., the other apostles]," 1 Cor. 15:10). While he placed great value on the importance of people, Paul also regarded them as trapped in a state of rebellion and alienation from God, a result of human sin and divine judgment.

THE PLIGHT OF HUMANITY

Paul's view of the general human situation is expressed in his phrase "slaves to sin" (Rom. 6:20). The phrase summed up his conviction that though people may be prone to think of themselves as masters of their own destiny, they are ultimately weak and powerless. But the phrase is also a statement of the kind of behavior and orientation Paul regarded as typical of humanity's situation.

While people may think of themselves as desiring to know God and have a relationship with Him, Paul believed just the opposite is the case. Instead of seeking God and His truth, Paul saw people as suppressing the truth about God available to them (Rom. 1:18–19). Rather than people being concerned to find God, Paul held that "no one seeks God" (3:11). Rather than being solicitous of God and friendly toward Him, Paul stated that collectively and individually they are "God's enemies" (5:10).

Paul's portrait of the human condition was an altogether grim one, made doubly so by his belief that it was an impossible situation to change apart from God's initiative. As he told the Corinthians, "The man without the Spirit does not accept the things that come from the Spirit of God, for they are foolishness to him, and he cannot understand them, because they are spiritually discerned" (1 Cor. 2:14). For Paul, the human condition is characterized by a rejection of God and His revelation, being routinely marked by hostility toward Him. As a result, people are subject to the tyranny of sin that is impossible to escape outside of Christ.

The historical root of sin's tyranny. In Romans Paul addressed the problem of universal sin, beginning his discussion with the affirmation that "sin entered the world through one man, and death through sin, and in this way death came to all men, because all sinned" (Rom. 5:12). Paul saw Adam's disobedience as an act with appalling consequences for all those who followed him. He portrayed sin in personified language as a power presently reigning in the world, exercising authority over all Adam's descendants (5:21).

Paul's conviction that sin and death entered the world through Adam's disobedience is clear enough, but the meaning of the phrase "because all sinned" (5:12) is variously interpreted. Earlier in Romans Paul stated that "all have sinned" (3:23), and it is possible that the phrase in 5:12 recapitulates that affirmation, namely, that all people voluntarily reject God and all fail to live in light of His revelation. However, later in this passage Paul said that "through the disobedience of the one man many were made sinners" (5:19). Because the verb translated "were made" (*kathistēmi*) points toward a consequent state of affairs and often carries a judicial connotation,[13] it seems that Paul regarded people after Adam not only as sinners by virtue of their manner of life but also as sinners because they are recipients of divine judgment. Thus the statement "because all sinned" (5:12) may mean more than that all people disobey God as Adam did. It may mean additionally that all people share the judicial consequence of Adam's sin. Later in this same letter Paul said all creation is "subjected to futility" (8:20 NASB), a situation likewise due to the judgment issued as a consequence of Adam's sin (Gen. 3:17–19). Humanity's plight is thus a matter of both human rebellion and also divine judgment.

This interaction of human responsibility and divine authority runs like a constant thread through Paul's theology. While at one point he emphasized divine activity and at another point human behavior, he believed that both factors defined his theology and ministry, even though he never attempted to specify precisely the nature or boundary of that interaction. Attempts by subsequent interpreters to explain that integration often end up diminishing or eliminating one aspect or the other. Paul asserted both that individuals were responsible and accountable for their actions and that God's authority was complete and not subject to qualification in any way. But he made no attempt to explain or integrate these affirmations. A passage of praise to God in his letter to the Romans no doubt reflected his own conviction on this matter: "How unsearchable [are] his judgments, and his paths beyond tracing out!" (Rom. 11:33b).

Death. Paul summed up humanity's plight in two short phrases: "death came through a man" (1 Cor. 15:21), and "in Adam all die" (v. 22). He referred to death also as a personified tyrant when he wrote that "death reigned from the time of Adam" (Rom. 5:14). The death spoken of in these passages is physical death, the end of earthly life, and spiritual death, the separation of the individual from relationship with God.

This idea of separation is basic to the meaning of the word "death." Thus Paul could say of Christians that "we died to sin" (6:2), meaning that they have been set free or separated from the power of sin that once dominated their lives as unbelievers. Paul used the word "death" with reference to both physical and spiritual realities when he described "the wages of sin" as death (6:23). Spiritual death is a condition of separation from God: "The mind of sinful man is death" (8:6). It is the present state of non-Christians which if unchanged ends in eternal death, a final separation from God. A life controlled by sin "leads to death" (6:16). Because all people are children of Adam, all begin life under the dominion of death (5:14).

Even Christians must contend with mortality, the separation of the soul and spirit from the body in physical death. There is the prospect that death one day will be vanquished when, as Paul said, "the perishable has been clothed with the imperishable, and the mortal with immortality" (1 Cor. 15:54). Until then, however,

---

13. James H. Moulton and George Milligan, *The Vocabulary of the Greek New Testament Illustrated from the Papyri and Other Non-Literary Sources* (Grand Rapids: Eerdmans, 1972), 313. Also see Albrecht Oepke, *Theological Dictionary of the New Testament,* trans. and ed. Geoffrey W. Bromiley (Grand Rapids: Eerdmans, 1964–76), s.v. *"kathistēmi,"* 3:445.

"we ourselves, who have the firstfruits of the Spirit, groan inwardly as we wait eagerly for our adoption as sons, the redemption of our bodies" (Rom. 8:23).

FLESH

When Paul used the word "flesh" (*sarx*), it could signify for him human life generally, or more particularly non-Christian life and practice. The general, neutral use of the word is illustrated by his profession to the Galatians: "The life I live in the body [*sarx*] I live by faith in the Son of God" (Gal. 2:20). As in his statement to the Corinthians, that "flesh and blood cannot inherit the kingdom of God" (1 Cor. 15:50), the word *sarx* refers to earthly, mortal life.

The more negative use of the word appears in contexts in which Paul discussed the aspirations, values, and behavior of people unaided and unenlightened by God's Spirit. In these passages flesh is contrasted with the Spirit to show how earthly orientation, values, and practices contrast with divine values and characteristics. Two passages in particular illustrate Paul's perspective on this matter. In Romans 8:5–13 and Galatians 5:13–26 he drew a series of contrasts distinguishing non-Christian experience and behavior from Christian life and practice.

In both of these passages the NIV translates the word "flesh" by the phrase "sinful nature." This is a satisfactory translation if it is kept in mind that "nature" primarily refers to a set of values and practices, that is, a capacity or disposition (in this case toward sin and away from God and His revelation, a characteristic of non-Christians), rather than a constitutional or material aspect of a person. In Romans 8 Paul regarded people as either controlled by the flesh or the Spirit (e.g., v. 9) in the same way a person could be either a Christian or a non-Christian. Paul left no middle ground in this passage; a person could not be both "in the flesh" and "in the Spirit."

Yet in his letter to the Galatians Paul seemed to speak of the flesh in the negative sense as a continuing reality for the Christian, a propensity or orientation toward sin and away from God's will that hounds a believer until the end of earthly life (the tense of the verbs "desires" and "in conflict" in 5:17, e.g., suggests an on-going struggle). The flesh is thus not an alien entity in the life of a Christian, but a disposition that expresses the goals, aspirations, values, and practices of people in the world, an orientation that Christians never escape entirely until they depart this earth.

It is also a disposition from which Christians cannot turn away apart from the enablement of the Spirit of God. But this anticipates a discussion of Romans 7 that has relevance to this question and may now be taken up (e.g., v. 18, "I know that nothing good lives in me, that is, in my sinful nature [*sarx*]. For I have a desire to do what is good, but I cannot carry it out").

The interpretation of Romans 7. The first six verses of Romans 7 deal with the relationship of Christians to the law and contribute to an understanding of Paul's anthropology. Nonetheless, the key text in the more narrow discussion about the flesh is Romans 7:7–25. The heart of the debate involves the meaning of the recurring first person pronoun "I" in the passage and the nature of its antecedent. For example, when Paul used the pronoun "I" did he intend it (1) to be a reference to himself (and to other Christians as well); (2) to describe his pre-Christian experience as a Jew in this passage, and in so doing define the situation of his fellow Jews also; or (3) to speak here as a child of Adam, reflecting through the use of "I" the experience of Adam that is consequently shared by both Jews and Gentiles, that is, by all people in the world? Good cases can be assembled in support of each of these views, and there are many variations and possible combinations of interpretations associated with each of them. At the same time, each view has problems dealing with particular statements or affirmations in the passage so that no interpretation has achieved general acceptance.

Many readers would assume that when Paul used the pronoun "I" he referred to himself and his situation as he wrote the letter. But several statements in these verses have made acceptance of such a straightforward reading difficult. Two verses can serve to illustrate the problem and at the same time provide an opportunity to consider factors that have influenced the development of alternative views.

In the first place Paul said, "Once I was alive apart from the law; but when the commandment came, sin sprang to life and I died" (v. 9). While it is difficult to see when this might fit into Paul's life, the situation of Adam alive in the Garden of Eden seems to correspond reasonably well to this statement. But a problem arises in the fact that the law-commandment Paul referred to in a preceding verse (v. 7) is from the Decalogue (the Tenth Commandment, "Do not covet," Ex. 20:17; Deut. 5:21), not the command of God from Genesis concerning eating from the tree of the knowledge of good and evil (Gen. 2:17; cf. 2 Cor. 11:3 as an illustration of Paul's familiarity with the Creation account).

The situation of Israel before and after the giving of the law at Sinai may then better fit the situation described by the statement. In this case the people of Israel were viewed as "alive" following their redemption from Egypt but "dead" after the giving of the law since it presented a standard they failed to keep (cf. Rom. 5:13). Though this explanation is consistent with Paul's previous statements in the letter about the negative effects of the law (e.g., 4:15; 5:20; 7:5), it blunts the neatness of the life-death contrast illustrated in the experience of Adam and relativizes the terms by applying them to a national group rather than an individual.

But the relativization of the terms is a problem also shared by the autobiographical view, though with a different sense attached to the words. If Paul wrote Romans 7 in terms of his Christian life, then verse 9 may describe a period following his conversion when he sought to live as a Christian in light of the stipulations of the law, a course that resulted in the death of his vitality in Christian experience and relationship. A further problem with this view is the general lack of supporting information about Paul's early Christian life, a fact underscored by the presence of a silent period spanning ten or more years when he lived in or near his birthplace, Tarsus (cf. Acts 9:28–30 and 11:25–26). So while Paul may have gone through such an experience, additional corroborating evidence is lacking.

Another problem facing a straightforward reading of Romans 7 as autobiography is the statement in verse 14, "I am unspiritual, sold as a slave to sin." The word translated "unspiritual" is an adjective of the word "flesh" (*sarkinos*). Earlier in this chapter (v. 5) Paul spoke of the flesh as a characteristic of life before his relationship with Christ ("we were controlled by the sinful nature"). And later (chap. 8) Paul described the person characterized by the flesh as not possessing the Spirit, and therefore a non-Christian (8:5–9). Equally difficult is the modifying clause, "sold as a slave to sin." In chapter 6 Paul affirmed that "we died.to sin" (v. 2) and that we had been "freed from sin" (v. 7). These seem to describe alternative and opposing situations and not conditions that could be experienced simultaneously. If that is so, the statement of 7:14 seems more easily defensible as a description of the situation of Adam following his disobedience (cf. 5:12–14; Gen. 3:17–19) or of Israel confronted with the stipulations of the law (cf. 8:3) than of Paul in his Christian experience.

Yet despite its problems, the autobiographical nature of this passage commends itself as the most likely reading of the letter. The response to the objection that this interpretation makes Paul the creator of a variety of conflicting affirmations regarding the Christian life is threefold. First, Paul believed in the progressive nature of Christian experience. He could speak of being redeemed (3:24) and also of awaiting redemption (8:23) because redemption is an experience that has a beginning and a consummation that may be separated by many years of earthly life. What is true of redemption applies as well to deliverance from sin, death, and the flesh. Though defeated by the work of Christ (in which the Christian shares), these powers have not yet been banished from the field of battle in which life in this world is lived. In fact, Paul described Christian experience until the redemption of the body as a time of "groaning inwardly" and "eagerly anticipating" this consummation (8:23). The anguished cry that concludes chapter 7, "Who will rescue me from this body of death?" (v. 24), gives voice to this longing.

Second, as the discussion regarding redemption shows, Paul's theology is sometimes presented in absolute and unqualified terms in one passage though it may be modifed subsequently by another affirmation elsewhere. Chapters 9–11 of this letter illustrate an unqualified description of God's sovereignty as it relates to salvation (e.g., 9:16) and an equally clear affirmation regarding the necessity of the individual's responsibility to believe in order to obtain that salvation (e.g., 10:13). These apparently conflicting propositions were affirmed but not specifically qualified nor systematically integrated by Paul anywhere in these letters (though readers are reminded that God's judgments are "unsearchable . . . and his paths beyond tracing out!" 11:33).

Third, Paul made no mention of the Spirit's ministry in Christian experience in the midst of the struggle described in Romans 7:7–25. The passage can thus be read as a vivid description of human powerlessness—that is true for Christians too—apart from the Spirit's enablement. The power of sin, the propensity of the flesh, even the jaws of death will be broken for the Christian, but only by the Spirit of God. Paul's portrait in these verses provides another perspective on the disciples' experience in Gethsemane and their consequent failure: though the spirit was willing, the flesh was weak (Mark 14:38; cf. John 15:5, "apart from me you can do nothing"). For the Christian as well, apart from divine resources provided by the Holy Spirit, powerlessness is a characteristic of life in this world.

FIGURES OF SPEECH AND PERSONAL REFERENCES

Heart. Paul sometimes referred to himself or others by using terms describing a part or aspect of the human body. For example, he used the word "heart" (*kardia*) to refer to decisions, emotions, and thoughts in connection with a person's mental, emotional, and volitional life. When he told the Thessalonians, "We are not trying to please men but God, who tests our hearts" (1 Thess. 2:4), he testified to a motive of his life and ministry that could be evaluated partially by others but which God alone could verify certainly. Similarly when he said that "it is with your heart that you believe" (Rom. 10:10), he described faith as an expression of the mind, emotions, and will. The summary profession "Jesus is Lord" testifies to this faith (10:9), but, ultimately, God alone knows the reality of the heart (8:27).

What distinguishes the heart of a Christian from the non-Christian (1:21) is the Holy Spirit's presence. Paul reminded the Corinthians that God had "set his seal of ownership on us, and put his Spirit in our hearts as a deposit" (2 Cor. 1:22). He told the Galatians, "Because you are sons, God sent the Spirit of his Son into our hearts" (Gal. 4:6). In the same vein he told the Romans that "God has poured out his love into our hearts by the Holy Spirit, whom he has given to us" (Rom. 5:5). The mind, emotions, and will are all influenced by the Spirit in the life of the Christian.

Spirit. This ministry of the Spirit is the creation of the capacity to have a relationship with God. Because Paul believed only Christians experience this ability to enjoy access to God, he used the word "spirit" (*pneuma*) in reference to Christians only. It serves as a general description of the essential, inner aspects of an individual, a virtual synonym for the word "heart," but it is used only with reference to the capacity of fellowship with God that the Holy Spirit creates in the life of a Christian. The "spirit" is then not a constitutional aspect of the individual in a physical, material sense but the ability to relate to God and experience communion with Him. Paul referred to this when he told the Romans that the Holy Spirit "testifies with our spirit that we are God's children" (Rom. 8:16).

Soul. Another word Paul used with reference to the immaterial aspect of individuals is the term "soul" (*psychē*). This word sums up what it means to be a living being in a comprehensive way, and was used by Paul as a general reference to humanity. In Romans 2:9, for example, he told his readers, "There will be trouble and distress for every human being [*psychē*] who does evil." It appears also in the quotation of Genesis 2:7 in 1 Corinthians 15:45, " 'The first man Adam became a living being.' "

The connection of the word "soul" to Adam illustrates a further aspect of Paul's thinking seen in his use of the adjective *psychikos,* often translated as "natural." In 1 Corinthians 2:14, for example, the "natural person" (*psychikos anthrōpos*) is the individual without the Holy Spirit, which is Paul's description of a non-Christian. An interpretive translation of these words is "the man without the Spirit" (NIV).

This is not to say that Paul refrained from using the word "soul" to refer to himself and other Christians. When he wrote the Thessalonians, for example, he said, "We loved you so much that we were delighted to share with you not only the gospel of God but our lives [*psychē*] as well" (1 Thess. 2:8). And in his concluding benediction for them he prayed, "May your whole spirit, soul and body be kept blameless at the coming of our Lord Jesus Christ" (5:23b). So while all people can be said to have a soul and body, corresponding to the material and immaterial parts of natural life, the Christian in addition has the capacity or ability to relate to God, a dimension called a spirit. Though Paul used the adjective "natural" to refer to a non-Christian, both the adjective and the noun "soul" are simply terms descriptive of earthly life. Even a Christian, for example, has a "natural body" (1 Cor. 15:44).

Body. Similarly, the word "body" (*sōma*) is a neutral word descriptive of physical or material life. Paul could use both "body" and "soul" with reference to the material or immaterial aspects of a person or to the individual as a whole without regard to particular components of personality (e.g., Rom. 12:1; 16:4). In contrast to a word like "flesh" that usually has negative connotations for Paul, the words "body" and "soul" are neutral, gaining either positive or negative implications from modifying words or the wider context in which they are used.

Conscience. Paul referred to "conscience" (*syneidēsis*) more often than did any other New Testament writer. Conscience is the capacity to evaluate acts or intentions as either right or wrong. Paul believed that all people have a conscience, and his description of its function is briefly stated in Romans 2:15. Because it serves as a moral mechanism, Paul usually advised people to live in light of the dictates of their conscience, even if the issue in question was addressed by the revelation of God. For example, when the Corinthians debated the question of whether it was right or wrong to buy meat that had been part of an idol sacrifice, Paul told people that to eat or not to eat this meat was a matter of moral indifference (1 Cor. 8:8). Unlike the prohibitions concerning certain foods under the old covenant (e.g., Deut. 14:3–21), nothing that God created was to be regarded as unclean in the era of the new covenant (1 Cor. 10:25–26; Rom. 14:14). But Paul recognized that the conscience is formed by a variety of factors and complex associations. Matters of conscience are not just intellectually based but have emotional roots that may slow the process of change in individual thinking and behavior. So he advised people to act according to their conscience (Rom. 14:5). He also warned individuals not to do anything that might cause another person to act in a way contrary to his or her conscience, either by example (1 Cor. 8:10) or argumentation (Rom. 14:1, 22). Paul may have thought that it was a short step from acting against one's conscience to acting against God's revealed will. At any rate, he saw an act against the conscience as a step of serious consequence that could end in an individual's destruction (1 Cor. 8:11).

Overall, Paul's view of the human situation is not a positive one. He regarded humanity as trapped by an array of more powerful hostile forces. Sin, death, and the flesh exercise authority that people cannot escape. Though more opposition was hardly needed, Paul likewise saw evil spiritual forces at work in the world. They were bent on frustrating the advance of the gospel and the work of God in Christians generally, while holding non-Christians in their sway. Because he regarded the human situation as desperate and inescapable, Paul saw divine intervention as the only hope for deliverance.

SOTERIOLOGY

The theological word commonly used to describe a biblical writer's teaching and belief about the subject of salvation is soteriology, based on the Greek word for salvation, *sōtēria*. To appreciate Paul's soteriology it is necessary to understand his anthropology, particularly his conviction that people are enslaved to sin and unable to free themselves from its dominion. As a result, though Paul believed strongly in an individual's responsibility to receive and participate in salvation, much of what he had to say about it concerns what God had done, was doing, and would do.

GOD'S PLAN OF SALVATION

Paul stated that the plan of God concerning salvation was all-encompassing, for it relates to both individuals and national groups. The most extensive statement of his belief is found in Romans 9–11, in which he addressed the question of Israel's status as the people of God and her relation to the Gentiles.

As Paul's readers well knew, the great majority of the Jewish people had been and continued to be unresponsive to the gospel, to Jesus as the Messiah, and to Paul's preaching about Him. Since much of the New Testament was being produced during this era of Paul's writing and ministry, the New Testament was not yet available as a collected source of guidance and instruction for the church. As a result, the common Bible for the early Christians was the Old Testament. What was evident to these readers of the Old Testament was that God had made certain promises to Israel about her status as a chosen people, a people whom He would not forget (Isa. 49:14–15). These assurances coupled with Israel's unresponsiveness to the gospel understandably raised questions about God's plan of salvation as it pertains to Israel and indirectly raised questions about God's faithfulness to the church.

Paul, for example, had ended Romans 8 with a stirring affirmation about the assurance of God's love and the impossibility of a Christian ever being separated from it. Yet while readers found in the Old Testament similar passages of assurance given to Israel, the Jewish people seemed for the most part to be cut off from God and separated from the benefits of salvation available in Christ. This fact, which seemed to contradict the assurance Paul so strongly affirmed, required a response.

Paul's summary reply was made in Romans 9:6, "It is not as though God's word had failed. For not all who are descended from Israel are Israel." So Paul explained from the Old Testament that the temporary rejection of Israel and the wide-scale responsiveness of Gentiles are in keeping with God's plan of salvation. The apostle also stated that even as God extends His salvation to broad people groups like Israel in the past or Gentiles in the present, His plan calls for the response of individual Jews and Gentiles to God as well. This was his point in the second half of 9:6, that not every individual in the nation of Israel experienced salvation any more than every member of the Gentile nations presently experiences it. This selectivity too is a part of God's plan of salvation.

This divine choice of some people for salvation, commonly called election (9:11), was (and is) understandably troublesome to people, raising questions about God's justice and fairness. Sensitive to this concern, Paul posed two questions in this passage to address it (vv. 14, 19). First he asked candidly, "Is God unjust?" (v. 14). The presumption behind this question is based on the description in the preceding verses (vv. 10–13) of God's choice of Isaac and not Esau. There Paul had boldly stated that God's plan was made "before the twins were born or had done anything good or bad—in order that God's purpose in election might stand: not by works but by him who calls." In other words, God's choice was not based on the kind of life the brothers had or would live. Paul did not state that God looked down the corridors of time, as it were, and chose the more noble of the two brothers based on the decisions and deeds that would characterize their respective lives. No doubt neither Paul nor his readers would have had a question about God's fairness or justice if His choice had been made in this way. But Paul apparently believed just the opposite was in fact the case, namely, that God's choice was not based on the perceived merits or demerits of the brothers' respective lives. And thus arises the obvious point of tension expressed in the question, "Is God unjust?" (v. 14).

Paul's answer is consistent with his anthropology, his view that all people find themselves on a path running away from God and toward a sure and certain destruction. Paul found in ancient Israel an illustration of that tendency and a statement of God's response that was his answer to the issue of election. Following the redemption of Israel from slavery in Egypt, they came into the Sinai Peninsula where God communicated to Moses His will for the people. While Moses was absent from the people and in God's presence, the Lord told him the people had turned to idolatry (Ex. 32:7–9). He then told Moses, "Now leave me alone so that my anger may burn against them and that I may destroy them. Then I will make you a great nation" (Ex. 32:10). But Moses interceded for the people and appealed to God for mercy on their behalf. In God's response to Moses Paul found the answer to the question of election: "I will have mercy on whom I have mercy, and I will have compassion on whom I have compassion" (Ex. 33:19; Rom. 9:15).

Paul's description of human society in Romans 1 parallels Israel's behavior described in Exodus. In both cases the people rejected the truth of God and turned to idolatry (Rom. 1:18–23), and in both cases it meant they stood as a people justly condemned ("men are without excuse," v. 20). Paul's solution to this desperate situation is God's intervention in electing some to salvation. In other words, from Paul's perspective justice is served if all are condemned. But mercy and grace are seen in God's intervention to save some.

Now, however, the question may be raised, "Why some and not all?" This question is related to the second question mentioned by Paul: "Why does God still blame us? For who resists his will?" (Rom. 9:19). Some may answer that God does not regard anyone as blameworthy in the final analysis and that ultimately all people will be saved. Though one might wish Paul had answered that way, he did not. The following verses clearly show that people follow one of two paths. Some begin and end on a path whose end is destruction, a final separation from God ("objects of wrath," v. 22). Others are rescued from this path ("the objects of his mercy") and are destined for glory, eternal fellowship with God (v. 23). These same alternative destinies are mentioned when Paul described people who would believe a lie and "be condemned" (2 Thess. 2:12), in contrast to those whom "from the beginning God chose . . . to be saved" (v. 13).

On the other hand, in some passages Paul seemed to look forward to the salvation of all people, the belief that is sometimes called universalism. Near the end of Romans 11, for example, he wrote, "God has bound all men over to disobedience so that he may have mercy on them all" (v. 32). Similarly, he compared the effect of Adam's sin on humanity with the effect of Christ's sacrifice: "Just as the result of one trespass was condemnation for all men, so also the result of one act of righteousness was justification that brings life for all men" (5:18). The parallel statement in the letter to the Corinthians seems equally comprehensive: "For as in Adam all die, so in Christ all will be made alive" (1 Cor. 15:22). Even Romans 3:23–24 may be thought to support a universalistic view of salvation: "for all have sinned and fall short of the glory of God and are justified freely by his grace through the redemption that came by Christ Jesus."

Each of these passages, however, is qualified by human responsibility, the other aspect essential to an understanding of Paul's view of God's plan of salvation. Though Paul believed strongly that God would authoritatively accomplish His will, he also believed with equally firm conviction in the necessity of individuals receiving the gospel by faith. In Romans 5, for example, the only phrase that breaks the sharply stated universal alternatives in the passage is the phrase "those who receive" in verse 17: "For if, by the trespass of the one man, death reigned through that one man, how much more will those who receive God's abundant provision of grace and the gift of righteousness reign in life through the one man, Jesus Christ." Though the word "receive" is a brief qualifier, it represents the essence of Paul's view concerning human responsibility.

A failure to believe also answers, for Paul, the question concerning Israel's present status as a people partially and temporarily rejected by God. Why did so many in Israel fail to obtain righteousness, that is, the salvation available in Christ to those who believe the gospel? Because, as Paul said, "they pursued it not by faith but as it were by works. They stumbled over the 'stumbling stone'" (i.e., Jesus the Messiah, Rom. 9:32, alluding to Isa. 28:16).

Even in this passage focusing on human responsibility, however, Paul included his conviction that God's plan was going forward as it was set forth in the Old Testament Scriptures. He cited in the following verse (v. 33) two passages from the prophet Isaiah (8:14; 28:16), joined to illustrate both God's divine purpose with regard to Israel ("As it is written: 'See I lay in Zion a stone that causes men to stumble and a rock that makes them fall' "), and human responsibility to believe in Jesus as the Messiah (" 'but the one who trusts in him will never be put to shame' ").

As Paul showed in Romans 11, only a few of his fellow Jews believed in Jesus as the Messiah. He described these Jewish Christians as "a remnant chosen by grace" (v. 6). The great majority of his kinsmen, he said, "were hardened" (v. 7) in accord with the Scriptures (vv. 8–10). Did that mean that Israel would never again enjoy the blessing of God as the beneficiary of His promises? Absolutely not! As Paul put it, "Did they stumble so as to fall beyond recovery? Not at all! Rather, because of their transgression, salvation has come to the Gentiles to make Israel envious. But if their transgression means riches for the world, and their loss means riches for the Gentiles, how much greater riches will their fullness bring!" (vv. 11–12).

Paul looked forward to the day when God's purposes for the salvation of the Gentiles would come to an end, when "the full number of the Gentiles has come in" (v. 25). Shortly thereafter he anticipated that Israel would respond to Jesus as her Messiah, "and so all Israel will be saved" (v. 26).[14] Paul also supported the fact of this consummation of God's plan of salvation by referring to Old Testament Scriptures (vv. 26–27).

One might think that anyone who held such divergent convictions about divine authority and human responsibility, and had such a grand vision of the progress of salvation as it reached both Jews and Gentiles, would hardly know where to begin in terms of practical ministry. But Paul apparently never suffered an idealist's or visionary's paralysis of ministry. He prayed and preached with equal vigor (Rom. 10:1, 14–15; 15:17–20), and he told the Corinthians with undisguised candor, "I worked harder than all of them" (i.e., the other apostles, 1 Cor. 15:10). As he said to the Romans, "I am not ashamed of the gospel, because it is the power of God for the salvation of everyone who believes: first for the Jew, then for the Gentile" (Rom. 1:16).

THE WORK OF CHRIST

If God the Father is regarded by Paul as the central person in the planning of salvation, the key person in achieving salvation is God the Son, Jesus. The preexistence of the Son was implied by Paul in his statement to the Corinthians concerning their commitment to contribute to the collection for the poor in Jerusalem. He reminded them of the "grace of our Lord Jesus Christ, that though he was rich, yet for your sakes he became poor, that we through his poverty might become rich" (2 Cor. 8:9). The riches Jesus gave up were His prerogatives as deity. The riches Christians enjoy as a result include both present and future experiences such as entering into a relationship with God and sharing with Jesus some of the rights and privileges that belong to Him—intimated by Paul in his phrase "heirs of God and

14. For more discussion of these verses see, Johnson, "Evidence from Romans 9–11," in *A Case for Premillennialism,* 211–23.

co-heirs with Christ" (Rom. 8:17). The poverty of which Paul spoke involved the self-sacrificial life Jesus lived and the awful death He died on behalf of sinful people. One way to grasp Paul's multifaceted view of Christ's work in salvation is to look at the terms he used to describe it.

Atonement. Romans 3:21–26 is a key passage for insight into Paul's understanding of Christ's work. In verse 25 Paul wrote, "God presented him [Jesus] as a sacrifice of atonement, through faith in his blood." The phrase translated, "sacrifice of atonement," renders a single word (*hilastērion*). Paul's readers would have often seen this word in the Septuagint. It referred to the lid that covered the ark of the covenant (the rectangular box that contained the tablets of the Ten Commandments; its construction is described in Ex. 25:10–16). The specifications for constructing the lid were given in Exodus 25:17–22, where the term is translated "atonement cover" (e.g., v. 17,) or "mercy seat" (NASB). According to this account in Exodus, God told Moses, "There, above the cover between the two cherubim that are over the ark of the Testimony, I will meet with you and give you all my commands for the Israelites" (v. 22). Elsewhere God told Moses about the nature of His presence at this place of meeting: "I appear in the cloud over the atonement cover" (Lev. 16:2).

This place of meeting was the focus each year of the Day of Atonement, when the high priest sprinkled sacrificial blood for himself and the people on the covering lid (Lev. 16:1–34), "because on this day atonement will be made for you, to cleanse you. Then before the Lord you will be clean from all your sins" (v. 30). The covering over the ark became the place where the holy God and sinful people could meet.

In the era of the new covenant, which Jesus made through His death on the cross, the sacrifice of atonement enables the holy God and sinful people to meet. Because of Jesus' sacrifice on the cross, cleansing for sin was achieved. As people receive by faith the benefits of Jesus' sacrifice, they receive forgiveness for sin and enter into a relationship with God. God and sinners can now come together, not because of the annual sacrifice of the Day of Atonement but because of the abiding sacrifice of Jesus' death for sin (cf. Heb. 8–10; 1 Pet. 2:24).

The English word "atonement" is a term whose meaning can be seen by an analysis of its parts. It is the condition ("ment") of being "at one" with another person. It is possible for people to be at one with God because the sin that formerly separated them is forgiven in the same way a debt is paid. This idea is related to Paul's ironic statement that "the wages of sin is death" (Rom. 6:23). He meant that the fair compensation for sin is death, separation from God. But this just recompense was paid by Christ by means of His death. This made it possible for individuals to escape the separation from God produced by sin and instead to enjoy a relationship with Him. Paul reminded his readers that this work of Christ was a part of God's plan, for "God presented him as a sacrifice of atonement" (3:25).

Reconciliation. "Reconciliation" is closely related to atonement since it too means that a broken relationship is restored. The kinship of these words is illustrated in an early English version of the Bible. When William Tyndale made his translation of the New Testament in 1526 he rendered 2 Corinthians 5:18 this way: "God . . . hath given unto us the office to preache [*sic*] the atonement."[15] This is a conceptually accurate translation, though the word Paul used is better translated as "reconciliation," the restoration or establishment of a friendly and harmonious relationship.

That the work of Christ achieved reconciliation between God and humanity is a distinctive emphasis of Paul and is discussed primarily in Romans and 2 Corinthians.[16] In those letters he made it clear that God took the initiative in this reconciliation. As he told the Corinthians, "All this is from God, who reconciled us to himself through Christ and gave us the ministry of reconciliation: that God was reconciling the world to himself, not counting men's sins against them" (2 Cor. 5:18–19). Even more emphatic was his statement to the Romans: "when we were God's enemies, we were reconciled to him through the death of his Son" (5:10; cf. Eph. 2:1–10). The hostility of humanity was overcome by the love of God (cf. the statement of Jesus, "Love your enemies and pray for those who persecute you, that you may be sons of your Father in heaven," Matt. 5:44–45).

The combination of divine authority and human responsibility that was a part of Paul's presentation of God's plan of salvation is also a feature of his statements about reconciliation. God has acted to reconcile the world (Rom. 11:15; 2 Cor. 5:19), but it is necessary for individuals to receive this experience (Rom. 5:11). Paul, in fact, summarized his message in the phrase, "Be reconciled to God" (2 Cor. 5:20). As Paul sometimes spoke about God's plan of salvation in universal terms, here too universal implications are a part of his discussion about reconciliation. In this case it is the world, a reference to people generally, which God has reconciled to Himself. Does this mean everyone will be saved? No. Instead the answer is that Paul believed the benefits of Christ's atonement were universal in their scope. Yet these benefits were experienced only by individuals who received them by believing the message of the gospel (see also the discussion of 2 Peter 2 in this volume).

Redemption. Another important term related to Paul's understanding of Christ's work in salvation is "redemption." Though the New Testament uses several words to refer to this idea, the noun Paul used in these letters (*apolytrōsis*) expresses the idea of being set free from enslavement, while the verb (*agorazō*; 1 Cor. 6:20; 7:23) reminds readers of the price that was paid for this freedom, namely, Christ's life. In Romans 3:24 Paul wrote of people being "justified freely by his grace through the redemption that came by Christ Jesus." Since to be justified means to be declared not guilty by God, the aspect of redemption in view in this verse is the freedom from the penalty of sin that Christ's death gained for guilty sinners.

---

15. *The Oxford English Dictionary,* 13 vols. (Oxford: Clarendon, 1933), 1:539.

16. Paul used the noun *katallagē* four times (Rom. 5:11; 11:15; 2 Cor. 5:18–19) and the verb *katallassō* six times (Rom. 5:10 [twice]; 1 Cor. 7:11; 2 Cor. 5:18–20). Reconcilation is also mentioned in the letters to the Ephesians (2:16) and Colossians (1:20, 22), using the verb with the intensive prefix *apo* each time.

Later in this letter Paul referred to the hope that Christians have for "the redemption of our bodies" (8:23). Earlier in the passage he had written of a future time when "the creation itself will be liberated from its bondage to decay" (v. 21). For the Christian this "bondage to decay" manifests itself in the mortality of the body. A part of the redemption that Christ achieved was the prospect of an immortal body, "liberated from its bondage to decay." Paul thus saw Christ's redemption as an act that had implications for both the present and the future experience of Christians.

But though Paul may have viewed the benefits of redemption from different vantage points, he regarded the liberation that Christ gained as a seamless whole since it is rooted in the person of Christ Himself. With this in mind he told the Corinthians that Christ had become redemption for them (1 Cor. 1:30), or stated otherwise, He has become their Redeemer.

In a similar vein Paul also described Christ as a Deliverer. Because Christians are free from the penalty of sin through Christ's redemption, Paul described Jesus to the Thessalonians as the One "who rescues us from the coming wrath" (1 Thess. 1:10). This same confidence was expressed in the answer to the anguished cry for a redeemed body in the soliloquy of Romans 7:24–25, "Who will rescue me from this body of death? Thanks be to God—through Jesus Christ our Lord!" Finally, it was to this Deliverer that Paul looked for the redemption of his kinsmen in Israel. Paul believed that Jesus Himself was the Deliverer who will come one day from Zion (11:26) to accomplish redemption for Israel.

Substitutionary death as a sin offering. The concept of Jesus' death as a substitute for the sin of others has been discussed above, particularly in connection with Paul's view of the Atonement. However, it may be beneficial to consider further several passages that address this point of Jesus' death as a sin offering. For example, in Romans 8:3 Paul wrote about God "sending his own Son in the likeness of sinful man to be a sin offering." The phrase "sin offering" translates the Greek words "for sin" *(peri hamartias)*, but since these words referred routinely in the Septuagint to the sin offering[17] (e.g., Lev. 5:6–7) the NIV translation is well taken. The same idea is expressed in the statement of 2 Corinthians 5:21, "God made him who had no sin to be sin [or 'to be a sin offering'[18]] for us." This is a development of his previously written affirmation that Christ "died for all, that those who live should no longer live for themselves but for him who died for them" (2 Cor. 5:15). Paul also had this idea in mind when he told the Galatians, "Christ redeemed us from the curse of the law by becoming a curse for us" (Gal. 3:13). That this was an essential part of the gospel from the beginning of Paul's ministry is clear from his summary statement to the Corinthians about his message: "I passed on to you as of first importance: that Christ died for our sins according to the Scriptures" (1 Cor. 15:3).

17. Of fifty-four occurrences of the phrase in the Septuagint, forty-four times it refers to the sin offering (Douglas Moo, *Romans 1–8* [Chicago: Moody, 1991], 512).

18. Bauer, Arndt, and Gingrich, *A Greek-English Lexicon of the New Testament,* 43.

Paul regarded Christ's death as the event that broke sin's power or authority and ultimately, to speak in Paul's personified terms, sealed sin's doom. As he told the Romans, "The death he died, he died to sin once for all" (6:10). Later he said that by means of the death of Christ God "condemned sin in sinful man" (8:3). This judgment on sin is based on Jesus' death. Sin as a penalty has been eliminated for the Christian (8:1). Sin as a power has been broken for the Christian (6:6, 18, 22). Sin as a presence will be removed for the Christian (6:7; 8:23). Sin will ultimately be banished when the Christian receives a glorified body (8:30), but both the banishment ("condemned," v. 3) and the reception ("glorified," v. 30) are such certain events that Paul used a past tense verb to describe them.

RESURRECTION

For Paul, Christ's resurrection was God's affirmation that Jesus' death did indeed pay the penalty for sin. As he told the Corinthians, "If Christ has not been raised, your faith is futile; you are still in your sins" (1 Cor. 15:17). This same point was made succinctly when he said that Christ "was delivered over to death for our sins and was raised to life for our justification" (Rom. 4:25). The resurrection testified to the fact that Jesus' death made possible acquittal from sin's penalty, escape from sin's power, and ultimate deliverance from sin's presence.

Jesus' resurrection also initiated His role as Lord. He now exercises authority at God's right hand. Paul referred to this when he said that Jesus "was declared with power to be the Son of God by his resurrection from the dead: Jesus Christ our Lord" (1:4). One expression of this authority is Jesus' ministry of intercession in behalf of Christians, a reason Paul could declare confidently that "there is now no condemnation for those who are in Christ Jesus" (8:1). When later in this passage he posed the rhetorical question, "Who is he that condemns?" (8:34a), the understood reply is "No one." For as Paul answered, "Christ Jesus, who died—more than that, who was raised to life—is at the right hand of God and is also interceding for us" (v. 34b).

Paul also regarded Christ's resurrection as typical of what Christians will experience. "Christ has indeed been raised from the dead, the firstfruits of those who have fallen asleep" (1 Cor. 15:20). In a similar vein he wrote to the Romans, "And if the Spirit of him who raised Jesus from the dead is living in you, he who raised Christ from the dead will also give life to your mortal bodies through his Spirit, who lives in you" (Rom. 8:11). The resurrection is then not so much a work that Christ did as it is a work of God the Father and the Spirit. Yet Paul regarded the resurrection as integrally related to Jesus' present ministry and an essential aspect of a Christian's future experience.

IN CHRIST

The combination of the present and the future was a frequent feature of Paul's discussions about the work of Christ and salvation. This is illustrated by the way in which he used the prepositional phrase "in Christ" (*en Christō*) in these letters. For example, he told the Corinthians that "if anyone is in Christ, he is a new creation; the old has gone, the new has come!" (2 Cor. 5:17). The "new creation" Paul spoke of here is the experience of salvation, an experience that is a process with a beginning and end. But Paul was so confident that the process of salvation would be brought to a triumphant conclusion that he sometimes spoke of it as a completed fact. In the preceding context of 2 Corinthians 5, for example, Paul referred to his great anticipation for the glorified body to come: "Meanwhile we groan, longing to be clothed with our heavenly dwelling . . . so that what is mortal may be swallowed up by life" (vv. 2, 4). Paul had not forgotten this longing, for a few verses later he wrote "the new has come!" (v. 17). He simply expressed his confidence that a relationship with Christ guaranteed that his longing would be fulfilled.

Similarly, when Paul asserted that "there is now no condemnation for those who are in Christ Jesus" (Rom. 8:1), he did not preclude the fact that he and all other people would one day stand before the judgment seat of God. On the contrary, later in this letter he reminded his readers that "we will all stand before God's judgment seat . . . and each of us will give an account of himself to God" (14:10, 12). It was not the avoidance of judgment but the certainty of the verdict that Paul spoke about with such assurance, because of his relationship with Christ.

The phrase "in Christ," then, unites the present and the future aspects of salvation for Christians. The expression encapsulated Paul's confidence that the work of Christ once begun was certain of completion and would end one day in Christians' being "heirs of God and co-heirs with Christ" (8:17).

THE WORK OF THE HOLY SPIRIT

Paul saw the Holy Spirit as the enabling Agent of salvation, the member of the triune God who is personally present in Christians from the beginning to the end of the salvation process. This presence of the Spirit in individual experience is the hallmark of the ministry of the new covenant (2 Cor. 3:3).

Faith and the ministry of the Spirit. Though Paul believed strongly in the necessity of proclaiming the gospel to all people (Rom. 1:14), he recognized that a response of faith to this message was possible only because of the Spirit's ministry. As he told the Corinthians, "No one can say 'Jesus is Lord,' except by the Holy Spirit" (1 Cor. 12:3). Or as he had written earlier in this same letter, "The man without the Spirit does not accept the things that come from the Spirit of God, for they are foolishness to him, and he cannot understand them, because they are spiritually discerned" (2:14). While there is a mystery in the interrelationship between the individual's responsibility to believe and the Spirit's enabling to make that faith response to the gospel, it is an enigma that Paul left unexplained in these letters. Nevertheless, the necessity of the Spirit's ministry in the response and profession of faith is consistent with Paul's anthropology and his general conviction regarding the inability of people to do God's will unaided.

The Spirit as guarantee. Webster defines guarantee as "an assurance for the fulfillment of a condition." In salvation the Spirit's presence guarantees the fulfillment of that process. Paul told the Corinthians that God had "anointed us, set his seal of ownership on us, and put his Spirit in our hearts as a deposit, guaranteeing what is to come" (2 Cor. 1:21b–22). When later in this same letter he expressed a longing for the completion of the process of salvation, "so that what is mortal may be swallowed up by life" (5:4), he went on to affirm that "it is God who has made us for this very purpose and has given us the Spirit as a deposit, guaranteeing what is to come" (v. 5).

Though Paul used different terms elsewhere in these letters to affirm this belief, he associated the ideas of ownership and assurance with the work of the Spirit. In writing to the Romans he said, "if anyone does not have the Spirit of Christ, he does not belong to Christ" (Rom. 8:9). The Spirit marks out those who belong to Christ. Later in this passage he referred to the Spirit's ministry of assurance regarding the status of Christians as members of God's family. "For you did not receive a spirit that makes you a slave again to fear, but you received the Spirit of sonship. And by him we cry, 'Abba, Father.' The Spirit himself testifies with our spirit that we are God's children" (vv. 15–16).

The leading of the Spirit. Related to the fact of the Holy Spirit as a guarantee of salvation is Paul's view that the Spirit's ministry leads the Christian through the process of salvation that culminates in the glorification of the body. He told the Romans that "those who are led by the Spirit of God are sons of God" (8:14). His use of the passive verb ("are led," *agontai*) emphasizes the Spirit's ministry in leading all Christians to the goal determined by God, stated later as being "conformed to the likeness of his Son" (v. 29). The Spirit is able to reach this goal because, as Paul wrote earlier in this passage, "the law of the Spirit of life set me free from the law of sin and death" (v. 2). Paul used the word "law" here similar to the way someone might speak of the "law of gravity" as a principle or power at work in a consistent and uniform way. The power of the Spirit is contrasted with the power of sin and death. The latter power pulls people away from God to their destruction. But the greater power of the Spirit breaks Christians free from the pull of sin and death and guarantees that the Spirit's leading will bring them to their intended destination.

Though Paul called attention to the Spirit as the determinative Agent in the process of salvation, he did not disregard or eliminate human responsibility. His viewpoint on the necessity of personal response was expressed in the appeal to "live by the Spirit" (Gal. 5:16). The word "live" is a good translation of Paul's idea, but it veils the verbal connection Paul made between the Spirit's leading and individual response. Paul often used the verb "walk" (*peripateō*), but he did so against the backdrop of the Old Testament where this verb refers to behavior in keeping with God's will (the Hebrew word *hālak* has the same meaning). As the Spirit "leads," the Christian "walks" by following God's will in dependence on the Spirit's enabling. This interplay of descriptive words is further illustrated by another appeal to the Galatians: "Since we live by the Spirit, let us keep in step with the Spirit" (5:25). In a similar vein in Romans, Paul had referred to people "who walk in the footsteps of the faith that our father Abraham had" (4:12). "Keeping in step" or "walking by the Spirit" for Paul meant believing God and acting in accord with His will, the human response to the Spirit's leading.

The Spirit and the law. Related to Paul's view about the ministry of the Spirit generally, and the leading of the Spirit in particular, is his understanding of the role and function of the law in the experience of salvation. When Paul referred to the law, he usually meant the stipulations and guidelines for behavior that were given to Israel by God through Moses. These stipulations are contained primarily in the first five books of the Old Testament (Genesis–Deuteronomy) though they were repeated and adapted in later Old Testament writings.

A significant question for early Christians concerned to what extent, if any, these stipulations to Israel applied to them as well, particularly since the Bible they read and studied was the Old Testament. Though portions of the New Testament seem to support those who wish to continue living in accord with the Old Testament laws (e.g., passages in Matthew and James, along with some recorded events in Acts), these letters of Paul have a different emphasis.

An instructive passage in this regard is in Galatians where he wrote, "If you are led by the Spirit, you are not under law" (5:18). Since Paul viewed all Christians as led by the Spirit (Rom. 8:14–15), it follows that he did not believe the stipulations of the law applied to them. This conclusion might be denied on the grounds that a qualification of some sort needs to be attached to Paul's statement about not being under law, such as "you are not under the Law's condemnation" or "you are not under a legalistic misinterpretation of the Law." While qualifications such as these are not unreasonable interpretations of Paul's view, they suffer from the fact that they are not qualifications Paul himself made.

When, for example, the apostle addressed this issue in Romans, he began by saying, "Do you not know brothers—for I am speaking to men who know the law—that the law has authority over a man only as long as he lives?" (7:1). Does Paul mean to say, "I am speaking to people who know that the condemnation of the Law has authority over a man only as long as he lives" or that "the legalistic misinterpretation of the Law has authority over a man only as long as he lives"? Few would think so. Yet a few verses later in this passage Paul said, "You also died to the law" (v. 4) and "by dying to what once bound us, we have been released from the law so that we serve in the new way of the Spirit, and not in the old way of the written code" (v. 6).

Paul made a similar sort of contrast with regard to faith in Christ and observance of the law. To the Galatians he wrote, "the law was put in charge to lead us to Christ that we might be justified by faith. Now that faith has come, we are no longer under the supervision of the law" (Gal. 3:24–25). And to the Romans he said, "Christ is the end of the law so that there may be righteousness for everyone who believes" (Rom. 10:4).[19]

One should not conclude that Paul saw the Old Testament and its stipulations as an irrelevant body of revelation. On the contrary, the law served to showcase human sinfulness, recognition of which is an essential first step in responding to the gospel. As he told the Romans, "through the law we become conscious of sin" (3:20). He also saw the church as the people of God as analogous to Israel in many respects, so that the successes and failures of Israel are instructive for the church (e.g., Rom. 15:4; 1 Cor. 10:1–10).

Yet Paul regarded Israel and the church as different groups. The old covenant, epitomized by the Mosaic legislation, was made with Israel (2 Cor. 3:12–14). For Christians, the old covenant has been superseded by the new covenant instituted by Christ (1 Cor. 11:25–26). This did not mean there was no continuity between the covenants. Paul cited four of the Ten Commandments, for example (Rom. 13:9), and parallels to a further five could be made. But the sign of the old covenant, the observance of the Sabbath (Ex. 20:8–11), is never applied to the church. To the contrary, Paul made it clear that observance of particular days was a matter of individual conscience (Rom. 14:5–6).

This does not mean that the new covenant contains no stipulations. The letters of Paul, in fact, included many commands. But when Paul told the Corinthians that "circumcision is nothing and uncircumcision is nothing. Keeping God's commands is what counts" (1 Cor. 7:19), this statement makes sense only in light of the new covenant superseding the stipulations of the old covenant (Gen. 17:14). The work of Christ and the ministry of the Spirit are the heart of the superiority of the new covenant. As Paul told the Romans, "what the law was powerless to do in that it was weakened by the sinful nature, God did by sending his own Son . . . in order that the righteous requirements of the law might be fully met in us, who do not live according to the sinful nature but according to the Spirit" (Rom. 8:3–4).

JUSTIFICATION

Paul sometimes portrayed the process of salvation in terms of past and present experience and future anticipation. For example, he commended the Thessalonians for the testimony of their faith, "how you turned to God from idols [past] to serve the living and true God [present], and to wait for his Son from heaven [future]" (1 Thess. 1:9–10). But usually he referred to only one aspect of salvation in any given verse.

The first phase of the experience of salvation is often called justification. The word refers to the acquittal from the penalty of sin that God gives to those who have faith in Christ (Rom. 3:26). The noun (*dikaiōsis*) occurs only twice in the New Tes-

19. For further discussion of this subject generally and this verse in particular, see David K. Lowery, "Christ, the End of the Law in Romans 10:4," in *Dispensationalism, Israel and the Church*, ed. Craig A. Blaising and Darrell L. Bock (Grand Rapids: Zondervan, 1992), 230–47.

tament, both times in Paul's letter to the Romans in relation to the work of Christ and its benefit for Christians (4:25; 5:18). In the use of the verb different temporal aspects of justification are seen. Paul told the Corinthians, for example, "you were justified in the name of the Lord Jesus Christ and by the Spirit of our God" (1 Cor. 6:11). This statement illustrates the idea that justification is a declaration of acquittal made by God at the moment of an individual's faith in Christ. Elsewhere Paul referred to God as the "one who justifies those who have faith in Jesus" (Rom. 3:26).

But Paul also could speak of justification with a future tense, as a declaration that will be made at the judgment. He told the Romans that "it is not those who hear the law who are righteous in God's sight, but those who obey the law who will be declared righteous (2:13).[20] Later in the letter he stressed Christ's work in connection with a Christian's righteousness, but retained the future point of view with regard to its application: "through the obedience of the one man the many will be made righteous" (5:19). A similar future orientation was a part of Paul's statement to the Galatians when he said "by faith we eagerly await through the Spirit the righteousness for which we hope" (5:5).

These last examples also illustrate how the idea of righteousness may include both an objective sense describing God's declaration of acquittal and a subjective sense relating to the development of character that accords with His will and character. Thus Paul told the Romans, "You have been set free from sin and have become slaves to righteousness" with the result that Christians should act as a people "in slavery to righteousness" (6:18–19).

That righteousness can be thought of as virtually equivalent to salvation is shown by a statement like that in Romans 5:17 in which Paul said that "those who receive God's abundant provision of grace and of the gift of righteousness [will] reign in life through the one man, Jesus Christ." The life referred to is the same as that mentioned in 6:23, "the wages of sin is death, but the gift of God is eternal life in Christ Jesus our Lord." This interplay of righteousness and salvation is found in Romans 9:30–10:13 as well. Paul described how the Gentiles obtain righteousness by faith in Christ (9:30) and then professed that "my heart's desire and prayer to God for the Israelites is that they may be saved" (10:1). Later he epitomized his message this way: "if you confess with your mouth, 'Jesus is Lord,' and believe in your heart that God raised him from the dead, you will be saved. For it is with your heart that you believe and are justified, and it is with your mouth that you confess and are saved" (10:9–10). Running through this passage is the equation of justification and salvation, a reminder that when Paul discussed salvation the part and the whole were often interchanged.

---

20. Paul did not think anyone could obey the law and thus merit salvation (Rom. 3:20). He believed God's righteousness was a gift (v. 24; 4:5).

SANCTIFICATION

Such a part-whole interchange is also true with regard to Paul's view of sanctification. This aspect of salvation is often regarded as the phase that extends between the beginning (justification) and the end (glorification) of the process of salvation. It could be called the "extended middle" experience of Christian life and practice since both justification and glorification can be viewed as experiences accomplished by God's declaration and therefore realized immediately. Sanctification, however, usually describes the experience of being set apart by God to belong to Him and be used by Him.

Paul summarized sanctification's goal in his letter to the Thessalonians when he told them, "It is God's will that you should be sanctified; that you should avoid sexual immorality. . . . For God did not call us to be impure, but to live a holy life" (1 Thess. 4:3, 7; the words "holy" and "holy life" translate *hagiosmos*, a term describing "sanctification"; cf. Titus 2:11–14; 3:4–7). The opposite of holiness, "impurity," could refer to immorality generally (1 Thess. 2:3), though Paul often used it to describe sexual immorality in particular (e.g., Rom. 1:24).

The manner of life that should characterize the experience of sanctification is seen in Paul's exhortation to the Romans: "Just as you used to offer the parts of your body in slavery to impurity and to ever-increasing wickedness, so now offer them in slavery to righteousness leading to holiness" (6:19). In a similar vein he said to the Corinthians, "Let us purify ourselves from everything that contaminates body and spirit, perfecting holiness out of reverence for God" (2 Cor. 7:1).

As a specific example of the kind of life Paul envisioned for Christians, he asked his readers to imitate his manner of life and adopt his values and behavior which, in turn, he traced to Christ. He urged the Corinthians, "Follow my example, as I follow the example of Christ" (1 Cor. 11:1). Earlier in this same letter, after describing his own self-sacrificial manner of life and the suffering he had endured as an apostle (4:8–12), he said, "I urge you to imitate me" (v. 16). He then spoke of sending Timothy who would "remind you of my way of life in Christ Jesus, which agrees with what I teach everywhere in every church" (v. 17). He commended the Thessalonians because, he wrote, "You became imitators of us and of the Lord; in spite of severe suffering . . . and so you became a model to all the believers" (1 Thess. 1:7).

The ultimate model for the Christian life and the process of holiness, however, is Christ Himself. As a summary of the manner of Jesus' earthly life, Paul reminded the Romans that Christ "did not please himself" (15:3). He epitomized love for God and love for others and thus modeled the manner of life Paul urged his readers to follow.

But, though there is a strong emphasis on human responsibility in Paul's statements about sanctification, he also reminded his readers of the divine interaction in this process when he stated that "from the beginning God chose you to be saved through the sanctifying work of the Spirit and through belief in the truth" (2 Thess. 2:13). The Spirit's role in this process is also brought out when Paul spoke about his proclamation of the gospel "so that the Gentiles might become an offering acceptable to God, sanctified by the Holy Spirit" (Rom. 15:16). God's work is even more accentuated in his prayer for the Thessalonians: "May God himself, the God of peace, sanctify you through and through" (1 Thess. 5:23a).

The continuation of this prayer suggests that Paul was thinking of future sanctification, especially the completion of the process of salvation: "May your whole spirit, soul and body be kept blameless at the coming of our Lord Jesus Christ" (v. 23b). So that no one would doubt his confidence in God to answer this prayer affirmatively he added further, "the one who calls you is faithful and he will do it" (v. 24).

Yet elsewhere Paul wrote of sanctification as if it were a past experience. At the beginning of 1 Corinthians he described his readers as "those sanctified in Christ Jesus" (1 Cor. 1:2). Later he said, "you were washed, you were sanctified, you were justified in the name of the Lord Jesus Christ and by the Spirit of our God" (6:11). As in the case of justification, then, Paul regarded sanctification as an aspect of salvation that can be spoken of as past, present, and future. When used in the past tense, it describes the experience of being cut off from a former non-Christian way of life, including the beliefs and practices that were a part of it, to a life marked by faith in Christ that now belonged to God and was to be lived for His glory. Discussion about sanctification in the present time focuses on the outworking of this new faith and the manner of life that corresponds to God's will. The future perspective looks forward to the consummation of this process when the life of faith will come to an end. Then the believer finally obtains what is hoped for, experiencing complete holiness or conformity to God's will along with the enjoyment of perfect fellowship with Him.

GLORIFICATION

The goal of the Christian experience of salvation is sharing and participating in the glory of God. As Paul told the Romans, "we rejoice in the hope of the glory of God" (5:2). This hope includes the transformation of mortal life to immortal or eternal life. Paul told the Corinthians that he looked forward to the body being "raised in glory" (1 Cor. 15:43). The "hope of the glory of God" also includes the prospect of unimpaired fellowship with Him, the direct experience of His presence, and completed knowledge of Him. Paul compared Christians' present experience to the perfect future in this way: "Now we see but a poor reflection as in a mirror; then we shall see face to face. Now I know in part; then I shall know fully, even as I am fully known" (1 Cor. 13:12).

As in the case of justification and sanctification, what Paul said about glorification was closely linked to Christ as well. He told the Romans that Christians are "co-heirs with Christ, if indeed we share in his sufferings in order that we may also share in his glory" (Rom. 8:17). The process of sanctification advances in the context of suffering, as Christ Himself suffered, and culminates in the experience of glory that Christ Himself now experiences. In similar fashion, the apostle told the Thessalonians that God had called them "through our gospel, that you might share in the glory of our Lord Jesus Christ" (2 Thess. 2:14).

Glory and suffering are often collocated in Paul, as when he testified, for example, "I consider that our present sufferings are not worth comparing to the glory that will be revealed in us" (Rom. 8:18). Elsewhere he expressed his conviction that "our light and momentary troubles are achieving for us an eternal glory that far outweighs them all" (2 Cor. 4:17).

In this aspect of salvation too, Paul stressed God's activity in bringing this phase of salvation to completion. He was so confident of this fact that he used the past tense of the verb to describe this experience as already done for Christians: "those he called . . . he also glorified" (Rom. 8:30). Later he referred to Christians as "the objects of his mercy, whom he prepared in advance for glory—even us whom he also called" (9:23–24). Paul's confidence in this is rooted in his view of God's faithfulness, the assurance that God will do what He promised.

FAITH AND OBEDIENCE

In the interplay of human and divine action in the process of salvation, Paul's view on human responsibility might be summed up in the verbs "believe and obey." People need to believe the message of salvation Paul proclaimed and to live in light of it. Several passages illustrate that believing and obeying are two sides of the same coin. For example, Paul told the Romans, "we received grace and apostleship to call people from among all the Gentiles to the obedience that comes from faith" (Rom. 1:5). The verbs for believe (*pisteuō*) and obey (*hypakouō*) are paralleled later when he referred to the unbelief of many in Israel by saying, "Not all the Israelites accepted (*hypakouō*) the good news. For Isaiah says, 'Lord, who has believed (*pisteuō*) our message?'" (10:16).

A similar parallel is seen when comparing Paul's initial and final words of commendation to the Romans. In the first part of the letter he said, "First, I thank my God through Jesus Christ for all of you, because your faith is being reported all over the world" (1:8). Near the close of the letter he expressed his appreciation this way: "Everyone has heard about your obedience, so I am full of joy over you" (16:19).

That Paul also used the negative corollary "disobey" (the verb, *apeitheō*; the noun, *apeitheia*) to mean both disobedience and unbelief is another illustration of the interplay of faith and obedience in his thought. In Romans, he described the changed situation of Jews and Gentiles before God this way: "Just as you who were at one time disobedient to God have now received mercy as a result of their disobedience, so they too have now become disobedient in order that they too may now receive mercy" (11:30–31). Later he solicited the Romans' prayer that "I may be rescued from the unbelievers [the participial noun of the verb *apeitheō*] in Judea" (15:31), as earlier he had described people worthy of judgment as those "who reject the truth" (2:8; using the same participial noun [translated "the unbelievers"] as in 15:31).

These examples point toward the fact that Paul regarded faith as a response of the whole person to the gospel, a response of the mind, emotions, and will that manifests itself in speech and action. This is not to say that Paul believed salvation was in any way earned, gained, or merited by particular behavior. His brief statement to the Romans summed up his view: "to the man who does not work but trusts God who justifies the wicked, his faith is credited as righteousness" (4:5). But faith is not passive acknowledgment of the truth of the gospel; it is active response to that truth. As he told the Romans, "thanks be to God that, though you used to be slaves to sin, you wholeheartedly obeyed the form of teaching to which you were entrusted. You have been set free from sin and have become slaves to righteousness" (6:17–18).

ASSURANCE AND ENDURANCE

Paul's belief in the certainty of salvation can be seen from his statements about its future aspects which were described as if they were already completed (e.g., glorification). Assurance of salvation is also rooted in Paul's view of God's faithfulness to do what He promises. But several passages provide another perspective on Paul's conviction about Christian assurance.

One of them is in Romans, in which Paul linked Christ's death to salvation's assurance. For Paul, gaining justification is the most difficult or challenging aspect of salvation, in comparison to which the completion of salvation was easily accomplished: "Since we have now been justified by his blood, how much more shall we be saved from God's wrath through him!" (Rom. 5:9). As Paul saw it, the difficult part had already been done (Jesus' death). That being so, what could hinder the accomplishment of the easier part (salvation)? This idea is repeated in the following verse: "For if when we were God's enemies, we were reconciled to him through the death of his Son, how much more, having been reconciled, shall we be saved through his life!" (5:10).

Later in Romans this same thought (though lacking the phrase, "much more") found similar expression. Here Paul first stated the fact that God "did not spare his own Son, but gave him up for us all" and then asked, "how will he not also along with him, graciously give us all things?" (8:32). The "all things" refers to everything pertaining to the process of salvation, the gamut of experiences described in the preceding verses (vv. 29–30), ending with glorification. This is a statement of assurance since the rhetorical question was often a way of making an affirmation, as here: God has done the former (given His Son), so He will certainly do the latter (save believers completely).

But this issue of assurance is also related to questions about Christian endurance or perseverance in the experience of salvation. One such question may be stated this way: Does the fact that Paul believed in assurance mean that he also believed that Christians would persistently endure in faithful obedience through the course of their experience of salvation? That is, though assurance of salvation is certain because it is grounded in God's character, was Paul equally confident that the corresponding human side of this experience—faithful obedience in doing the will of God—would be evident?

Paul's statements about this suggest the answer is yes. A word Paul often used to describe this response is *hypomonē* ("patience," "endurance," "steadfastness," or "perseverance"). For example, in describing God's judgment he spoke of two groups of people: "those who by persistence in doing good seek glory, honor and immortality, he will give eternal life. But for those who are self-seeking and who reject the truth and follow evil, there will be wrath and anger" (Rom. 2:7–8). Paul expressed thanks to God for the Thessalonians' "work produced by faith, your labor prompted by love, and your endurance inspired by hope in our Lord Jesus Christ" (1 Thess. 1:3).

Endurance or perseverance is clearly seen in the context of Christian suffering. To the Romans he referred to suffering and its place in Christian experience by saying, "suffering produces perseverance; perseverance, character; and character, hope" (Rom. 5:3–4). Paul commended the Thessalonians for "your perseverance and faith in all the persecutions and trials you are enduring" (2 Thess. 1:4). He encouraged the Corinthians in their "patient endurance of the same sufferings we suffer" (2 Cor. 1:6). He urged the Romans to be "patient in affliction" (Rom. 12:12) and reminded them that in the experience of salvation "we hope for what we do not yet have, we wait for it patiently" (8:25). Patient endurance in carrying out God's will is the human response to the assurance that God will accomplish the promised salvation.

Though these statements on the subject might lead a reader to answer, "Yes, Paul did believe that patient endurance in the will of God would characterize Christian experience," his discussion about practical matters in the Corinthian church shows the issue's complexity and the necessity of qualifying a simple affirmative answer.

One example occurs in the context of directions Paul gave about proper conduct in observing the Lord's Supper (1 Cor. 11:17–34). Their commemoration took place in the context of a communal meal, similar to the setting in which Jesus instituted this remembrance of His death in the midst of the Passover meal. The Corinthians, however, apparently did not practice the communal sharing that characterized the Jewish Passover, in which rich and poor all ate the same meal. The Lord's Supper had become instead an occasion for self-indulgence for some, shown all the worse against the backdrop of deprivation experienced by others. As Paul observed, "One remains hungry, another gets drunk," with the result that the rich "humiliate those who have nothing" (vv. 21–22).

Because the Corinthians had been indifferent to correcting this injustice, God intervened in discipline. As Paul explained, "that is why many among you are weak and sick, and a number of you have fallen asleep" (v. 30). But even this intervention was a testimony to salvation's assurance since, as Paul said, "when we are judged by the Lord, we are being disciplined so that we will not be condemned with the world" (v. 32). In this case, the severity of the discipline led to death ("a number of you have fallen asleep"). But the ultimate consequence was salvation, not condemnation. Nevertheless, it is clear that some Christians in the Corinthian church were not demonstrating faithful endurance in doing the will of God that Paul elsewhere described as the human corollary to assurance.[21]

21. Another example is the factious and divisive Corinthians whom Paul called "worldly" (or "carnal," *sarkinos, sarkikos*) in 1 Cor. 3:1–3.

The Corinthian situation is a reminder that the model of Christian experience was not uniformly achieved. As in other aspects of salvation, the interplay of divine enablement and human appropriation produces different responses. Paul stated the ideal in his letter to the Corinthians: the love that the Spirit produces "always perseveres" (1 Cor. 13:7). The Scriptures are a stimulus to that end for, as Paul mentioned, "everything that was written in the past was written to teach us, so that through endurance and the encouragement of the Scriptures we might have hope" (Rom. 15:4). But ultimately endurance, like every other characteristic of Christian experience, depends on God's enabling. For this reason Paul prayed, "May the Lord direct your hearts into God's love and Christ's perseverance" (2 Thess. 3:5). God and Christ are both examples and sources of these needed virtues. Paul's prayer for the Romans expressed this reality: "May the God who gives endurance and encouragement give you a spirit of unity among yourselves as you follow Christ Jesus, so that with one heart and mouth you may glorify the God and Father of our Lord Jesus Christ" (15:5–6).

ECCLESIOLOGY

In Paul's ecclesiology, the discussion concerns his belief about the church (*ekklēsia*) and his views on how the church should function. Each of Paul's letters includes directions of a practical nature related to church life and practice, but the letters to the Corinthian church, in particular (especially 1 Corinthians), provide insight into some of the problems that developed in the early church and the measures Paul used in dealing with them.

THE LOCAL AND UNIVERSAL CHURCH

The local or regional church. The references to the church in these letters of Paul usually focus on a local or regional group of Christians. When these believers came together for worship, instruction, and fellowship, they apparently met in someone's home. When, for example, Paul wrote to the Corinthians from Ephesus he passed along greetings from two former members: "Aquila and Priscilla greet you warmly in the Lord, and so does the church that meets at their house" (1 Cor. 16:19). While staying in Corinth on his third journey, he mentioned again the hospitality of these friends who were then living in Rome and were using their home once more as a meeting place for the church: "Greet Priscilla and Aquila, my fellow workers in Christ Jesus. . . . Greet also the church that meets at their house" (Rom. 16:3–5). Later in this letter he mentioned his host in Corinth whose home also may have been the meeting place of the church: "Gaius, whose hospitality I and the whole church here enjoy, sends you his greetings" (16:23).

Whether there were multiple meeting places of the church in a city is uncertain. Paul usually addressed the church as a single entity in his letters. However, he did refer to groups of churches at various times, either in ethnic or regional terms. For example, when he mentioned the self-sacrifice of Priscilla and Aquila and their ministry (in cities like Corinth and Ephesus) he referred to the churches in terms of their ethnic majorities: "They risked their lives for me. Not only I but all the churches of the Gentiles are grateful to them" (Rom. 16:4). Elsewhere he referred to the churches of particular regions like Galatia (Gal. 1:2), Asia (1 Cor. 16:19), or Macedonia (2 Cor. 8:1). Both geography and Jewish ethnicity probably come together in his testimony to the Galatians that "I was personally unknown to the churches of Judea that are in Christ" (Gal. 1:22).

The universal church. But the most comprehensive references by Paul are those that encompass all the churches without regional or ethnic distinction. When he advised the Corinthians about order in their meeting, he prefaced his stipulation by saying, "As in all the congregations of the saints" (1 Cor. 14:33b). Other passages also seem to refer to the universal church. When, for example, Paul advised the Corinthians, "Do not cause anyone to stumble, whether Jews, Greeks or the church of God" (1 Cor. 10:32), the last phrase seems to be a reference to all Christians.

In a similar way his references to Christians being members of one body suggest a unity that extends beyond the local church: "The body is a unit, though it is made up of many parts; and though all its parts are many, they form one body. So it is with Christ. For we were all baptized by one Spirit into one body—whether Jews or Greeks, slave or free—and we were all given the one Spirit to drink" (12:12–13). Comments about different ministries in the church point in this same direction. "And in the church God has appointed first of all apostles, second prophets, third teachers" (v. 28). This could be read as a statement about the local Corinthian church (Paul used the same term [*apostoloi*] for those who carried the Gentile Christians' monetary gift to the poor in Jerusalem [2 Cor. 8:23, translated "representatives of the churches" in the NIV]). But the previous defense of his apostleship ("Am I not an apostle? Have I not seen Jesus our Lord?" 1 Cor. 9:1) and a subsequent reference to Jesus' appearance to all the apostles ("Then he appeared to James, then to all the apostles, and last of all he appeared to me also," 15:7–8) suggest that in 12:28 Paul had in mind the narrow definition of apostle (limited to those who had been Jesus' associates in His first coming) and the universal church. This is probably also the case in a similar passage in the letter to the Romans when he said, "in Christ we who are many form one body, and each member belongs to all the others" (Rom. 12:5), though the gifts mentioned subsequently are all understandable in a local first-century church (vv. 6–8).

ORGANIZATION AND ADMINISTRATION

Congregational order. Reading these letters one gets the impression that the churches Paul addressed operated by congregational consensus. It is possible that when Paul gave directives using plural verbs he was addressing an appointed council or group of leaders rather than the congregation as a whole, though such an interpretation of the evidence is difficult to support. When, for example, he reprimanded the Corinthians for tolerating a member's continued involvement in an immoral relationship, he seemed to have the whole church in mind as he described the setting for disciplinary action: "when you are assembled in the name of our

Lord" (1 Cor. 5:4). The whole church seems to be addressed also when he advised the Corinthians about handling disputes among members. He told them to "appoint as judges even men of little account in the church! I say this to shame you. Is it possible that there is nobody among you wise enough to judge a dispute between believers?" (6:5).

The impression that congregations were self-governing is reinforced by Paul's advice that the meeting of the church should be marked by order and self-discipline. No particular individuals are charged with implementing these directions. Rather, personal responsibility and congregational consensus seem to be converging factors in bringing about the desired results. He told the Corinthians that only two or three people should speak in a tongue, "one at a time, and someone must interpret. If there is no interpreter, the speaker should keep quiet in the church and speak to himself and God" (14:27b–28). In the same way only two or three prophets should speak "in turn so that everyone may be instructed and encouraged. The spirits of prophets are subject to the control of prophets" (vv. 31b–32).

Yet he also referred to "those with gifts of administration" (12:28) and said that if someone's gift is "leadership, let him govern diligently" (Rom. 12:8). He also urged the Thessalonians to "respect those who work hard among you, who are over you in the Lord and who admonish you" (1 Thess. 5:12). The verb in the phrase, "who are over you," is *proistēmi*, translated "leadership" in Romans 12:8. So some carried out leadership and administrative responsibilities in the church. But what authority they brought to their tasks is uncertain. Possibly these leaders primarily fulfilled the decisions of the congregation.

Paul and other apostles. One voice of authority in these letters belongs to the apostle himself. He told the Thessalonians, "I charge you before the Lord to have this letter read to all the brothers" (1 Thess. 5:27). And "if anyone does not obey our instruction in this letter take special note of him" (2 Thess. 3:14). Warning the Corinthians that arrogant talk was no substitute for power, he asked them, "Shall I come to you with a whip, or in love and with a gentle spirit?" (1 Cor. 4:21). Though not intended as an illustration of his authority, he went on to say about an immoral member in the congregation that, "I have already passed judgment on the one who did this, just as if I were present" (5:3).

Yet Paul did not hold the office of apostle alone. He referred to other apostles beyond the Twelve in his letter to the Corinthians (1 Cor. 9:4–6; 15:5–7) and acknowledged the authority of the Jerusalem apostles in his letter to the Galatians, calling James, Peter, and John, "those reputed to be pillars" (2:9). He also warned the Corinthians about false apostles who had come to them, "masquerading as apostles of Christ" (2 Cor. 11:13). So while these letters give few indications of a developed hierarchy of leadership in local churches, there was reference to and recognition of apostolic authority.

Hierarchy in the husband-wife relationship. Paul did, however, describe a hierarchy of sorts in the church, based on the husband-wife relationship. He told the Corinthians, "I want you to realize that the head of every man is Christ, and the head of the woman is man, and the head of Christ is God" (1 Cor. 11:3). There is considerable debate among Pauline interpreters about both what his directions to the churches meant and how they were applied. For example, expositors debate to what extent Paul's admonitions about the relationship of husbands and wives particularly, and men and women generally, in the church correspond to common viewpoints and practices about these relationships in first-century culture. One illustration of the controversy related to this discussion concerns Paul's directive to the Corinthians about women praying and prophesying with their heads covered (vv. 5–16).

Most interpreters see Paul telling the Corinthian women who participated in the worship of the church (by praying or prophesying publicly) to do so with a material covering over their head, either covering head and face in the manner of a veil, or more simply as the hood on the common cloak pulled up over the back and top of the head (see esp. v. 10).[22] Paul apparently saw this as the appropriate means by which women could both contribute to the meeting of the church through the exercise of their gifts and also distinguish themselves from men to whom they were complementary.

Though there is some debate about the nature of the covering,[23] more important discussion concerns the significance of this manner of participation in light of first-century society. Should Paul's directive be regarded simply as an expedient measure intended to mitigate criticism and eliminate impediments to evangelism that culturally unacceptable or unusual behavior might create (cf. his advice about speaking in tongues at meetings of the church, particularly in the presence of visitors; 1 Cor. 14:23)? Or was it an abiding policy for all churches then and now who acknowledge the authority of Paul's writings as Scripture? This is not an easy question to answer since Paul buttressed his directive by referring to creation (11:9), which suggests to some the universality and abiding relevance of this rule of worship. But it must be kept in mind that the Sabbath observance was an ordinance also established by reference to creation (Ex. 20:11), though most Christians do not regard the sanctity of Saturday as certainly established for all time because of it.

An additional point of tension in interpreting Paul's directives about the role of men and women in worship is his instruction later in the same letter about the silence of women, at least in the matter of questioning a speaker (1 Cor. 14:35). He stated the general policy that "women should remain silent in the churches" (v. 34). But since he had earlier stipulated circumstances in which women might pray or prophesy (11:5), most interpreters regard Paul's guideline in 14:34 as limited to direct interaction with a public speaker during the church meeting. This is because Paul added, "If they want to inquire about something, they should ask their own husbands at home" (v. 35).

22. A minority opinion is that a woman's hair is her covering. See, for example, James Hurley, "Did Paul Require Veils or the Silence of Women? A Consideration of 1 Cor. 11:2–16 and 1 Cor. 14:33b–36," *Westminster Theological Journal* 35 (1973): 190–220.

23. Further discussion and citation of ancient literature relevant to this issue may be found in David K. Lowery, "1 Corinthians," in *The Bible Knowledge Commentary, New Testament*, ed. John F. Walvoord and Roy B. Zuck (Wheaton, Ill.: Victor, 1983), 528–30.

This last proviso could be interpreted as a further circumscription of silence, applying it only to married women (the Gk. term for "wife" or "woman" is the same, *gynē*) who enjoyed the representation of a husband at the meeting of the church. These married women were not to usurp or bypass their husband's representative role as head of the family by speaking on their own behalf. As Paul maintained, "They are not allowed to speak, but must be in submission, as the Law says" (v. 34). Though he did not cite any text, he may have had in mind the statement in Genesis 3:16 to Eve: "Your desire will be for your husband, and he will rule over you." This second clause can be read as an affirmation of the husband's authoritative role. In sum, these prescriptions to the Corinthians enabled women to have some participation in church meetings without provoking additional controversy that could have jeopardized the freedom the church enjoyed to preach the gospel in the first-century patriarchal society of which it was a part.

That Paul regarded women as able partners in the proclamation and practice of the gospel is clear from his recommendations and commendations. He urged unmarried women in Corinth to consider remaining single so that they could "be concerned about the Lord's affairs" (1 Cor. 7:34). He sent greetings to Tryphena, Tryphosa, and Persis, describing them as "women who work[ed] hard in the Lord" (Rom. 16:12; cf. also Mary, v. 6). And he commended to the Roman church "our sister, Phoebe, a servant [*diakonos*] of the church in Cenchrea . . . for she has been a great help to many people, including me" (16:1–2). That Paul esteemed the gift of prophecy as especially beneficial to the church (1 Cor. 14:1–5) and women as among those who exercised this gift (11:5), says much about his appreciation for the contribution of women to the life of the church.

SPIRITUAL GIFTS, ESPECIALLY PROPHECY

In two places in these letters Paul addressed the role that spiritual gifts and their exercise played in the church. The most extensive discussion is in 1 Corinthians 12–14, in which Paul promoted the use of gifts for the benefit of the church as a whole, especially the gift of prophecy. He had no corrective agenda in mind when he wrote to the Romans about the contribution of gifts (Rom. 12:3–8), but what he said about their distribution and use coheres with his message to the Corinthians.

The Greek term for gift is *charisma,* a word that reminded readers that the various abilities were an expression of God's grace (*charis*) and were to be used for the benefit of others as an extension of God's kindness to the church (1 Cor. 12:4–6). Paul believed that every church member was endowed with a gift. As he told the Corinthians, "Now to each one the manifestation of the Spirit is given for the common good" (v. 7). He also believed that who received which gift was a decision made by the Holy Spirit, not a matter of individual selection, development, or pleading: "All these are the work of one and the same Spirit, and he gives them to each man, just as he determines" (v. 11).

Paul referred to a variety of gifts in these two passages (Rom. 12:6–8; 1 Cor. 12:8–10, 28–30), though the importance of prophecy appears in both (mentioned first in the list in Romans). This is more evident in 1 Corinthians, where Paul wanted to curb the congregation's enthusiasm for speaking in tongues and to encourage the church to provide more opportunity for those with the gift of prophecy to speak in their meetings (1 Cor. 14:1–5). According to Paul, "Two or three prophets should speak, and the others should weigh carefully what is said. And if a revelation comes to someone who is sitting down, the first speaker should stop. For you can all prophesy in turn so that everyone may be instructed and encouraged" (vv. 29–31). There was clearly a measure of spontaneity in these meetings, since a revelation might come to one prophet even as another was speaking. Paul provided a glimpse at the possibilities in his advice to the Corinthians: "When you come together, everyone has a hymn, or a word of instruction, a revelation, a tongue or an interpretation. All of these must be done for the strengthening of the church" (v. 26).

It is important to recall, once again, that the Bible of these early churches was the Greek translation of the Old Testament. Those with the gift of teaching (Rom. 12:7; 1 Cor. 12:29) might offer lessons of instruction and encouragement based on its message. As Paul told the Romans, "Everything that was written in the past was written to teach us, so that through endurance and the encouragement of the Scriptures we might have hope" (Rom. 15:4). But the revelation of New Testament prophets served to complement the message of the Old Testament and provided a specific word from God to people in the church. There was much to be learned from what God had said to Israel, and the similarities in role between Israel and the church meant there were many helpful applications for Christian life and ministry. Still the message of the New Testament was more than a repetition of God's word to Israel. Yet the writing of the New Testament was a gradual process, probably not completed until near the end of the first century. The revelations spoken by the New Testament prophets served to bridge the gap between God's will spoken to Israel and His will revealed to the church. These revelations thus served an essential function in the life of the early church.

How long the gift of prophecy continued in the church is debated. In light of the completion of the canon by the end of the first century (though general agreement about which writings should be included was not finally agreed on until in the fourth century), it is possible that prophecy was spoken less frequently even during the first generation of the church. Paul did write about a time when prophecy would come to an end: "where there are prophecies, they will cease. . . . For we know in part and we prophesy in part, but when perfection comes, the imperfect disappears" (1 Cor. 13:8–10). Some have interpreted the coming of "perfection" as a reference to the completion of the New Testament. But the fact that Paul went on to say in this passage, "now I know in part; then I shall know fully, even as I am fully known" (v. 12) gives reason to question this interpretation. Paul seemed rather to look forward to a time when all earthly limitations will have finally passed away and intimacy with God will be complete. Thus while historical considerations like the formation of the New Testament may imply that foundational gifts such as prophecy ceased within the church's first generation, there is no clear evidence in these letters that Paul regarded the gifts as inoperative at any time soon in the immediate future.

FREEDOM AND RESPONSIBILITY

Paul's advice about how the Corinthians should conduct their church meetings illustrates the interplay of issues like individual freedom and responsibility for the well-being of others that runs through many of his directives about practical matters. He believed, for example, that Jewish convictions and practice did not apply to the church, even though cases like circumcision could be tied to Old Testament stipulations. Those roots made no difference in light of the gospel. When there was danger of confusion about this fact, as in the Galatian church, for example, he was unmistakably blunt: "Mark my words! I, Paul, tell you that if you let yourselves be circumcised, Christ will be of no value to you at all" (Gal. 5:2).

But if the practice of the Old Testament stipulations and Jewish customs were viewed as lifestyle choices based on personal scruples or on account of missionary interests, Paul's concerns were minimal or nonexistent. As he told the Corinthians, he himself often lived in accord with Jewish scruples: "To the Jews I became like a Jew, to win the Jews" (1 Cor. 9:20; cf. Acts 21:17–26). And he told the Romans that decisions about what kinds of food to eat and whether and how to observe particular religious days were matters of personal decision before God (Rom. 14:5–6). It was not the business of the church to dictate standards of behavior to its members in these matters, for to do so would replace the authority of God with human authority (14:4; cf. vv. 9–10) and serve only to repeat the error of the Pharisees and their forebears (Mark 7:7–9).

Yet interwoven with this theme of personal freedom was a clear message about the responsibility to act with regard to the well-being of others both inside and outside the church. As he told the Romans, "Each of us should please his neighbor for his good, to build him up" (Rom. 15:2), and "Let us therefore make every effort to do what leads to peace and to mutual edification" (14:19). At the same time, Paul did not imagine that the church was without any kind of law or that it lacked specific stipulations regarding the will of God. He regarded himself as "under Christ's law" (1 Cor. 9:21) and urged the Galatians to "carry each other's burden, and in this way you will fulfill the law of Christ" (6:2). He also included many commands and guidelines that serve as law ("You know what instructions we gave you by the authority of the Lord," 1 Thess. 4:2). They ranged from comprehensive statements such as, "It is God's will that you should be sanctified" (v. 3), to specific instructions like, "If a man will not work, he shall not eat" (2 Thess. 3:10).

Though there are many points of similarity between these commands to the church and the law given to Israel, they are also often characterized by a variety of differences in application. In the case of material giving, for example, Paul exhorted these churches to give to the poor. He personally spearheaded a collection from predominantly Gentile Christians for the needs of mostly Jewish Christians in Jerusalem. Yet when he specified the manner in which giving was to be done, he did not follow the Old Testament pattern of a fixed tithe. Rather, he told the Corinthians that "each one should set aside a sum of money in keeping with his income" (1 Cor. 16:2), suggesting proportional giving but leaving the decision about degree or extent to individual determination. In a later letter he reminded them that "each man should give what he has decided in his heart to give, not reluctantly or under compulsion, for God loves a cheerful giver" (2 Cor. 9:7).

Many of these similarities are due to the fact that the church, like Israel, is composed of people whom God has redeemed and called to be His representatives. But the differences are a reminder that the church and Israel are not one and the same. Paul did not believe that the temporary ascendancy of the church as the people of God meant that Israel had ceased to be a people called by Him, nor did it mean that the promises made to Israel were now valid only for the church. Though the church shares, for example, in the benefits of the new covenant promised to Israel, Paul compared the church to a wild olive branch grafted into a cultivated tree (Rom. 11:24). The church no more displaces Israel than the branch displaces the tree (vv. 17–18). In the same way, many of the distinctive characteristics of Israel are not applied to the church though both people of God share the benefits of His mercy (v. 32).

ESCHATOLOGY

Eschatology refers to the belief and teaching about the final events (the word *eschatos* means "last") and aspects of God's work in salvation at the end of the world. What Paul believed about the culmination of individual salvation is relatively clear. The particular order of some of the events that are a part of the culminating sequence are less clear, but some idea of his mind on these matters can be determined from statements in these letters.

GLORIFICATION

The culmination of salvation for individuals is glorification. God's plan regarding salvation is summarily stated by Paul this way: "those he predestined, he also called; those he called, he also justified; those he justified, he also glorified" (Rom. 8:30). Glorification involves several aspects, including deliverance from the presence of sin and all its pernicious effects at death (1 Cor. 15:55–56) into the presence of God.

Entrance into God's presence at death. Though Paul did not write explicitly about the circumstance of Christians entering into the presence of Christ and God immediately at death, an understanding of this sort is implied by his word of assurance to the Thessalonians that "God will bring with Jesus those who have fallen asleep in him" (1 Thess. 4:14). The verb "fall asleep" (*koimaō*) was sometimes used to refer to death by both biblical and nonbiblical writers, but Paul frequently employed it to describe the death of Christians (e.g., 1 Cor. 15:6, 18, 20, 51).

Related to this issue is the understanding that Paul's anthropology included the conviction that people are composed of material and immaterial parts. He told the Romans that "if Christ is in you, your body is dead because of sin, yet your spirit is alive because of righteousness" (Rom. 8:10). The spiritual aspect of a believer enters at death into the Lord's presence. In 2 Corinthians 5 Paul wrote in terms of the two spheres of mortality and immortality (without discussion of any phases in that experience).[24] Still his profession that he would "prefer to be away from the body and at home with the Lord" (v. 8) can be applied to the circumstance of those Christians he described in 1 Thessalonians 4:14. Thus the first phase of the experience of glorification is entrance into the presence of the Lord at death.

Resurrection of the body. But the process of glorification for the individual Christian that begins at death with the spiritual aspect of the believer is completed at the resurrection with the transformation of the Christian's body. As Paul assured the Thessalonians, "According to the Lord's own word, we tell you that we who are still alive, who are left till the coming of the Lord, will certainly not precede those who have fallen asleep . . . the dead in Christ will rise first" (1 Thess. 4:15–16).

Paul discussed the resurrection most extensively in 1 Corinthians 15. As he told the Corinthians, the resurrection of Christians will follow the pattern of Jesus' resurrection (v. 20). But defining the nature of the resurrected body was no easy task. Paul's depiction was more suggestive than descriptive (vv. 35–57) and has produced discussion and debate among interpreters even in the present.[25]

For example, he compared the mortal body to a seed. As a seed is sown in the ground, so the body is laid in a grave. But the flower that emerges from that seed is remarkably different and grander than the lowly seed that was sown. As Paul put it, "it is sown in dishonor, it is raised in glory; it is sown in weakness, it is raised in power; it is sown a natural body, it is raised a spiritual body" (vv. 43–44).

When Paul described the resurrected body as a "spiritual body," did he mean it was nonmaterial? Probably not. As in the case of the references to "glory" and "power," "spiritual" identifies the resurrection body with the Holy Spirit's work. In salvation the Holy Spirit is the Agent who begins and completes the process of transformation. But to conclude that Paul envisioned that Christians would become like the Holy Spirit with a nonmaterial existence is an overinterpretation of Paul's point.

Paul, in fact, explicitly likened the Christian's resurrected body to Christ's resurrected body (vv. 20, 45–49). If he regarded Christ's resurrected body as a non-material mode of being, like that of the Holy Spirit, he expressed this in a remarkably oblique manner. What distinguished the Son from the Father and from the Holy Spirit was His incarnation. If Paul meant to say that the incarnate Son became again a purely spiritual being at His resurrection, and Christians likewise will gain this mode of being, his words to the Corinthians about the necessity of a resurrection seem curiously beside the point. Though it is clear that Paul did not articulate precisely the nature of Christ's resurrected body with all its glorious differences, he conceived of it, nonetheless, as a corporeal form of existence.

---

24. For further discussion about this and the question of an "intermediate state," see David K. Lowery, "2 Corinthians," in *The Bible Knowledge Commentary, New Testament,* 565–66.

25. See, e.g., the discussion and debate about the nature of the resurrection body carried on by Murray J. Harris, *Raised Immortal* (Grand Rapids: Eerdmans, 1985) and *From Grave to Glory* (Grand Rapids: Zondervan, 1990); and Norman L. Geisler, *The Battle for the Resurrection* (Nashville: Nelson, 1989) and *In Defense of the Resurrection* (Clayton, Calif.: Witness, 1991).

This bodily transformation would also be experienced by Christians living at the time of Jesus' return. As Paul told the Corinthians, "We will not all sleep, but we will all be changed. . . . the dead will be raised imperishable, and we will be changed. For the perishable must clothe itself with the imperishable, and the mortal with immortality" (vv. 51–53). Thus the experience of glorification for those alive at Christ's return begins at His appearing (cf. 1 Thess. 4:17).

Earlier in this letter to the Corinthians Paul compared the present experience of salvation with the future this way: "Now we see but a poor reflection as in a mirror; then we shall see face to face. Now I know in part; then I shall know fully, even as I am fully known" (13:12). The heart of glorification is this enjoyment of God's presence and the unimpaired fellowship with Him that will exist. Paul envisoned the end of all things as a state in which "God may be all in all" (15:28), in which no opposition will remain and His people will live completely in His presence.

THE SEQUENCE OF FINAL EVENTS

While there is some discussion and disagreement about the nature of the resurrection body and related aspects of the experience of glorification, it is a debate that involves less diversity of interpretation than the question about Paul's understanding of the sequence of events that usher in the end of the present world. In part, this diversity in viewpoint may be due to the fact that Paul's perception of the order of these events may itself have been indefinite. Or it may be that his readers had a better understanding of his view based on teaching previously received from him. When, for example, he wrote the Thessalonians with a word of clarification about these matters he asked, "Don't you remember that when I was with you I used to tell you these things?" (2 Thess. 2:5). Whatever the case may be, what follows is one interpretation that attempts to integrate Paul's various statements about culminating events and also mention alternative points of view about Paul's meaning.

The Day of the Lord. Paul's letters to the Thessalonians are a good place to begin this discussion since questions about the resurrection of the dead and the transformation of living Christians at Jesus' return were issues of great concern to that community. In his second letter to them Paul said, "Concerning the coming of our Lord Jesus Christ and our being gathered to him, we ask you, brothers, not to become easily unsettled or alarmed by some prophecy, report or letter supposed to have come from us, saying that the day of the Lord has already come" (2 Thess. 2:1–2). Whether Paul had in mind two or three different avenues of testimony about the Day of the Lord is uncertain. He knew that each of them was false, but the convergences of these witnesses (cf. Deut. 19:15) understandably upset the Thessalonians, particularly if Paul had taught them that Christians were destined to escape God's judgments associated with the Day of the Lord.

References to this day are found in various statements of the Old Testament prophets. Although these references sometimes depict the time as one of blessing for God's people and judgment for others (e.g., Joel 2:28–32; Zeph. 3:8–20), the emphasis is more often on the day as a time of God's wrath. Zephaniah said, "The great day of the Lord is near . . . a day of wrath, a day of distress and anguish . . . because they have sinned against the Lord. . . . Neither their silver nor their gold will be able to save them on the day of the Lord's wrath. In the fire of his jealousy the whole world will be consumed, for he will make a sudden end of all who live in the earth" (Zeph. 1:14–18). As Joel summarily described it, "Alas for that day! For the day of the Lord is near; it will come like destruction from the Almighty" (Joel 1:15).

Given these catastrophic descriptions of that time, it may seem strange that the Thessalonians could entertain the notion that "the day of the Lord has already come" (2 Thess. 2:2). However, Paul had advised them earlier that "the day of the Lord will come like a thief in the night" (1 Thess. 5:2), and he told them in the meantime to "be alert and self-controlled" (v. 6). Understandably, they may have thought themselves remiss in one or both of these areas, lacking in faithfulness or self-control. And because they were experiencing persecution (2 Thess. 1:4), they were susceptible to doubts and questions about the timing of God's deliverance.

The time of deliverance. In his first letter to the Thessalonians Paul had twice assured them that they would not experience God's wrath. He described them as people who "wait for his son from heaven . . . Jesus, who rescues us from the coming wrath" (1 Thess. 1:10). He later affirmed that "God did not appoint us to suffer wrath but to receive salvation through our Lord Jesus Christ" (5:9). It is not the fact of deliverance that is questioned by interpreters of Paul, but its timing.

This deliverance is often referred to as the Rapture, an old word meaning "the act of conveying a person from one place to another, esp. to heaven."[26] It is used to describe Paul's conviction that "we who are still alive and left will be caught up . . . in the clouds to meet the Lord in the air" (4:17). Interpreters of Paul generally place this deliverance at either the beginning of the time of God's wrath, in the middle of it, or near the end.

Those who believe the Rapture will occur before the day of wrath regard this as the view most in accord with Paul's statements about deliverance from wrath. Those who believe that the Rapture will occur in the middle of this period read what Paul said about a "man of lawlessness" in 2 Thessalonians 2:3–4 in light of Daniel's prophecy about "one who causes desolation," whose decisive action at the midpoint of a particular era precipitates desolation (Dan. 9:27; 11:36). Those who believe the Rapture will occur at the end of this time of wrath see no compelling reason to separate it temporally from Christ's second coming. They believe the view that Christians will meet Christ in the air and then accompany Him as He returns to vanquish all opposition on the earth is the most likely reading of Paul's message.

A case can be made for each of these views, and each has certain problems as well. Those who separate the Rapture from the Second Coming (i.e., those who see it occurring before or those who see it occurring in the middle of the time of wrath)

26. *The Oxford English Dictionary,* 8:153.

are hard-pressed to find this distinction expressed anywhere else in Paul's writings. But those who link the Rapture and the Second Coming must struggle to defend the view that Paul did not have in mind the assumption of Christians directly to heaven in 1 Thessalonians 4:17, but rather their return with Christ to the earth. As a recent commentator has observed, there is no indication in the passage that the resurrected and raptured accompany Christ to the earth. On the contrary, Paul's statement "suggests that both dead and living Christians will return to heaven with the Lord, not only to enjoy continuous fellowship with him, but also, in terms of 1:10, to be saved from the coming wrath of God."[27]

THE JUDGMENT OF GOD

Paul's belief in the certainty of God's judgment is clear from his various statements in these letters. The most extensive discussion is in Romans 2, where he affirmed that the judgment of God would be according to truth (v. 2), that it would be based on behavior representative of a person's life, whether good or evil (vv. 6–10), and that it would be without partiality (v. 11). These principles of judgment apply to all people, though Paul knew that humanity left to its own devices would incur certain condemnation (3:10–20), the essence of which was ultimate separation from God's presence. He told the Thessalonians that God "will punish those who do not know God and do not obey the gospel of our Lord Jesus. They will be punished with everlasting destruction and shut out from the presence of the Lord" (2 Thess. 1:8–9).

The only escape from the sentence of condemnation and the penalty it brings is the gift of righteousness ("This righteousness from God comes through faith in Jesus Christ to all who believe," Rom. 3:22). Paul affirmed for Christians that "there is now no condemnation" (8:1). This does not mean that Paul had abandoned the principles of judgment he had stated earlier in his letter to the Romans. Rather, it is by means of the Spirit that Christians are able to enter the category of those "who by persistence in doing good seek glory, honor and immortality" (Rom. 2:7; cf. 8:4).

When he wrote to the Corinthians, Paul reminded them that "we must all appear before the judgment seat of Christ, that each may receive what is due him for the things done while in the body, whether good or bad" (2 Cor. 5:10), a statement also consistent with the principles found in Romans 2. Similarly, he told the Romans, "we will all stand before God's judgment seat . . . so then, each of us will give an account of himself to God" (14:10, 12). The alteration of Christ and God on the judgment seat reflects Paul's conviction that "God will judge men's secrets through Jesus Christ" (2:16). As he told the Corinthians, "Judge nothing before the appointed time; wait till the Lord comes. He will bring to light what is hidden in darkness and will expose the motives of men's hearts" (1 Cor. 4:5).

27. Charles A. Wanamaker, *Commentary on 1 & 2 Thessalonians* (Grand Rapids: Eerdmans, 1990), 175.

The fact that Paul thought in categorical terms of Christians "doing good" did not preclude his recognition that believers sometimes could be seriously remiss in their manner of life. He reminded the Corinthians that God's judgment was not only a future reality. Some in the church had brought the judgment of God on themselves, even as Paul wrote: "That is why many among you are weak and sick, and a number of you have fallen asleep. . . . When we are judged by the Lord, we are being disciplined so that we will not be condemned with the world" (11:30, 32).

The experience of these Corinthians is similar to the situation of Christian ministers described earlier in this letter (3:10–15). The result of a minister's service to the church "will be shown for what it is, because the Day will bring it to light. It will be revealed with fire, and the fire will test the quality of each man's work. If what he has built survives, he will receive his reward. If it is burned up, he will suffer loss; he himself will be saved, but only as one escaping through the flames" (vv. 13–15). Like the minister in Paul's admonition, the disciplined Christians described in chapter 11 are saved ("not . . . condemned with the world," v. 32), but they are like those escaping through the flames.[28]

For Christians characterized by faithfulness, there is a reward at the judgment. According to Paul, "At that time each will receive his praise from God" (4:5). This commendation of God may well have summarized the essence of reward for Paul. However, he did refer later in this letter to Christians who will judge angels and the world (6:2–3). This may be a case in which the verb translated "judge" (krinō) meant something closer to "govern" or "rule."[29] It also may be an aspect of what it means for Christians to be "co-heirs with Christ" and "share in his glory" (Rom. 8:17). But this is an instance in which the original readers of his letters probably knew more than readers today know about Paul's thought on this subject.

THE CONSUMMATION OF ALL THINGS

Like the Old Testament prophet Isaiah (Isa. 65:17–25), Paul looked forward to a radical change in the natural world, a virtual emancipation of creation itself (Rom. 8:18–21). When Christians enter into their glorification then "the creation itself will be liberated from its bondage to decay and brought into the glorious freedom of the children of God" (v. 21). This renewal will take place at Christ's return.

Whether this renewal will immediately give way to the eternal state or will usher in a time during which the expectations of the Old Testament prophets will find fulfillment (e.g, Isa. 11:6–9) is debated. Paul's letters are indecisive on this point, but if he envisioned such an era before the advent of the eternal state, he has given only a vague indication of it in 1 Corinthians 15:23–24. There he described the order of the resurrections as "each in his own turn: Christ, the firstfruits; then, when he comes, those who belong to him" (v. 23). The first stage, Christ's resurrection, has occurred. But nearly 2,000 years have elapsed, and the second stage

---

28. In 1 Corinthians 3:17 the one who "destroys God's temple" is apparently an unbeliever.

29. Bauer, Arndt, and Gingrich, A Greek-English Lexicon of the New Testament, 452.

has yet to be fulfilled. It is possible that a third stage is described in v. 24, "then the end will come, when he hands over the kingdom to God the Father after he has destroyed all dominion, authority and power." On this reading, the resurrection of all people will take place in a third stage after the earthly renewal anticipated by the Old Testament prophets is fulfilled and judgment against all the enemies of God is completed: "For he must reign until he has put all his enemies under his feet. The last enemy to be destroyed is death" (vv. 25–26, cf. Rev. 20:1–15).[30]

Paul stated that Christ's authority will be universally acknowledged and His judgment comprehensively applied. When that is completed, the Son Himself will defer to the Father's authority in whose stead and power He had acted. That submission of the Son will be the last act of history. Then will begin the eternal state that Paul cryptically described as God being "all in all" (1 Cor. 15:28).

---

30. For a recent presentation of this view, see D. Edmond Hiebert, "Evidence from 1 Corinthians," in *A Case for Premillenialism*, 225–34.

6

A THEOLOGY OF
PAUL'S PRISON EPISTLES

Darrell L. Bock

When one reads the New Testament, and most especially the epistles of a complex writer like the apostle Paul, a question (which often hides a touch of frustration) frequently surfaces. It is, "Why did not God reveal His Word in strict propositions and within a logical order, like a systematic theology?" The thought usually assumes that such a revelation would have solved many problems we have in theologizing today. However, that question ignores a fact about the New Testament. It was not written as an exercise in abstraction nor as an attempt to answer philosophical questions. It was a pastoral theology, formulated to deal with the issues and situations of everyday first-century life.[1]

1. J. Christiaan Beker (*Paul the Apostle: The Triumph of God in Life and Thought* [Philadelphia: Fortress, 1980], esp. 3–36) has called the tension between the essence of Paul's thought and its application in specific situations Paul's "coherence-contingency" hermeneutic. Beker argues that there is a central fulcrum, a "coherence," to Paul's thought but that he applies it "contingently," that is, in differing situations. This means that he could emphasize justification in Romans and wisdom in 1 Corinthians, though both categories reflect the same inner essence. Beker finds this center in an apocalyptic mind-set: "Paul's apocalyptic with its Jewish and Old Testament roots is able to secure the abiding importance of Old Testament themes for Christian theology. Contrary to our common conception of a *Christocentric* promise-fulfillment scheme, Paul refuses to spiritualize the Old Testament promises. His hope in a transformed creation makes his Christological thought subservient to the God who is faithful to his promises, that is, to the theocentric fulcrum of Paul's thought which centers on the question of the public manifestation of God's sovereignty" (xiv). This is a helpful way of looking at how Paul did his theologizing and where the center of his theology lies.

DARRELL L. BOCK, B.A., Th.M., Ph.D., is professor of New Testament studies at Dallas Theological Seminary.

PAUL: A PASTORAL THEOLOGIAN

Paul's epistles are applied theology, and even in his most abstract portions, his goal is to have his readers see the world and how they live before God in terms of specific concrete categories and concerns. The danger in describing Paul in abstract, logical statements is that the real life settings of his teachings may be lost and his teaching may become sterilized, robbing it of its vitality in terms of genuine experience and meaningful exhortation. There is no better example of the pastoral nature of Paul's teaching than his Prison Epistles.[2] Uncertain of his own fate as he wrote these four letters, Paul communicated a trust in the sovereign God and a certainty of triumph, regardless of what might happen to him in this life. In a situation where many would despair, Paul rejoiced, knowing that nothing could destroy what God had done in Jesus Christ, both for the new community God created in the church, as well as for those individuals who are members of that community (Ephesians). Paul also knew that Christ shares in this divine sovereignty and as Mediator serves as the believer's Enabler, so that all one needs for honoring God in this life is available now (Colossians). In fact, Jesus transforms relationships at every social level, as life is lived in light of forgiveness and reconciliation, the essence of fellowship (Philemon). So Paul could rejoice and call on all believers to recognize that their citizenship is a heavenly one that transcends any circumstances and suffering they may face in this life (Philippians).

COLOSSIANS: THE PRIMACY OF JESUS CHRIST
HE ALONE IS OUR DELIVERER, HOPE, AND ENABLER

Though short in length and written to a church Paul did not plant, Colossians stands tall in highlighting the centrality of Jesus Christ as the Mediator of God's saving activity. The epistle emphasizes that those who belong to Jesus need nothing more to find the fullness of God's blessing other than to draw on the resources God has already provided through Jesus. Its major concern was to exhort believers in Colosse in the face of false teaching, which emphasized ascetic practice as a means of experiencing God's presence in a more meaningful way. Paul outlined the blessings of God who acts through the Mediator-Enabler Jesus, who is the Lord. By doing so, the apostle refuted the false teaching and laid the basis for articulating the church's call. The four themes of God, Jesus, the heresy, and the church's task are

2. A defense of introductory issues lies beyond the scope of this essay. Suffice it to say that all these letters are regarded as genuinely Pauline and as reflecting a Roman imprisonment. Of the four letters to be discussed, the most debated are Ephesians and Colossians. For defenses of non-Pauline authorship for Colossians, see Eduard Lohse, *Colossians and Philemon,* Hermeneia (Philadelphia: Fortress, 1971); and for the same in Ephesians, see A. T. Lincoln, *Ephesians,* Word Biblical Commentary (Dallas, Tex.: Word, 1990). For a defense of Pauline authorship of Ephesians, see Marcus Barth, *Ephesians,* The Anchor Bible, 2 vols. (Garden City, N.Y.: Doubleday, 1974), while P. T. O'Brien defends the Pauline authorship of Colossians in *Colossians and Philemon,* Word Biblical Commentary (Dallas, Tex.: Word, 1982). On Philippians, see P. T. O'Brien, *Commentary on Philippians,* The New International Greek Testament Commentary (Grand Rapids: Eerdmans, 1991), which also includes a full overview of the debate over the epistle's setting, a discussion that applies to all these letters.

the center of Paul's teaching in this book, as he sought to carry out the ministry God had given him (1:24–2:5).

THE ACTIVE GOD WHO SAVES

God's initiative in salvation. The letter begins with a note of thanksgiving for the Colossians, who reflected the faith and love that draws its vitality from the sure hope God has provided in the gospel (1:3–8). The hope expressed here is not a "wish," but a concrete hope that awaits them in heaven. This is why it is "stored up" for them there. That hope is the realization of full fellowship with God (3:3). This gift reflects God's gracious activity and is at the center of the gospel message (1:6–8). Then after his note of thanksgiving, Paul described this activity in more detail. In discussing God's saving process, Paul used the language of warfare, noting that God "rescued" believers out of Satan's dark domain and "transferred" them into the kingdom of His beloved Son (1:13–14). It was God's pleasure to work through the mediatorial effort of His Son, who is made in His image and in whom all the fullness of deity resides (1:15, 19; 2:9). In fact, God's desire was that the Son have preeminence in all things, as is seen in the Son's work in creation and redemption (evidenced especially by His resurrection; 1:15–20). The Son has preeminence in creation, but He uses that authority to reconcile the entire creation to God. The presence of such power is wielded not as a club over creation, but in service toward her as God seeks to restore what sin lost.

God's initiative in transformation. God's work extends beyond rescue to transformation. He is also active in giving believers the fullness of life He has graciously bestowed on them (2:10). This transfer is pictured as a "circumcision" God performs as He buries them in baptism and raises them to new life through faith (2:11–12). This highly symbolic description of salvation portrays the "new birth" and "new life" God gives and effects. Thus God "makes alive" by forgiving the sinner, by canceling out the debt of sin as revealed through the demands of the Law, and by defeating those who stand opposed to humanity through Christ and the cross (2:13–15). As a result, all growth comes through one's relationship to Christ and not through any series of rules or religious disciplinary practices (2:19).

Paul said it another way, when he stressed that the believer's life "is hidden" in God (3:3). This is why Paul could exhort the readers as "God's elect," since He is the active agent in their salvation from start to finish. This is also why God should be praised (1:3, 12; 3:17) and is the object of intercession (4:2–4). God's power, provision, and sovereignty were central for Paul.

God's initiative in directing Paul. Of course, God is active in another way. He is the one who directed Paul's ministry (1:1, 25). So Paul was called to reveal the riches God has made available to the saints and especially to Gentiles (1:26–29). Paul called these riches a mystery, the hope of glory, which is Christ in the believer (1:26–27). Such mystery is presented as newly revealed truth in Colossians (see also Eph. 3:4–6; while the term "mystery" in Rom. 16:25–27 describes revelation in continuity with Old Testament promise). Christ, the focus of God's work, is the means of both maturity and glorification for believers (Col. 2:2; 3:3–4).

JESUS CHRIST—THE MEDIATOR, ENABLER, AND LORD

Into His kingdom through deliverance. From the beginning of the letter, the centrality of Jesus is emphasized. Paul was His apostle (1:1) and the brothers and sisters in Colosse found their set-apart status in Him (1:2). Christ is the Object of faith and the Source of the concrete future hope that awaits them from heaven (1:4–5; 3:3–4). When God acted to rescue them, He took them out of the grip of Satan and placed them into a personal relationship with Christ and His rule (1:13–14). The past tenses in 1:13 show that this transfer has already taken place, though its implications extend into the future toward things which are yet to occur (*errysatō*, "He rescued"; *metastēsen*, "He transferred," 3:3–4). This discussion of the benefits that come from Christ is important to the letter, because before Paul even treated the problem the Colossians were facing, he exposed them to the rich benefits they already possessed.

Preeminent in creation and redemption. How great is the One into whose kingdom believers have come? The answer to this question is the goal of the great hymnic section of Colossians 1:15–20. This passage has roots in the wisdom tradition of Judaism and its great confessions of the role of God in creation (Gen. 1:1; Prov. 8:22; Job 28:23–28; Pss. 95:6–7; 100:3; Wisd. Sol. 7:22–27; Ecclus. 24). Wisdom is not found mainly in Torah, but in the one who is "the image of the invisible God" (*eikōn tou theou tou aoratou*). Jesus incarnates God's attributes and bears divine authority as One who participated in the Creation itself. As "the firstborn of all creation" (*prōtotokos pasēs ktiseōs*; cf. Ps. 89:27), He is preeminent among all rulers. Everything in heaven and earth, visible and invisible, no matter at what level of spiritual authority, was created by and is subject to Him. He is the sustainer of creation. He rules the kingdom to which the saints belong. Jesus serves as the sovereign Mediator of creation, exercising divine prerogative.

Later in the letter, Paul made the same point by pointing out that Jesus is at God's right hand (3:1). To understand what God is doing and why, one need only look to Jesus (2:2–3).

The hymn in 1:15–20 not only considers Jesus' role in Creation, but it also considers His mediatorial role in redemption. Christ does not exercise His power as a capricious selfish dictator, but He serves the creation as He seeks and provides for its total redemption. Such redemption involves more than human beings; it extends to the entire creation of both heaven and earth (1:18–20). Such authority finds its initial expression in the church, where Christ functions as its Head (*hē kephalē*), its leader, the beginning (*archē*), the firstborn to rise from the dead (*prōtotokos ek tōn nekrōn*). He is the first to manifest the characteristics of a new humanity, redeemed into newness of life. His preeminence extends into all areas, for not only did He create the cosmos and sustain it; He also is the means and example of its redemption. Such authority reveals God's desire that Jesus reflect the presence of divine fullness (1:19). Such reconciliation came through the cross.

When Paul considered such redemptive activity at a personal level rather than a cosmic one, he noted that estranged and hostile sinners were reconciled through Jesus' death so that those who abide by faith might be set apart as special before God (1:21–23). Besides being Mediator, Jesus is also Enabler. When one is in Him, he has the foundation needed for experiencing the fullness of God's blessing.

United with His body, the church. The church is so identified and united with Christ that it is called His "body." In fact, Jesus procured benefits for this new community with His very own death. For Paul to suffer on behalf of this church was for him to "fill up Christ's afflictions" (1:24), because when the church suffers (as Christ's body), Christ suffers (cf. Acts 9:1–6). Such a corporate identification can also be expressed as Christ indwelling the community, the great mystery of God (Col. 1:29). Those who are members of this new community live no longer for themselves but instead they live for and represent Him (3:1–17).

The Source and Center of growth. To be in Christ means one should pursue the maturity that comes from Him (1:28). As believers do this, the church experiences greater love and unity. These truths about Christ mean that faith can have orderliness (2:2–4). But when one turns away from focusing on Christ, trouble follows (2:8). So Paul called for a walk "according to Christ" (2:8). He is the one they received as Lord and with Him as Lord they are to continue to walk, since He is the Source of their enablement, wisdom, and knowledge (2:2–6). That is also why believers can be described as "Christ's circumcision," since they are set apart for Him (2:11). All through 2:9–15, Paul repeatedly stated that growth comes to those who are "in," "with," or "through" Christ. Christ is substantive life, while others teach practices that are merely shadows (2:17).

Dying and rising with Christ. The believer's existence is so identified with Jesus that Paul wrote of dying with Christ to the elemental spirits of the world and being raised with Him (2:20–3:11). This language repeats the imagery of 2:9–15. It reflects a change of identity and allegiance, so that the standards, methods, and created forces of the world no longer define life. Instead God, who rescued them in Christ, directs and defines it. So to be heavenly minded is not to escape or withdraw, but to reflect the divine characteristics of the new life God makes available to the believer (3:1–17).

The new man. Jesus formed the "new man" or new humanity in which people from various nations dwell and find renewal according to the image of God (3:10–11). The new man is Messiah incorporate. The new man/old man contrast describes a person's life in terms of two periods in two different worlds. First, there is the "old man," that is, the old community where the believer dwelt before coming to Christ and which was shed at conversion like old clothes (3:9). Having left the old world behind, believers are exhorted to leave old practices behind. Second, there is life as it is lived in Christ, the life of the new community in which old social and racial distinctions have been obliterated into oneness and where transformation into the image of God is taking place (3:10–11).

Summary. So Christ is Mediator and Enabler, the Source of life. Responding to that reality means that peace before God can reign in the heart (3:15), the Word of Christ can dwell richly in the life (3:16), and everything that is done occurs with the recognition that one is His (3:17). His lordship governs the believer's relationships, whether at home with one's spouse, as child or parent, or as slave or master (3:18, 20, 24). Sharing in the gracious benefits of His rule means honoring His rule with one's life. Christology is the theological center of Colossians that leads to the formation of a new community, whose commitment to love, knowledge, wisdom, and unity should allow Christ's followers to counteract false teaching (2:4). But what exactly was the problem that Paul dealt with through this Christology?

THE COLOSSIAN HERESY

The first hint of a problem appears in 2:4. Paul spoke of beguiling speech and the threat of delusion. The believing Colossian community was a healthy one (2:5), and Paul did not want anything to distract it from being on course. But this false teaching was particularly subtle, because it drew on a person's religious enthusiasm. It promised a deeper experience with God, allegedly one greater than even Jesus provided (2:16–23). But one must prepare for such an experience, for it required discipline and denial. On the surface such an opportunity for a closer experience with God would be attractive to a people who desire to know Him. But Paul regarded such a claim as a delusion. It was based on the standards and the forces of this world, and was not according to Christ (2:8).

Its nature. Scholars have debated extensively whether the heresy in view here was Hellenistic or Jewish. Those who see it as Hellenistic in nature appeal to Gnostic or mystery religion influence. It is probably best to see the heresy as eclectic, combining features of both cultures. The reference to observing Sabbaths (2:16) indicates a Jewish flavor, while the emphasis on ascetic practice and heavenly mediaries, like the angels, is Hellenistic. The key to understanding the heresy lies in 2:18, a much-debated verse. Two readings are popular and the choice between them is difficult to make. The question pertains to the phrase "worship of the angels" (*thrēskeia tōn angelōn*).

Does this refer to the heretics' desire "to worship angelic beings"? Taken in this sense, the heresy has a Hellenistic background, for a Jewish monotheist would be unlikely to worship mediatorial spirits. It is also this emphasis that makes the view unlikely. Would it be attractive to a church initially committed to Jesus?

The other view takes the phrase to mean "seeing the worship of angels." In other words, the teaching emphasized having visions which included observance of heavenly worship by the angelic host, which claimed to offer the adherents a direct experience of the heavenly presence of God. To enter God's presence in this way, one had to prepare for the experience through prayer, fasting, and rigorous disciplined worship. The offer of such a direct experience with God would be attractive to believers who desired to be close to Him. Those who have criticized this view have argued that Jews would not be drawn to a teaching that elevated the angelic realm so highly, but this misunderstands the view. The presence of angels—but not the worship of them—reflects one's presence before God. There is no demeaning of monotheism in this view; rather, what the false teachers sought was a heightened experience of it! This option seems the more likely understanding of 2:18.

Precedent for this approach to spirituality in Judaism is seen in a movement that came to be known as "Merkabah mysticism." The Merkabah refers to Ezekiel 1 and the throne chariot of God that Ezekiel saw. This teaching spoke of days of fasting to prepare for a journey to the heavens to see God and have a vision of Him and His angelic host in worship (Philo, *Die Somniis* 1.33–37; *De Vita Mosis* 2.67–70; 1QH 6:13; 1 Enoch 14:8–25; 2 Baruch 21:7–10; Apocalypse of Abraham 9:1–10; 19:1–9; Ascension of Isaiah 7:37; 8:17; 9:28, 31, 33). One could withdraw and eventually go directly into God's presence. Thus this false teaching emphasized the humility of ascetic practice, visions, the rigors of devotion, treating the body harshly, and rules about what should not be eaten or what days should be observed (2:16–23). All this activity was aimed to help prepare individuals for the experience that took them beyond what Jesus had already provided, so they could see God and His angels in heaven.

The heresy rebuked. Paul condemned such an invitation to super spirituality. He said that would disqualify them from receiving the full benefits of life Christ offered (2:18). It was a shadow (2:17). In fact, since it failed to check the flesh, it was of no value (2:23). It ignored Christ, the Source of growth for the body (2:19). That is why Paul called it a philosophy that came from human tradition and the world, one that was really deceitful (2:8). Paul's complaint about philosophy was not an attack on the syllogisms of atheism, but on a movement that had in view God and divine things, but in a way that distorted what Christ provided.

The remedy and the call. This desire "to experience heaven" also shows why Paul used so much "heavenly" language in describing what Christ has done. The concept of being raised with Christ and setting one's mind on the things above means that the believer already has a relationship with the God of heaven, so that a "trip" into His presence is unnecessary. God has not called His church to withdraw and await a future great experience of Him, but to engage the world with a lifestyle typical of those who are related to God (3:1–17). They can do this boldly, because they know that one day God will complete what He has started and will take them to Himself in glory (3:3). Asceticism is not the way to heaven; faith in Jesus is. Thus Paul came to focus on the call of the church to know God's will and to reflect what it means to belong to the "new man" or "the new humanity."

THE NATURE AND TASK OF THE CHURCH:
A NEW COMMUNITY THAT LIVES ETHICALLY

The body of Christ. Primary to Paul's view of the new community is his description of the church as "the body of Christ" (cf. 1:18). It indicates that the church is so identified with Him that she can be said to be a part of Him. This description also reflects part of the Son's authority associated with God's kingdom program (1:12–20). His presence and authority pervade the new community. God's kingdom program involves more than the church, but the church is a part of it. In the church God's rule and attributes are reflected to the world, since it functions as light, a subpoint made more explicit in Ephesians (Eph. 1:19–23; 5:7–14) than in this epistle. God is honored when He expresses His rule through the transformed lives of church members, who are shining as light (Matt. 5:14–15).

The new man. A second description of the new community is that it is the "new man" or "new humanity," the incorporation of a new community before God in Christ, where there is no "Greek or Jew, circumcised or uncircumcised, barbarian, Scythian, slave or free, but Christ is all, and is in all" (3:10–11). The "new man" is not an internal attribute of the person (i.e., the new nature), but a place where formerly separate peoples reside. This means that the church was formed to be a community with values distinct from the world, reflecting a distinct character in it and where one's identity is not determined by race or social status, but by being united to Jesus. Believers are to identify with the new community and reflect its values. There is a relational, ethical dimension to associating with Christ and this new community. This explains the ethical exhortations in Colossians 3:5–4:6, which all have strong relational dimensions. Paul did not envision a community living in isolation. Rather, it is to live differently, because God has transformed her members into a different kind of people, who know themselves as chosen of God (3:12).

The task: to be filled with and reflect the experiential knowledge of God. This background helps explain Paul's prayer at the beginning of the letter (1:9–14). He wanted the Colossians to be filled with the knowledge of God's will. God's will is not facts about God, nor is it deciding where God would have one be or what one should do. In this text God's will referred to the kind of person one is, because he or she experiences the benefits God made available to believers. This experience of God's will means that believers not only complete the work God gives them to do but they also bear fruit while doing it (1:10). The bearing of fruit refers not to the completion of a task but how the task is done. What character is manifested as the task is carried out? Such experience leads to an increase in one's knowledge of God (1:10). Also it enables one to go through life with endurance, patience, and joy (1:11), since one understands that being God's child means being different from the way the world lives. In addition, it is a life filled with gratitude to the Father for His rescuing work (1:12–14). Such is the life Paul prayed believers would have. He desired that they would live worthy of the Lord, being fully pleasing to Him, as those who are filled with the knowledge of His will. So central is this goal in the Colossian letter that Paul's coworker, Epaphras, also prayed for it when he interceded for the Colossians (4:12). There it is called maturity and being fully assured in the will of God.

SUMMARY

Ultimately, Colossians is about the work of the Father in the Son on behalf of a people whom He calls to manifest His message and presence on earth. This new community, the church, is to realize that the benefits God has given are all that is needed to lead a God-honoring life. To suggest that someone needs something more than what Christ already makes available is a delusion. Blessing comes from God through Christ alone, and a life that pleases God draws on what the Mediator and Enabler provides.

PHILEMON: FULL FELLOWSHIP IN CHRIST
RELATIONSHIPS TRANSFORMED BY FORGIVENESS AND RECONCILIATION

This short epistle is actually a private letter to Philemon, a slave owner. It is Paul's appeal on behalf of Philemon's slave, Onesimus, who had abandoned his master, had come into contact with the apostle, and had come to Christ in the process. Even the greeting in the epistle shows that the relationship between a slave and a master takes on new significance and different dynamics when both are Christians (vv. 1–3). So Paul included Apphia, Archippus, and the church in the greeting and the conclusion to help show the accountability and linked relationship that exists in the church.

FELLOWSHIP

The major concept of the letter is "fellowship" (*koinonia*; for a variation of this term, see v. 17). Philemon 6 is syntactically a difficult verse, a feature which renders its meaning unclear, even though the verse introduces the letter's major theme.[3] What is clear is that fellowship is more than mere association. The term itself means "participation," and it is especially participation in Christ that brings them into a new level of sharing and involvement with each other. This idea is much like the reconciliation triangle that Ephesians 2:11–22 discusses and the humility Philippians 2:5–11 exhorts the church to have. The church is a new humanity whose relationships transcend social barriers, when the knowledge of Christ is applied to those relationships. Unity with Christ and the fact that Christians' identity and status come only from what He provides allows for this transformation of relationship. In verse 6 Paul prayed that the "participation involved with faith would become effective to the point of understanding and practicing the good that sharing in Christ means" (author's paraphrase). In this way knowledge of Christ is promoted. Paul had in mind here much more than the mere propagation of teaching; what he was calling for from Philemon was promotion of teaching through its demonstration. The rest of the letter details how such fellowship manifests itself. True fellowship means mutually participating in Christ so that reconciliation, forgiveness, and harmony become possible.

THE GOOD INVOLVES EXCHANGING
PERCEPTIONS AND ACTING ACCORDINGLY

Another key idea is the promotion of the good. Paul came back to this later in the letter. He appealed to Philemon's goodness, which would manifest itself in a

---

3. For details about this verse, see Norman T. Wright, *The Climax of the Covenant: Christ and Law in Pauline Theology* (Philadelphia: Fortress, 1992), 41–55, and "Putting Paul Together Again: Towards a Synthesis of Pauline Theology (1 and 2 Thessalonians, Philippians, and Philemon)," in *Thessalonians, Philippians, Galatians, Philemon*, vol. 1 of *Pauline Theology*, ed. Jouette Bassler (Philadelphia: Fortress, 1991), 203–5.

direct response from his own will (v. 14). Paul then explained how an appropriate response meant seeing things differently. No longer was this situation a matter of a master "holding all the cards" because the slave did wrong. Rather, everyone's role, including Paul's, was changed because they were all in Christ. Now Onesimus should be received "no longer as a slave, but more than a slave, as a beloved brother" (v. 16). Even more than that, Paul said the slave should be received as if he were Paul himself, since the slave had ministered to Paul for Philemon (vv. 13, 17). Paul would take responsibility for any debts the slave owed. So Paul, as the apostle, took the position of and responsibility for the slave! In fact, in this situation he explicitly refused to use his apostolic authority (vv. 8–10), for Onesimus had become Paul's child in Christ and as such, the slave had come to have new worth (vv. 10–11). Paul also reminded Philemon that the master was in the apostle's debt for his own spiritual life (v. 19b), so the way to return the favor was to treat the slave (or better, the new family member!) with forgiveness and reconciliation. In Christ, though believers occupy different roles and have different functions, they are equally responsible to display the reality of being part of a community of reconciled people.

THE DEBT

A final feature of Paul's teaching in the book of Philemon is the use of commercial metaphors to express these relationships (vv. 15–20). All the references to debt, to charging to one's account, and to the promise to repay speak of the mutual accountability and responsibility believers have to each other. When Paul called for obedience to his plea (v. 21), he was asking that Philemon continue to display the love and faith he heard Philemon had (v. 5). Such a faithful display would refresh Paul (v. 20), just as Philemon's previous acts of love had refreshed the saints (v. 7). To love Jesus Christ means to transform the way relationships function between members of His body. Such transformed relationships reflect a fellowship that is really mutual participation in one another's lives.

EPHESIANS: TOWARD THE SUMMING UP OF ALL THINGS IN CHRIST
GOD'S POWER IN THE NEW COMMUNITY OF JEWS AND GENTILES

Ephesians details the rich provision God has given His people through Christ. It probably was a regional letter, rather than a letter written to one locale, since certain verses indicate that some of Paul's readers did not know him personally nor did he know them, even though the church at Ephesus was founded by him (Eph. 1:15–16; 3:1–6). Besides explaining what God has done through Christ, Ephesians also describes the new community God has formed by bringing Jews and Gentiles together (2:11–22). In fact, a major focus of this letter and of the Prison Epistles in general is the corporate nature of those who are in the body of Christ. Believers do not have a private faith; they have corporate relationship and responsibility to each other. God has taken the initiative to form a new people through Jesus, as His plan moves toward summing up all the creation in Him. People in that new community should reflect the unity they have in Christ and walk in a manner that pleases the one who forgave them. As they walk in a world that lives by different standards, they should realize that God is committed to expressing His presence and character through them.

PRAISE FOR GOD'S INITIATIVE IN SALVATION

Praise for blessing in Christ. The letter starts with a major note of thanksgiving. In fact, Ephesians 1:3–14 is one of the longest psalms of the New Testament, and it is a praise psalm in its form.[4] Paul raised this upbeat note, because God has taken and is taking the initiative in forming His new community and providing them with a vast array of spiritual blessings in Christ, blessings whose source is heaven (1:3). Throughout the hymn (as in in the doctrinal section of Col. 2:6–3:3), the phrases "in Him," "through Him," or "in Christ" appear, showing that Jesus mediates those blessings. The hymn gives the general praise in Ephesians 1:3 and then mentions three specifics in verses 4–14.

Praise for election. First, God initiated the process in the past through His election of believers in Christ (1:4). The selection took place before the world was established, but just as important as its timing is its goal. The selection took place not merely to deliver the lost, but also to transform them (v. 5). The goal is holiness and blamelessness. When God finishes what He has started, those who were lost in darkness (2:1–3) will stand faultless before Him, totally changed. This process occurs because God has foreordained the believer for adoption (*huiothesian*). Election and foreordination is a teaching that is much discussed in theology, but for Paul it was a positive concept because of what it meant to the believer who graciously received it. Knowing God's character, Paul was comfortable resting in God's sovereign exercise of authority. For Paul, election led to praise, because it reflected God's commitment to the grace He bestows in Christ, the beloved One (1:5–6).

Praise for a redeemed relationship. Second, Paul praised God for the initiative He takes in bringing believers into a redeemed relationship (1:7–10). Redemption means that one has been set free. Paul expressed the idea here in a unique way. Some think of redemption only as having occurred in the past, but Paul wrote of it here as a present possession (*echomen*, "we have"). Believers' current relationship with God takes place in the context of deliverance, the forgiveness of sins. For Paul, redemption does not occur in a moment, but is the platform for an abiding relationship with God. That is why Paul spoke about God's lavishing of His grace on the community. Paul also stressed the access to God's revelation of the mystery that revealed what God has done in Christ, a plan whose goal is to sum up all things in Christ (1:9–10). Such cosmic reconciliation was already noted in Colossians 1:18–20. Paul indicated that there is more to the plan in the future, "the fullness of time," though Paul did not detail here exactly what is involved. First Corinthians 15:20–28 looks forward to the day when Christ will manifest His authority over all things before handing all authority back to the Father. The book of Revelation re-

4. Other examples are Luke 1:46–55 and 1:67–79.

fers to these periods as the 1,000-year reign of Christ and the new heavens and the new earth.

Praise for unifying Jews and Gentiles in a new community. Third, Paul was grateful for Jew-Gentile union (1:11–14). The essence of the new community is that old racial barriers are broken down as reconciliation takes place not only between people and God, but also between individuals (2:11–18). All this activity takes place in the context of the exercise of God's sovereign will (vv. 5, 9, 11). So the "first to have hoped in Christ," the Jews, as well as the many Gentiles in Ephesus, are brought together into a new entity that God is forming, sealing them in this relationship by the Spirit. The "we-you" contrast that appears throughout the book (1:11–14; 2:1–3; 2:11–13, 17–18) refers to Jews and Gentiles. This new union exists so that God may be praised for His grace. God has committed Himself to it, by sealing them with the Spirit, whose presence is an "earnest" (*arrabōn*) of the rest that is to come. So whether looking at God's initiative from the standpoint of the past (election), the present (redemption and Jew-Gentile union), or with an eye to the future (summing up all things in Christ and the Spirit as earnest), God is to be praised as He graciously provides salvation.

BLESSING IN CHRIST:
SALVATION AND POWER FOR TRANSFORMATION

Power for the believer available through the exalted Christ. For Paul, understanding salvation also meant understanding the access believers have to spiritual power through Christ. Such power allows them to live in a way that honors God. This explains Paul's two prayers in the letter (1:15–23; 3:14–19), as well as the doxology in 3:20–21.

The combination of blessing and provision is highlighted in Paul's initial prayer. He desired that the Ephesian Christians understand three things God had graciously given them: the hope, the riches of their inheritance, and the great power at work in all who believe. The hymn of praise in 1:3–14 expressed the hope of ultimate redemption, as well as highlighting the inheritance as a product of adoption into sonship. In the prayer of Ephesians 1:15–23, however, Paul concentrated on power, since promise means nothing without the ability to deliver it. An understanding of these three basic provisions motivates the believer and defines one's identity in Christ, but power is key since it drives the entire process and makes realization possible.

Paul illustrated the power available to believers by referring to the power that raised Jesus. But the parallel is more than an illustration, for it sets forth the book's basic teaching, namely, the significance of Jesus' exaltation, a central theme of the New Testament (e.g., Acts 2:30–36; Heb. 1:3–14; Rev. 1:4–20). Because of His exaltation, Jesus sits at God's right hand. From that position, He has authority over every force in creation. Paul went to great length to show that every conceivable form of authority is placed under Him. A full range of terms was used to refer to such forces including "rule, authority, power, and dominion" (Eph. 1:21). In fact, there should be no doubt that Jesus' rule applies to the current age as well as in the age to come (v. 21). Some object to this reading by citing Hebrews 2:5–10. But that passage speaks only of subjection not yet completed for humanity (note the allusion to Ps. 8), while pointing out that Jesus is already in a glorified position. That point does not contradict Paul's point in Ephesians. The two passages are simply an example of the New Testament's emphasis on salvation in process, so that it can be expressed in "already" (Eph. 1:19–23) and "not yet" (Heb. 2:5–9) terms. Jesus' position and authority are already established, but the full manifestation of that authority awaits the age to come.

Jesus' present authority. The events described in Ephesians 1:20–22 make it clear that Paul was highlighting Jesus' current authority. He noted Jesus' resurrection, he mentioned that Jesus is seated at God's right hand (Ps. 110:1), and he wrote that Jesus is Head over the church. All three of these events have occurred, so it is natural to expect that Paul also intended the submission of all things (Eph. 1:22) to be understood as something God has already done through Christ. Had Paul intended this submission to refer to something in the future, he would have mentioned it last and changed from the aorist (past) tenses he used throughout this list to the future tense. Paul's point was that what God has started and put in place through Jesus Christ, He will also bring to pass. Paul expressed this idea of "triumph-submission" as something that had already occurred (and also in Col. 2:14–15), in addition to his looking forward to its fuller realization in the future (1 Cor. 15:24–28). Such an "already" element in Paul's teaching about Jesus' rule is not the same as the "overrealized reign" teaching he condemned in Corinth (1 Cor. 4:8). This is because the erroneous Corinthian concept of reign was not a rule in progress, but a rule fully realized, not even needing a resurrection hope, as the warning of 1 Corinthians 15 makes clear. Paul taught that Christ already is triumphant and he also spoke of a future greater realization of that rule. Nevertheless, the battle against sin still needs to be waged in this life (Eph. 6:10–18), though believers engage in it knowing that the power of the one on their side is greater than and has triumphed over the forces opposed to them.

So in Ephesians 1:19–23 Paul argued that as a result of Christ's exaltation, all things are submitted to Him and He serves as Head over the church. Jesus' role within the church is primarily an expression of His authority in the present era. In this context it is clear that "headship" refers not to origin, but to Christ's preeminent position within the church. Headship pictures authority, but it is not raw power; rather, the term emphasizes service, since Jesus pours Himself into the church. Paul returned to the theme of exaltation in 4:7–10, where he showed that the gifts of the church reflect Christ's victory gained in the exaltation, a view similar to Acts 2:30–36. So exaltation leads to Christ pouring Himself into the church (1:23), as well as gifting it (4:7–10). The One with authority continues to serve through giving of Himself, just as He had in giving His life (Mark 10:42–45).

God's power already exercised for salvation and transformation. Most people break the prayer at 1:23, but that is not wise since Ephesians 2:1 (NASB) begins with "and" (*kai*), thereby extending the example of the prayer. In 2:1–10, Paul gave a second description of Christ's exercise of power for believers and their formation as a community (note the *syn* prefixes in 2:5–6). Every believer has already experienced a decisive and defining exercise of God's power. Salvation is a rescue out of a life directed by Satan, the world, and the flesh. God extends great life-forming power when one is made alive out of the death that results from sin and is seated together with Christ (2:4–7). Though this language is highly abstract, the point is that the believer was graciously made alive (i.e., born again) and has a position that is now inseparably linked to Christ. To the person who believes, God gives newness of life and citizenship in heaven. No longer is the believer associated with and allied to earthly forces. In the cosmic struggle between God and the forces that oppose Him, the believer has changed sides and has access to the King. This is a more elaborate way of expressing what Paul said about rescue in Colossians 1:12–14 and citizenship in Philippians 3:20–21. In fact, what is true of any single believer is true of all of them as a community. They share their benefits "together" (2:5–6 NASB). What God did for one, He did for all. This is the ground of their unity in Christ (4:1–6).

The goal of salvation in this life. Access to such power is a result of grace and results in a fundamental new goal for believers, as well as a new identity. They have become God's new creation (2:10). The phrase describing the new creation (*autou gar esmen poiēma,* "for we are His creation," author's trans.), is emphatic since the pronoun "His" begins the clause. We are, indeed, His creation! And that creation has a purpose. God through Christ calls believers to good works (2:10). He has prepared those works for them, so they may walk in them. Since "walk" becomes the dominant metaphor of Ephesians 4–6, it is clear that Ephesians 2:10 is a key transition verse for the book. Paul emphasized that the believer has access not only to God, but also to the ability to carry out the call (2:18–22; 3:14–19; 6:10–18). The power Paul has in mind here is one that directs and transforms a person who has experienced God's gracious renewal into new life. The good news of God's grace is not only that it saves but that it also transforms.

Understanding God's power: the key to reflecting His character. Paul's second prayer involves a similar theme (3:14–19). Christ should be so trusted and resident in a person's life ("Christ may dwell in your hearts through faith") that the believer comes to appreciate the depth of His love. After mentioning love, Paul spoke again of power. This time he referred to it as a capacity to comprehend what God is doing, as a key to spiritual growth. To understand what God has done and what He is capable of doing should lead believers to rely on Him to bring it to pass. So the goal of this understanding is that one might be filled with God's fullness, another major theme of the book.

Filling and fullness. The theme of fullness is a key idea is this book. Ephesians 1:23 makes the point that the church is being filled with Him, that is, Christ. Ephesians 3:19 declares that a goal of the spiritual life is to be "filled up to all the fullness of God" (NASB). Ephesians 4:10 speaks of the expectation that Christ will fill all things. Ephesians 5:18 makes a call for believers to be filled with the Spirit. The point of all these images is that God through Christ, and by the Spirit, is "pouring Himself and the manifestation of His presence" into the creation, especially into the church and her members. The prayer of Ephesians 3 is a call to believers to experience the love of God in Christ so deeply that Christ resides in and directs their lives. In turn, His direction means that one's life reflects the presence and attributes of God. It is significant that for Paul such concrete spiritual goals are the basis of his prayer requests. For Paul, character matters more than circumstances, so this is what he prayed for and desired (Phil. 1:12–26). Ephesians 4–6 specifies the walk that grows out of this filling and which produces the work of God's transforming power in the life. The language here reminds one of Paul's description of salvation in Romans 1:16–17, where he called the gospel the "power of God." Then in Romans 1–8 he described how one is brought out of sin into newness of life through the provision of the Spirit's powerful, transforming presence.

The doxology of Ephesians 3:20–21 also focuses on power. It speaks of God's capacity to do beyond what His followers ask or think. In context, the point is not a *carte blanche* to believers to ask for whatever they want, but an affirmation that God will make available to them the power to transform, as described in Ephesians 1–3. This goal is one of God's primary concerns as He works in and for believers.

The Holy Spirit. A major agent in making this power real is the Holy Spirit. In this letter, the Spirit is an "earnest" payment of God's commitment to believers (1:13–14). As such, the Spirit is the initial down payment on a commitment to redeem. He is the source of unity among the believers, as well as an agent of protection (2:18–22; 4:3–4; 6:17). He is the conduit for revelation of the mystery (3:5). Whatever takes place in the church, whether good or bad, He observes (4:30). And He guides the believer into reflecting God's character, into praise, and into relating to other believers in mutual submission (5:18–20). The Spirit's presence makes the new community of God's people a new holy temple (2:18–22), as God goes about the task of building it up in Christ.

Christ our peace forms the one new man. In summing up all that God has done through Jesus in salvation, Paul called Christ the source of peace (2:14–18). In the context of Ephesians, this does not mean that Christ is the source of inner peace, but that He is the bridge of reconciliation between Jews and Gentiles and between members of the new community and God. The goal of salvation is not merely to make individuals right with God, but to make them right with each other. As God brings both Jews and Gentiles together through Christ, reconciliation operates in a triangle among the three. As they enter the new community, they do not cease to be who they were, but now they can function together side by side as evidence of God's transforming, reconciling love (1 Cor. 7:17–24; Rom. 14–15). This reconciling work stands as the foundation for the new community God is building through Christ. This is why throughout Ephesians 2:11–22, the dominant repetitive term is the prefix *syn* ("together"). God has formed a new unit, in which He is said to have created out of the two "one new man" (*ena kainon anthrōpon*). Once again, themes noted in Colossians reappear in Ephesians.[5]

---

5. Also see the discussion on the new man in the Colossians section above.

In addition, Paul noted that what God has done is greater than the evidence of His presence in the Old Testament. This new community that incorporates Christ is a new holy temple (2:19–22). Paul liked to strike this note (corporate in 1 Cor. 3:16–17 and individualized in 1 Cor. 6:19–20). This is a temple in progress, growing to maturity to reflect the oneness it possesses already in its position (Eph. 4:10–16; also 1 Cor. 3:10–17). In this new "house" God is performing His special work, as He seeks to show His presence in a more vital and visible way than He did through the temple of old. Now His presence is dispersed, not localized. Now His presence is incarnated, instead of confined behind a veil. Christ (i.e., the Messiah) serves as the Cornerstone of this house, and He holds it together through the energizing power of God's Spirit (Eph. 2:20–22). For Paul, there is no more important or sacred institution in the current era than the new "humanity" God is building in Jesus Christ. That is why Paul compared the church to a holy temple.

PAUL AND THE APOSTLES' MINISTRY OF THE MYSTERY

The new community. The inclusion of believing Jews and Gentiles into one new community is the focus of God's new work. Ephesians 2:11–22 makes it clear that the new community He has formed is not simply a matter of moving Gentiles into Israel, so that the church replaces Israel. Rather, it is a new work of God where both Jews and Gentiles are placed into a new institution though which God is currently at work. That is why Paul called the church a "new man."[6] This new institution does not dissolve ethnic distinctions, but displays reconciliation, with every believer equally qualified to share in the benefits of salvation and peace that emerge from the uniting of Jews and Gentiles into a new living community.

Paul and the mystery. Paul's ministry to the Gentiles is a stewardship he received from God (3:3). In describing the mystery he spoke of believing Gentiles as fellow heirs, fellow members, and fellow partakers of the body.[7] The term "mystery" is key. Its roots in Judaism go back to the revealing of the *râz* (the mystery) by God in differing situations (cf. Dan. 2:19, 30; also 1QH 5:36; 1QpHab 7:4–5; 1Q27 1:1, 2–4).[8] Mystery refers to a now-revealed teaching that God has made known or developed. Both Ephesians 3 and Colossians 1:26 mention this mystery, with each passage expressing different aspects of its teaching. Colossians empha-

6. For more detail on this passage, see Carl Hoch, Jr., "The New Man of Ephesians 2," in *Dispensationalism, Israel and the Church: The Search for Definition,* ed. Craig A. Blaising and Darrell L. Bock (Grand Rapids: Zondervan, 1992), 98–126. In Colossians, Paul spoke of the new community as a holy place. He could say this because Christ's indwelling of the community members is at the center of the divine mystery now operating in God's plan of the ages (Col. 1:24–2:4). On the clearly distinct relationship between Israel and the church in Paul's theology, see Beker, *Paul the Apostle,* 315–17, 328–47. Beker defends the view that for Paul the church is not viewed as the "true Israel," though he erroneously suggests that the equation did exist for John, Matthew, and Luke, as well as for the writer of Ephesians, who Beker wrongly says is someone other than Paul. Hoch's article corrects Beker's imbalance at this point.

7. Note the repeated use yet again of the prefix *syn* to make this point in verse 6.

8. Robert L. Saucy, "The Church as the Mystery of God," in Blaising and Bock, *Dispensationalism, Israel and the Church,* 137–51.

sizes the mystery as the Messiah indwelling Gentiles ("Christ in you"), while Ephesians stresses the equality Gentiles have in the body God has formed in Christ. Christology and ecclesiology merge here. Both these texts stress the newness of the revelation. These details of God's plan were not known previously in other times or generations.

A third crucial Pauline reference to mystery appears in Romans 16:25–26 and goes in a different direction. Here the revelation of the mystery is related to the preaching of the gospel as a whole. Romans stresses that the mystery has connection to the "sacred writings," an allusion to the Old Testament (also Rom. 1:2–4 refers to the gospel). This means that though aspects of mystery revelation are new, other aspects have roots that reach back into Old Testament promise and represent its development. Colossians 2:2 helps explain this diversity with its mix of continuity and discontinuity, for it affirms that ultimately the mystery is Christ Himself. With the revelation of Him, the rich treasures of promise begin to be revealed and realized more fully. This helps explain why Paul, when he preached in Acts, emphasized that what he preached was in line with and represented the initial fulfillment of Old Testament hope and promise (Acts 24:14–15; 26:22–23).

The apostles' and prophets' message and Paul's mission. Paul's ministry task and his understanding of the mystery were not his alone. The mystery he preached was also revealed to the other apostles and to New Testament prophets (Eph. 3:5). When Paul summarized the contents of his message, he wrote of the "unsearchable riches of Christ" (3:8). His goal was to preach this message to Gentiles and to let all (including Jews) know of the plan or stewardship (*oikonomia*) of the mystery of God for the ages.[9] God's dispensational plan is a unity that seeks to reconcile and unify the creation. In this unification, God's wisdom in reconciling people to Himself and to one another becomes manifest in the church before the spiritual forces who reside in heaven (3:10). In other words, the church is to be an audio-visual display of God's reconciling work. In this primary way she testifies to God's grace and wisdom. So Paul encouraged living life in Christ in such a way that reconciliation is the dominant feature of church life.

THE WALK OF THE NEW COMMUNITY:
THE CALL FOR CHANGED ETHICS

A unified faith to be maintained. Paul placed the life of the new community in the context of God's call. Diligence in maintaining the unity of the faith is part of the saint's calling (4:1–6). This is what Paul considered a life worthy of the calling. Such a walk takes patience and forbearance, but it is grounded in the essential unity He has provided through the one body, one Spirit, one hope, one Lord, one faith, one baptism, and one God. The assumption in this exhortation is that relationships take work and can yield disappointment; but in the context of God's forgiveness

---

9. From the term *oikonomia* is derived the theological term "dispensation," which has a Latin origin. Its occurrence in Ephesians 3:9 is the one technical use of this term that comes close to its theological force. In Ephesians 3:2 *oikonomia* is used only of Paul's particular stewardship within the larger plan of God.

and reconciling work, believers are still called to mirror His forgiving love (4:31–5:2).

Diversity of teaching gifts for edification, maturity, and unity in experience. Spiritual gifts are benefits poured out as a result of Christ's triumphant victory in resurrection (4:7–10). The diversity of teaching functions (apostle, prophet, evangelist, pastor-teacher) is designed to equip the saints for ministry. Paul's teaching in 4:11–16 is central to his philosophy of how ministry occurs in the church and how she is to grow. Teaching equips all the saints to minister. Then the equipped saints exercise their gifts in works of ministry which produce growth in the church. The goal is to attain to the unity of the faith. This might be confusing in light of 4:3, where unity is said to exist already. However, the unity in view in 4:15–16 is an experienced one. Paul was saying that a test of maturity is the manifestation of unity. Attaining to the fullness of Christ is not merely knowing about Him, or teaching concerning Him, but so knowing Him that the body reflects the unity she possesses. In other words, maturity means not being tossed from side to side by false teaching, but instead so manifesting Christ that the community is "truthing in love." This is not merely speaking the truth in love, as many English translations render 4:15a, but it is living authentically, or as 4:24 puts it, wearing "the new self, which in the likeness of God has been created in righteousness and holiness of the truth" (NASB).

Living unlike the Gentiles: the two humanities. The apostle urged believers to follow a lifestyle that does not reflect the empty, sensuous way of the Gentiles (4:17–19). Such is the life of the former humanity, what Paul called the "old self" in 4:22 (NASB). That way of life is to be shed. Rather, truth is found in Jesus; thus one should live authentically as a transformed person who belongs to the new community. That means shedding the old clothes of the former life, being renewed constantly, and putting on the new clothes of the new, renewed community and its transformed lifestyle (4:22–24).[10] For Paul there are two worlds and thus two citizenships: one is that of the world (or what Romans 5 calls being "in Adam"), while the other is a heavenly citizenship of being a member of Christ's body or being "in Him." This contrast forms the basis of Paul's exhortations to walk not as the Gentiles do in 4:17–24. He says, in effect, that in learning Christ (i.e., in coming to Him) they changed countries and allegiances, so they should wear the characteristics of the new community they represent. Colossians 3:1–17 has a similar exhortation.

The specifics of the new walk. The new ethics means that truth, reconciliation, labor, gracious speech, kindness, and generosity should characterize the believer (4:25–5:2). Falsehood, lingering anger, stealing, bitter speech, and slander

10. The infinitives for "putting off" and "putting on" are in the summarizing aorist tense, but the infinitive for "renewing" is in the present tense, suggesting a continual need to renew. It is debated whether verses 22–24 refer to position (you have put off; you are being renewed; you have put on) or are exhortations (put off; be continually renewed; put on). Either is possible, but the order of the infinitives suggests that exhortations are probably present. If position were the point, one would expect continual renewal to be mentioned after one came into his position in Christ.

should be shed as remnants of an old lifestyle to be left behind. God's example of love and forgiveness, along with a desire not to grieve the Holy Spirit, serve as motivations for this walk. The call is to imitate the Father, as a loving child would a parent. So immorality and greed are left behind as unfitting, while thanksgiving and service become the qualities one should manifest (5:1–6). In fact, such sinful activity is what brings God's wrath on the unbeliever, so God's child should not engage in such activity (5:5–6).

Light exposing darkness. In writing of an ethic that is distinct from that of the world, Paul compared the believer's walk to functioning as light in the midst of darkness (5:7–14). The image of the Christian as light is a common New Testament theme and is drawn from the connection the believer has to Christ (Luke 1:78–79; John 8:12; 2 Cor. 6:14) or God the Father (1 John 1:5–10). Paul's expectation was not that believers withdraw from involvement with the outside world, but that they live differently than the world, sharing the positive characteristics noted in Ephesians 4:25–5:4. The nonassociation Paul referred to in these verses is not a separatism of contact, but of practice. The walk of the children of light yields the fruit of goodness, righteousness, and truth, that is, the characteristics of ethical integrity that stand out in contrast to the licentious, immoral practices of the world (4:17–19). The unfruitful deeds of darkness are to be avoided.

In fact, the call is to live in such a way that unrighteous activity is exposed by the light of a life filled with moral integrity. The call to arise from the dead in 5:14 could be taken in one of two ways. If directed to a lethargic believer, it would mean to wake up and walk with renewed commitment to the Lord. But more likely, the verse gives the appeal of those in the light to those in darkness, a call to enter into new life through coming to the light. In the exposure of sin and need is also the invitation of forgiveness and life. A commitment to a life lived before God as light means that one never ceases to point others toward it.

Walking with care. The call to a contrastive lifestyle means that believers need to walk carefully, because the potential of falling into evil is always present (5:15–20). Such a life requires the direction of the Spirit of God. Such direction guides, and it also encourages the heart so that singing and thanksgiving are present. In addition, relationships with other believers occur in a context of mutual service. Whether husband or wife, child or parent, slave or master, the goal is to serve faithfully before God (5:21–6:9).

Serving others. In referring to marital, family, and master-slave relationships, Paul was looking at the impact of Christ on three of the most basic relationships of the first century. For Paul, the Christian faith was not an abstract exercise in theological discourse. Instead it called for a different way to relate to others.

Thus the marriage relationship was not defined in terms of the exercise of power among the partners, but was seen in terms of mutual service practiced in the context of mutually connected roles that mirror how Christ relates to the church (5:21–33). To understand headship and submission, one must understand the relationship and function of both Christ and the church. To speak in terms of functional equality for husband and wife erroneously removes the complementary quality of the relationship and invalidates the comparison to Christ and the church, who are not functionally equal. So the husband as head is to love the wife, but this "headship" was not a mere appointment to authority. In fact, the passage says nothing about the exercise of authority toward the one who has responsibility for it. Rather, the exemplary "head," Christ, served in this role, being the Savior of the body. Paul concentrated on the picture of Christ the servant, who saves the church by dying for it and who nourishes the church through the washing that comes through the Word. The husband is to love the wife like his own body, just as Christ and the church are mysteriously one body. In fact, the reality of oneness means that the husband and wife are not to function as "you and me," but as "us." This does not mean a dissolution of individual personalities, but it does mean that the loving husband and the submissive wife function harmoniously and sensitively as they pursue holiness in life together. They look out for each other and for the unit, not for themselves. So the husband loves, while the wife submits and respects (5:22–24, 33). In doing so, they show how a cooperative relationship works as they also mirror how Christ relates to the church.

A similar service occurs as the child honors the parents and the father nurtures (*ektrephete*) the child (6:1–4). Parental nurturing means that provoking a child is excluded. Responsible authority does not wield power; it serves with it.

Service in the slave-master relationship means integrity in labor, not eye service or the use of threats (6:5–9). When the master is told to do the same as the slave in 6:9, Paul's point is that the slave should be treated with honesty and integrity, just as he asked the slave to do toward the master. This leveling of the social "playing field" between slave and master shows how Christ impacts relationships. Of course, the great first-century Christian example of such leveling is the message of Paul's letter to Philemon.

THE COMMUNITY ABLE TO STAND:
THE ARMOR OF GOD

In the end, Paul saw believers equipped to resist the enemy (6:10–20). To oppose the evil forces with which they do battle they need to wear the protection God has supplied. The image of the cosmic struggle or confrontation with evil is frequent in the book, but it hits its high point here (1:19–23; 2:1–7; 4:7–10; 5:7–14, 17). Such strength comes from the Lord and consists of reflecting the true lifestyle God makes available through Jesus ("girded your loins with the truth," 6:14 NASB; cf. 4:15, 21, 24; 5:9). Truth in this passage, just as in the earlier verses is not just knowledge, but a lifestyle that reflects the truth, that which is the fruit of the light. Wearing the armor also means wearing righteousness, which in the context of Ephesians refers not so much to justification, but to a life of righteousness (4:24; 5:9). In addition, protection comes from reflecting the unity that the gospel provides within the community ("shod your feet with the preparation of the gospel," 6:16, looks back to 2:11–22; it is not a reference to evangelism). In fact, faith is a shield against the devil, while additional protection comes from salvation and the Spirit of God, who wields great power through the Word. The reference to salvation means that believers are to draw on all the benefits it provides, something Paul also alluded to in 1:15–23 when he prayed that believers understand the hope and riches they possess in Jesus. In addition, diligent prayer is encouraged, especially for Paul's own evangelistic efforts. By wearing these characteristics, the wrestling match (*hē palē*) with spiritual forces will result in victory. To be strong in the Lord is to wear the character He enables believers to possess.

SUMMARY

Ephesians is ultimately about how God has powerfully equipped the church to experience blessing in Christ, by creating a new community that is able to honor God and resist the forces of evil. No longer does one's Jewish or Gentile identity dominate. They are part of a new, reconciled community, a reconciliation that involves not only God but also one another. All enablement in this new sacred community is rooted in what the exalted Christ has provided for His people. That is why believers can have hope, since they have begun participation in a wealth of benefits distributed from heaven.[11] The church's members are citizens raised and seated with Jesus in a heavenly citizenship, though they represent Him now as light on the earth, fully enabled for the task. In all of this, God is taking steps toward the ultimate summation of all things in Christ.

PHILIPPIANS: KNOWING CHRIST AND LIVING AS CITIZENS OF HEAVEN IN A FALLEN WORLD

In this prison epistle Paul wrote to a church he established (see Acts 16:9–34). It was a good church, but there was a threat to its health (Phil. 3). Paul was probably writing from Rome after much communication with this congregation.[12] In fact, Paul also wrote for other reasons. He wished to thank the Philippians for their monetary gift to support him (Phil. 4:10–18), as well as to give them news about his situation. This letter is known as the epistle of joy, a description that may

11. Stress on activity from heaven is shown by the use of the term *epouranios* ("heavenlies") in Ephesians. Five of the nineteen uses in the New Testament come in this book. Ephesians 1:3 summarizes all these blessings as heavenly ones, and 1:20 makes the point that Christ's exalted authority is in the heavenlies. In 2:6 Paul argued that believers are now seated in the heavenlies. In 3:10 he pointed out that the cosmic forces in the heavenlies observe God's wisdom through the church, while in 6:12 he mentioned that the community's battle is against heavenly forces. Thus this cosmic imagery serves to underscore the battle-citizenship motif in the book and underscores that the believers' benefits come from the God of heaven. One suspects that Matthew's use of the phrase "kingdom of heaven" is making a similar point.

12. For a full discussion of the setting of this letter and the difficult choice of whether it was written from Rome (Acts 28) or Caesarea, where Paul was for two years (Acts 23:35–24:27), see O'Brien, *Commentary on Philippians*, 19–26. O'Brien correctly prefers Rome, but for the view on Caesarea, see Garald Hawthorne, *Philippians*, Word Biblical Commentary (Waco, Tex.: Word, 1983), xxxvi–xliv. In Caesarea Paul's life was not really in danger as he waited a decision; only Rome could condemn him. Yet Philippians seems to suggest Paul's uncertainty about whether he would live, thus suggesting an incarceration that threatened his life (Phil. 1:18–25).

elevate this idea to too central a role, but it is a major theme, and it is significant that these notes come when Paul was in prison, uncertain of his future. Such a setting reveals the extent of Paul's trust in God and gives credibility to his exhortation to this church to suffer and live in a way that rests in God's sovereign work, honors Him, and reflects the heavenly citizenship believers possess (1:27–30).

THE SOVEREIGNTY OF GOD

Toward the Philippians. Despite being in prison after a worldwide ministry, Paul was confident of God's control whether for himself or the Philippians. In 1:6, Paul expressed his confidence that God would finish what he started in Philippi. In fact, Paul regarded such confidence as fully appropriate in light of their participation (*sygkoinōnous*) with him in his own tribulations (1:7–8) and because of his love for them. For Paul, this participation exemplifies the love that the church possesses. It is to abound in conjunction with knowledge, so that righteousness results and God is praised for His great transforming work. Paul's view of fellowship in this letter is much like the type of "participation" in life that he exhorted for Philemon.

In Philippians 2:12–13, Paul noted a second example of his awareness of God's work for the Philippians. As he exhorted the community to work out their salvation with fear and trembling, that is, to apply themselves fully to their growth, he reassured them that God was at work within them so His good pleasure could be accomplished. Paul understood that what God asks believers to do in spiritual growth and character, He enables them to accomplish. Failure comes because one does not draw on what God makes available. Thus they must hold fast to the Word of life (2:16), since that will enable them to be blameless and to function as lights in the world (2:15).

Finally, when Paul dealt with the threat of false teaching, he reminded the Philippians of the example of God's activity in his own life. God issues the call to grasp the prize that comes through Jesus Christ, and Paul was confident that God would reveal the right way for the Philippians to proceed (3:14–15).

In Paul's ministry. Another example of Paul's reliance on God's sovereignty is his attitude toward his incarceration and the gospel preaching that had occurred in his absence (1:12–26). Though some preached with hostile motives toward Paul, the apostle was comfortable in the fact that Christ was proclaimed and the gospel was advanced. Some who preached knew that Paul had been put in prison for the defense of the gospel. The implication of Paul's language is that he was put there by God. Limiting the scope of Paul's outreach was not a matter for defeat, but was God's design, as his ministry penetrated into the praetorian guard.

When Paul thought of God's sparing of Epaphroditus, he also saw His sovereign mercy at work (2:27). Such evidences of God's hand helped Paul in good circumstances or bad to rest in His care and rely on His strength (4:10–13).

With Paul's life. Paul rested the fate of his life and ministry in the care of God. For him, life was defined in one of two paths—either he would continue to serve Christ in ministry or he would die and live with Him (1:20–24). He was comfortable with either option; whatever God chose for him was acceptable. Though it was personally better for Paul to go be with the Lord, he knew that it was better for the Philippians that he continue to minister. So after some deliberation Paul was confident that he would be spared. Thus his approach to God's direction in his life is exemplary of his trust in and desire to serve Him with honor, something he exhorted the Philippians to do as well (1:27–30).

God's activity is at the center of Paul's exhortation in this letter. His sovereign, gracious activity is the base for all theological teaching. But God the Father (1:2) does not work alone. The Mediator of blessing is Jesus Christ.

CHRIST AT THE CENTER OF BLESSING

The Source of blessing. Paul's prayers often raised central themes in his letters. Philippians 1:3–11 is no exception. As Paul expressed his affection for the Philippians and his confidence that God would complete His work in them, he also noted that purity and blamelessness of character come through being filled with the fruit of righteousness. Love, knowledge, and discernment produce such fruit, but the basis for being able to love unconditionally with knowledge and discernment is understanding the work and example of Christ (2:5–11).

This central role of Jesus as the hub of blessing caused Paul to say later that he desired a righteousness that is not based on his own activity in the context of law, but that comes through faith in Jesus Christ (3:9). Paul wished to know Christ and the power of His resurrection, even to share in His sufferings. So Paul recognized that Jesus is not only the Source of blessing, but that He is also the example of how to attain it. Faith in Jesus means not only looking to Him, but also walking down His path. In this sense, Paul's remarks are like those of Jesus where He called disciples to "come after me" (Luke 9:23). Paul's words also recall in part why the earliest Christians called themselves "the Way" (Acts 9:2). They saw themselves not only on a journey to God but on a journey *with* Him.

The subject of the message. It is Christ who is preached by all, since He is at the center of the gospel (Phil. 1:15–17). His centrality is so great that even if Paul was mistreated by others as they preached Christ or if they preached Him to dishonor the apostle, he still rejoiced that Christ was proclaimed. Because of Christ, Paul was in prison (1:13). In fact, one is struck by how often the title "Christ" appears in 1:12–26 (nine times!). The promised Anointed One of God stands as the center of blessing and as the subject of the gospel. As long as He is served, God could use Paul wherever and however He desires.

The reference point for life and death. The reason Paul could rest in God's care while in prison becomes clear in one of the more defining remarks in all of his epistles. The apostle's statement that to live is Christ and to die is gain (1:21) supports his earlier remark that he desired that Christ be honored in his body, whether by life or by death (1:20). Paul's personal identity and motivation were defined by Jesus and the relationship he had to Him. To live was to serve Christ, while death meant being with Him. Hawthorne has stated the force of 1:21 very well. "Life is summed up in Christ. Life is filled up with, occupied with Christ, in the sense that everything Paul does—trusts, loves, hopes, obeys, preaches, follows . . . and so on—is inspired by Christ and is done for Christ. Christ and Christ alone gives inspiration, direction, meaning and purpose to existence."[13] Such desire to glorify Christ and let Him define life was expressed repeatedly by Paul (1 Cor. 11:31; Gal. 2:20; Col. 3:17). Paul's hope for the future, centered as it was in Jesus, kept him from making too much of his current circumstances. This hope enabled him to reassess his circumstances, not by suppressing his emotions, evident throughout this letter, but by relating them to God's sovereignty and to Jesus' centrality in life.

Jesus the example of service and humility. No passage in Philippians is as well known or discussed as extensively as 2:5–11. Here Jesus is set forth as an example, as Christology takes on a practical and exemplary turn.[14] In this passage Paul uniquely combined high Christology with a call to practical living.

For Paul, Jesus existed in the "form" of God (*morphē theou*). Does this refer to Jesus' humanity or His divinity? Is Jesus made in God's image like Adam, or does He uniquely bear God's form? To answer these questions, the next phrase needs to be interpreted. It reads, *ouk harpagmon to einai isa theo* ("He did not consider equality with God something to be held to self-advantage," author's trans.).[15] This clause could mean that Jesus sought to get hold of something He did not previously possess. However, against this is the linguistic evidence for *harpagmos*, which refers to "the attitude one will take towards something which one already has

---

13. Hawthorne, *Philippians*, 45. Though many make a point of the contrast of the present tense *zēn* and the aorist *apothanein*, the contrast in tense is natural because of the nature of living and dying. Life is by nature a progressive activity, while death is an act of a moment. The concepts, not the tenses, are key to the meaning here. See discussion in Moisés Silva, *Philippians*, Wycliffe Exegetical Commentary (Chicago: Moody, 1988), 82–83.

14. The literature on this passage is voluminous. The most well-known English monograph on this passage is Ralph P. Martin, *Carmen Christi: Philippians 2:5–11 in Recent Interpretation and in the Setting of Early Christian Worship* (Cambridge: Cambridge Univ., 1976). Martin does not believe that Jesus serves as an example in this text, but this is a decidedly minority position. The most significant article on the disputed term *harpagmos* in the passage is R. W. Hoover, "The HARPAGMOS Enigma: A Philological Solution," *Harvard Theological Review* 64 (1971): 95–119, which in turn develops work by W. Jaeger, "Eine stilgeschichtliche Studie zum Philipperbrief," *Hermes* 50 (1915): 537–53. The discussion in this section is heavily indebted to Norman T. Wright, *The Climax of the Covenant: Christ and the Law in Pauline Theology* (Philadelphia: Fortress, 1992), 56–98. It is the best recent discussion of this text and defends in detail the view that Jesus is an example. Wright sees in the passage a second Adam motif and Servant imagery, as well as an affirmation of Jesus' preexistence. As the Servant of Yahweh, Jesus contrasts with and reverses the sin of Adam, not by using His divine status to self-advantage but by serving others.

The question of the possible hymnic origin of Philippians 2:5–11, though interesting, is irrelevant in determining the theology of its function in Philippians and therefore is not treated here. Also helpful on these disputed matters is the discussion of O'Brien, *Philippians*, 186–271, which has several interesting excursuses. Also see C. F. D. Moule, "Further Reflections on Philippians 2:5–11," in *Apostolic History and the Gospel: Biblical and Historical Essays Presented to F. F. Bruce on His 60th Birthday*, ed. W. Ward Gasque and Ralph P. Martin (Exeter: Paternoster, 1970), 264–76.

15. The results and conclusions of many complex exegetical questions are summarized here. For a defense of this view, see Wright and O'Brien as noted above in n. 14.

and holds and will continue to have and hold."[16] In addition, the following phrase in verse 7, the emptying of Himself by *morphēn doulou labōn* ("taking on the form of a slave") must mean that He took on something He did not previously possess, namely, humanity. In fact, this second phrase in verse 7 clearly stands in contrast to the debated *morphē* phrase in verse 6. Therefore the "form of God" must refer to His equality with deity, not His humanity. Wright clearly states the three options of force that could result from such a reading of the hymn. Either (1) there are two gods (but this is untenable; see 1 Cor. 8:5–6),[17] or (2) Jesus was absorbed into divinity (but this is excluded from His clear, distinct identity in the postresurrection period), or (3) correctly, "Jesus, in being exalted to the rank described in 2:9ff, is receiving no more than that which was always, from the beginning of time, his by right."[18] Or as Wright also puts it, "Jesus—or more accurately, the one who became Jesus—must have been from all eternity 'equal with God' in the sense of being himself fully divine."[19] So Jesus as a divine figure emptied Himself.

But what was the emptying? For many the *kenōsis* (from *kenoō*, "to empty") means that Jesus divested Himself of divine attributes of omniscience and other such qualities. But the text says nothing about leaving anything behind; it gives no grammatical object for what is emptied. Rather, the emptying denotes taking on a new, lower status. Jesus emptied Himself, *"by taking on the form of a slave"* (2:7).[20] It was subtraction by humble addition, not exchange. His deity and commitment to reflect divine love required that He take up the redemptive cause and become a man who suffered and died (Rom. 5:6–8). As the God-Man, Jesus fulfilled His vocation. By taking the form of a slave (explained in the next phrase, "becoming in the likeness of men," i.e., becoming a man through birth), He renounced His divine seat in heaven and descending, took on life in the sinful world. In His slav-

16. See Wright, *Climax of the Covenant,* 78, citing the detailed work of Hoover. Three Latin phrases summarize the debate on this term, though ten major views exist! (1) *Res rapta* means that something has been seized. So Christ did not regard divine equality as something that needed to be seized, *since it was His by divine right.* He did not seek to usurp God's authority. This view is concerned with how Christ possessed His divine status. So the event took place *before* the other events. The Latin Fathers preferred this option. (2) *Res retinenda* means that Christ did not regard His divine equality, which He already possessed, as something to be greedily clung to. The Greek Fathers opted for this sense. (3) *Ras rapienda* means something to be newly grasped, so that Christ did not regard the deity *that He did not currently possess* as something He had to reach out and take. This view looks at how Christ would come to His great status *after* the events described. The view adopted above argues that an idiom is used and that none of these Latin phrases adequately summarizes its force.

17. Paul's Jewish monotheism would not allow him to believe in multiple gods.

18. Wright, *Climax of the Covenant,* 94.

19. Ibid. Wright's remark about the "one who *became* Jesus" simply denotes that He was not named Jesus nor was He incarnate until He was born of woman.

20. That the emptying is the humbling is shown by the verb-participle connection in 2:7. The participle explains how the emptying takes place. Since the New Testament (John 1:1–18) speaks of God incarnate, He cannot have left divine attributes behind and still be deity incarnate. The emptying has to do with His humble way of bearing and serving, rather than with His wielding authority.

ery as a man, He served God and died on the cross for all humankind. Jesus embraced the divine call to serve for the interest of others, rather than in self-interest. So Jesus humbled Himself, even unto death (Phil. 2:8).

The story of Jesus continues. God exalted Him and "graced" (*echarisato*) Him with the name above all names, so that all creation will someday bow before Him (2:9–10). Jesus would now be confessed and worshiped with the name Lord (*kyrios*). His sovereignty involved the whole of creation. The language of verse 11 comes from a Greek version of Isaiah 45:23. This Old Testament verse described the honor God would receive, but here Paul said such honor is given to Jesus. The hymn of Philippians 2 depicts a "reverse parabola," which begins and ends in heavenly glory after His having descended into the sinful earth to redeem it (John 1:14–17). Jesus receives honor through the gate of humility, death, and faithful service. Here Jesus functions as Adam should have and as the Servant of Yahweh was called to do.

Paul presented this high Christology not for its own sake, but to make one practical point. Christians should live with the same attitude of humble service as that of Christ (Phil. 2:1–5, 12–18). Power and privilege are not to be wielded like a club, but are to be put to positive, edifying use in humble service to others (Mark 10:42–45). The one who loves as Jesus did, will serve as He did, like a humble servant. Is this yet another way to express what Jesus called "the greatest commandment" (Mark 12:28–31)? This might explain why Paul often referred to himself as "a slave of Jesus Christ." In serving the one who exemplified service as a slave, he was proud to regard himself as a bondservant of Jesus Christ.

The One who judges and transforms. Jesus is also the center of the judgment to come. Paul refers to this as "the day of Jesus Christ," the time of the return of Jesus (Phil. 1:6; 2:16; 3:20–21; 1 Thess. 4:17; 1 Cor. 15:51). Elsewhere Paul referred to this event as "the day" (Rom. 13:12; 1 Cor. 3:13; 1 Thess. 5:4), "that day" (2 Thess. 1:10 NASB), "the day of the Lord" (1 Cor. 5:5; 1 Thess. 5:2), and "the day of our Lord Jesus [Christ]" (1 Cor. 1:8; 2 Cor. 1:14). "The day" is a variation of the reference to "the day of the Lord" in the Old Testament, a time of judgment, but Paul was confident that for the Philippians "the day of Jesus Christ" would be a positive experience. He looked forward to that time when he would stand proud, knowing that his work had not been in vain, since the Philippian believers had shone as lights in the world (2:15). Paul longed to see in his converts the fruit of his ministry, all to the praise of God.

So Paul longed for Jesus' return not just to judge the unrighteous, but to save and transform the righteous. This is why Christians eagerly await the Savior and the time when He will transform them out of their lowly bodies of fleshly limitation into glorious bodies of sinlessness (3:20–21; 1 Cor. 15: 35–49; 2 Cor. 5:1–10; 1 Thess. 1:10; Titus 2:13). This is but a part of the eventual redemption of all creation (Rom. 8:18–25).

The hope. Jesus is the center of hope, which is expressed in confident terms in Philippians 1:6, 10; 2:16; and 3:20–21. Such transformation will be the cause for the Philippians to glory in Jesus Christ (2:16) and praise for God (1:10). Philippians

2:10–11 looks to a similar time and reaction. The righteousness Paul looked forward to having is that which comes through Jesus, the source and center of blessing (3:9). This is Jesus' upward call, not just to new life, but to eventual transformation into complete holiness.

THE HOLY SPIRIT

The Spirit is not mentioned often in this book. But He is seen as one who helps in prayer (1:19) and who is a source of fellowship, that is, He participates in believers' lives (2:1). Such aid and support recalls the function of the Spirit described in John's gospel (John 14:15–17). The participial form of the verb for "help" or "support" (*epichorēgeō*) appears in Galatians 3:5 in reference to God supplying the Spirit to them through faith, while in Colossians 2:19 the verb refers to what *Jesus* supplies to His body, the church, to make it grow. The verb is also used in Philippians 1:19 of what the *Spirit* does in prayer (Rom. 8:26). Thus as a Pauline theological term, it describes the activity of the Godhead. The Spirit also is the source of one's life of worship (Phil. 3:3), a sign that believers are the true circumcision of God (cf. Rom. 2:28–29).

PAUL'S MINISTRY AND IMPRISONMENT

Responses of others to his ministry. Much of this epistle focuses on Paul's ministry and its progress. The value of Paul's ministry and imprisonment led to confidence and boldness for most of the believers (1:14). But two factions were present and the motives for their preaching differed. Nonetheless, it is clear that these factions were within the church, since they both preached Christ and Paul referred to them all as "brethren" (1:14–17).

The first group preached Christ from pure motive and good will because they knew that Paul was in Rome to defend the gospel. The second group was acting out of envy and rivalry, supposing they would bring tribulation to Paul in his incarceration. Paul's differing descriptions of the rationale for the two groups distinguishes accurate from inaccurate responses, but he was not concerned about the attitudes of others toward him. Christ was preached and that was all that mattered.

The group Paul referred to negatively here is not the same group he castigated in Philippians 3:2, 18–19.[21] The opposition to Paul here was personal and did not seem to be fueled so much by theological error as by personal animosity against the apostle. Paul was able to transcend the enmity, because for him what mattered was that all these ministries sought to proclaim Jesus.

His goals in ministry. Paul had various goals for his ministry. First, he wished to honor Christ through his body, whether in life or death (1:20). Second, he desired to have fruitful labor in this life on behalf of the Philippians (1:22–25). Third, he wished to avoid shame (*aischynthēsomai*, 1:20) as he ministered for Jesus. Accomplishing this goal would take courage as he offered himself in service to

---

21. O'Brien notes six options which scholars raise about this second group. He also defends the distinction between these two groups *(Philippians,* 101–6).

Jesus. As he was confident that God would work for the Philippians (1:6), so he had the expectation and hope that he would not be ashamed in his labor, even as he faced the possibility of death. As Paul sought to be bold, he asked the same of the Philippians (1:28).

His attitude in ministry. Paul approached his ministry with one point of reference—to be used by God however he willed, wherever He led (1:19–26). Paul rejoiced in his dire situation, knowing that God intended it for him and that through it he had been able to witness to people he might otherwise never have had the opportunity to reach so intimately (1:12–13). So in life or death, Paul was content.

His ministry as a libation. Paul considered his ministry an offering poured out to God (2:17). The verb *spendō* ("poured out") is used only twice in the New Testament (here and in 1 Tim. 4:6). In the Septuagint, it was used of the poured-out portion of an offering associated with a burnt or cereal offering (Num. 15:3–10). In Philippians, Paul held out the possibility that he might die, but in doing so he would have spent himself as a holy offering to God. Such was the total sacrifice he was willing to make in his ministry. In fact, he was glad to do so (2 Cor. 12:15).

His ministry as an example. In all these attitudes, Paul presented himself to others as an example (3:17; 4:9). In challenging the Philippians to imitate him, he especially had in mind the running of the race to attain the upward call of Jesus Christ (3:7–16), a theme to be examined later in relation to the citizenship the Philippians possessed. The second time Paul mentioned their imitating Him (4:9) was after he spoke of virtues they should pursue, a list that recalls the fruit of the Spirit (Gal. 5:22–23), as well as the clothes of the new man (Col. 3:9–17). The ability to engage in such imitation means pursuing Christ and relying on Him in both thought and prayer (Phil. 4:6, 8). This is the essence of what it means for believers to live out their citizenship as members of the heavenly commonwealth and to run the race of experiencing all God offers His own (3:8–11, 20–21).

THE CITIZENSHIP AND THE RACE

Heavenly citizenship and unity. Paul's cosmic and apocalyptic view of reality is highlighted by the concept of the believer's heavenly citizenship (1:27–30; 3:20). In Philippians 1, this concept surfaces in the verb *politeuesthe* ("live as citizens"). Its cognate, *politeuma* ("commonwealth"), appears in Philippians 3. The term suggests relationship to the *polis* ("city-state"), that is, the new community of Christ whose origin is heaven. Thus Paul wrote, "Our commonwealth [citizenship NIV] is in heaven" (3:20, author's trans.).[22] Paul stated that this citizenship currently exists; it is not only a future hope. As such the term expresses a fundamental orientation and identity of believers.

---

22. The emphatic position of the pronoun *hēmōn* ("our") shows that this heavenly Christian citizenship stands in contrast to the earthly citizenship of Paul's opponents. For the term "commonwealth" in everyday Greek, see 2 Maccabees 12:7; *The Letter of Aristeas* 310; and Josephus, *The Antiquities of the Jews* 12.108. O'Brien (*Philippians,* 460) argues that it is comparable to the way other New Testament texts use the term *basileia* ("reign" or "kingdom").

Yet even this seemingly abstract image also has a practical focus. Philippians 1:27–30 makes the point that the believer's life is to be worthy of such an origin; it is to be worthy of its relationship to the gospel of Christ. That means that unity should be pursued, as the community stands in one mind for the gospel. In fact, opponents need no longer be feared, even though the call of this new community is both to believe and suffer. By engaging in this call, the Philippians would share in the same struggle (*agōna*) Paul was currently engaged in, and they would thereby have fellowship with him and show their unity with him and with Christ in humble service (1:29–2:11). Their allegiance was so wedded to identity with the God of heaven that they would stand firm in the battle against opponents who were committed to the fallen perspectives and desires of the earth (3:19). The saints' hope is that heaven will complete the process and deliver them, by changing their "lowly bodies" (3:21) to be like His glorious body. Then Jesus will once again exercise great power on their behalf and make them like Himself. Here is an example of Paul's view of God's apocalyptic activity of redemption and transformation. It provides a base for ethical exhortation to stand firm until He completes the task that Paul was confident God would bring to pass (1:6).

Behind this declaration of heavenly citizenship stands the recognition of God's saving and exalting activity in redemption, what Paul elsewhere called dying and rising with Christ (Col. 2:9–15; Rom. 6:1–11), or what he portrayed as God making the sinner alive and raising him or her out of death to His side in heaven (Eph. 2:1–7). This explains why their citizenship is heavenly. Both its origin and its destiny are with God in heaven. So allegiance and faithfulness should be directed there. This perspective is another way of saying that the believer should "set your minds on things above" (Col. 3:1–17). For Paul, heavenly citizenship has its privileges and responsibilities, as well as being a hope that puts present events in their proper place.

An example of this call to stand firm and be unified is Paul's brief exhortation to Euodia and Syntyche (Phil. 4:1–3). He asked the "loyal yokefellow" (4:3) to aid in their reconciliation. Though many have speculated as to who this individual might be (Timothy, Epaphroditus, Luke Silas, or Syzygos, taking the Greek term for "yokefellow" as a personal name), others see the appeal to the Philippian church, which is viewed as an individual unit.[23] Whatever the meaning, Paul was concerned that unity be restored to the body and that others work hard to make it happen.

Shining as lights. As God works, so too are the saints to labor in the task of living out what salvation asks of them (2:12–13). Life should be pursued without grumbling (2:14), and the goal is to live blamelessly and innocently in the midst of a crooked and perverse generation, to shine as lights in the world (2:15). Paul's exhortation makes it clear that blamelessness is not only a goal of the future life; it is to be pursued in this life. To shine as lights is to live righteously (Eph. 5:9; Matt.

---

23. Hawthorne opts for the church (*Philippians,* 179–80), as does Silva (*Philippians,* 222), while O'Brien prefers an individual whose name is not revealed in the letter (*Philippians,* 479–81). Silva notes that Paul did use the second person singular to refer to the community of believers (Rom. 2:1, 17; 1 Cor. 12:12–26; Eph. 4:15–16; Col. 2:18–19).

5:14–16). Paul wrote that such a life comes by "holding fast the word of life" (Phil. 2:16 NASB). Such a life will result in full joy on the day of Christ, as the ministry of Paul would realize its goal of producing a community where the life of faith is manifested (2:16–18).

Genuine righteousness. The ultimate goal of salvation is eternal redemption (3:20–21), but Paul was also concerned that meanwhile, as the day of Christ draws near, the Philippians would understand their task. So he prayed that their love may abound more and more (1:10–11). The goal of pursuing such love is that they may approve what is excellent and may be pure and blameless for the day of Jesus Christ, filled with the fruit of righteousness. Now this prayer is not about God's giving the believer a perfect, glorified body in the future, which thus reflects blamelessness. The phrase, "filled with the fruit of righteousness," shows that Paul had in mind the produce of one's activity in this life. The pursuit of what is excellent is also restated in Philippians 4:4–9, where Paul also urged them to rest in God's care through prayer. The goal can be stated simply: pursue genuine righteousness.

In Philippians 3:14–15, Paul illustrated this goal more graphically, using himself as the example and describing life as a race. Here he contrasted his philosophy of life in Christ to what he could have had (and did have when he was a Jew). Before, he rested on his laurels in the flesh, his great accomplishments, and rich heritage (3:4–6). His righteousness was his own and came with reference to the law. But in Christ all this had changed. As a result of Him, he viewed those accomplishments as being as worthless as human dung (the meaning of *skybala*)[24] in comparison to the surpassing worth of knowing Him and experiencing what he now saw as genuine righteousness (3:8–11). Paul wanted to "gain Christ," that is, to have a righteousness not of his own based on law, but which results from faith in Jesus Christ. This means it is not a life of self-attainment, but of giving and serving from the heart. To know the power of the resurrection is to live a life (a new, transformed life) in which one can even share in sufferings like those Christ experienced and honor God (3:10–11). To become like Him is to serve like Him in humility and perhaps even at cost of one's life, as did Jesus (2:5–11).

Paul sought to run the race of the Christian life, looking and stretching forward toward the goal. This goal was the "prize" of God's call in which Paul was asked to be like the One who now resides in heaven, what Paul called the "upward call of God in Christ Jesus" (3:12–15 NASB). Therefore, Paul did not look back, but always moved forward toward that goal. This is not a claim to perfectionism, but is a reminder that when God saves us His plan is to transform us and make us more like Himself, even to the point of death (3:10; Eph. 2:8–10). Paul was so convinced of this approach to life that he argued that those who are mature will be of like mind, and if one does not think this way God will reveal it (Phil. 3:15).

24. The choice of this graphic term is often softened in English translations to avoid giving offense (e.g., "rubbish" in the NIV, NRSV, and NKJV or "refuse" in the RSV), but these weaken the mood and depth of feeling Paul had about his former life. The shocking effect of the imagery was to emphasize the total uselessness of his former way of life and attainments. Here the KJV has it right.

God's gift: belief and suffering. The desire to imitate Christ and reflect genuine righteousness helps explain Paul's remark earlier in the letter that it is God's gift to them not only that they believe on Him but also that they suffer for Him (1:29–30). To stand firm for God in a world that is hostile to His ways means opposition and suffering. For Paul, suffering is a part of every Christian's call as life continues in a world groaning for redemption from sin (Rom. 8:18–25). Thus Paul viewed the Christian life as a struggle (*agōna*, Phil. 1:30) that all believers share together as they stand firm to represent God in the face of opposition to Him.

Joy. Despite the call to pursue righteousness and suffer, Paul also made it clear that believers should rejoice. As already noted, joy is so prevalent that many see it as the major theme of the book. That is probably not the case, but there is no denying that as Christians engage in battle with the world and suffer for it, they are to be joyful, not morose. Numerous verses emphasize this point (1:19, 25; 2:18, 29; 3:1; 4:4, 10). The various causes for joy are that Christ is preached, that Paul could minister to them, that he could be poured out like a sacrifice for them, that friends in the Lord could be received, that they were in the Lord, and that they had concern for each other. For Paul, there was much to be thankful for in Jesus (1:3–5).

Thanks for their gift and their fellowship-partnership. A major reason Paul wrote to this church and was thankful for them was their concrete expression of support for him (4:10–18). This church had sent a gift of monetary support to Paul as he sat in prison (4:14–18). This gift Paul called their "partnership" with him, using the verb form (*ekoinōnēsen*, v. 15) of the Greek word for fellowship (*koinonia*). They fellowshiped with him by participating in his ministry through this concrete expression of love and concern. Paul did not expect or assume such support. He had learned to be content whatever his condition, whether in humble or bountiful circumstance. In fact, when Paul wrote that he could do all things through Christ who strengthened him (4:13), he meant that he could face every kind of circumstance or financial situation without losing sight of God's purposes for him. So he received their gift with gratitude, a gift that he said was a "fragrant offering" to God (4:18). Their concern caused Paul to assure them that God also will take care of them too (4:19).

Two examples: Timothy and Epaphroditus. Paul was not the only example to be emulated by the Philippians. Those whom Paul sent to update them on his situation were also commended for their ministry to Paul and the Philippians. As such, they too were examples of faith and maturity, examples of those who pursue genuine righteousness by following Christ's example. Timothy is described as genuinely anxious for the Philippians' well-being (2:20). Here is a positive use of the concept of anxiety, where it expresses a genuine love and concern for the welfare of another. But showing such outward concern, Timothy is an example of one who looks out for the interests not only of others but also of Jesus Christ Himself (2:21). In fact, Paul's connection to Timothy was so strong that the apostle compared it to a father-son relationship (2:22).

Epaphroditus was a fellow soldier with Paul, an image that suggests the idea of a battle (2:25). He, like Timothy, longed for the Philippians, and was even concerned that they were too worried about him when he fell seriously ill (2:26–27). The church should receive him back with joy and know that he had risked himself, even to the point of death, for them and for Jesus (2:29–30).

The danger. Not everyone, however, is exemplary. Some, like wild dogs, would seek to devour the believers (3:2). They argue for circumcision, but are really mutilators of God's way, in fact, evil workers. This group of opponents is not the same as those who preached Christ out of envy (1:15–18). The threat of this strongly rebuked group in 3:2 is sinister and is to be avoided at all costs. These Judaizers put confidence in the flesh and said that circumcision was necessary for salvation. This was an old and constant fight for Paul (Gal. 1–3; Acts 15). In contrast to those who trust in a religious rite to save are those of the true circumcision, those who worship God in spirit (John 4:24), who glory in Jesus Christ, putting no confidence in the flesh, that is, in human achievement as accomplishing saving merit before Him (Phil. 3:3). In contrast to this approach to life, Paul spoke of the "race" for Jesus (see above). When Paul returned to discuss this group, he called them enemies of the cross of Christ (3:18), rejecting Jesus and His substitutionary death. Their end is destruction, their god is their belly (i.e., their pursuit of self-satisfying merit which drives them as a passion), and their glory is actually their shame, as their minds are set on earthly things (3:19). This use of imagery concerning earthly things that bring shame is similar to Colossians 3:1–11, except that in Philippians pride is the prime target. To look to Jesus is to rest in His goodness and His hope for us, not in achievement that is designed to barter for righteousness before God.

Resting in His care. Paul concluded the exhortations of this epistle by highlighting that believers should rest in God's care with rejoicing and prayer, staying focused on those virtues that build genuine righteousness (4:4–9). By imitating Paul, who pursued being like Christ, they could attain what God desired for them (4:9; 3:8–11).

SUMMARY

Philippians is a call to reflect heavenly citizenship, by imitating the one who is the source of their new position. To pursue righteousness is to seek to serve through a life filled with virtue, where the goal is to give and to minister. To shine as lights is to reflect the truth in life, not just proclaim it in word. To hold fast to the Word means to live the truth, not just describe it. That is the walk that is worthy of the gospel. Obviously, then, Paul's theology not only instructs; it also urges and guides.

The Prison Epistles: Christ Is Victorious, So Receive Salvation and Live Differently

The Prison Epistles reflect Paul's wedding of deep theology with pastoral concern. God has triumphed in the cross and resurrection of Jesus. So the Father extends His deliverance toward those who come to Him in faith. That means that believers are part of what God is using to reflect the redemption of the entire creation. Such an ultimate hope means that life in this world also is transformed. Life means serving God (not self), reflecting a heavenly citizenship (not an earthly one), drawing on the enabling God gives to overcome sin and to shine as lights to a needy world, being willing to suffer and stand united before a dark world in need, while revealing God's gospel, goodness, and character in the way we relate to one another and to those who need God's redemptive work.

Paul was a theologian of great depth who wrote on themes of cosmic dimensions, but he was not so heavenly minded that he was no earthly good. He was a pastor shepherding the saints in their call. Paul's wish for believers is simple: Be a good citizen of heaven, and be so heavenly minded that you are of earthly good. He reminded believers that God had enabled them to perform the task and that as they stayed focused on Jesus, they could pursue the goal, united in their service for Him. They are never to forget that they are a new community in Him. In the context of God's sovereign work and in light of His victory and enablement, believers are to reflect His presence, love, and character until He brings the hope to realization and all things are summed up in the restoration that Christ will eventually bring.

7

A THEOLOGY OF
PAUL'S PASTORAL EPISTLES

MARK L. BAILEY

First Timothy, 2 Timothy, and Titus have been known as the Pastoral Epistles since they were first so-called by the German scholar, Paul Anton, in 1726.[1] Both because of what they contain and to whom they are addressed, this title has been appropriately retained. While the word "pastor" is not used in any of the three books, they do address the major issues facing those who are called to pastoral leadership positions within the church. The theological considerations in these epistles must be understood in light of the purpose statements of the epistles themselves. The books claim to be written by Paul to his associates, Timothy and Titus, with the purpose of encouraging them to stand firm in the gospel in the face of heretical challenges. Many scholars deny Pauline authorship of the Pastorals in favor of a pseudepigraphical author of the second century who wrote under the name of Paul as if he were writing to two of his colleagues. The arguments against Pauline authorship concern the historical, stylistic, and theological differences between the Pastoral Epistles and the other accepted Pauline writings. Recent exegetical and

---

1. Donald Guthrie, *The Pastoral Epistles,* Tyndale New Testament Commentaries (Grand Rapids: Eerdmans, 1957), 11.

MARK L. BAILEY, B.A., M.Div., Th.M., is associate professor of Bible exposition at Dallas Theological Seminary and a Ph.D. candidate.

expositional works provide adequate defense for Pauline authorship so there is no need to do so here.[2]

While specifically addressed to Timothy and Titus, evidence within the epistles reveals that Paul spoke "past" these two to the larger bodies of listeners within the churches (1 Tim. 2:8–11; 3:12; 5:3–8, 14–18; Titus 3:14).[3] Hence these letters are to be read by the whole church and not just its leaders.[4] All three books stress the need for Paul's associates to silence the threatening heresies, appoint qualified leaders in their respective churches, maintain the integrity of the gospel of grace, and train people to lead godly lives within their communities. At the theological center of the Pastorals is the need to defend the faith against encroaching errorists. The term "the faith" within these books is the objective truth of the gospel of God's grace which He has made available through the saving work of Christ, effected by the ministry of the Holy Spirit.

When studying the Pastoral Epistles, one cannot help but see the practical purpose for these books in addressing the issues facing the establishment of young churches. What is amazing is the extent of theological truth that undergirds the practical exhortations. Many efforts are made today to plant and organize churches without serious attention to genuine faith and commitment to sound doctrine. This is a far cry from what was modeled and mandated in these epistles. To rightly understand the theology of these letters properly, one must be acquainted with the historical threat of the false teachers in Ephesus and Crete. This background serves to explain the theological emphases in the work of the Trinity, the explication of the message of salvation, and the instructions concerning the leadership and lifestyles of the church. Therefore, to consider the error Paul combated helps us appreciate the truth Paul communicated to establish a healthy church.

2. For a defense of Pauline authorship, see W. Lock, *A Critical and Exegetical Commentary on the Pastoral Epistles,* International Critical Commentary (Edinburgh: T. & T. Clark, 1924); Guthrie, *The Pastoral Epistles,* 1957; J. N. D. Kelly, *A Commentary on the Pastoral Epistles* (Grand Rapids: Baker, 1981); C. Spicq, *Saint Paul: Les Épîtres Pastorales* (Paris: Gabalda, 1947); D. Edmond Hiebert, *Titus and Philemon,* Everyman's Bible Commentary (Chicago: Moody, 1957); Gordon D. Fee, *1 and 2 Timothy, Titus,* Good News Commentary (San Francisco: Harper & Row, 1984; Philip H. Towner, *The Goal of Our Instruction* (Sheffield: JSOT, 1989); T. D. Lea and H. P. Griffin, Jr., *1, 2 Timothy, Titus,* New American Commentary (Nashville: Broadman, 1992). For opposition to Pauline authorship, see P. N. Harrison, "Important Hypotheses Considered; III: The Authorship for the Pastoral Epistles," *Expository Times* 67 (1955): 77–81; Martin Dibelius and Hans Conzelmann, *The Pastoral Epistles,* Hermeneia, trans. P. Buttolph and A. Yarbo (Philadelphia: Fortress, 1972); C. K. Barrett, *The Pastoral Epistles* (Oxford: Oxford Univ., 1963); and A. T. Hanson, *The Pastoral Epistles,* New Century Bible Commentary (Grand Rapids: Eerdmans, 1982).

3. Other evidence includes the general wording of the leadership qualification lists in 1 Timothy 3:1–13; 5:9–13; and Titus 1:5–9 and the use of the plural "you" in the salutations of all three letters (1 Tim. 6:21; 2 Tim. 4:22; Titus 3:15).

4. For the historical, social, and religious background of Ephesus, see Lea and Griffin, *1, 2 Timothy, Titus,* 78–80.

THE HERESY: THE DANGER OF DECEIT AND DEPARTURE

The heresy Paul addressed sets the background for the theology and exhortations Paul offered the churches. Two major trends in interpretation of the heresy in the Pastorals exist. One interpretation identifies the error as a syncretism between Jewish and a preemergent Gnosticism.[5] The other view follows a pseudonymous authorship of the Pastorals and suggests the letters were a second-century paradigm for dealing with all kinds of heresy. Support for this second view stems from the letters themselves which describe the heretical threat as both present (1 Tim. 1:3, 20; 2 Tim. 2:20; Titus 1:10–16) and future (1 Tim. 4:1; 2 Tim. 3:1).[6] But the content of the letters suggests one need not choose between the historical and paradigmatic views, nor must one accept a late, post-Pauline setting for these letters. The books arose out of historical need, and they also contain prophetic warnings for the the present age as well.

Paul's strategy in dealing with the heretics at Ephesus and Crete involved attacking the false teachers more for their moral deficiencies (and the destructive effects that such teaching would produce on the unsuspecting hearers) than for the flaws in the doctrinal content. Doctrinal refutation became Timothy's and Titus's responsibility rather than being undertaken by Paul directly.

THE DEFICIENCY OF CHARACTER

A series of descriptive phrases used throughout the Pastoral Epistles highlight the lack of proper ethical standards. First, the false teachers coveted the role of teacher in order to be viewed as authoritative, especially as it related to interpretations of the law. Paul's words, "They want to be teachers of the law, but they do not know what they are talking about or what they so confidently affirm" (1 Tim. 1:7), possibly reflect a premature desire for some to move into leadership positions before they were ready.

Second, Paul called them "hypocritical liars, whose consciences have been seared"[7] (4:2). As Fee summarizes, "They liked the visible expressions, the ascetic practices, and the endless discussions of religious trivia, thinking themselves to be obviously righteous because they were obviously religious."[8] Consequently, they left themselves vulnerable to the deceit and doctrines of demons (4:1–3). One of Satan's tactics is the attempt to hinder the message of the gospel and the application of the truth in the lives of Christians (Matt. 13:1–9; 2 Cor 4:4; 11:3, 13–14).

A third passage in the Timothy correspondence expresses a set of characteristics of those who were communicating error at Ephesus (1 Tim. 6:3–5). Since they were ignorant even about that which they pontificated, they were called conceited

---

5. Dibelius and Conzelmann, *Pastoral Epistles*, 39–41.

6. P. Trummer, *Die Paulustradition der Pastoralbriefe* (Frankfurt: Lang, 1978), 185–86.

7. The term *seared* translates the Greek word *kekausteriasmenon*, which can mean "to cauterize." It is used only here in the New Testament, and it means that one is "insensible to the distinction between right and wrong" (Kelly, *Commentary on the Pastoral Epistles*, 94).

8. Fee, *1 and 2 Timothy, Titus*, 270.

(*tetyphōtoi*, "swollen-headed") and they had a perverted interest in stirring up controversies.[9] The underlying motivation for such behavior was surfaced by the apostle as the greedy desire to make a profit from their preaching (v. 5).

A fourth passage, 2 Timothy 3:1–9, presents a vice list.[10] In discussing this passage, Hanson notes, "If we begin at the last word of Rom. 1:29, 'gossip,' we can trace quite a close parallel with the list in 2 Tim. 3:2–4, down to the end of Rom. 1:31; most of the vices in the author's list have an exact or fairly close parallel in Paul's list."[11] Unfortunately, in Romans Paul described pagan society, whereas in 2 Timothy he was predicting a future trend in the church. After warning of the extensive catalog of sins that would mark "the terrible times in the last days,"[12] Paul summarized the root issues when he said the people would be "lovers of pleasure rather than lovers of God—having a form of godliness but denying its powers" (2 Tim. 3:5; cf. Titus 1:16). Then, as now, all false teaching at its heart, is hedonistic and rationalizing (2 Tim. 4:3–4). Rather than finding fulfillment in a dynamic relationship with God, the selfish pursuit of pseudointellectual religious thought becomes the dominant desire. Paul further described this as "always learning and never able to acknowledge the truth" (3:7).

Paul warned that as the end of the age approaches, such evil men and imposters (v. 13)[13] would only get worse and their numbers would increase. The cause for this was that they were deceiving and being deceived by what they themselves were teaching. Thus the error was propagating itself in homogeneous communities that were being founded for the self-serving reinforcement of one another and the doctrines they were advocating (4:3–4).

The book of Titus contains a couple of statements that exposed the moral failure of the errorists on Crete. Especially appropriate (but unfortunate) was Paul's emphasis on the deception; it is appropriate because his statement coincided with the reputation that "Cretans are always liars, evil brutes, lazy gluttons" (Titus 1:12), but it is unfortunate because that particular element in the culture had begun to invade the churches on the island.[14] This false teaching was similar to the errors at

---

9. Kelly translates the word "controversies" (*diaparatribai*), as "persistent wranglings" (*Commentary on the Pastoral Epistles*, 135).

10. For other vice lists in Paul's writings see 1 Timothy 1:9–10; Romans 1:29–31; 1 Corinthians 6:9–10; and Galatians 5:19–21.

11. Hanson, *Pastoral Epistles*, 144. As can be inferred from this quotation, Hanson is skeptical of Pauline authorship of the Pastorals. See n. 2 above.

12. Concerning the use of the future tense in this passage, Kelly wrote, "Since he is availing himself of prophetic material current in the Church, he naturally uses the future tense, but it soon becomes plain that his gaze is fixed in the present, in which these predictions are being only too accurately realized" (*Commentary on the Pastoral Epistles*, 193). Here, as in 1 John 2:18, the presence of the same spirit that will become more prominent and personalized in the last days is seen as already at work.

13. The term *goētes*, which the NIV translates as "imposters," may be a reference to the practice of the magical cults at Ephesus. See the discussion by Kelly, *Commentary on the Pastoral Epistles*, 200.

14. For the history of this quotation of Epimenides, see Fee, *1 and 2 Timothy, Titus*, 179.

Ephesus, as Paul warned Titus of the corrupted consciences and facade of godliness of such teachers (Titus 1:15–16).

THE DEPARTURE FROM THE TRUTH

All false teaching has one trait in common: a departure from revealed truth. Besides being deficient in personal morality, the errorists ended up where they did because of what they left behind. They left what was true to pursue what was false (1 Tim. 1:3; 6:3). Paul used a series of graphic words to impress his readers with such deviation.

Wandering. The Greek word *astocheō* in 1 Timothy 1:6 portrayed the idea "wide of the mark or to shoot past the goal."[15] This is a fitting expression since, in the previous verse, Paul had stated that the goal of his instruction was love from a "pure heart and a good conscience and a sincere faith" (v. 5). The false teachers had obviously bypassed this defining purpose as they "wandered" away to other interests.

Rejecting. Equally graphic is the term for their "rejection" of faith and a good conscience (1 Tim. 1:19). This term (*apōtheō*) was used for violent and willful rejection in Acts 7:39; 13:46; and Romans 11:2. Even the result in the immediate context of 1 Timothy 1:19 illustrated such violence since it caused the "shipwreck" of the faith of Hymenaeus and Alexander (v. 20). The future expectation, as predicted by Paul, did not look any brighter.

Apostatizing. By the revelation of the Spirit of God, Paul predicted a moral and spiritual apostasy (*apostasia,* 1 Tim. 4:1) as the last days approach. What began as a departure from the truth will result in the seduction by demons and their doctrines (vv. 2–3). According to Paul, this had already begun among some gullible women at Ephesus (2 Tim. 3:6) and men such as Hymenaeus and Philetus (2 Tim. 2:17–18).[16]

Bankrupt. As a result of being led away by the controversial heresies, some were "robbed of the truth" (1 Tim. 6:5). As Guthrie commented, "When reason is morally blinded, all correctives to unworthy behavior are banished, and the mind becomes destitute . . . of the truth."[17] First Timothy 6:10 and 21 further comment that the false teachers "wandered away from the faith" for the pursuit of monetary gain and the profession of an elitist claim of superior spiritual insight.[18] The danger of such a "turning away" was illustrated in 2 Timothy 4:4 where Paul used a medical term, *ektrepō,* that meant in everyday Greek to wrench a limb out of joint.[19]

15. Lea and Griffin, *1, 2 Timothy, Titus,* 69.

16. The verb *astacheō,* used in 2 Timothy 3:18, was introduced in 1 Timothy 1:6 and 6:21. These are the only three occurrences of this verb in the New Testament.

17. Guthrie, *Pastoral Epistles,* 112. As Fee observes, "Believers have come to know the truth (2:4; 4:3; 2 Tim. 2:25); these men have been robbed of it (cf. 2 Tim. 2.18; 3:7–8; 4:4)" (*1 and 2 Timothy, Titus,* 142).

18. More will be said about this "so-called knowledge" under the discussion of the nature of the false doctrine.

19. This verb also appears in 1 Timothy 1:6; 5:15; 6:20; and Hebrews 12:13.

Ironically, the first and last reference to departure refers to the myths into which the false teachers veered. When truth is sacrificed, only what is mythological is left to be invented or investigated.

THE DIVISIVE DOCTRINES

Evidence in the Pastoral Epistles suggests the error was not a fully developed system of thought.[20] The message of the false teachers seems to have been a mixture of Jewish tradition and Gnostic asceticism. "While there were undoubtedly minor differences between the false teaching in Ephesus and Crete, the features seem to be common, and there is strong justification for regarding them as separate manifestations of a general contemporary tendency."[21]

The Jewish flavor. The Jewish flavor of the heresy emerges in their devotion to the study of genealogies and myths and their desire to be teachers of the law (1 Tim. 1:3, 7; Titus 3:9). Scholars interpret these terms as referring to either fictitious Jewish speculations about the Pentateuch, especially the genealogies, or the Gnostic doctrine about origins. "Viewed in this light, the errorists are Judaizers who concentrate on far-fetched minutiae of rabbinical exegesis to the detriment of the gospel."[22] They were also identified as "those of the circumcision group" (Titus 1:10).[23]

The Gnostic trend. Early Gnostic influences were reflected in their prohibitions against marriage and certain foods (1 Tim. 4:3) and the pursuit of what Paul said is "falsely called knowledge" (6:20; cf. 1:4, 6; 4:7; 6:4).[24] As was true with most Gnostic variations, this teaching led to asceticism on the one hand and it excused greed and sensual indulgence on the other. Both extremes are always the logical ends of such a philosophy. Marriage was forbidden and certain distinctions between clean and unclean foods were reinstituted (4:3, 8; 5:23; Titus 1:15) under the guise that such practices insured a higher form of holiness. One significant doctrine which had to be adjusted to fit their views was the Resurrection. Hymenaeus and Alexander went so far as to deny the resurrection of the body by advocating it

20. Guthrie, *Pastoral Epistles,* 28; Kelly, *Commentary on the Pastoral Epistles,* 10–12; and J. B. Lightfoot, "The Date of the Pastoral Epistles," in *Biblical Essays* (London: Macmillan, 1893), 412.

21. Guthrie, *Pastoral Epistles,* 35. For the differences between the Gnostic trends addressed in the Pastoral Epistles and the more formalized Gnosticism of the second century, see Guthrie, *Pastoral Epistles,* 36–38.

22. Kelly, *Commentary on the Pastoral Epistles,* 45.

23. Scholars debate whether the reference to the "circumcision group" is a reference to teachings about the practice of circumcision or a Pauline epithet for a Jewish-oriented sect claiming special understanding or status (Gal. 2:12; Acts 11:2; Col. 4:11). For the arguments for both sides, see Arlund Hultgren, *I–II Timothy, Titus,* Augsburg Commentary on the New Testament (Minneapolis: Augsburg 1984), 45–46.

24. These ascetic practices were similar to those addressed in Colossians 2:16, 20–22. For other problems with food, see 1 Corinthians 8–10 and Romans 14.

had been spiritually fulfilled (2 Tim. 2:17–18).[25] They were also engaged in argumentation over the meaning of words (2:14, 16, 23; 4:4; Titus 3:9). Some have suggested they may have even gone so far in their degeneration as to have been involved in the Ephesian mystery rites (1 Tim. 4:1; 2 Tim. 3:13).

Meaningless value. The great masquerade in the false teaching involved superficial claims to godliness, which Paul viewed as hypocritical (2 Tim. 3:2–5). Paul's condemnation of the teaching surfaces in the pejorative words Paul used to expose them. Their discussions were meaningless (1 Tim. 1:6) and godless (6:10; 2 Tim. 2:23). Worse than everything else, all the false teaching contradicted the sound instruction and godly teaching of the Lord Jesus Christ (1 Tim. 6:3). Furthermore, throughout these letters Paul used the word "myths" (*mythois,* 1 Tim. 1:4; 4:7; 2 Tim. 4:4; Titus 1:14) to describe their teaching as devoid of truth and Christian reality.

THE DESTRUCTIVE RESULTS

The teachers' corrupting influence became one of the major reasons for Paul's taking so much time to expose this error. Their immoral character and the inroads their doctrine was beginning to have within the church demanded Paul's urgent attention. Such unwanted elements produced confusion and promoted controversies diametrically opposed to God's work and message of grace through faith (1 Tim. 1:4). Both those who taught and those who listened were adversely affected. If not stopped, the imposters would only proceed from bad to worse, spreading like gangrene (2 Tim. 2:17; cf. 3:13), becoming more and more ungodly (2:16), with the inevitable grief and judgment they had invited on themselves (1 Tim. 6:10).

Equally dangerous was the effect on those who listened to deception. Paul stated that quarrels were generated (2 Tim. 2:23) which resulted in strife, suspicion, and schisms (1 Tim. 6:4–5). Such quarrels over words ruined the hearers because it tended to undermine their faith (2 Tim. 2:14, 18). At Ephesus, the extent of the influence was exposed. The false teachers had wormed their way into the houses of weak-willed women (2 Tim. 3:6) to such an extent that some were already viewed as having followed Satan himself (2 Tim. 5:15).

THE DRASTIC TREATMENT

Both Timothy and Titus needed to take a strong stand against the false teachers (1 Tim. 1:3; 2 Tim. 2:14; Titus 1:13).[26] Paul's counsel ranged from the need to be alert all the way to exercising the final stages of church discipline. These young

25. Towner believes that the false views of the Resurrection arose from a misunderstanding of eschatological realism from Paul's promise of living with Christ as in Romans 6:8 (*Goal of Our Instruction,* 31–32).

26. As for the charge that Paul dealt differently with the false teachers in the Pastoral Epistles than he did in Colossians, one needs to remember that in the Pastorals the apostle was speaking to his associates who knew the content of the Christian faith, whereas in Colossians he was refuting the errors of the heretics for the benefit of the church members.

leaders needed to encourage action by those who might be affected and to take action toward the false teachers themselves. Warnings were given for the immediate as well as the eschatological expectations. For those in the church, Paul advocated avoiding the teachers (2 Tim. 3:5, 9) as well as their "godless chatter" (1 Tim. 6:20; 2 Tim. 2:16) and "stupid arguments" (2 Tim. 2:23; cf. Titus 3:9). Three specific reasons were given for the latter: (1) the chatter and quarreling led to further ungodliness (2 Tim. 2:16); (2) it spread like gangrene (2 Tim. 2:17); and (3) it was unprofitable (Titus 3:9). Warning the Ephesians about the present and future deviations that would precede the eschatological judgment could help stem the tide (1 Tim. 4:1–3). Second Timothy 4:15 warned the Ephesian church to be on guard. Both Timothy and Titus should protect the church by disallowing (silencing) the false teachers from promoting their errors (1 Tim. 1:3; Titus 1:11). The method of silencing them was outlined for Titus in 1:11–13 and 3:10–11. First the errorists must be rebuked sharply with a view toward restoration (Titus 1:11). If after two warnings there was still no response, the divisive person was to be shunned (Titus 3:10–11). Ultimately, they were to be "handed over to Satan" in order to prevent the presence of such blasphemy (1 Tim. 1:20).

CONCLUSION

Towner is right when he says, "it is clear from the verbal assault that the false teachers rejected, undermined, diluted, or otherwise perverted the apostolic gospel."[27] To answer such hostile attacks, Paul set forth for his associates and their communities a foundational understanding of the essential connections between God, Christ, the Holy Spirit, and the basics of the message of salvation.

GOD: SOVEREIGN AND CO-SAVIOR WITH CHRIST

GOD, THE SOVEREIGN CREATOR AND SUSTAINER OF ALL THAT LIVES

Critics of Pauline authorship believe the Pastorals present God as distant and uninvolved. While there is a high and lofty portrait of God, He is also shown to be intimately involved with His creation. God's sovereignty surfaces in His identifying titles, His creation, and the providential care and control He exercises in the universe. Nowhere is this intimate work of God more evident than in His direction of Christ's appearances and His gracious provision of salvation for sinful humanity. God is Sovereign in His essence, plan, and works. Two doxologies (1 Tim. 1:17; 6:15–16) and two of the seven major liturgical passages within the book serve as basic sources for the theology of God in these epistles.

His essence. In contrast to all pagan deities, God is the living God (1 Tim. 3:15; 4:10) in whose sight or presence the ministries of the church are carried forward (5:21). This assumes His omnipresence and omniscience. Paul reflected his Jewish/Christian monotheism when He spoke of God being the one and only eternal

27. Towner, *Goal of Our Instruction,* 25.

God (1:17; 2:5).[28] God is immortal, invisible (1:17), and personally inaccessible (6:16). Were it not for His own self-disclosure, His creation would not experience His grace. He is called "the King" (1:17), and "the only Ruler, the King of kings and Lord and lords" (6:15). The affirmation that eternal life is grounded in a God who cannot lie led the readers to assurance of their faith (Titus 1:2) and served as a contrast to the Cretans who had earned a reputation for persistent lying (1:12–13).

His plan. That God acted in the past and will continue to act in the future is fundamental. His sovereignty extends even to the "appointed season" which He determined for the arrival of the Messiah (1 Tim. 2:5–7; Titus 1:3; cf. Gal. 4:4; Rom. 5:6; Eph. 1:9–12; 3:4–11). Even before time God planned to provide the grace essential for salvation through Christ (2 Tim. 1:9). As Lea puts it, "The coming of Christ into human history constitutes the visible fulfillment of God's promise of eternal life for humanity."[29]

His works. Three times in these letters Paul credited God with being the Creator and Sustainer of everything (1 Tim. 4:4; 6:13, 15). Because everything comes from Him, all is good as He has made it, and therefore all should be received and used with thanksgiving. What God created is to be valued as a rich provision given by Him and intended for humankind's enjoyment (1 Tim. 4:3–4; 6:13, 17).[30] The Creation account, including belief in Adam and Eve's historicity, was affirmed (1 Tim. 2:13–14; 4:2–4; cf. Titus 1:15). This had major implications for the refutation of the ascetic and exclusionary practices of the false teachers who were threatening the church with their doctrines. As an example, Paul did not see the material world as something to be avoided, as it was part of God's creation. The foods He has provided are to be enjoyed (1 Tim. 4:3). People should function within the social structures of family, church, and society under the control of human government, and not in isolation from them. Marriage is encouraged and children are a blessing from the Lord (3:2–5; 5:10, 14). Even wealth must have a righteous use (6:17–18). With the recognition that evil does exist in the world (1:9–10; 2 Tim. 3:13), and with it the very real expectation of persecution (2 Tim. 3:12–13), retreat to monastic settings with ascetic lifestyles is not to be tolerated.

GOD, THE CO-SAVIOR WITH CHRIST AND FATHER OF HIS FAMILY, THE CHURCH

Co-savior with Christ. The title "Savior" occurs ten times in the Pastoral Epistles. Six of these references are designations of the Father (1 Tim. 1:1; 2:3;

---

28. Towner notes, "Interestingly, while other NT writers know and apply the formula (Matt 23:8ff; Mark 12:29, 32; John 8:41; James 2:19; 4:12), it is a uniquely Pauline thrust that uses it to pin the universal access to salvation on the *heis theos* of God" (*Goal of Our Instruction,* 51).

29. Lea and Griffin, *1, 2 Timothy, Titus,* 271.

30. The doctrine of God as the Creator and Sustainer of all is rooted in the Old Testament (Job 10:8–9; 32:4; 37:1–13; Ps. 139:13; Isa. 40:28–29; 44:24; 45:5–7, 9–11), the teaching of Jesus (Matt. 5:45; 6:25–33; 10:29; Luke 12:22–31; John 5:17), and elsewhere by Paul (1 Cor. 8:6; Col. 1:15–17).

4:10; Titus 1:3; 2:10; 3:4).[31] The Father's role in salvation first includes His will for all people. His desired will is for everyone to "be saved and come to a knowledge of the truth" (1 Tim. 2:4).[32] This unrestricted emphasis counters the Jewish notion that God has willed the destruction of sinners and the Gnostic notions that salvation belongs only to the spiritually elite.[33] Before the beginning of time, God decided to provide grace for salvation in Christ (2 Tim. 1:9). Salvation is the result of a divine call according to the purpose, grace, mercy, and peace that are sourced in God (1 Tim. 1:2; 2 Tim. 1:2; Titus 1:1). To call God "blessed" is unique to the Pastorals (1 Tim. 1:11; 6:15). Kelly interprets this to mean that all blessedness is found in His person and He bestows it upon other people.[34] In addition, a central gift from Him is repentance, which leads one to the truth, and faith and love (1 Tim. 1:14; 2 Tim. 2:25).[35]

Father of His house. The references to God as Father primarily reflect New Testament theology. Only fifteen times was God referred to as the Father in the Old Testament. Where it does occur, it is used of the nation Israel or to the king of Israel. Never was God called the Father of an individual or of human beings in general (though isolated instances occur in second temple Judaism, Sirach 51:10). In the New Testament numerous references to God as Father can be found.[36] The designation of God as Father expresses His relationship with those who by faith have become His children (1 Tim. 1:2; 2 Tim. 2:1; Titus 1:4). The church is His family (1 Tim. 3:5) and therefore constitutes His household (3:15). Its ministers also belong to Him (6:11; 2 Tim. 3:17).

Trainer of His children. All Scripture is said to be "God-breathed" (*theopnuestos,* 2 Tim. 3:16).[37] Its profitability includes its place in the salvation, transfor-

---

31. The other four references (2 Tim. 1:10; Titus 1:4; 2:13; 3:6) speak of Christ. For the Old Testament background for God as Savior, see Isaiah 45:15, 21; and Psalm 62:2, 6. Guthrie raises the question of whether the term *Savior* was used of God in contrast to Nero. He sees it more probably as the result of Paul's drawing an expression from his Jewish background (*Pastoral Epistles,* 55–56).

32. This also seems to be the best way to handle the statement in 1 Timothy 4:10 that He is "the Savior of all men." Neither elsewhere nor in the Pastorals did Paul advocate universalism. God's desire and provision for all to be saved does not imply that all will be saved. This is evident from the qualifying phrase, "especially of those who believe" which limits the benefits of salvation to those who trust God through faith in Jesus Christ. Lock states, "His will to save is as wide as His will to create and protect" (*Commentary on the Pastoral Epistles,* 2). This teaching is like that in 2 Peter 3:9.

33. Kelly, *Commentary on the Pastoral Epistles,* 63.

34. Ibid., 51.

35. Faith and love often occur together in the Pastorals (1 Tim. 2:15; 4:12; 6:11; 2 Tim. 1:13; 2:22; 3:10; Titus 2:2).

36. For a more complete discussion, see H. F. D. Sparks, "The Doctrine of the Divine Fatherhood of God in the Gospels," in *Studies in the Gospels: Essays in Memory R. H. Lightfoot,* ed. D. E. Nineham (Oxford: Blackwell, 1955), 241–62; and J. Barr, "Abbā Isn't Daddy," *Journal of Theological Studies* 39 (1988): 28–47.

37. With the use of the unique word, *theopneustos,* every Scripture can be said to be the result of the breath or Spirit of God. The parallel passage in 2 Peter 1:20–21 would argue for the latter.

mation, and equipping processes of the believer. The Scriptures are designated as the "word of truth" (2 Tim. 2:15) and are "free" from the "chains" or circumstances that seek to hinder its application (2 Tim. 2:9). They are, however, "able to make you wise for salvation" (3:15). Because of these characteristics, the Scriptures play a vital role in both salvation and the spiritual life. In their role in salvation, they should be preached to all (4:2, 5, 17). Because they have their origin in God, they are profitable for transforming and equipping believers to do the work and will of God (3:16–17). In the future God Himself will judge the way His "word of truth" is handled, and people will be held accountable for the diligence commanded for its proper use (2 Tim. 2:15).[38]

THE RIGHT RESPONSE TO GOD

Because God is who He is, He should be worshiped with honor and glory as the only real God and not be blasphemed (1 Tim. 1:16–20; 2:10; 6:1, 15–16; 2 Tim. 1:3; 2:19, 22).[39] As the Planner, Initiator, and Sustainer of life and salvation, He is the only suitable object of hope (1 Tim. 5:5; 6:17). His commands should be obeyed (2 Tim. 1:3), and He is worthy of all service (1:8; 4:5). For such obedience and service, God called and gifted people for ministry (1:3, 6). God can be pleased through prayers for others, especially governmental leaders (1 Tim. 2:1–3) and through the family care given to needy relatives, such as widows (5:4). Paul urged a variety of prayers toward God, including intercession, thanksgiving (2 Tim. 1:3–4), and various kinds of petition (1 Tim. 5:5). Since God called believers to salvation and holy living (2 Tim. 1:9), one should serve "with a clear conscience" (1:3). As the omniscient and omnipresent God, Paul invoked Him to witness the truthfulness of the charges and apostolic warnings for his readers. So Paul exhorted believers to maintain a godly lifestyle and ministry that will honor and glorify Him (2:14).

CHRIST JESUS:
CO-SAVIOR WITH THE FATHER AND MEDIATOR FOR HUMANITY

What was said of the Father can be also said of Christ. Since the salvation theme is central to the Pastorals, an exalted Christology is an indispensable part of Paul's presentation. Since all ministry occurs for the benefit of Christ (1 Tim. 4:6) and in His sight (5:21), to understand these descriptions of Christ is crucial.

THE MESSIANIC LORD

The name "Christ Jesus" appears in twenty-five out of thirty-two references to Christ in the Pastoral Epistles, so these letters present an exalted Christology

---

38. For an excursus on the inspiration, infallibility, inerrancy, and authority of Scripture, see Lea and Griffin, *1, 2 Timothy, Titus*, 238–41.

39. For other doxologies of Paul, see Romans 11:36; 16:27; Galatians 1:5; Philippians 4:20; Ephesians 3:21.

where His role as Messiah is stressed.[40] He is the Lord (*kyrios*, 1 Tim. 1:2, 12; 6:3, 14; 2 Tim. 1:2), a title that also expresses the idea of exaltation. This term is especially useful for Paul. "Lord" refers to Him to whom the believers should pray and from whom the church should receive her commands. The coming parousia and judgment are also linked to these titles. Because He is a descendant of David according to the flesh (2 Tim. 2:8), saints will one day reign with Him (2:12). His future appearing will result in believers being rescued from all evil and brought safely into His heavenly kingdom (4:1, 8). As the Lord, He has the authority to send apostles (1 Tim. 1:1; Titus 1:1); enlist and commission "soldiers" for sacred duty (cf. 2 Tim. 2:3); and delegate, empower, and then evaluate such ministry (1 Tim. 4:6).

CO-SAVIOR WITH THE FATHER

The title "Savior" appears ten times in these three epistles. Six times it is a reference to God (1 Tim. 1:1; 2:3; 4:10; Titus 1:3; 2:10; 3:4), and the remaining four occurrences apply to Christ (2 Tim. 1:10; Titus 1:4; 2:13; 3:6). While salvation is willed by the Father, it is provided by Christ. That "Christ Jesus came into the world to save sinners" was a major affirmation by Paul (1 Tim. 1:15). Paul was more emphatic in the book of Titus when He called Christ "Jesus our Savior" (Titus 1:4) and "our great God and Savior,[41] Jesus Christ" (2:13).

Salvation in the Pastorals is both a present experience and an eschatological rescue. The problem of sin has been solved and eternal life is a sure promise (1 Tim. 1:16). As Co-Savior with God the Father, Christ shares in being the Source of grace, mercy, peace, faith, and love (1 Tim. 1:1, 14; 2 Tim. 1:2, 9, 13; 2:1; Titus 1:4), the Object of hope (1 Tim. 1:1), and "the promise of life" (2 Tim. 1:1). Salvation for sinners is the demonstration of His "unlimited patience" (1 Tim. 1:16). Simply stated, the elect "obtain the salvation that is in Christ Jesus" (2 Tim. 2:10). This exalted view of Christ may account for the absence of any reference to His sonship or to Christological subordination themes in the Pastoral Epistles.

THE APPEARANCE OF GOD'S GRACE

The word *epiphany* is used both in its nominal (*epiphaneia*) and verbal (*epiphainō*) forms to highlight various stages in Christ's ministry. Three such stages may be distinguished.

First, the term was used for the incarnation of Christ (1 Tim. 3:16; 2 Tim. 1:10; Titus 2:11).[42] The Incarnation was physical in that Christ came in a human

---

40. I. Howard Marshall, *The Origins of New Testament Christology* (Downers Grove, Ill: Inter-Varsity, 1977), 94.

41. The absence of the pronoun before "Savior" argues for a single person rather than a reference to both the Father and the Son.

42. Since the word is used in connection with "Savior," there may be an intended swipe at the pagan imperial cult (Hanson, *Pastoral Epistles*, 153) in which the word *epiphanē* was used for the king's birthday, coronation, or return from a journey (Kelly, *Commentary on the Pastoral Epistles*, 145).

body. This stress on the physical body (*sarx*) may have been a necessary rebuttal of the beginnings of Gnostic dualism present in the false teaching, a problem 1 John also treats. The manifestation of Christ in the flesh was in reality a manifestation of God's grace. Grace comes through Christ. In other words, Jesus is the personification, or better, the embodiment of the grace of God. This grace is given in Christ before time (2 Tim. 1:9–10), but was manifested in the Incarnation (1 Tim. 3:16; cf. Eph. 1:11; 2:5–10; 3:11; Rom. 16:25–26). By this, Paul affirmed both Christ's preexistence and God's precreation plan to provide salvation through Him. The appearance of grace "brought to light" the revelation of life and immortality made available through Christ's death and resurrection. The work of the incarnate Christ as an appearance of grace is the core of the gospel (2 Tim. 1:10; 2:10). Paul said "the grace of God that brings salvation has appeared to all men" (Titus 2:11). The prayer for all individuals, the will of God for all humankind, and the ransom for everyone correlates with the grace that has appeared to all.

Second, the word *epiphaneia* refers to the appearance of the grace of God at the time of individual salvation (Titus 3:4–5). What Paul had earlier termed "grace" was also said to be the appearance of "the kindness and love of God our Savior." What is significant about this passage is the appearance's timing. The circumstantial clause ("when the kindness and love of God our Savior appeared") is tied to the main clause which says "He saved us" (v. 5).[43] The time of the appearance is related to the time of the salvation. In other words, His grace makes an appearance whenever a person is saved. The basis of salvation is His mercy, and the saving process comes through rebirth and the renewal of the Holy Spirit. The results include justification by grace, the hope of eternal life, and the promise of an inheritance.

Third, the term *epiphaneia* is used of the return of Christ at His second advent (1 Tim. 6:14; 2 Tim. 4:1, 8; Titus 2:13). Paul commonly used the Greek term *parousia* for the return of Christ. In 2 Thessalonians 2:8 both terms, *epiphaneia* and *parousia,* appear together. The future appearance of Christ will result in His kingdom's consummation, the judgment of the living and the dead, and the bestowal of rewards for faithfulness and expectant waiting (2 Tim. 4:8).

THE RANSOM FOR ALL

The only occurrence of the word "ransom" (*antilytron*) in the New Testament is in 1 Timothy 2:6.[44] A ransom speaks of the price paid to free someone who has been held captive. The preposition *hyper,* which follows the word "ransom," stresses the substitutionary nature of Christ's work. While such substitution is potential for all, it is effective ("especially") for those who believe (1 Tim. 4:10).

---

43. For this emphasis, see Fee, *1 and 2 Timothy, Titus,* 203, who also notes that the two expressions "kindness" and "love" were used together in Hellenism and Hellenistic Judaism as the highest virtues of both deities and human rulers. Here Paul countered that the highest expression of both of these is the gracious salvation only God could provide in Christ.

44. The root *lytron* is used in Mark 10:45 followed by the preposition *anti* for a similar emphasis. Paul may have coined the term in this context from the truth in the Mark passage as a more formalized theological expression.

The sacrifice's voluntary character is underlined by the words, "gave Himself" (1 Tim. 2:6), thereby reflecting an undisputed Pauline idea (cf. Gal. 1:14; 2:10; Eph. 5:21; Titus 2:14).[45]

THE MODEL OF RIGHTEOUS SUFFERING

In 1 Timothy 6:13 the reference to God who gives life to everything may speak more of protection of life than the source of life, in light of the following statement about the testimony of Jesus at His trial before Pontius Pilate. Jesus Christ Himself provided the example for Paul to exhort Timothy. "Take hold of the eternal life to which you were called when you made your good confession in the presence of many witnesses" (v. 12). The audience for the charge was God the Father and Christ Jesus (v. 13), who far outrank any earthly procurator. The innocence with which Christ suffered is remembered in the charge for Timothy "to keep this command without spot or blame" (v. 14). Paul showed Timothy that his confession of faith in the death of Christ was a confession of the very center of the gospel message, and Christ's faithfulness before His death became the model for faithfulness for all ministry thereafter.

THE MEDIATOR BETWEEN GOD AND MAN

The term "mediator" (*mesitōs*) reflects the role of a go-between or negotiator who brings together two parties who either had no previous relationship, or having had one, found themselves at enmity. The need for a mediator presupposes the universal depravity of all humanity. The provision must come from someone who is satisfactory to God and can meet the needs of humanity at the same time. The reference to Christ as Mediator speaks more to His function than as a particular title. Inherent in the idea of a mediator is someone who "establishes a relationship which would not otherwise exist."[46] An emphatic connection exists between the humanity of Christ and His role as sole Mediator between God and the rest of humankind. This eliminates any thought of angelic or intermediary deities envisioned by Jewish-Christian Gnosticism. As the Mediator, Jesus, through His death and resurrection, established a new relationship between God and humanity. All that separates the Creator and His creatures was removed in Christ. Lea sees in the word "mediator" a link to the concept of covenant.[47] Similarly Hebrews contains three references to this term to speak of Christ's role in relationship to the new covenant (Heb. 8:6; 9:15; 12:24). Concerning the relationship of Christ to God in the immediate passage, Becker states, "the unity or oneness of the Mediator not only reaffirms the universality of access to salvation implied by the *heis theos* formula, but also stresses

45. For an extended discussion of the substitutionary atonement, see Leon Morris, *The Atonement* (Downers Grove, Ill.: InterVarsity, 1983), 106–31; and idem, *The Apostolic Preaching of the Cross* (Grand Rapids: Eerdmans, 1956), 9–59.

46. Albrecht Oepke, *Theological Dictionary of the New Testament*, trans. and ed. Geoffrey W. Bromiley (Grand Rapids: Eerdmans, 1964–76), s.v. "μεσιτας," 4:601.

47. Lea and Griffin, *1, 2 Timothy, Titus,* 90.

the sole means of salvation is the Christ-event."[48] A new arrangement has been established by Christ the "negotiator."

The designation "man" in reference to Christ in 1 Timothy 2:5 is meant to contrast Jesus as the Second Adam from the First Adam. As the Second Adam, He is the Head of a new humanity.[49] Paul indicated elsewhere that the reason for the incarnation of Christ was His redemptive death (Rom. 8:3; Gal. 4:5; Phil. 2:7–8; 1 Tim. 1:15). Also Hebrews 2:14 states, "Since the children have flesh and blood, he too shared in their humanity so that by death he might destroy him who holds the power of death—that is, the devil."

THE JUDGE OF THE LIVING AND THE DEAD

Reference to Jesus as Judge of the living and the dead is found in a context where eschatological judgment is motivation for authentic ministry. In light of the defections that will increase as the end of the age approaches, Paul exhorted Timothy to practice a bold ministry of the Word (including preaching, being prepared, correcting, rebuking, and encouraging) with patience and careful instruction (2 Tim. 4:1–2). As Judge, Christ will evaluate the ministries of those entrusted with the gospel. Believers will be judged and rewarded for their faithfulness, and unbelievers will be judged for their lack of faith.

The kingdom's consummation for the elect will follow the judgment at the end of the age (2 Tim. 2:12; cf. 1 Thess. 2:12; 2 Thess. 1:4–5; Gal. 5:21; 1 Cor. 6:9–10; 15:50; Eph. 5:5). Jesus' resurrection guarantees and qualifies Him to be not only the Judge of all the living and the dead, but also the Ruler of His kingdom. This may also have been behind the association of His descendancy from David with His resurrection in 2 Timothy 2:8 (cf. Acts 13:33; 17:31; Heb. 1:3; 10:12–13).

OTHER MINISTRIES OF CHRIST

In addition to the benefits of eternal life, Christ bestows other blessings and responsibilities on believers. Since He is God and cannot deny His own character, He will never be unfaithful (2 Tim. 2:11–13). Therefore, He can be a constant source of comfort and strength to Christians (4:22; 1 Tim. 4:6). Under His direction apostles were selected, strengthened, and appointed to service (1 Tim. 1:1, 12: 4:6; 2 Tim. 1:1; 2:2; Titus 1:1), and under His watchful "ever-presence" they served in their respective ministries (1 Tim. 5:21). Jesus will dispense eternal rewards for such faithful ministries when He returns (2 Tim. 4:8).

THE HOLY SPIRIT: THE AGENT OF REBIRTH AND INDWELLING ENABLER FOR MINISTRY

The Holy Spirit is mentioned only five times in the Pastorals directly (1 Tim.

---

48. O. Becker, *New International Dictionary of New Testament Theology* (Grand Rapids: Zondervan, 1975), s.v. "Covenant, Guarantee, Mediator," 1:375.

49. Lea and Griffin, *1, 2 Timothy, Titus,* 91; and Kelly, *Commentary on the Pastoral Epistles,* 63.

3:16; 4:1; 2 Tim. 1:7, 14; Titus 3:5).[50] Paul seemed to assume a familiarity with the Spirit's work, and the references indicate His role in the whole of salvation and service. The part played by the Spirit in Jesus' resurrection was labeled as *vindication* (1 Tim. 3:16). The vindication by the Spirit in this verse's poetical structure surfaces the connection with and contrast to Christ's incarnation. The emphasis argues for both the humanity and deity of Christ. If Romans 1:4 and 8:11 can be seen as true parallels, Christ's life and message were vindicated by the Holy Spirit when He raised Christ from the dead. Through resurrection, all that Christ had predicted and all that God provided through Him was shown to be trustworthy.

First Timothy 4:1 focuses on the Spirit's work of *revelation*. The Spirit warns of the apostasy that will afflict the church in the latter times. As discussed later, Paul saw these trends as present in the church when he wrote. The present tense of the verb "says" (*legō*) and the parallel "the Scripture says" (1 Tim. 5:18) give an indication of the role of the Spirit in inspiration. What the Holy Spirit "says" becomes Scripture. Paul knew that the Spirit was the Source of the prophetic message.[51]

In 2 Timothy 1:7 the Spirit's role as the *enabler* for ministry contrasts with one's deficiency without Him.[52] Paul urged Timothy not to be ashamed of his testimony or his association with those who, like Paul, were suffering for the gospel. In such circumstances the human spirit apart from God can easily suffer from "timidity" (*delias*). The Spirit of God gives the Christian various virtues of "power" (*dynameōs*), "love" (*agapēs*), and a "sound mind" (*sōphronismou*).[53] These virtues are essentials in the Christian walk of faith. Paul exhorted Timothy to have an assertive leadership in the power of the Spirit, in which love would be balanced with the wisdom needed in decision-making. Hence the Spirit enables the believer to think and serve boldly in the defense of the gospel (2 Tim. 1:8). While some have said verse 7 refers to ordination or to the Spirit's gifts for service in the church, it seems likely that it speaks of receiving the Spirit (because of the verb "give"). The Spirit given at conversion is the same Spirit who is operative in the believer's life, whether at ordination or in service.[54]

The Holy Spirit is also essential for the *preservation* of the gospel message (2 Tim. 1:14). "The standard of good words" Timothy was commanded to "retain" (2 Tim. 1:13) was also to be "guarded" with the help of the Holy Spirit (1:14; cf. 1 Tim. 6:20). The Spirit who had been "given" to them (2 Tim. 1:7) also

50. Some have debated whether the Holy Spirit is the referent in 1 Timothy 3:16 and 2 Timothy 1:7.

51. For other references to the prophetic function of the Spirit, see Acts 8:29; 21:11; Revelation 2:7, 11, 17, 29; 3:6, 13, 22.

52. Throughout the writings of Paul, "the spirit" the believer "receives" is always a reference to the Holy Spirit (Rom. 5:5; 8:15; 1 Cor. 2:2; 12:7; 2 Cor. 1:22; 5:5). See Knight (*Commentary on the Pastoral Epistles,* 371) for other arguments for identifying "the spirit" in this passage as the Holy Spirit.

53. Whereas this form is unique to the New Testament, other forms of the same word group are sprinkled throughout the Pastorals (1 Tim. 2:9, 14; 3:2).

54. For a defense of this position, see Towner, *Goal of Our Instruction,* 57.

"dwells within" (*enoikountos*) them to enable living for the gospel and to protect it as a "good deposit" (*kalēn parathekēn*) from God.

The Spirit's role in *regeneration* and *renewal* (Titus 3:5) will be discussed in the section on salvation. The Spirit who was active in Christ's ministry and in giving the Scriptures is the same Holy Spirit who empowers believers to protect and proclaim the gospel. The Holy Spirit, the personal Agent of God, is active in regenerating sinners, bringing them into a life of renewed relationship with God.

SALVATION, THE GOSPEL OF GRACE

The portrayal of God the Father and Christ the Son as Savior has shown that salvation is a central theme in the Pastorals. Seven liturgical passages reflect a crystallization of teaching which outlines the essentials of the doctrine of salvation. Whether originating in the hymnody of the early church or in catechistic summaries, these formulae of salvific statements serve to define the gospel, which was to be inherited, guarded, and transferred from Paul to his associates. Salvation in these epistles can best be understood by examining the seven central passages that most completely set forth the concepts involved.[55]

1 TIMOTHY 1:15:
CHRIST'S INCARNATION FOR SALVATION

As the first formalized statement in the Pastorals, 1 Timothy 1:15 briefly captures the message of salvation.[56] First Timothy 1:12–16 forms a larger unit in which the history of salvation is linked with Paul's own personal experience as the prototype (*hypotypōsis*) for the salvation of sinners. The statement brings together the work of Christ and the salvation He provides. Verse 15 summarizes the purpose of the incarnation of Christ to save sinners. The preceding context (vv. 13–14) roots this salvation in the mercy and grace of God and the faith and love that are in Christ Jesus. Paul used himself as a prototype to show that salvation has been extended to anyone regardless of the extent of his or her sinful past. The means by which that salvation is received is through belief that rests on Jesus Christ (v. 16). The experience of salvation begins at the point of faith but will not be complete until its future consummation in eternal life.

1 TIMOTHY 2:5–6:
ONE GOD AND ONE MEDIATOR FOR ALL

The theme of salvation dominates the entire context of 1 Timothy 2:1–7. The prayer, title, will of God, and work of Christ in these verses all support the universal interest of salvation. The "testimony" phrase, which concludes this section, demonstrates the traditional or liturgical nature of this passage. The passage has

---

55. See Towner, *Goal of Our Instruction*, 75–119 for an excellent exegetical analysis of these central passages.

56. This is the first of five "faithful sayings" (cf. 1 Tim. 3:1; 4:9; 2 Tim. 2:11; Titus 3:8). For an extended treatment of these five passages, see George Knight III, *The Faithful Sayings in the Pastoral Epistles* (Grand Rapids: Baker, 1979).

a threefold emphasis on "all men" as observed in the prayers that should be prayed, the will of God, and the ransom Christ provided (vv. 1, 4, 6). The phrase "all men" was also quite possibly used to oppose the false teacher's spiritual elitism. Further evidence against the teaching of the apostates emerges in the use of the term "one" for God and for Christ the Mediator. Jews and Gentiles alike are related to God through the work of Christ. The inclusivity of "all men" is balanced by the exclusivity of the "one" and only way to be reconciled to God (John 14:6). "The universally accessible God has provided an equally accessible Mediator."[57] Salvation originates in the will of God who "wants all men to be saved and come to a knowledge of the truth" (1 Tim. 2:4; cf. 2 Tim. 1:9; Titus 1:2; Gal. 1:4; Eph. 1:5, 9). Christ's substitutionary death is the means by which He accomplishes His role as the sole Mediator between God and humanity (1 Tim. 2:5; cf. the previous discussion on the ransom ministry of Christ).

1 TIMOTHY 3:16:
THE MYSTERY OF GODLINESS, CHRIST'S SAVING CAREER

Creatively designed in six poetical lines is this statement of the "mystery of godliness." When Paul used "mystery" (*mysterion*) in reference to salvation, he had in mind the eternal plan of God to provide His grace through the historically revealed work of Jesus Christ (Rom. 16:25; Eph. 1:9–10; Col. 1:24–27). "Godliness" (*eusebia*, in the phrase "the mystery of godliness") is defined by Kelly as "Christian life and faith."[58] The six lines of poetry contain the content of the mystery, which is a composite of antitheses centering around salvation made available in Christ. The first antithesis contrasts the "revelation" of the Incarnation ("He appeared in a book"), which culminated in the crucifixion and "vindication" of His resurrection "by the Spirit." The second antithesis contrasts the realm of humanity ("the nations") with that of the angels, since both were witnesses of the salvation provided by Jesus Christ. What was revealed in the events described in the first two lines was witnessed by those mentioned in the next two lines. The third set of antithetical lines speaks of the proclamation of the Christ-provided salvation, with its contrast between the world and heaven ("glory"). The argument through all three sets of lines explains that what was effected through Christ was proclaimed, and what was proclaimed was believed. The thrust of verse 16 explains that what took place in history became the message to be preached. The only right response to the message is faith.

2 TIMOTHY 1:9–10:
GOD'S GRACE GIVEN IN CHRIST JESUS

As another passage that explains the gospel, these verses are bracketed with references to the grace of God in verses 8 and 11. As this section occurs in an exhortation to Timothy, the theme of preaching is repeated throughout the pericope.

---

57. Towner, *Goal of Our Instruction*, 86.
58. Kelly, *Commentary on the Pastoral Epistles*, 89.

God's purpose before time and His provision within time are two major notes sounded in this section. The goal of God's "calling" in salvation is a holy life, a theme repeated throughout these letters to Timothy and Titus. Salvation is not merited by humankind, but is grounded in God's attributes and purpose (Eph. 2:8–9; Rom. 9:11–12). To reinforce this, Paul stated that God purposed to provide grace through Christ "before the beginning of time" (2 Tim. 1:9). The eternal past was thereby connected to the temporal manifestation of "our Savior Christ Jesus." The effects of the "gospel" events were the destruction of death and the revelation of immortality and life (1:10). Christ's resurrection defeated death and made both the quality and the extent of eternal life a possible reality.

2 TIMOTHY 2:8–13:
CHRIST'S RESPONSE TO BELIEVERS

The theme of salvation occurs in 2 Timothy 2:8, 11–13. Verse 8 describes the work of Christ in two statements: His resurrection and His role as a Descendant of David. This reversal of the order of these two events may be explained by the wider context (v. 18) where Paul referred to a tenet of the false teachers, namely, the belief that the resurrection of believers had already taken place.

The stress in this passage is that the salvation of the elect has been made available "in Christ Jesus" (v. 10). The testimony of suffering for the gospel and the continual need for it to be preached form the backdrop for a series of "if" and "then" clauses in verses 11–13, all of which are designed to motivate faithfulness in the face of persecution or opposition. The first two (vv. 11–12a) are positive, and the second two (vv. 12b–13) anticipate potential negative experiences. The protasis of each statement considers a believer's action, while the apodosis contemplates an appropriate response by Christ. In the first condition, identification with the death of Christ assures participation in the resurrected life (v. 11). In the second conditional statement, endurance in the present promises a co-reign with Christ in the future (v. 12). Third, the warning against denial of Christ (perhaps a reference to the contemporary problem of apostasy at Ephesus) is the danger of eschatological denial by Christ (v. 12). Fourth, the abiding hope for enduring in the face of external pressures is that, even if one might fall into unfaithfulness, Christ will remain faithful to both His nature and His people and will not withdraw His faithfulness from them (v. 13). The third condition seems to warn against one that may not even have a genuine relationship with the Lord (James 2:14–26), and the fourth condition speaks to a more momentary lapse. In this way Paul was warning the church of the apostates' fate and was discouraging those who may have begun to follow them.

TITUS 2:11–14:
GRACE'S CALL TO HOLINESS AS BELIEVERS AWAIT HIS RETURN

While Titus 2:11–14 describes the benefits of salvation through the work of Christ, these verses also function as an exhortation to live the Christian life. This passage is a single sentence in the Greek text which has as its subject the grace of God. Parallel to what Paul said in 1 Timothy 2:3–6 and 6:14, what has actually appeared is the One in whom "the grace of God that brings salvation has appeared" (Titus 2:11; 1 Tim. 1:9–10). The references to the "epiphany" in Titus 2:11, 13 frame the instructions of "present-tense Christianity" with the first and second advents of Christ. The epiphany of God's grace brought salvation "to all men" at the first advent of Christ, and the epiphany of God's glory will come at His second advent at the end of the present age. Between these two advents the salvation provided by Christ is to be experienced personally and practically.

The apostle's heartbeat centers on the ethics of holiness. Before Paul mentioned salvation's provision he stressed what is to be renounced (ungodliness) and what is to be pursued (self-control and godliness). The connection of salvation with instruction is noteworthy. There is no thought that salvation can be experienced without the expectation of living a different kind of life. The ethic of denial includes ungodliness (*asebia*) and worldly passions (*kosmikas epithymias*). The three virtues of self-control (*sōphronōs*), uprightness (*dikaiōs*), and godliness (*eusebōs*) coordinate with one's relationship with self, others, and God respectively. The Christian life in the "present age" is to be consistent with the eschatological expectation. Salvation is meant to transform the Christian's present life, while waiting for the "glorious appearing of our great God and Savior, Jesus Christ" (v. 13). The salvation initiated by Christ's first coming will be completed at the Second Advent (cf. 1 Tim. 1:16; 4:8; 6:12, 14; 2 Tim. 1:12, 18; 2:12; 4:1; Titus 1:2). Redemption's substitutionary nature is highlighted by Christ's self-sacrifice for (*hyper*) those He saves. Two reasons for His saving people appear in Titus 2:14, which reflects the Old Testament passages of Psalm 129:8 and Ezekiel 37:23. Redemption's purposes are to redeem from sin and to cleanse a people for His own use, "eager to do what is good" (Titus 2:14). That God and Christ can be seen cooperating in the salvation process is typical of these epistles.

TITUS 3:3–7:
GOD'S GRACE THROUGH FAITH ALONE UNTO GOOD WORKS

The final "faithful saying" in the Pastorals is found in Titus 3:3–7. Verses 4–7 are a single sentence in the Greek text. Verse 3 describes the condition of humanity apart from God's grace. The need for salvation always serves as a background for a proper appreciation of its provision. Fee argues that this passage has a twofold function: a capsulization of the gospel of grace which is unmerited by works, and an encouragement at the same time that the purposeful end of salvation includes good works.[59] The major truths brought forward in this passage are God's grace and the Holy Spirit's work as they each contribute to the process.

The *basis* of salvation is stated in typically Pauline terminology. The appearance of Christ is paraphrased by the attributes of "kindness" and "love."[60] Both the negative and the positive are truths with which to be reckoned. "He saved us"

---

59. "More likely this is an early creedal formulation that presents Pauline soteriology (the doctrine of salvation) in a highly condensed form" (Fee, *1 and 2 Timothy, Titus*, 202–3).

60. The term used here is *philanthrōpia*, which expresses the special love God has toward humanity, which motivated the giving of His Son.

not because of the righteous activities of human merit (v. 5; cf. Rom. and Gal. where law-keeping is discounted), but because of His grace, mercy, and love (1 Tim. 1:12–16; Titus 3:5). Lea has rightly captured this truth when he affirmed, "Salvation depends solely and completely on God's grace, displayed in 'his mercy,' revealed and achieved by his Son, Jesus Christ, and applied to humankind by the Holy Spirit."[61] This is the only passage in the Pastorals where all three members of the Trinity are referred to together.

The *meaning* of salvation is found in this pericope in three metaphors: rebirth, renewal, and justification.[62] The word for "rebirth," *palingenesia,* in verse 5, is used only here and in Matthew 19:28. In Titus, the reference is to the present experience of new life granted to the individual. Matthew's reference seems to relate to Israel's rebirth in the era to come, since the emphasis there is on Christ's future reign on His glorious throne when the twelve apostles will sit alongside Him judging the twelve tribes of Israel. Thus present salvation and future eschatology are again linked in Pauline fashion.

The absence of the preposition *dia* before the word for "renewal" (*anakainōsis*) indicates that a single event is more likely in view rather than a sequence of them. The "rebirth and renewal" are a work "done by the Holy Spirit." The renewal is one of reconciliation whereby the saved person is granted access to the Father by the Spirit (Eph. 3:18). Differing interpretations surface for the concept of "washing," which precedes the above two terms.[63] It seems most consistent to take "washing" as a reference to the spiritual cleansing which is effected through the ministries of the Holy Spirit.

Justification is the third metaphor for salvation in the passage. Justification is when God, solely because of His grace and mercy, declares righteous the sinner who responds to His grace with faith in the Lord Jesus Christ (cf. Luke 18:13–14; Rom. 5:1, 9). Justification is a favorite theological concept of Paul (Rom. 3:24; 5:1, 9; 1 Cor. 6:11; Gal. 2:16–17; 3:24).

The *results* of God's salvific work will ultimately be fully realized in the eschaton. Three are mentioned in this passage. Believers are qualified through salvation for a future inheritance ("become heirs," Titus 3:7; cf. Gal. 4:7; Rom. 8:17). The logical connection from being a member of the family to being an heir is suggested throughout the New Testament (John 1:12; Rom. 8:14, 17; Gal. 4:6–7; Eph. 2:6; Heb. 6:17–20; James 2:5). As Lea concludes, "Christian salvation results in adoption into God's family, which in turn makes believers 'heirs.'"[64] While awaiting that inheritance, the saved have "the hope of eternal life." This phrase spells out the two other results or benefits of salvation. A present benefit is their hope which is both in Christ as their Savior as well as *for* Christ at His coming, which

61. Lea and Griffin, *1, 2 Timothy, Titus,* 322.

62. Fee sees both the newness of the relationship with God and the newness of the recreated inner man as the thrust of these metaphors.

63. See Fee, *1 and 2 Timothy, Titus,* 204–5, for a sampling and evaluation of the various views.

64. Lea and Griffin, *1, 2 Timothy, Titus,* 325.

will result in ultimate deliverance. The third part of the package is both the present and future experiences of eternal life (1 Tim. 1:16; 6:12; Titus 1:2).

CONCLUSION

In each of the formulaic statements, the theme of salvation is central to the citations. God's provision of salvation in the work of Christ on earth serves to refute the errorists, as well as to crystallize the gospel as the "sound teaching" which is to be received, guarded, and then entrusted to each succeeding generation of the church. The purpose and grace of God has made salvation available to humans who can receive eternal life by faith in the person and work of Jesus Christ. Through His death and resurrection, the ransom for sin has been paid, the believer redeemed, and a mediated relationship with God has been established with the promise of life and ultimate immortality. The salvation provided in the past can be experienced in the changed life of the present, while awaiting the future consummation.

THE CHURCH: THE HOUSE AND FAMILY OF GOD

The church's roles and relationships in these Pastoral letters stress the family connections within the community of faith. This emphasis may have been because of what was being done to family units by the false teachers and their heresies. Paul employed a series of illustrative phrases to place the church in a proper frame of appreciation and to elevate the importance of the conduct of its members in relationship to God and the truth.

THE ROLE OF THE CHURCH

The household of God. Some see this word "household" as a reference to the temple imagery of the believer (1 Cor. 3:16; 6:19; 2 Cor. 6:16; Eph. 2:21–22). However, the weight tips in the Pastorals toward domestic imagery (2 Tim. 2:21; cf. 1 Cor. 4:1; 9:17; Gal. 6:10; Eph. 2:19). Speaking of the church as the "household of God" (1 Tim. 3:15), Paul highlighted the family relationship shared by the believer and the heavenly Father (Gal. 6:10; 1 Peter 4:17; 1 Tim. 3:4–5). The applicational instruction therefore takes the shape of fulfilling stewardships, taking proper responsibility, and maintaining proper order. Support for this conclusion is the parallel in 1 Timothy 3:5 where the elder is qualified to rule the "house of God" by the way he manages his own household. Furthermore, the illustration of the need for pure and clean vessels in 2 Timothy 2:20 argues for the identity of the church as the house of God. This metaphor served to elevate the community of believers as the "location" of God's presence on earth. The church has become His base of operation in the world.

The church of the living God. God calls the church to be His people. As the Exodus event in the Old Testament served to call out a people for God (Deut. 5:2–6; 7:6–9), the work of Christ established the church of God as the people of God in the New Testament (1 Cor. 3:11; Eph. 2:20; 4:4–6; 1 Peter 2:4–8). In contrast to the pagan deities of Ephesus, the phrase "the living God" (1 Tim. 3:15) demanded that Christians understand their participation in the church and reflects the dynamic relationship between them and God. He established the church, so it belongs to Him. Therefore, every activity within the church is of great importance to Him and should be carried out at His direction.

The pillar and foundation of the truth. According to 1 Timothy 3:15 and 2 Timothy 2:19 the church functions as a stable platform for the message of the gospel. The term *pillar* (*stylos*) carries the idea of strength and support, as does the term for foundation (*hedraiōma*). The two form a hendiadys to express the same basic idea. The church is to be the "unshakable repository of the truth."[65] Since the gospel is "the truth," it must be upheld at all costs. As Lock put it, "Each local church has in its power to support and strengthen the truth by its witness to the faith and by the lives of its members."[66]

The people of God's own possession. A similar echo of Old Testament ideas is found in the phrase, "a people that are His very own" (Titus 2:14; cf. 2 Tim. 2:19). The first reference highlights the purity which should characterize God's people, while the second reference (2 Tim. 2:19) stresses their identity. The church as the people of God today, like Israel in the Old Testament, should be holy and pure as she represents that identification with God. The citation of Numbers 16:5 in 2 Timothy 2:19 is appropriate since both passages deal with the recognition of true leaders as distinct from false intruders.

THE RELATIONSHIPS WITHIN THE CHURCH

The strategic purposes for the church in the world have obvious implications for the lives of its members. First Timothy 3:15 states that Paul thought it important that believers know "how to conduct themselves in God's household, which is the church of the living God." A living God demands living patterns that accurately present to the community the difference a life with Him can make.

The motive of testimony. Sprinkled throughout the passages exhorting believers to display godly characteristics are a series of motivational statements pertaining to the church's testimony in the community. Not only must the church uphold the doctrinal content of the faith, but its members' lifestyles should make an impact on the world. As a leader, Timothy was to live in such diligence that "everyone might see . . . [his] progress" (1 Tim. 4:15). Instructions concerning widows were ordered "so that no one may be open to blame" (5:7). Instructions concerning younger widows and master-slave relationships were designated "so that God's name and our teaching may not be slandered" (6:1; cf. 5:14). Younger women, in the way they functioned at home, were to insure that "no one will malign the word of God" (Titus 2:5). Young men were to conduct themselves in such a way as to eliminate the criticism of the opposition (2:8). These negatives are balanced with a final positive motivation to slaves to serve their masters "so that in every way they will make the teaching about God our Savior attractive" (2:10). In keeping with the major

65. Towner, *Goal of Our Instruction,* 132.

66. Lock, *Pastoral Epistles,* 44.

themes of the Pastoral Epistles, character enhances the potential effects for the message of the gospel to be heard by the unsaved. Godly character is exhorted regardless of sex or socioeconomic status. How various segments of the church are to act and how they are to be treated were of concern to Paul. Since the church is God's household, and each believer is a member of His family, it is not surprising that family roles are the basic metaphor of illustration. Men and women are given general instructions that are gender-specific, but not age-restricted.

The prayers of men. Four different words were used (1 Tim. 2:1) to describe the kinds of prayer men were to pray: request (*deēsis*), prayer (*proseuchē*), intercession (*enteukis*), and thanksgiving (*eucharistia*). The concerns of prayer are both external and internal. The external concerns are for all people in general and governmental leaders in particular (2:1–2). The specific goal in prayer for others is their salvation, since that is the will of God (2:4). The internal concern is for believers to lead peaceful and quiet lives. Christians will be in position to be God's agents of evangelism if they are not living in antagonism or hostility with the community at large. As Towner states, "Moreover, providing a peaceful and orderly society was the state's domain, so prayer for it was calculated to ensure that the best possible conditions for spreading the gospel were obtained."[67] Hence the church's prayers for the world and recognition of the authority of the state are fundamental to the church's evangelistic mission. This kind of prayer life was to be carried out in holiness before God and in harmony with other people (2:8).

The propriety of women. Paul's instructions to women in general are related to their attire and their attitude. Moderation and modesty are to characterize their dress as they come to the assembly. Their works rather than their wardrobe are to be their reputation builders (1 Tim. 2:9–10). Both 1 Timothy 2:9–10 and 1 Peter 3:1–6 seek to protect women from being more identified with their culture than with Christ.

A second concern pertains to the submission of women to the leadership of the church. First Timothy 2:11–15 has been the subject of much debate, especially in recent years. One view sees the restrictions on women as timeless, while the other sees them limited to the local situation at Ephesus. The passage contains a chiasmus (inverted parallelism). The section opens and closes with the phrase "in silence" (*en hēsychia*). The silence is not absolute but the demonstration of a meek and quiet spirit (1 Peter 3:4), which is teachable and submissive, without challenging their leaders' authority.[68] The immediate occasion for prohibitions regarding the Ephesian women was due to their gullibility and instability (1 Tim. 5:11–13; 2 Tim. 3:6–7). Another reason might be that some women were possibly neglecting their roles as wives and mothers (1 Tim. 5:11–15).

The phrase "in all submission" describes the manner in which women are to learn. The idea of learning is contrasted with teaching, and submission is the opposite of exercising authority. Thus the central thrust is that teaching and ruling with authority is to be done by qualified men, with the women adopting a posture of sub-

67. Towner, *Goal of Our Instruction*, 203.
68. For a brief excursus on women in the ministry, see Lea and Griffin, *1, 2 Timothy, Titus*, 103–5.

mission. The meaning of the phrase "to have authority" (*authenteō*, a word that occurs only here in the New Testament) has been a matter of significant debate. Whether the verb means "to exercise authority" or "to usurp authority" is debated, as is the question whether the teaching involved false teachers or correct content. Also at issue is whether the two infinitives, "to teach or to have authority" refer to separate actions or a singular concept.[69]

The supporting statements in verses 13–15 must inform these questions. The illustrations of creation and the Fall both seem to give evidence that male leadership was not the result of the errors at Ephesus, but was designed by God from the beginning, as both illustrations show. The order of creation and deception at the Fall argue for male responsibility in different ways. The order of creation is plain enough. At the Fall, both the deception of Eve and the fact that responsibility still rested with Adam argue again for male leadership. Though Eve sinned first and was deceived, sin was passed on to the human race through Adam (Rom. 5:12). Hence the chronological priority of creation and the reversed chronology of the Fall were Paul's argument for why women are to be learners and not teachers, and to be in submission and not in authority. First Corinthians 11:2–16 also cites the creation order in clarifying the differing roles of men and women. These roles have nothing to do with the question of equality as the illustration from the order and roles within the Trinity in the Corinthian passage demonstrates.

The meaning of "will be saved through childbearing" (1 Tim. 2:15) is another highly debated portion in this text. Some have suggested that it means a woman lives out her spiritual salvation by her godly behavior.[70] Others see a reference to the birth of Messiah.[71] The NIV and the marginal reference in the Good News Bible suggest that a woman is promised safety "through" the act of childbearing.[72] In the context it seems preferable to interpret this phrase to mean that a woman will be saved from the error of Eve (usurping the leadership of the man) by carrying out her God-ordained role as a godly mother. This fits better with the entire pericope which functions as a "role" clarification for church gatherings. Her role is spiritual and is significant to the proper function of the church.

More specific instructions are given on the basis of gender, age, and social circumstances. Desired qualities for the *older men* of the congregation were that that they be temperate, worthy of respect, self-controlled, and sound in their faith, love, and endurance (Titus 2:2). They are not to be spoken to in harshness, for they deserve to be treated as one should treat his father (1 Tim. 5:1). *Younger men* are

69. For a survey and discussion, see G. W. Knight, "'AUΘENTEW in Reference to Women in 1 Tim. 2:12," *New Testament Studies* 30 (1984): 143–57, and A. C. Perriman, "What Eve Did, What Women Shouldn't Do," *Tyndale Bulletin* 44 (1993): 129–42. Also see Ann Bowman, "Women in Ministry: An Exegetical Study of 1 Timothy 2:11–15," *Bibliotheca Sacra* 149 (April–June 1992): 193–213.

70. Fee, *1 and 2 Timothy, Titus,* 76–77; and Lea and Griffin, *1, 2 Timothy, Titus,* 102.

71. The problem is that the death of Christ, not His birth, is said to be the means of salvation. Also it is the action of "childbearing," not the noun "childbirth," which is emphasized.

72. The problem here is that some godly women do die in childbirth. Also a different word is used in the Pastorals for physical deliverance (1 Tim. 3:11; 4:18).

exhorted to be self-controlled and follow good examples of integrity, seriousness, and soundness of speech (Titus 2:6). In keeping with their age they are to be related to as brothers (1 Tim. 5:1).

Older women should possess reverent behavior which should be free of slanderous speech and addictions (Titus 2:3). One of the strategic roles they play is in their instruction of younger women (1 Tim. 5:2). Paul urged Timothy to instruct the church to treat older women with respect like that shown to a mother. In their ministry they are to model how the home should function. *Younger women* are to be instructed by the older women to love their husbands and children. Like the younger men, they are to be self-controlled with a stress on purity. Their homes and families are to be a major preoccupation where they are to demonstrate kindness and submission to their husbands (Titus 2:4–5). As expected from the previous relationships, a young woman should be treated as a sister (1 Tim. 5:2).

Paul wrote in some length regarding the care the church was to give to widows (1 Tim. 5:3–16). Widows who have children or grandchildren are to be cared for by their own families because it is fair as a form of repayment to them, and it is pleasing to God as a means of making one's faith practical. *Needy widows* were to be qualified by the church for support by reason of age, need, and character. The need came in the absence of any supporting family. The age was set by the apostle as sixty and above. The list of character qualities included her dedication to God (hope and prayers), her husband (faithful to one man), and her sensitivity to the needs of others (acts of hospitality and goodness). *Younger widows* were encouraged to get married, have children, and manage their homes in order to avoid the split loyalties that come with the mixture of motives and temptations.

Slaves were taught that their masters were worthy of "full respect" and believing masters ought to receive service which is even "better," because of the personal relationships as believers (1 Tim. 6:1–2). Such submission should not be selective nor retaliatory (i.e., back talk and theft). The instructions recognized that bosses might be believers (6:1) or unbelievers (6:2). Submission was exhorted regardless of the spiritual disposition of their masters. Slaves were to earn the trust of their bosses with the goal of attracting them to the Savior (Titus 2:9–10). Thus the exhortations to the slaves fit the central thrust of the salvation theme in the Pastoral Epistles. Guthrie comments with regard to slavery that for Paul "it was more important . . . to avoid reproach against the name of God and his doctrine . . . than to make an abortive revolutionary attempt to undermine the social structure."[73]

The *rich* were given counsel about how they could use their money as a source of blessing. Paul counseled believers to be unemotionally attached to their wealth. The attitudes one should have toward money should be governed by the realities of the life in the age to come (1 Tim. 6:19; cf. Matt. 6:20). Two temptations the rich should avoid are pride and the speculative notion that wealth will always be available (1 Tim. 6:17). Instead, all hope is to be grounded in God, and money is to be used generously for good deeds and needy causes (6:18). This will keep one's

73. Guthrie, *Pastoral Epistles*, 109.

perspective on life more balanced and will help secure eternal treasures (6:19; cf. Luke 12:15).

CHURCH LEADERSHIP:
RESPONSIBLE PEOPLE WITH CHARACTER

The discussion of church leadership is distinguished in the Pastorals more by the emphasis on character qualifications than by the descriptions of official functions. In fact, contrary to the notion that the central thrust of the Pastorals was to establish the order of the church, 2 Timothy does not include a single reference to church offices or its leaders' qualifications. The positions of leadership described were not the hierarchical positions reflected in the first few centuries following the New Testament, nor were they the capacities filled by Paul's associates sent to help clarify and qualify other men for the leadership of their assigned churches. Rather, the functions described most closely resemble the early church at Jerusalem where the Twelve served with a body of "presbyters" (Acts 11:30; 15:2) and when Paul and Barnabas appointed elders in the churches of Cilicia (14:23). Two dominant themes emerge from the Pastorals: first, the church is best served by leaders who model lifestyles of integrity; and second, a major responsibility of the leadership is to uphold the sound doctrine of the gospel of the grace of God.

THE OFFICES OF THE CHURCH

The term *presbyteroi* was used nontechnically of older men (1 Tim. 5:1; Titus 2:2) and technically as an official title of leadership within the church. The terms used for the official leadership positions in the church were probably adapted from previous use in other institutions. For example, the term "elder" had a rich heritage in the Jewish community (Acts 11:30; 15:2, 4, 6, 22–23; 16:4; 21:18; James 5:14; 1 Peter 5:1). The qualifications of the offices of the elder/overseer and deacon receive the greater prominence. Some distinguish between the elders (*presbyteroi*) and the bishop (*episkopos*), and others have argued for a separate office of a class of widows. The fact that the term "bishop" is found only in the singular and "elders" is always in the plural (with the exception of 1 Tim. 4:14) can be explained within their respective contexts, depending on whether the reference is to the qualification of a single leader or to the group as a functioning body. Further, it seems best to see the two terms as referring to the same office and function in light of their interchangeability in Acts 20:17–28 and especially Titus 1:5–9. In Acts 20:17 they are called "elders" and in verse 28 they are designated "overseers." Paul told Titus to appoint "elders" (Titus 1:5), but when their qualifications were outlined, the term "elder" appears in verse 6 while "overseer" is the title in verse 7. Aspiring to the office of an elder is a noble pursuit (1 Tim. 3:1). While a specific age requirement was not set forth, a certain level of natural and spiritual maturity was expected. Illustrations of this are seen in the qualifications that refer to marital and parental functions and the fact that a novice was not to be appointed (1 Tim. 3:4; Titus 1:6).

Though the origin of the office of deacon is not clear, both Philippians 1:1 and 1 Timothy 3:8–10 argue for its existence in the early days of the church. Acts

6:1–6 may be the background of its origin since in that passage the verb *diakoneō* ("to serve") describes the function of those selected to relieve the apostles, but this is less than certain since the term for service is a generic one for ministry. The recognition of the office, the association with the elders, and the promises of reward for excellent service all argue for the presence of the office by the time of the Pastorals.

Functions of the elder. Elders/overseers are responsible for instruction in and defense of the faith (1 Tim. 3:9; 4:11–13; 5:17; 2 Tim. 2:2; 3:16–17; Titus 1:9; 2:1, 15), the administration of worship and related activities (1 Tim. 2:1–8; 5:3–16), oversight of the discipline and restoration of sinning members (1 Tim. 5:20, 22), and the successful transfer of the ministry to a new generation of faithful men (2 Tim. 2:2). Some may have a more concentrated role of communicating the Word of God than others (1 Tim. 5:17).

Respect for the office. Three specific instructions describe the treatment of those who hold the office of an elder. First, those who direct the church's affairs are worthy of double honor, especially if accountable for the preaching and teaching of the Scriptures (1 Tim. 5:17).[74] Second, accusations against elders were to be screened and considered only after adequate verification by two or three witnesses.[75] The public rebuke for those exposed not only serves to correct the sinning elder but also warns the whole congregation of God's serious approach toward sin. A third admonition stipulates that various treatments of leaders should be done with equity rather than favoritism (5:21).

Ordination. The Pastoral Epistles are not clear on whether ordination was or should be practiced. Some say ordination is implied by the phrase "the prophecies once made about you" (1 Tim. 1:18) and the mention of the gift given to Timothy where the elders "laid their hands upon you" (4:14). It is difficult to know whether this practice was limited to the charismatic era of New Testament apostles and prophets, was something that applied to Timothy alone, or whether it indicated a practice that can continue today. On the question of succession, Hanson is correct when he states, "The nature of succession in the ministry was certainly present, but it was regarded as primarily a succession of teaching or tradition rather than as an 'apostolic succession' of ordination reaching back to the apostles."[76]

QUALIFICATIONS OF CHURCH LEADERS

The contrasts in the Pastorals between the false teacher's character and teachings and what should be the church servant's character and teachings is quite obvious and is undoubtedly intentional. If the errorists could be identified by their behavior, how much more important it was for church leaders to validate their min-

---

74. Opinions are divided on whether remuneration or simply rights of honor are intended by the phrase "double honor." For a brief discussion see Fee, *1 and 2 Timothy, Titus,* 128–30.

75. This reflects the Old Testament system of justice (Deut. 19:15) and the teaching of Jesus (Matt. 18:15–20).

76. Hanson, *Pastoral Epistles,* 37.

istry by their conduct. The virtue lists of the elders related to their private and public lives. How they acted at home and in the community would be some indication of how they would act within the church. The following definitions of these offices are offered, and, where appropriate, the virtues required of an elder are contrasted with those vices Paul exposed in the false teachers.

To be "above reproach" translates the words *anepilēmpton* (1 Tim. 3:2) and *anegklētos* (Titus 1:6) and connotes the fact that an elder should be one who is free from any deficiency of character that could call into question his ability to lead the church.

"The husband of but one wife" (*mias gynaikos andra,* 1 Tim. 3:2) has been interpreted in a variety of ways.[77] At minimum it called for a husband to be singularly focused on his wife and devoted to her. The parallel phrase that is used of the widow in 1 Timothy 5:9 is the same with only the genders reversed and may indicate a marital history of one mate. Regardless of the choices or one's interpretation of this phrase, an unquestioned testimony in one's marital life is the point. There is no question that marriage is not only permitted, contrary to the false teachers who were forbidding marriage (1 Tim. 4:3), but also an elder's marriage is one of the qualifying evaluations for leadership.

An elder "must manage his own family well" (*idiou oikou kalōs proistamenon,* 1 Tim. 3:4; cf. Titus 1:6). Leadership within the home, especially in relationship to his children, help indicate whether a leader is able to lead God's children in His household. The logic is stated in the immediate context. "If anyone does not know how to manage his own family, how can he take care of God's church?" The verb carries the idea of "standing before" others with the skills of effective leadership.

Contrary to the false teachers who were "conceited" (*tetyphōtai,* 1 Tim. 6:4; *tetyphōsmenoi,* 2 Tim. 3:3), "arrogant" (*hyperōphanoi,* 2 Tim. 3:2), "self-lovers" (*philautoi,* 3:2), and "boasters" (*alazones,* 3:2), an elder must refrain from being "overbearing" (*mē authadē*), literally, "not self-willed or stubborn," Titus 1:7). Church authority rests in Christ as the head of the church. Therefore, an elder must serve Christ, the Head, and must have the body of the church as his highest interest.

An elder should not be "quick tempered" (*mē orgilon,* Titus 1:7). While anger may be inevitable, the Scriptures call anger sin when it rises quickly, is left unresolved, broods into bitterness, is human-centered, or has revenge in mind (cf. James 1:20; Eph. 4:26–27; Col. 3:8). In ministry people can try an elder's patience. The root issues of selfishness, insecurity, and feelings of inferiority need to be addressed to slow a quick temper.

---

77. Interpretations include the prohibition of polygamy, the necessity of marriage, the prohibition of remarriage, disqualifying a divorced man, and a faithful husband. For an extended discussion, see Eldon Glasscock, " 'The Husband of One Wife' Requirement in 1 Timothy 3:2," *Bibliotheca Sacra* 140 (1983): 255. For further discussion on marriage and divorce issues in general, see C. E. B. Cranfield, "The Church and the Divorce and Remarriage of Divorced Persons in Light of Mark 10:1–12," in *The Bible and the Christian Life* (Edinburgh: T. & T. Clark, 1985), 229–34.

Freedom from "drunkenness" (*mē paroinon,* 1 Tim. 3:3; Titus 1:7) is imperative to preserve the clear judgment required of those who make churchwide decisions. While absolute abstinence is not commanded, preoccupation with drink is. By application, all addictive behaviors that might lure one away from the high calling of leadership must be avoided.

Not being a "violent" man (*mē plēktēn,* 1 Tim. 3:3; Titus 1:7) is another essential qualification. Striking out at others surfaces a lack of self-control. In both passages where this characteristic is mentioned, it follows the reference to wine. This may indicate a cause-effect relationship. Impaired judgment may result in impaired actions. The false teachers were described as "brutal" (*anēmeroi,* 2 Tim. 3:3) and "rash" (*propeteis,* literally, "reckless," 3:4). Neither is desirable in an elder.

Besides the warning against drunkenness, a more general requirement of being "temperate" (*nēphalian,* 1 Tim. 3:2) is advocated as well. Soberness from all physical and spiritual excesses enables the leader to be self-restrained under all circumstances. Balance, whether in diet or doctrine, is critical to effective shepherding.

Elders should avoid "pursuing dishonest gain" (*mē aischrokerdē,* Titus 1:7). This is an obvious contrast to the false teachers "who think that godliness is a means to financial gain" (1 Tim. 6:5). Elders may be remunerated, but the purest motives, when it comes to money, must be maintained. Because the "love of money is a root of all kinds of evil" and "some people eager for money, have wandered away from the faith and pierced themselves with many griefs" (1 Tim. 6:10), one cannot be too careful here to maintain an "above reproach" attitude regarding money.

The countering solution (*alla*) to the greediness implied in the previous requirement is for the elder to be "hospitable" (*philoxenon,* 1 Tim. 3:2; Titus 1:8). Entertaining strangers or guests not only guards from greed; it also serves as an invitation for opening the door of opportunity to model and communicate the gospel message. Exhortations throughout the Scriptures reveal hospitality should extend to believers and to those still in the world. Hospitality is "love expressed."

Whereas the false teachers masqueraded their desire for money beneath the mask of ministry (1 Tim. 6:5, 10; 2 Tim. 3:2), Paul said a leader could not be a lover of money (*aphilargyron,* 1 Tim. 3:3), since the "love of money is a root of all kinds of evil" (6:10). The ministry is no place to get rich or be consumed with the desire for more money. Contentment in whatever financial condition one finds himself is what Paul modeled and taught for all.

An elder is also "one who loves what is good" (*philagathon,* Titus 1:8). The errorists were "not lovers of good" (*aphilagathoi,* 2 Tim. 3:3). What is wholesome and worthwhile deserves the leader's highest loyalties. What a man thinks about (Phil. 4:8) determines his life's direction. Godly leaders should point their congregations to noble causes which have redeeming and eternal values.

Effective leadership demands that elders be "self-controlled" (*sōphrona,* 1 Tim. 3:2; Titus 1:8). This term suggests being able to think with a "sound mind."

There is no replacement for a level-headedness in the ministry which protects the church from the excesses, extremes, and tangents that could pull the church in all the wrong directions. Having self-control is the opposite of being "lovers of pleasure" (*philēdonoi*, 2 Tim. 3:4) and "without love" (*astorgoi*, 2 Tim. 3:3).

One who would lead the church should also be "upright" (*dikaion*, Titus 1:8). This word means to rule righteously without partiality or prejudice. This is the opposite of being "slanderous" (*diaboloi*, 2 Tim. 3:3). God's righteous standard is the principle of rule in His house. As leaders pattern their lives after God, they provide the church with an appropriate model to be imitated.

In contrast to being "unholy" (*anosioi*, 2 Tim. 3:2) with "seared" (*kekaustēriasmenōn*, 1 Tim. 4:2) consciences, is the quality of being "holy" (*hosion*, Titus 1:8). This means to be pleasing to God by having an unpolluted life. This term reflects a practical rather than a positional holiness before God. It is the visible expression of invisible righteousness (cf. 1 John 3:7).

A "disciplined" (*enkratē*, Titus 1:8) elder is one who is allowing God to exercise control of his life. This quality is the fruit of walking by the Spirit (Gal. 5:23). It is a necessary additive to faith for an effective and productive ministry (2 Peter 1:6). Mind, emotions, and will need to be kept in submission under God's mighty hand.

While a dominant description of the end times will be a "falling away" from the faith (*apostēsontai*, 1 Tim. 4:1), the teaching responsibility of an elder demands that he "must hold firmly to the trustworthy message as it has been taught" (*antechomenon tou kata tēn didachēn pistou logou*, Titus 1:9). Support of the truth is to be the church's and pastor's burden (cf. 1 Tim. 3:15). A different term is used in 1 Timothy 3:2 (*didaktikon*) to stress the ability necessary to handle the Word of God, which is the guideline for all preaching, teaching, and counseling.

The word "respectable" translates the Greek *kosmian* (1 Tim. 3:2). This relates to orderliness and matches what Paul wrote elsewhere on how the church should be administered (1 Cor. 14:40). A careless pastor will produce a careless people. Neither are options for God's church.

In dealing with people, the elder should always be "gentle" or reasonable (*epieikē*, 1 Tim. 3:3). This is a quality of gentleness and forbearance that allows the overseer to handle difficult and trying times without losing control or becoming frustrated with those difficult people he serves.

Linked to being reasonable is the requirement not to be "quarrelsome" (*amachon*, 1 Tim. 3:3). A leader of God's people cannot be prone to fighting or quick to engage in contention. Constant debate and arguments hinder the peacefulness that reflects godly wisdom (James 3:17). One of the most pronounced denunciations of false teaching was its promotion of "controversies" (*ekzētēseis parechousin*, 1 Tim. 1:4; cf. 6:4; 2 Tim. 2:14–16, 23; Titus 3:9).

An elder called to exercise oversight over God's flock "must not be a recent convert" (*mē neophyton*, 1 Tim. 3:6). The idea within the imagery of this Greek term is "not newly planted." The temptations to pride and self-deceit are too great. The possibility of a church's ministry being disrupted becomes more likely when a convert is elevated to a position of leadership too quickly. Leadership demands mentoring, and mentors earn the title by earning respect over a period of time.

Finally, the elder should "have a good reputation with outsiders" (*matyrian kalēn echein apo tōn exōthen,* 1 Tim. 3:7). Like other age-groups in the church, the instructions Paul gave with regard to elders ends with a word of motivation by one's testimony. Excellence of reputation with the unbelieving community protects one from falling "into disgrace and into the devil's trap." The world needs no ammunition which can be aimed toward the church as an excuse for their unbelieving responses. Protecting the reputation of the gospel continues to be a priority emphasis in the Pastoral Epistles.

THE PROPER HONOR OF ELDERS

The elder is worthy of "double honor" for serving well in preaching and teaching the Word of God (1 Tim. 5:17). Remuneration is based on the principle from Deuteronomy 25:4 and the statement of the Lord in Luke 10:7. Bringing charges against an elder should not be tolerated without proper corroboration.[78] The purpose of public discipline is for the warning of the entire church.

THE DEACON

The office. The word "deacons" is used only in 1 Timothy 3:8 and Philippians 1:1 (along with the singular "deacon" in 1 Tim. 3:12) to refer to a church office. The references to Phoebe (Rom. 16:1) and Paul (Col. 1:23) as servants probably relate more to function than office. The office of deacon most likely developed out of the needs of the church. Acts 6:5–6 never called the seven "deacons," but the need and the service provided in Jerusalem may have been a forerunner to the office as it was later developed.

The qualifications of deacons. The requirements for deacons (1 Tim. 3:8–10; 12–13) bear many similarities to those for elders. Their personal, family, and church life also qualify them for service. Deacons are to be "worthy of respect" (*semnous,* 1 Tim. 3:8) because of their exemplary character. The nature of their serving among the people of the church demands that they be sincere (*mē dilogous,* literally, "not double-tongued," 1 Tim. 3:8). Somewhat less stringent than the elder requirement, a deacon cannot be "indulging in much wine" (*mē oinō pollō prosechontas*). Like the elder, the deacon cannot be guilty of "pursuing dishonest gain" (*mē aischrokerdeis*) in dishonest or shady money-making schemes. Instead, one must "keep hold of the deep truths of the faith with a clear conscience" (*echontas to mystērion tēs pisteōs in kathara syneidēsei*). Again like elders, deacons must have a model family life by being "irreproachable" (*anenklēoi,* 3:10), "the husband of but one wife" (*mias gynaikos,* 1 Tim. 3:12), and able to manage "his children and his household well" (*teknōn kalōs proistamenoi kai tōn idōn oikōn,*

---

78. The "two witnesses" requirement in accusations is rooted in Deuteronomy 17:6 and 19:15 (cf. Matt. 18:15–17).

3:12). Distinct from the elder, the deacon is promised honor in a more long-range perspective: "Those who have served well gain an excellent standing and great assurance in their faith in Christ Jesus" (v. 13).

For a certain group of women, 1 Timothy 3:11 interjects a list of qualifications almost identical to those of the deacons. Some writers interpret "women" (*gynaikas*) as a reference to the office of deaconess, whereas others say it refers to deacons' wives. In the Pastorals Paul used the noun *gynē* for both women (1 Tim. 2:9–12, 14) and wives (1 Tim. 3:2, 12; 5:9; Titus 1:6). The fact that in 1 Timothy 3:2 and 10 the word refers to the wives of elders and deacons respectively seems to argue for that option as the best interpretation for verse 11.[79] Furthermore, the qualifications of these women are treated separately from the men who serve as deacons. This would thus argue against seeing them as identical in role. Discussing them along with the deacons, however, suggests the women did serve in some capacity. This then called for their having four characteristics: being "worthy of respect" (*semnas*), "not malicious talkers" (*mē diabolous*), "temperate" (*nēphalious*), and "trustworthy in everything" (*pistas in pasin*). Their involvement in serving with their husbands requires a commensurate maturity. Regardless of how one interprets 1 Timothy 3:11, it is interesting to note Paul's respect for Phoebe, who is called a servant (*diakonon*) of the church (Rom. 16:1). This might argue for a more formal capacity of service for women within the early church. In addition, the early church soon established an office for deaconesses. These passages must have served some justification for such a practice.[80]

THE CHRISTIAN LIFE: TRUTH INCARNATE

In the Pastoral Epistles, Christian experience is carefully balanced between the responsibilities for what one believes and how one behaves (1 Tim. 4:16). Two foci form the fusion of a life and ministry of integrity: a commitment to the truth of the gospel and a life so managed that one's conscience and testimony for the sake of the gospel are pure (1:18–19).

A commitment to the truth. A ministry of integrity centers around the truth. Various descriptions point up the content side of the ministry. The message is defined as "the glorious gospel of the blessed God" (1 Tim. 1:11). The revelation that God has extended grace to sinners and offers eternal life through His Son Jesus Christ is the heart of the gospel. The gospel is called "the faith,"[81] "the truth,"[82]

79. Knight, *Commentary on the Pastoral Epistles,* 171, further advances that the absence of any marital status or fidelity requirement as with the other deacons argues for them being the wives of the deacons already addressed. This would explain as well their insertion in the deacon qualification list.

80. See Kelly, *Commentary on the Patoral Epistles,* 83–84.

81. First Timothy 1:2, 9; 3:9; 4:1, 6; 5:8; 6:10, 12, 21; 2 Timothy 3:8; cf. Galatians 1:23; Philippians 1:25, 27.

82. First Timothy 2:4; 4:3; 2 Timothy 2:18, 25; 3:7; Titus 1:1; cf. Galatians 5:7; 2 Thessalonians 2:12.

"sound teaching,"[83] and "or godliness."[84] The faith's objective content is more in the foreground than the subjective response of belief in the message. This can be explained by the circumstances that prompted the correspondence. Paul assumed his readers were familiar with the right personal response of faith in the gospel, but they needed to be reminded of its centrality to life and its cruciality to a defense against error.

Paul used various verbs to validate this observation. Exemplary phrases like "pointing out" (1 Tim. 4:6 NASB); "brought up in" (4:6); "training" (4:8); "command and teach" (4:11); "devote yourself to the public reading of Scripture, to preaching and teaching" (4:13); "keep reminding" (2 Tim. 2:14); "rightly handling" (2:15); "equipped" (3:17); "continue" (3:14); "preach . . . be prepared . . . correct, rebuke, and encourage . . . careful instruction" (4:2); and "rebuke" (Titus 1:13) are all variations of the advice Paul gave to Titus, "You must teach what is in accord with sound doctrine" (Titus 2:1).

To summarize, the truth was to be held on to personally (1 Tim. 3:9), guarded carefully (6:20; 2 Tim. 1:4), preached boldly (1 Tim. 4:11–13; 2 Tim. 4:2), and entrusted to others faithfully (2 Tim. 2:2). Such actions assumed that the gospel message would be preserved and protected for future generations in the church.

The commitment to character. The opening statement of purpose in 1 Timothy 1:5 frames the entire ethic of the Pastoral Epistles: "The goal of this command is love, which comes from a pure heart and a good conscience and a sincere faith." These kinds of loving relationships have already been discussed. What remains is to consider the essential virtues that are given repeated emphasis in these letters.

A "good" (1 Tim. 1:5, 19) and "clear" (3:9; 2 Tim. 1:3) conscience is appropriate for believers as opposed to the false teachers' "seared" (1 Tim. 4:2) or corrupted (Titus 1:15) consciences. In the case of the latter, their rejection of truth resulted in their immoral behavior. In all references to a right conscience, faith and sound doctrine are seen as close associations.

The words that cluster around the theme of faith are also instructive. The verb "believe" (*pisteuō*) is used to reflect the necessary prerequisite for a relationship with Christ (1 Tim. 1:16; 3:16; 2 Tim. 1:12) or God (Titus 3:8). Those without salvation in Christ Jesus are without faith. The noun "faith" (*pistis*) was used for both the subjective acceptance of the message of Christ (1 Tim. 1:4–5; 2 Tim. 1:13; Titus 1:1) or the ongoing virtue of the Christian life (1 Tim. 1:4; 19; 4:12; 2 Tim. 1:5; 2:22; 3:10). By far the most common use of the term was for the objective message of the gospel. The adjective "faithful" (*pistos*) occurs eight times. The active sense always refers to one's relationship to Christ (1 Tim. 4:3, 10, 12; 5:16; 6:2). In the passive sense the term denoted faithfulness (1 Tim. 1:12; 3:11; 2 Tim. 2:2).

Eusebia ("godliness") is the word used in the Pastorals to describe authentic Christian experience. Both the negative descriptions of the false teachers and the apostle's positive instructions with respect to this term showed a necessary connec-

83. First Timothy 1:10, (NASB); cf. 6:3; 2 Timothy 1:13; 4:3; Titus 1:9; 2:1.

84. First Timothy 3:16; 4:7–8; 6:5–6; Titus 1:1.

tion between one's relationship to God and the behavior one demonstrates in good works. "Godliness" has been defined as "the manner of life in Christ that a knowledge of the truth produces."[85] The reason for such a linkage lies in the problem with the false teachers. They wrongly said godliness centered in knowledge (2 Tim. 3:5), while they were motivated by greed (1 Tim. 6:5). Their claim to godliness did not produce the result in good works which a genuine *eusebia* always does. False claims to esoteric knowledge were fundamentally at odds with the genuine walk that comes from the true knowledge of saving faith.

Paul viewed *eusebia* as the bridge between faith and good works. Good works flow from genuine faith. The necessity of good works is mentioned fourteen times in the Pastorals. Though salvation is not based on such works (2 Tim. 1:9; Titus 3:5), they are, nevertheless, the purpose or goal of salvation (Titus 2:14). Therefore, the apostle's imperatives in Titus 3:8 are worth rehearsing: "This is a trustworthy saying, and I want you to stress these things, so that those who have trusted in God may be careful to devote themselves to doing what is good. These things are excellent and profitable for everyone."

---

85. Towner, *Goal of Our Instruction*, 152 (cf. Titus 1:1).

8

A THEOLOGY OF HEBREWS

BUIST M. FANNING

Effective Christian preachers have a compelling vision of Jesus Christ which they communicate forcefully to their listeners to lead them to view their circumstances differently and to respond with strengthened faith and commitment. This is the model exemplified in the Epistle to the Hebrews, which is not so much an epistle as a sermon in written form (a "word of exhortation" as the writer described it in 13:22; cf. Acts 13:15). This sermon was addressed to Christians who were under great pressure because of their allegiance to Christ.

The central vision of Christ presented by the "preacher" who wrote Hebrews is a striking one, based squarely on the Old Testament (especially Psalm 110) and on an accurate knowledge of Jesus' earthly life, death, and resurrection, and deepened by inspired theological reflection on the meaning of these things for Christian faith and life. The writer's compelling view of Christ is that of God's Son and High Priest exalted now to the position of greatest honor in God's presence. This picture of Christ gives the right perspective for seeing who He is and all that He fulfilled in God's eternal purpose by following the path of obedience set out for Him. It also gives a clear view of what He meant for the readers in their situation. With this view of the exalted Son, they could look in a fresh way at their own difficult circumstances and move forward with renewed hope along the trail He blazed for them.

BUIST M. FANNING, B.A., Th.M., D.Phil., is professor of New Testament studies at Dallas Theological Seminary.

This view of Christ is also the central point at which the major theological themes of Hebrews converge.[1] In the following pages, the theology of Hebrews will be presented in three major sections: Christ and His Mission, From Old to New, and The Christian Life. The picture of Christ as exalted Son and High Priest appears prominently in each of these.

CHRIST AND HIS MISSION

Christology is the central focus in all the theology of Hebrews, and two titles of Christ are central to its Christology: Son of God and High Priest. Around these two focal points all the major ideas in Hebrews concerning Christ's person and work can be located. Christ as High Priest is actually the more distinctive and important idea in the theology of the book, but Christ as Son of God is foundational.

JESUS CHRIST AS SON OF GOD

References to Jesus as "Son" or "Son of God" occur frequently in Hebrews, and they reveal Him in three vital stages of Sonship,[2] which are distinguishable theologically but are intermingled quite freely in the argument of the epistle. These stages and their interconnections may be seen in microcosm in the finely crafted introductory sentence, Hebrews 1:1–4. There Jesus Christ is portrayed as the *preexistent, eternal Son* who from eternity past shared fully in the divine nature and activity of God. As such He became the full and final revelation of God in His role as *incarnate, earthly Son,* who provided complete purification for sin. Because of His obedience to God's saving purpose, He has been made heir of all, *exalted Son of God,* seated in the position of greatest honor in God's heavenly presence. In the following discussion of these stages of sonship, other passages and Christological themes that do not explicitly use the term "Son" but present similar ideas will also be considered.

Preexistent, eternal Son. As mentioned, the opening sentence of Hebrews introduces Jesus Christ as the Son of God in three senses, but its presentation of Him as the preexistent, eternal Son shows that this stage is the indispensable basis and anchor of the other two. Jesus' mission and accomplishments as incarnate and then exalted Son were rooted in the fact that, as the eternal Son, He shared fully in the divine nature and activities of God during His preexistent state. In Hebrews, the Son's ontology and function are inseparable.[3]

1. Cf. David J. MacLeod, "The Doctrinal Center of the Book of Hebrews," *Bibliotheca Sacra* 146 (1989): 291–300.

2. Cf. George Milligan, *The Theology of the Epistle to the Hebrews with a Critical Introduction* (Edinburgh: T. & T. Clark, 1899), 74–88; William R. G. Loader, *Sohn und Hoherpriester: Eine traditionsgeschichtliche Untersuchung zur Christologie des Hebräerbriefes* (Neukirchen-Vluyn: Neukirchener, 1981); and Mikeal C. Parsons, "Son and High Priest: A Study in the Christology of Hebrews," *Evangelical Quarterly* 60 (1988): 200–208.

3. See the comments on this interplay in Richard N. Longenecker, *The Christology of Early Jewish Christianity* (London: SCM, 1970), 154–55; and Geerhardus Vos, *The Teaching of the Epistle to the Hebrews* (Grand Rapids: Eerdmans, 1956), 73–83.

The first verse and a half of Hebrews emphasize the change from old to new: God spoke in various ways but incompletely in earlier days, but now He has spoken fully and uniquely in His Son. The phrase "in a Son"[4] is the fulcrum point of the opening paragraph (1:1–4), because it culminates the striking initial statement about God's revelation and then becomes the focus for seven descriptions of the Son which follow in verses 2b–4. These descriptions show why the revelation through Him has completely superseded all earlier forms. Taken together they communicate forcefully the author's compelling and central vision of Christ as exalted Son and High Priest, because they are skillfully arranged in a ring structure which begins and ends with His exaltation.[5] Starting in verse 2b with Christ's appointment as heir of all (a reference to His exalted status after the Resurrection and Ascension), the author backed up to show the basis for this in the Son's preexistent activity in Creation (v. 2c), His sharing in the very essence of God (v. 3a), and His ongoing providential activity (v. 3b). The author then began to come back around the circle with a mention of the Son's purification of sins (v. 3c)—as a quick summary of the themes of His earthly life, suffering, and high priestly accomplishment—which were developed extensively in later chapters. Finally, the descriptions come full circle with references to the Son's session at God's right hand and His inheritance of an exalted name (vv. 3d–4). In this section attention is given to the three descriptions of the Son's protological nature and activity. The statements about His earthly and exalted status will be discussed later.

The Son's preexistence is clearly seen in the statement of His role in the creation of the world: He was the agent or mediator through whom God created the universe in all its dimensions of time and space (1:2c). This theme is developed also by John and Paul (John 1:3, 10; Rom. 11:36; 1 Cor. 8:6; Col. 1:16). In Hebrews the specific contextual link with the preceding description (Heb. 1:2b) emphasizes how fitting it is for Christ to become heir of all things based on His work of redemption and subsequent exaltation, since He was the one involved in the creation of all things as well. But the wider theological truth evoked here is the Son's existence prior to all created things (His "protological preexistence"[6]) and His participation with the Father in divine works. The interpretation of this verse offered by Athanasius long ago appears to be correct: "When the sacred writers say, 'Who exists before all the ages,' and 'by whom He made the ages,' they clearly proclaim the eternal and everlasting being of the Son and designate Him as God Himself."[7]

---

4. The Greek noun is cited without an article, which as elsewhere in Hebrews (3:6; 5:8; 7:28) stresses the inherent character of the one who is Son. The descriptions that follow elaborate on the details of His character.

5. John P. Meier, "Structure and Theology in Heb 1:1–14," *Biblica* 66 (1985): 168–89.

6. This refers to the person or thing in question existing before creation, not just before his own manifestation, see R. G. Hamerton-Kelly, *Pre-existence, Wisdom and the Son of Man* (Cambridge: Cambridge Univ., 1973), 21.

7. Athanasius, *Orations against the Arians* 1.12, cited in Philip Edgcumbe Hughes, *A Commentary on the Epistle to the Hebrews* (Grand Rapids: Eerdmans, 1977), 40.

Jesus' role in Creation as the preexistent Son is mentioned in other verses in Hebrews in addition to the opening sentence. In 1:10 the words of Psalm 102 are cited as referring to the Son: "In the beginning, O Lord, you laid the foundations of the earth, and the heavens are the work of your hands."[8] The quotation of the psalm is then continued (1:11–12) to bring out the eternal existence entailed by this role in Creation: "They will perish, but you continue . . . they will be changed, but you are the same and your years will never end." While Jesus' everlasting existence asserted here is explicitly focused on *future* eternity, there is an implicit inclusion of eternity past as well, in verse 10 and in the phrases "you continue" and "you are the same" (vv. 11–12). Later in the epistle (3:2–6) by a complex analogy the faithfulness of Jesus in God's house is compared to that of Moses, and His honor is shown to be superior to that of Moses in the same way a Son's honor surpasses a servant's in the house (3:5–6). But His honor is also likened in 3:3 to the superior honor afforded to the *builder* of a house compared to the house itself. This point is anchored by the reminder in verse 4 that God is the builder of all things. These verses also then allude to the role the Son played in Creation and the divine status which this implies for Him.[9]

After citing the Son's role in Creation, the author of Hebrews moved back a step in his cycle of descriptions to portray the Son as sharing eternally in the divine nature of the Father (1:3a). This is communicated in two phrases that form the predicates of a participle expressing timeless existence (*ōn,* present participle of the verb *eimi*): "being the radiance of God's glory and the exact representation of His essence." The first of these phrases employs a word suggesting the "shining forth" of the sunlight (*apaugasma* from *augēs,* "sunshine"), denoting not the passive "reflection" of God's glory but the active "radiance, shining forth" of one who in Himself possesses the divine perfections.[10] To use a similar illustration, the idea is that the Son shines forth with God's glory in the way the sun radiates its own light, not in the way the moon reflects that of the sun. Similar statements about the Son are made in John 1:14; 17:4–5; and 2 Corinthians 4:6.

8. This is supported by the use of *pros* in 1:7–8. Cf. Walter Bauer, William F. Arndt, and F. Wilbur Gingrich, *A Greek-English Lexicon of the New Testament and Other Early Christian Literature,* 2d ed., rev. F. Wilbur Gingrich and Frederick W. Danker (Chicago: Univ. of Chicago, 1979), 710.

9. This conclusion is resisted by Harold W. Attridge, *The Epistle to the Hebrews: A Commentary on the Epistle to the Hebrews,* Hermeneia, ed. Helmut Koester (Philadelphia: Fortress, 1989), 110, on the ground that Jesus is not explicitly labeled "the builder," but he is unable to give a satisfying sense to the verses without it. For arguments in favor of the view taken here, see Mary Rose D'Angelo, *Moses in the Letter to the Hebrews,* SBL Dissertation Series 42 (Missoula, Mont.: Scholars, 1976), 164–77.

10. Henry George Liddell and Robert Scott, *A Greek-English Lexicon,* revised and augmented by Henry Stuart Jones, with the assistance of Roderick McKenzie, with a supplement edited by E. A. Barber (Oxford: Clarendon, 1968), 274. See also Gerhard Kittel, *Theological Dictionary of the New Testament,* trans. and ed. Geoffrey W. Bromiley (Grand Rapids: Eerdmans, 1964–76), s.v. *"augazō, apaugasma,"* 1:507–8; and R. P. Martin, *The New International Dictionary of New Testament Theology* (Grand Rapids: Zondervan, 1975), s.v. *"apaugasma,"* 2:289–90.

The second phrase in Hebrews 1:3a changes the image but makes the same point: the Son is the "exact representation of his being." The predicate here (*charaktēr*) can be used of the impression or mark made by a die in minting coins,[11] and so the phrase is rightly translated "the exact representation of His nature" (NASB), or "he bears the very stamp of his nature" (RSV), or "he is the perfect copy of his nature" (JB). The Greek word translated "nature" (*hypostasis*) is also significant to note, since it denotes here the "substantial nature, essence, actual being"[12] of God, which the Son is thus said to reproduce exactly.

What then is the point of these clauses describing the Son's nature? Cullmann has summarized it well in saying that these attributes "express the Son's complete participation in the deity of the Father."[13] This conclusion is disputed, however, by Rissi, who interprets the present participles ("being the radiance . . ." and "upholding . . .") of verse 3 as describing not preexistence but the *present* essence of the Son, not His eternal existence but His meaning for the community in the present.[14] Of course these descriptions have a bearing on the Son's present significance for the church, but the eternal dimension cannot be excluded, and the latter is the essential foundation for the former.[15] Wilckens also misreads the structure of thought expressed by the participles in verse 3 when he attributes these qualities to Jesus only as the *exalted* Son: "Since God's glory has impressed itself on Him as the One exalted by God, He is its reflection and image."[16] But this verse patently moves through the three stages of sonship emphasized in Hebrews and does not picture His exalted status only: "who *being* the radiance of his glory and the impress of his essence, . . . *having made* purification of sins, *sat down* at the right hand."[17]

The Son's full participation in the nature of the Father and unique relationship with Him is, of course, very significant in a statement on His revelatory role, which is the larger point of 1:1–4. Who could better reveal the Father fully than the Son who reflects His essence exactly? This connection is elaborated elsewhere in the New Testament, most notably by John (John 1:14–18; 14:8–9; Col. 1:15).

11. J. Gess, *The New International Dictionary of New Testament Theology*, s.v. "*charaktēr*," 2:288–89.

12. Bauer, Arndt, and Gingrich, *A Greek-English Lexicon of the New Testament*, 847; Helmut Köster, *Theological Dictionary of the New Testament*, s.v. "*hypostasis*," 8:585.

13. Oscar Cullmann, *The Christology of the New Testament*, rev. ed., trans. Shirley C. Guthrie and Charles A. M. Hall (Philadelphia: Westminster, 1963), 304.

14. Mathias Rissi, *Die Theologie des Hebräerbriefs: Ihre Verankerung in der Situation des Verfassers und seiner Leser* (Tübingen: Mohr [Paul Siebeck], 1987), 46.

15. The present or imperfect of *eimi* is often used, as here, not of exclusively *present* circumstances but of absolute, *eternal* existence, especially when placed in contrast to an aorist of *ginomai*, as here in verses 3–4. See John 1:1–6; 8:58; Colossians 1:15–18; Revelation 1:4; 1:8; 4:8; 11:17; and comments by Brooke Foss Westcott, *The Epistle to the Hebrews*, 2d ed. (London: Macmillan, 1892; reprint, Grand Rapids: Eerdmans, 1984), 9, 17.

16. Ulrich Wilckens, *Theological Dictionary of the New Testament*, s.v. "*charaktēr*," 9:421.

17. This point is made, on the basis of the tenses involved and the overall thought-structure, by Meier, "Structure and Theology in Heb. 1:1–14," 179–82.

The final description of the eternal Son in the descriptive cycle of Hebrews 1:1–4 is the reference to His ongoing relation to the creation: "sustaining all things by his powerful word" (1:3b). This phrase expresses the cosmological role of the Son in sustaining and maintaining His created work (as in Col. 1:17), but includes also His providential activity of carrying the creation forward toward its God-ordained end.[18] This also shows the Son's identity with the Father, since such providential activity was attributed to God in the Old Testament (Isa. 46:3–4).

These three descriptions of the protological nature and activity of the Son (Heb. 1:2–3) share a common conceptual background which requires further theological inquiry. All three clauses utilize expressions that occurred commonly in Hellenistic Judaism to describe "wisdom" or the "Word." This usage is sourced ultimately in the Old Testament, where, for example, Proverbs 8:22–31 portrays wisdom in personified terms as existing with God before and at Creation. In intertestamental Judaism such phrasing became commonplace. In the Wisdom of Solomon, wisdom is said to be "the fashioner of all things" (7:22; 8:6), "present when God made the world" (9:9), "a pure emanation of the glory of the Almighty. . . . a reflection [*apaugasma*] of eternal light . . . an image of his goodness" (7:25–26), and the one who pervades and penetrates all things and orders the whole universe (7:24, 27; 8:1). Eternal existence is ascribed to wisdom in Sirach 24:9. The Word, especially in Philo, is described as the image of God, His agent in Creation, His firstborn son, the exact representation [*charaktēr*] of divine power, and the one through which God sustains all things.[19] It is clear that Hebrews 1:2–3 describes the Son by means of language drawn from this conceptual background, but this is not new with Hebrews, since as already noted, John and Paul used similar phrasing to characterize Jesus' relation to God and the world. What has come under debate recently is how this "Wisdom Christology" should be interpreted in Hebrews.

Robinson and Dunn have advanced the interpretation that wisdom language like that in Hebrews 1:2–3 is a "way of speaking" about Jesus which does not assert His *personal* preexistence and sharing of the divine nature, but simply that the preexistent Wisdom of God came to be embodied so completely in the human Jesus that these things could be said of Him as the bearer of divine wisdom. In Dunn's words,

> *Christ alone so embodies God's Wisdom, that is, God's creative, revelatory and redemptive action, that what can be said of Wisdom can be said of Christ without remainder. . . .* It is the act and power of God which properly speak-

---

18. Westcott, *Epistle to the Hebrews,* 13–14.

19. For these and other references in Philo, see Attridge, *Epistle to the Hebrews,* 40–45 or Hugh Montefiore, *Commentary on the Epistle to the Hebrews* (San Francisco: Harper and Row, 1964), 36. Other references of this sort to wisdom are surveyed in John F. Balchin, "Paul, Wisdom and Christ," in *Christ the Lord: Studies in Christology Presented to Donald Guthrie,* ed. Harold H. Rowden (Downers Grove, Ill.: InterVarsity, 1982), 208.

ing is what preexists; Christ is not so much the preexistent act and power of God as its eschatological embodiment.[20]

Though it is helpful to be aware of the background of wisdom-language, it is plainly wrong to see impersonal wisdom as the topic here. The verses clearly speak of a specific person, the Son, Jesus, of whom these things are predicated.[21] To dismiss the statements of the text as merely "a way of speaking" is simply forced exegesis to fit the demands of a larger case which Dunn and Robinson try to trace through the New Testament.[22] In fact, wisdom terminology as a way of reflecting on Jesus' person and mission is important in several strata of New Testament theology,[23] and it seems clear that it should be traced to Jesus' own teaching about Himself as the full and personal expression of God's wisdom and essence. In Matthew 11:16–30 (also see 23:34, and parallels in Luke 7:34–35; 11:49), Jesus identified Himself as God's wisdom and as God's Son who alone can reveal the Father, and then called people to come and learn from Him, just as wisdom (personified) called for followers in Judaism (see Prov. 8:1–21; 9:1–6; Wisdom 6:12–20; 9:17–18; Sirach 6:18–31; 24:19–22; 51:13–30, esp. 51:23, 26).[24]

There are two other ways in which the personal preexistence and eternality of the Son are implicitly reflected in Hebrews. One of these (to be discussed in more detail in the next section) can be seen in references to His "becoming incarnate" (2:9, 14) and "coming into the world in a body prepared for him" (10:5–9). These patently portray the Son as a preexistent, heavenly Being who entered this world and took on a human nature at a certain point in history in fulfillment of God's plan of salvation. While this was the beginning of His earthly and human existence, it was clearly not the start of His existence; it was not His absolute beginning.

20. James D. G. Dunn, *Christology in the Making: A New Testament Inquiry into the Origins of the Doctrine of the Incarnation* (Philadelphia: Westminster, 1980), 209. See also John A. T. Robinson, *The Human Face of God* (London: SCM, 1973), 149–61; L. D. Hurst, "The Christology of Hebrews 1 and 2," in *The Glory of Christ in the New Testament: Studies in Christology in Memory of George Bradford Caird*, ed. L. D. Hurst and N. T. Wright (Oxford: Clarendon, 1987), 156; and George B. Caird, "The Development of the Doctrine of Christ in the New Testament," in *Christ for Us Today*, ed. W. Norman Pittenger (London: SCM, 1968), 75–80.

21. Cf. John P. Meier, "Symmetry and Theology in the Old Testament Citations of Heb 1:5–14," *Biblica* 66 (1985): 531–32. See also Charles F. D. Moule, "Jesus of Nazareth and the Church's Lord," in *Die Mitte des Neuen Testaments: Einheit und Vielfalt neutestamentlicher Theologie: Festschrift für Eduard Schweizer*, ed. Ulrich Luz and Hans Weder (Göttingen: Vandenhoeck & Ruprecht, 1983), 184. Moule considers the view of Jesus as simply the human bearer of divine wisdom/Word to be an "oversimplification" which does not do justice to the reality reflected in the New Testament.

22. Robinson professes to be conscious of the danger of "adapting the biblical writers' view of pre-existence to one that we can find acceptable" (*Human Face*, p. 152, note), but he seems intent on doing just that.

23. In regard to Pauline thought, see Balchin, "Paul, Wisdom and Christ," 204–19.

24. Felix Christ, *Jesus Sophia: Die Sophia-Christologie bei den Synoptikern* (Zürich: Zwingli-Verlag, 1970), 80, 99, 119, 153–54. Suggs shows how this wisdom Christology is central to Matthew's presentation of Jesus (M. Jack Suggs, *Wisdom, Christology, and Law in Matthew's Gospel* [Cambridge, Mass.: Harvard Univ., 1970], 44–61, 95–97).

The other reflection of the Son's preexistence and eternality is found in statements about His indestructible life and His continuing forever. In Hebrews
7:15–17, Jesus' eternal sonship is seen as the essential foundation for His priesthood: He became a Priest not by physical descent from Aaron but "by the power of
an indestructible life."[25] The author found this idea reflected in Psalm 110:4 ("You
are a priest forever in the order of Melchizedek"). He connected it to Jesus' sonship
in 7:3 by the pattern found in the Melchizedek of Genesis 14, who was "without
father or mother, without genealogy, without beginning of days or end of life," and
in a reverse typology, "like the Son of God" in His unending priesthood.[26] In a section of practical exhortations, Hebrews 13:8 portrays Jesus Christ in His unchanging constancy as the focus of their faith: "the same yesterday and today and
forever." This verse, like 1:10–12, points not only to His constancy into an unending future, but connects that also to His prior existence which stretched back
through the lives of their leaders (13:7) and His own faithful earthly life into eternity
past,[27] and thus gives assurance of His eternal constancy in providing for His people
at any time (cf. 4:14–16; 7:23–25).

In summary, the theme of the preexistent, eternal Son in Hebrews presents a
picture of Jesus as sharing fully in God's divine nature and activity. With this backdrop, it is easy to see why Hebrews in at least one instance explicitly labels the Son
as "God." As Cullmann states, "Jesus can be addressed as God just because of the
unique sonship which implies his deity."[28] Citing Psalm 45:6–7, Hebrews 1:8 says
of the Son, "Your throne, O God, will last for ever and ever." While various questions about other matters attend the full exegesis of this verse, most interpreters
agree that the author of Hebrews here applied the title *theos* to the Son in recognition of His divine status.[29] Thus, in the words of Cullmann, "Jesus' deity is more
powerfully asserted in Hebrews than in any other New Testament writing, with the

---

25. Büchsel imposes his dogmatic views on the text when he uses Hebrews 9:14 to strip 7:16 of its
plain sense. "The eternal Spirit of God who is at work in Him is the power of indestructible
life in the man Jesus. . . . Hence He does not have the power of an indestructible life in Himself, e.g., because He has a divine nature. He has it in fellowship with God" (*Theological
Dictionary of the New Testament*, s.v. "*akatalytos*," 4:338–39). Büchsel has sidestepped the
clear theological implication of 7:16 because of a dogmatic presupposition.

26. Milligan, *Theology of the Epistle to the Hebrews*, 75; George Barker Stevens, *The Theology of
the New Testament*, 2d ed. (Edinburgh: T. & T. Clark, 1918), 503.

27. Filson rightly emphasizes the past *historical* dimensions of the reference to "yesterday" in
13:8, but he cuts the frame too short in denying a past *eternal* dimension (F. V. Filson, *"Yesterday": A Study of Hebrews in the Light of Chapter 13*, Studies in Biblical Theology 2:4
[London: SCM, 1967], 30–35).

28. Cullmann, *Christology of the New Testament*, 310.

29. Attridge, *Epistle to the Hebrews*, 58–59. See Murray J. Harris, "The Translation and Significance of *ho theos* in Hebrews 1:8–9," *Tyndale Bulletin* 36 (1985): 129–62; and Leslie C.
Allen, "Psalm 45:7–8 (6–7) in Old and New Testament Settings," in *Christ the Lord*,
220–42. However, K. J. Thomas, "The Old Testament Citations in Hebrews," *New Testament Studies* 11 (1964–65): 303–25 and Hurst, "The Christology of Hebrews 1 and 2,"
159–60, dispute this conclusion.

exception of the Gospel of John."[30] The remarkable feature of the Christology of Hebrews is that at the same time, it pays close attention to the true, earthly *humanity* of Jesus, and it is to this topic that we now turn.

Incarnate, earthly Son. As mentioned above, the opening verses of Hebrews emphasize that God has spoken fully and finally in these last days in His Son. Because the Son shares fully in the divine essence, He could be the complete and unique revealer of the Father. But of course this revelation had to be accomplished by a new stage of Sonship: the preexistent, eternal Son needed to become the incarnate, earthly Son, and as 1:3 emphasizes, this ultimately led Him to suffering and death in order to "make purification for sins."

One of the hallmarks of Hebrews is this portrait of the costly humility of the Son of God: His earthly suffering, His tested obedience, His self-sacrifice to do God's will and accomplish the work of revelation and redemption set out for Him. Hebrews, more than any other New Testament book except the Gospels themselves, pays close attention to the earthly life of the historical Jesus, including His descent from Judah (7:14), His fully human temptations and sinless obedience (4:15), His struggle in Gethsemane (5:7), and His sacrificial death outside Jerusalem (13:12).[31] This is coupled with repeated theological reflection on His shared humanity and solidarity with humankind and the necessity of partaking fully in human likeness in order to follow the mission set out for Him by God (2:10–18; 4:14–5:10; 10:5–10). This paradoxical path of the heavenly Son of God who came to earth to accomplish our cleansing is captured best in Hebrews 5:8–9: "Son though he was, he learned obedience from the things which he suffered; and being made perfect, he became the source of eternal salvation to all who obey him." These great themes can best be traced out in detail by developing the thought of one central passage (2:5–18) and bringing other key texts (4:14–16; 5:7–10; 10:5–10; 12:1–11) into that discussion along the way.

This central passage on the incarnate, earthly Son (2:5–18) can be divided into two sections, the first of which (vv. 5–9) considers the significance of the Son by means of a quotation and brief exposition of verses from Psalm 8. The quotation from this psalm reflects on the astonishing status of humankind, who, though seemingly insignificant in God's magnificent creation, have been given great dignity ("crowned with glory and honor") and a great destiny (dominion over all things). Psalm 8 itself looks back to Genesis 1:26–28 and the bestowal of God's image and His commission of humans to rule over the whole earth. But in a pattern common for him and in good exegetical fashion,[32] the writer of Hebrews pondered the sense

30. Cullmann, *Christology of the New Testament,* 305.

31. Erich Grässer, "Der historische Jesus im Hebräerbrief," *Zeitschrift für die neutestamentliche Wissenschaft* 56 (1965): 63–91; and Bertram L. Melbourne, "An Examination of the Historical Jesus Motif in the Epistle to the Hebrews," *Andrews University Seminary Studies* 26 (1988): 281–98.

32. See George B. Caird, "The Exegetical Method of the Epistle to the Hebrews," *Canadian Journal of Theology* 5 (1959): 47–49, for a masterful treatment of the author's pattern in exegeting four central Old Testament texts (Pss. 8; 95; 110; and Jer. 31), each of which reveals the "self-confessed inadequacy of the old order" (p. 47).

of the biblical text that says "all things" are subject to humans (Ps. 8:6). He concluded that this commission is obviously *not yet* fulfilled in the way it was intended by God, since "we do not see everything subject to him!" (Heb. 2:8c). As Caird says, "The Old Testament expresses an aspiration and a vision to which it was unable to furnish the fulfillment."[33]

Reflecting on other details of Psalm 8, the author of Hebrews pointed to the One in whom the pattern suggested in the psalm is replicated: Jesus, who was "made for a little while lower than the angels," and now has been "crowned with glory and honor" (Heb. 2:9) so that in Him the exalted destiny of humankind has begun to be fulfilled and will in the future be consummated.[34] This exposition of the psalm is based not on a directly messianic understanding (as though the psalm meant Christ exclusively), but on the observation of a theological pattern or typological connection between humanity in general and Christ in particular.[35] The author thus expressed, without developing it overtly, an Adam-Christology in which Christ as representative man secures the fulfillment of the God-given dominion for humanity which the first Adam forfeited.[36]

What is not made explicit in Hebrews 2:9 is the path by which this is accomplished: it was by the Son's (a) coming to earth in incarnation ("made for a little while lower than the angels"), (b) suffering death for those in whose humanity He thus came to share ("by God's grace tasting death for everyone"), and as a result (c) being exalted to His present status of glory and honor at God's right hand ("crowned with glory and honor because of the suffering of death"). The correspondences between humankind in Psalm 8 and Jesus' fulfillment of the pattern are thus explicated by means of paronomasia, in which the key phrases are given an extended sense from that which they carried in the psalm. However, far from misreading these phrases, the author of Hebrews in this way deftly pointed to the larger sense in which Jesus fulfills them. So the phrase "made a little lower/made lower for a little," which in Psalm 8:5 pointed to the noble position of humanity just a little below "God" (so MT; LXX and Hebrews have "angels"), has become by play on words a reference to the humiliation of Jesus' incarnation: "made for a little while lower than angels." Second, the phrase "crowned with glory and honor" (Ps. 8:5b, denoting humanity's continued bearing of God's image as in Gen. 1:26–27) is shifted to denote Jesus' exaltation after death. Finally, even the phrase

33. Ibid., 49.

34. Richard N. Longenecker, *Biblical Exegesis in the Apostolic Period* (Grand Rapids: Eerdmans, 1975), 181.

35. Donald R. Glenn, "Psalm 8 and Hebrews 2: A Case Study in Biblical Hermeneutics and Biblical Theology," in *Walvoord: A Tribute,* ed. Donald K. Campbell (Chicago: Moody, 1982), 46–47; Leonhard Goppelt, *Theology of the New Testament,* trans. John E. Alsup, ed. Jürgen Roloff, 2 vols. (Grand Rapids: Eerdmans, 1982), 2:244–46; and Longenecker, *Biblical Exegesis in the Apostolic Period,* 171–74, 181.

36. C. F. D. Moule, *The Origin of Christology* (Cambridge: Cambridge Univ., 1977), 101; Hamerton-Kelly, *Pre-existence, Wisdom and the Son of Man,* 247–48; and Erich Grässer, "Beobachtungen zum Menschensohn in Hebr 2:6," in *Jesus und der Menschensohn: für Anton Vogtle,* ed. Rudolf Pesch and Rudolf Schnackenburg (Freiburg: Herder, 1975), 411–13.

"son of man," which in Psalm 8:4b meant simply "man" (by synonymous parallelism with 8:4a), becomes an elegant[37] reference to Jesus as the Son of man,[38] with contextual emphasis on His incarnation, human nature, vicarious death, and subsequent vindication by God.[39]

The three thoughts quickly made in Hebrews 2:9 are then filled in by further theological reflection in 2:10–18. They are not taken up in distinct sections but are interwoven in the argument of the paragraph. For convenience, the three themes are examined separately to facilitate correlation with similar ideas presented elsewhere in Hebrews.

The first theme then to be observed in Hebrews 2:10–18 is that Jesus as God's Son came to earth to share fully in our humanity and thus to establish His solidarity with all people. Implicit in Jesus' fulfillment of Psalm 8 is His true humanity, and so the exposition in Hebrews 2:9 points out that the preexistent, eternal Son "was made lower for a time" by coming to earth and partaking in flesh and blood. The divine One became incarnate and thus humbled Himself to a human, earthly existence for a time. The theological elaboration in 2:14a stresses His full participation in human nature: "Since therefore the children are sharers in flesh and blood, he also likewise partook of the same." The emphasis of this verse is that the preexistent, eternal Son willingly *entered into* human, earthly life. The tenses of the Greek verbs are vital to notice in order to construe the sense correctly: "the children *have shared/are sharers*" (a perfect tense stressing their present state of existence) versus "he partook" (an aorist verb with ingressive sense focusing on the event of entering into this condition).[40] This alludes to the fact that Jesus had not always existed in this human condition, but at a certain point in history He became a man. His share in human physical nature is alluded to also in 5:7, in the reference to "the

---

37. With great delicacy of style the author allowed this point to carry itself without laboring it by explicit development.

38. Whether this phrase is a title for Jesus in Hebrews 2:6 is much disputed, and the author does not develop it as such. But this can be explained in terms of his style, as suggested in the previous note. Moreover, since "Son of man" was presumably recognized in his circles as a messianic title and he develops themes related to such a sense, it is clear that he intends it to be read in this way, as noted by F. F. Bruce, *The Epistle to the Hebrews: The English Text with Introduction, Exposition and Notes,* New International Commentary on the New Testament (Grand Rapids: Eerdmans, 1964), 35. See also Francis J. Moloney, "The Reinterpretation of Psalm VIII and the Son of Man Debate," *New Testament Studies* 27 (1981): 656–72. Moloney argues that the Targum's interpretation of "son of man" in Psalm 8 as individual and messianic suggests the existence of these ideas in pre-Christian Judaism and prepared the way for the widespread New Testament reading of it in reference to Jesus.

39. Francis J. Moloney shows that these themes are combined also in the Johannine use of the title "Son of Man" for Jesus (*The Johannine Son of Man* [Rome: Libreria Ateneo Salesiano, 1976], 211–20).

40. Bruce, *Epistle to the Hebrews,* 41 n. 55; Geoffrey W. Grogan, "Christ and His People: An Exegetical and Theological Study of Hebrews 2:5–18," *Vox Evangelica* 6 (1969): 62; and John W. Pryor, "Hebrews and Incarnational Christology," *Reformed Theological Review* 40 (1981): 46. See this writer's discussion on the distinction between the perfect and aorist tenses when used with this sort of verbal idea (Buist M. Fanning, *Verbal Aspect in New Testament Greek* [Oxford: Clarendon, 1990], 136–40).

days of his flesh," but there it is viewed from the perspective of His later exalted status (vv. 5–6).

The emphasis on His physical incarnation is repeated in 10:5–10, where His *coming to earth* and *assumption of a physical body* in order to do God's will are also made explicit. Here the author saw David's expression of full devotion in Psalm 40 as fulfilled typologically in the Son's incarnation and sacrificial death.[41] The wording of the psalm is skillfully introduced and adapted to highlight the larger significance of Christ's fulfillment. There can be no doubt that Hebrews 10:5 ("when he comes into the world") envisions the preexistent Son entering human life, and the phrasing from Psalm 40 is compressed in order to highlight "doing God's will" as the purpose of this entrance. In addition, the wording of the Greek version of the psalm ("a body you have prepared for me"), which is a free rendering of the Hebrew original ("my ears you have opened"),[42] is exploited as the most appropriate way to describe the Son's full devotion to God's will. It was through His voluntary, bodily sacrifice of Himself that Jesus Christ accomplished our sanctification in the fulfillment of God's will (Heb. 10:5, 10). A full incarnational Christology is very clear in both passages (2:5–18 and 10:5–10).

On this very point, however, there has been much dispute. The picture of a "Christology from above"—that of the heavenly, preexistent Son coming into the world and becoming fully human—is rejected by some, who insist that a Christology from below is more truly the picture given in Hebrews. As Hurst says, "The first two chapters of Hebrews are not concerned primarily with a preexistent figure who lowers himself to *become* man; they focus rather upon a human being who is *raised* to an exalted status."[43] Robinson argues for a similar view of the whole book.[44] The textual support for this approach is the stout emphasis in Hebrews on the real humanity of Jesus. But emphasis on Jesus' humanity must not be used to distort the verses in Hebrews which so clearly teach His heavenly preexistence and incarnation.[45] As noted above, Hebrews uniquely combines both humanity and deity in its Christology.

41. S. Lewis Johnson, *The Old Testament in the New* (Grand Rapids: Zondervan, 1980), 53–67.

42. The legitimacy of this interpretive paraphrase, produced by understanding the part (ears) for the whole (body), is ably defended by Walter C. Kaiser, "The Abolition of the Old Order and Establishment of the New: Psalm 40:6–8 and Hebrews 10:5–10," in *Tradition and Testament: Essays in Honor of Charles Lee Feinberg*, ed. John S. Feinberg and Paul D. Feinberg (Chicago: Moody, 1981), 19–37.

43. Hurst, "Christology of Hebrews 1 and 2," 152. In this he is summarizing George B. Caird, "Son by Appointment," in *The New Testament Age: Essays in Honor of Bo Reicke*, ed. William C. Weinrich, 2 vols. (Macon, Ga.: Mercer Univ., 1984), 1:73–81.

44. Robinson, *Human Face of God*, 155–61. Pryor responds to Robinson's views and concludes that preexistence and incarnation cannot be excluded from the Christology of Hebrews ("Hebrews and Incarnational Christology," 44–50). See a similar conclusion in Ronald Williamson, "The Incarnation of the Logos in Hebrews," *Expository Times* 95 (1983): 4–8.

45. See, e.g., the non sequitur in John Knox, *The Humanity and Divinity of Christ: A Study of Pattern in Christology* (Cambridge: Cambridge Univ., 1967), 61–70, 73, 93–95, 106. He argues in effect, "since Jesus was fully human, then He could not have been divine or pre-existent." This suggests the need for C. E. B. Cranfield's reminder, in response to a similar

This then leads to the other element of this first theme in 2:10–18—the Son's true incarnation established a vital link with all humankind so that we may become His "brothers." The theme of "the Son and sons" is uniquely developed in Hebrews as a way of expressing the solidarity established in the incarnation between the Savior and those He came to save. This theme of course comes directly from the Adam-Christology seen by the author in Psalm 8: Jesus as true Man fulfilled the God-given destiny for humankind which Adam lost and secured redemption for those whose humanity He came to share.

The theme is picked up immediately in Hebrews 2:10 where God's action in Christ is described as "bringing many *sons* to glory." This thought is expanded in 2:11–13, which emphasizes Jesus' work for them: "he who sanctifies and those who are sanctified are from one" (NASB; cf. NIV: "are of the same family"). The family motif is continued—"So Jesus is not ashamed to call them brothers"—and supported by Old Testament quotations that highlight the relationship between God's leader and the community of God's people whom he leads (Ps. 22:22; Isa. 8:17–18). They are His brothers, the children God has given to Him. In Hebrews 2:14–18, this solidarity with believers is seen to be a necessity because of the redemptive mission the Son came to accomplish: "Since the children have flesh and blood, he too shared in their humanity . . . . For surely it is not angels he helps, but Abraham's descendants. For this reason he had to be made like his brothers in every way." In these verses the breathtaking truth of Christianity shines forth again: the eternal Son did not serve from afar but came to be one of us and to walk the costly path of obedience which leads us to glory!

The second theme in Hebrews 2:10–18 to develop Jesus' fulfillment of Psalm 8 is that in God's plan Jesus had to undergo suffering and death in order to provide salvation for humankind. Two phrases in the exposition given in Hebrews 2:9–10 should attract attention initially: "*by God's grace* Jesus experienced death for everyone," and "*it was fitting* for God to perfect the champion of our salvation through suffering." These have reference, in part, to what *God* was doing in and through Jesus' suffering, and to what may be seen of God's character in Jesus' vicarious death.[46] In this way they allude to the point of 1:1–4: God has spoken fully and uniquely in His Son, so as to supersede all previous revelation of Himself. Reflections of 10:7, 9–10 can also be seen: Jesus came to do God's will and it is by that will that His sacrifice sanctifies believers. The point is that God was working out His plan of salvation through Jesus' suffering and death, and Jesus for His part was obedient to the path laid out for Him, even though it involved suffering.

The element of salvation history (i.e., God working out His plan of salvation) is continued and the theme of "Son and sons" is picked up by the term "author" or

argument by Dunn, that the distinction between *full* humanity and *true* humanity is worth preserving in Christological discussion ("Some Comments on Professor J. D. G. Dunn's Christology in the Making with Special Reference to the Evidence of the Epistle to the Romans," in *The Glory of Christ in the New Testament*, 271 n. 6).

46. William Manson, *The Epistle to the Hebrews: An Historical and Theological Reconsideration* (London: Hodder and Stoughton, 1951), 101–2.

"pioneer" (*archēgos*) used of Jesus in 2:10. This term is variously translated and it has a cluster of nuances difficult to communicate in English by only one word.[47] The sense of hero or representative victor can easily be seen in this context, since in 2:14b–15 He is said to have stripped the devil of his power and thus has delivered from death all those held as slaves in fear of its power. And, of course, His fulfillment of Psalm 8 involves a representative victory for all humankind. The term carries with it a salvation-historical perspective because it points to Jesus' role in breaking through to a new stage in God's dealing with humanity. Jesus, as the Founder of our salvation, has inaugurated the fulfillment of redemption which earlier ages could only foreshadow.[48]

The term *archēgos* is also vitally connected with the theme of "Son and sons" because of its meaning of pathfinder, trailblazer, leader. This nuance comes to the fore in the language of 12:1–2, where Christians are urged to run their race with endurance by fixing their gaze on the *archēgos* who has gone before and reached the goal despite the shame and suffering of the Cross. While the suffering of Christians is different in quality, they too are called to follow in His path of suffering and then glory, humiliation and then honor. As verses 3–4 urge, believers must learn obedience in the face of real temptation, endurance in the harsh reality of sinful, earthly life. Though we are God's children we are not exempt from faith-testing difficulties, just as Jesus, Son though He was, learned obedience through suffering (5:8).

More importantly, it must be emphasized that Hebrews teaches the necessity of Jesus' suffering and death as the way of providing salvation and victory for humankind. In God's grace the Son experienced death for everyone (2:9), and, of course, this required His incarnation and true humanity in order to free His fellows by His vicarious death from their slavery to the fear of death (2:14–15). How could He achieve the dominion over all things intended for humans (2:6–8; Ps. 8:4–6) unless this enemy is brought into subjection? As Paul argued also from Psalm 8, Christ's death and resurrection signals the final victory over every enemy, including death, for all who are His people (1 Cor. 15:20–28). (Further treatment of the meaning of the Son's death will be given in the later section on Jesus as High Priest.)

The third theme developed in Hebrews 2:10–18 is that because of His obedience in carrying out God's redemptive plan despite severe temptation, Jesus has been exalted to the honored position in God's very presence as the believers' perfected High Priest. This is the final step in the path of the Son seen in Psalm 8: incarnation, then suffering, then glory. The goal is portrayed in the exposition in Hebrews 2:9 ("because of the suffering of death crowned with glory and honor") and is elaborated in two significant ways in 2:10 and 2:17–18. These are more easily developed here in reverse order.

47. See George Johnston, "Christ as *Archēgos*," *New Testament Studies* 27 (1981): 381–85 for a presentation of various lines of meanings. He prefers the sense "Prince."

48. Cf. J. Julius Scott, "*Archēgos* in the Salvation History of the Epistle to the Hebrews," *Journal of the Evangelical Theological Society* 29 (1986): 47–54.

In verses 17–18 the point is made that His incarnation (and consequent suffering) served the purpose of making Him a merciful and faithful High Priest. He was shown to be *faithful* in that His obedience despite temptation enabled Him to make full propitiation for the sins of His people (v. 17b). This path made Him a *merciful* High Priest because His sufferings and death as a man qualified Him for sympathetic dealings with those who are tempted and in need (v. 18; 4:14–16).

In 2:10 the same points are in mind but are presented in the form of a theme quite distinctive of the Epistle to the Hebrews: the author of salvation was *perfected* through sufferings. This is striking phraseology in a book which began by attributing a full share of the divine nature to this one (1:1–4) and which insists in several places on His sinlessness (4:15; 7:26–28; 9:14). It is clear that His perfecting did not involve a change from sinful to sinless.[49] Instead, as many have observed, this perfection focused on His qualification or preparation for priestly service. The Greek words for perfecting are used in a similar way in the LXX in connection with ordaining or consecrating priests (Ex. 29:9, 29, 33; Lev. 8:33, 21:10),[50] and the link with high priestly service appears in each of the contexts in Hebrews in which Jesus is said to have been perfected (Heb. 2:10; 5:9; 7:28).

In this perfecting, Jesus was qualified or given credentials demonstrating His worthiness to act as High Priest. He became the perfect High Priest in the sense that He showed His sinlessness by full obedience to God's will despite temptation (5:7–10; 7:26–28); He became sympathetic through His identification with humanity in incarnation, temptation, and suffering (2:17–18; 4:14–16); and He ultimately went to the cross and offered Himself as the fully effective sacrifice for sin (2:9–10, 17; 5:7–10; 7:26–28).[51]

The process by which the Son was perfected is laid out in a particularly vivid way in 5:7–10 (in a context establishing His qualifications to be High Priest). Verse 7 graphically portrays His experience in Gethsemane as a picture of the trials and sufferings He encountered in earthly life, namely, His dependence and human limitation, and His anguish in prayer as He cried out to God for deliverance. It is clear

---

49. Anthony A. Hoekema, "The Perfection of Christ in Hebrews," *Calvin Theological Journal* 9 (1974): 31.

50. Gerhard Delling, *Theological Dictionary of the New Testament*, s.v. *"teleioō,"* 8:82–83; R. Schippers, *New International Dictionary of New Testament Theology*, s.v. *"telos,"* 2:60. Peterson does not agree that *teleioō* has this cultic sense in Hebrews, because the LXX uses an idiomatic phrase *teleioun tas cheiras* ("to fill the hands") in various ways related to priestly ordination, while Hebrews uses only the verb (David Peterson, *Hebrews and Perfection: An Examination of the Concept of Perfection in the "Epistle to the Hebrews,"* SNTS Monograph Series 47 [Cambridge: Cambridge Univ., 1982], 26–30). Transfer of the cultic sense from the phrase to the verb alone is not automatic. However, since the noun *teleiōsis* is used numerous times by itself in the LXX for such ordination (and the verb is used alone in Lev. 21:10) and since the contexts in Hebrews consistently make this connection, the sense seems valid. See Moisés Silva, "Perfection and Eschatology in Hebrews," *Westminster Theological Journal* 39 (1976): 60–62 for further validation of this sense.

51. Cf. Hoekema, "Perfection of Christ in Hebrews," 32–33. This nuance of earthly sonship (obedience to the Father and carrying out His mission) is emphasized by Cullmann, *Christology of the New Testament*, 275–84, 305.

that the Son of God garnered no special treatment or exemption from normal human weakness! Yet the experience in Gethsemane also brings into focus Jesus' genuine struggle with strong temptation. Facing the temptation to be untrue to God's will, He proved His obedience in the ultimate way by giving Himself on the cross (cf. 10:5–10).

The next verse (5:8) traces the paradox of the *Son of God* learning obedience in such a school: "Son though he was, he learned obedience through the things which he suffered." The Greek original highlights this path to learning by a proverbial wordplay: He learned (*emathen*) obedience by what He suffered (*epathen*). What this meant for the Son was not that He "learned to obey" but that He learned by experience all that obedience in earthly life entails. He set out on the path of obedience to God (10:5–10) and never left it, but along the way He learned in the harsh reality of sufferings what that involved.[52]

This evidences once again the true humanity of the Son, because it indicates the inner development and growth through experience which is part of all human existence. This was not a change in His case from prior imperfection, but the filling out in human experience of that mind-set of obedience which He possessed all along.[53] His fully tested faith and obedience can thus be cited as the most powerful exhortation imaginable for His people who must endure their earthly pilgrimage in the face of stern difficulties and temptation (2:18–3:6; 4:14–16; 10:19–39; 12:1–2).

This proven obedience then led to His perfection as the source of eternal salvation for His people (5:9) and as the divinely appointed High Priest (v. 10), a position of great honor and glory (cf. vv. 4–5 and 2:9–10).

The theme of perfection is extended in Hebrews to describe not only Jesus as the perfect High Priest, but also His work of salvation and the condition to which He brings His people as a result (7:11, 19; 9:11; 10:1, 14; 12:23). These elements will be developed in later sections.

As seen repeatedly, it was Jesus' suffering and obedience as the incarnate, *earthly* Son which qualified Him to be raised to the position of *exalted* Son. This is the view of Him to which attention is directed in the next section.

Exalted Son. The opening lines of Hebrews (1:1–4) begin the focus on Jesus as exalted to God's right hand, the central vision of Him in the entire book. The title "High Priest" is often associated with His exalted status, as will be seen later. But the title "Son" is used of His exaltation in a number of verses as well, and these verses portray a third stage of His sonship. The third stage adds a new dimension to Jesus' position as God's Son, but it could not have been reached except by the One who was first the preexistent, eternal Son and then the incarnate, earthly Son.

This new stage of sonship is most clearly seen in 1:3b–14, where the introduction's sevenfold description of the Son is concluded and His superiority to angels is presented through a catena of Old Testament citations. His exaltation to a high position after His sacrificial death is stated in 1:3b: "having accomplished purification for

---

52. Westcott, *Epistle to the Hebrews,* 128; and Bruce, *Epistle to the Hebrews,* 103–4.

53. Hoekema, "Perfection of Christ in Hebrews," 35–36; and Cullmann, *Christology of the New Testament,* 97–98.

sins, he sat down at the right hand of the majesty on high." "Sitting at the right hand" is patently an allusion to Psalm 110:1, which is quoted near the end of this section (Heb. 1:13).

The explanation of this exalted position given in 1:4 is surprising at first because it speaks of the Son *becoming* better than the angels and *inheriting* a better name: "having come to be as much superior to the angels as the name which he has inherited is superior to theirs." This speaks of a stage of honor not reached before, bestowed on Him because of His obedient suffering in providing purification for sin (as in 2:9). The sense becomes clearer in 1:5, which states that the superior name (and position) He has inherited is that of "Son."[54] But in what way is this to be understood, since He already was called Son in His preexistent and then incarnate relationship to God (cf. 1:2; 5:8)? The sense must be seen in the use of the title Son in Psalm 2:7 and 2 Samuel 7:14, the two significant Old Testament verses quoted in Hebrews 1:5. In their Old Testament contexts these refer to the Davidic king, installed by God as His theocratic ruler and enjoying a special relationship with God, which is pictured as "sonship."[55] By applying these verses to Jesus, the writer to the Hebrews pointed to His enthronement as the promised Davidic King. No angel ever enjoyed the status Jesus has now inherited! As Son in this new sense, He has been "begotten" or installed as the anointed Ruler over all the kings of the earth, with the pledge that all the nations will be His inheritance and the ends of the earth His possession (Ps. 2).[56] As such, He began to fulfill the covenant with David, God's pledge that His house and kingdom will endure forever (2 Sam. 7).[57] This then reinforces a similar reference which began the ring structure in Hebrews 1:2b: the appointment of the Son as Heir of all. The close association of regal sonship with inheritance in Psalm 2:7–8 ("you are my son . . . . I will give you the nations as your inheritance and the ends of the earth as your possession") suggests that this should be understood as another dimension of His exaltation as Davidic King after His resurrection and ascension.

The language of becoming, inheriting, and begetting used in 1:4–5 of this third stage of Jesus' sonship must not be misunderstood as "adoptionist Christol-

---

54. As Meier points out, this is emphasized by the skillful arrangement in 1:5 of quotations from Psalm 2:7, which *begins* with the name "Son," and from 2 Samuel 7:14, which *ends* with it ("Structure and Theology in Heb. 1:1–14," 187 n. 63). Such inclusion or bracketing is a favorite rhetorical device in Hebrews.

55. See John H. Eaton, *Kingship and the Psalms,* 2d ed. (Sheffield: JSOT, 1986), 146–49, for discussion of this motif in the Psalms. The Davidic King or Messiah is spoken of as God's son (or God is said to be his father) in Psalms 2:7, 12; 72:1; 89:26–27.

56. The "begetting" referred to in Psalm 2:7 is interpreted similarly of Jesus' resurrection/exaltation in Acts 13:33. It is foreign to the context to interpret this as the "eternal generation" of the Son, as suggested by Charles Caldwell Ryrie, *Biblical Theology of the New Testament* (Chicago: Moody, 1959), 236; Montefiore, *A Commentary on the Epistle to the Hebrews,* 44–45; and Donald Guthrie, *New Testament Theology* (Downers Grove, Ill.: InterVarsity, 1981), 362.

57. The promise is repeated in more spectacular terms in Isaiah 9:1–7; 11:1–12:6; Jeremiah 23:5–8; Ezekiel 37:1–28; and Amos 9:11–15.

ogy."[58] It is clear from Hebrews that Jesus did not become God's Son for the first time at His exaltation nor is He called Son only in view of His exaltation.[59] Jesus' three stages of sonship portrayed in Hebrews are distinguishable but vitally connected. He was always the Son in the preexistent sense (1:1–3; 7:3), He became the Son in earthly, incarnate terms as He learned obedience in suffering (2:5–18; 5:7–10; 6:6), and He was exalted to a new stage of sonship (1:4–5; 5:5). Thus it is wrong to label this "adoptionist" in any true sense, since He was already the Son before His exaltation. There is no indication in Hebrews that one who was *not* God's Son at all has been exalted to that relationship because of earthly obedience. Jesus was appointed to a new stage of sonship, not made Son for the first time at His exaltation to this royal status.

Both Psalm 2 and 2 Samuel 7 graphically portray the *earthly* aspects of the messianic rule (Ps. 2:1–2, 6, 8, 10; 2 Sam. 7:10–11). The future, earthly dimension of Jesus' rule as Davidic King is pictured in Hebrews 1:6 in connection with another quotation demonstrating His superiority to angels: "let all the angels of God worship him" (Deut. 32:43; Ps. 97:7). The significance of this is seen in the setting for such worship provided by the introduction to the quotation in Hebrews 1:6a: "when he brings the firstborn into the inhabited world, he says. . . ." Two terms are crucial to understand this phrase. "Firstborn" in this context must be given the sense it carries in Psalm 89:26–27, another Old Testament text picturing the Davidic ruler as God's son, even His "firstborn," appointed to be above all the kings of the earth. The reference to leading Him into "the inhabited world" (*hē oikoumenē*) seems at first glance to refer to the Incarnation, when the Messiah was brought into this earthly life. But the worship of all the angels is difficult to connect with that event (despite Luke 2:8–14), since Hebrews 2:5–9 views the Incarnation as the event that made Jesus *lower* than angels for a time. It is the latter passage, in fact, which clarifies the sense of 1:6 by picking up the contrast with angels, because it uses the key term again, this time with an added description and a reference back: "It is not to angels that he has subjected the coming inhabited world [*tēn oikoumenēn tēn mellousan*], of which we are speaking" (2:5). As the paragraph then shows, *the world to come* is subjected to Jesus as Son of Man (2:6–9).[60]

58. Robinson, *Human Face of God*, 155–61; Dunn, *Christology in the Making*, 51–56; and Caird, "Son by Appointment," 73–81, emphasize the so-called adoptionist language in Hebrews.

59. Ernst Käsemann's idea that the earthly Jesus was called Son only by "a proleptic application of the title," that is, in view of His later exaltation to sonship (*The Wandering People of God: An Investigation of the Letter to the Hebrews*, trans. Roy A. Harrisville and Irving L. Sandberg [Minneapolis: Augsburg, 1984], 97–101) does not do justice to the presentation of the Son in Hebrews.

60. The interpretation of *hē oikoumenē* in 1:6 and 2:5 as the earthly realm over which the Messiah rules is defended by George Wesley Buchanan, *To the Hebrews: Translation, Comment and Conclusions*, The Anchor Bible (Garden City, N.Y.: Doubleday, 1972), 17–18, 26–27, 64–65. Also see Otto Michel, *Theological Dictionary of the New Testament*, s.v. "*hē oikoumenē*," 5:159.

The next three Old Testament quotations in the catena of 1:5–14 pick up the reference to the Son's exalted kingship by contrasting the angels' transitory and ephemeral status (v. 7, quoting Ps. 104:4) with the Son's eternal kingdom (vv. 8–9, quoting Ps. 45:6–7) and unending existence (vv. 10–12, quoting Ps. 102:25–27). These quotations highlight the interrelatedness of the three stages of Jesus' sonship. In them the author alluded to the eternal sonship by addressing the Son as God (Heb. 1:8a) and pointing to His role in creation (v. 10) and His unchanging existence in contrast to all created things (vv. 11–12). The Son's obedience in earthly testing is seen in verse 9a as the path which led to His anointing and exaltation above His companions in verse 9b. These are complemented by the explicit mention of the Son's throne and the righteousness of the scepter of His kingdom (v. 8).

The culminating quotation in the catena, however, is from Psalm 110:1, the verse which is so central to the epistle's view of Jesus Christ. In this psalm, David spoke of his son, King Solomon, as the one whom Yahweh had enthroned as His vice-regent with the divine promise to subdue his enemies before him.[61] But in the light of God's continuing revelation of His work of salvation, Hebrews, in common with much of the New Testament,[62] sees the psalm as fulfilled in a typical-prophetic fashion ultimately and uniquely in Jesus. The pattern of God's exaltation of the Davidic king is seen in Solomon, but is fulfilled ultimately in Jesus. He was exalted to God's right hand not just metaphorically, but literally after His resurrection and ascension. He is the Davidic King and "lord" in the ultimate sense.[63] That the exalted kingship of Psalm 110 also included a cultic role as "king-priest" (v. 4) is developed with great insight later in Hebrews (4:14; 5:5–6, 10; 7:1–3; 8:1; 10:12–13).

So in this third stage of sonship, Jesus is portrayed in Hebrews as the King who will fulfill the promise to David. But is He reigning *now* in all the regal dignity which the divine plan intends, or is His Davidic rule to be instituted only in the *future*? The answer in Hebrews seems to be that this is a false dichotomy. Like the larger scheme of eschatology in Hebrews,[64] the Son's royal rule is viewed in an "already/not yet" contrast. In His resurrection, ascension, and exaltation,[65] He has

61. Herbert W. Bateman IV, "Psalm 110:1 and the New Testament," *Bibliotheca Sacra* 149 (1991): 438–53.

62. Matthew 22:44; 26:64; Mark 12:36; 14:62; 16:19; Luke 20:42–43; 22:69; Acts 2:34–35; 7:55–56; Romans 8:34; 1 Corinthians 15:25; Ephesians 1:20; Colossians 3:1; 1 Peter 3:22; Revelation 3:21.

63. Cf. Darrell L. Bock, *Proclamation from Prophecy and Pattern: Lukan Old Testament Christology,* Journal for the Study of the New Testament, Supplement Series 12 (Sheffield: JSOT, 1987), 128–32.

64. C. K. Barrett, "The Eschatology of the Epistle to the Hebrews," in *The Background of the New Testament and Its Eschatology,* ed. W. D. Davies and D. Daube (Cambridge: Cambridge Univ., 1956), 364.

65. The Resurrection is mentioned separately in Hebrews only at 13:20 and the Ascension in 4:14. But these are to be assumed in the references to Jesus' exaltation, which is a consistent focus in Hebrews. The epistle simply assumes the first two steps and goes on quickly to the final one.

been appointed king (1:5) and has assumed His royal throne in order to exercise righteous rule over His kingdom (v. 7). He has been seated in the position of regal dignity as God's ultimate vice-regent (v. 13). To Him all things have been subjected (2:8a–b). Yet in spite of such expressions of His present kingly role, other verses in the same paragraphs look to a future sense in which His rule will be consummated. The inhabited world which has been subjected to the Son and not to angels is described as the *coming* world (2:5), because we do *not yet* see all things subjected to Him, though we do see Jesus in whom the fulfillment has begun (v. 8b). In 1:6 angelic worship directed toward the Son when He is brought into this world as the royal Firstborn is portrayed as a future event.[66] Even in 1:13, the words of Psalm 110:1 express at the same time the installation of the King and the existence of enemies yet to be subjected to His rule (also Heb. 10:12–13). Jesus' Davidic kingship is thus portrayed in Hebrews in two dimensions: a rule presently in effect, inaugurated yet invisible; and a visible rule on this earth which is yet to consummated but certain of fulfillment.[67] Other details of the eschatology of Hebrews will be filled in later.

JESUS CHRIST AS HIGH PRIEST

The picture of Jesus Christ as High Priest is the most distinctive theme of Hebrews, and it is central to the theology of the book. As already stated, its doctrine of sonship is foundational to its teaching about Christ's priesthood. Likewise its view of salvation, of the Christian life, and of salvation-history are all vitally connected to the theme of His high priesthood.

Background for the theme of Christ's High Priesthood. Various ideas in Judaism and Christianity may have influenced the author of Hebrews in conceiving his view of Jesus as High Priest, but the particular lines of development appear to be distinctly his, worked out through inspired reflection on Old Testament texts and on Jesus' death, resurrection, and exaltation.

Some antecedents may be found, for instance, in the Old Testament examples of a priestly function for Israel's king, offering prayers and sacrifices on behalf of the people (e.g., 2 Sam. 6:12–23; 24:21–25; 1 Kings 3:4; 8:22–53, 62–64; 12:32–33; Ezek. 45:17–46:17).[68] Subsequent to this, there developed in intertestamental Judaism an expectation that the future Messiah would exercise a priestly

---

66. The clause with *hotan* and the aorist subjunctive indisputably refers to a *future* occurrence (cf. Westcott, *Epistle to the Hebrews*, 22), but future from what point? The reference point is clearly the time of the epistle, despite Hughes's suggestion otherwise (*A Commentary on the Epistle to the Hebrews*, 58).

67. For a similar treatment of Jesus' Davidic kingship, see Erich Sauer, *The Triumph of the Crucified* (Exeter: Paternoster, 1951), 24–25, 45–46, 51–52, 152–53, and *From Eternity to Eternity* (Exeter: Paternoster, 1954), 185–94; and Darrell L. Bock, "The Reign of the Lord Christ," in *Dispensationalism, Israel and the Church: The Search for Definition*, ed. Craig A. Blaising and Darrell L. Bock (Grand Rapids: Zondervan, 1992), 37–67.

68. For evidence from the Psalms, see the section, "The King as God's Chief Cultic Minister," in Eaton, *Kingship and the Psalms*, 172–77.

role. This was expressed in differing degrees, from a concept of one Messiah with priestly and royal functions, to an expectation of two Messiahs, one priestly and one royal, to a focus primarily on a priestly Messiah over the royal one.[69] In the New Testament, explicit indications of a priestly role for Jesus are quite muted outside of Hebrews. But the related motifs of Jesus' sacrifice for others (Gal. 2:20; Eph. 5:2, 25; 1 Peter 2:24; 3:18) and His intercession (Matt. 10:32; Rom. 8:34; 1 John 2:1–2), mediation (1 Tim. 2:5), and supersession of the temple and its sacrifices (Matt. 12:6; Mark 14:58; John 2:19–21) are found quite clearly in other places,[70] and are almost certainly rooted in Jesus' own teaching that a priestly role was part of His mission.[71] In Hebrews, however, these are pulled together in a unique way.

Without minimizing the influence of these antecedents, it must be said that the most significant catalyst for the high priestly Christology of Hebrews appears to be Psalm 110. While Psalm 110:1 is commonly cited with Christological import in the New Testament (some sixteen times outside of Hebrews, the most frequently cited Old Testament verse), this epistle alone brings 110:4 into the picture (ten references), in addition to five citations of 110:1.[72] As the writer to the Hebrews reflected on Jesus' life, death, and resurrection, Psalm 110:4 (a priest forever in Melchizedek's line) helped him to grasp the wider significance of 110:1 (exaltation to God's right hand).[73] The theological implications following on this insight were astounding: what did it mean for Jesus' priestly work that He was exalted to glory after His atoning death, that He is now in God's very presence, that He is seated there? What did it mean for the old covenant and its priesthood that the Son was a Priest of a different order, not based on human descent but on the power of an indestructible life and God's oath of appointment? What does it mean for the Christian life that believers have such a High Priest? The central themes of Hebrews come directly out of these reflections. It would be an exaggeration to hold that all of Hebrews is simply a theological exposition of Psalm 110,[74] but it would not be far off!

---

69. The order in which these ideas developed is not clear, and it seems that a mixture of these existed in different communities of intertestamental Judaism. For survey of this topic, see Longenecker, *Christology of Early Jewish Christianity,* 113–19; and James R. Schaefer, "The Relationship between Priestly and Servant Messianism in the Epistle to the Hebrews," *Catholic Biblical Quarterly 30* (1968): 362–70.

70. A survey of these themes can be found in Olaf Moe, "Das Priestertum Christi im NT ausserhalb des Hebräerbriefs," *Theologische Literaturzeitung* 72 (1947): 335–38.

71. Cf. Montefiore, *Commentary on Hebrews,* 95–96.

72. See David M. Hay, *Glory at the Right Hand: Psalm 110 in Early Christianity,* Society of Biblical Literature Monograph Series 18 (Nashville: Abingdon, 1973), 163–66 for a summary of quotations and allusions to this psalm.

73. "In a sense, the whole theological achievement of the author rests on the fact that he alone among NT writers read 'theologically' beyond the first verse of Psalm 109 [110] . . . noticed the claim of v. 4, connected it with v. 1, and drew out the implications for Christology and soteriology" (Meier, "Structure and Theology in Heb. 1:1–14," 184 n. 55).

74. Cf. Buchanan, *To the Hebrews,* xix.

Christ's qualifications to be High Priest. The connection of Christ's high priesthood with His sonship and with Psalm 110:4 can be seen in the first major exposition of this theme in Hebrews 4:14–5:10. Following an exhortation to steadfastness based on Jesus' sympathetic high priesthood (4:14–16), the author cited two general qualifications met by the Aaronic high priests and showed that Jesus also fulfilled those requirements (5:1–10). The two qualifications are a shared nature, giving the priest ability to sympathize with those for whom He offers sacrifice, and divine appointment to minister in this way in things pertaining to God. There is an interchange here between the sympathy of Jesus for human weakness, since He experienced the full range of human temptation and yet was without sin (4:15), and the ability of Old Testament priests to deal gently with sinners, since they were sinners themselves and had to offer sacrifice for their own sins as well as for the peoples' (5:1–3). Also, the Old Testament priests were not self-appointed but were called to their service by God (vv. 1, 4), and similarly (vv. 5–6), Jesus did not exalt Himself but was designated as High Priest by God's appointment, as expressed in the words of Psalm 110:4, "You are a priest forever after the order of Melchizedek." The important connection of sonship with priesthood is seen in the fact that Psalm 2:7 is coupled with 110:4 to substantiate Jesus' appointment to priesthood. This underscores the dual role of King-Priest which Hebrews envisions Jesus fulfilling in His exalted status.

The significant treatment in Hebrews 5:7–10 of the path of costly obedience trod by the earthly Son then returns to repeat the point (from 4:15) that He shared fully in human weakness and thus is qualified as the sympathetic High Priest (cf. also 2:17–18). In 5:9, Jesus is said to have been "made perfect" and so became the source of eternal salvation to all who obey Him. As discussed in an earlier section, this "perfection" Jesus attained is vitally related to His high priestly ministry. It focuses (here in 5:8 and also in 2:10; 7:28) on His sinless obedience to God's plan for Him, His full experience of human temptation and suffering, and His accomplishment of eternal salvation for His people. Jesus' credentials to serve as High Priest are well established. These verses (5:7–10), with their explicit description of Jesus' earthly struggles, give evidence that the author's doctrine of high priesthood was influenced not only by Psalm 110, but also by reflection on Jesus' teaching that the Cross was central in His God-given mission and on Jesus' obedience to that mission despite the cost.[75]

Melchizedekan priesthood and the Levitical order. The presentation of Jesus' qualifications to be High Priest ended in 5:10 with words drawn from Psalm 110:4: "having been designated by God a high priest according to the order of Melchizedek." The author was torn at that point by the need to give his readers an explanation of the sense of this verse and the realization they would only with difficulty grasp or accept such an exposition. So he interposed the hortatory section, 5:11–6:20, before coming around again to the same expression in 6:20, "having become a high priest forever according to the order of Melchizedek."

---

75. Manson, *Epistle to the Hebrews,* 109–11, 121.

In chapter 7 the author then went back to Genesis 14 in order to explain the sense of Psalm 110:4. As Caird has argued, the treatment of Melchizedek in Hebrews 7:1–10 is not so fanciful and bizarre as many have alleged. Instead, the author followed a very sound exegetical procedure:

> The psalm was written at a time when the temple cultus was in the hands of the levitical priests. Why should anyone dream of a new order of priesthood unless he felt the present order to be deficient? . . . He carries us back to the story of Genesis 14 not to compose a fanciful and allegorical midrash on that chapter after the manner of Philo, but rather because he wishes to answer the very modern question: "What did the words 'priest forever after the order of Melchizedek' mean to the psalmist who wrote them?"[76]

In examining what Genesis 14:18–20 contributes to answering this question, the author treated the narrative as historical fact (not merely the vehicle for allegory as Philo does in *Legum allegoriae* 3.79–82). In addition, he looked theologically at Genesis 14 for the nature of Melchizedek's priesthood which would make the psalmist choose him as the model for the Davidic king-priest described in Psalm 110. In his exposition (Heb. 7:1–10) the writer made three points about Melchizedek.

First, Melchizedek was a *king-priest*. The author emphasized this by citing the titles used of Melchizedek in Genesis 14:18: king of Salem and priest of the Most High God (Heb. 7:1). In 7:2 he cited the interpretation of the personal name Melchizedek, "king of righteousness," and repeated the title king of Salem with an interpretation of the place name, "king of peace," as a way of highlighting the royal status further. Though people in the Western world are inclined to follow Shakespeare's dictum, "That which we call a rose by any other name would smell as sweet," such attention to the etymological significance of proper names was almost universal in antiquity as a way of understanding the true nature of a person or thing. The combination of royal and priestly dignity in one person is noted here because the author wanted his readers to recall the same point about Jesus' exalted status. He is at the same time the royal Son and High Priest, as 5:5–6 communicates by linking Psalms 2:7 and 110:4.

Second, the author observed indications in Genesis 14 that the Melchizedekan order would be an *eternal* priesthood. The text in Genesis recounts nothing about Melchizedek's genealogy, records no father or mother, and gives no glimpse of his beginning or death. So Melchizedek amazingly prefigures the eternal order of priesthood to which Jesus has been appointed: "made like the Son of God, he remains a priest forever." The enigmatic king of Salem was not an angelic figure, as

---

76. Caird, "Exegetical Method of the Epistle to the Hebrews," 48.

one of the Qumran documents (11Q Melchizedek) apparently understands him.[77] Nor was he a theophany of the preincarnate Son, as suggested by some patristic writers and early modern interpreters.[78] There is no reason to think that Melchizedek was anything more than an ancient historical king-priest who interacted in significant ways with Abraham. But Genesis 14 is silent on any beginning, end, or genealogy for Melchizedek. What is the meaning of this silence, when viewed from the perspective of Psalm 110 and the exalted present position of the Son of God? It is that Melchizedek in this regard perfectly prefigured the eternal priesthood which Jesus now exercises.[79] The absence of genealogy was especially noticeable in contrast to the Levitical order for which proper descent from priestly stock was all-important. This contrast with Jesus' priesthood is made clear in Hebrews 7:13–16 (not based on physical descent but on the power of an indestructible life).

Third, the events of Genesis 14 demonstrate the *superiority* of Melchizedek's order to the Levitical priesthood (7:4–10). This is borne out by two significant incidents in Melchizedek's interaction with Abraham: he received tithes of the battle spoils from Abraham, and he pronounced blessing on Abraham. Both were indications in ancient culture of superior status ("how great this man was to whom the patriarch gave a tithe," v. 4). And to extend the argument, a father may be seen to act for his descendants, and so through Abraham Levi also is subordinate to Melchizedek. This superiority has wide-reaching ramifications, since the law itself was bound up with the Levitical order, as verse 5 intimates. The theological ripples that come from this are then developed in verses 11–28.

Having developed the sense of Psalm 110:4 by an exposition of Genesis 14:18–20, the author then drew out the theological ramifications of Jesus' service as a Melchizedekan Priest (7:11–28). These can be mentioned here quickly, since they are developed in other sections before and after. The first theological implication is that the description of another priesthood in Psalm 110:4 entails not only a change in God's program from the Levitical priesthood but also a change from the law with which it is bound up (Heb. 7:11–14). The Mosaic regulations focused on genealogical succession to the priestly office, yet this no longer holds since Jesus, descended from Judah, is a Priest nonetheless. Second, the shift from a priesthood based not on genealogical succession but on the resurrected life of Jesus Christ signifies the change to a better, eternally effective priestly work, which gives sure ac-

---

77. In favor of the angelic view see M. de Jonge and A.S. Van der Woude, "11Q Melchizedek and the New Testament," *New Testament Studies* 12 (1965–66): 301–26; and Richard N. Longenecker, "The Melchizedek Argument of Hebrews: A Study in the Development and Circumstantial Expression of New Testament Thought," in *Unity and Diversity in New Testament Theology: Essays in Honor of George E. Ladd,* ed. Robert A. Guelich (Grand Rapids: Eerdmans, 1978), 161–85. Horton argues against the angelic view (F. L. Horton, *The Melchizedek Tradition: A Critical Examination of the Sources to the Fifth Century* A.D. *and the Epistle to the Hebrews,* Society for New Testament Studies Monograph Series 30 [Cambridge: Cambridge Univ., 1976], 164).

78. See Bruce, *Epistle to the Hebrews,* 137, and Attridge, *Epistle to the Hebrews,* 195, for citation of examples.

79. Cf. the discussion in Vos, *Teaching of Hebrews,* 105–7.

cess to God (vv. 15–19). Third, God's oath in appointing Jesus as Melchizedekan Priest (Ps. 110:4) guarantees the superiority and continuance of His priesthood over the former order (Heb. 7:20–22). Fourth, the priestly succession required under the old priesthood by the deaths of generation after generation of priests is no longer necessary, since Jesus by His unending life continues forever in His service (vv. 23–25). So as verse 25 concludes, "he is able to save completely those who come to God through him, because he always lives to intercede for them." Fifth, verses 26–28 summarize the superiority of Jesus' priesthood by noting His sinlessness, His once-for-all, effective sacrifice of Himself, and the authority of His priesthood to supersede the law, as seen in God's oath appointing "the Son made perfect forever." Further implications as to the salvation-historical change in God's program are developed in Hebrews 8. These will be discussed in the later section, "From Old to New."

Day of Atonement typology and Christ's sacrifice. The epistle's writer paused in 8:1 to emphasize the striking picture he had developed. "The point of what we are saying is this: we do have such a high priest, who sat down at the right hand of the throne of the Majesty in heaven." In explaining the ministry Christ has taken up in His exalted position, the writer focused on a distinction between the *true* sanctuary, in which Christ is now present and active in heaven, and the earthly sanctuary, which is the mere *shadow* of the heavenly (8:2–5). This contrast is left undeveloped in 8:6–13, where Christ's role is explained in terms of inaugurating the new covenant. In 9:1–10:18, however, the author went back to this contrast of earthly and heavenly sanctuaries in order to elaborate on the significance of Christ's high priestly ministry. In effect, what the author did was to answer the questions (both reflections on Ps. 110:1, 4), "What priestly work did Christ accomplish in order to come to His present exalted position?" and "What priestly work is He now carrying out in that heavenly realm?" He answered these questions by tracing the role of the Old Testament high priest in the Day of Atonement ritual (Lev. 16) as the pattern followed also by Christ in accomplishing our eternal redemption.

The author mentioned first the arrangement and furnishings of the earthly tabernacle with its two chambers (Heb. 9:1–5). He then summarized the daily service of the priests in the outer chamber and the yearly entrance of the high priest alone into the inner chamber, taking the blood of a sacrificial animal as an offering for Himself and the people. This situation, he stated, is the Holy Spirit's indication that the earthly tent was ineffectual and pointed forward to the present fulfillment in Christ (vv. 6–10).

The Day of Atonement ritual, however, gives the pattern for understanding the significance of Christ's high priestly work, as verses 11–14 make clear. Christ also as High Priest entered the heavenly sanctuary, but He did so once for all, not repeatedly, and not by means of the blood of sacrificial animals, but by means of His own blood. And much more than effecting a ritual cleansing of the flesh, Christ's sacrifice purifies the *conscience,* giving full forgiveness for sins as the fulfillment of the new covenant promise (cf. 8:12; 10:18). The contrasts in verses 11–14 between the work of Christ and that of the Old Testament high priest are designed to present to the readers the full significance of Christ's priestly work. Four contrasts are touched on in several places in the following verses (9:15–10:18).

The first of these contrasts is that Christ as High Priest entered not into a sanctuary of this creation, but into heaven itself, into the very presence of God (9:11, 23–24). So the approach to God has been perfected, not just in shadow but in reality (10:1–2), and Christ has thus opened up full access to God's presence. As mentioned in other places in the epistle (4:16; 10:19–25), Christians may now draw near to God in faith to find mercy for every time of need as a result of Christ's high priestly work.

The second contrast speaks of the effectiveness of Christ's priestly work: His sacrifice and entrance into the heavenly sanctuary occurred not repeatedly but *once for all.*[80] The Old Testament high priests repeated their work year after year because it was never effective in dealing with sin (9:25; 10:1–2, 11). Christ, on the other hand, in God's plan offered Himself once for all as the perfect Sacrifice for sin and thus accomplished eternal redemption and full forgiveness (9:12; 9:26–28; 10:12–14). Another way in which this effectiveness is emphasized is the contrast concerning the posture of the priest (10:11–12). The Old Testament priest continually *stood* while serving, but Christ was able to sit at God's right hand because His offering was perfect. This contrast in effectiveness demonstrates that Christ's priestly offering focused on the cross, not on His ongoing ministry now that He is in heaven.[81] Hebrews 9:12 should not be mistaken to indicate that Christ entered heaven *with* His blood, as though to offer it there once or continually in the heavenly sanctuary.[82] The Greek preposition *dia* used in verse 12 clearly carries the sense of means or instrument (through, by means of), not accompaniment (along with, together with). Christ's high priestly sacrifice was accomplished once for all on the cross as the perfect sacrifice, so that "there is no longer any sacrifice for sin" (10:18).

The third contrast focuses on the nature of Christ's sacrifice. He entered the sanctuary not by means of the blood of sacrificed animals but by means of His own blood, since He offered Himself on the cross by the will of God (9:12–13, 25–28;

80. The Greek words *hapax* and *ephapax* are used six times in Hebrews of Christ's work (7:27; 9:12, 26, 28; 10:2, 10); also *mian* and *miāi* are used in 10:12, 14 to emphasize His single sacrifice. There is also an invariable contrast in Greek tenses to support this distinction: the present of *prospherō* is used nine times of the repeated Old Testament offerings (and once of Christ but negated, 9:25), while the aorist is used four times to speak in these contexts of Christ's single act of giving Himself.

81. See the full discussion in Wilfred Stott, "The Concept of 'Offering' in the Epistle to the Hebrews," *New Testament Studies* 9 (1962–63): 62–67; and Philip Edgcumbe Hughes, "The Blood of Jesus and His Heavenly Priesthood in Hebrews, Part II: The High Priestly Sacrifice of Christ," *Bibliotheca Sacra* 130 (1973): 195–212.

82. This is the view of Walter Edward Brooks, "The Perpetuity of Christ's Sacrifice in the Epistle to the Hebrews," *Journal of Biblical Literature* 89 (1970): 205–14, but it is a misreading of Hebrews. The analogy with the Old Testament priest sprinkling the blood in the holy of holies (cf. Heb. 9:7) does not hold in regard to Christ's work, and so in no place does Hebrews speak of Christ as taking His blood with Him into heaven or making an "offering" in the heavenly realm. The emphasis is completely the other way.

10:5–10). The ceremonies of the old covenant established the principle that blood sacrifice was required for forgiveness of sins (9:18–22). Shedding of blood was necessary to inaugurate the covenant itself and to purify the tabernacle and its accoutrements; in fact, as 9:22 says, "The law requires that nearly everything be cleansed with blood, and without shedding of blood there is no forgiveness." This was a type of Christ's true atoning sacrifice which was to come. The presentation of His sacrifice in this section shows that it was understood, as in early Christianity in general, as a voluntary and vicarious sacrifice.

The voluntary nature of Christ's sacrifice is made clear by repeated statements that He offered His own blood or Himself (vv. 12, 14, 25, 26). This is also emphasized by the contrast with the sacrifices of bulls and goats, which were of course involuntary (v. 12; 10:4). In addition, Psalm 40 is quoted in Hebrews 10:5–10 with emphasis laid on Christ's commitment to do God's will, even though this meant "the offering of his body once for all" (10:10).[83] The references in these chapters to offering of "blood" have led to much discussion over the exact meaning of such wording. Some have argued that the blood speaks of the *life* of the sacrificial victim, so that in Christ's case what is offered is His life, and His life is thus made available to others through His sacrifice.[84] This seems true but it does not go far enough. Others understand "blood" in such passages to focus on the violent *death* of the victim or the life as given over in death.[85] This is certainly the sense in Hebrews, where references to Christ's blood are contextually associated with His suffering and death (cf. 2:14, 9:13–16, 10:19–20, 13:12).

The vicarious or substitutionary nature of Christ's sacrifice is seen in several elements of the presentation in 9:15–10:18 (as well as in 2:9; 7:27). One is the typological relationship of His death with the Old Testament sacrificial system (9:18–22; 10:1). In the Old Testament ritual, forgiveness was associated with the death of an innocent victim, which provided atonement for the sins of the priest and the people.[86] In the fulfillment of the type, however, Christ served as both Priest and victim in that He "offered himself without blemish to God" to provide forgiveness for others (9:14, 25–27; 10:10). A second way in which Christ's death is shown to be substitutionary is in the illustration of the testament given in 9:15–18. In a play on words with the term "covenant" (*diathēkē,* which also denotes a last will or testament), the author evoked the picture of someone dying so that others may receive benefit. A covenant is not valid until the death of the testator. But in this case His

83. See the earlier discussion of this passage in connection with Jesus' incarnation.

84. Westcott, *Epistle to the Hebrews,* 294; William Milligan, *The Resurrection of Our Lord* (London: Macmillan, 1881), 263–78; and Vincent Taylor, *The Atonement in New Testament Teaching,* 2d ed. (London: Epworth, 1945), 121–23, 198.

85. Leon Morris, *The Apostolic Preaching of the Cross,* 3d ed. (London: Tyndale, 1965), 112–28; Johannes Behm, *Theological Dictionary of the New Testament,* s.v. *"haima,"* 1:173–74; A. M. Stibbs, *The Meaning of the Word "Blood" in Scripture* (London: Tyndale, 1954); and Philip Edgcumbe Hughes, "The Blood of Jesus and His Heavenly Priesthood in Hebrews, Part I: The Significance of the Blood of Jesus," *Bibliotheca Sacra* 130 (1973): 107–9.

86. Cf. Morris, *Apostolic Preaching of the Cross,* 160–78.

death was necessary all the more, because the benefit to be provided included complete forgiveness of sins for those whose iniquities deserved punishment instead (cf. Jer. 31:34, quoted in Heb. 8:12 and 10:17–18).[87] But most importantly, Hebrews 9:15–18 portrays Christ's death in terms drawn from the description of the suffering servant in Isaiah 53:3–12, which speaks of the innocent one taking on himself the guilt of sinners and suffering for their well-being (Heb. 9:14, 26–28).[88]

The fourth contrast moves into the realm of effects or results of Christ's high priestly work. It sanctifies not just in some external, ceremonial way but cleanses the conscience and provides the full and eternal forgiveness that the new covenant promised (9:13–14, 15–22; 10:1–4, 14–18). Actually the effect of Christ's work is described with various terms, which give a full-orbed picture of its results. It is spoken of in these chapters as eternal redemption (9:12), cleansing of the conscience (vv. 13–14; cf. 10:2), removal of sin (9:26), perfecting of the worshiper (10:1, 14), sanctification (vv. 10, 14), and forgiveness of sins and lawless acts (v. 18). But in the context of chapters 9–10, the author tied together these different elements by coming back again and again to the new covenant's promise of complete forgiveness. The larger structure of chapter 9, of course, is the comparison of Christ's work with the Old Testament ritual of the Day of Atonement, and the patent argument is that Christ has superseded the old covenant's provision for sin. This is made even clearer by the repetition at the beginning of this comparison (8:6, 12), in the middle (9:15), and at the end (10:15–18) of the promise of eternal forgiveness in the new covenant. The mediatorial function of the high priest (cf. 5:1) is fulfilled by Christ in that by His high priestly work He became the Guarantor (7:22) or Mediator of the new covenant (8:6, 9:15, 12:24; whenever Hebrews speaks of Christ's mediatorial work, it is connected with the new covenant). In this way, His priestly work is seen again, as in the first mention in the epistle (1:3), in vital connection with the salvation-historical change which God had undertaken through Christ.

Christ's present ministry in heaven. The final dimension of Christ's high priestly role to be developed here is His present ministry in heaven. This integrates in a number of ways with the other features of His priestly work. It also is drawn directly from theological reflection on Psalm 110. What can be learned about Jesus' present role in heaven when He is seen as the One who is now exalted to God's right hand (Ps. 110:1), after experiencing all the temptations of earthly life? What does it mean if after His sacrificial death, He is seated in God's very presence as a Priest forever in a new priestly line (Ps. 110:4)?

Hebrews begins to trace Jesus' present ministry for believers as early as 2:14–18 and 4:14–16, where His high priestly role is first mentioned. There His traits as a merciful and sympathetic High Priest are emphasized in connection with His full participation in humanity. Because of His incarnation, temptation, and suffering, He is able to help those who are weak and in need. So in their present suffer-

87. Ibid., 107–11.

88. Schaefer, "Relationship between Priestly and Servant Messianism," 377–81.

ings, believers are urged to approach the throne of grace with confidence that mercy and grace are available in their struggles. But the office of high priest requires not merely sympathy toward sinners but also divine appointment (5:1–10), and this is where the insights from Psalm 110 provide the backdrop for what was said about Jesus as High Priest in the earlier passages.

Jesus, who was obedient to God's will even to the point of sacrificial death, was appointed by God as High Priest forever in a new order of priests (5:8–10). Thus He has entered on behalf of believers into the inner sanctuary, into God's very presence as the Melchizedekan High Priest (6:19–20). In contrast to the old priesthood, this new order has an eternal quality about it (7:3), and Jesus has become a priest based on the power of an indestructible life (vv. 16–17). Clearly these references are to Jesus' eternal nature as God's Son and to the confirmation of it in His resurrection. Because He lives forever in a permanent priesthood, He is able to save His people completely (vv. 23–24a). At this juncture in chapter 7 a significant feature of Jesus' present ministry is cited: He always lives to *intercede* for His people (v. 24b).

Jesus' high priestly intercession is not described explicitly in this verse. However, it is clearly linked to what He knows of human needs (since He is fully sympathetic),[89] and it is based on His exalted position (seated at the Father's right hand after offering Himself once for all as our perfect sacrifice). Hebrews 9:24 complements the picture of Jesus' intercession: "He entered heaven itself, now to appear for us in God's presence." His presence with God is a constant reminder of the work of sacrifice which He accomplished and which God accepts.[90] Jesus' presence with God *for* us assures us that grace and mercy is available for whatever distress believers may encounter.

The thought in Hebrews thus seems to be similar to that of Romans 8:31–39. (In the New Testament the verb "intercede" appears only in Rom. 8:27, 34; and Heb. 7:25.) The common threads are these: (1) Christ's death demonstrates God's love for humankind in the ultimate way. (2) Believers can be sure then that God will freely provide for their needs. (3) No one can accuse them, since Christ is at God's right hand and appeals to Him on their behalf. (4) Therefore, they may be sure that no trial or any other circumstance can separate them from God's love in Christ.

This line of thought shows, of course, that there is no concept of the Son persuading a reluctant Father to show grace to believers. Instead it was by God's grace that He went to the cross (Heb. 2:9), and His presence with God is the full demonstration that God has accepted believers completely and that they may have confidence about the future, no matter what the circumstances.[91]

89. Cf. Cullmann, *Christology of the New Testament*, 102–3.
90. Leon Morris, "The Cross in the Epistle to the Hebrews," in *The Cross in the New Testament* (Grand Rapids: Eerdmans, n.d.), 284; and Westcott, *Epistle to the Hebrews*, 230.
91. Cf. Philip Edgcumbe Hughes, "The Blood of Jesus and His Heavenly Priesthood in Hebrews, Part III: The Present Work of Christ in Heaven," *Bibliotheca Sacra* 131 (1974): 32–33.

FROM OLD TO NEW: SALVATION-HISTORY IN HEBREWS

One of the most distinctive themes in the theology of Hebrews is the change from old to new in God's dealings with humankind. In Jesus Christ a decisive shift in salvation-history has occurred according to God's plan. What was provisional and ineffective has been superseded by the final and full salvation in the Son of God, a change anticipated in the Old Testament itself. This focus in Hebrews is often traced by highlighting the ways in which Jesus is said to be "better" than what the Old Testament provided. The theme is, however, more pervasive in Hebrews, and some of its wider dimensions will be traced in this section.

FROM SHADOW TO SUBSTANCE

Central to the thought of Hebrews is the idea that the Old Testament foreshadowed the decisive days of fulfillment that have now begun in Jesus Christ. Three lines of argument are used in Hebrews to make this point.

The Son as the final revelation of God. Hebrews emphasizes this theme from the very first paragraph. Hebrews 1:1–4 traces the decisive change in God's revelation: in earlier days God spoke in various ways but incompletely in the prophets, but now He has spoken fully and uniquely in His Son (vv. 1–2a), especially in the incarnation, life, sacrificial death, resurrection, and exaltation of the One who shared the Father's nature (vv. 2b–4). These are significant assertions, though many Christians have perhaps become so accustomed to the ideas that they no longer seem remarkable. One important assertion is the fact of *progress* in God's revelation: valuable as they were, the prophets' words were not God's final message to His people. Moving beyond the Old Testament, God has revealed His purpose and character climactically in His Son. But the writer asserted here a significant *continuity* in revelation as well: it is God who spoke then and now to reveal His eternal plan. This is typical of Hebrews: a new stage in God's salvation has been reached, but it was prepared for and foreshadowed by what has come before. Of significance is the phrase "in these last days," which describes the present age. This wording is reminiscent of Old Testament prophecy, but here the point is that the fulfillment of prophecy has begun in Christ.[92] All that was spoken before pointed to the "end" which is revealed in the Son.

The superiority of Christianity to the old covenant. A striking feature of Hebrews is the repeated assertion of the Son's superiority to various aspects of Old Testament religion. Words denoting "better" are used thirteen times in Hebrews, always of this comparison in some way.[93] In other places the same comparison is

---

92. The phrase in the LXX is *ep' eschatou (-ōn) tōn hemerōn.* See this in Genesis 49:1; Numbers 24:14; Joshua 24:27; Jeremiah 23:20; 30:24; 49:39; Ezekiel 38:16; Daniel 2:28; 10:14; Hosea 3:5; Micah 4:1; and similar wording in Deuteronomy 4:30; 31:29; 32:20; Isaiah 2:2. Hebrews adds the demonstrative *toutōn* to focus on the present. Bruce rightly says that the phrase "implies an inaugurated eschatology" (*Epistle to the Hebrews*, 3), and this idea will be defended in the section on eschatology.

93. Cf. forms of *kreittōn* in Hebrews 1:4; 7:7, 19, 22; 8:6 (twice); 9:23; 10:34; 11:16, 35, 40; 12:24, and of *kreissōn* in 6:9.

made using different wording (2:2–4; 3:3–6; 5:4–10; 10:27–28; 12:25).[94] The superiority of the Son to the old order is the backbone of the author's exhortations for his readers to hold on to their Christian confession, despite the difficulties it may bring.

The author did not argue the superiority of Christianity only against the Judaism of his day or against some perverted observance of Old Testament religion in earlier days. The comparison is always focused on the Mosaic order itself as revealed by God. Moreover, the points compared are not secondary matters, but things central to religious life, such as hope, covenant, ministry, promises, and sacrifice for sin.[95] And in making this argument, remarkably, the author cited Old Testament Scripture as valid revelation from God, to show that it has been fulfilled in Jesus Christ. The point is that *God* established something better through the Son, which was prefigured in the old order. The new has superseded the old according to God's plan.

"The self-confessed inadequacy of the old order."[96] Closely related is a third line of argument in Hebrews concerning the relationship between the testaments. This theme was treated with insight by Caird years ago, and he calls it "the main argument of the epistle."[97] He points out that the Old Testament is treated as valid, but is cited to show "its constant disclaimer of finality."[98] He writes:

> It is not the purpose of the author to prove the superiority of the New Covenant to the Old, nor to establish the inadequacy of the old order. His interest is in the confessed inadequacy of the old order. . . . His argument falls into four sections, each having as its core an Old Testament passage which declares the ineffectiveness and symbolic or provisional nature of the Old Testament religious institutions. All other scriptural references are ancillary to these four (Pss. 8, 95, 110, and Jer. 31), which control the drift of the argument.[99]

The proof that God is working out His salvation in the old order and the new is found in this very thing: the same God who has spoken in Christ provided anticipations of this fulfillment throughout the Old Testament. As Caird puts it, "The Old Testament provides aspirations to which only Christ supplies the fulfillment, questions to which only Christ furnishes the answers. . . . it enables [the writer] to present Christ as the climax of the ongoing, historic purpose of God."[100] The Old Testament prefigured the days of fulfillment that have now begun in Christ.

94. William L. Lane, *Hebrews 1–8*, Word Biblical Commentary (Dallas: Word, 1991), cxxix.

95. Ibid., cxxix; and W. Klassen, "To the Hebrews or against the Hebrews? Anti-Judaism and the Epistle to the Hebrews," in *Anti-Judaism in Early Christianity*, ed. S. G. Wilson (Waterloo, Ont.: Wilfred Laurier Univ., 1986), 7.

96. This phrase is quoted from Caird, "Exegetical Method of Hebrews," 47.

97. Ibid.

98. Ibid., 46.

99. Ibid., 47.

100. Ibid., 51. See the same point made by Goppelt, *Theology of the New Testament*, 2:245–47.

THE NEW COVENANT

A second topic in Hebrews which focuses attention on the shift from old to new in God's program is the new covenant. This theme has many ties with Christ's priesthood and sacrifice, but its connection with salvation history will be treated here. Hebrews argues that the new covenant has superior benefits and that in God's plan it was to supersede the old covenant and its law.

The need for the new covenant and its superior provisions. As already stated, Hebrews often cites the Old Testament's own reflections of its provisional character. This appears unmistakably in Hebrews' treatment of the need for a new covenant with better promises to replace the old.

The old covenant's provisional character is seen initially in the discussion of Christ's Melchizedekan priesthood in Hebrews 7. Verse 11 of that chapter reasons that if the Levitical priesthood (associated specifically with the law) had been adequate, why would God speak in Psalm 110:4 of a priest arising from a different order? The chapter goes on to argue that such a change in priesthood entails also a shift away from the law and the covenant associated with the old order. The connection of priesthood with "covenant" is made explicit in 7:22. "Because of this oath [of Ps. 110:4], Jesus has become the guarantee of a better covenant." Linked to this reasoning is the contrast between the "weakness and uselessness" of the former order with its impermanence (vv. 18, 23) and the better hope, better covenant, and eternal provision Jesus has inaugurated (vv. 19–22).

In chapter 8 the same line of reasoning is repeated and linked explicitly with Jeremiah's prophecy of the new covenant. Jesus' ministry as Priest is superior to the old order of priests just as the covenant He has mediated is better and based on better promises (8:6). The argument of verse 7 supports this statement (cf. the Gk. causal conjunction *gar*) by mirroring the argument of 7:11[101] to the effect that "if the old had been adequate, a replacement would not have been needed." But the wording of 8:7 anticipates the exegetical insight the author of Hebrews drew from Jeremiah's prophecy itself and developed explicitly in 8:13. Hebrews 8:7 emphasizes that God's introduction of a *second* covenant indicates inadequacies in the *first*. This comes from the author's attention to the wording of Jeremiah 31:31. The promise of a new covenant through Jeremiah demonstrates the Lord's intent to replace the old and make the first covenant obsolete (Heb. 8:13).[102] The argument makes clear that Jeremiah promised not a *renewed* covenant but a second, new one which replaces the old. The new covenant is thus discontinuous with the old and provides something better.

101. Both verses contain a contrary-to-fact conditional statement arguing the inadequacy of the old order. See Attridge, *Epistle to the Hebrews,* 226–27; and Lane, *Hebrews 1–8,* 208.

102. "Here is a perfectly sound piece of exegesis. Jeremiah predicted the establishment of a new covenant because he believed the old one to be inadequate for the religious needs of sinful men. The sacrifices of the old covenant were a perpetual reminder of sin and of man's need for atonement, but what men needed was the effective removal of sin, so that it could no longer barricade the way into the inner presence of God" (Caird, "Exegetical Method of Hebrews," 47).

The particular old covenant weakness, emphasized in Hebrews 9–10, is its ineffective provision for forgiveness of sins and access to God. The repeated sacrifices under the old order could never take away sins or give open access to God (9:9; 10:1, 11). In contrast, two covenant-provisions from Jeremiah 31 are emphasized in Hebrews. These are forgiveness of sins and the implanting of God's laws on human hearts (the internalizing of God's precepts). These provisions are repeated in Hebrews 10:15–18, and a focus on them appears also in more subtle ways.[103] Under the new covenant mediated by Christ in His death (9:15–16), there is full and eternal forgiveness (9:12; 10:12–18), just as God promised through Jeremiah ("I will remember their sins no more," Jer. 31:34d). In addition, Christians now have open access to God by faith so they may confidently draw near in worship (Heb. 10:19–22). This theme of divine access is related to the new covenant provision of internalized law, in that God's people are given a cleansed conscience and a sincere heart in order to approach Him with full assurance (v. 22). The reference to "having our hearts sprinkled to cleanse us from a guilty conscience" (v. 22) seems to allude to Ezekiel's presentation of the new covenant in 36:25–27, in which sprinkling with pure water is linked to bestowing a new heart and putting the Spirit within so that God's people will observe His statutes.[104] The new covenant inaugurated by Christ's death is superior because it provides eternal forgiveness and transforms individuals so they may draw near to God with a clear conscience.

The abrogation of the law. God's redemptive purpose was being worked out in this change from the old covenant with its ineffective sacrificial system to the new covenant blessings through Christ. God used the old order for good, but it was always provisional, intended as a foreshadowing of the coming order that would replace it.[105]

The author of Hebrews found insight into this shift through his exegetical reflection on another Old Testament text, Psalm 40. That psalm presents a contrast between the "sacrifices and offerings" in which God takes no delight and "coming to do your will" through "a body prepared for me" (cited in Heb. 10:5–7). The exposition of this in verses 8–9 specifically associates these "sacrifices" with the law ("which are offered in accordance with the law," v. 8b, author's trans.) and "doing God's will" with Jesus' sacrifice of Himself. The working out of God's redemptive purpose in history can be seen in this contrast. The conclusion from this is stated in verse 9b, "He abolishes the first in order to establish the se-

103. Attridge, *Epistle to the Hebrews,* 226.

104. David Peterson, "The Prophecy of the New Covenant in the Argument of Hebrews," *Reformed Theological Review* 38 (1979): 78; and Homer A. Kent, "The New Covenant and the Church," *Grace Theological Journal* 6 (1985): 294. The working of the Spirit is one of Paul's emphases in his discussion of the new covenant ministry in 2 Corinthians 3–4.

105. See the summary of the role of the law in Hebrews in Susanne Lehne, *The New Covenant in Hebrews,* Journal for the Study of the New Testament Supplement Series 44 (Sheffield: JSOT, 1990), 26–27 (cf. also pp. 22, 78). The law provided limited, temporary cleansing and access to God, and, more important, it foreshadowed categories important to the new covenant order. But there is no "new law" envisioned under the new covenant.

cond."[106] Here the Greek neuter singular is used to speak more generally of "the first matter/thing" (*to protōn*) and "the second matter/thing" (*to deuteron*), referring not to covenant alone or sacrifices alone but to the entire old order associated with the sacrifices and the entire new order established by Christ's offering of Himself. In doing God's will on the cross, He abolished the one and established the other.

As Ellingworth points out, Hebrews 10:9b uses a strong word to describe the end of the old order: "*Abolishes* [Gk. *anairei*] is the strongest language the writer ever uses, perhaps the strongest he could use, about the end of the old order. . . . he is pointing to an act by which God put an end to a system which he had himself set up."[107]

Similar wording about the abrogation of the law is found in chapter 7. In 7:12 and 18, two words are used to describe the "change" (*metathesis*) in the law and "setting aside" (*athetēsis*) of the commandment. These words denote not merely an amendment or alteration of the law, but its abrogation, annulment, or supersession.[108] This is stated in a context that argues that various aspects of the old order are interconnected: the priesthood, sacrifices, covenant, law or commandment, and hope. So when the priesthood changes, as God's oath in Psalm 110:4 signifies, the law and other features of the old order associated with it are changed also according to God's plan.[109]

The point is not that the sacrificial system and the priesthood alone are set aside, while the law itself is retained. Nor is it that only the cultic or ceremonial aspects of the law were abrogated.[110] This sort of limitation is never given. Instead the author took pains to associate the law itself with the sacrificial system and the Levitical priesthood in the very contexts where he argued for abrogation. This can be seen in the parenthetical comments of 7:11, 18–19 and 10:8. Having explicitly linked the law to the sacrifices and priesthood, the author then affirmed that these interconnected features of the old order have been superseded in God's program by the new covenant provisions through Christ.

Another support for this view is the line of thought advanced in 7:28. Here the author presented the law and its high priests as a temporary provision to be su-

---

106. Cf. Kaiser, "Abolition of the Old Order and Establishment of the New," 33–34; and William L. Lane, *Hebrews 9–13*, Word Biblical Commentary (Dallas: Word, 1991), 264.

107. Paul Ellingworth, *The Epistle to the Hebrews*, Epworth Commentaries (London: Epworth, 1991), 89. See also Otto Michel, *Der Brief an die Hebräer*, Kritischexegetischer Kommentar über das Neue Testament, 12th ed. (Göttingen: Vandenhoeck & Ruprecht, 1966), 338. He cites Hellenistic uses of this word that refer to making laws "invalid."

108. See Attridge, *Epistle to the Hebrews*, 201, 203; Bauer, Arndt, and Gingrich, *A Greek-English Lexicon of the New Testament*, 21, 511; and Christian Maurer, *Theological Dictionary of the New Testament*, s.v. "*tithēmi*," 8:158–59, 161–62. The nouns are used in the New Testament only in Hebrews. *Athetēsis* is used in 9:26 of the "removal" of sin, and *metathesis* is used in 11:5 of Enoch's translation from earth and in 12:27 of the "removing" of created things which can be shaken so that the eternal things may remain.

109. Bruce, *Epistle to the Hebrews*, 145–48.

110. Cf. wording to this effect in Herbert Braun, *An die Hebräer*, Handbuch zum Neuen Testament 14 (Tübingen: Mohr [Paul Siebeck], 1984), 201, 226, 298; Kaiser, "Abolition of the Old Order and Establishment of the New," 33; and Lane, *Hebrews 1–8*, 182.

perseded by God's later provision. The oath of Psalm 110:4 "came after the law" to appoint Jesus as the eternal and perfect High Priest. As Bruce says, "This supersession came into effect when the Messiah appeared and vindicated his high-priestly title on the basis of a perfect sacrifice."[111] Just as Paul argued in Galatians 3:15–29 (somewhat differently) that the law was a temporary arrangement designed to lead to Christ, the author of Hebrews pictured the work of God in the Son as the culminating event in salvation-history, marking the fulfillment and abrogation of the law.[112] This event marks the inauguration of the new covenant, as chapter 8 then states.

The work of God in Christ inaugurates a new era in the fulfillment of God's plan, but some aspects of that plan are yet to be fulfilled.

ESCHATOLOGY IN HEBREWS

Dualism and cosmology in Hebrews. From a study of certain verses and forms of expression in Hebrews, many have concluded that the epistle is strongly influenced by Platonic philosophical ideas. These ideas were perhaps mediated through Philo or the wider Hellenized Judaism of Alexandria and elsewhere, but a background of Platonic or Philonic concepts of reality is thought by many to be central in this epistle. Moffatt, for example, wrote that "the philosophical element in [the author's] view of the world is fundamentally Platonic. Like Philo and the author of *Wisdom*, he interprets the past and present alike in terms of the old theory that the phenomenal is but an imperfect, shadowy transcript of what is eternal and real."[113]

The expressions that seem most strongly to indicate this background are in three places: 8:5 (the earthly sanctuary as "a copy [*hypodeigma*] and shadow [*skia*] of what is in heaven"); 9:23–24 ("It was necessary, then, for the copies [*hypodeigmata*] of the heavenly things to be purified with these sacrifices, but the heavenly things themselves with better sacrifices than these. For Christ did not enter a man-made sanctuary that was only a copy [*antitypos*] of the true one [*alēthinos*]; he entered heaven itself"); and 10:1 ("The law is only a shadow [*skia*] of the good things that are coming, not the very form [*eikōn*] of the things themselves"). These expressions seem to reflect a Platonic cosmology: a vertical dualism contrasting what is earthly, derivative, and insubstantial with what is heavenly, real, and eternal. If this view of reality is predominant in Hebrews, then a horizontal, eschatological perspective would be less significant in its theology.[114]

---

111. Bruce, *Epistle to the Hebrews*, 160.

112. See the comparison of new covenant themes in Paul and Hebrews given by Lehne, *New Covenant in Hebrews*, 73–80. Kent discusses how national Israel and the church relate to the new covenant ("New Covenant and the Church," 296–98).

113. James Moffatt, *A Critical and Exegetical Commentary on the Epistle to the Hebrews*, International Critical Commentary (Edinburgh: T. & T. Clark, 1924), xxxi. A detailed case for Philonic influence was made by Ceslas Spicq, *L' Épître aux Hébreux*, 2 vols. (Paris: Lecoffre, 1952–53).

114. The most recent detailed defense of this approach is James W. Thompson, *The Beginnings of Christian Philosophy: The Epistle to the Hebrews*, Catholic Biblical Quarterly Monograph Series 13 (Washington, D.C.: Catholic Biblical Society of America, 1982).

However, the Platonic interpretation of these phrases is by no means necessary. The discussion of shadow, type, pattern, and true form can just as easily be drawn from eschatological sources and refer to the temporal dualism of Jewish-Christian apocalyptic. As Barrett argued in a classic essay, the predominant framework of thought in Hebrews is eschatological, not Platonic. "Apocalyptic supplies the notion of both a heavenly temple, and an eschatological temple; these were normally combined in the belief that, in the age to come, the heavenly temple would be manifested and established on earth."[115] Hurst has shown that the features that have been read in a Philonic way are better understood as Old Testament ideas developed by the author of Hebrews in an apocalyptic framework.[116]

This conclusion about the background of thought is supported in the context of the verses from Hebrews cited above. The contrasts of shadow versus reality and earthly versus heavenly in 8:5; 9:23–24; and 10:1 are framed by the contrast between the old and new covenants in chapter 8 and the old and new priesthoods in chapter 9. They concern the good things to come (10:1) and are linked to the setting aside of the old system in order to establish the new (10:9). The dominant framework in Hebrews is the outworking of God's salvation in history, not a Platonic cosmology.[117]

The already/not yet tension. The outworking of God's salvation is seen by Hebrews in an already/not yet tension, as in the New Testament in general. The decisive era in the fulfillment of God's promises has been reached or inaugurated in Christ, so that in some sense the fulfillment is already present. But the consummation has not yet come, and significant events in God's program are eagerly expected in the future.[118]

The "already" can be seen in Hebrews from the very first paragraph. Hebrews 1:2 contrasts earlier forms of God's revelation with the decisive revelation given "in these last days"[119] in His Son. In fulfillment of Psalm 8 and 110, the Son has taken His seat at the Father's right hand (1:3, 13; 8:1; 10:12) and thus has been crowned with glory and honor (2:9), though He awaits the full subjection of His

115. Barrett, "Eschatology of the Epistle to the Hebrews," 386. See also R. J. McKelvey, *The New Temple: The Church in the New Testament,* Oxford Theological Monographs (Oxford: Oxford Univ., 1969), 25–41.

116. L. D. Hurst, *The Epistle to the Hebrews: Its Background of Thought,* Society for New Testament Studies Monograph Series 65 (Cambridge: Cambridge Univ., 1990), 7–42; and idem, "Eschatology and 'Platonism' in the Epistle to the Hebrews," in *Society of Biblical Literature 1984 Seminar Papers,* ed. Kent Harold Richards (Chico, Calif.: Scholars, 1984), 41–74.

117. Goppelt, *Theology of the New Testament,* 2:246–47; George Eldon Ladd, *A Theology of the New Testament* (Grand Rapids: Eerdmans, 1974), 572–77; and William Robinson, "The Eschatology of the Epistle to the Hebrews: A Study in the Christian Doctrine of Hope," *Encounter* 22 (1961): 41–44, 49–51.

118. Barrett, "Eschatology of the Epistle to the Hebrews," 384, 391; Robinson, "Eschatology of the Epistle to the Hebrews," 44–45; Thompson, *The Beginnings of Christian Philosophy,* 41–42; and Lehne, *New Covenant in Hebrews,* 79.

119. See n. 92 about the LXX background of this phrase.

enemies under His feet. To be in the Christian community is to experience already the powers of the age to come (6:5). Christ by His death has become the Mediator of the new covenant (8:6–13; 9:15) prophesied by Jeremiah. The old, imperfect sacrificial rituals looked forward to the "time of the new order" which has now been reached (9:10) because of Christ's sacrifice "at the end of the ages" (9:26). The sacrifices of the law were only a shadow of the coming good things now available to the worshiper through Christ (10:1). God's plan was that the heroes of faith of earlier days would be made perfect only in connection with believers of this era (11:39–40). The prospect of the eschatological shaking of all creation should make Christ's followers thankful, since they are already receiving an unshakable kingdom (12:28).

The "not yet" dimension of the eschatology of Hebrews can be seen in numerous verses. Several verses mention without discussion such future events as the resurrection of the dead (6:2; 11:35), future judgment (6:2; 10:27, 31; 12:23), and giving an account for one's ministry (13:17). Other future events are more significant to the argument of Hebrews: the inhabited world to come which will be subject to Christ (2:5); the subjecting of all enemies to the Son in fulfillment of messianic promises (1:13; 2:8; 10:13);[120] the Sabbath-rest which may be entered through enduring faith (4:9, 11);[121] the end of the age until which the believer must hold fast his or her hope (3:6, 14; 6:11); the reception of future blessing or inheritance (9:15; 10:36; 11:14, 16; 13:14); Christ's second coming (9:28; 10:37), the Day of the Lord or of judgment (10:25); and the eschatological shaking of all the creation (12:26–29).

A detailed eschatological scheme is not laid out, but it is clear that Hebrews looks forward to significant events in the future which will consummate God's work of salvation. The author exhorted his readers to faith and endurance based on the prospect of these future events.

THE CHRISTIAN LIFE: CALL TO FAITH AND ENDURANCE

Hebrews is marked by a unique intermingling of doctrine and exhortation. The rich theology of the epistle provides the basis for urging Christians to live in faith and obedience. This mix of theology and exhortation is the writer's pastoral response to the situation his readers were facing: a situation of grave spiritual danger. In this setting the writer communicated vital truths about living the Christian life in the face of weakness and difficulty.

THE SPIRITUAL CONDITION OF THE READERS

The readers had begun their Christian experience when they heard the message of salvation from godly people who had heard Jesus Himself (2:1–4; 13:7).

---

120. This is one of the most significant future events mentioned in Hebrews: the consummation of Jesus' Davidic kingship in a visible rule on earth. See the treatment of this in the section "Jesus as Exalted Son."

121. See the development of this theme in the next section.

Later they had endured a hard struggle of suffering and persecution by showing exemplary faith, joy, and self-giving love (10:32–34). They had labored for God and lovingly served His people and were continuing to do so (6:10). But now they were at great risk. They seemed to be caught in a kind of spiritual lethargy and infancy (5:11; 6:12). They were in danger of drifting away or shrinking back from their commitment to Christ (2:1; 10:39). Their confidence in God's promises had been shaken, and they were on the verge of hard-hearted unbelief and rebellion against God (3:6–14; 4:1, 11; 10:35–36; 12:25). These readers were apparently tempted to abandon their Christian confession and pull back into the protective fold and familiar religious practices of Judaism.[122] They had not yet taken such a step, but they were greatly tempted.

Their spiritual problems were due in part to the threat of further persecution for their faith in Christ (10:32–39; 13:3, 13). Identification with Christianity had exacted too high a price and Judaism offered a safe haven. There is also evidence that the readers had struggled with a troubled conscience and the shock of leaving behind old ways of approaching God in worship. Lindars has argued that the readers must have been troubled by their continued struggles with human frailty and sinfulness, and they naively longed for the sense of immediate, tangible cleansing available through the Jewish sacrificial ritual. The epistle's emphasis on the superiority of the new covenant to the old and of Christ's perfect sacrifice compared to the ineffective offerings of the old order was designed to answer such a problem.[123]

Instead of reverting to Judaism, the readers desperately needed to focus on Jesus Christ and grasp the meaning of His high priesthood. He alone provides the full and eternal forgiveness that God had promised in the new covenant, a forgiveness and cleansing of the conscience never available under the old order. Jesus is the merciful High Priest who fully identified with human weakness and made mercy and grace available for every need they had. The emphasis on Jesus' true humanity also plays a large role in the writer's exhortation to his readers: Christ's example of fidelity to God despite human suffering sets the pattern for all Christians to follow in their times of adversity. Jesus, though He was God's Son, "learned obedience from what he suffered" (5:8) and remained faithful even to the point of "enduring the cross" (12:2). So also Christians as God's children cannot expect to escape hardships but must endure them in faith, with the assurance that these represent the Lord's fatherly discipline to train them in righteousness (12:4–11).

The readers' precarious spiritual condition provides the setting for the epistle's teaching on the Christian life. An understanding of this teaching requires an exploration of the well-known warning passages in Hebrews.

---

122. This is the conclusion of many. See especially Bruce, *Epistle to the Hebrews,* xxiii–xxx; Barnabas Lindars, *The Theology of the Letter to the Hebrews* (Cambridge: Cambridge Univ., 1991), 4–5; Attridge, *Epistle to the Hebrews,* 10–13; and J. Dwight Pentecost, *A Faith That Endures* (Grand Rapids: Discovery House, 1992), 11–13, 26–31.

123. Lindars, *Theology of Hebrews,* 10–15.

THE WARNINGS AGAINST APOSTASY

The warnings to the readers of Hebrews constitute some of the most perplexing passages in the epistle. These sections are 2:1–4; 3:6–4:13; 5:11–6:12; 10:26–39; and 12:12–29.

Approaches to these passages. Interpreters have followed four major approaches in seeking to make sense of the theology of these texts. Each approach has strong and weak points.

In the Arminian approach the warnings are viewed as addressing genuine Christians who may fall away from salvation and thus incur eternal judgment. Adherents differ over the nature of the apostasy in view and over the possibility of reconversion after falling away. Support for this approach comes from the description in 6:4–5 of those who fall away, since this seems to reflect a genuine experience of Christian conversion. The warnings of judgment in 6:7–8 and 10:26–31 also fit this view since these seem to speak of eternal condemnation for apostates.[124] The problem with this approach is that it conflicts with passages that clearly teach the security of the believer (John 10:25–30; Rom. 8:28–39; 1 Peter 1:3–9), including passages in Hebrews (7:25; 8:12; 9:14–15; 10:14). Another difficulty for some is that it proves too much: restoration of one who falls away is impossible (6:4–6), a position opposed by much of Arminian theology.

The normal Calvinist approach understands these passages as addressed to participants in the Christian assembly, who by rejecting what they know of Christ would fall into eternal judgment and show that they never had a genuine faith in Him at all. This view gives the most natural interpretation of the verses describing judgment (6:7–8; 10:26–31) and those that imply security (7:25; 8:12; 9:14–15; 10:14), but has difficulty with the descriptions in 6:4–5, since they appear to present genuine Christian experience rather than mere profession of Christianity.[125]

Another approach with Calvinist roots is the hypothetical one. On this reading the warnings are given to shock the readers by presenting the awful judgment that would come if a genuine believer rejected Christ. But the writer did not consider this possible; he simply used the argument to show the folly of the action his

---

124. Cf. I. Howard Marshall, *Kept by the Power of God: A Study of Perseverance and Falling Away* (London: Epworth, 1969), 132–54; and Grant Osborne, "Soteriology in the Epistle to the Hebrews," in *Grace Unlimited,* ed. Clark H. Pinnock (Minneapolis: Bethany Fellowship, 1975), 144–66.

125. Cf. Philip Edgcumbe Hughes, "Hebrews 6:4–6 and the Peril of Apostasy," *Westminster Theological Journal* 35 (1973): 137–55; Roger Nicole, "Some Comments on Hebrews 6:4–6 and the Doctrine of the Perseverance of God with the Saints," in *Current Issues in Biblical and Patristic Interpretation: Studies in Honor of Merrill C. Tenney,* ed. Gerald F. Hawthorne (Grand Rapids: Eerdmans, 1975), 355–64; and Stanley D. Toussaint, "The Eschatology of the Warning Passages in the Book of Hebrews," *Grace Theological Journal* 3 (1982): 67–80. Scot McKnight's phenomenological view seems to fit best here, but the logic of his position is not entirely clear ("The Warning Passages of Hebrews: A Formal Analysis and Theological Conclusions," *Trinity Journal* 13 [1992]: 21–59).

readers were tempted to take.[126] This view makes good sense of the descriptions of 6:4–6 and the verses on security, but the warnings about judgment ring hollow when read hypothetically.

Another approach common in evangelical circles is that these passages warn genuine believers about loss of reward or God's disciplinary judgment for those who are unfaithful. This view holds to the security of the believer against eternal condemnation, but understands these as real warnings about some lesser judgment the readers were in danger of incurring.[127] This approach makes good sense of 6:4–5, but it has difficulty with the severity of judgment described in 6:7–8 and especially 10:26–31.

Before a conclusion can be drawn about these approaches, three important themes in the warning passages must be examined. It is important to draw evidence from all the passages to get a composite picture of these themes.

Nature of the apostasy. The first theme to examine is the nature of the "falling away" about which the readers were being warned.

The passages give evidence that the readers were currently in a kind of spiritual lethargy and infancy (5:11; 6:12). They were not making spiritual progress as they ought. Also they were spiritually exhausted, weakened, and lame (12:12–13). They needed renewed strength to run their race with endurance (10:36; 12:1–2) and to hold fast to the hope they had confessed (3:6, 14). What they were warned against, however, was worse than lethargy and weakness.

The passages describe the next step in frightening terms. The readers had not taken this step yet, but they were on the verge of it. They are said to be in danger of drifting away from or neglecting the gospel of salvation (2:1, 3), of throwing away their confidence or shrinking back from faith (10:35, 38–39). They were on the verge of hard-hearted unbelief (3:12, 19), disobedience (3:18; 4:6, 11), and refusing God and turning away from Him (12:25). They were warned against being hardened by sin's deceitfulness (3:13) and sinning willfully after having the knowledge of the truth (10:26). They were threatened by spiritual failure and falling short of God's promises and His grace (4:1, 11; 12:15). Finally, they were in danger of falling away from their current spiritual status (6:6) or turning away ("apostatizing") from the living God (3:12).

These references to "falling away" or "apostatizing" employ words that occur elsewhere to denote a willful rejection of salvation and rebellion against God and His ways (Luke 8:13; Acts 21:21; 2 Thess. 2:3; 1 Tim. 4:1). Hebrews itself paraphrases what it means to fall away by describing it as a repudiation of Christ

---

126. Homer A. Kent, *The Epistle to the Hebrews: A Commentary* (Grand Rapids: Baker, 1972), 113–14; and Thomas Hewitt, *The Epistle to the Hebrews: An Introduction and Commentary,* Tyndale New Testament Commentaries (Grand Rapids, Eerdmans, 1960), 110–11. A variation on this is given by Ryrie, *Biblical Theology of the New Testament,* 256–58.

127. Zane C. Hodges, "Hebrews," in *The Bible Knowledge Commentary: New Testament,* ed. John F. Walvoord and Roy B. Zuck (Wheaton, Ill.: Victor, 1983), 786–89, 794–96, 805–6; and Joseph C. Dillow, *The Reign of the Servant Kings: A Study of Eternal Security and the Final Significance of Man* (Miami Springs, Fla.: Schoettle, 1992), 433–66.

and His sacrifice: crucifying the Son of God all over again and subjecting Him to public disgrace (6:6) and trampling the Son of God under foot, treating the blood of the covenant that sanctified him as an unholy thing, and insulting the Spirit of grace (10:29). This indicates that the apostasy in view was not the sort of struggle with sin and temptation that was the common plight of God's people. Christ as merciful High Priest stood ready to provide mercy and grace for this kind of weakness. Instead the readers were warned against a knowledgeable, willful rejection of Christ and His sacrifice. To repudiate Him was to refuse the only effective sacrifice for sins, and only severe judgment could follow after such an act (10:26–27).

Negative consequences. What sort of consequences are said to be the fate of those who apostatize in this way? The warning passages speak of these in foreboding terms. The readers cannot hope for escape if they neglect God's salvation in Christ (2:3). To provoke God by unbelief means to fall under His anger as the wilderness generation did and to be estranged from the living God (3:8, 10–12, 16–17). Thus they would fail to enter the promised rest (3:18–4:11).[128] It would be impossible to renew them to repentance once they fall away, and instead they would be like land that bears no fruit: worthless, cursed, and left for burning (6:6–8). No provision for sin can be expected, but only a terrible and fiery judgment as the vengeance of the living God against His enemies (10:26–31). There could be no blessing, no repentance, and no escape for one who profanely refuses the awesome God who will shake the whole creation, who Himself is a consuming fire (12:14–29).[129]

As Toussaint has argued, these consequences can hardly be some sort of disciplinary judgment or loss of rewards. Instead they describe eternal damnation.[130] This is especially clear in the references to estrangement from the living God and coming under His wrath (3:10–12), no sacrifice availing for sin (10:26; cf. the contrast to the eternal effectiveness of Christ's sacrifice), and the prospect of fiery judgment (6:8; 10:27).

Positive response. The third important theme in the warning passages is the response the author urged his readers to make in their precarious condition. His exhortation is consistent and centers on virtues they sorely needed: faith and endurance.

The need to hold firmly to their confidence in God and endure patiently through whatever suffering may be necessary is the constant theme of the warning

128. The "promised rest" in Hebrews refers to earthly, millennial blessings as well as the believer's eternal future in heaven. For this association see George Wesley Buchanan, *The Consequences of the Covenant* (Leiden: Brill, 1970), 70–80; Otfried Hofius, *Katapausis: Die Vorstellung vom endzeitlichen Ruheort im Hebräerbrief* (Tübingen: Mohr [Paul Siebeck], 1970), 59–74; 144–53; and Neils-Erik Andreasen, *Rest and Redemption* (Berrien Springs, Mich.: Andrews Univ., 1978), 109–15.

129. The judgment on those who reject God's work in Christ will be immeasurably worse than what the wilderness generation suffered, as the writer showed by his "how much more" arguments in 2:3; 10:29; and 12:25.

130. Toussaint, "The Eschatology of the Warning Passages," 67–80. See also McKnight, "The Warning Passages of Hebrews," 33–36.

passages. The writer explicitly instructed them in 10:36, "you have need of endurance [*hypomonē*]," and they are urged to "run their race with endurance," as Jesus their Pioneer did when He endured sinners' hostility and ultimately endured the cross in following God's will for Him (12:1–3). Related to this is the call to exercise patience or longsuffering (*makrothymia*) in faithfully awaiting God's promises to be fulfilled (6:12, 15). A similar theme is that of "holding on" or "holding firm" (*katechō, krateō*) to their confession of faith in Christ, seen in a number of texts (3:6, 14; 4:14; 10:23). This is expressed in different terms in 2:1, where they are warned against "drifting away" and are told to pay closer attention to what they have heard about salvation in Christ. The exhortation to make every effort to enter the promised rest expresses the same need for constancy and diligent attention to God's message (4:11). The call to "hold on" is linked consistently with references to Christian hope or confidence in God (cf. 3:6; 6:11; 6:18; 10:23; 11:1). Assurance of God's care and of the fulfillment of His promises is what they must hold to firmly. This is coupled with repeated calls to respond to God and His promises with faith and to avoid unbelief (3:12, 19; 4:2–3; 6:12; 10:22, 38; 11:1–39; 12:2; 13:7).

So the warning passages urge the readers to continue in faith toward God and not fall into judgment by turning away from His full and perfect provision for sins through the Son and High Priest, Jesus Christ. But how can these elements of the warning passages be put together in a coherent way?

The interpretive paradigm. The pattern for making sense of these warnings is to be found in two conditional sentences in the first lengthy warning passage, 3:6–4:13. These two significant statements are in 3:6 and 3:14: "But Christ is faithful as a son over God's house. And we are his house, if we hold on to our courage and the hope of which we boast." "We have come to share in Christ if we hold firmly till the end the confidence we had at first."

Careful attention to the wording shows that these lines do not cite what *will* be true if they hold on, but what is *already* true of them, and which is to be evidenced by their endurance through temptation. The writer asserted that their continuance in faith will demonstrate that they *are* (present tense in Gk.) members of God's household, not that it will make it so in the future. Holding on to their confidence will reveal the reality they already *have* come to share (perfect tense) in Christ, not what they will share. By continuing in faith, they demonstrate the work Christ has already begun and will certainly accomplish in them (7:25; 8:12; 9:14–15; 10:14). The warnings about falling away and exhortations to endure are designed to make this point.

This paradigm for reading the warning passages is a common one in the New Testament: continuation in faith is the evidence of a genuine relationship with God, while failure to continue is the sign of false profession.[131] This is seen clearly in Jesus' words, "I never knew you," addressed to people who profess to be His followers and to do miracles in His name, but who practice lawlessness (Matt. 7:21–23). It is not that they fell away but that they never had a true relationship with

---

131. "Continuance in the Christian life is the test of reality" (Bruce, *Epistle to the Hebrews,* 59). See similar comments in Kent, *Epistle to the Hebrews,* 67, 74–75.

Him at all. Similarly 1 John 2:19 speaks of some whose failure to continue showed their true status: "They went out from us, but they did not really belong to us. For if they had belonged to us, they would have remained with us; but their going showed that none of them belonged to us."[132]

This pictures the crisis point reached by the readers of Hebrews. In their time of severe temptation, would they hold fast to the hope they had professed and thus show that they genuinely were God's people and partakers in Christ (3:6, 14)? The writer was confident they would endure and would remain faithful (cf. 6:9–12; 10:39). But he was careful to warn them against the alternative. They had been exposed firsthand to the truth of the gospel and the supremacy of Christ's saving work. Up to this point, they have given every evidence of true Christian experience. But they must continue in faith and obedience. To shrink back from Christ now would be a willful repudiation of the only way of salvation, and severe judgment would be certain for them.

This interpretation of the warning passages makes the best sense of the evidence of Hebrews itself and of broader New Testament theology. The difficulty for this approach is the description in 6:4–5 of those who fall away, since these verses seem to reflect a genuine experience of Christian conversion, rather than a description of false profession. The answer to this problem is to realize that in these verses the writer was describing the phenomena of their conversion: what their Christian experience has looked like outwardly. He portrayed them in distinctly Christian terms to emphasize how close they had been to the faith. From all that anyone could tell (and from how they viewed themselves), there would be those who would hold on and show the genuineness of their confession, and this was what the writer expected (6:9–12; 10:39). Nevertheless, he needed to warn them in strongest terms not to abandon their hope and repudiate Christ.

FAITH AND SOJOURNING

Many Christians think immediately of the great "hall of faith" in Hebrews 11 when they think of this epistle. They are correct to do so, because faith is one of the primary motifs in the epistle's teaching. There is also something distinctive about this, because Hebrews gives a unique coloring to faith compared to other New Testament books. But this uniqueness should not be distorted. Faith is often associated in Hebrews with the theme of sojourning or pilgrimage, and these will be discussed together.

Faith in Hebrews. Hebrews' teaching about faith is said by many to be distinctive in three ways compared to other New Testament writers like Paul or John. First, faith in Hebrews, according to some writers, is not focused on justification or soteriology but has become an ethical category, the quality of steadfastness. Sec-

---

132. Paul and James also wrote of people who profess a connection with the Christian faith, but who subsequently fail to continue and thus show they are not genuine believers (1 Cor. 5:11; 6:9–11; 2 Cor. 13:5; Col. 1:21–23; James 2:14–26). For elaboration of this view see D. A. Carson, "Reflections on Christian Assurance," *Westminster Theological Journal* 54 (1992): 16–20.

ond, Christ is said to be not the content or object of faith in Hebrews, but its model, the supreme example of faith in God. Third, the orientation of faith in Hebrews is said to be consistently future and to be almost synonymous with hope, while Paul, for example, oriented faith toward the past (the cross of Christ) or the present (as the means of mystical union with Christ).[133]

These distinctives have a measure of truth to them, because they reflect aspects of faith that are emphasized more in Hebrews than in other books. However, they can be distorted and may misrepresent what is said about faith, both in Hebrews and in other New Testament books. The distinctions stated above should not be forced into either/or dichotomies in Hebrews or elsewhere.[134] Three observations may be made.

First, Hebrews speaks of faith more broadly than just "initial faith" or the response of faith at the point of conversion. Faith encompasses also the continuing response of trust, obedience, and endurance which results from that conversion. As Lindars has said, faith in Hebrews "is always an active virtue, embracing acceptance, obedience, trust and perseverance. . . . It is not incompatible with the Pauline concept of faith, but Paul's special issue of justification does not arise in Hebrews."[135] This can be seen in the first warning passage (3:6–4:13), which calls for persevering faith in God and His word, instead of the unbelieving disobedience of the wilderness generation. It also shows up clearly in the exhortations of Hebrews 10:32–39, which carry over into the examples of faith in chapter 11. The Old Testament illustrations demonstrate that faith is infused with moral courage; it acts on its conviction and stands up for God and His ways in spite of adversity or persecution. They also show that faith is rooted in a personal relationship with God, a knowledge of Him and His character that enables the believer to rest in God's care, whatever His calling may mean in terms of earthly success or failure.

Second, while it is true that Hebrews emphasizes Christ's role as the supreme example of faith in God, it also presents Him as the object of the Christian's faith. This is not done with explicit formulas (e.g., "faith in Christ") as in other books, but it is communicated in the implicit logic of the epistle's exhortations. The careful portrayal of Jesus' true humanity and full deity and the superiority of His high priestly ministry is designed to bolster enduring faith in Him. As Hurst argues, Hebrews "focus[es] on Christ's high priestly work as the basis of the Christian's confidence."[136] It is significant to note that failure to continue in faith is regarded as an

---

133. Goppelt, *Theology of the New Testament*, 2:262–63. On these points Goppelt is following Erich Grässer, *Der Glaube im Hebräerbrief* (Marburg: Elwert, 1965) and Gerhard Dautzenberg, "Der Glaube im Hebräerbrief," *Biblische Zeitschrift* 17 (1973): 161–77.

134. See Dennis Hamm, "Faith in the Epistle to the Hebrews: The Jesus Factor," *Catholic Biblical Quarterly* 52 (1990): 270–91; and Thompson, *Beginnings of Christian Philosophy*, 53–80.

135. Barnabas Lindars, "The Rhetorical Structure of Hebrews," *New Testament Studies* 35 (1989): 386 n. 4. Hurst has also shown that Paul and Hebrews are not as far apart on this point as some have insisted (*Epistle to the Hebrews*, 119–24).

136. Hurst, *Epistle to the Hebrews*, 119. Cf. Cullmann, *Christology of the New Testament*, 98.

insult to the Son of God and His crucifixion (6:6; 10:29). The same sort of implicit focus on Christ as the object of faith can be seen in 13:7–8, where the exhortation to imitate the faith of their beloved leaders is followed by a statement of Christ's trustworthiness: "Jesus Christ is the same yesterday and today and forever."[137]

Third, Hebrews often orients faith toward the future and connects it with hope, but not to the exclusion of its past and present dimensions. The future perspective is more explicit in Hebrews, but as seen above, reliance on Christ's work in the past is implicit in much of the argument of the epistle. Also, Hebrews uses cognate concepts to speak of faith in its present orientation: for example, confidence and boldness are closely associated with faith in Hebrews and capture the present dimension of faith quite graphically (cf. 3:14, 4:16, 10:19, 11:1). It is true, however, that faith is most commonly future-looking in Hebrews, because it is so often focused on trust in God's promises of future blessing (cf. 4:1–11; 6:11–20; 10:22–23; esp. 11:1, 8–19). This also explains why faith is so often linked with hope, as in 3:6, 12; 6:11–12; 10:22–23; and most notably in the well-known description of faith in 11:1: "Now faith is being sure of what we hope for and certain of what we do not see." This future orientation may be inevitable in a book written to people undergoing persecution; urging them to endure and count on God's promise of a brighter future is very natural as well as biblical in such a setting.

Christian living as a pilgrimage. Faith's future orientation and its certainty concerning unseen realities (11:1) provides an easy transition to the other prominent theme in Hebrew's view of the Christian life: the motif of sojourning or pilgrimage.[138] This idea is seen in vivid terms in several examples of faith cited in chapter 11. Abraham, being called to go out to a place which he would inherit, obeyed God and went out, even though he did not know where he was to go (11:8–10). Ironically, he lived as a stranger in the land of promise, without owning more than a grave plot, yet he looked forward to the permanent city prepared by God for him. All these people of faith (vv. 13–16) viewed themselves as aliens and foreigners on earth, but longed for the heavenly homeland, though they never experienced its fulfillment in their lifetimes. Other faithful ones were persecuted on earth and wandered in inhospitable places, but this world was not worthy of them (vv. 37–38). In spite of such hardships in the visible creation, these people of faith had insight into the unseen realities of God's promises and were convinced that He was at work no matter what their outward circumstances (vv. 1, 6).

The idea of God's people as pilgrims journeying by faith to a promised land is reflected more subtly in the rest of Hebrews as well. It is related to the image of Jesus as the Pioneer (*archēgos;* 2:10; 12:2) and Forerunner (*prodromos,* 6:20) and to the motif of "Son and sons" (2:5–18). Christ has gone before and blazed a trail of obedience and faith in spite of temptation, and Christians are called to follow in His path. This will certainly involve suffering as God's people in a sinful world, but

---

137. Hurst, *Epistle to the Hebrews,* 119–20.

138. Käsemann, *The Wandering People of God,* 17–48; and Thompson, *The Beginnings of Christian Philosophy,* 76–77.

Christians must run the race with endurance and look with faith to Jesus who has gone before and opened the way to God (6:20; 12:1–2). As for Jesus, so for Christians the pattern of their pilgrimage is suffering and then glory, humiliation and then honor (2:9; 12:2). In this way, God works through the Son "to bring many sons to glory" because Jesus shared their humanity, suffered and died for each one, and thus gained the victory over the devil for all humankind (2:9–18).

Christians are also viewed as journeying, like Israel did in the wilderness, toward the fulfillment of God's promise of rest (4:1–11). This rest remains as a promise yet to be fulfilled for Christians, and they must enter it by faith (4:1, 3, 6, 11). Along the way, they are called to regard earthly possessions and loyalties as unimportant in comparison with the future and lasting blessings God has promised for those who identify with Jesus Christ (10:34; 13:13–14).

SERVICE AND COMMUNITY

A final truth from Hebrews about living the Christian life concerns the importance of the Christian community. The need for mutual support and a concern for others is especially important when believers are faced with weakness and suffering.[139]

Mutual support and exhortation. Like the rest of the New Testament, Hebrews insists that the Christian life cannot be lived in isolation from other believers. Christians are urged repeatedly to support and encourage one another, especially in the midst of the pressures of persecution and temptation which they face.

The warning passage of chapter 3 takes this corporate perspective when it calls on the readers to be concerned for one another: "Take care, brethren, lest there be in any one of you an evil, unbelieving heart, in falling away from the living God. But encourage one another every day, as long as it is called 'today,' that none of you may be hardened by the deceitfulness of sin" (3:12–13).[140] The support of the community of faith is essential for Christians to endure temptation and enter into God's promised rest.

A more positive presentation of the same need is given in 10:24–25 (also in a context of warnings to hold fast): "Let us consider how to stimulate one another to love and good works, not abandoning our assembling together, as is the habit of some, but encouraging one another, and all the more as you see the Day drawing near." A Christian should think not only of his or her own concerns, but must give careful thought and attention[141] to supporting fellow believers and spurring them on in Christian character and service. This kind of mutual support can come only from meeting together regularly and taking thought for the welfare of others in the community, as these verses instruct. Another way in which the community operates can

---

139. Cf. Milligan, *Theology of Hebrews,* 185–86; and Käsemann, *Wandering People of God,* 21–22.

140. Similar wording is found in Hebrews 12:15.

141. The verb in Hebrews 10:24 (*katanoōmen,* "Let us consider") is the same as in 3:1 (*katanoē-sate,* "fix your thoughts on" Jesus).

be seen in 12:1–2, where Old Testament saints and Jesus Himself are cited as examples of fidelity to God. This illustrates the powerful stimulus that comes from seeing others living the life of faith and resisting sin despite temptation and suffering (cf. also 13:7–8).

Service and worship. Hebrews also gives powerful testimony to the need for Christians to reach out to others in loving service and to respond to God in heartfelt worship. Being under personal pressure and temptation is no excuse for living a self-absorbed and thankless existence.

The main teaching on Christian service comes in a series of exhortations in the final chapter of Hebrews.[142] Some are standard instructions about Christian living needed anywhere, but most reflect the particular situation of the readers. These are exhortations to brotherly love, hospitality, care for prisoners and the persecuted, financial contentment, and spiritual stability in the face of heterodoxy and opposition (13:1–14). All of these are especially necessary for a community undergoing difficulty. But they reveal the particularly Christian orientation of caring for the needs of others and actively seeking their good, rather than becoming absorbed in self-interest or self-pity. The writer urged the readers to such responses in the midst of their own suffering because he had already impressed on them the example of Jesus, the merciful and faithful High Priest. The readers are asked simply to follow the path of love and sacrifice modeled by their Pioneer (cf. 2:9–18; 4:14–5:10).

Worship is a natural concomitant of service to others, as Hebrews 13:15–16 shows: "Through Jesus then let us continually offer a sacrifice of praise to God, that is, the fruit of lips that acknowledge His name. Do not neglect to do good and to share with others, for God is well-pleased with such sacrifices." The grace to serve others is vitally connected with the wholehearted focus on God's majesty and goodness which constitutes worship.[143] Both require setting aside self-interest and self-sufficiency. Hebrews shows that these are essential features of Christian character.

In addition to this important passage in chapter 13, allusions to worship are pervasive throughout Hebrews. The basic attitude of worship is reflected in the constant focus on Jesus as Son and High Priest. In His earthly life and sacrificial death Jesus fulfilled the plan of God for the salvation of humankind, and Hebrews repeatedly points its readers to consider Him, follow Him, and trust in Him. He alone is the source of hope and help in their time of need. Looking to Him in faith and devotion is the central theological and practical message of Hebrews.

142. Many of the themes surface earlier in the letter, as commendations for the readers' behavior in times past. See Hebrews 6:9–12 and 10:32–34.
143. This connection can be seen also in Hebrews 10:19–25, which urges holiness and reverence in approaching God in worship, as well as vital relationships with fellow believers.

9

A THEOLOGY OF JAMES

Buist M. Fanning

The Epistle of James is known and loved for its penetrating exhortations about practical Christian living. It is not often thought of for its theology. In fact, one prominent commentator states that James "has no 'theology.' "[1] It is true that James does not emphasize theological themes as some other writers do. For example, the epistle has no explicit mention of Jesus' incarnation, cross, or resurrection. There is perhaps no mention of the Holy Spirit (James 4:5 is debated), very little about new life in Christ, no clear doctrine of the church, and little on God's plan of salvation working out in history. What James did give is clear exhortation and this is to be expected in light of the purpose he indicated in his epistle. He wrote not to correct doctrinal problems, but to urge Christians to act on what they believe, to "be doers of the word, and not hearers only" (1:22 NKJV). But while James emphasized practical Christian living, he revealed his theological foundations and contributed distinctive insights to Christian theology.

Temptation, Sin, and Human Nature

The opening theme in James, which comes up again in several important places in the epistle, is that of temptation, sin, and the nature of humankind. This

---

1. Martin Dibelius, *James: A Commentary on the Epistle of James,* Hermeneia, ed. Helmut Koester, trans. Michael A. Williams, rev. Heinrich Greeven (Philadelphia: Fortress, 1976), 21.

Buist M. Fanning, B.A., Th.M., D.Phil., is professor of New Testament studies at Dallas Theological Seminary.

was certainly prompted by the situation his readers were facing: they were undergoing difficulties and James focused their attention on the theological significance of such trials in the Christian life.

TRIALS AND TEMPTATIONS

The difficulties Christians encounter in the world are discussed in three places in James (1:2–4, 12–15; 5:7–11). These adversities are described in turn as trials, temptations, and sufferings in the three passages. The descriptions are significant for understanding different facets of the Christian's experience of trials. The common element in all three passages is the call to endure such difficulties in a faithful way.

In the first passage (1:2–4), James called his readers to be joyful in the midst of trials (*peirasmoi*). The reason Christians can be joyful despite difficulties is that God uses such adversities in a positive way in their spiritual development: "because you know that the testing of your faith develops perseverance" (v. 3). Perseverance or endurance (*hypomonē*) in turn leads to full-orbed Christian character: "that you may be mature and complete, not lacking anything" (v. 4). This positive result helps to shed light on the sense of the word translated "trial" or "temptation" (*peirasmos*) in James.

The Greek noun *peirasmos* and the cognate verb *peirazō* are used in two related senses in the New Testament, one positive and one negative. The positive sense denotes "testing, trial, putting to the test" with the intent of confirming and strengthening the virtue of someone. This is the sense in which God tested Abraham in asking him to offer up Isaac his son (Gen. 22:1–12; Heb. 11:17). The negative meaning is "temptation, enticement to sin." In this sense Jesus was tempted by the devil (Matt. 4:1–11; Mark 1:12–13; Luke 4:1–12), and the devil is specifically called "the tempter" in his efforts to lead astray both Jesus (Matt. 4:3) and Christians (1 Thess. 3:5; cf. 1 Cor. 7:5).[2]

The positive sense of *peirasmos* appears in James 1:2–4. God allows adversity in the lives of His people as a means of confirming and strengthening their character. This idea is reinforced by the word translated "testing" (*dokimion*) in verse 3 ("the testing of your faith develops perseverance"). The Greek noun and adjective *dokimion* and *dokimos* refer to the process of testing something to show its genuineness and thus to pronounce it approved. It is used invariably with the positive connotation of "approval, approved."[3]

James's teaching then is that the adversities Christians face in this sinful

2. Walter Bauer, William F. Arndt, and F. Wilbur Gingrich, *A Greek-English Lexicon of the New Testament and Other Early Christian Literature*, 2d ed., rev. F. Wilbur Gingrich and Frederick W. Danker (Chicago: Univ. of Chicago, 1979), 640–41; and W. Schneider and C. Brown, *The New International Dictionary of New Testament Theology* (Grand Rapids: Zondervan, 1975), s.v. *"peirasmos,"* 3:798–804. Douglas Moo presents this distinction as "the inner enticement to sin" versus "external afflictions" (*James,* Tyndale New Testament Commentaries, rev. ed. [Grand Rapids: Eerdmans, 1987], 59).

3. Bauer, Arndt, and Gingrich, *A Greek-English Lexicon of the New Testament*, 203.

world are paradoxically to be welcomed. This is true not because suffering is good in itself, but because God uses it to test and deepen the character of His people as they learn to depend on Him in greater ways. When believers respond to such trials with joy, faith, and endurance, their Christian experience is no longer just intellectual or theoretical. They develop proven faith (v. 3), full and complete character (v. 4), and the kind of practical obedience James called for throughout his epistle. The corollary to this is that a faith that is not tested by adversity will always remain shallow and incomplete. A fully developed Christian experience includes living by the Word as well as hearing it (1:22–27), doing as well as believing (2:14–20), obeying what is right as well as knowing what is right (4:17), even when pressed by adversity.

The second passage on testing is James 1:12–15. Here James's teaching about trials shifts by a play on words from the positive to the negative connotation of the word *peirasmos*. In verse 12 the positive sense appears again, picking up strands of thought from 1:2–4: "Blessed is the man who perseveres under trial [*peirasmos*], because when he has stood the test [i.e., has become approved, *dokimos*], he will receive the victor's crown" (author's trans.). However, in verses 13–14, the thought changes to the darker side of testing, the allure of temptation. When enticed to sin, no one should blame God, since He has no connection with temptation: "God cannot be tempted by evil, nor does he tempt anyone" (v. 14).

James's insistence that God is not the source of temptation was a common idea in ancient Judaism. The Jewish teaching was that God leads men to righteousness, not disobedience. He brings His people into situations where their faithfulness is tested, but He does not lead them to go astray. Even in a time of trial, God's influence is toward obedience and "He gives no one permission to sin."[4] If someone gives in when tempted, he or she must not blame God or assume that there was no chance to escape since God was doing the testing (see Paul's similar teaching in 1 Cor. 10:13).

The fault in temptation and sin lies not with God but with the nature of humanity, as James explained in 1:14–15. These ideas will be discussed in the next section.

The third passage about trials is James 5:7–11, where they are presented as hardships or suffering which must be endured faithfully. The theme of endurance or perseverance (*hypomonē*) is continued from the earlier passages and is supplemented by commands to show patience or longsuffering (*makrothymia*) in the face of difficulties or persecutions. In spite of suffering, Christians must not lose faith in God or attack one another (cf. v. 9), but must continue faithful to Him and wait for His purposes to be fulfilled.

What is new in this passage is the perspective that God's people will inevitably encounter suffering or hardship in this world. Like the prophets of old and righteous Job (vv. 10–11), Christians are not exempt from difficulties, but they must imitate the patience and endurance of such people of faith from the Old Testament. God's blessing will come on those who are steadfast and patiently wait for Him.

4. See Sirach 15:11–20, from which this quotation is taken.

The way the passage begins suggests a specific hardship which Christians may suffer. "Therefore" in verse 7 (NASB) connects these verses to the woes pronounced on rich people who cheat their laborers out of the pay they deserve and live in self-indulgent pleasure at their expense. The connection to verse 6, which describes the oppression and even murder of an innocent or righteous person, is especially clear. God's people may often suffer by being outside this world's circles of power and wealth. This theme of wealth and poverty in James will be discussed later.

As elsewhere in the Bible, there is an eschatological dimension to this teaching about suffering: Christians undergo hardship in the present age, but they look forward expectantly to the Lord's coming when their suffering will be ended. His coming is imminent, and so they must be patient and steadfast until His gracious deliverance arrives (vv. 7–8, 11b). Also the perspective of the Lord's judgment to come gives believers a standard of righteousness and mercy by which to measure human behavior—their own as well as others'—in this age. This point is assumed in James 5:7–12 but made explicit in 2:5–12.

SIN AND HUMAN NATURE

As might be expected from a book with the practical emphasis of James, this epistle contains clear teaching on human nature and the sinful forces that influence it. But not all James wrote about humankind is negative. He reminded his readers that man is made in God's likeness (3:9), an assertion of man's nobility and value. To praise God and curse one's fellow human with the same tongue is totally inconsistent, because of the human likeness to God (3:9–10). More neutral but realistic is the teaching in James 4:14 about the ephemeral nature of earthly human life: "Why, you do not even know what will happen tomorrow. What is your life? You are a mist that appears for a little while and then vanishes." So even the Christian must rest in God's providence and not assume a boastful or self-sufficient attitude.

James is especially rich, however, in insights concerning sin and its influence on human nature. True to his focus on practical living, James was realistic about people and their failings. "We all stumble in many ways," he acknowledged in 3:2, and in particular, he exclaimed, "No man can tame the tongue" (v. 8). What is the inner dynamic that explains this bent toward moral failure in humans? James delved into this in his most distinctive teachings about man, which center around the two concepts of double-mindedness and evil impulse.

The human tendency to be "double-minded" (*dipsychos*) is first described explicitly in connection with faith and doubt in prayer to God (1:5–8). In adversity one should ask God for wisdom, but one must ask in faith, not doubting. Double-mindedness is introduced as a further description of the person who doubts (v. 8). Such a person "is like a wave of the sea, blown and tossed by the wind," and "unstable in all he does" (vv. 6, 8). This inconstancy is caused by a division in the innermost self, an "inner disunity of heart."[5] Doubt is not equivalent to double-mindedness, but is simply a manifestation of this deeper problem. In this sense humanity's plight is not merely that our outward behavior is sometimes good and sometimes evil, but that we have no inward wholeness, no integrity of heart and mind. In addition, such double-mindedness is not simply hypocrisy or lack of consistency between inner conviction and outward behavior. Instead even the inner conviction is divided. Thus humans are subject to all sorts of influences which drive them this way and that. This is a problem in prayer for the man addressed in 1:6–8 because not only is he unsure of God's faithfulness but he is "not sure he really wants what he asks for."[6]

This sense of double-mindedness is reinforced in James 1 by the contrast with God's singleness and constancy. He is "the Father of heavenly lights, who does not change like shifting shadows" (v. 17). More immediately (v. 5), God is said to give "generously" to all. The word rendered generously (*haplōs*) comes from a root meaning single, simple, sincere.[7] When used to describe giving, it denotes generosity, but this is because the giving is thus without reservation, wholehearted. God's response to prayer is rooted in His unchanging, undivided character of holiness and grace.[8] Human nature in contrast is unstable, equivocal.

Human moral duplicity surfaces again in James 3:9–12, though the term "double-minded" is not used. With the same tongue, people bless God and "curse men" (v. 9). Such inconsistency does not appear in illustrations from the rest of God's creation (spring of water, fig tree, grapevine) and it should not be true of humankind (vv. 10–12). When James does repeat the term "double-minded" (4:8), it appears in a context critical of the human attempt to be friends with God and the world at the same time (4:4). The epithet "double-minded" is parallel to "sinners" in 4:8 perhaps because James regarded this as the root and essence of human sinfulness.[9] It is instructive also to note that the command James gave to double-minded people is to "purify your hearts" (4:8), which gets to the core of the problem with people.

James's doctrine of humanity's double-mindedness is rooted ultimately in his other significant insight into human nature, his teaching that people have an evil impulse within them (1:13–15; 4:1–3). This is actually the continuation of prominent Old Testament and Jewish ideas about human nature. For example, Genesis 6:5 and

---

5. Oscar J.F. Seitz, "Antecedents and Significance of the Term *Dipsychos*," *Journal of Biblical Literature* 66 (1947): 215. Seitz establishes this meaning for the term *dipsychos* from usage in Hermas, 1 and 2 Clement, and similar concepts in rabbinic literature. Also see Seitz, "The Relationship of the Shepherd of Hermas to the Epistle of James," *Journal of Biblical Literature* 63 (1944): 131–40; and Wallace I. Wolverton, "The Double-minded Man in the Light of the Essene Psychology," *Anglican Theological Review* 38 (1956): 166–75.

6. Arthur Temple Cadoux, *The Thought of St. James* (London: James Clarke, 1944), 54–55, 59, 62 (quotation taken from p. 62).

7. Bauer, Arndt, and Gingrich, *A Greek-English Lexicon of the New Testament*, 85–86.

8. This contrast between man and God in James is well-presented in Sophie Laws, "The Doctrinal Basis for the Ethics of James," *Studia Evangelica* 7 [= *Texte und Untersuchungen* 126] (1973): 299–305.

9. Laws, "The Doctrinal Basis for the Ethics of James," 301.

8:21 speak of the evil inclination (Heb. *yēṣer*) of man's heart. Sometimes in Old Testament usage the *yēṣer* is portrayed as a positive impulse, showing that the basic frame of mind can be turned toward good under divine influence (1 Chron. 28:9; Isa. 26:3). But it is usually seen as an evil bent opposed to God, but allowed and even created by God as part of His sovereign plan for His creation (Ps. 103:14; cf. a later expression of this in Sirach 15:14). The same concepts were common at Qumran and in intertestamental and rabbinic literature.[10]

James's point about the evil impulse (James 1:13–15) is that it is a capacity within the individual, and something belonging to one personally, which is responsive to evil. Thus temptation takes hold not just because it is an external influence, but because the person's own inner desire responds to the enticement. And no one else can be blamed for the fault—it is one's *own* evil impulse which captures a person and leads to sin (James 1:14). Then follows the three-step sequence of evil pictured as the process of conception and birth (1:15): "After desire has conceived, it gives birth to sin; and sin, when it is full-grown, gives birth to death." The starting point for sin and death in humans is the evil impulse.

This evil desire within the individual is cited again in James 4:1–5, as the source of struggles and quarrels among people and the seat of envious yearning. According to James these outward manifestations of evil come from the inward passions, lusts, or covetous impulses waging war within the person and influencing his behavior (vv. 1–3). This idea is reinforced when, in an extremely difficult verse to interpret (v. 5), James described the God-given human spirit as one that yearns strongly toward envy or jealousy: "The spirit he caused to live in us envies intensely" (v. 4b NIV; NEB is similar).[11]

However, this context also gives a clue about the Christian's hope for victory over the evil impulse, a countervailing force from God to overcome evil desire. The contextual clue is the treatment of heavenly versus earthly wisdom in the preceding paragraph (3:13–18) and the parallel effects of earthly wisdom and the evil impulse. The effects of both are strife, bitterness, envy, disorder, quarreling, and so forth. On the other hand, the fruit of heavenly wisdom is the opposite: purity, peace, kindness, submissiveness, and such. The point is that one's life needs to be infused with God's wisdom in order to overcome the evil impulse within. God's wisdom comes in the form of insight into life and how to live skillfully, based on instruction in the Word of God and obedience to it (cf. James 1:22–25 and similar themes in

10. The Jewish background is surveyed in Joel Marcus, "The Evil Inclination in the Epistle of James," *Catholic Biblical Quarterly* 44 (1982): 606–21.

11. It is possible to understand "spirit" in verse 5 as the Holy Spirit and to take God as the subject of "yearning," as the NASB does, "He jealously desires the Spirit which he has made to dwell in us" (RSV is similar, and most commentators take this interpretation). But the word *phthonos,* denoting jealousy or envy, consistently has an evil sense rather than the positive sense of "zeal, holy jealousy," and the contrast of verse 6a suggests the interpretation given above. See Marcus, "The Evil Inclination in the Epistle of James," 608–9; Luke T. Johnson, "James 3:13–4:10 and the Topos *peri phthonou,*" *Novum Testamentum* 25 (1983): 327–47; and James B. Adamson, *James: The Man and His Message* (Grand Rapids: Eerdmans, 1989), 330–33.

Old Testament wisdom literature). As James 1:18 and 21 point out, Christians have been born of God through His Word and that Word is now planted within them. If they welcome its truth and live by it, it serves as a counterforce within them to oppose the evil inclination. There is a life-transforming power in God's wisdom as found in His Word and this can overcome the evil impulse and produce the harvest of righteous fruit God desires.[12]

James 4 suggests two other influences toward evil that compete for human loyalty. The world exerts an influence that opposes God, and so friendship with the world and complicity with its selfishness and indulgence automatically set a person against God (4:4). The pollution of the world must be resisted if one's religion is to be truly pure and unstained (1:27). The other external influence on humans is the devil (4:7b). Christians must resist or stand against him, and James offered the assurance that he will flee in the face of such resistance. The context shows that submission and humility before God is the attitude that accompanies this victory over the devil (4:6–10).

FAITH AND WORKS

The most controversial theological topic in the Epistle of James is its doctrine of faith and works, especially in comparison with Paul's teaching in Romans and Galatians. This issue is explicit in James 2:14–26, but surfaces in other passages as well.

THE NATURE OF SALVATION IN JAMES

A question that is sometimes skipped over in treatments of faith and works in this epistle is the nature of the salvation spoken of in James 2:14. This has almost universally been taken as a reference to eternal salvation, deliverance from condemnation for sin. But a different view of it has been vigorously advanced and debated in recent years.[13] This alternative approach understands salvation in James to be pri-

---

12. Many have noticed the parallels between James's teaching on wisdom and Paul's discussion of the role of the Spirit in overcoming the power of the flesh in the life of the Christian (Gal. 5:16–26; Rom. 8:1–17). See J. A. Kirk, "The Meaning of Wisdom in James: Examination of a Hypothesis," *New Testament Studies* 16 (1969): 24–38; and Peter H. Davids, *The Epistle of James: A Commentary of the Greek Text*, New International Greek Testament Commentary (Grand Rapids: Eerdmans, 1982), 52–56. Divine wisdom and the Holy Spirit were often associated in ancient Judaism, so the connection is not surprising. It may be that James thought of the Spirit and wisdom together in a context such as 3:13–4:3. But since he does not cite the Spirit explicitly, we cannot be sure, however suggestive the parallels may be.

13. See three works by Zane C. Hodges, *The Gospel Under Siege: A Study on Faith and Works* (Dallas: Redención Viva, 1981; 2d ed., 1992); *Dead Faith: What Is It? A Study on James 2:14–16* (Dallas: Redención Viva, 1987); and *Absolutely Free! A Biblical Reply to Lordship Salvation* (Grand Rapids: Zondervan, 1989). A similar view is advanced by R. T. Kendall, *Once Saved, Always Saved* (Chicago: Moody, 1983), 207–17. Disputing Hodges's view specifically is John F. MacArthur, Jr., *The Gospel According to Jesus* (Grand Rapids: Zondervan, 1988), "Faith According to the Apostle James," *Journal of the Evangelical Theological Society* 33 (1990): 13–34, and *Faith Works: The Gospel According to the Apostles* (Dallas: Word, 1993). G. Z. Heide also argues against Hodges's view in "The Soteriology of James 2:14," *Grace Theological Journal* 12 (1991): 69–97.

marily "preservation of the physical life from death," focusing on "the temporal life and the preserving of it."[14] Hodges argues that this sense can be seen in all the references to salvation in James (1:21; 2:14; 4:12; 5:15, 20). He compares James with the wisdom books of the Old Testament (e.g., Prov. 10:27; 11:19; 12:28; 13:14; 19:16), in presenting "the death-dealing effects of wickedness and the life-saving effect of righteousness."[15]

Several lines of evidence must be examined in order to evaluate Hodges's view of salvation in James. The New Testament usage of the verb translated "save" in James 2:14 (*sōzō*) is not by itself determinative, since it can refer to physical or spiritual deliverance, depending on the context in which it occurs.[16] For example, in James 5:15 the word is used of healing or rescuing someone from physical sickness by prayer. However, apart from contexts in which physical sickness or natural danger is in view, the words "save" and "salvation" in the New Testament predominantly denote deliverance from condemnation in hell, and as will be shown, this is the interpretation that best fits the usage in James 1:21; 2:14; 4:12; and 5:20.[17]

An important line of evidence to examine is the sense of the phrase "to save the soul/life" (*sōsai tēn psychēn*) in James 1:21.[18] Since this is the first mention of salvation in the epistle and introduces important themes in the letter, it will help clarify the sense of salvation in 2:14. References to saving the life or to killing or destroying the life occur about a dozen times in the New Testament. In several places the phrase denotes saving or losing the physical life (Mark 3:4; Luke 6:9; healing is in view in these passages).[19] But in other contexts the soul's eternal salvation or destruction is in view. John 12:25, for example, explicitly connects preserving the soul with eternal life, and Matthew 10:28 warns that God can destroy both soul and body in hell.

This gives the key for interpreting the well-known saying of Jesus about saving or losing one's *psychē* (Mark 8:35; parallels in Matt. 16:25 and Luke 9:24): "For whoever wants to save his life [*psychēn*] will lose it, but whoever loses his life for me and for the gospel will save it." This saying captures both senses (physical and spiritual) in describing the paradox of being a disciple of Jesus. Following Him may require martyrdom or various lesser sacrifices of one's own desires leading up to that ultimate sacrifice. In the face of such sacrifice a person may desire to

---

14. Hodges, *Dead Faith*, 12–13. Since Hodges himself (*Absolutely Free*, p. 206) commends this book as his "full, documented treatment" of the issue, it will be cited in this section more than his more recent works.

15. Hodges, *Dead Faith*, 12–13, 29–30; quotation on p. 12.

16. Cf. Bauer, Arndt, and Gingrich, *A Greek-English Lexicon of the New Testament*, 798–99.

17. J. Schneider, *The New International Dictionary of New Testament Theology*, s.v. "*sōzō*," 3:216.

18. Hodges's interpretation of this expression is presented in *Grace in Eclipse: A Study on Eternal Rewards*, 2d ed. (Dallas: Redención Viva, 1987), 27–33.

19. This appears also in Greek Old Testament usage, as Hodges points out (*Grace in Eclipse*, 115). He cites Genesis 19:17; 32:30; 1 Samuel 19:11; Job 33:28; Psalms 31:7; 72:13; 109:31; and Jeremiah 48:6 as illustrations.

preserve his or her physical life by denying Jesus, but the tragic result would be spiritual destruction: condemnation for sin. On the other hand, one who loses physical life for Jesus' and the gospel's sake will save his or her soul spiritually and will enjoy eternal life.[20] This reference to spiritual salvation appears as well in 1 Peter 1:9, in which "the salvation of your souls" is stated to be "the goal of your faith," arrived at through endurance in the face of trials, and identified contextually as "a salvation ready to be revealed in the last time" (1:5 NASB).

Many have shown that James's theological and ethical instructions are strongly influenced by the teaching of Jesus, and his choice of words to express these is often similar to the wording of the Synoptic Gospels, especially Matthew.[21] It is best then to understand "salvation of the soul" in James 1:21 to continue the sense of Jesus' words in referring to spiritual salvation.

So the promise of ultimate spiritual deliverance is held out in James 1:21 as a motivation for the readers to continue in obedience to the Word of God, already implanted in their hearts at their conversion (v. 18). James insisted that they become doers of this Word and not mere hearers, because only hearing the Word is self-delusion and lacks the blessing of God (v. 22–25). In fact, failure to live out one's religious convictions is plainly a matter of self-deception and such religion is worthless, no matter how much the person may think he or she is religious (v. 26). A person's true religion is expressed by showing mercy to those in need and resisting the pollution of the world (v. 27).

Continuing this line of thought in chapter 2, James cautioned his readers that faith in Jesus Christ and favoritism toward the rich and against the poor are not compatible. Living out their faith required love, not partiality, toward others. James concluded by warning that God's judgment will be merciless on someone who has not shown mercy (2:13). This reflects Jesus' warning that God will treat individuals in judgment as they have treated others (Matt. 6:12, 14–15; 18:32–35). Those who refuse forgiveness to others have not felt God's great mercy themselves. In the context of warning against this judgment, James then discussed the kind of faith that "saves" in 2:14–26. This continues the argument from 1:21 in denoting deliverance from eternal condemnation for sin. Spiritual salvation is in view also in 4:12 and 5:20.[22]

FAITH IN JAMES

References to faith in James appear predominantly in the central passage on faith and works in chapter 2 (vv. 14–26). Faith is mentioned in two other places

20. John D. Grassmick, "Mark," in *The Bible Knowledge Commentary, New Testament,* ed. John F. Walvoord and Roy B. Zuck (Wheaton, Ill.: Victor, 1983), 141, 169; and Colin Brown, *The New International Dictionary of New Testament Theology,* s.v. *"sōzō,"* 3:212–13. See the same sense in Matthew 10:39 and Luke 17:33.

21. Franz Mussner, *Der Jakobusbrief,* Herders theologischer Kommentar zum Neuen Testament 13:1, 4th ed. (Freiburg: Herder, 1981), 47–52; and Davids, *The Epistle of James,* 47–50.

22. James 4:12 clearly alludes to Jesus' words in Matthew 10:28: "Fear Him who is able to destroy both body and soul in hell" (NASB). Cf. Ralph P. Martin, *James,* Word Biblical Commentary (Waco, Tex.: Word, 1988), 164, 219–20.

describing the Christian's faith expressed in prayer (1:6; 5:15) and in one verse on the Christian endurance that is developed when faith is tested (1:3). It also appears in two verses early in chapter 2 (vv. 1, 5). These last two verses have significance for the central passage, because James indicated (v. 1) that the focus of the Christian's faith is "our glorious Lord Jesus Christ," a reference to Jesus' exalted position to which He ascended after His crucifixion and resurrection. Faith in such a one is the content of Christian faith, as elsewhere in the New Testament. In addition, James insisted that such faith is incompatible with prejudice against the poor. Further on (v. 5), James pointed to God's initiative in making people His own through faith: "Has not God chosen those who are poor in the eyes of the world to be rich in faith and to inherit the kingdom he promised to those who love him?"

In the central passage (2:14–26), the terms "faith" or "believe" occur fourteen times. These are divided between descriptions of a faith that James approved of and a faith he regarded as inadequate. In the positive vein, James made reference to a faith that is demonstrated by works (v. 18), that operates together with works (v. 22a), and is made complete by works (v. 22b). This kind of faith is exemplified by Abraham, whose obedience in offering Isaac constituted a fulfillment of Genesis 15:6, describing his faith in God (v. 23).

On the negative side, James referred repeatedly to a faith "without works" or "not having works" (vv. 14, 17, 18, 20, 26). This is faith "by itself" or functioning "alone" (vv. 17, 24). James ironically compared this to the faith of demons, who acknowledge a perfectly true doctrinal proposition ("God is one"), but whose accompanying action is merely to tremble with fear in the face of their certain condemnation (v. 19 NASB). James's verdict on this kind of faith is that it is without benefit and useless (vv. 14, 16, 20). Such faith is "dead" (vv. 17, 26). More significantly for the sense of James's discussion is the way he began the passage in verse 14: "if a man claims to have faith." This is a professed faith, one which a person claims to have. This description sets the tone for his discussion, and James specifically avoided stating that the person actually *has* faith. It is merely a claim to faith, which needs to be evaluated in the ways suggested in the passage. Is it lived out in deeds of love and obedience or not?

This is an important point to stress in order to grasp James's teaching in the passage. He explicitly began the discussion by focusing on the claim someone may make about faith. Verse 14, which functions iike a topic sentence, clearly signals that a profession of faith will be discussed.[23] This is, of course, a natural sequel to the theme of religious self-deception that James began to develop in 1:22, 25–26. Someone who hears the Word but fails to act on it or who "considers himself religious" (1:25) but does not live it out is plainly self-deceived and does not have true religion at all, despite his claim. A similar disjunction between outward profession or even boasting and the actual truth of the matter is seen in 3:13–16.

So the references in 2:14–26 to faith without works or not having works,

---

23. C. E. B. Cranfield, "The Message of James," *Scottish Journal of Theology* 18 (1965): 338–42; and John Calvin, *Institutes of the Christian Religion,* The Library of Christian Classics, ed. John T. McNeill, trans. Ford Lewis Battles (Philadelphia: Westminster, 1960), 3.17.11., 815.

faith by itself or alone, faith that is useless, without benefit, and dead must be understood in the light of this initial premise.[24] This is not true Christian faith, despite what someone may claim. Such a claim is false, according to James; that person is deceived and his religion is worthless. And the most tragic way in which it is worthless is shown in verse 14: it cannot save from eternal condemnation for sin. As verse 13 indicated, such a person will be judged without mercy.

The description of faith as "dead" (vv. 17, 26) must be understood in the same framework of false profession James introduced in verse 14. It is not faith that once was alive and now has become inactive, but faith that has no life and has never had true life, despite someone's claim. The analogy of the body in verse 26 should be interpreted in keeping with the theme James himself introduced rather than vice versa.[25] This is confirmed by the way "dead" is contextually defined at its initial mention in verse 17. There is no benefit in faith without works (vv. 14, 16), it cannot save (v. 14), it is useless or unproductive (v. 20). Dead faith then is one which, despite an outward claim to genuineness, does not produce the intended results of faith. Similarly, a body without a spirit may look vital enough outwardly, but it is actually dead and produces no signs of true life.[26]

WORKS IN RELATIONSHIP TO FAITH

What did James mean when he spoke of works accompanying faith (2:14–26), and what is their relationship to faith? The nature of the works is illustrated in the immediate context as acts of compassion toward those in need (2:15–16). Doing deeds of mercy and kindness was already mentioned in 1:27 as one of the evidences of true religion, and the law of love toward one's neighbor was cited in 2:8–13 as the appropriate behavior to accompany faith in Christ (rather than favoritism, 2:1, 9). But deeds of love and kindness, significant as they are, were not all the works James had in mind.[27] The examples of Abraham and Rahab (2:21–25) demonstrate that acts of obedience and commitment to God were also in view. The illustrations should also include basic Christian traits like self-control, humility, and so on (cf. 1:26; 3:2, 13, 17–18).

The significant point to note about these works, however, is that James viewed them as the expression or outworking of true faith and of new life in Christ,

24. It throws things all out of proportion to understand, with Hodges (*Dead Faith*, 11–15), that this dead faith secures eternal salvation and deliverance from any condemnation for sin, but that James called it useless, without benefit, and dead because it lacks works and so cannot ensure rescue from the temporal consequences of sin.

25. Hodges's approach (*Dead Faith*, 7–9) of starting the explanation of 2:14–26 with the analogy of the body in verse 26 actually turns the passage on its head and enables him to avoid exposition of the phrase with which James himself began in discussing faith: "if someone *says* that he has faith." It is wrong for Hodges to mention the view that the passage discusses false profession and then state that "there is nothing in James's text to suggest" such an interpretation (pp. 9–10; see also p. 20). In fact, the passage plainly begins with this premise.

26. Cf. Cranfield, "The Message of James," 342; and Adamson, *James: The Man and His Message*, 296 n. 150.

27. Moo, *James*, 102.

not the means of gaining these blessings. They demonstrate faith (2:18), are the completion and fulfillment of faith (2:22–23), and constitute living out the Word that was already implanted by God when He gave spiritual birth to the Christian (1:18–21).

This is the central distinction between the works James described and the works Paul spoke of in Galatians and Romans. To put it another way, the distinction is between postconversion deeds and preconversion deeds.[28] James insisted that true faith necessarily produces works of love and obedience. Paul argued that no works can serve as a basis for gaining God's righteousness or God's favor (Gal. 2:16; Rom. 3:28; 10:1–8).[29] However, the two approaches are clearly compatible, since Paul also called for godly living as the expression of true faith (Rom. 6:22; Gal. 5:6; Eph. 2:8–10; Phil. 1:11),[30] and James for his part attributed salvation to God's gracious initiative in the lives of people, not to their merit (1:17–18; 2:5, 12–13).[31]

JUSTIFICATION IN JAMES

The final issue to be resolved here is the meaning of justification in James 2, especially in comparison with Paul's use of this concept. It is here that Paul and James seem most at odds with each other, since parallel verses can be found that appear to say exactly opposite things.

"For we maintain that a man is justified by faith apart from works of Law" (Rom. 3:28 NASB). "For if Abraham was justified by works, he has something to boast about, but not before God" (Rom. 4:2 NASB). "Was not Abraham our father justified by works, when he offered Isaac his son upon the altar?" (James 2:21). "You see that a person is justified by works and not by faith alone" (James 2:24).

Even though these verses seem difficult to reconcile, the foundation for a proper understanding has already been laid in the earlier discussion of faith and works. The distinction of preconversion works versus postconversion works is significant in this regard, and this suggests other differences between the two writers. Writing in forensic terms, Paul denied that works can have any merit in God's initial act of declaring a sinner righteous. Such justification is completely a gift of His grace apart from works for all who believe in Jesus Christ (Rom. 3:20–26). James spoke of works being done as the fruit of faith by those whose initial justification is already accomplished. This is seen in the double reference to Abraham's justifica-

28. Ibid., 46. James and Paul simply looked at the question from different but complementary perspectives.

29. The difference, as Moo argues (*James,* pp. 44–46, 101–2), is not one of self-righteous or legalistic works (Paul) versus deeds of love (James). It is not just self-righteous or legalistic deeds that cannot save; no human works can merit or accomplish salvation. See also Douglas J. Moo, " 'Law,' 'Works of the Law,' and Legalism in Paul," *Westminster Theological Journal* 45 (1983): 84–90.

30. Leonhard Goppelt, *Theology of the New Testament,* trans. John E. Alsup, ed. Jürgen Roloff, 2 vols. (Grand Rapids: Eerdmans, 1982), 2:209–10.

31. George Barker Stevens, *The Theology of the New Testament,* 2d ed. (Edinburgh: Clark, 1918), 286–87.

tion in James 2:21, 23. He was justified by works when he offered up Isaac (v. 21), but this was the fulfillment of the truth that Abraham had already believed God and his faith was reckoned as righteousness (v. 23).[32] But the nature of this justification must be clarified further.

One way to interpret the justification of James 2 is to read it as final justification, "God's ultimate declaration of a person's righteousness" which occurs at the future judgment.[33] This perhaps alludes to Jesus' teaching (Matt. 12:36–37), "I say to you, that every careless word that men shall speak, they shall render account for it on the day of judgment. For by your words you will be justified, and by your words you will be condemned." In the judgment God will confirm the righteousness attained by His people, who were justified initially and sanctified by His grace. This interpretation suits the general statement in verse 24 quite well, but it does not fit the descriptions of Abraham and Rahab, who "were justified" in a particular historical situation. This can hardly be read as final judgment, and James said nothing to connect it explicitly with final justification.[34]

The better way to understand justification in this passage is to see it as the demonstration of a righteous standing before God. The verb *dikaioō* is sometimes used in the sense of "vindicate, show to be righteous" (e.g., Rom. 3:4; 1 Tim. 3:16).[35] In this sense Abraham's obedience and Rahab's hospitality demonstrated their righteousness for anyone to see.[36] This fits better with these historical illustrations. It also suits the general statement of James 2:24. A person's righteous standing cannot be seen only from his or her faith, but is shown by one's acts of love and obedience, which others may witness. This interpretation also reinforces the theme of demonstrating the genuineness of faith, which runs through 2:14–26.

THE LAW AND THE WORD IN JAMES

Ryrie has written that James's theology is preeminently a theology "of the Word."[37] This is not because James discussed bibliology extensively, but because he emphasized the practical significance of God's truth in the regeneration and spiritual growth of the Christian. Also his epistle is saturated with allusions and cita-

32. G. C. Berkouwer, *Faith and Justification,* trans. Lewis B. Smedes (Grand Rapids: Eerdmans, 1954), 129–39, esp. 135–36.

33. Joachim Jeremias, "Paul and James," *Expository Times* 66 (1954–55): 370–71; Bo Reicke, *The Epistles of James, Peter, and Jude,* The Anchor Bible (Garden City, N.Y.: Doubleday, 1964), 34–35; Davids, *The Epistle of James,* 132; and Moo, *James,* 109–11.

34. See the discussion in Robert V. Rakestraw, "James 2:14–26: Does James Contradict the Pauline Soteriology?" *Criswell Theological Review* 1 (1986): 39–42. He takes justification here to be God's approval or declaration of a person's righteousness during his lifetime.

35. Bauer, Arndt, and Gingrich, *A Greek-English Lexicon of the New Testament,* 197–98; and Gottlob Schrenk, *Theological Dictionary of the New Testament,* trans. and ed. Geoffrey W. Bromiley (Grand Rapids: Eerdmans, 1964–76), s.v. "*dikaioō,*" 2:213–14.

36. Calvin, *Institutes of the Christian Religion,* 3.17.12, 816–17; Colin Brown, *The New International Dictionary of New Testament Theology,* s.v. "*dikaiosynē,*" 3:370; and Donald Guthrie, *New Testament Theology* (Downers Grove, Ill.: InterVarsity, 1981), 506.

37. Charles Caldwell Ryrie, *Biblical Theology of the New Testament* (Chicago: Moody, 1959), 136.

tions from the Old Testament as well as the teaching of Jesus. The Word assumed a large place in James's exhortations toward practical Christian living.

The law and the Word of God should be treated together because James himself associated them closely. This can be seen in 1:18–25, where James described the spiritual birth of the Christian, which is accomplished "through the word of truth" (v. 18), a reference to the true message, the gospel about Christ, to which they had responded in their conversion (cf. 2:1). In keeping with his emphasis in this letter, James insisted that Christians live out the implications of this spiritual position. They should humbly accept the "implanted word" (1:21 NKJV), by acting on it. They must be quick to hear its instruction (v. 19), but beyond hearing it they must be careful to do what it says (v. 22). The comparison with a person who looks in a mirror and then quickly forgets what he has seen illustrates the need to live out the Word and not merely hear it.

But after four references to the "word," James substituted a new expression in the midst of the mirror illustration, explaining how "the perfect law of liberty" brings blessing to the person who looks intently into it and perseveres in acting on what he learns (v. 25 NKJV). The word of truth and the perfect law of liberty are parallel in James's thought, but the exact connection between them needs to be explored.

The description of the law in James 1:25 as the "perfect law of liberty" reveals a distinctive pattern in the way James spoke about this law. In his first two references to law he added important descriptive phrases: "perfect law of liberty" (1:25; cf. "law of liberty" also in 2:12 NASB) and "royal law" (2:8). This indicates that James did not have in mind a reference to the Mosaic Law alone. He specified further to distinguish this law from the Old Testament Law per se.[38]

The descriptions of law in James 1:25 and the association with the implanted word that gives new life, go a long way toward clarifying what James had in mind. Mitton has suggested that the promise of the new covenant (Jer. 31) is in view. The law of James 1:25 is one that is planted within God's people, written on their hearts rather than merely external (Jer. 31:33). It is perfect (*teleios*) in that it is part of the culmination of God's plan of salvation. It completes the work of providing personal knowledge of God and full forgiveness of sins, which the old covenant could not give (Jer. 31:32, 34). In this way it is a "law of liberty," setting people free from sin and providing the inner dynamic to obey God's commands.[39]

James's other distinctive description of the law is found in 2:8. There he called for observance of the "royal law according to the Scripture" and quoted the

---

38. W. Gutbrat, *Theological Dictionary of the New Testament,* s.v. *"nomos,"* 4:1081; and M. J. Evans, "The Law in James," *Vox Evangelica* 13 (1983): 34.

39. C. Leslie Mitton, *The Epistle of James* (London: Marshall, Morgan & Scott, 1966), 71–74. See also Goppelt, *Theology of the New Testament,* 2:203–4. In this sense, "the law that gives freedom" (NIV) is not contradictory to Paul's association of the law with bondage (Gal. 4:21–5:1). Instead, it exactly complements his words about freedom in Christ for faith to work through love and fulfill the whole law by love for one's neighbor (Gal. 5:6–14). The Christian is free from the law (Rom. 6:14–15; 7:1–4), though "not being without law of God but under the law of Christ" (1 Cor. 9:21 NASB; cf. Gal. 6:2).

command "Love your neighbor as yourself" from Leviticus 19:18. The adjective "royal" (*basilikos*) is at first ambiguous, but the reference to the kingdom (*basileia*) in James 2:5 helps clarify it. James meant the law related to the kingdom and to its King.[40] The emphasis on the command to love adds to this sense, since Jesus is the One who taught that love for God and for one's neighbor are the sum and heart of the law. But it should be noticed that the "law of the king" is not some entirely new code but includes the commands of the Old Testament (the Decalogue as well as Leviticus 19), though the ethical principles and heart attitude of the commands are emphasized.[41]

If James intended to associate law with Jesus in this way, it may shed further light on the what he meant by "perfect law" in 1:25. In the Sermon on the Mount, which James knew well,[42] Jesus taught that Christians should love their neighbors as Leviticus 19 said, but He called for a radical extension to include love for enemies as well (Matt. 5:43–47; Luke 6:27–36). This is associated with His instruction for them to be perfect (*teleioi*), as their heavenly Father is perfect (5:48). Jesus began that sermon (Matt. 5–7) by insisting that He had come not to abolish the Law and the Prophets but to fulfill them and that whoever keeps the law's commands will be great in the kingdom (Matt. 5:17–20). While endorsing the law and indicating that He would fulfill it, Jesus nevertheless deepened its meaning, focused on love as the heart of the law, and transcended it by His own authority (Matt. 5:21–48; 7:12; 12:8; 22:34–40).[43]

So what James seems[44] to have meant by the "perfect law of liberty," "the royal law focusing on love," is the Old Testament ethic as taught and fulfilled by Jesus Christ. It is the Old Testament read in the light of Jesus' teaching and culminated by the salvation He provided.[45] In this way it can be cited as parallel to the message of the gospel, the word of truth by which God graciously gives new life (1:17–18, 21–25). And because of this connection, the law of liberty can be cited as the basis by which Christians will be judged (2:11–12). What they know of God's mercy through Christ should be reflected in how they treat others.[46]

40. Luke T. Johnson, "The Use of Leviticus 19 in the Letter of James," *Journal of Biblical Literature* 101 (1982): 400–401; and Moo, *James*, 49.

41. Johnson shows that James drew from various specific commands in the wider context of Leviticus 19:18, as explications of the law of love ("The Use of Leviticus 19 in the Letter of James," 394–400).

42. Davids lists twenty-five parallels between this epistle and Matthew 5–7 (*Epistle of James*, 47–48).

43. On Jesus and the law in Matthew, see Douglas J. Moo, *Dictionary of Jesus and the Gospels* (1992), s.v. "Law," 458–59.

44. This is phrased tentatively because James was not explicit about these connections with Jesus' life and teaching, so one cannot be sure. But this interpretation makes better sense of his wording than any other. See Evans, "The Law in James," 36–37, for a similar caveat.

45. Cadoux, *The Thought of St. James*, 72; Ryrie, *Biblical Theology of the New Testament*, 138; Davids, *Epistle of James*, 47–50, 114; and Moo, *James*, 50.

46. Goppelt, *Theology of the New Testament*, 2:207.

In chapters 2 and 4, James added another significant point about this law. Even though it contains various commands, it should be viewed as a unit. To violate even one part of it constitutes lawbreaking because it all stands together (2:10–11). The reason for this unity is the single source for all its provisions: the same one who prohibited adultery also prohibited murder (2:11). James was not saying that every detail of the ritual law of the Old Testament must be followed, but that the ethical demand of all of God's law as summed up in the law of love must be lived out.[47] So to show partiality toward the wealthy and to dishonor the poor is a violation of the royal law. So also to commit slander against a brother is to disobey the law of love and sit in judgment over the whole law (4:11–12). This must not be done because it is a refusal to submit to the one Lawgiver and Judge whose will and character this law expresses (4:7, 10, 12). Instead, Christians are expected to be "doers of the law" (4:11) and "doers of the word" (1:22). God's law as taught and fulfilled through Jesus Christ must be heard and obeyed.

OTHER TOPICS

Two other themes do not require lengthy discussion but deserve mention here.

PRAYER, CONFESSION, AND HEALING

Prayer is another theme for which this epistle is well known.[48] James urged Christians to pray in any situation: in trials, troubles, sickness, or rejoicing (1:5; 5:13–14). God's people can go to Him in prayer, even when confused and perplexed by trials or suffering, because He provides wisdom and grace, no matter what their circumstances or frame of mind (1:5). But one's basic attitude in prayer must be faith and not doubt; the doubter cannot expect any response to his or her prayer (1:6–8). James's contrast between faith and doubt is concerned with the Christian's basic attitude about God, not the size or purity of one's faith.[49] The point James emphasized in context is the character of God. He is the God who gives generously, without reproaching anyone for asking His favor (1:5). Every good and perfect gift is from Him, and He is the Creator and Sovereign of the universe, unchanging in His perfections (1:17). He graciously gives new life in Christ so that Christians can be His beloved children (1:18). In James's view the bedrock of prayer is what a person believes about God.

James was also concerned about what Christians ask for in prayer (4:2–3). Sometimes believers fail to experience the blessings God is ready to give them because they do not ask for them in prayer. James's sobering statement is, "You do

---

47. Stevens, *Theology of the New Testament*, 284–85; Goppelt, *Theology of the New Testament*, 2:205–6; and Moo, *James*, 48–49.

48. C. Richard Wells gives a comprehensive treatment of prayer in James and effectively shows how prayer is integrated into the theology of the epistle ("The Theology of Prayer in James," *Criswell Theological Review* 1 [1986]: 85–112).

49. Jesus taught that faith the size of a mustard seed is enough to move mountains (Matt. 17:20). See the attitude of the man in Mark 9:23–24: when Jesus told him all things are possible to the one who believes, he said, "I do believe; help me overcome my unbelief."

not have, because you do not ask God" (v. 2d). In context this statement includes situations in which someone is too proud or self-confident to turn to God for help, since the later verses emphasize the need for humility before God (vv. 6–7, 10). But its straightforward meaning also includes simple prayerlessness: failure to ask God because of neglect or preoccupation with other things.

Another problem Christians experience in prayer is asking for the wrong things or asking out of selfish motives (v. 3). Like a wise and loving father, God does not answer such requests from His children. Instead, James implied that godly prayer involves a searching of one's own motives before God, a readiness to learn from Him about what to ask, and sometimes a struggle to bring one's own desires into line with His desires and timing. But this is, of course, just what Christ experienced in Gethsemane, when He sought the Father three times in prayer asking that the cup might pass from Him, but all along submitting His will to God's (Matt. 26:36–46; Mark 14:32–42).

In his final paragraph about prayer (James 5:13–18), James emphasized the amazing effectiveness of prayer. The main point is stated in verse 16b: "The prayer of a righteous man is powerful and effective."[50] Prayer can accomplish much because of the greatness and power of God. The biblical illustration of prayer's great impact is Elijah (vv. 17–18). The earlier verses on healing, confession, and forgiveness also give a specific example of how effective prayer can be (vv. 13–16a). In these verses James encouraged one who is sick[51] to call for the elders of the church, as spiritual leaders and those who gave pastoral care, to anoint the individual and pray for healing.[52]

In writing about prayer for a sick believer, James urged the elders to deal with spiritual or moral problems that may be present as well as the physical sickness (vv. 15–16). Spiritual and physical health are often linked. If sins are present in a believer's life, they should be confessed to the elders and to God and one will find forgive-

50. A Greek participle (represented in the NIV as "and effective") is taken correctly in this rendering as adverbial ("in its working, in its effects") rather than as an attributive, "the effective prayer" (as in the NASB).

51. Daniel R. Hayden understands the "sickness" in verses 14–16 to be not physical illness but discouragement, depression, or spiritual weariness from the believer's struggle against sin ("Calling the Elders to Pray," *Bibliotheca Sacra* 138 [1981]: 258–66). Wells agrees with this in part, suggesting that the healing of verse 15 is "deliverance from the psycho-spiritual effect of illness, rather than the illness itself" ("Theology of Prayer in James," 105–6). Hayden shows that this sense is possible for the key terms James used, but there is nothing in the passage that requires such a reading. The more normal sense of physical sickness is preferable, though spiritual and psychological effects may be included as well. As Psalm 32:1–5 and other passages show, these are often intermingled.

52. The anointing with oil "in the name of the Lord" seems to be symbolic of God's power and blessing being applied in the person's life. John Wilkinson takes anointing to refer to the application of good medicine along with prayer ("Healing in the Epistle of James," *Scottish Journal of Theology* 24 [1971]: 338–40), but the wording is too terse to carry that sense clearly and the phrase "in the Lord's name" more naturally fits a spiritual, symbolic meaning. See Gary S. Shogren, "Will God Heal Us—A Re-examination of James 5:14–16a," *Evangelical Quarterly* 61 (1989): 99–108, for discussion of the issues and support for the interpretation adopted here.

ness. In verse 16 James urged that this kind of mutual confession and prayer support should be the common practice of Christians who share spiritual life together in a local body of believers. Not all sickness is connected with sin, of course, as Jesus made clear in John 9:1–3. James's point is simply that both must be dealt with when they are linked.

But the remarkable statement in James 5:15 must be discussed: "The prayer offered in faith will make the sick person well; the Lord will raise him up." James's intent was to encourage prayer for healing. Physical illness brings great suffering, but prayer can make a difference. The point is that God can do amazing things in response to prayer offered in faith to Him. But James's encouragement must not be misunderstood as a guarantee of healing in every case. The earlier verses on prayer in the epistle indicated that the "prayer of faith" fundamentally expresses trust in the God who is all-loving and generous, but who is also all-wise and sovereign. Faith then involves leaving requests even for healing in His hands and submitting to His will and timing in the matter. It is especially important to refuse the logic that says a person is not healed because he or she did not have enough faith. James 5 has in view the faith of those who pray for the sick person. Also there are clear biblical examples of people who were not healed even though their faith was perfectly strong. For example, Paul prayed three times for healing of a physical affliction and God did not heal him (2 Cor. 12:7–10). But God showed Paul that His grace was sufficient to sustain him, and He would use the affliction for significant spiritual purposes in his life.[53]

WEALTH AND POVERTY

James had much to say about the economic condition of his readers and how God's truth applied to their situation. In this he asserted the priority of eternal values over temporal ones. Earthly wealth will fade away and the rich person without God will be wretched when the judgment comes (James 1:10–11; 5:1–3). But Christians, though poor in this world, can rejoice in their exalted status because God's grace has made them rich in faith and heirs of the promised kingdom (James 1:9; 2:5). As Jesus taught, a person who gains the whole world but loses his soul has no profit at all (Matt. 16:26; Mark 8:36; Luke 9:25).

The contrast of earthly versus eternal values and the situation of his readers strongly influenced James's approach to wealth and poverty. His readers were predominantly poor,[54] and they had suffered greatly at the hands of rich people who

---

53. D. Edmond Hiebert, *The Epistle of James: Tests of a Living Faith* (Chicago: Moody, 1979), 322, among others, understands the faith described in James 5:15 to be a special God-given assurance that it is His will to heal in a specific case. This would be similar to the use of "faith" in 1 Corinthians 12:9—a kind of special faith beyond ordinary Christian trust. But the reference to faith in James 5:16 is so simple and unqualified that it seems better to understand that James was referring to the same sort of faith already described in 1:5–8 and implied in 4:2–3.

54. But the participation of the wealthy in their church meetings was an expected thing (2:1–4), and James exhorted the (probably wealthy) Christian businesspeople to trust God in their pursuits and avoid self-sufficiency and pride (4:13–17). The warnings of 5:1–6, however, are addressed to non-Christian rich people (see Moo, *James,* 159 for reasons why James may have addressed them in his epistle).

had misused their wealth and power. The rich had exploited the poor Christians, used the legal system to oppress them (2:6), failed to pay the wages due to their workers, and even condemned and killed the righteous (5:4–6). The rich were living in luxury and indulgence at the expense of others who were in need (5:5). Beyond all this, the rich showed contempt for the name of Christ (2:7).

In this context, James emphasized the evils of misused wealth. On the other side he viewed the poor as righteous and the special objects of God's favor. This is consonant with the Old Testament, Jewish traditions, and Jesus' teaching about the poor.[55] It is not meant to deny that Christians may be rich and use their wealth in godly ways or that poor people may be unrighteous. But it did address the abuses of wealth in James's situation and continues to have relevance for the believer who, rich or poor, seeks to live in a godly way.[56]

Finally, in keeping with the theme and emphasis of his epistle, James insisted that Christians live out these convictions concerning wealth and poverty. They must trust God in their poverty and look patiently to Him for ultimate deliverance (5:7–11). Those who have faith in the Lord Jesus Christ should not allow economic status to affect the way they treat people, either in exalting the rich or dishonoring the poor person in their midst (2:1–9). They must live out the law of love by resisting partiality. This "royal law" also compels action in response to a fellow believer who is ill-clothed or in need of daily food (2:15–16). Acts of love and kindness, not mere words, are the way for Christians to live out their faith and become doers of the Word.

---

55. See the background survey on wealth and poverty in Mussner, *Der Jakobusbrief,* 76–84; Davids, *Epistle of James,* 41–47; and Moo, *James,* 53–55.

56. For more on this topic, see Robert Lee Williams, "Piety and Poverty in James," *Wesleyan Theological Journal* 22 (1987): 37–55; and Pedrito U. Maynard-Reid, *Poverty and Wealth in James* (Maryknoll, N.Y.: Orbis, 1987).

10

A THEOLOGY OF
PETER AND JUDE

Buist M. Fanning

The two epistles by Peter are discussed together because of their common authorship, although they have different emphases since they were written to address distinct problems.[1] Jude's themes, of course, are similar to those of 2 Peter.[2]

CHRISTOLOGY

These three epistles give invaluable teaching about who Jesus Christ is, and many of the other important theological topics, especially in 1 Peter, relate closely to what is said about Christ.

---

1. The Petrine authorship of these epistles is disputed, especially that of 2 Peter. See Werner Georg Kümmel, *Introduction to the New Testament,* trans. Howard Clark Kee, rev. ed. (Nashville: Abingdon, 1975), 421–24, 430–34. For defense of their authenticity, see Michael Green, *The Second Epistle General of Peter and the General Epistle of Jude: An Introduction and Commentary,* Tyndale New Testament Commentaries (Grand Rapids: Eerdmans, 1968), 13–35; and Donald Guthrie, *New Testament Introduction,* 3d ed. (Downers Grove, Ill.: Inter-Varsity, 1970), 773–90, 820–48. Since 1 Peter is longer, its teaching will predominate in the discussion given here, but for some themes 2 Peter and Jude will be more prominent.

2. These two epistles are clearly related in their themes and literary composition. But no decision is necessary here concerning which of the two came first. For discussion of these issues, see Guthrie, *New Testament Introduction,* 919–27; and Richard J. Bauckham, *Jude, 2 Peter,* Word Biblical Commentary (Waco, Tex.: Word, 1983), 141–43.

Buist M. Fanning, B.A., Th.M., D.Phil., is professor of New Testament studies at Dallas Theological Seminary.

In general terms Peter communicated his Christology simply by recounting the course of Christ's life. Christ suffered while in the flesh, though He Himself was innocent and trusted God the Father (1 Peter 2:21–23; 3:17–18; 4:1). He died on a cross, bearing the sins of others (1:18–19; 2:24). God raised Him from the dead and gave Him glory and authority at His right hand in heaven (1:7, 21; 3:22). Soon He will be revealed from heaven in glory and power, with blessing for all who are His (1:7, 13; 4:13; 5:4; 2 Peter 1:11) and judgment for His adversaries (1 Peter 4:5, 17; 2 Peter 2:9; 3:3–13). Peter's straightforward outline of events was shared by other New Testament writers.[3] These events go a long way toward identifying who Jesus Christ is. But Peter's Christology must be filled out by specific details from this outline which he developed further.

First, it is significant to see that the life of Jesus on earth was central for Peter's Christology. The dichotomy between the Jesus of history and the Christ of faith, so prominent in some modern theologies, was foreign to Peter's thought.[4] He was an eyewitness of Jesus' life and ministry (1 Peter 5:1; 2 Peter 1:16), and he included reflections of this in his teaching about Him. He recounted especially the opposition, suffering, and death Jesus endured (1 Peter 2:21–24; 3:18; 4:1; 5:1). He recalled His sinless life (1:19; 2:22; 3:17–18), His glory at the Transfiguration (2 Peter 1:16–18), and His trust in God and refusal to retaliate against His persecutors (2:22–23).[5] He recalled also Christ's resurrection and specifically cited Christ's ascension to heavenly glory (1 Peter 1:3, 21; 3:18, 21–22; 2 Peter 1:16–18). In various places Peter's instruction to his readers mirrors the wording of Jesus' own teaching, which he had heard for himself (e.g., cf. 1 Peter 2:20 with Luke 6:32–34).[6] Like the rest of the New Testament, these epistles anchor Christianity in the historical events of Jesus' life and work on earth.[7]

But Peter, like the other New Testament writers, saw God's eternal plan being worked out in the historical events of Jesus' life. The God of heaven was at work in those earthly happenings. Peter affirmed that Christ "was foreknown before the creation of the world, but was revealed in these last times for your sake" (1 Peter 1:20). "The God and Father of our Lord Jesus Christ" showed His mercy in granting new life and a living hope "through the resurrection of Jesus Christ from the dead" (v. 3). This salvation through Christ and the grace it brought to Christians was prophesied in Old Testament days as "the Spirit of Christ" working through the prophets foretold "the sufferings of Christ and the glories that would

---

3. Cf. Acts 13:23–31; Philippians 2:6–11; Hebrews 2:9–18; 5:7–10.

4. This is the point of José Oriol Tuñí, "Jesus of Nazareth in the Christology of 1 Peter," *Heythrop Journal* 28 (1987): 292–304.

5. P. E. Davies, "Primitive Christology in 1 Peter," in *Festschrift to Honor F. Wilbur Gingrich*, ed. E. H. Barth and R. E. Cocroft (Leiden: Brill, 1972), 115–22.

6. Robert H. Gundry, "'Verba Christi' in 1 Peter: Their Implications Concerning the Authorship of 1 Peter and the Authenticity of the Gospel Tradition," *New Testament Studies* 13 (1966–67): 336–50, and "Further Verba on Verba Christi in First Peter," *Biblica* 55 (1974): 211–32.

7. For example, Luke 1:1–4; Acts 2:22–24; Romans 1:2–4; 1 Corinthians 15:3–8.

follow" (vv. 10–11). The same "Holy Spirit sent from heaven" was active through those who had evangelized Peter's readers (v. 12). God's will was worked out in Jesus' suffering and death, and so Christians also can entrust themselves to a faithful Creator in their suffering according to the will of God (2:15, 19–25; 3:17–18; 4:14–19).

The doctrine of the Incarnation is implicit in Peter's presentation of Jesus Christ, because along with an emphasis on Christ's suffering in the flesh (2:21–25; 3:18; 4:1) and earthly life are references to His preexistence. That Christ existed before His manifestation on earth is indicated in the parallelism of 1 Peter 1:20, "He was chosen before the creation of the world but was revealed in these last times for your sake." Christ was chosen (literally, "foreknown" or "predestined by God"[8]) before the foundation of the world to provide redemption and then was manifested on earth in the times of fulfillment witnessed by Peter and his readers. The two contrasting temporal phrases are reinforced by Greek conjunctions (*men . . . de*) designed to highlight the contrast of two significant stages in God's plan of salvation through Christ, namely, His pretemporal purpose and His historical execution of that purpose through Christ. Some have argued that this foreknowledge of Christ indicates merely an ideal preexistence in the mind and purpose of God, especially since Peter's readers were also said to be foreknown by God (1:2).[9] But this ignores the different context of verse 20 compared to verse 2. The "foreknowledge of Christ before creation" is not mentioned in isolation but is contrasted with His "manifestation in the last times" for the sake of the readers.[10] While he did not develop the point, Peter clearly thought of Christ as preexistent before His appearance on earth to suffer in the flesh and shed His blood for redemption.[11]

Peter's mention of Christ's preexistence raises the question of how he conceived of Christ's relationship with God the Father. This issue is suggested also by the first several verses of 1 Peter. In 1:2, Peter associated Jesus Christ with God the

---

8. For the sense of *proginōskō* here, see J. N. D. Kelly, *The Epistles of Peter and Jude,* Harper's New Testament Commentaries (New York: Harper & Row, 1969), 42–43, 75–76; and Wayne A. Grudem, *The First Epistle of Peter: An Introduction and Commentary,* Tyndale New Testament Commentaries (Grand Rapids: Eerdmans, 1988), 50, 85.

9. James D. G. Dunn, *Christology in the Making: A New Testament Inquiry into the Origins of the Doctrine of the Incarnation* (Philadelphia: Westminster, 1980), 236–39; and Earl Richard, "The Functional Christology of First Peter," in *Perspectives on First Peter,* ed. Charles H. Talbert (Macon, Ga.: Mercer Univ., 1986), 130–32.

10. George Barker Stevens, *The Theology of the New Testament,* 2d ed. (Edinburgh: T. & T. Clark, 1918), 298–301; Ceslas Spicq, *Les Épîtres de Saint Pierre,* Études bibliques (Paris: Gabalda, 1966), 32–33; Charles Caldwell Ryrie, *Biblical Theology of the New Testament* (Chicago: Moody, 1959), 271; and Kelly, *Epistles of Peter and Jude,* 76.

11. Christ's preexistent activity may be described in 1 Peter 3:19–22, but see the discussion of this passage later. The reference to "the Spirit of Christ" active in the Old Testament prophets (1 Peter 1:11) almost certainly describes the Holy Spirit bearing witness to Christ, rather than the preexistent Christ Himself as a Spirit. It may mean "the Spirit sent from Christ," implying preexistence. See J. Ramsey Michaels, *1 Peter,* Word Biblical Commentary (Waco, Tex.: Word, 1988), 43–44; and Peter H. Davids, *The First Epistle of Peter,* New International Commentary on the New Testament (Grand Rapids: Eerdmans, 1990), 62–63.

Father and with the Spirit in a Trinitarian allusion, and in verse 3 he blessed "the God and Father of our Lord Jesus Christ." Jesus' sonship is implied by these associations, but Peter did not develop this common title of "Son" for Christ. He did not use "Son" for Christ at all in 1 Peter, and in 2 Peter it occurs only in the citation of the words spoken at the Transfiguration (1:17, "My beloved Son in Whom I am pleased"). However, Peter associated Jesus Christ with the work of God in a unique way in these and other verses, and he located blessing and life particularly in Him (1 Peter 1:3–5; 1:18–21; 3:18–22; 4:11; 5:10). It should also be noted that in 2 Peter 1:16–17, when Peter cited God's approbation of Jesus as His beloved Son, he reinforced the larger significance of that title by noting the shared divine majesty of Father and Son. Peter did this by using the same word group to refer first to the majesty of Jesus Christ and then to the majesty of God the Father: "we were eye-witnesses of his majesty [*megaleiotētos*]. For when he received honor and glory from God the Father and the voice was borne to him by the Majestic Glory [*tēs megaloprepous doxēs*], 'This is my beloved Son, with whom I am well pleased'" (1:16b–17). In biblical Greek these words were used consistently of divine splendor or majesty.[12] Using this repetition, Peter indicated that Jesus Christ shared the divine glory of God the Father.

This is seen also in the titles Peter used of Christ. Peter's favorite terms for Him in 1 Peter were "Christ" (used thirteen times by itself), "Jesus Christ" (seven times), and "Lord" (four times, including "Lord Jesus Christ" in 1:3). Peter never used "Jesus" by itself. In 2 Peter the title "Lord" is more common, being used three times as "our Lord Jesus Christ," four times as "our Lord and Savior Jesus Christ," and once as "Jesus our Lord." The use of "Lord" is significant, because in two places Peter cited an Old Testament passage originally referring to God the Father (Yahweh) and applied the title to Jesus as Lord (1 Peter 2:3; 3:15).[13] This prepared the way for the bolder ascription of full deity to Jesus Christ given in 2 Peter 1:1, "our God and Savior Jesus Christ."[14] The more common phrase in 2 Peter is "our Lord and Savior Jesus Christ" (used four times, in 1:11; 2:20; 3:2, 18). Peter saw that Jesus Christ so shared and exerted the glory and authority of God the Father that He could be addressed by the same titles.[15]

ATONEMENT AND SALVATION

One of the most important contributions of these epistles is their teaching about the salvation that Christ provided. It is significant that Peter especially came

---

12. Walter Bauer, William F. Arndt, and F. Wilbur Gingrich, *A Greek-English Lexicon of the New Testament and Other Early Christian Literature*, 2d ed., rev. F. Wilbur Gingrich and Frederick W. Danker (Chicago: Univ. of Chicago, 1979), 496–97.

13. Kelly, *Epistles of Peter and Jude*, 86, 142.

14. See discussion in Oscar Cullmann, *The Christology of the New Testament*, rev. ed., trans. Shirley C. Guthrie and Charles A. M. Hall (Philadelphia: Westminster, 1963), 313–14; and Murray J. Harris, *Jesus As God: The New Testament Use of* Theos *in Reference to Jesus* (Grand Rapids: Baker, 1992), 229–38.

15. See Cullmann, *Christology of the New Testament*, 234–37.

to emphasize the need for the Messiah to suffer and die in accomplishing God's will (1 Peter 1:11), since the apostle had strenuously resisted Jesus' forewarning about this (Mark 8:31–33). "He, who had wanted to hear nothing of it during the lifetime of Jesus, made Jesus' suffering and death the very centre of his explanation of Jesus' earthly work."[16]

THE SIGNIFICANCE OF CHRIST'S DEATH

Three passages express Peter's central teaching about Christ's suffering and death.

First Peter 1:18–21. This passage describes Jesus' death as the sacrifice that provided redemption from the futile ways of sin to a life of faith and hope in God. The key word is the verb "redeem" in verse 18 (*lytroō*, "ransom, set free"), which denoted release from slavery by payment of a ransom. This word group was used in the Greek Old Testament and in secular Greek in the literal sense of the ransoming of slaves or hostages.[17] But the more influential Old Testament usage was the common occurrence of the verb to describe God's deliverance of Israel out of slavery in Egypt. God "brought them out with a mighty hand and redeemed them from the land of slavery" (Deut. 7:8; cf. Ex. 6:6; 15:13; Deut. 9:26; 13:5; 15:15; 24:18; 2 Sam. 7:23; 1 Chron. 17:21; Ps. 78:42).[18] The metaphor of God's mighty deliverance of a people for Himself from evil oppression lies behind the New Testament doctrine of redemption. But more important is Jesus' teaching about His role in God's redemption: "For even the Son of Man did not come to be served, but to serve, and to give his life as a ransom [*lytron*] for many" (Matt. 20:28; Mark 10:45).

This is the point Peter also emphasized by contrasting the corruptible earthly price of redemption ("not with perishable things such as silver or gold") over against the costly means that God chose to redeem ("with the precious blood of Christ, a lamb without blemish or defect"). The blood of Christ was already mentioned in 1 Peter 1:2 ("chosen . . . for obedience to Jesus Christ and sprinkling by his blood"). There the reference to His blood is an allusion to the ceremony of covenant ratification in Exodus 24:5–8. Moses signified the inauguration of the Mosaic covenant by sprinkling the blood of the sacrifices on the altar and on the people, who pledged obedience to what the Lord commanded in the law. As Jesus taught in the institution of the Lord's Supper (Matt. 26:27–28; Mark 14:23–24; Luke 22:20), His blood was the ratification of the new covenant, since it was the basis for the

---

16. Ibid., 74.

17. Colin Brown, *The New International Dictionary of New Testament Theology* (Grand Rapids: Zondervan, 1975) s.v. *"lytron,"* 3:189–95; and Leon Morris, *The Apostolic Preaching of the Cross*, 3d ed. (London: Tyndale, 1965), 11–64.

18. O. Procksch, *Theological Dictionary of the New Testament*, trans. and ed. Geoffrey W. Bromiley (Grand Rapids: Eerdmans, 1964–76), s.v. *"luō,"* 4:328–35; and Eugene H. Merrill, "A Theology of the Pentateuch," in *A Biblical Theology of the Old Testament*, ed. Roy B. Zuck (Chicago: Moody, 1991), 68, 87.

complete forgiveness of sins promised in Jeremiah 31:31–34.[19] Here in 1 Peter 1:19 Christ's blood signifies His life poured out on the cross as the price for the Christian's redemption. The vicarious nature of this death is reinforced by the comparison with that of a blameless sacrificial lamb (v. 19). It is not clear whether the background for this is the unblemished Passover lamb (Ex. 12:5), the lamb without defect required in the regular sacrificial rituals (Lev. 22:17–25; Num. 28–29), or the innocent lamb led to slaughter, as mentioned in Isaiah 53:7.[20] In any case, the image is one of vicarious sacrifice, the blameless victim dying for the sake of others.

Peter concluded this explanation of Christ's death by anchoring it in the eternal plan of God (1 Peter 1:20), showing God's acceptance of the sacrifice by resurrecting and exalting Christ (v. 21) and bringing the discussion back to its starting point by noting its effects: the readers' relationship with God (v. 21; cf. v. 17).

First Peter 2:21–25. In this passage Peter described Christ's death as "suffering,"[21] one of the words characteristic of 1 Peter. The verb is used four times in 2:19–23 (out of eleven occurrences in the epistle). It is clear that the suffering in view was the agony Christ endured before and on the cross. Peter's purpose in this description is seen in verse 21 and the wider context of instruction to Christian slaves: to present Christ as an example of innocent but patient suffering. Christians are called (v. 21a) to suffer injustice without retaliation, and in this they follow in Christ's steps (v. 21b). Peter emphasized the exemplary significance of Christ's death (which will be developed further in the section on the Christian life). But the meaning of His death is not limited to this.

Peter's basic statement in verse 21, "Christ suffered *for* you," suggests the larger significance of Christ's suffering, which is made explicit in subsequent verses. Jesus died as a substitutionary sacrifice. He was not put to death for any guilt of His own, but bore the penalty of sin for others. Peter emphasized this point by quoting from and alluding to the description of the Suffering Servant in Isaiah 53 and showing that Jesus fulfilled that role in His death.[22]

Peter quoted Isaiah 53:9 almost exactly in 1 Peter 2:22 to show Christ's innocence, "He committed no sin, and no deceit was found in his mouth." Alluding to Isaiah 53:7 in 1 Peter 2:23, Peter described perhaps what he had personally witnessed of Christ's behavior before the cross: "When they hurled their insults at

19. Edward Gordon Selwyn, *The First Epistle of St. Peter,* 2d ed. (London: Macmillan, 1946), 120–21; Kelly, *Epistles of Peter and Jude,* 44; and Donald Guthrie, *New Testament Theology* (Downers Grove, Ill.: InterVarsity, 1981), 474.

20. See discussion in Michaels, *1 Peter,* 65–66; and Davids, *First Epistle of Peter,* 72–73.

21. A textual variant reads "Christ died for you" instead of "Christ suffered for you," but the latter has superior external and internal evidence.

22. Peter's sermon in Acts 3 (vv. 13, 26) and the prayer made during his imprisonment in Acts 4 (vv. 27, 30) also identify Jesus with the Servant of Isaiah 53. For discussion of other New Testament uses see Joachim Jeremias, *Theological Dictionary of the New Testament,* s.v. "*pais theou* in the New Testament," 5:700–717; O. Michel, *The New International Dictionary of New Testament Theology,* s.v. "*pais theou,*" 3:610–13; and Richard N. Longenecker, *The Christology of Early ˸ vish Christianity* (London: SCM, 1970), 104–9.

him, he did not retaliate; when he suffered, he made no threats. Instead, he entrusted himself to him who judges justly." Jesus suffered undeservedly and without resisting, submitting Himself to God's will and justice. The reason for His innocent death was to provide for others: "He himself bore our sins in his body on the tree . . . by his wounds you have been healed" (v. 24, quoting portions of Isa. 53:4–5, 12). As Kelly observes, the theme of God's Servant suffering for others runs through Isaiah's Song "like a refrain,"[23] and Peter saw the central importance of this in Christian salvation.

The sense of the key phrase in 1 Peter 2:24, "He himself bore our sins in his body on the tree," is debated. It may be understood as the removal of sins as Christ carried them up and put them on the cross where they were destroyed.[24] The alternative is a reference to Christ's carrying or enduring the penalty for sins in His death on the cross, in the sense that "the Lord has laid on him the iniquity of us all" (Isa. 53:6). The background in Isaiah 53 and the phrase "in his body" makes a stronger case for the latter understanding.[25] The allusion to Deuteronomy 21:23 in the phrase "on the tree" (cf. Gal. 3:13) added the note of divine penalty or judgment for sin. In the will of God Christ died not because of His own sin, but because of the burden of guilt He carried as a penal substitute for others.[26]

The passage also presents, in unmistakable terms, the transformation that Christ's work on the cross is designed to produce in the lives of those who become Christians. "He bore our sins . . . that we may depart from sin and live for righteousness" (1 Peter 2:24b). "You were straying like sheep, but now you have turned to the Shepherd and Overseer of your souls" (v. 25). This final verse implies the resurrection of Christ by showing that He is alive and active in the care of those who are His.

First Peter 3:18. This verse also emphasizes the substitutionary nature of Christ's death. He "suffered[27] once for all concerning sins, the just for the unjust." Again the note of innocent suffering is sounded: He was righteous and thus suffered not for any misdeeds of His own but as a substitute for those who were unrighteous, who justly deserved punishment for sin. The description of Christ as "Righteous" seems to be taken from the portrayal of the Servant of Isaiah 53:11–12 ("by his knowledge my righteous servant will justify many, and he will bear their iniquities. . . . he was numbered with the transgressors, for he bore the sin of many"). The need for His suffering is expressed by the phrase "concerning sins" (*peri hamartiōn*). This was used of sin offerings in the Old Testament (e.g., Lev. 5:6–7;

---

23. Kelly, *Epistles of Peter and Jude,* 122.

24. The prepositions used in this expression may imply this idea. See Murray J. Harris, *The New International Dictionary of New Testament Theology,* s.v. "Prepositions and Theology in the Greek New Testament," 3:1195–96 for this view.

25. See Grudem, *First Epistle of Peter,* 131–34, for a defense of this approach.

26. Selwyn, *First Epistle of St. Peter,* 180.

27. There is a textual variation here between "suffered" and "died," but the former reading is preferred on external and internal grounds. See Davids, *First Epistle of Peter,* 135 n. 17.

6:30; Ps. 40:6 [quoted in Heb. 10:6, 8]; Isa. 53:10),[28] and in the New Testament it shows that Christ's death was a sacrifice to deal with sin and its penalty (Rom. 8:3; Heb. 5:3; 10:18, 26; 1 John 2:2; 4:10).[29]

When the guilt of sin is dealt with, access to the holy God is opened up. Peter stated that this was an express purpose of Christ's suffering: "to bring you to God" (1 Peter 3:18b). This is a vivid portrayal of Christ's mediatory role in opening the way to God. Paul referred to the same work of Christ in Romans 5:2; Ephesians 2:18; 3:12, and the author of Hebrews described it in different terms in Hebrews 4:16; 7:25; 10:19–22.

In elaborating on Christ's work of bringing people to God, Peter referred again to His death and resurrection. This is done by parallel, contrastive participles, "having been put to death in the flesh but made alive in the spirit" (1 Peter 3:18c). There is no question that the contrast between "put to death" and "made alive" refers to the death and resurrection of Christ. What is not so clear is the sense of the "flesh" and "spirit" contrast and its logical connection with the participles. "Flesh" is often used in 1 Peter of the physical, earthly dimension of life, especially in contrast to an eternal, heavenly mode of existence (1:24; 3:21; 4:1–2, 6) and this makes sense here. Then "spirit" in contrast would not distinguish between parts of Christ's person (material versus immaterial), since He died and was raised not in part but as a whole person. Instead the contrast concerns two modes of existence: the realm of unregenerate earthly life versus eternal heavenly life.[30] Christ suffered and died in the earthly mode of life, but in regard to the spiritual heavenly realm of existence He is alive and glorified (3:22). Two other New Testament passages have a similar contrast (Rom. 1:3–4; 1 Tim. 3:16). The reference was not to the Holy Spirit directly, though He would be thought of in the background, since the Spirit permeates and characterizes the spiritual mode of existence.[31]

The meaning of the verses that follow (3:19–22) will be discussed in a later section.

---

28. Harris, *The New International Dictionary of New Testament Theology,* s.v. "Prepositions and Theology in the Greek New Testament," 3:1203; and Davids, *First Epistle of Peter,* 135.

29. The same focus on atonement for sin is expressed by the prepositions "on account of" (*dia*) and "for the sake of" (*hyper*) with sin as the object. See Romans 4:25; 1 Corinthians 15:3; Galatians 1:4; and Hebrews 10:12.

30. This is the consensus of most recent works. See Kelly, *Epistles of Peter and Jude,* 150–51; Davids, *First Epistle of Peter,* 136–37; and William Joseph Dalton, *Christ's Proclamation to the Spirits: A Study of 1 Peter* 3:18–4:6, Analecta Biblica, 2d ed. (Rome: Pontificio Instituto Biblico, 1989), 138–41.

31. Thus Peter did not make the Spirit the agent of resurrection, as the NIV has it: "He was put to death in the body but made alive by the Spirit." The New Testament associates the Spirit with "making alive" (*zōopoieō*) in the sense of giving new life to unregenerate people (John 6:63; 1 Cor. 15:45; 2 Cor. 3:6), but "making alive" carries a different sense when used of Christ's resurrection in 1 Peter 3:18.

SALVATION APPLIED

God provided for the spiritual deliverance of humankind through the death and resurrection of Jesus Christ. How that work is applied to individuals is another important topic in the epistles of Peter and Jude.[32]

God's initiative in salvation.[33] These epistles pay special attention to God's sovereignty in the outworking of salvation. In general terms, all three epistles see the events of this world as the fulfillment of God's sovereign will. No matter what happens, God is working out His plan and Christians may depend on His goodness and power (1 Peter 2:15; 3:17, 20; 4:2, 19; 5:6; 2 Peter 1:3–4; 2:4–9; 3:5–13; Jude 5–6, 14–15, 24–25). But God's sovereignty may be seen as well in the more specific events of salvation history.

On the one hand, God foreordained Jesus Christ before the foundation of the world to be the atoning sacrifice (1 Peter 1:20). Christ is the living Stone, "rejected by men but chosen by God and precious to him" (2:4), the chosen and precious cornerstone that God laid in Zion so that "the one who trusts in Him will never be put to shame" (2:6; Isa. 28:16; Rom. 9:33; 10:11). The Spirit speaking through the Old Testament prophets predicted the grace that would come to people through this salvation, the sufferings that Messiah would endure to provide it, and the glories He would attain for Himself and His people (1:10–11; 5:10). The Holy Spirit guided the prophets so that they spoke God's words and not merely their own (2 Peter 1:20–21). Thus, the fulfillment of God's will could be seen in the events of Christ's life and ministry, and they confirmed the truth of the Old Testament predictions (2 Peter 1:16–19).

In addition, God's initiative in the salvation of individuals is made clear in these epistles. Peter described Christians individually as elect or chosen (*eklektos*) according to God's foreknowledge or predestination (1 Peter 1:1–2). Collectively believers in Christ are a chosen nation (2:6), because of their relationship to Him, the chosen cornerstone (2:4). In addition, these epistles often speak of Christians as called by God (*kaleō, klētos*). This divine "summons" is God's working to bring people into a relationship with Himself. It involves a call to live holy lives, since He who called them is holy (1:15). It is a call out of darkness into His amazing light

---

32. This distinction between the *provision* of Christ's saving work and its *application* to individuals is significant in Peter's teaching, though not developed in detail. It arises from the description of false teachers in 2 Peter 2:1. The description in verses 1–3 makes it clear that they will go into eternal destruction, yet they are said to deny "the Lord who bought them." The best understanding of this is to see that Christ's death on the cross *provided* redemption for all humankind, even for those who will never respond to the gospel and ultimately are condemned. But Christ's atonement is *applied* and effected in the lives of those whom God has chosen, called, and begotten in the way described in this section. See Edwin A. Blum, "2 Peter," in *The Expositor's Bible Commentary,* ed. Frank E. Gaebelein (Grand Rapids: Zondervan, 1981) 12:276–77; Kenneth O. Gangel, "2 Peter," in *The Bible Knowledge Commentary, New Testament,* ed. John F. Walvoord and Roy B. Zuck (Wheaton, Ill.: Victor, 1983), 870; and Andrew D. Chang, "Second Peter 2:1 and the Extent of the Atonement," *Bibliotheca Sacra* 142 (1985): 52–63.

33. The subpoints in this section are suggested by Donald G. Miller, "Deliverance and Destiny: Salvation in First Peter," *Interpretation* 9 (1955): 413–25.

(2:9). It calls them to innocent suffering like Christ's (2:21), but also to inherit blessing in following His example (3:9). Ultimately, it is a call to God's eternal glory in Christ (5:9). By living out the Christian character that God has put within them, believers make their calling and election sure and receive a rich welcome into Christ's eternal kingdom (2 Peter 1:10–11; cf. 1:3–4). Their calling is assured because they are beloved in God the Father and kept for Jesus Christ (Jude 1) by God the Savior who is able to guard them from falling and to present them blameless before His glorious presence with great joy (Jude 24–25).

New Birth. According to Peter another evidence of God's initiative in salvation, as well as the first step in its application to the individual's life, is the new birth. Peter portrayed the beginning of the Christian life as a birth from God, using the verb "to beget again, cause to be born again" (*anagennaō*).[34] Peter described God as "the One who according to His great mercy caused Christians to be born again to a living hope" (1 Peter 1:3). This new birth was brought into effect in their lives by the preaching of the gospel to which they responded. Using the same verb for "born again," Peter wrote, "For you have been born again, not of perishable seed, but of imperishable, through the living and enduring word of God. . . . and this is the word that was preached to you" (1 Peter 1:23, 25). The same imagery appears in 2:2 in urging them to go on in the Christian life. "Like newborn babies [*hōs artigennēta brephē*]," Peter urged, "crave pure spiritual milk, so that by it you may grow up in your salvation."[35]

Growth. As just mentioned, Peter followed references to the Christian's new birth in 1 Peter 1 with the imagery of growth in the Christian life (2:2). The sense is that spiritual birth or conversion is just the beginning and must be followed by a process of development or maturing in character and understanding. The growth should be seen, however, as simply the process of working out the potential already bestowed on the believer in the new birth. This is shown in part by the connection between the seed through which the Christian is born again (1:23–25) and the pure, spiritual milk by which growth occurs (2:2). Even though a mixed metaphor results (since the figure changes), both of these refer to the Word of God, God's truth, or the gospel. This is clear in 1:23 ("through the living and enduring word of God") and is implied in 2:2 by the adjective "spiritual" (*logikos,* related to the noun "word," *logos*). While the adjective carries the sense "spiritual" in 2:2, it makes the association with God's word in 1:23–25 and shows that this is the "pure milk" Peter had in mind.[36] The birth and the growth are along the same line.

This is the point of the other verse in Peter's writings where the picture of growth is used. In 2 Peter 3:18 Peter closed his letter by urging his readers to "grow in grace and in the knowledge of our Lord and Savior Jesus Christ." This growth is the antidote to the influence of false teachers (verse 17) and concerns not esoteric things but the basics of Christianity: maturing in grace and in knowing Jesus

---

34. Bauer, Arndt, and Gingrich, *A Greek-English Lexicon of the New Testament,* 51.

35. The theme of new birth in Peter is similar to that of John 1:13; 3:3–8; Titus 3:5; and James 1:18, though different terminology is used in each passage.

36. Kelly, *Epistles of Peter and Jude,* 85; and Grudem, *First Epistle of Peter,* 95–96.

Christic.[37] It is likely that Peter closed his letter in the same way he began, because 2 Peter 1:3–11 seems also to picture a process of growth in Christian character. To the basic experience of conversion and initial faith (vv. 3–5a), the Christian should give diligent effort to developing a series of Christian traits: virtue, knowledge, self-control, perseverance, godliness, brotherly affection, and love (vv. 5–7).

The imagery of new birth and growth is related in Peter's teaching to the call for a change in behavior from the old to the new now that a person is a Christian. This can be seen especially in 1 Peter 1:14–16 (not conformed to the former lusts but holy in all conduct, as God is holy) and 2:1–3 (putting aside various evils and longing for spiritual growth). The Christian's change from old to new is connected also with the pattern of Christ's death and resurrection in 2:24 and 4:1–3. Since Christ suffered for sin and has been raised, Christians also should be done with sin and live for righteousness. This connection has similarities with Paul's teaching in Romans 6 and elsewhere, but Peter articulates it simply as God's purpose in Christ's suffering (2:24) and as a pattern to be followed (4:1–3), rather than a salvation-historical identification of the Christian with Christ, as in Paul.

Consummation. While Peter's teaching on how salvation is applied gave attention to the beginning and continued process of living as a Christian, the actual words for "salvation" have a predominantly future orientation in 1 Peter.[38] "Salvation," in strict terms, is the future culmination of the Christian's experience, though it is the guaranteed end of a process already begun. For example, Peter taught in 1:3–5 that regeneration is toward a living hope[39] and an imperishable inheritance kept in heaven for those "who are protected by the power of God through faith for a salvation ready to be revealed in the last time." The same future orientation is seen in verses 9–10, where the goal of the readers' faith is said to be the salvation of their souls.[40] This future "reception" of salvation is simply the culmination of what God is already doing in a believer's life. Peter's reference to Christian growth in 1 Peter 2:2 identified the goal of such development as "unto salvation" (*eis sōtērian*).[41] Final deliverance is the end product of the new birth and Christian growth.[42]

---

37. "Knowledge" of God or Jesus Christ is a characteristic idea of 2 Peter (1:2–3, 5–6, 8; 2:20–21; 3:18). This knowledge comes to the Christian because God has revealed Himself uniquely through the gospel of Jesus Christ. In accepting the gospel, the believer acquires true knowledge of God and a personal relationship with Him. This is his possession from the beginning of faith, but he must grow in understanding and obedience.

38. J. Schneider, *The New International Dictionary of New Testament Theology*, s.v. "*sōzō*," 3:215; and Davids, *First Epistle of Peter*, 20.

39. Three references to "hope" in 1 Peter focus on the culmination of personal salvation as something Christians can confidently expect in the future (1:3, 13; 3:15).

40. The present participle "obtaining" in this verse should be taken in a futuristic sense: it is a process that is under way but not fulfilled until the coming of the future events described in verses 5 and 7. See Buist M. Fanning, *Verbal Aspect in New Testament Greek* (Oxford: Clarendon, 1990), 221–23, 413.

41. See Bauer, Arndt, and Gingrich, *A Greek-English Lexicon of the New Testament*, 229–30. The preposition *eis* may denote "reference or respect," but this is not as likely as the more common use showing the goal, especially with a verb of change such as "grow."

42. Two other references to salvation in Peter's epistles also relate to the future (1 Peter 4:18;

This is the culmination envisioned by Peter in 2 Peter 1:3–11. As believers grow in Christian virtues (vv. 5–7) they are simply living out what God has put within them at the moment of their conversion (vv. 3–4). This confirms their calling and election by God and ensures a rich welcome into Christ's eternal kingdom (vv. 10–11).[43]

CHRIST'S PREACHING TO THE SPIRITS

Two perplexing passages related to Peter's teaching about salvation are 1 Peter 3:19–22, which speaks of Christ's preaching to certain "spirits in prison," and 4:6, which refers to the gospel being preached to the "dead." These passages are not necessarily connected, except by the broad theme of some sort of proclamation.

As might be expected, a number of interpretations have been offered for such puzzling words. Some of them are clearly at variance with the theology of the New Testament and of 1 Peter itself. For example, the idea that these verses speak of offering a second chance for salvation to the unconverted dead[44] directly contradicts the New Testament's teaching that salvation comes to the ungodly only through faith in Christ and that eternal judgment is the fate of those who reject God's salvation in this life (Matt. 7:13; Luke 16:23–31; John 3:36; 17:12; Rom. 2:1–3; Phil. 1:28; 3:19; 2 Thess. 1:8–10; Heb. 9:27–28; 10:39; Rev. 20:11–15). In addition, it is inconceivable that Peter would urge people to suffer in this life for the sake of the gospel if he believed that mercy would be extended to all the dead in the hereafter (1 Peter 4:1–5, 12–19; cf. 2:7–8; 2 Peter 2:1–3; 3:7). This suggests that 1 Peter 4:6a is better taken to mean "the gospel was preached even to those who are now dead," referring to the prior evangelization and conversion of certain believers who had then passed on in death.[45] Though to human eyes they suffered judgment in this earthly life (i.e., they died, in the midst of physical abuse from the ungodly and taunts that Christianity would do them no good after all), they will enjoy life from God in the spiritual, heavenly realm because of the gospel (v. 6b). Thus they, and not their enemies, will ultimately be vindicated when Christ judges the living and the dead (v. 5).[46]

---

2 Peter 3:15). First Peter 3:21 makes a generic present statement: "Baptism now saves you." As the verse shows, "baptism" is used here not of the physical rite, but as a metaphor for God's saving work and the individual's response to it ("the appeal of a good conscience toward God"). See Grudem, *First Epistle of Peter*, 163–64. The "now" contrasts the present dispensation of Christ with the deliverance of Noah's time.

43. Cf. Blum, "2 Peter," in *The Expositor's Bible Commentary*, 270–71.

44. Charles Bigg, *A Critical and Exegetical Commentary on the Epistles of St. Peter and St. Jude*, International Critical Commentary, 2d ed. (Edinburgh: T. & T. Clark, 1902), 170–72; Francis Wright Beare, *The First Epistle of Peter: The Greek Text with Introduction and Notes*, 3d ed. (Oxford: Blackwell, 1970), 172, 182; and Anthony Hanson, "Salvation Proclaimed: [Part] I. 1 Peter 3:18–22," *Expository Times* 93 (1982): 100–105.

45. It is common to speak of events in someone's past while referring to his or her present status. To say "the President was born here" does not imply he was president when born!

46. See the defense of this interpretation in Kelly, *Epistles of Peter and Jude*, 172–76; Edwin A. Blum, "1 Peter," in *The Expositor's Bible Commentary*, 12:245; Grudem, *First Epistle of Peter*, 170–72; and Dalton, *Christ's Proclamation to the Spirits*, 225–41.

Apart from the question of how to read 1 Peter 4:6, the interpretation of 3:19–22 is still perplexing. The main issues about "Christ's preaching to the spirits" center on the audience (who are these spirits?), the content (what was His message?), and the occasion of this preaching (when did it occur?).[47] Possible answers to each of these questions are numerous and the arguments for and against different options go far beyond what can be discussed here. But two main lines of interpretation can be mentioned and evaluated briefly.

The most common interpretation takes "the spirits in prison" to be evil angels who were "disobedient in the days of Noah" in that they cohabited with women on earth and fathered a race of giants by them in the days before the Flood (Gen. 6:1–4). For this they were confined by God in a place of punishment, awaiting final judgment in the end times (cf. 2 Peter 2:4–5; Jude 6–7; Matt. 25:41; Rev. 20:10–15; 21:8). After Christ's resurrection, probably as part of His ascension, He went to them and proclaimed His triumph over all the forces of evil (cf. 1 Peter 3:22). Though this interpretation may seem strange to modern readers, it fits the language and immediate context of the passage quite well. It also has many parallels with common intertestamental Jewish ideas about Genesis 6, fallen angels, and future judgment.[48] In the wider context of 1 Peter these verses are designed to encourage suffering believers that victory is ultimately theirs in Christ. All the ungodly and the enemies of the gospel will be defeated, while Christians, though they suffer now, will be delivered and will share in Christ's glorious triumph in the future.[49]

The other major line of interpretation understands "the spirits in prison" to be unrighteous humans, now dead and confined in hell, who lived in the days of Noah. In the spiritual realm Christ went in those days and preached to them a message of repentance through Noah, a preacher of righteousness (2 Peter 2:5). But they resisted God's longsuffering mercy during the building of the ark and were destroyed in the Flood. This interpretation also fits the wording and immediate context of the passage very well. The reference to human disobedience leading right up to the judgment of the Flood is consistent with the emphasis of Genesis 6 (cf. also Matt. 24:37–39; Luke 17:26–27; Heb. 11:7; 2 Peter 2:5), and the picture of Christ being active through the Spirit in Old Testament days is similar to 1 Peter 1:11. There are also parallels in extrabiblical literature portraying Noah's preaching to his

---

47. See the summary of issues in Blum, "1 Peter," in *The Expositor's Bible Commentary*, 241; and Grudem, *First Epistle of Peter*, 203.

48. These ideas are found commonly in books like 1 Enoch, Jubilees, Testaments of the Twelve Patriarchs, and 2 Baruch, as well as in the writings of Josephus, Philo, and the Qumran community. See the literature cited in note 49 for specific references. The most striking parallels are with 1 Enoch 6–21 (and scattered references in later chapters): fallen angels are called spirits, are linked to disobedience in Noah's day, are said to be in prison, and Enoch goes to them to announce their judgment.

49. This is the general interpretation of Kelly, *Epistles of Peter and Jude*, 151–64; R. T. France, "Exegesis in Practice: Two Samples," *New Testament Interpretation: Essays on Principles and Methods*, ed. I. Howard Marshall (Grand Rapids: Eerdmans, 1977), 264–81; Blum, "1 Peter," in *The Expositor's Bible Commentary*, 241–43; Dalton, *Christ's Proclamation to the Spirits*, 143–88; and Davids, *First Epistle of Peter*, 138–43.

generation during the ark's construction and the mocking he received for obeying God.[50] According to this view, these verses fit the wider context of 1 Peter by encouraging Christians to stand for righteousness and to try to influence their contemporaries for the gospel in spite of the resistance and suffering that may come to them. Judgment is near and the outcome will be bleak for the ungodly, but in Christ there is deliverance.[51]

Both of these are plausible readings of the passage, but the latter interpretation seems marginally better. While many points could be compared and debated,[52] two factors favor the reference to Christ's preaching through Noah. One is the Greek participle of verse 20, translated "who disobeyed" in the NIV. The grammatical characteristics of this construction (participle in predicate position to an articular noun) indicate that the participle is adverbial in sense rather than adjectival (not "who disobeyed," but "as they disobeyed") and that it describes the time of the main verbal idea, "he preached," in verse 19.[53] The sense then is "Christ went and preached to them, as they long ago disobeyed when God's patience waited in the days of Noah while the ark was being built." This strongly supports the reference to Christ's preaching through Noah.

The other factor supporting this view is the marginally better way in which it fits into the argument of 1 Peter. As developed in the next section, Peter wrote to Christians suffering for their faith in a hostile environment. Peter urged them as God's people to live in a consistently righteous way and to seek to have an influence for Christ on the evil world around them (1 Peter 2:9–12). In spite of insults and outright beatings, they must trust themselves to God and communicate their hope in Christ by their conduct and speech (2:18–21; 3:1–2; 14–17; 4:1–4). They can do this because they bear the name of Christ and God's Spirit rests on them (4:14, 16). This is all the more urgent because the time of judgment is near, when deliverance will come only to Christians out of all the mass of humanity (4:5, 7, 12–19). Because of Christ's death, resurrection, and ascension, their salvation and glory is assured (1:3–7; 3:21–22; 5:9–10). Into this argument it is most appropriate to insert a reference to Christ's work through Noah, who lived and preached righteousness in the midst of an evil generation. Despite mocking and difficulty, Noah did God's will, and he and all who identified with him were saved from judgment. This sort of encouragement to Peter's readers is more appropriate in the larger argument than the reminder of Christ's victory over evil angels suggested by the alternate view.[54]

50. See references in Grudem, *First Epistle of Peter,* 216.

51. This is the approach of Roger M. Raymer, "1 Peter," in *The Bible Knowledge Commentary, New Testament,* 851–52; Guthrie, *New Testament Theology,* 841–43; Grudem, *First Epistle of Peter,* 203–39; and John S. Feinberg, "1 Peter 3:18–20, Ancient Mythology, and the Intermediate State," *Westminster Theological Journal* 48 (1986): 303–36.

52. For specific issues see the literature cited already.

53. There are almost no exceptions to this pattern. See Friedrich Blass and A. Debrunner, *A Greek Grammar of the New Testament and Other Early Christian Literature,* trans. Robert W. Funk from the 9th-10th German ed. (Chicago: Univ. of Chicago, 1961), § 270; and the discussion in Grudem, *First Epistle of Peter,* 233–36.

54. See Grudem's discussion of the context in *First Epistle of Peter,* 230–33.

THE CHRISTIAN LIFE: IMITATING CHRIST'S SUFFERING

We have said much here already about living the Christian life.[55] But two topics regarding Christian behavior must be discussed more specifically since they are distinctive themes of 1 Peter.[56]

SUFFERING IN IMITATION OF CHRIST

"Running through the whole letter, sometimes overtly expressed but never far below the surface"[57] is the awareness that the readers of 1 Peter were threatened by trials and suffering for their faith. There are no indications that the persecutions yet involved imprisonment or martyrdom, but the Christians were certainly suffering general hostility and resentment, false accusations and suspicion, personal animosity and harassment, verbal abuse, and sporadic physical beatings because of their allegiance to Christ.[58] This topic occupied much of Peter's attention as he wrote. Words for suffering occur sixteen times in 1 Peter (out of fifty-seven New Testament occurrences), in addition to other expressions describing such difficulties.[59]

Peter's response to the readers' situation was to encourage and instruct them with Christ's example of suffering and glory in order to strengthen their faith in God's providence and ultimate victory. In some of the most distinctive and best-known passages in the epistle, Peter mingled references to Christ's suffering with exhortations to the readers about their own difficulties.[60]

In 1 Peter 2:18–20, Peter encouraged Christian slaves by pointing out that patient endurance of unjust treatment from a harsh master brings God's favor. This would especially be true when they are submissive to their master regardless of his disposition (v. 18), endure ill-treatment "for the sake of conscience toward God" (v. 19 NASB), and suffer perhaps even physical beatings "for doing good" (v. 20). Peter pointed them beyond such difficult circumstances to see that God's favor rests on those who may suffer in that way. But the encouragement was immeasurably strengthened when Peter cited Christ as the example to follow in such suffering

---

55. See the section on atonement and salvation.

56. Cf. George Eldon Ladd, *A Theology of the New Testament* (Grand Rapids: Eerdmans, 1974), 601.

57. Kelly, *Epistles of Peter and Jude*, 5.

58. See Kelly, *Epistles of Peter and Jude*, 5–11, for a survey of evidence for persecution in these churches.

59. Davids argues that "suffering" and "sickness" are treated differently throughout the New Testament and that "suffering" in 1 Peter concerns persecution from outsiders and not human illness or the grief caused by death (*First Epistle of Peter*, 30–44). He seems right about suffering in 1 Peter, but his further discussion on sickness and healing in the New Testament should cause hesitation. While he acknowledges that healing is not always granted, he comes close to saying that physical healing in answer to prayer is the norm of Christian experience, which is contrary to New Testament teaching.

60. See the surveys of this topic given in Randy Hall, "For to This You Have Been Called: The Cross and Suffering in 1 Peter," *Restoration Quarterly* 19 (1976): 137–47; and Gordon E. Kirk, "Endurance in Suffering in 1 Peter," *Bibliotheca Sacra* 138 (1981): 46–56.

(vv. 21–25): He suffered innocently, not because of His own misdeeds; He did not retaliate or threaten in the face of insults and harsh treatment; He entrusted Himself to God the righteous Judge; and He died while remaining faithful to God's purpose. In all these ways Christ is the example for suffering and the Christian must "follow in His steps" (v. 21b NASB). Peter also included a subtle reminder of God's providence in the believer's godly suffering ("to this you were called," v. 21a) and of God's ultimate judgment of such mistreatment (trust in God "who judges justly," v. 23b).

Christ is the example also in 1 Peter 3:13–22, which speaks more generally about Christians suffering for what is right. In the midst of such a threat, Christians must not be fearful (v. 14b) but must maintain their reverence for Christ and be prepared to testify respectfully to anyone of their hope in Him (v. 15). Perhaps their persecutors will see their exemplary behavior and grow ashamed of any attempt to mistreat them (v. 16). Nevertheless, if in God's will a Christian should suffer for what is right and good, that person will experience His blessing (vv. 13–14, 17). The cardinal example of this is Christ, who suffered to accomplish God's redemptive purpose, but has now been made alive and exalted to the ultimate position of authority at God's right hand (vv. 18, 22; cf. 1:11, 20–21).

The same themes about Christian suffering are sounded in 1 Peter 4:12–19 and 5:8–10, but the reference to Christ's example of suffering and glory is more subtle (e.g., 4:13; 5:10). Suffering is seen as the expected lot of God's people in this world (4:12; 5:9), as part of His will and calling for them (4:19; 5:10), and as the pathway to blessing for those who endure faithfully (4:14; 5:10). Christians must be careful not to incur suffering as evildoers but as those committed to Christ (4:15–16), and in such difficulties they can be confident of God's care for them (4:19; 5:10). What is emphasized more in 4:12–19 than earlier is a call to rejoice in the midst of suffering (4:13, 16)[61] and a solemn warning about the imminent eschatological judgment God will inflict on the ungodly, including those who persecute His people (4:17–18).

The note of imminent judgment appears in another passage about the Christian's suffering (1 Peter 4:1–6). These verses mention first the purifying effect that suffering can have in the life of the Christian (vv. 1–2). Here again Christ's suffering is cited as an example: just as He suffered in the flesh, the Christian must adopt the same attitude of commitment to God's will no matter what the cost. The experience of suffering has a purging effect, resulting in a greater resolve to live for God and set aside the sins of the former life. But this change in lifestyle may subject the Christian to abuse from former associates in sin. However, they will have to give account to Christ who is "ready to judge the living and the dead" (v. 5),[62] and this may happen shortly, because "the end of all things is near" (v. 7). The positive side of this eschatological feature appears in a brief phrase in 1 Peter 1:6 and 5:10, in which suffering is said to be "now for a little while," after which God's eternal blessing and glory will rest on those who suffer faithfully.

---

61. This theme also appears in 1 Peter 1:6, the first passage on suffering in the epistle.

62. On Jesus as Judge, see Cullmann, *Christology of the New Testament*, 157–59.

SUBMISSION AND GOOD DEEDS IN SOCIAL RELATIONSHIPS

Conduct or behavior is one of the key words in Peter's instructions for Christian living. The Greek words *anastrophē* and *anastrephō* are used ten times in 1 and 2 Peter (and only twelve times elsewhere in the New Testament) to describe a way of life or pattern of conduct, usually the behavior a Christian should display. In most of the verses behavior in relationship to other people is in view.

Relationship to the godless world. Peter shared with much of the New Testament the conviction that Christians live as sojourners and pilgrims in a godless world (1 Peter 1:1, 17; 2:11).[63] Without Christ people live in spiritual ignorance (1:14), emptiness (1:18), aimless wandering (2:25), and moral debauchery (4:3–4). Christians have a new citizenship and identity as God's people (2:9–10) and are thus no longer in the moral and spiritual darkness of the unconverted world, but are in His wonderful light (2:9). They still live among the ungodly, but they must not settle down and mirror the lifestyles around them. Instead they are called to be holy in all their conduct, since God is holy (1:14–16). They must proclaim His virtues in a dark world (2:9), abstain from destructive lusts, and maintain good behavior that will bring their detractors to glorify God (2:11–12).[64] Peter's view of how the Christian should live in a hostile environment was remarkably positive and outward-looking. Far from counseling his readers to withdraw or blend in, he urged them to live consistently as God's people and exert an influence on others.[65]

The foundation for this approach was Peter's ecclesiology, as shown in 1 Peter 2:4–10. Christians, because of their faith in Jesus Christ as the chosen living Stone, are built together as living stones to constitute a spiritual house, a new temple in which God dwells (vv. 4–5a). They are a holy priesthood, a community in which God is worshiped through Jesus Christ (v. 5b). The three messianic "stone" citations from the Old Testament in verses 6–8 substantiate the description of Jesus as the living Stone in verse 4. He is the ultimate of the Davidic kings established by God in Zion, and faith in Him brings deliverance (v. 6b; Isa. 28:16). He was rejected by the world but exalted to be the cornerstone of God's work of salvation (v. 7; Ps. 118:22), and those who stumble over Him in disobedience to the gospel fall into judgment ordained by God (v. 8; Isa. 8:14). But the point of 1 Peter 2:6–8 is to demonstrate the honored status believers have because of their relationship with

---

63. Cf. John 17:14–18; 2 Corinthians 5:6–9; Philippians 3:20; Hebrews 11:13–16, 38; 13:14. The sociological approach to 1 Peter exemplified by John H. Elliott (*A Home for the Homeless: A Sociological Exegesis of 1 Peter, Its Situation and Strategy* [Philadelphia: Fortress, 1981]) has made too much of a supposed sense of social alienation and need for group identity on the part of the readers. Peter's concept of sojourning is more a theological conviction than a rhetorical strategy, more moral and spiritual than sociological, though these are not at odds. See the evaluation of Elliott's treatment by Moses Chin, "A Heavenly Home for the Homeless: Aliens and Strangers in 1 Peter," *Tyndale Bulletin* 42 (1991): 96–112.

64. Cf. Matthew 5:13–16.

65. See the discussion of this point in Leonhard Goppelt, *Der erste Petrusbrief,* Kritisch-exegetischer Kommentar über das Neue Testament, 8th ed., ed. Ferdinand Hahn (Göttingen: Vandenhoeck & Ruprecht, 1978), 155–63; and I. Howard Marshall, *1 Peter,* IVP New Testament Commentary (Downers Grove, Ill.: InterVarsity, 1991), 77–83.

Christ.[66] As the messianic community, their identity and destiny are completely different from the unbelieving world around them. They are the people of God in this age, "a chosen people, a royal priesthood, a holy nation, a people belonging to God" (v. 9). They were once not a people, but now they are "the people of God" (v. 10). These titles were used of Israel in the Old Testament in its relationship to Yahweh (Ex. 19:5–6; Isa. 43:20–21; Hos. 1:9; 2:25). Christians now fulfill the same pattern in their relationship to God through Christ, but it is important to note that Peter did not call the church the new or true Israel. The church does not replace Israel in God's program, though Christians now live as God's people in this world in the way Israel was intended to live and someday will live in fulfillment of God's promises.[67]

Relationship to the state, masters, and spouses. The need to maintain reputable conduct and exert influence as God's people within a hostile world (1 Peter 2:11–12) leads to the call for submission and doing good in three vital social relationships. The command "be subject to every human institution" (2:13)[68] is the general principle, with specific illustrations of such subjection developed in the following paragraphs running through 1 Peter 3:7. Submission should be given to governmental authorities (2:13–17), to masters (2:18–25), and to husbands (3:1–6). Within each of these relationships Peter also called for Christians to "do good" in their conduct toward others.

Peter's command for "submission" (*hypotassomai*) in each of these relationships (2:13, 18; 3:1) was a call for acceptance of the leadership of another under whose authority the Christian has been placed.[69] In New Testament usage this word clearly denotes subordination in a relationship of authority or ordered hierarchy. Sometimes the New Testament asserts that the order of authority has been established by God (Rom. 13:1; Eph. 1:22; Eph. 5:22–24 and 1 Tim. 2:11–14 with 1 Cor. 11:3, 7–12; Heb. 2:5, 8).[70] In the case of slavery, the New Testament calls for submission to the existing order, but nowhere defends it as God-ordained and instead implies its limited validity (Titus 2:9–10; cf. 1 Cor. 7:21–23; Eph. 6:5–9; Col. 3:22; 1 Tim. 6:1–2; Philem. 15–16). In either case, those under authority must

66. W. Edward Glenny, "The Israelite Imagery of 1 Peter 2," in *Dispensationalism, Israel and the Church: The Search for Definition,* ed. Craig A. Blaising and Darrell L. Bock (Grand Rapids: Zondervan, 1992), 163–68; and John Hall Elliott, *The Elect and the Holy: An Exegetical Examination of 1 Peter 2:4–10 and the Phrase βασίλειον ἱεράτευμα* (Leiden: Brill, 1966), 33–38.

67. Glenny, "Israelite Imagery of 1 Peter 2," 169–87.

68. The translation "every human creature" is preferred by Werner Foerster, *Theological Dictionary of the New Testament,* s.v. *"ktizō,"* 3:1034–35; F. Neugebauer, "Zur Deutung und Bedeutung des 1. Petrusbrief," *New Testament Studies* 26 (1979–80): 85–86; Davids, *First Epistle of Peter,* 98–99; and Michaels, *1 Peter,* 124. But this does not fit the phrase or the context as well as the sense given above. See Grudem, *First Epistle of Peter,* 118–19, for discussion.

69. Gerhard Delling, *Theological Dictionary of the New Testament,* s.v. *"hypotassō,"* 8:43–45.

70. In these cases, submission is "keeping a divinely willed order," or "acquiescence in a divinely willed order," as Delling argues (ibid., 43).

yield to or accept the leadership of the one to whom they are subject. Sometimes this is a forced submission (cf. 1 Cor. 15:27–28; Eph. 1:21; Phil. 3:21; Heb. 2:5, 8; 1 Peter 3:22). On the other hand, in this part of 1 Peter and similar contexts, it refers to the voluntary subordination of oneself to a rightful authority (1 Cor. 14:34; Eph. 5:21–6:9; Col. 3:18–4:1; 1 Tim. 2:11; Titus 2:5, 9; 3:1; Heb. 12:9; James 4:7; 1 Peter 5:5). The verb *hypotassomai* may sometimes be translated "obey,"[71] since this is how submission is displayed and obedience is often associated with it in New Testament usage (cf. Eph. 6:1; Col. 3:20, 22; 1 Peter 3:6). But submission and obedience are not synonyms since submission is the more general attitude and implies the structure of relationships in which obedience takes place.

By extension from the more common usage, "submission" is called for in one verse (Eph. 5:21) in the New Testament within the mutual relationship of believers and so outside of the framework of an order of authority: "Submit to one another out of reverence for Christ." Here submission takes the form of self-giving deference, concern for others more than for self, a "readiness to renounce one's own will for the sake of others, i.e., *agapē*, and to give precedence to others."[72] This is important to mention because some avoid the hierarchical idea by understanding submission throughout this section of 1 Peter to mean "general Christian deference" or considerate behavior toward others, allowing the sense of Ephesians 5:21 to control the meaning here.[73] But the orders of authority evident in 1 Peter 2:13–3:6, as well as the common meaning of *hypotassomai* in the New Testament, show that the hierarchical element cannot be dispensed with in this context.[74]

Another variation on this is the interpretation of Goppelt, who specifically denies the hierarchical sense and takes it as a command for involvement of Christians in society. Speaking of the term submission (*hypotassomai*), he writes,

> We hear the word automatically in terms of the prefix "sub" (under). In the New Testament, however, the accent did not fall on the prefix but on the root *taxis* (order) or *tassesthai* (to order itself or oneself). At its core the directive did not address itself in opposition to rebellion but to the flight of emigration. It wanted to say primarily: enlist yourselves in the given institution![75]

71. Bauer, Arndt, and Gingrich, *A Greek-English Lexicon of the New Testament*, 847–48. See Luke 2:51 and 2 Corinthians 9:13.

72. Delling, *Theological Dictionary of the New Testament*, s.v. "*hypotassō*," 8:45. This is like the humility called for in Romans 12:10; Ephesians 4:2–3; and Philippians 2:1–4. See James B. Hurley (*Man and Woman in Biblical Perspective* [Grand Rapids: Zondervan, 1981], 142–44) for a different view of submission in Ephesians 5:21. He argues that submission is "not yielding to the needs of another but rather yielding to the authority of another" (p. 142), so this verse is the general heading for the "yielding to authority" which is specified in the following verses: wives to husbands, children to parents, and slaves to masters.

73. Michaels, *1 Peter*, 123–24; and Davids, *First Epistle of Peter*, 98–99, 115, 121–22.

74. See Grudem, *First Epistle of Peter*, 118, 125, 135–37; and Hurley, *Man and Woman in Biblical Perspective*, 152–57.

75. Leonhard Goppelt, *Theology of the New Testament*, trans. John E. Alsup, ed. Jürgen Roloff, 2 vols. (Grand Rapids: Eerdmans, 1982), 2:168.

In his view the word denotes "attentive personal engagement" or "an enlisting of oneself."[76] While there is truth in the idea that Peter called for meaningful involvement in society, this is a distortion of the meaning of *hypotassomai.* The command to submit denotes more than that in 1 Peter 2:13–3:6.

So Peter urged his readers to accept the leadership of those rulers, masters, and husbands under whose authority they had been placed. However, he added a new dimension to the concept of submission. He showed that in Christ these relationships can be lived out in a new spirit because they are motivated and governed by Christian values, even if only on one side of the relationship. Throughout these paragraphs it is clear that the higher loyalty must be to the Lord rather than to any earthly authority (cf. Peter's words in Acts 4:19–20). The general command in 1 Peter 2:13 gives the motive for submission as "for the Lord's sake." This certainly means submission characterized by the kind of behavior and influence described in 2:11–12. But it also implies that conduct contrary to the Lord's teaching must be resisted, even if commanded by an earthly authority.[77] This truth is taught also in 2:19 which inserts "conscience toward God" into the discussion of suffering injustice from harsh masters. God's approval comes to those servants who resist immoral acts, even at the cost of personal suffering. Finally, the same truth comes out more positively in the counsel to wives in 3:1. Submission to a husband in the first century usually would mean adopting his religion, but the Christian wife's submission is expressed differently: by quietly winning her husband to Christ with respectful and pure behavior.

These ideas are reinforced by Peter's repeated instructions to do good in these relationships and in their general lifestyle. References to doing good, seeking what is good, having a good conscience, or maintaining good conduct occur fifteen times in 1 Peter (compounds of *agathos,* twelve times; and of *kalos* three times). Sometimes they denote doing what is right as opposed to sin or evil (2:14, 20; 3:11, 17, 21; 4:19). In other places the sense is doing what is beneficial or pleasing, what is helpful and fulfills the Christian's responsibility toward others (2:12, 15; 3:6, 13, 16; 4:10). This sort of behavior should bring commendation from the authorities (2:14). It is part of his instruction that they must not suffer for doing wrong or give any grounds for accusation by their opponents (2:12, 15; 3:16). If it is necessary to suffer, let it be for doing what is good and right rather than any sort of deserved punishment (2:20; 3:17). "Good conduct" is tied in ultimately with Peter's urging that Christians must live responsibly and morally and exert an influence for God in the unconverted world around them (2:11–12; 3:15–16).

Relationships within the Christian community. In two passages Peter gave instructions about how believers should relate to each other in the church. He emphasized the mutuality of their relationship by giving "one another" commands. Loving one another fervently and with forbearance must take highest priority (1 Peter 4:8). They must show hospitality to one another without complaint (v. 9). And

76. Ibid., 168 n. 7.
77. Davids, *First Epistle of Peter,* 18.

whatever spiritual gift each one has received should be used in God's strength to serve the others in the community (vv. 10–11).

Peter also urged the elders (the official leaders in the church[78]) to shepherd or care for their "flock" with eager willingness because God had entrusted people to their oversight (5:1–2a). They must do this without greediness or a domineering spirit, but as examples of Christian virtue (vv. 2b–3). Their reward will come when Jesus appears as the Chief Shepherd, under whose authority they serve (v. 4). The younger believers must be in submission to the leadership of these elders in the church (v. 5a). Finally, humility toward one another and faith in God's care for them must be their constant attitude (vv. 5a–7).

CHRISTIAN TRUTH: SCRIPTURE, ORTHODOXY, AND HERESY

Christian truth is a topic frequently discussed in 2 Peter and Jude, because these epistles were addressed to churches plagued by false teachers. A similar situation is found in the Pastoral Epistles. This topic appears in 1 Peter, but not as often since the occasion for writing was different.

CHRISTIAN ORTHODOXY

In response to the threat of false teachers, Peter and Jude emphasized the need to maintain and defend God's truth as revealed through the apostles. God's truth communicated to humankind is mentioned in various places in these epistles under different terms: "truth," "word" or "message," "faith," "commandment," and "Scripture." These terms are almost interchangeable in these letters to refer to what God has communicated.

In 1 Peter, apart from any concern about false teaching, Peter showed what was at stake in regard to God's Word. Christians must maintain their commitment to the truth revealed from God, because it alone is eternal and life-giving. The gospel, which was proclaimed to them and by which they were born again, is the living and abiding Word of God (1:23, 25). A person's response to God's message is all important. Obeying this truth brings purification from sin at conversion (v. 22), but disobeying God's Word means to reject Jesus Christ in unbelief (2:7–8; cf. 3:1). There is thus a basic division in humanity between those who come in faith to Jesus as God's chosen "Living Stone" and are built on Him as living stones to be God's people, and those who show that they are not God's people by stumbling over Him in unbelief (2:4–10).

Because the truth of God makes such a difference, Peter stressed the need to preserve God's truth more urgently when he wrote in 2 Peter to Christians struggling against false teaching. Peter understood that the readers always needed to be reminded about vital truths concerning their salvation, Christian growth, and future events (1:3–12). But he commended them that they already knew and were established in what he called "the truth you now have" (v. 12b). This last phrase is liter-

---

78. Compare Philippians 1:1 and 1 Timothy 3:1–7 with Acts 14:23; 20:17, 28; 1 Timothy 5:17–25; and Titus 1:5–9.

ally "the present truth," meaning the truth of God they received at their conversion and in subsequent Christian instruction. As the content of verses 3–11 suggests, this truth included basic concepts about the gospel as well as wider theological issues and covered ethical as well as theological instruction.[79]

Second Peter 1:12 refers to their stability ("firmly established") in holding to God's truth. This was important, because the false teachers were unstable in doctrine (3:16) and preyed on people who were unstable (2:14). Thus at the conclusion of the letter Peter again warned them to be on guard and not be carried away by such error and in turn lose their steadfastness in holding to God's truth (3:17). This is similar to Jude's exhortation to "build yourselves up in your most holy faith" (v. 20), and his urging to help others who were in danger of slipping: "Be merciful to those who doubt; snatch others from the fire and save them; to others show mercy, mixed with fear, hating even the clothing stained by corrupted flesh" (vv. 22–23). Jude added the comforting doxology in verses 24–25 about "the only God our Savior . . . through Jesus Christ our Lord," who is "able to keep you from falling and to present you before his glorious presence without fault and with great joy."

One of the reasons for Peter's letter was to make available a reminder of this teaching for them after his death (2 Peter 1:13–15). Like other apostles, Peter realized his own significant role as a witness to Jesus Christ and a revealer of God's truth to His people (1 Peter 5:1; 2 Peter 1:16; cf. Acts 1:21–23; 2:32; 3:15; 4:20, 33; 5:32; 10:39; 13:31; 1 Cor. 9:1–2; 1 John 1:1–5). Jesus Himself had warned that false teaching would arise and so He put them on guard against it (Matt. 7:15; 24:11, 24; Mark 13:22; Luke 21:8). Paul issued a similar warning to the Ephesian elders (Acts 20:28–31). Because of the apostles' vital role, the early church devoted itself to their teaching (Acts 2:42). The apostles received some teaching by direct revelation from God (Gal. 1:11–12, 16; Eph. 3:2–12; 2 Peter 1:18); some came from consultation with others who heard the Lord (1 Cor. 11:34; 15:3); other instruction came through a process of Spirit-guided reflection on what was already revealed in the Old Testament and in the teaching and work of Christ (John 14:17, 26; 16:12–15; 1 Cor. 2:13; 7:12, 25). But however received, apostolic teaching was authoritative because its ultimate source was God (1 Cor. 7:40; 11:34; 14:37; 1 Thess. 4:1–2, 8; 2 Peter 3:2). The apostles were not creators of truth, but channels through whom God communicated His truth to the churches. This is expressed clearly in 2 Peter 3:2: "remember . . . the commandment of the Lord and Savior through your apostles." Also appearing in 2 Peter 3:1–2 is the need for reminders of apostolic teaching after the apostles themselves have died (cf. 1:12–15; Jude 17). The apostles' teaching then served as the standard by which the churches sought to live.

The picture of "handing over," "entrusting," and "receiving"[80] apostolic

---

79. Thus, Christianity could also be described as the way of truth (2 Peter 2:2), the straight way (v. 15), and the way of righteousness (v. 21), from which the false teachers deviate.

80. The primary Greek words are *paradidōmi, paradosis,* and *paralambanō.* These refer to the passing on and receiving of religious tradition or authoritative instruction. The words *paratithēmi* and *parathēkē* express a similar idea, denoting a deposit or entrustment of truth. See Bauer, Arndt, and Gingrich, *A Greek-English Lexicon of the New Testament,* 614–16, 619, 623.

tradition is common in the New Testament, in early and late books (Acts 16:4; 1 Thess. 4:1–2; 2 Thess. 2:15; 3:6; 1 Cor. 11:2, 23; 15:1–3; also 1 Tim. 6:20; 2 Tim. 1:13–14; 2:2). God was the ultimate source of apostolic teaching, and so Christians were expected to hold firmly and specifically to it (Acts 20:26–32; Rom. 6:17; 16:17; Gal. 1:6–12; 2 Tim. 1:13–14; 2 John 9–11). The concept of handing on authoritative Christian truth appears twice in these epistles (2 Peter 2:21; Jude 3). Both are significant expressions of the need to hold to the norm of apostolic teaching. In 2 Peter 2:21 the apostle described apostates as people who knew the way of righteousness but turned back "from the holy commandment delivered [*paradidōmi*] to them." Here Christian truth is viewed from the standpoint of God's demand for faith and obedience and is called "the holy commandment" (3:2 uses commandment in a similar way).

Similarly Jude urged his readers to "contend for the faith that was once for all entrusted [*paradidōmi*] to the saints" (v. 3). "Faith" in this expression has an objective sense: "what is believed," "the body of faith or belief" which is passed on in apostolic teaching.[81] Bauckham, however, suggests that "belief" has a narrower scope, referring to the gospel or "the central Christian message of salvation through Jesus Christ," rather than a broader body of orthodox or normative Christian belief.[82] But in the New Testament "the message of salvation through Jesus Christ" can hardly be held to a limited scope. And in light of other uses of *paradidōmi* in such contexts, it is hardly correct to limit "faith" to the gospel narrowly conceived; what was passed on by the apostles was the wide range of Christian doctrine and ethics. Also other New Testament uses of "faith" in the objective sense are better taken with a broad meaning (Acts 6:7; Gal. 1:23; Phil. 1:27; 1 Tim. 1:19; 3:9; 4:1, 6; 5:8; 6:10, 11, 21; 2 Tim. 4:7; Titus 1:13). In the absence of limiting qualifiers in this context, "the faith" must be understood as the Christian faith, the body of truth Christians believe, the teaching passed on by the apostles as normative for Christian belief. The word has the same sense in Jude 20.

This faith was delivered to the saints "once for all" (Jude 3) in the sense that it focused on the historical particularity of the incarnation, teaching, death, and resurrection of Jesus Christ and the truth God revealed about Him through the apostles (cf. Rom. 6:10; Heb. 9:26–28; 1 Peter 3:18). No other foundation could be laid except Him (1 Cor. 3:11), and continued revelation was not expected after the passing of the apostles (cf. 2 Tim. 2:2; 3:14; true apostolic succession is following what the apostles taught and passing it on to others). What Jude called for was the active propagation and defense of this faith (similar to Phil. 1:27). The verb "contend" in

---

81. Bauer, Arndt, and Gingrich, *A Greek-English Lexicon of the New Testament,* 664; Rudolf Bultmann, *Theological Dictionary of the New Testament,* s.v. *"pisteuō,"* 6:213–14; and Green, *Second Epistle General of Peter,* 47. Stevens suggests that *faith* carries the subjective sense here: "the steadfast confidence of the Christian considered as a gift of God" (*Theology of the New Testament,* 312). But *paradidōmi* would not be used of giving in that sense.

82. Bauckham, *Jude, 2 Peter,* 32–33. He offers this interpretation in answer to those who see early Catholic teaching in Jude. But see the following discussion of early Catholicism for a different approach to this issue.

Jude 3 denotes a struggle in which every effort is expended both for Christian truth and against those who oppose it. As the context of Jude shows, this includes the doctrinal content of Christianity as well as its moral demands.[83]

It is clear that 2 Peter and Jude speak about the importance of God's truth given through the apostles and the need to hold to it as a norm for Christian faith and practice.[84] But this has been attacked by many who are unsympathetic to that approach to Christian truth. These epistles are castigated as a later, regrettable development within Christianity which lost the theological freedom and creativity found in the earlier days of the church. In this view these letters are a significant step along the way toward the dead orthodoxy and traditionalism of the later Roman Catholic Church. The common description of this tendency is "early Catholicism," and these epistles along with the Pastoral Epistles and Acts are cited as prime examples.[85]

While references to early Catholicism can often be found in New Testament studies, this view of early Christian development has come under widespread criticism more recently, especially its forced dichotomies between supposed earlier and later books of the New Testament.[86] The validity of this approach can only be maintained by distorting and overemphasizing certain ideas in the supposed later books and ignoring or minimizing the same features in earlier books. For example, as discussed above, the importance of God's truth revealed through the apostles and the idea of a body of apostolic teaching passed on to the churches and considered to be normative for faith and practice is found not only in the Pastorals, 2 Peter, and Jude, but also in Galatians, 1 and 2 Thessalonians, and 1 Corinthians.[87] Ultimately it goes back to what Jesus charged His followers to do in Matthew 28:18–20 (teach people to observe all He commanded). This is given more attention in 2 Peter and Jude only because the truth was under threat from false teaching and the apostles would soon be gone from the church. But as in all "occasional" literature like the

---

83. Bauckham, *Jude, 2 Peter,* 32–34.

84. Ladd, *Theology of the New Testament,* 604.

85. See Ernst Käsemann, "An Apologia for Primitive Christian Eschatology," in *Essays on New Testament Themes,* Studies in Biblical Theology, trans. W. J. Montague (London: SCM, 1964), 169–95, and "Paul and Early Catholicism," in *New Testament Questions of Today,* trans. W. J. Montague (Philadelphia: Fortress, 1969), 236–51, for classic expressions of this concept. James D. G. Dunn presents a good summary of this supposed tendency and discusses 2 Peter and Jude as examples of it (*Unity and Diversity in the New Testament: An Inquiry into the Character of Earliest Christianity* [Philadelphia: Westminster, 1977], 341–66).

86. See Martin Hengel, *Acts and the History of Earliest Christianity* (London: SCM, 1979), 121–22; and I. Howard Marshall, " 'Early Catholicism' in the New Testament," in *New Dimensions in New Testament Study,* ed. Richard N. Longenecker and Merrill C. Tenney (Grand Rapids: Zondervan, 1974), 217–31.

87. Blum, "2 Peter," in *The Expositor's Bible Commentary,* 272; Green, *Second Epistle General of Peter,* 47, 159; E. Earle Ellis, "Prophecy and Hermeneutic in Jude," in *Prophecy and Hermeneutic in Early Christianity: New Testament Essays* (Grand Rapids: Eerdmans, 1978), 233. For a comparison of ideas in 2 Peter and Galatians, see William R. Farmer, "Some Critical Reflections on Second Peter: A Response to a Paper on Second Peter by Denis Farkasfalvy," *Second Century* 5 (1985–86): 32–34.

New Testament epistles, topics are discussed in proportion to their need; many accepted and foundational ideas are not made explicit unless they are threatened. Finally, critics have observed that the whole theory of early Catholicism is based on judgments about what is valid for Christianity that are rooted not on the New Testament itself but on the preferences of liberal Protestantism.[88] Such an approach distorts rather than gives a valid interpretation of books like 2 Peter and Jude.[89]

THE AUTHORITY OF SCRIPTURE

God's word, the truth, and the apostolic faith are closely linked in 2 Peter with "the Scriptures." This is especially true of 2 Peter 1:19–21, the primary passage about Scripture in these epistles. Here in a space of ten verses there are references to the truth Christians possess, apostolic reminders for the church (vv. 12–15); apostolic witness to Christ, God's voice from heaven (vv. 16–18); the prophetic word, prophecies of Scripture, and prophets speaking from God by the Holy Spirit (vv. 19–21). These are intertwined in the argument of the verses, because Peter was supporting the validity of apostolic teaching about the second coming of Christ (v. 16) by citing his eyewitness account of the Transfiguration[90] and the confirmation of Old Testament Scripture (vv. 17–21). The false teachers had rejected Christian teaching about the Second Coming as simply human invention ("concocted fables," v. 16), and Peter needed to reassert its divine source.[91] After citing the personal experience of the apostles as eyewitnesses of Christ's majesty at the Transfiguration (v. 16) and as hearers of the heavenly voice attesting His messianic status (vv. 17–18), Peter added the testimony of Scripture in verses 19–21.

The sense of verse 19a and the connection it expresses between the Transfiguration account and the Old Testament is much debated. The common interpretation has come to be "we have the prophetic word made more certain" (cf. RSV, NIV, NASB). The intent of this is that the Transfiguration experience confirmed and reinforced the validity of the prophetic message about the Second Coming.[92] While this interpretation has much to commend it, the high view of Scripture given in verses 20–21 indicates that Peter was not looking for confirmation of Scripture or

88. Denis Farkasfalvy, "The Ecclesial Setting of Pseudepigraphy in Second Peter and Its Role in the Formation of the Canon," *Second Century* 5 (1985–86): 25–29; and Tord Fornberg, *An Early Church in a Pluralistic Society: A Study of 2 Peter*, Coniectanea Biblica, NT Series (Lund: Gleerup, 1977), 3–6.

89. Jerome H. Neyrey, "The Form and Background of the Polemic in 2 Peter," *Journal of Biblical Literature* 99 (1980): 407, 430–31; and Roman Heiligenthal, *Zwischen Henoch und Paulus: Studien zum theologiegeschichtlichen Ort des Judasbriefes* (Tübingen: Francke, 1992), 64–70.

90. The Transfiguration has bearing on Christ's second coming in power because it prefigured His coming glory. See W. L. Liefeld, "Transfiguration," in *Dictionary of Jesus and the Gospels*, ed. Joel B. Green and Scot McKnight (Downers Grove, Ill.: InterVarsity, 1992), 834–41.

91. Bauckham, *Jude, 2 Peter*, 205, 213–15, 221–22; Jerome H. Neyrey, "The Apologetic Use of the Transfiguration in 2 Peter 1:15–21," *Catholic Biblical Quarterly* 42 (1980): 506–9.

92. For evaluation of various options, see Bauckham, *Jude, 2 Peter*, 223–27; Green, *Second Epistle General of Peter*, 86–87; and Neyrey, "Apologetic Use of the Transfiguration," 514–16.

comparing its certainty to that of the Transfiguration. Instead he made a strong statement about the authority of Scripture: "we possess the prophetic word as something altogether reliable."[93] The reference to "the prophetic word" in this verse certainly includes Old Testament prophecy about Christ's glorious coming in the future. But in the first century the whole Old Testament was regarded as the product of the Holy Spirit and thus as "prophecy." This was especially true in Christianity, since Jesus Christ was understood to be predicted throughout the Old Testament (Luke 24:27; John 5:46). So "the prophetic word" included all of Hebrew Scripture.[94]

Because the Scripture's validity was so sure, the readers must pay attention to it in their struggles against the false teachers (2 Peter 1:19b). In a further description, which fit their situation perfectly, Peter portrayed the Scriptures as "a light shining in a dark place" (cf. Ps. 119:105). In a world spiritually ignorant and resistant to the truth, the Scriptures must be heeded. They are the Christian's guide until their light is eclipsed by God's full revelation at the coming of Christ (2 Peter 1:19c).[95]

Peter anchored his statement about Scripture's reliability (v. 19) by giving one of the classic Christian statements about the inspiration of Scripture (vv. 20–21).[96] In context these verses were meant to emphasize that Scripture is not a mere human product but comes from God. Thus the false teachers who rejected apostolic teaching about Christ's coming will face God's judgment rather than apostolic censure alone.

The emphasis on God as the source of Scripture is clear in verse 21 ("not from men . . . but from God"). But it should be seen also in the statement of verse 20, "no prophecy of Scripture came about by the prophet's own interpretation." The last part of this statement has been translated and interpreted in various ways. The RSV and NASB have "no prophecy of scripture is a matter of one's own interpretation" (KJV's "private interpretation" is similar), and the NEB says, "no one can interpret any prophecy of Scripture by himself." In this way the phrase is taken to mean that no one should interpret Scripture independently of the wider church and

93. This is the translation of Bauer, Arndt, and Gingrich, *A Greek-English Lexicon of the New Testament*, 138. See also Neyrey, "The Apologetic Use of the Transfiguration," 515–16. This takes the comparative in an elative sense ("very reliable"), a grammatical use found often in Hellenistic Greek, as shown in Blass-Debrunner-Funk, *A Greek Grammar of the New Testament*, §§ 60–61, 244.

94. Bauer, Arndt, and Gingrich, *A Greek-English Lexicon of the New Testament*, 724; Erik Sjöberg and Eduard Schweizer, *Theological Dictionary of the New Testament*, s.v. "*pneuma*," 6:381–86, 398, 407–9, 454, and Gerhard Friedrich, "*prophētēs*," 6:856–57; Kelly, *Epistles of Peter and Jude*, 321; and Bauckham, *Jude, 2 Peter*, 224. See also Acts 2:30; 3:18–26; 13:16–41; and Hebrews 1:1.

95. Green, *Second Epistle General of Peter*, 87–89.

96. These verses emphasize that Scripture is God's Word by describing the *mode* of inspiration: "men spoke from God" under the guidance of the Spirit. Second Timothy 3:16–17 is complementary but refers to the *result* of inspiration: Scripture is "God-breathed" and useful for Christian living.

its authority or guidance. This is often the view of those who are inclined to see in 2 Peter "early Catholicism" or the regulated magisterium of the later Catholic Church.[97] A variation of this is the idea that proper interpretation of prophecy must be widely accepted or part of apostolic tradition, not idiosyncratic or based only on someone's private judgment.[98] This fits the context of 2 Peter quite well, since the false teachers were apparently guilty of distorting Scripture to use it to their advantage (3:16).

But several important considerations show that 2 Peter 1:20 is not concerned with the later *explanation* of prophecy but with its *origination*. The verb of verse 20b (*ginetai*) fits this sense much better: it usually means "comes to be, comes about," rather than "is." The word translated "one's own" or "private" (*idios*) occurs frequently in ancient Greek usage in passages discussing the origination of a message. In these passages the consistent use of "one's own" is to contrast a mere human message (i.e., someone speaks "on his own") with one coming from God.[99] So the meaning is not "private" versus "widely accepted," but "a human's" message versus "God's." Finally, the key word "interpretation" (*epilyseōs*) is the strongest evidence for the idea of a later explanation of what the prophet has written. Yet when this word is studied in specific contexts describing prophecy (as in 2 Peter 1:20), a different sense emerges. In contexts describing prophetic activity, this term is often used of the second step in God's revelation to the prophet. The first step is a vision, dream, or sign God gives to the prophet. This is vital, but its significance must be understood before God's message is grasped. The second step then is for God to reveal the *interpretation* of the vision or sign.[100] The prophet must have God's explanation of the sign before he can truly proclaim God's message. In this way the entire prophecy originates from God, both the prophetic vision and its interpretation to the prophet himself. By extension, the God-given interpretation can be used as a short-hand expression for the entire prophecy or for a prophecy which has no distinct sign or vision. Thus to state that "no prophecy of Scripture arises from one's own interpretation," is to insist that the prophetic Scripture originated not from a merely human source but from God.[101]

97. Käsemann, "Apologia for Primitive Christian Eschatology," 189–91; Kelly, *Epistles of Peter and Jude*, 324 (not as strong as Käsemann); Dunn, *Unity and Diversity in the New Testament*, 358 (also tentative); and Henning Paulsen, *Der zweite Petrusbrief und das Judasbrief*, Kritischexegetischer Kommentar über das Neue Testament (Göttingen: Vandenhoeck & Ruprecht, 1992), 123–24.

98. Bauer, Arndt, and Gingrich, *A Greek-English Lexicon of the New Testament*, 369; F. Büchsel, *Theological Dictionary of the New Testament*, s.v. "luō," 4:337, and Gerhard Friedrich, "*prophētēs*," 6:833; and Blum, "2 Peter," in *The Expositor's Bible Commentary*, 275. The idea that no prophecy can be understood on its own in isolation from other prophecies is a very unlikely interpretation in this context.

99. For example, Jeremiah 23:16 and Ezekiel 13:3. See other references listed in Bauckham, *Jude, 2 Peter*, 229–30.

100. See Genesis 40:8; 41:8, 12; Amos 7–8; Jeremiah 1; Zechariah 1–6; Daniel 7–8.

101. This view is presented in a fine treatment by Bauckham, *Jude, 2 Peter*, 228–35. It is also found in Stevens, *Theology of the New Testament*, 320–21; Green, *Second Epistle General of Peter*, 89–92; and D. Edmond Hiebert, "The Prophetic Foundation for the Christian Life: An Exposition of 2 Peter 1:19–21," *Bibliotheca Sacra* 141 (1984): 164–65.

Verse 21 then reiterates the same point because it was so important to Peter's argument against the false teachers, "For prophecy never had its origin in the will of man, but men spoke from God as they were carried along by the Holy Spirit." The reference to "prophecy" (v. 21) and to a "prophecy of Scripture" (v. 20) is again a way of describing the entire Old Testament, as argued above in connection with "the prophetic word" in verse 19. The reason Jews and Christians spoke of the Old Testament as "prophetic" in a broader sense was their belief in the inspiration of the entire Scripture (v. 21b). Peter had written earlier about the Spirit's ministry in the Old Testament prophets as they predicted the sufferings and glory of Christ (1 Peter 1:10–12). But in 2 Peter 1:21 he described the Spirit's inspiration of the Scriptures more specifically.

The basic proposition of verse 21 is "men spoke from God." The Old Testament authors did not produce their "prophetic" writings by means of human will or insight alone. Instead, the source for what they communicated was God. The means by which this was accomplished is expressed by the participle "being moved" or "carried along" (*pheromenoi*) by the Holy Spirit. The figurative meaning of the verb in 2 Peter 1:21 is illustrated by literal uses in Acts 27:15, 17 of a ship being driven along by wind and storm.[102] As they communicated their message, these men were impelled or influenced by the Holy Spirit in such a way that what they said was "from God" rather than "by human will." As a result, the Old Testament is "altogether reliable" (2 Peter 1:19), Peter's main point throughout this passage.

This verse then teaches in a succinct but powerful way the doctrine of "concursive inspiration."[103] This is the teaching that the Scriptures are the product of a divine and human authorship, and both play their appropriate roles. It was human beings who communicated as they wrote Scripture, and they reflect their own style of writing, religious background, and historical and cultural situation. But the Spirit guided their writing so that what they produced was not their own exposition—not by their will or insight alone—but was from God. The verse is clear that men spoke, but did so under the influence of the Holy Spirit. This influence is not conceived of in a Greek fashion, in which the author is merely the ecstatic organ of God's dictation, completely overpowered by the Spirit's impulse.[104] This was Philo's view and became the rabbinic idea of inspiration, but as Schrenk argues from New Testament evidence, "There is a greater sense of the persons of the authors in early Christianity than in Judaism, and therefore a greater regard for the natural and historical mediation of the divine utterance. Yet this does not in any way weaken

---

102. Bauer, Arndt, and Gingrich, *A Greek-English Lexicon of the New Testament*, 855.

103. See D. A. Carson, "Recent Developments in the Doctrine of Scripture," in *Hermeneutics, Authority, and Canon*, ed. D. A. Carson and John D. Woodbridge (Grand Rapids: Zondervan, 1986), 5–48. His definition of concursive inspiration is: "God in His sovereignty so superintended the freely composed human writings we call the Scriptures that the result was nothing less than God's words and, therefore, entirely truthful" (p. 45; cf. p. 29).

104. This is the view of Colin Brown (*The New International Dictionary of New Testament Theology*, s.v. "*pneuma*," 3:705). On Greek inspiration, see Hermann Kleinknecht, *Theological Dictionary of the New Testament*, s.v. "*pneuma*," 6:343–52.

the basic conviction that it is God who speaks in Scripture."[105] The New Testament consistently views the Old Testament as a divine-human product (e.g., Matt. 1:22; 2:15; 22:43; Mark 12:26, 36; Acts 1:16; 3:18; 4:25; 28:25).

So Peter's teaching about inspiration was the conviction that the Spirit guided the writers of Scripture in such a way that what they wrote was truly God's Word. What the Scriptures say, God says. This was the common view of Scripture held by Jesus and by the early church.[106] Sometimes the force of verses like 2 Timothy 3:16 and 2 Peter 1:21 are evaded by alleging that this view of inspiration was not representative and was taught only in the "marginal" books of the New Testament.[107] It is true that the clearest explicit formulations of the doctrine of inspiration are given in 2 Timothy 3:16 and 2 Peter 1:21, but the same conviction is presupposed in other verses. As Schrenk says on this very point, "all emphasis upon the fact that God speaks in Scripture . . . or that the *kyrios* speaks by the prophets . . . testifies at root to exactly the same point as is at issue in the doctrine of inspiration."[108]

Because the Scripture is God's Word, Peter and Jude could cite it directly or allude to it in their instruction and count on its authority. Peter cited Scripture explicitly in 1 Peter nine times and alluded to it another twenty times, a remarkably large number for an epistle of its length.[109] Second Peter and Jude also draw on Old Testament accounts in the sections arguing the certainty of judgment (2 Peter 2:4–10, 15–16; Jude 5–7, 11–13) and elsewhere (2 Peter 3:4–13; Jude 9, 22–23). Jude alluded to an account in one apocryphal book (Assumption of Moses in v. 9) and quoted from another one by name (1 Enoch 1:9 in vv. 14–15). The fact that he quoted from a noncanonical book is not problematic in itself. Several times Paul quoted from Greek secular writers, because their specific words were appropriate to his point, without in any way validating the inspiration or authority of their entire work (Acts 17:28; 1 Cor. 15:33; Titus 1:12). But Jude seemed to accept the historicity of the account that "Enoch the seventh from Adam" was the one who spoke in the book of 1 Enoch and that it was an inspired prophecy. Jewish traditions about Enoch were rich and varied in the first century, and many involved his insight into heavenly matters and God's plan for the world's future, since Genesis 5:24 records,

105. Gottlob Schrenk, *Theological Dictionary of the New Testament,* s.v. *"graphē,"* 1:757–58. He cites the following verses from Matthew in which specific attention is paid to the human authors: 2:5, 17, 23; 3:3; 4:14; 8:4, 17; 12:17; 13:14, 35; 22:24; 24:15; 27:9.

106. John W. Wenham, *Christ and the Bible,* 2d ed. (Grand Rapids: Baker, 1984), 11–37, 84–108. This was also the view of Judaism in the first century. "According to the later Jewish view, Scripture has sacred, authoritative, and normative significance. It is of permanent and unassailable validity. . . . The implication of the doctrine of inspiration is that the revealed truth of God characterises [*sic*] every word" (Schrenk, *Theological Dictionary of the New Testament,* s.v. *"graphē,"* 1:755).

107. James Barr, *Beyond Fundamentalism* (Philadelphia: Westminster, 1984), 4–5.

108. Schrenk, *Theological Dictionary of the New Testament,* s.v. *"graphē,"* 1:757. He cites these verses in support: Matthew 1:22; 2:15; 15:4; 19:5; 22:31, 43; Mark 12:26, 36; Acts 1:16; 3:18; 4:25; 28:25; 1 Corinthians 14:21; 2 Corinthians 6:17; Romans 12:19; Ephesians 6:17; Hebrews 3:7; 9:8; 10:15.

109. See the list of references in Davids, *First Epistle of Peter,* 24–25.

"Enoch walked with God; then he was no more, because God took him away." Jude accepted the legitimacy of this tradition, without ascribing canonicity or divine authority to 1 Enoch as a whole.[110]

In one other significant passage about Scripture, Peter referred to Paul's letters in support of his eschatological argument (2 Peter 3:15–16). What is unusual in these verses is that Peter placed Paul's letters in the category of "Scripture," on a par with the Old Testament as authoritative writings.[111] Peter noted that the false teachers had misused Paul's letters just as they had the Old Testament (and perhaps other writings now contained in the New Testament): "His letters contain some things that are hard to understand, which ignorant and unstable people distort, as they do the other Scriptures, to their own destruction" (v. 16b). In the same passage Peter alluded to the divine source of Paul's teaching by referring to "the wisdom given to him" (v. 15b). This is almost certainly the so-called "divine passive," meaning wisdom given by God.[112] Also, Peter's citing of Paul in his argument indicates the authoritative status Paul's letters held for Peter and his readers, and apparently also for the false teachers.

Viewing Paul's letters as Scripture and as divinely authoritative is simply the logical extension of Peter's (and the early church's) thinking traced above. If the apostles played a significant role in communicating God's truth to the church, and if the Spirit's guidance set the Old Testament writings apart as God's prophetic Word, then Paul's letters would have been valued from the very start as authoritative. Paul himself had an awareness of the unique authority of his words (1 Cor. 2:13; 7:25, 40; 14:37; Gal. 1:11–12, 16; Eph. 3:2–12; 1 Thess. 4:1–2, 8) and desired his letters to be used for the church's instruction (Col. 4:16; 1 Thess. 5:27). It was only natural for the early congregations to value Paul's letters as authoritative from the very start and to begin to distribute and collect copies of his letters for the whole church to possess. These verses from 2 Peter attest to the existence of a collection of Pauline letters very soon after they were written ("in all his letters," 3:16a) and of the high regard in which they were held. The process that led to the acceptance of an authoritative canon of New Testament Scripture was begun very early.[113]

---

110. For other suggestions about this issue, see George Lawrence Lawlor, *Translation and Exposition of the Epistle of Jude* (Nutley, N.J.: Presb. & Ref., 1972), 101–2 (Jude cited an Enoch tradition without knowing the book of 1 Enoch); Ellis, "Prophecy and Hermeneutic in Jude," 224–25 (Jude's citation is an extension of the principle that valid interpretations or expansions of Scripture are equal to Scripture in authority, though not canonical); and Walter M. Dunnett, "The Hermeneutics of Jude and 2 Peter: The Use of Ancient Jewish Traditions," *Journal of the Evangelical Theological Society* 31 (1988): 289 (Jude accepted 1 Enoch 1:9 as "inspired, apparently historical, and true").

111. A similar thing is done in 1 Timothy 5:18, which quotes Deuteronomy 25:4 and Luke 10:7 after the introductory formula "the Scripture says."

112. Bauckham, *Jude, 2 Peter,* 329.

113. Green, *Second Epistle General of Peter,* 28–30, 148; and David G. Dunbar, "The Biblical Canon," in *Hermeneutics, Authority, and Canon,* 318–23.

RESPONSE TO HERESY

Much is said in 2 Peter and Jude about heresy. The primary factor guiding the authors' reaction to the false teachers in these epistles was their rejection of orthodox truth, as described above. They must be resisted because they depart from God's truth communicated through the apostles and in the Scriptures. Those who deny apostolic teaching and distort the Scriptures thereby oppose God and bring destruction on themselves and any who follow their error. Their judgment for this is sure, though it has not come yet. Christians must resist these false teachers and maintain Christian truth because so much is at stake (2 Peter 1:12–15; 2:1–3, 21; 3:16–18; Jude 3–4).[114]

The specific nature of the false teaching opposed in 2 Peter and Jude is not so important for this discussion,[115] but the general characteristic of heresy as departure from apostolic truth should be noted. The false teachers departed from Christian truth in both theology and ethics, both belief and behavior. They regarded apostolic teaching, especially concerning the second coming of Christ, to be cleverly concocted myths rather than divine truth (2 Peter 1:16). They rejected the Lord Jesus (2:2; Jude 4), probably in the sense of refusing to acknowledge His divine majesty (2 Peter 1:16) and the need for His redemption ("denying the Lord who bought them," 2:2). They also apparently refused to recognize Jesus Christ as the future Judge, spoke harshly against Him in that role (Jude 14–15), and resisted any idea of divine judgment (2 Peter 2:3–10; Jude 5–7, 13).[116] In addition to mocking the doctrine of future judgment, they scoffed at the idea of Christ's coming again to interrupt the continuity of earthly life (2 Peter 3:3–4). In general, they taught falsehood and error (2:1, 3; 3:17) and gained a hearing in the community under false pretenses (2:1; Jude 4). They promised great things to their followers but miserably failed to provide any benefit (2:19; Jude 12).

They also lived in error (2 Peter 2:15; Jude 11) and caused the Christian lifestyle to be reviled (2 Peter 2:2). Their behavior was marked by outrageous licentiousness, and they enticed others to live in crass sensuality also (2:2, 10, 13–14,

---

114. Thus, the motivation for urging resistance to the heretics is not a self-serving attempt to maintain power on the part of autocratic leaders in the churches, as Michel Desjardin alleges ("The Portrayal of the Dissidents in 2 Peter and Jude: Does It Tell Us More about the 'Godly' than the 'Ungodly'?" *Journal for the Study of the New Testament* 30 [1987]: 89–102). This is a gross distortion of 2 Peter and Jude as well as the New Testament's view of truth in general.

115. For discussion of the details, see Bauckham, *Jude, 2 Peter*, 11–13, 154–57; D. J. Rowston, "The Most Neglected Book in the New Testament," *New Testament Studies* 21 (1974–75): 555–57; and Neyrey, "The Apologetic Use of the Transfiguration," 504–19. Both epistles are probably more general in order to address the situation in more than one church. But it is clear from the epistles that specific false teachers are in view and not just a stereotyped polemic against heresy, as Frederik Wisse argues ("The Epistle of Jude in the History of Heresiology," in *Essays on the Nag Hammadi Texts in Honour of Alexander Bölig*, ed. Martin Krause [Leiden: Brill, 1972], 133–43).

116. Cf. Neyrey, "Form and Background of the Polemic in 2 Peter," 407–31; and Carroll D. Osburn, "The Christological Use of 1 Enoch 1:9 in Jude 14–15," *New Testament Studies* 23 (1976–77): 334–41.

18; 3:3; Jude 4, 7, 16, 18). They were ungodly and lawless people (2 Peter 2:6; 3:7, 17; Jude 4, 15), living on the purely natural plane, and lacking the Holy Spirit (Jude 19). Their influence on others was motivated by greed and self-interest (2 Peter 2:3, 14; Jude 12, 16). In addition to rejecting Christ's lordship, they resisted all authority, were boastful, and provoked divisiveness (2 Peter 2:10; Jude 8, 11, 16, 19). Here, as is often true, doctrinal error was accompanied by moral turpitude and these fed on each other (Rom. 16:17–18; 1 Tim. 1:6, 19; 4:1–2; 6:3–5; 2 Tim. 3:1–9).

Some have expressed disbelief that such godless heretics would actually have been tolerated in a Christian church.[117] But as these epistles state, the false teachers did not enter the churches with the announced intent of subverting apostolic doctrine and behavior. They slipped in secretly (Jude 4; cf. Gal. 2:4) as itinerant preachers, a common part of first-century religious life (cf. Acts 13:15; 2 John 7–11; Didache 11.1–12; 13.1–7). Or they arose within the community itself and later quietly brought in heretical teachings from outside (2 Peter 2:1; cf. Acts 20:29–30; Rom. 16:17–18). In either case, the false teachers became accepted and began to have an influence, though they were false brethren all along (cf. Gal. 2:4), under God's condemnation (2 Peter 2:1–3; Jude 4). By the time their true reprobate status became obvious, they had already established a foothold in the community, especially among the unstable and uncommitted (2 Peter 2:14, 18). The false teachers and any who follow them will suffer a worse condemnation because, having been exposed to the truth, they rejected Christianity in favor of false teaching (2:17–22).[118]

The appearance of false teachers in those churches is the fulfillment of a pattern: just as false prophets arose among God's people in the Old Testament, so Christians can expect evil forces to oppose God's truth and trouble His people in their time. In this way Peter could speak of false teachers coming in the future (2:1–3; 3:3) and already present among his readers (2:10–22). Since their appearance fulfills a pattern seen in the Old Testament, the pattern of sure judgment visited against those who opposed God in earlier days also guarantees the certainty of judgment on these false teachers (2 Peter 2:1–22; Jude 3–16).[119]

ESCHATOLOGY AND JUDGMENT

The eschatology of these epistles focuses on the certainty of judgment, because of the response given to the false teachers in 2 Peter and Jude. But several other eschatological themes appear and have a significant place in the theology of Peter and Jude.

---

117. Wisse, "Epistle of Jude in the History of Heresiology," 136–37. Actual ministry experience or just reading a daily newspaper should have convinced Wisse that this is all too believable.

118. Blum, "2 Peter," in *The Expositor's Bible Commentary,* 282–83. For a different view (that vv. 20–22 describe not apostates but new Christians who fall back into sinful ways), see Duane A. Dunham, "An Exegetical Study of 2 Peter 2:18–22," *Bibliotheca Sacra* 140 (1983): 40–54.

119. J. Daryl Charles, " 'Those' and 'These': The Use of the Old Testament in the Epistle of Jude," *Journal for the Study of the New Testament* 38 (1990): 109–24.

The present as a time of eschatological fulfillment is an important theme in these epistles as in much of the New Testament. By looking back on salvation history, it can be seen that the present dispensation is a time of decisive prophetic fulfillment. The end times have begun in the coming of Christ. God predestined Him before the foundation of the world to provide redemption and now He has been manifested "at the end of times" for the sake of Christians (1 Peter 1:20). When the Old Testament prophets predicted the sufferings and glory of the Messiah, they were describing the grace and salvation now enjoyed by believers (vv. 10–12). In several other verses Peter explicitly used the term "now" to highlight the present as the time of fulfillment in contrast to the previous dispensation (2:10, 25; 3:21). But the present blessings also look forward to a consummation yet to come in the future. Believers enjoy salvation as a present possession, yet they await the future completion of their deliverance (1:4–5, 9, 13). Jesus Christ has already been raised and given heavenly glory and dominion at God's right hand (1:21; 3:22), but His glory is yet to be revealed on earth (4:13) and His people suffer in anticipation of sharing His glory in the future (1:7; 5:1, 4, 10).[120]

So there is a consummation yet to come, and it is imminent according to these epistles. Peter's use of "now" sometimes contrasts the present with what is yet to occur (1:6, 8), and the present sufferings are just "for a little while" until God's deliverance comes (v. 6; 5:10). In fact, persecution of believers and opposition by false teachers are expected in the last days and are signs that the Day of the Lord could come at any time (4:12–19; 2 Peter 3:2–4, 10; Jude 17–18).[121] Christians await the revelation or appearing of Jesus Christ in glory (1 Peter 1:7, 13; 4:13; 5:4) and His coming in judgment and power (2 Peter 1:16; 3:3; Jude 14). "The end of all things is near" (1 Peter 4:7), their final salvation is "ready to be revealed in the last time" (1:5), Jesus is "ready to judge the living and the dead" (4:5), and "it is time for judgment to begin" for the righteous and the ungodly (4:17–18). The judgment has not come yet because God's timing is different from human's, and He is patient and merciful in wanting others to come to repentance (2 Peter 3:8–9).

The coming events include the blessings of final salvation for believers, as mentioned above. These blessings are simply the culmination of the process of redemption already operating in their lives, guarded and guaranteed for them by God (1 Peter 1:3–5, 8–9, 13; 2 Peter 1:3–11; Jude 21, 24–25).[122] Believers look forward to an unfading heavenly inheritance (1 Peter 1:4), a share in Christ's messianic glory (4:13; 5:1, 4, 10), a rich welcome into the eternal kingdom of Jesus Christ (2 Peter 1:11), deliverance from all evil in the new heavens and new earth (3:13), and enjoyment of eternal life by the mercy of the Lord Jesus Christ (Jude 21).

120. Edward Gordon Selwyn, "Eschatology in 1 Peter," in *The Background of the New Testament and Its Eschatology,* ed. W. D. Davies and D. Daube (Cambridge: Cambridge Univ., 1956), 394–401.

121. Davids, *First Epistle of Peter,* 15–16; and Selwyn, "Eschatology in 1 Peter," 399. Selwyn notes that Jesus warned of persecution in the end times (Matt. 10:16–26; Mark 13:9–13).

122. "Our author, therefore, conceives of the end as organically linked with what has already occurred . . . the culmination of something already experienced and known" (Selwyn, "Eschatology in 1 Peter," 397).

For unbelievers, on the other hand, judgment is waiting, and it cannot be denied or avoided. In his first epistle Peter warned in somewhat general terms of the judgment to come on all who persecute believers and disobey the gospel (1 Peter 2:12; 3:16; 4:4–5, 17–18). In 2 Peter and Jude the warnings became pointed and specific, because the opponents taught that there would be no judgment. They were eschatological skeptics, perhaps because they (1) doubted that God would intervene in the natural continuities of the universe (2 Peter 3:4), (2) believed all eschatology had already been realized in the present (2 Peter 1:16), or (3) lived in licentiousness and could not permit themselves to envision future accountability before a righteous God (cf. 2:2, 10, 13–14, 18; 3:3; Jude 4, 7, 16, 18).[123] This is why these two epistles stress the certainty of judgment on the heretics and their followers and reinforce it by Old Testament examples of God's judgment on ungodliness and unbelief (2 Peter 2:1–22; Jude 4–16). Their judgment is certain because it was predetermined long ago (2 Peter 2:3; Jude 4) and because the sovereign God is reserving a time and place of punishment for them, just as He has kept fallen angels in hell until the judgment of the great Day yet to come (2 Peter 2:4, 9, 17; 3:7; Jude 6, 13). Because of the nature of this false teaching, 2 Peter and Jude emphasized the future punishment and destruction which God will visit on the earth and all ungodly beings (2 Peter 2:1, 3, 9; 3:7, 10, 12, 16; Jude 6, 7, 13, 15, 23). Picking up the important Old Testament theme of the Day of the Lord or the Day of God (which is identical), these epistles focus almost entirely on the judgmental aspects of the Day (2 Peter 2:9; 3:7, 10, 12; Jude 6). The judgments include the fiery destruction of the present universe (2 Peter 3:10–12), but that will be followed by the promised appearance of new heavens and a new earth (3:12), as Isaiah 65:17; 66:22; and Revelation 21:1–5 also describe.[124]

Understanding the background of the false teaching just described and seeing how 2 Peter and Jude responded to it demonstrates how inappropriate some of the common expositions of their eschatology are. It is frequently argued that 2 Peter especially shows the fading of the church's eschatological hope and illustrates the crisis it experienced because of the unexpected delay of the Parousia.[125] However, far from showing that the later New Testament church had given up its imminent expectation of the end and had settled into an increasingly comfortable existence on earth, these epistles (1 Peter as well as 2 Peter and Jude) illustrate just the opposite. They demonstrate a continued anticipation that Christ could come at any time and a conviction that Christians are pilgrims and strangers in a world that could soon pass

---

123. E. M. B. Green, *II Peter Reconsidered* (London: Tyndale, 1960), 25; Charles H. Talbert, "II Peter and the Delay of the Parousia," *Vigiliae Christianae* 20 (1966): 141; Ladd, *Theology of the New Testament*, 606; Neyrey, "Form and Background of the Polemic in 2 Peter," 407–31; and Bauckham, *Jude, 2 Peter*, 154–57.

124. For discussion of when these things will occur in relation to other future events, see R. Larry Overstreet, "A Study of 2 Peter 3:10–13," *Bibliotheca Sacra* 137 (1980): 354–71.

125. Dunn, *Unity and Diversity in the New Testament*, 350–51; Käsemann, "Apologia for Primitive Christian Eschatology," 170, 178–85, 193–95.

away.[126] The issue of the delay of the Parousia often centers on 2 Peter 3:3–4 (scoffers who say, "Where is the promise of His coming?" NASB). But as discussed above, this does not speak of the whole church struggling with Christ's delay and trying to give some answer to their disappointment. Instead it reflects false teachers who try to deny that judgment will ever come by noting that it has not come yet.[127]

As elsewhere in the New Testament, the eschatological teaching of these epistles carries a moral and practical import. It brings comfort, as in 1 Peter 4:19, in which teaching about impending judgment is the basis for encouraging suffering believers to entrust themselves to God's faithfulness and to continue in their righteous conduct despite the persecution it may bring. In 2 Peter 3:11–12, after describing the future destruction of the existing creation, Peter urged the believers to live in holiness and godliness, watching expectantly and zealously for the eschatological culmination.[128] How useless to live for earthly things when they are so clearly limited in comparison with eternal values! The reference to the righteous character of the new heavens and the new earth (v. 13) also provoked an exhortation to perseverance and purity (vv. 14–15). Jude also offered comfort in a context describing fiery judgment on sin (vv. 22–23). His concluding doxology emphasizes God's ability to keep Christians from falling and to bring them into His glorious presence without fault and with great joy (vv. 24–25).

126. A. L. Moore disputes Käsemann's view of the eschatology of 2 Peter and shows that it parallels that of Mark 13 and 2 Thessalonians 2, preserving rather than abandoning the characteristic themes of earliest Christian expectation (*The Parousia in the New Testment* [Leiden: Brill, 1966], 151–56). See also Fornberg, *An Early Church in a Pluralistic Society,* 60–78; and Bauckham, *Jude, 2 Peter,* 8–9, 151–52.

127. This is carefully argued by Talbert, "II Peter and the Delay of the Parousia," 137–45. See also Moore, *The Parousia in the New Testment,* 151–56.

128. The verb in the phrase "speeding its coming" (NIV) or "hastening the coming of the Day of God" (NASB) should be taken to mean "to strive for" or "be zealous for." It reinforces the first verb in the verse, "looking forward to" in describing the Christian's anticipation and desire for God's eschatological program to be accomplished. See Bauer, Arndt, and Gingrich, *A Greek-English Lexicon of the New Testament,* 762; and Christian Maurer, *Theological Dictionary of the New Testament,* s.v. *"prosdokaō,"* 6:726 n. 7.

INDEX OF
SUBJECTS

INDEX OF PERSONS